DK SMITHSONIAN HANDBOOKS

HERBS

SMITHSONIAN
HANDBOOKS

HERBS

LESLEY BREMNESS

Photography by
NEIL FLETCHER
MATTHEW WARD

Editorial Consultant
HOLLY H. SHIMIZU

A Dorling Kindersley Book

LONDON, NEW YORK, MUNICH,
MELBOURNE, and DELHI

Important Notice

The recommendations and information in this book are appropriate in most cases. However, the advice this book contains is general, not specific to individuals and their particular circumstances. Any plant substance, whether used as food or medicine, externally or internally, can cause an allergic reaction in some people. During pregnancy, avoid taking any new or unknown substances without consulting a physician. Neither the author nor the publishers can be held responsible for claims arising from the mistaken identity of any herbs, or the inappropriate use of any remedy or healing regimen. Do not try self-diagnosis or attempt self-treatment for serious or long-term problems without consulting a medical professional or qualified practitioner. Do not undertake any self-treatment while undergoing a prescribed course of medical treatment without first seeking professional advice. Always seek medical advice if symptoms persist.

Project Editor Charlotte Davies
Project Art Editor Colin Walton
Assistant Editors Lucinda Hawksley, Lesley Malkin
Illustrations researched and commissioned by Mustafa Sami
Production Controller Adrian Gathercole
Series Editor Jonathan Metcalf
Series Art Editors Peter Cross, Spencer Holbrook
U.S. Consultant Holly H. Shimizu
U.S. Editor Charles A. Wills

First American Edition, 1994
Reprinted with corrections, 2000
Second American Edition, 2002
2 4 6 8 10 9 7 5 3 1

Published in the United States by
Dorling Kindersley, Inc.
375 Hudson Street
New York, New York 10014

ISBN 0-7894-9391-8

Computer page makeup by Colin Walton Graphic Design, Great Britain
Text film output by The Right Type, Great Britain
Reproduced by Colourscan, Singapore
Printed and bound by Kyodo Printing Co., Singapore

Contents

FOREWORD

Herbs are plants that connect us to the past, present, and future. We associate them with appetizing food, natural scents, gentle healing, peaceful gardens, beneficial crafts, intriguing history, and sacred activities. Each subject in this colorful tapestry enriches the others, but through the threads the background remains green, because the basis of all these delights is the plants themselves.

ALL ACROSS America renewed interest in herbs has created a tremendous need for a reassessment of their worth. A recognized necessity for closer contact with nature, a renewed approach to preventive health, an appreciation and interest in Native American uses of plants, in traditional Chinese medicine, and in the value of essential oils and aromas have all contributed to this new awareness. Herbs are now familiar and much valued friends to both professional and amateur gardeners, and their importance as garden plants is growing. For all these reasons, those who share an interest in herbs must join in a world-wide effort to ensure that these valuable plants are not threatened with extinction, their potentially life-enhancing uses lost to the world forever.

ANCIENT CURE
As long as 200,000 years ago, Euryale ferox *seeds were eaten by early humans in China. Many centuries later, its medicinal uses were recognized, and it appears in early Chinese herbals.*

GLOBAL INFLUENCES

America's ethnic diversity means that fresh herbs and spices are available in markets that may not be found in the herb references on our bookshelf. Neighbors, coworkers, and our daily newspapers often enlighten us with special recipes that call for our newly discovered food enhancers. In ethnic restaurants our palates have been introduced to unusual herbs such as Epazote (*Chenopodium ambrosioides*) mixed with black beans, or Rau Ram (*Polygonum odoratum*) sometimes used in Vietnamese chicken dishes. In addition to these culinary herbal experiences, one of the exciting by-products of the ethnic mix of American society is the informational

COWSLIP
Many European wild flowers like Cowslip hold forgotten herbal secrets. It is sedative when taken fresh or in a tea.

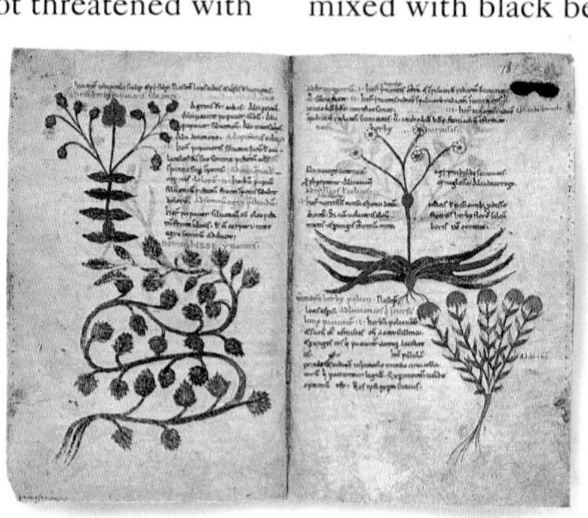

MONASTIC HERBAL
Herbals such as this, an Apuleius text copied by Canterbury monks around AD *1100, spread botanical medical knowledge across continents. Despite botanical inaccuracies, recent archaeological finds suggest monastic herbal medicine was highly sophisticated.*

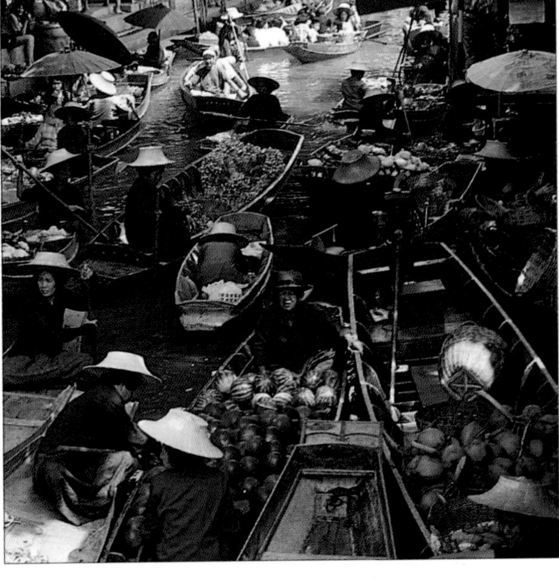

FLOATING MARKET
Among the melons in Thailand's floating markets are Lime leaves, Lemongrass, Galangal, and Betel leaf bundles. All have medicinal and culinary uses. Also for sale are medicinal Centella and Lotus root, and Jasmine garlands for temple offerings. Some are cultivated; others are collected from the wild.

exchange on herbs which is taking place on a regular basis. Herbs gathered from far corners of the world are being discussed in the hopes of discovering the significance, meaning, and uses of a particular genus. Not coincidentally, this global sharing has shown that a herb's uses are often similar on different continents and, through the test of time and experience, these plants have proven their worth. One example is illustrated in the genus *Podophyllum*. Both the indigenous American species (*P. peltatum*) and its Asian counterpart, the Himalayan species (*P. hexandrum*) have been used in their respective areas for centuries, by the native peoples, in the treatment of cancer. The Asian species was used to develop the drug, Vepeside, a treatment for lung and testicular cancer. In 1990, the Asian species of *Podophyllum* was listed in the Convention on International Trade in Endangered Species (CITES). In that same year, sales of Vepeside topped 100 million dollars here in the United States.

The *Podophyllum* case exemplifies the urgent need for professional botanists and horticulturists to join others in facing up to the many challenges of conservation. In response to this need, drug companies such as Shaman Pharmaceuticals in San Francisco have made a commitment to the preservation of natural areas by producing drug plants under cultivated conditions. Moreover, these enlightened companies are dedicated to preventing the exploitation of the areas and people where new drugs or plant treatments are discovered.

POISONOUS PLANTS

The Glory Lily (*Gloriosa superba*, see right) is an Asian suicide herb, but in tiny doses it can treat leprosy. Curare arrow poison from *Chondrodendron* species is also a major muscle relaxant for surgery and now saves lives. However, toxic plants must be used only by experts. To avoid poisoning from an unfamiliar herb, accurate identification is vital – both for plants from the wild and those bought in shops. An herbalist's instructions must be followed precisely. If adverse reactions occur, stop the treatment and consult a qualified herbalist again.

Rich Resources

Leaders in America's herbal arena are encouraged by recent successes in recognizing the unlimited potential of herbs. Dr. James Duke, a well known authority on herbs and an ethnobotanist with the U.S. Department of Agriculture, is growing four plants on his farm that could be starter material for major drugs (that is those worth more than 20 billion dollars in annual sales) in this country. These familiar plants, Mayapple used to produce Vepeside, Yew used to produce Taxol, Yam used to produces steroids, and Blood Root to produce Viadent, all thrive on his farm. He also grows Ginseng, America's largest crude drug with annual sales of over 75 million dollars.

Moreton Bay Chestnut
Unusual alkaloids in the seeds of this plant have stimulated new research into the immune system, AIDS, and cancer.

Processing Plants
Herbal laboratories use the whole herb to prepare remedies preferred by herbalists. They offer slower-acting, but gentler and safer healing than the potent, patentable drugs made from isolated ingredients that have stronger side effects.

These and hundreds of other useful plants are described in this unique volume, with information on herbs, including recent Chinese research and native plant uses. As a compilation of herbal knowledge, it will be valued by herb growers and users alike.

Conservation of Plants for the Future

Only 5 percent of all flowering plants have been researched, and yet within the next 50 years a quarter of this 5 percent may become extinct. Apart from being a moral issue, the preservation of species also has an economic importance – native peoples who have always practiced conservation should share in the rewards of any commercialization of their herbal knowledge.

Conservation Checklist

- Identify plants carefully. Never pick rare or endangered species.
- Choose the right plant part and gather plant parts in the correct season.
- Do not take more than you will use.
- Leave some of the reproductive parts (root or seeds) to ensure future growth.
- Avoid disturbing the plant's habitat.

Amazon Rain Forest
Full of untapped herbal potential, the rain forests are also the "lungs of the world." Their survival determines our own future.

HOW THIS BOOK WORKS

THIS BOOK is divided into six parts according to major plant type (see p.10): trees, shrubs, herbaceous perennials, annuals and biennials, vines, and other herbs (including fungi and non-seed-bearing plants). Within each section the entries are arranged alphabetically by their scientific names. The page below shows a typical entry.

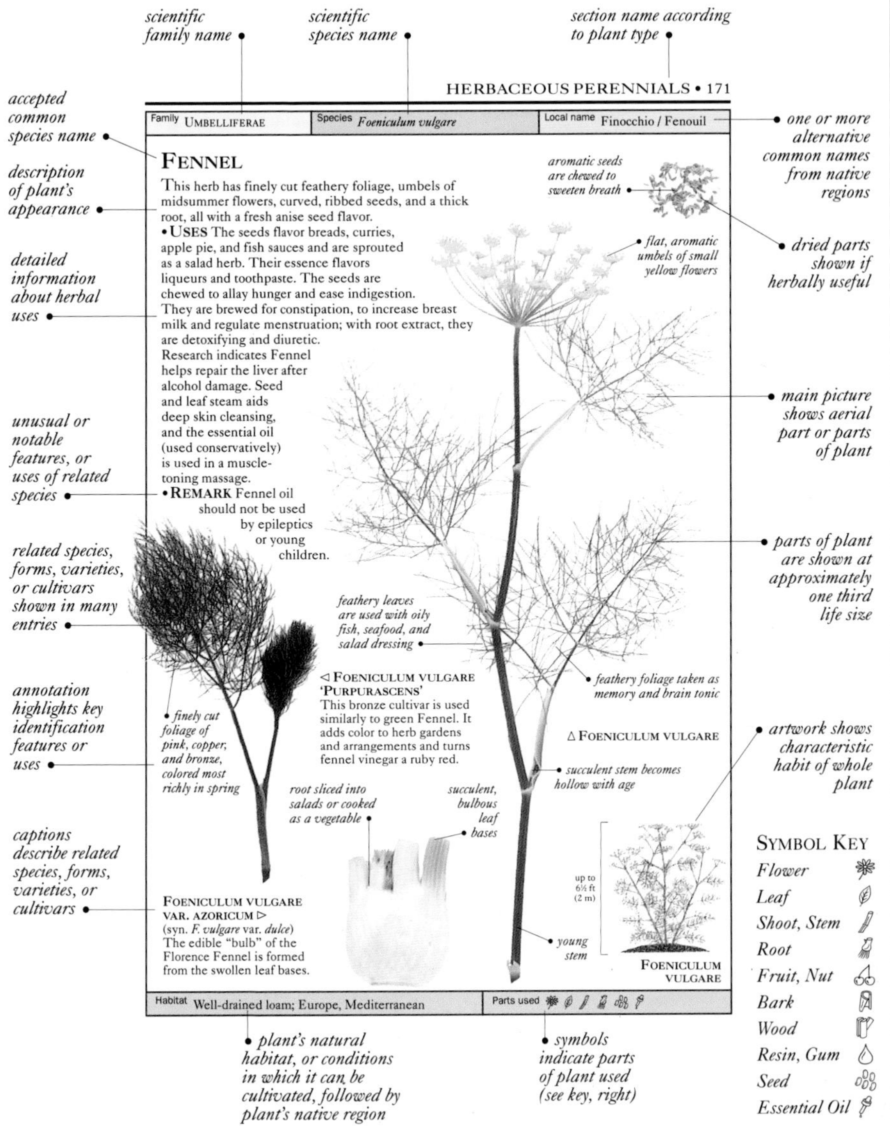

scientific family name
scientific species name
section name according to plant type
HERBACEOUS PERENNIALS • 171
accepted common species name
Family UMBELLIFERAE
Species Foeniculum vulgare
Local name Finocchio / Fenouil
one or more alternative common names from native regions
description of plant's appearance
FENNEL
This herb has finely cut feathery foliage, umbels of midsummer flowers, curved, ribbed seeds, and a thick root, all with a fresh anise seed flavor.
• USES The seeds flavor breads, curries, apple pie, and fish sauces and are sprouted as a salad herb. Their essence flavors liqueurs and toothpaste. The seeds are chewed to allay hunger and ease indigestion. They are brewed for constipation, to increase breast milk and regulate menstruation; with root extract, they are detoxifying and diuretic. Research indicates Fennel helps repair the liver after alcohol damage. Seed and leaf steam aids deep skin cleansing, and the essential oil (used conservatively) is used in a muscle-toning massage.
• REMARK Fennel oil should not be used by epileptics or young children.
aromatic seeds are chewed to sweeten breath
dried parts shown if herbally useful
flat, aromatic umbels of small yellow flowers
detailed information about herbal uses
main picture shows aerial part or parts of plant
unusual or notable features, or uses of related species
parts of plant are shown at approximately one third life size
related species, forms, varieties, or cultivars shown in many entries
feathery leaves are used with oily fish, seafood, and salad dressing
◁ FOENICULUM VULGARE 'PURPURASCENS'
This bronze cultivar is used similarly to green Fennel. It adds color to herb gardens and arrangements and turns fennel vinegar a ruby red.
feathery foliage taken as memory and brain tonic
annotation highlights key identification features or uses
finely cut foliage of pink, copper, and bronze, colored most richly in spring
△ FOENICULUM VULGARE
artwork shows characteristic habit of whole plant
succulent stem becomes hollow with age
root sliced into salads or cooked as a vegetable
succulent, bulbous leaf bases
captions describe related species, forms, varieties, or cultivars
FOENICULUM VULGARE VAR. AZORICUM ▷
(syn. F. vulgare var. dulce)
The edible "bulb" of the Florence Fennel is formed from the swollen leaf bases.
young stem
up to 6½ ft (2 m)
FOENICULUM VULGARE
Habitat Well-drained loam; Europe, Mediterranean
Parts used
plant's natural habitat, or conditions in which it can be cultivated, followed by plant's native region
symbols indicate parts of plant used (see key, right)
SYMBOL KEY
Flower
Leaf
Shoot, Stem
Root
Fruit, Nut
Bark
Wood
Resin, Gum
Seed
Essential Oil

WHAT IS AN HERB?

FROM EARLIEST TIMES, humans have divided plants into two groups, the useful and the not useful, the former being the broadest definition of an herb. Those regarded as useful depend on the environment and society in which one lives – an Amazon healer might consider 500 plants to be useful, and therefore "herbs," whereas a city dweller might know only five. Thus "herb" is a cultural rather than a botanical definition.

In this book we define them more narrowly, as we omit fuel, timber trees, and most food plants (although 100 years ago vegetables were still called "pot herbs"). Exceptions have been made for the growing number of food plants now known to have medicinal or cosmetic benefits; hence several fruits, vegetables, and grains are included.

HERBS IN THE PLANT KINGDOM

Most people assume herbs are annual or herbaceous plants, such as Basil, or perhaps Ginseng, but in fact herbs span the breadth of the entire plant kingdom, from giant conifers to tiny yeasts. Herb plants are found among mosses, ferns, conifers, and even algae, as well as the more familiar higher flowering plants.

PLANT GROUPS

Botanical divisions within the plant kingdom are based on each plant's method of reproduction. In this book, however, plants have been grouped according to the more easily visible size and shape of growth, rather than according to the formal botanical divisions.

TREES
Woody perennials with a single main stem, usually branching well above the ground to create a crown.

SHRUBS
A loose term for woody perennials with multiple branches from the base; generally smaller than trees.

HERBACEOUS PERENNIALS
Perennial plants that die back to roots in autumn and grow new shoots in spring.

ANNUALS AND BIENNIALS
Annuals germinate, seed, and die in one year. Biennials complete their cycle in two years, flowering in the second year.

VINES
Vines and clambering plants with a tendency to climb (by adaptations of stems, leaves, or roots), to twine, or to grow tendrils or suckers.

OTHER HERBS
Herbal plants and fungi that do not reproduce by seed: mainly the ferns (above left) and fungi (above right). This group also includes mosses such as Sphagnum and primitive plants such as Horsetail (which reproduce by means of spores) and seaweeds, such as Bladderwrack.

ALGAE
Some algaes are used in cosmetics.

Whatever family they belong to, all herbs used in this book contain one or more chemically defined active ingredients that have a specific use.

ACTIVE INGREDIENTS

- **ALKALOIDS** are active organic compounds containing at least one nitrogen atom, potent but often toxic (e.g. morphine). Alkaloids provide many important drugs and are the focus of most pharmaceutical research.
- **BITTERS** are diverse compounds that have a bitter taste and stimulate the appetite.
- **ENZYMES** are organic catalysts, essential for biochemical functions, and are found in all plants.
- **ESSENTIAL OILS** are aromatic plant essences extracted by distillation, organic solvents, or pressing.

ALKALOIDS
Quinine alkaloids are a cure for malaria.

- **GUMS** are sticky substances, insoluble in organic solvents, often produced in response to wounding of the plant.
- **GLYCOSIDES** are substances that can be broken down by specific enzymes to yield a sugar and a therapeutically active, often toxic, "aglycone."
- **MUCILAGE** is a viscous gum that swells into a gel in water. It is used to soothe irritated or inflamed skin.
- **SAPONINS** are emulsifying, often irritating or toxic, glycosides, similar to soap and chemically akin to steroids, which yield sex hormones.
- **TANNINS** are astringent compounds that cause proteins in blood to coagulate.
- **VITAMINS AND MINERALS** are required for various metabolic functions but, unlike enzymes, are not catalysts.

△ GUM
Liquidambar orientalis *is expectorant.*

SCIENTIFIC NAMES

The species is the basic plant group, classified by the structure of its flowers, fruit, and other organs. Species are grouped into genera and families and may be subdivided into subspecies, hybrids, varieties, forms, and cultivars.

FAMILY
A family contains a single genus or several related genera. The mints shown here all belong to the Labiatae family.

GENUS
A genus contains one species or several related species. The name appears in italic type, e.g. *Mentha*.

SPECIES
Species members are similar. The name consists of the genus name and the species epithet printed in italic type ◁ e.g. *Mentha aquatica*.

HYBRID
A hybrid is produced when two species cross together. This is indicated by a multiplication sign, e.g. *Mentha* x *villosa*. ▷

VARIETY, FORM, & SUBSPECIES
Varieties (var.), forms (f.), and subspecies (subsp.) are minor subdivisions of a species. The names are written in italic and roman type, e.g. *Mentha pugelium* var. *erecta*. ▷

CULTIVAR
A cultivar is a type of plant that has been produced artificially, e.g. *Mentha spicata* 'Crispa.' ▷

LEAVES AND STEMS

THE LEAF is the most frequently used part of an herb and its activity, photosynthesis, is fundamental to human existence, forming the basis of our food chain. During photosynthesis, the pigment in leaves, chlorophyll, absorbs red and blue light to convert water and carbon dioxide into sugars and oxygen; green light is reflected, making leaves appear green. Variegated leaves contain less chlorophyll than nonvariegated leaves and may contain smaller amounts of active ingredients. Chlorophyll is antiseptic and deodorizing. Its ability to clear toxins formed the basis of an entire healing system. Photosynthesis

PERILLA ▷
Perilla frutescens *var.* crispa
antibiotic leaves are used fresh in sushi to reduce bacteria poisoning, and dried to treat flu, coughs, and nausea.

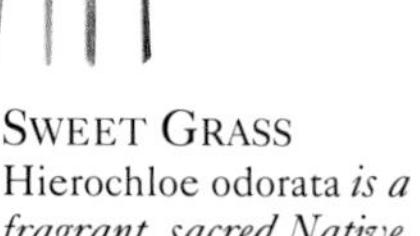

• *dried leaves keep scent*

SWEET GRASS
Hierochloe odorata *is a fragrant, sacred Native American incense plant.*

PALE CATECHU
In China, a decoction of Uncaria rhynchophylla *thorns treats dizziness, hypertension, and children's convulsions.*

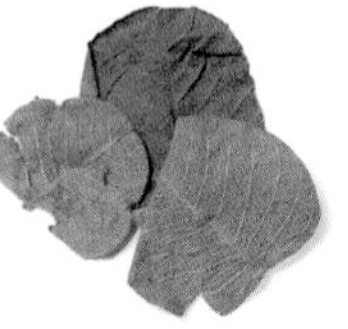

COIN LEAF CLOVER
The leaves of Desmodium styracifolium *treat colic, gallstones, and hepatitis.*

LEMONGRASS
The lemon-flavored culinary stems of Cymbopogon citratus *also have medicinal and aromatic uses.*

LEAF ANATOMY

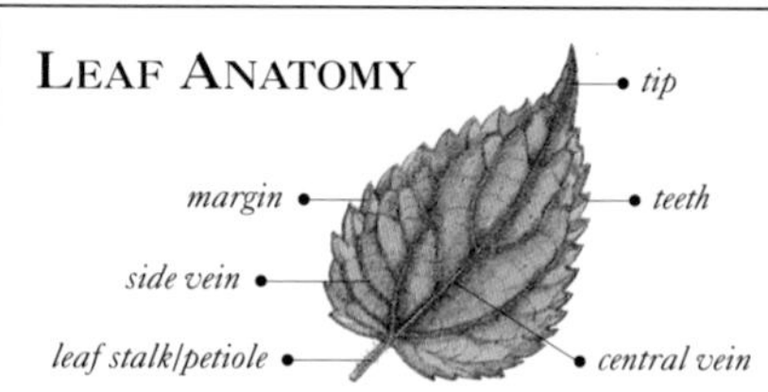
tip
margin
teeth
side vein
leaf stalk/petiole
central vein

LEAF ARRANGEMENTS

WHORL

OPPOSITE

ALTERNATE

SIMPLE LEAF SHAPES

OVATE

OBOVATE

ELLIPTIC

COMPOUND LEAF SHAPES

PALMATE

PINNATE

BIPINNATE

decreases in autumn, and nutrients are exported from the leaves, thus reducing their flavor and therapeutic value. Leaf chemistry gives rise to a variety of culinary flavors, perfumes, and medicines. Leaves also produce oxygen as a by-product of photosynthesis, so indoor plants improve stale air.

Stems transport nutrients and support the plant. Many yield useful sap and supply strong, flexible fibers, such as flax and hemp, used in the manufacture of linen, rope, and paper.

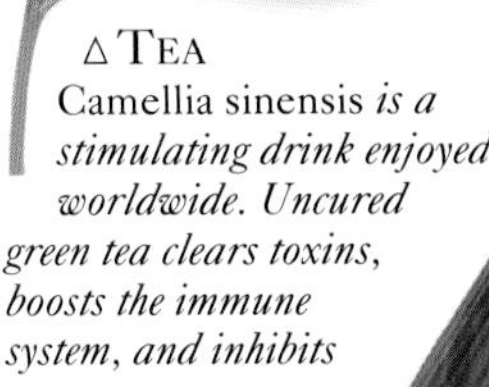

△ TEA
Camellia sinensis *is a stimulating drink enjoyed worldwide. Uncured green tea clears toxins, boosts the immune system, and inhibits some cancers.*

SWEET BAY ▷
Laurus nobilis *has evergreen leaves used all year round as a flavoring and symbol of attainment.*

◁ TRAVELERS' PALM
Ravenala madagascariensis *aids travelers because the leaves fan out to indicate east and west, and the leaf stalks hold an emergency water supply.*

STEVIA
Stevia rebaudiana *is a tropical annual with very sweet leaves that yield the substance "stevioside." This white crystalline powder is 250–300 times sweeter than sucrose.*

FIDDLEHEAD FERN
The emerging leaves and stalks of Pteridium aquilinum *are cooked or pickled. Bulk raw enzymes destroy vitamin B_1 (thiamine).*

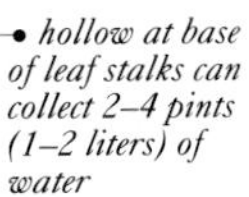

hollow at base of leaf stalks can collect 2–4 pints (1–2 liters) of water

HARVESTING LEAVES

For maximum value of most species, pick clean, dry, undamaged leaves or sprigs at midmorning, just before flowering. Freeze immediately, or dry in bunches in warm, dust-free, circulating air, out of sun, until brittle (4–10 days). Store in dark, airtight jars.

HEMLOCK △
Conium maculatum *is extremely poisonous, with a mousy, fetid smell. It is used in the witches' brew in Shakespeare's* Macbeth.

Flowers

Answering the call to reproduce, many plants evolved a flower, and each flower part can be used herbally. In the center of a basic flower is the female organ, the pistil, consisting of the ovary below and style and stigma above, surrounded by a ring of male stamens (each made up of a filament and an anther). Around the center is the corolla, or petals, whose color, scent, and nectar evolved to entice bees and other insects to aid pollination. The outer ring – the calyx or sepals – protects the flower when in bud.

Cross fertilization occurs when pollen released by the stamens of one flower reaches the ripe stigma of another, and travels down into the ovary to fertilize an ovule. This can sometimes create interesting new varieties or, less happily from an herbal point of view, muddy blends.

The flowers of pungent-leaved herbs often have a milder flavor than the leaves, and many flowers, such as Mint, Rosemary, and Chive florets, are delicious eaten raw. Indeed, many flowers in this book are enjoyed in cuisines worldwide. However, flowers from poisonous plants should be avoided in food and drinks.

Fragrance from flowers is captured in potpourri, and in perfumes such as the popular

△ Elderflower
The creamy flower clusters of Sambucus nigra *have a muscatel flavor used with gooseberries in fool and in refreshing elderflower "champagne" or "lemonade."*

Passion Flower ▷
The distinctive shapes of Passiflora incarnata *invited symbolism. It is used with the leaf and stem as a non-addictive, nondepressant sedative.*

Calendula ▷
The edible golden petals of Calendula officinalis *rejuvenate skin, are antiseptic and antifungal. They heal cracked skin, sunburn, and eczema.*

Flower Anatomy & Arrangements

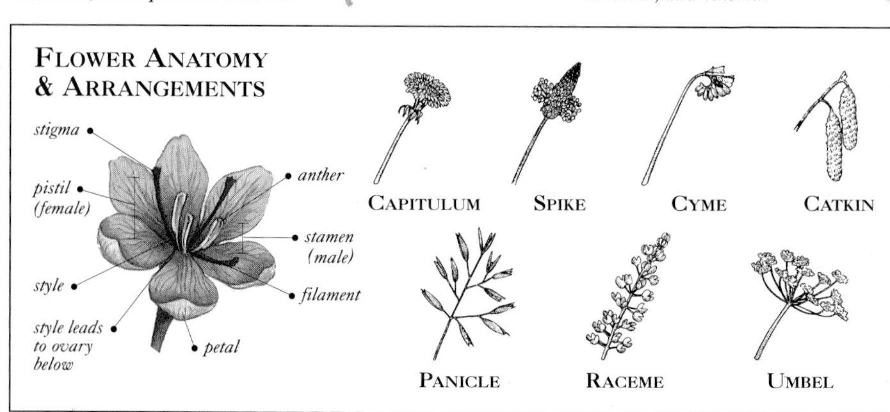
stigma
pistil (female)
style
style leads to ovary below
petal
anther
stamen (male)
filament
Capitulum
Spike
Cyme
Catkin
Panicle
Raceme
Umbel

Hindu champac from *Michelia champaca*. Medicinal flowers include the world's largest (*Rafflesia keithii*), a liana parasite, considered to be an aphrodisiac.

HARVESTING FLOWERS

Flowers contain the most active ingredients when they first open fully. Collect unblemished flowers of good shape in dry weather at midday. Pick flowering stems and avoid touching the petals. Discard soiled flowers as washing spoils the texture. Transport loose in open baskets.

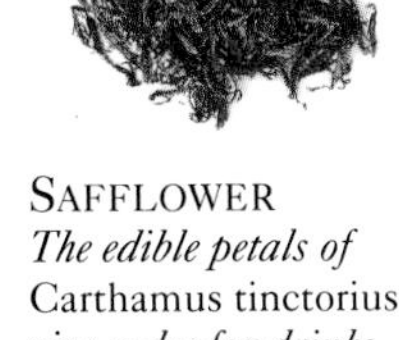

SAFFLOWER
The edible petals of Carthamus tinctorius *give a dye for drinks and cosmetics.*

KING-GUY-SOYI
The flowering stems of Schizonepeta tenuifolia *treat boils, rashes, and itching.*

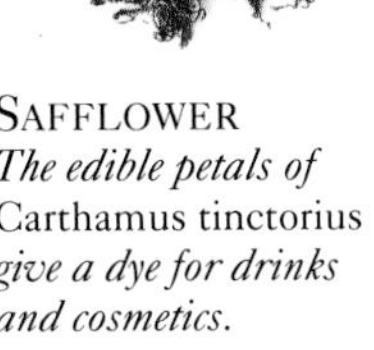

△ ROSE PETALS
Fragrant roses are the traditional main ingredient of potpourri, blended with other aromatic flowers, leaves, spices, and fixatives.

TEA CHRYSANTHEMUM
Cooling, antibiotic flower tea from Chrysanthemum morifolium *reduces blood pressure, and is a Taoist elixir.*

• flowers, leaves, and berries are a cardiac tonic

ENGLISH HAWTHORN
Crataegus monogyna *flowers improve damaged heart valves.*

MIMOSA
Acacia dealbata *is the florist's Mimosa.*

QUEEN OF THE NIGHT
The cactus flower Selenicereus grandiflorus *is a stimulant.*

TIGER FLOWER
The beautiful flower of Tigridia tenuifolia *was once a valued ancient Mexican fertility drug.*

DRYING FLOWERS

Spread out whole small flowers or thick petals of large flowers on paper or gauze, in warm, dust-free, circulating air for 1–3 weeks. Turn them once or twice. Dry roses and other large flower heads upright in mesh. Hang loose bundles of Lavender stems and remove the flowers later.

SEEDS, FRUITS, AND NUTS

SEEDS ARE PRODUCED by flowering and some nonflowering plants. Inside every seed is the genetic information for future growth, a store of food, and a dormant embryo that can grow into a seedling. The condensed nutrition in seeds supplies the world's major foods: cereals and pulses, such as rice, wheat, and soybeans. Many seeds have an extremely high fatty oil content (different from essential oil), which can be pressed out for cooking, cosmetics, medicines, and for craft and industrial uses.

A fruit is a ripe, developed flower ovary that can be succulent or dry. A

TANGERINE PEEL
Peel from Citrus reticulata *is used in Chinese medicine to break up body congestion, clear the liver, and ease abdominal pain.*

seed

peel

△ CHINESE CUCUMBER ▷
The seed and peel of Trichosanthes kirilowii *inhibit cancer cells. The root is used in AIDS research.*

△ GRAINS OF PARADISE
Aframomum melegueta *produces a hot, peppery West African condiment with a cardamom aroma.*

seeds nourish and lighten skin

BAOBAB
The acid pulp of Adansonia digitata *is used as cream of tartar, makes a lemonade-type drink, and is medicinal.*

△ WAX GOURD ▷
Benincasa hispida *contains anticancer terpenes; the fruits are eaten cold in Chinese meals to aid weight loss.*

FRUIT, NUT, AND SEED ANATOMY

Seeds develop in a flower's ovary; the ovary wall then develops into the fruit. In different species the fruit may be fleshy; a narrow pod with a row of seeds; or so thin it appears to be just a husk. A nut is a hard, dry fruit that does not split when ripe and contains one seed.

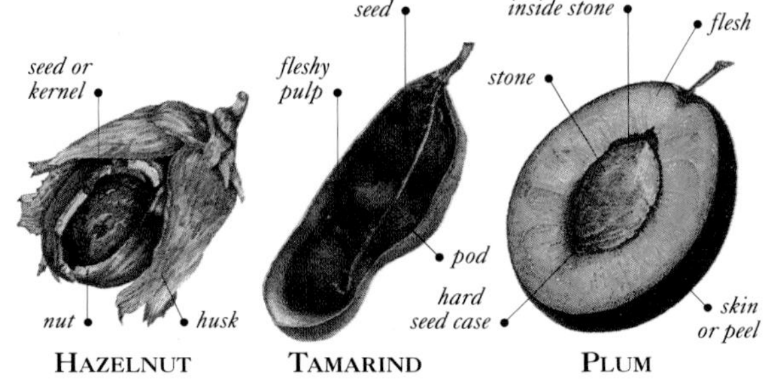
seed or kernel
nut
husk
HAZELNUT
seed
fleshy pulp
pod
hard seed case
TAMARIND
seed or kernel inside stone
flesh
stone
skin or peel
PLUM

succulent fruit is fleshy, like a plum or cherry. A nut is a type of dry fruit with a hard or woody pericarp (fruit wall), such as a hazelnut or chestnut.

◁ △ Billy Goat Plum
Terminalia ferdinandiana *is an Australian fruit rich in vitamin C.* T. chebula *seeds (above left) stimulate the appetite.*

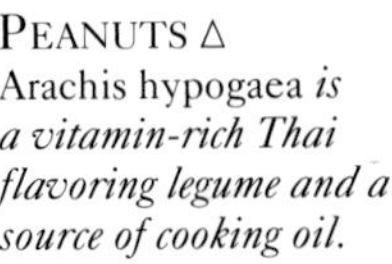

Peanuts △
Arachis hypogaea *is a vitamin-rich Thai flavoring legume and a source of cooking oil.*

Herbal Uses

Seeds and pods supply many spices, from anise to vanilla. They also yield the stimulant drinks coffee, cocoa, cola, and guarana; poppy seed capsules are the source of the drugs opium and morphine; the seeds of Job's Tears are made into beads; and the ivory nut provides Vegetable Ivory, a carving material. Fruits supply food, flavorings, dyes, cosmetic enzymes, perfumes, wax, and medicines. Fruits are usually used when fresh, but may also be dried or frozen.

△ Miraculous Berry
Dark red berries of the West African shrub Synsepalum dulcificum *stimulate the tongue so food tastes sweet for several hours.*

△ Tonka Beans
Dipteryx odorata *is an aromatic fixative for potpourri; the seed oil is given for earache.*

△ Guarana
Seeds from the Amazonian Paullinia cupana *give a stimulant, caffeine-rich drink.*

◁ Prickly Pear
Opuntia ficus-indica *is a Mexican cactus with succulent fruits that are nutritious, medicinal, and a source of alcohol.*

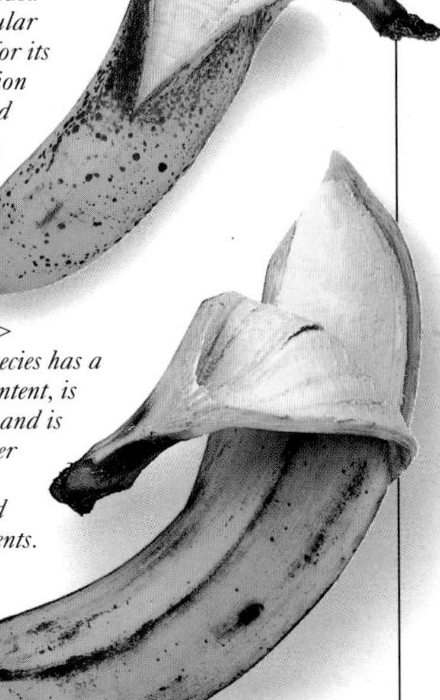

Banana ▷
The sweet, phosphorus- and carbohydrate-rich fruit of this Musa *species is popular with athletes for its quick conversion to energy. Used in face masks, its pulp softens skin.*

Plantain ▷
This Musa *species has a high starch content, is eaten cooked, and is brewed for beer and vinegar. It is also good for convalescents.*

Drying Seeds

Pick seeds when ripe from healthy plants on a warm, dry day. Shake into a paper bag or cut whole stalks. Lay seeds or stalks on paper or hang above an open box in a warm place for two weeks to ensure no moisture remains. Rub seeds from their stalks or pods; store in airtight jars.

ROOTS

ROOTS ARE THE underground parts of a plant. They hold the plant in the soil and absorb water and nutrients. Some are storage organs, containing concentrated active compounds. For example, the potency of the Ginseng root increases each year following the sharp frosts of autumn, when nutrients from the aerial parts of the plant return to the root for storage in winter. Roots are valued for a range of uses: Orris root is enjoyed for its long-lasting fragrance, Marsh Mallow roots are used in soothing skin creams, and Licorice for lozenges.

The underground storage organ may be a bulb, corm, or tuber – the Early Purple Orchid tuber contains the most nutritious plant substance known. Rhizomes are creeping, horizontal, under-

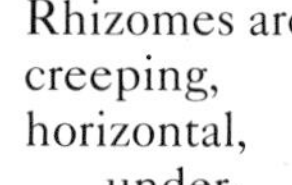

△ GOLDEN SEAL
Hydrastis canadensis *is a strong general tonic for the mucus membranes, liver, and uterus, and for venous circulation.*

◁ HORSERADISH
A pungent condiment, Armoracia rusticana *also stimulates the appetite. A root section left in the ground will regrow.*

△ SKUNK CABBAGE
The roots of Symplocarpus foetidus *treat asthma and headaches and stem blood flow. The root hairs reduce toothache.*

WHITE SQUILL ▷
Urginea maritima *bulbs are expectorant and diuretic. Red Squill is used as a rat poison.*

ROOT ANATOMY

The tiny hairs on roots absorb nutrients and water and may exude protective chemicals. Thick roots act as an anchor and as storage organs in dormant seasons. Root skin or bark may contain a different mixture of active compounds from the interior.

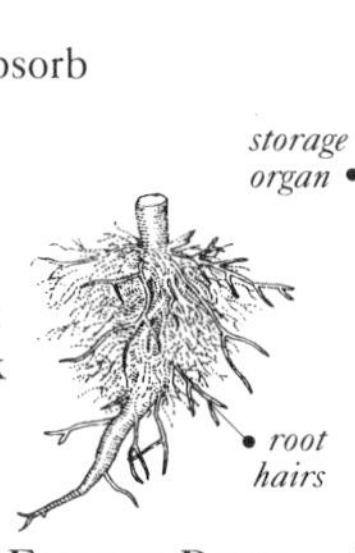
root hairs
FIBROUS ROOT

storage organ
TAPROOT

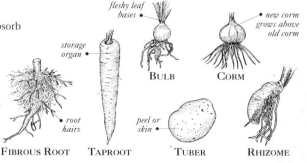

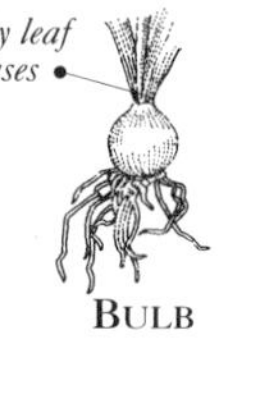
fleshy leaf bases
BULB

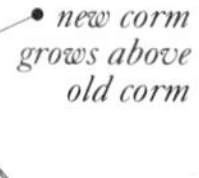
new corm grows above old corm
CORM

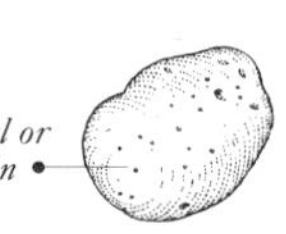
peel or skin
TUBER

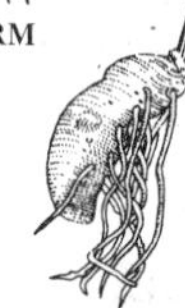
RHIZOME

ground stems from which roots and new shoots grow. Runners and stolons are both horizontal stems, not roots. Runners grow new plants where they touch the soil; stolons grow new plants at nodal joints (points with growing cells).

GREENBRIAR ▷
Smilax glabra *is a cooling, purgative tonic. It relieves itching and inflammation, treats boils and syphilitic lesions, and inhibits cancer cells.*

△ TI HUANG
A cooling yin tonic, Rehmannia glutinosa *beautifies hair and nourishes the blood.*

HARVESTING ROOTS

In seasonal climates, the best-quality roots are dug in spring before sap rises, or in autumn. The dry season is best in the tropics. If leaving some root for regrowth, cut cleanly with a knife.

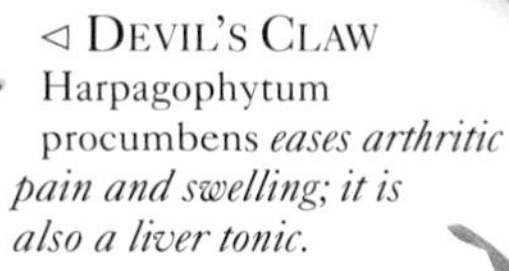

◁ DEVIL'S CLAW
Harpagophytum procumbens *eases arthritic pain and swelling; it is also a liver tonic.*

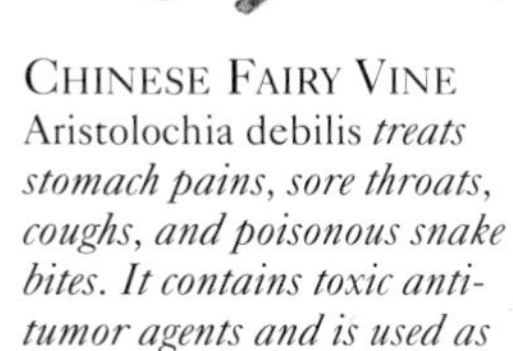

GREATER GALANGAL
Alpina galanga *root has a peppery, gingery flavor. It yields an essential oil,* essence d'Amali.

MAYAPPLE
The toxic, antiviral rhizome and resin of Podophyllum peltatum *are used in drugs for venereal warts, warts, and some cancers.*

CHINESE FAIRY VINE
Aristolochia debilis *treats stomach pains, sore throats, coughs, and poisonous snake bites. It contains toxic antitumor agents and is used as a painkiller for cancer.*

PREPARING ROOTS

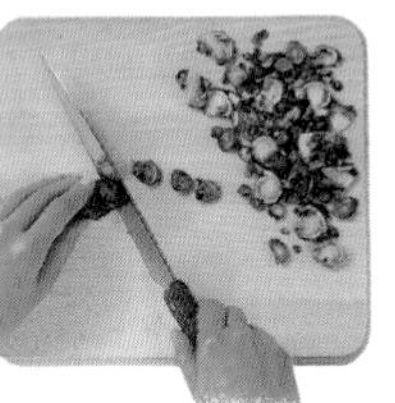

Shake or rub off soil, remove fibrous roots, and scrub clean. Chop, then spread to dry in a warm oven (120–150° F, 50–60° C) for 2–6 hours until brittle. Store in dark, airtight jars and label. Most roots prepared in this way will keep for years without absorbing moisture.

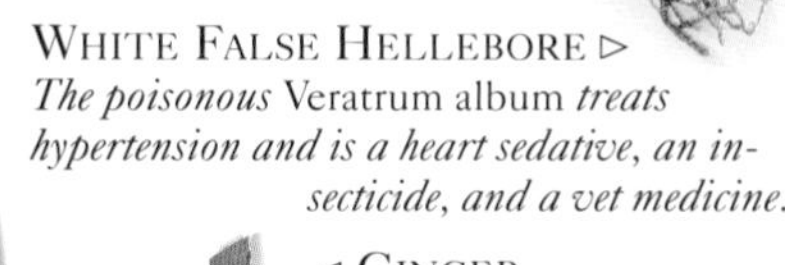

WHITE FALSE HELLEBORE ▷
The poisonous Veratrum album *treats hypertension and is a heart sedative, an insecticide, and a vet medicine.*

◁ GINGER
A popular spice, Zingiber officinale *reduces nausea from travel and from eating too much garlic.*

BARK, WOOD, AND RESIN

WOOD AND ITS protective layer of bark are found in the trunk, limbs, and roots of trees and shrubs. In spring, a ring of cells growing under the bark, the cambium layer, begins to divide, creating new sapwood to serve as vertical feeding channels for the plant. This hardens by the autumn. Outer bark, which is composed of dead cells, cracks or peels as the wood expands. Bark is continually replaced by the cambium layer, which means the inner bark stays moist and alive (see box below).

Bark is used in deodorizing charcoals, as cork, for soil improvement, and as a source of tannins and spices. Many bark drugs come from trees native to the Americas, like the malaria cure quinine (*Cinchona* spp.), and witch hazel.

Wood is primarily used in construction, and for fuel and paper pulp. But various woods have herbal uses, such as medicinal Lignum Vitae (*Guaiacum officinale*) and Quassia, which is also an insecticide. Aromatic woods have long been used as incense, and the essential oils they contain are antiseptic and kill airborne disease. Woods such as Sandalwood and Cedar hold their scent for years, which increases their value as perfumes.

Resins and gums are inflammable, sticky, often aromatic compounds, that are insoluble in water. Trees make them to protect themselves when damaged. Latex is a whitish juice or

CINNAMON ▽▷
The sweet, spicy quills (below) are the branch bark of Cinnamomum verum, *used in desserts; the robust red-brown trunk bark from* C. aromatica *(right) is known as Cassia, and flavors savory dishes. Sliced Cassia branches treat poor circulation and fever.*

sliced branches

Cassia inner bark

outer bark

quills

QUASSIA
The medicinal wood chips of Picrasma excelsa *also yield an insecticide for woolly aphids and greenflies.*

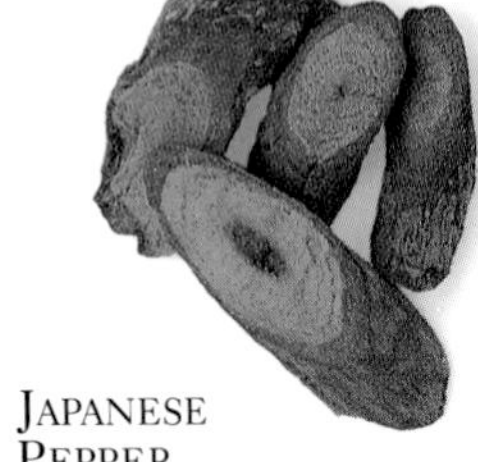

JAPANESE PEPPER
Piper futokadsura *stems treat lower back pain, stiff joints, and muscle cramps. In tests they inhibit cancer cells.*

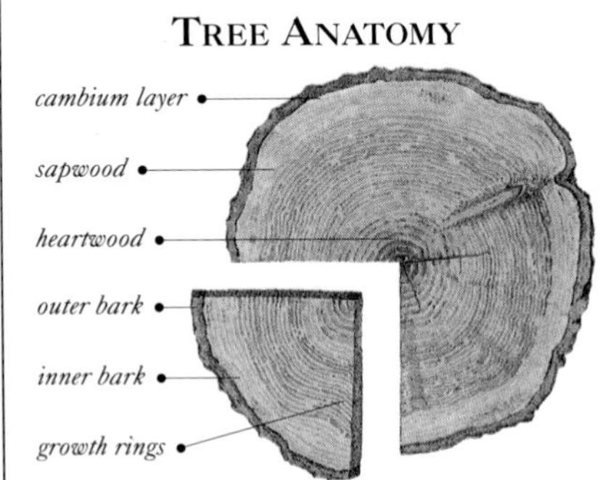
TREE ANATOMY
cambium layer
sapwood
heartwood
outer bark
inner bark
growth rings

MINDANO GUM
Eucalyptus deglupta *has colored, camphor-scented bark that peels in ribbons and is a folk medicine for fatigue.*

IRONWOOD
A sacred Buddhist tree, Mesua ferrea *has aromatic, astringent bark, given to induce perspiration.*

sap exuded for the same reason. Resin, gum, and latex are usually collected by cutting the bark (see box bottom right).

HARVESTING BARK AND WOOD

Bark is pried off in a tree's dormant season; wood is chipped and dried. All bark removal makes trees vulnerable; removing all the bark in a ring around a tree will kill it. When gathering bark, brush it clean, wash it, then spread it out to dry.

COPAL RESIN
The resin of Protium copal *is a sacred, protective, and medicinal Mayan incense.*

FRANKINCENSE
Boswellia carteri *resin makes a healing incense, which induces a meditative state.*

ALOE WOOD
The prized elusive scent of Aquilaria agallocha *exists only in resin-saturated diseased wood.*

PAU D'ARCO
Tabebuia impetiginosa *is an immune enhancer and fabled cure-all for cancer and candida.*

TRAGACANTH
Astragalus gummifer *gum, scentless until burned, is cosmetic, medicinal, an incense, and a fumigant.*

ANGOSTURA
Bitters is made from the resinous inner bark of Galipea officinalis, *a fragrant palmlike tree. It is a stimulant folk medicine and is added to sherry and gin.*

LIGNUM VITAE
Guaiacum officinale *wood has a laxative resin. The heated wood is aromatic.*

BORNEO CAMPHOR
Dryobalanops camphora *crystals are used in moth balls and are less toxic than camphor.*

BAOBAB
The spongy wood of Adansonia digitata *stores carbohydrates and water and is carved into panscrapers (above) and fishing floats. Its acid fruits thicken rubber latex.*

RESIN, GUM, AND LATEX EXTRACTION

Resin, gum, and latex are harvested by puncturing or cutting the bark in diagonal grooves, avoiding the cambium layer. It is collected later (as seen right, where latex is being tapped from the Rubber Tree, *Hevea brasiliensis*). Pine, copal, dragon's blood (from *Dracaena* species), dammar (from *Shorea* species), balsams, mastic, and storax are all collected in this way. Resin is also collected as naturally exuded "tears" from Frankincense, Myrrh, and Gum trees.

ESSENTIAL OILS

ESSENTIAL OILS, also known as volatile or ethereal oils, are the concentrated aromatic essences of plants. They are found in special cells of flowers, leaves, seeds, peel, and roots, and in the bark, resin, and wood of trees. More than 400 essences have been identified, of which about 50 are available to the public. The most expensive, Tuberose, comes from the flower *Polianthes tuberosa*. These essences provide antiseptic protection for the growing plant. They also give the herb its flavor and part of its health value, but their main attraction is their fragrance. This seductive scent lies behind the appeal of aromatherapy, in which oils are administered mainly via massage. A dramatic increase in public interest in essential oils has led to their greater accessibility, and there is now a growing demand for their use in aromatherapy courses and treatment.

These wonderful substances can be used to uplift, refresh, or relax the mind, body, and spirit, to soothe muscles, and to beautify the skin. They may also be used to treat common ailments, in room-sprays, in incenses, and in the bath.

USING ESSENTIAL OILS SAFELY

Users of essential oils must be extremely safety conscious. Essential oils should not be taken internally except when

ROSE OIL
Rosa damascena *is grown mainly in Turkey and Bulgaria for rose essential oil. This is usually extracted by solvents, but in this process valuable components are lost, so the more expensive method of "enfleurage" may be used, creating rose attar.*

PATCHOULI OIL
Distilled from leaves and shoots, this exotic fragrance of India became a symbol of the 1960s. The pure oil is less heavy than many Patchouli perfumes.

▽ PAU D'ANGOLA (*Mespilodaphne pretiosa*)

▽ TUCUMA (*Astrocaryum tucuma*)

△ PRIPRIOCA (*Cyperus odoratus*)

AROMATIC POWDERS
When essential oils exist in strong cells, such as in many woods and roots, they keep their scent for years and can be usefully stored in powdered form. Pau D'Angola, Priprioca, and Tucuma are all used in both perfumes and medicines.

EXTRACTING OILS FROM PLANTS

It takes 60,000 roses to make only 1 oz (30 g) of rose oil (see right), hence its very high price. Essential oils are extracted by distillation, expression, enfleurage, or by a solvent. The plant part used and the delicacy of the oil determine the method employed. Distillation is the most common, used for flowers little affected by heat, like Lavender, and for most leaves, seeds, and wood. In the expression method, oil is pressed out. Enfleurage, in which fat absorbs the perfume, is suitable for fragile petals. Alcohol is the solvent most often used, but a nonalcohol solvent system has recently been developed.

prescribed by qualified persons, and training is necessary to learn how to use oils safely. Some should be avoided during pregnancy, for example, or by sufferers of epilepsy or high blood pressure, or by people with sensitive skin. Essential oils should not be confused with *pressed* oils, usually from seeds, used in cooking.

FRANKINCENSE
Another source of frankincense resin *(see p.21)*, Boswellia thurifera *is distilled to produce oil used in rejuvenating creams for mature skin.*

COSTUS
The scented root oil of Saussurea lappa *treats skin disease and is added to Asian perfumes and hair dyes.*

◁ MYRRH
An ancient and sacred incense, the antiseptic, anti-inflammatory oil of Commiphora myrrha *was used for embalming. It is now found in toothpaste and perfume.*

ESSENTIAL OIL DOSES

Essential oil doses are measured in drops; for massage, 2 or 3 drops of essential oil are blended with 1 tsp (5 ml) of pressed or "carrier" oil, such as almond or grape-seed oil. Once mixed, their shelf life is reduced from years to months.

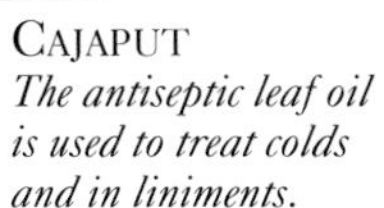

LEMON
Lemon peel oil is a bleach and immune system enhancer. Eighty-five lemons yield 1 oz (30 g) of oil.

CAJAPUT
The antiseptic leaf oil is used to treat colds and in liniments.

JASMINE
Jasmine flowers collected in the early morning yield expensive jasmine oil by enfleurage. It is an antidepressant and aphrodisiac, used in perfumes, dry skin care, and massage.

BUYING AND STORING OILS

Buy oils that have been tested for purity and extracted from organically grown plants. They should be sold in dark glass bottles with a dropper, and labeled with the botanic name, country of origin, and safety advice. Keep oils in a cool, dark place. They may be fatal if ingested, so store securely, away from children.

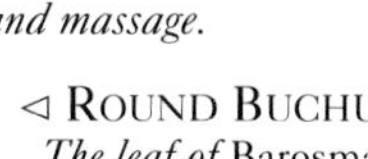

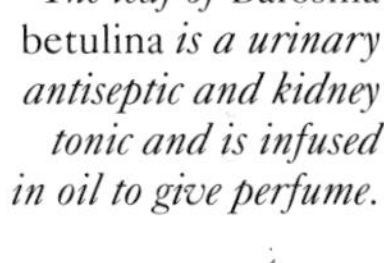

◁ ROUND BUCHU
The leaf of Barosma betulina *is a urinary antiseptic and kidney tonic and is infused in oil to give perfume.*

BOLDO ▷
Peumus boldus *is a digestive, liver tonic, and diuretic, and a weight-loss aid. When distilled, its sweet, refreshing leaf oil is popular in soaps and perfumes.*

Using Herbs in Cooking

HERBS TASTE GOOD and look good. They are the ingredients that can transform ordinary food and drinks into sumptuous meals. Greater travel opportunities and exotic cookbooks have introduced many new herbs to our diet, and long-forgotten edible flowers, buds, leaves, and roots are creeping back into common usage. Research has shown that culinary herbs can also have digestive, stimulant, or calming effects.

There are three basic ways of cooking with herbs. Some plants, such as Borage, are eaten fresh, as a garnish, or in drinks and salads. Mild herbs like Parsley are added toward the end of cooking to bring out flavor. Stronger tasting herbs and spices such as Garlic and Bay are added to dishes as cooking starts.

Useful Equipment

kitchen knives
mortar and pestle
rotary grater
citrus zester
double-handled knife
chopping board
garlic press
wheel

Herb and Spice Mixtures

Every cuisine has its favorite blends. The Chinese have five-spice with Star Anise, Fagara, Fennel, Cassia, and Cloves. Malay blends include Chili, Tamarind, Coconut, Galangal, Candlenuts, and Lime Leaf. Cajun mixes use Paprika, Mustard, Cumin, Chili, and Oregano. Pizza herbs are Basil, Sweet Marjoram, and Oregano, and the North American pumpkin pie mix is Nutmeg, Cinnamon, Allspice, and Ginger.

BOUQUET GARNI
An herb bundle is used in the cooking of soups and stews. It is tied for easy removal and traditionally includes three Parsley stalks, a small Thyme sprig, and a Bay leaf, with a range of extras from Lemon peel to a Celery stalk wrapping.

◁ CHAT MASALA
An Indian salad mix of Asafoetida, Ajowan, Cumin, Mint, Ginger, Cayenne, Mango, and Pomegranate seeds.

◁ HARISSA
A Tunisian paste for couscous stews, with red Chilies, Coriander seeds, Caraway, Garlic, Cumin, and Mint, in Olive oil.

QUATRE-EPICES ▷
A French blend for pork dishes with Black Peppercorns, Cloves, Ginger, Nutmeg, and occasionally Cinnamon.

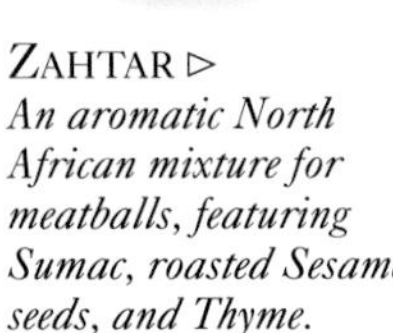

ZAHTAR ▷
An aromatic North African mixture for meatballs, featuring Sumac, roasted Sesame seeds, and Thyme.

STORING HERBAL FLAVORS

Many cooking ingredients absorb plant flavors. Unheated vegetable oil, heated vinegar, or warmed honey will assume the flavors of fresh herbs, fragrant flowers, or spices. The plants should be steeped in the liquid for about two weeks. For a stronger flavor, the process may be repeated with fresh herbs. Vanilla sugar is achieved by "dry infusion" with a Vanilla pod. Butter rolled in chopped herbs or covered in Rose petals overnight will absorb the taste and fragrance.

CAPERS
Pickled buds of Capparis spinosa.

HERBAL VINEGARS
White or red wine vinegars are made by adding fresh herbs and flowers, such as Dill, Chili, Marjoram, Rosemary, Elderflower, or Lavender, to cider or wine vinegar, in an airtight bottle. They add flavor to dressings and marinades.

DRINKS

From desert nomads to the Arctic Inuit, tribes worldwide find local plants to brew into drinks, like Mormon Tea (*Ephedra nevadensis*), Maté, and Guarana. Many of these, such as Tea and Coffee, are now widely used. Herbs steeped in tonic wines, liqueurs, and syrups create delights such as electuaries, cordials, and robs.

SARSAPARILLA
The roots of Smilax regelii (*syn.* Smilax officinalis) *flavor soft drinks and root beer; it is also an Amazonian tonic taken for skin disease and to restore virility.*

YERBA MATÉ
The leaves of Ilex paraguariensis *are brewed to make a South American caffeine-rich, stimulant tea.*

ROOIBOSCH
This South African fermented, red-leaf tea, from Aspalathus linearis, *is low in caffeine and reduces allergies.*

LABRADOR TEA
The slightly narcotic leaves of the Arctic evergreen shrub Ledum groenlandicum *are brewed as tea (steeped only, as boiling may release a harmful alkaloid) or beer. They are used by Canadian native peoples as an expectorant and cold remedy.*

HERBAL TEAS AND INFUSIONS

Place the fresh or dried leaf, flower, crushed seed, bark, or root in a teapot; add boiling water and brew for 5 minutes. Allow a teaspoon of dried herb or a fresh sprig of about 6–9 leaves per cup. Strain and serve.

YELLOW GENTIAN
Gentiana lutea *roots and the underground stem make gentian bitters and brandy (to aid digestion and stimulate appetite), and a nerve tonic used by the ancient Greeks as a poison antidote.*

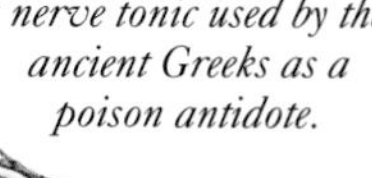

HEALING HERBS

TURNING TO PLANTS for healing is an instinct as old as human history and is mirrored in the behavior of animals. As humans evolved, so too did a variety of beliefs in what maintained life and the events or forces that could damage it. Many healing remedies that involved plants were selected by observation, inspiration, and experience, and skilled healers became highly valued members of tribes of all races.

CHINESE HERBALISM

Underlying Chinese herbalism is the Taoist philosophy, in which all phenomena result from the interplay of yin (feminine, cool, moist) and yang (masculine, hot, dry) as they create a spiral of continuous change. So early Taoists tasted each herb to feel its yin or yang effect, and linked each with a season, taste, emotion, and element (fire, water, wood, earth, or metal) to symbolize its way of creating change in the body. Taoists sensed three types of body energy: Jing – inherited instinct and growth, nurtured by food and herbs; Qi (Chi) – the life force in all things, adjusted through acupuncture and herbs; and Shen, which gives higher consciousness by meditation. All three energies are considered in the Chinese holistic approach to diagnosis. An herb is seldom used alone as a treatment but is combined with others to reinforce its action and to counter side effects.

DANG SHEN
Codonopsis pilosula *is a tonic, detoxifying, yin herb, one of 2,000 Chinese herbs tested over 4,500 years.*

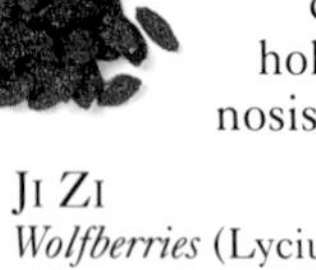

JI ZI
Wolfberries (Lycium chinense) *are a kidney tonic linked to the element earth.*

AYURVEDA

SANDALWOOD
It strengthens the brow chakra and cleanses and cools the blood.

Ayurveda, "the science of living," is an ancient Hindu healing system involving meditation, yoga, and about 500 herbs. Ayurvedics see three forces interacting with body systems: agni (fire), prana (breath), and soma (love). Ayurvedics believe that imbalance causes illness, so they use herbs to rebalance the whole system as well as to treat specific symptoms. Ayurveda links bodily energy with the energy of the universe through the chakras – seven points along the spine, each with specific associations. For example, the golden crown chakra is linked to the brain and pineal gland and is balanced with brain tonic herbs.

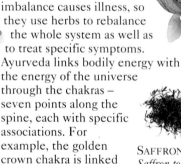

SAFFRON
Saffron tones the heart chakra and benefits both heart and skin.

NATIVE TRIBES OF THE AMERICAS

Each tribe uses local plants for healing, under the guidance of the shaman, or medicine man. He is taught to "listen" to the plants as teachers, and to divine cures using medicine wheel plant totems and incense. Saunalike sweat lodges are used for physical and mental purification.

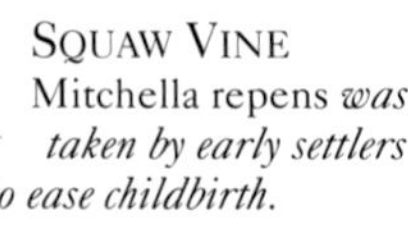

SQUAW VINE
Mitchella repens *was taken by early settlers to ease childbirth.*

Western Herbalism

Garlic
A daily ration for pyramid builders maintained their stamina.

Western herbal systems evolved from 3,000 BC in Sumer, Crete, Egypt, and Greece. In Greece, in 1,300 BC, Asklepios developed healing centers combining his diagnostic skills and unrivaled knowledge of herbs with music and sports. Asklepians became a noble order of healers and included Hippocrates, who emphasized self-healing. About AD 175, Galen codified Greek ideas of the four elements: earth, water, fire, and air, relating them to four humors and personality types. These formed the basis of European herbalism and Pakistani Unani medicine. The Roman "mechanistic" view took over from ancient Greek "holistic" ideas and dominated science until recently.

Mandrake
Poisonous, man-shaped, narcotic root, as used by Lucrezia Borgia.

Homeopathic Remedies

A recent interpretation of new physics principles suggests that all things, from light waves to plants and humans, are composed of patterns of energy. This may explain how homeopathy works: minute doses of plants, repeatedly diluted in alcohol, are given as treatment. In the most "potent" doses almost nothing of the plant remains, but as the remedies often work, one theory is that the plant's pattern of energy has left a kind of "echo" in the alcohol. A holistic approach is taken, considering physical and emotional symptoms and using plants that cause similar symptoms to stimulate the body's defenses. This is called "treating like with like."

Arnica
This immunostimulant is used in homeopathy to reduce bruises and jet lag.

The Bach, Californian, and Australian Flower Remedies, which come from wild plants, are prescribed to heal inharmonious states of mind.

Herbal Preparations

Herbal remedies require various preparation methods. Infusions are the most common (see p.25), but compresses, poultices, syrups, and powders can all be made at home, as well as decoctions, ointments, and tinctures. A standard infusion or decoction dose is 1 tsp (5 ml) of dried herb or a fresh sprig of 6–9 leaves to 1 cup (225 ml) of water.

Decoction
Bruise the root, bark, or seed; put in a pan of cold water; cover. Bring to boil; simmer until reduced to ¼ of the volume; strain.

Ointment
Melt 10 oz (250 g) petroleum jelly; add 1 oz (30 g) dried or 3 oz (90 g) fresh herbs. Simmer for up to 2 hours; strain.

Tincture
Put 4 oz (100 g) dried or 10 oz (250 g) fresh herbs in jar; add 1¼ pt (500 ml) of 60° proof alcohol. Stand for two weeks; strain.

Medicinal Meals

The Chinese have long recognized the therapeutic value of herbs and food combined. A Chinese medicinal meal is designed to rebalance conditions that cause illness, using cooling yin foods, such as Barley or Cucumber, or warming yang foods, such as Ginger or Red Pepper. Fat-reducing preparations include Dates, Oats, Mung Beans, and Lotus. Celery, Lotus seeds, Haws, and Parsley are used to slow the aging process. The ingredients shown here are for a tonic soup to build Qi and Jing, detoxify the blood, and tone the organs.

Lycium chinense

Dioscorea opposita

Astragalus membranaceus

Dimocarpus longan

Codonopsis lanceolata

Cordyceps sinensis

Modern Herbalism

Herbs offer hope for cures for modern diseases. Alkaloids that inhibit HIV have been discovered in Australia's Moreton Bay Chestnut (see p.43), Amazon Alexa trees, and Hogweed (see p.176). Diseases such as malaria, which are now resistant to some synthetic drugs, have been found to respond to treatment with traditional herb cures. The number of herbs believed to combat cancer grows daily – Suma (*Pfaffia paniculata*), the so-called "Amazon Ginseng," is now a patented cancer treatment – and more people are using tonics like the Chinese Sweet Tea Vine (*Gynostemma pentaphyllum*) to boost energy levels and strengthen the immune system.

The demand for accurate information about new herbal products is growing. In Europe, the scientific evaluation of 200 herbs now taking place will enable their medicinal actions to be legally quoted on packaging.

Poria Cocos
This fungus is given in fat-reducing meals in China. It also inhibits cancer cells.

False Indigo
A North American herb with indigo flowers and an antiseptic root, Baptista australis *is under research as a potential immune system booster.*

leaflets stimulate the appetite and aid digestion

Herba Sargassum
Sargassum fusiforme *is one of 300 Chinese antitumor herbs.*

Iceland Moss
The lichen Cetraria islandica *gives a brown dye and helps to fight tuberculosis.*

Astragalus Root
Astragalus membranaceus *boosts the immune system and generates anticancer cells in the body.*

HERBS FOR OTHER USES

HERBS TOUCH OUR DAILY LIVES in many ways, from the Mint in our morning toothpaste to the Cotton in our bed sheets. The herb plants in this book are described chiefly in terms of their culinary and medicinal virtues, but there are many more exotic and unusual ways to use plants. Some uses are widespread, others specific to certain countries or areas.

VEGETABLE IVORY
The seeds of Hyphaene benguellensis *replace ivory for carving and buttons.*

LOCAL SECRETS

Each culture discovers its own cosmetic plants. In Peru, dried Rhatany root (*Krameria triandra*) is used as a gum-tightening toothpaste that removes tartar and preserves teeth. The dried leaves of the South American shrub Jaborandi (*Pilocarpus jaborandi*) are used as a powerful but potentially hazardous hair tonic that opens skin pores to combat premature baldness. Sweet-scented carnauba wax from the leaf buds of *Copernicia* species is an ingredient in hair creams and mascaras. Plants are also used in many cultures to decorate and color the body. In Peru, the sap of the Genipa tree (*Genipa americana*) yields a blue body paint.

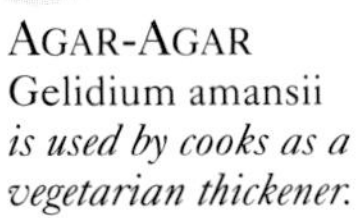

AGAR-AGAR
Gelidium amansii *is used by cooks as a vegetarian thickener.*

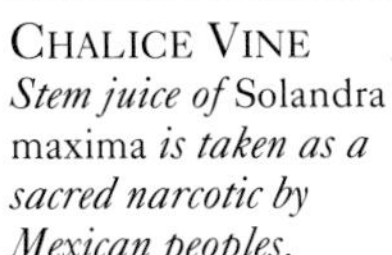

DAMIANA
The aromatic leaf of Turnera aphrodisiaca *is a flavoring, tonic, and aphrodisiac.*

CHALICE VINE
Stem juice of Solandra maxima *is taken as a sacred narcotic by Mexican peoples.*

◁ HENNA
Lawsonia inermis *is used for bridal hand-painting in India.*

MACADAMIA ▽
Macadamia integrifolia *nuts give supple skin.*

Plant aphrodisiacs often appear in the form of energizing herb tonics, such as the bark of Belize's Tree of Togetherness (*Anemopaegma arvense*). In the southern USA, Saw Palmetto (*Serenoa repens*) berries go into love potions with the root of Sweet Anise (*Osmorhiza occidentalis*), and in Ghana, the aphrodisiac leaf of Flakwa (*Vernonia conferta*) is added to palm wine.

TATOO PLANT
Eclipta prostrata *leaf juice makes an indigo skin dye.*

HERBAL PEST CONTROL

Some toxic herbs are used to stun fish for easy catching – with no ill effects when eaten. A few, such as certain *Derris* species, may also be used as organic insecticides. Fish Poison Plant (*Tephrosia vogelii*) has cleared the Bilharzia water snail from Africa's Lake Malawi.

DEVIL'S TOBACCO
The toxic leaves of Lobelia tupa *are smoked in the Andes as a hallucinogenic intoxicant.*

HERB GARDENS

THE CHARM and attraction of herbs are magnified in an herb garden. Herbs will bring grace, fragrance, and flavor to almost every site: herbaceous borders, alpine and wild gardens, conservatories, patios, and interiors. Certain plants grow particularly well alongside others; when they are planted together deliberately this is known as companion planting, and often herbs make suitable companion plants. Many gardeners believe that pungent herbs deter pests as a result of their strong aroma. Some believe that Chamomile exudes a tonic for its neighbors. Other herbs are thought to discourage weeds.

PRIVATE AND PUBLIC GARDENS

A separate site, where herbs can grow together in profusion, is often desirable for a private garden. It should be located to receive maximum sunlight (this brings out leaf and flower scents) and enclosed to focus attention on the sensory pleasures and enhance the feeling of a special space.

A disciplined, geometric path design is a perfect complement to the "cottage-garden" abundance of herbs, giving a strong pattern in winter and making herb-gathering easier in bad weather. Most herbs are adaptable and easy to grow, flourishing even in confined locations such as patio pots, hanging baskets, and window boxes.

Public herb gardens offer great potential benefit for local communities. The fragrance and soft textures of herbs delight the blind. The subtle shades of silver and pink flowers and foliage, and

◁ HERB POTS
Pots allow you to move aromatic herbs into sunlight or to bring half-hardy and tender plants indoors during cold spells. The soil will drain well, an essential growing condition for many species.

SECRET GARDEN ▷
An enclosed herb garden lures you into its peaceful space, creating a feeling of seclusion and encouraging a closer knowledge of each plant.

◁ AUTHOR'S GARDEN
A Yew hedge gives shelter to a traditional herb garden with a Rose arbor, Sage, Rosemary, and Bay growing in the foreground. There are scarlet Bergamot, Lilies, and yellow Foxgloves beyond.

◁ DECORATIVE HERBS ▷
A basket (see left) offers sharp drainage conditions in which this group of Thyme, Tarragon, Sage, and Savory flourish. A cartwheel (see right) is an attractive and practical means of displaying herbs. Here, a range of low thymes allow the spokes of the wheel to remain visible.

soothing aromas, can be a tonic to the stressed.

Many herbs are grown in places of worship, as they have sacred associations and aid contemplation and meditation. Schools, hospitals, and prisons could all benefit from their enriching influence.

PLANT PHARMACIES

Herb gardens in the past were frequently used as community chemists. From as early as AD 529, Europe's first monastery at Monte Cassino in Italy became a center for herb growing and first aid. In the 9th century, the usefulness of St. Gall's herb garden in Switzerland so impressed Holy Roman Emperor Charlemagne that he ordered duplicates to be built across his empire. In Asia, in AD 657, a Tang dynasty emperor commissioned botanical details and information on how to grow and use 844 medicinal herbs from all over China. This information was printed and distributed to every town, with orders to grow herbs for the local people. A similar system still exists in Vietnamese villages today. The abbey gardens of Bury St. Edmunds in England supplied plants to pharmacists from the 7th century until 1950. Many botanic gardens, such as two of Europe's first at Padua and Pisa in Italy, began life as herb gardens. Koishikawa, the oldest botanic garden in Tokyo, Japan, was planted as a physic garden to reduce the need for medicinal imports from China.

The plant labels used by many botanic gardens today list uses, and are a testimony to the role of these ancient herb gardens.

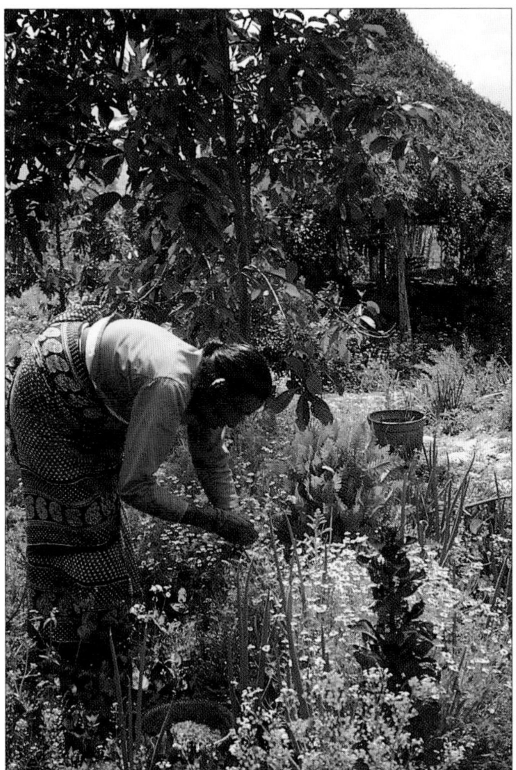

◁ NEPALESE HERB GARDEN
In this garden, Nepalese entomologist Kaminee Vaidya conducts organic pest control experiments. She uses different methods of companion planting based on a combination of Ayurvedic ideas (see p.26) and scientific theories.

TREES

Family PINACEAE	Species *Abies balsamea*	Local name Canada Balsam

BALSAM FIR

The 50 species of *Abies* are tall, evergreen conifers named from the Latin *abire*, to rise up. Balsam Fir has aromatic needles, scented purple cones, and bark covered in bubbles of valuable resin.

• **USES** The liquid resin taken from bark incisions is known variously as balm of Gilead, Canada turpentine, and, more recently, Canada balsam. It is one of the best gargles for sore throats. The resin is a treatment for sinus congestion and is applied as a poultice to help arthritis, cuts, and bruises. It has also been used to mount slide specimens and to make fine lacquer. Balsam gum is chewed. The resinous needles, cones, and winter buds are used to scent potpourri.

• **REMARK** *Abies alba* bark resin is distilled to make Strassburg turpentine. The buds and leaves are distilled to make the expectorant and antiseptic Silver Pine needle oil, which is used in cough drops and asthma inhalations, and to give pine scent to toiletries.

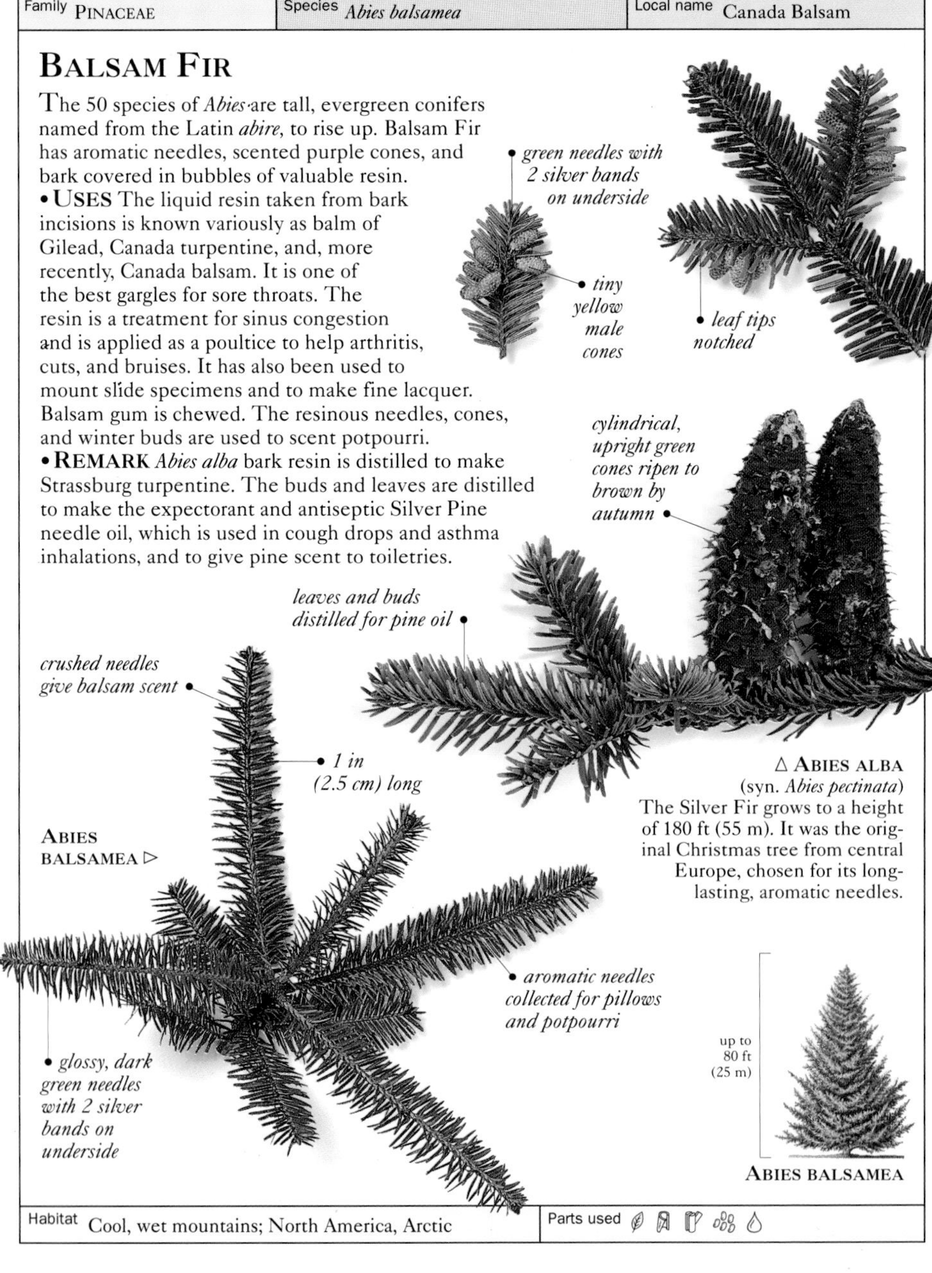
green needles with 2 silver bands on underside
tiny yellow male cones
leaf tips notched
cylindrical, upright green cones ripen to brown by autumn
leaves and buds distilled for pine oil
crushed needles give balsam scent
1 in (2.5 cm) long
aromatic needles collected for pillows and potpourri
glossy, dark green needles with 2 silver bands on underside
up to 80 ft (25 m)

ABIES BALSAMEA ▷

△ ABIES ALBA (syn. *Abies pectinata*)
The Silver Fir grows to a height of 180 ft (55 m). It was the original Christmas tree from central Europe, chosen for its long-lasting, aromatic needles.

ABIES BALSAMEA

Habitat Cool, wet mountains; North America, Arctic	Parts used

Family ACERACEAE	Species *Acer saccharum*	Local name Rock Maple

SUGAR MAPLE

The Latin word *acer* means hard or sharp and refers to the timber taken from this deciduous tree. The Sugar Maple has light gray bark, greenish yellow spring flowers, and winged autumn fruits.

• **USES** The sap, taken from the first spring flow until buds swell, can be drunk fresh, fermented for mild vinegar, or boiled and reduced to produce the sweetest of all maple syrups. The seeds are edible after removing the wings, soaking, boiling, and roasting. Flour from the inner bark was once used by Native Americans.

• **REMARK** The famous autumn leaf color is a popular tourist attraction in eastern Canada and New England.

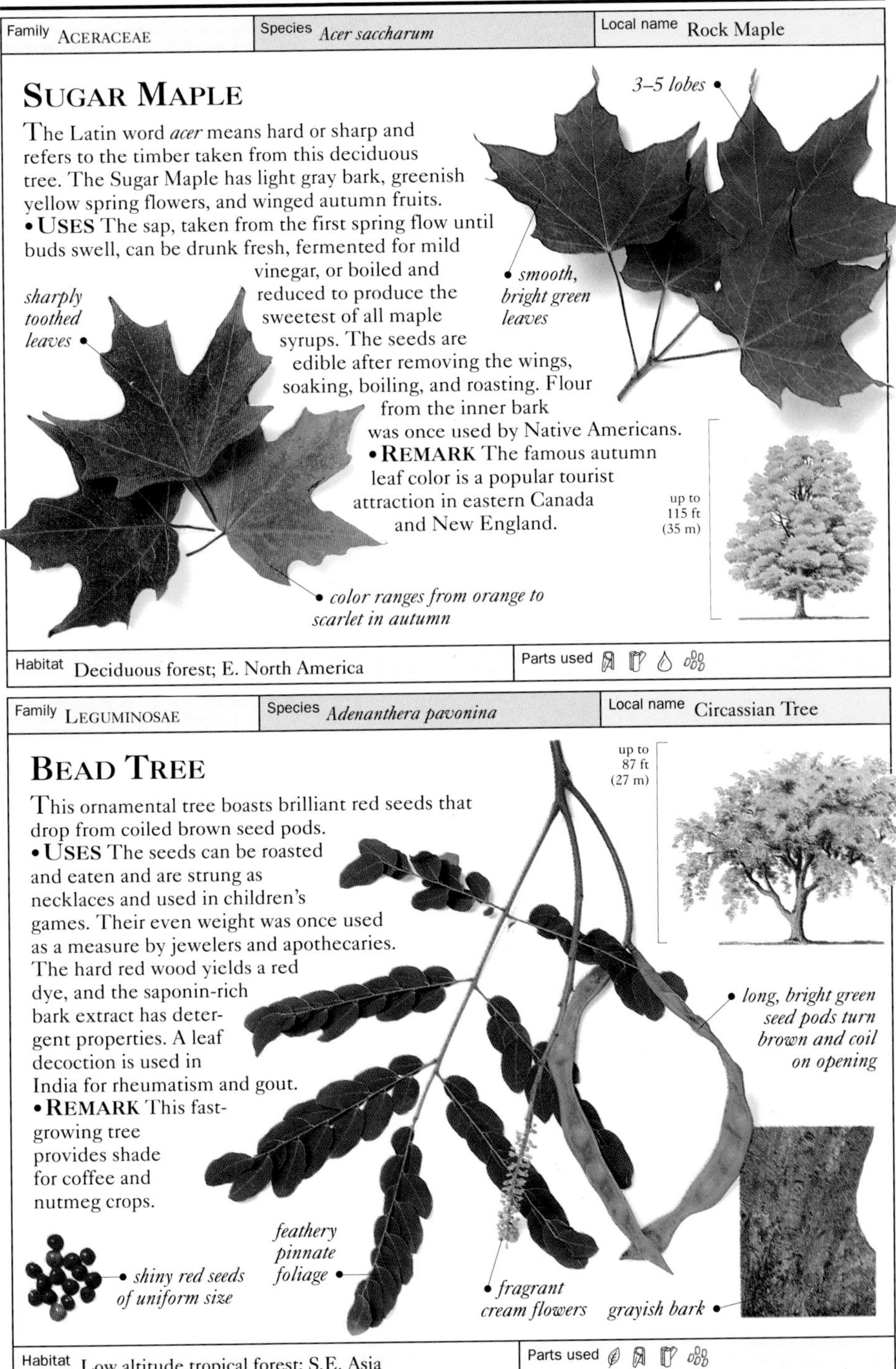
3–5 lobes
smooth, bright green leaves
sharply toothed leaves
color ranges from orange to scarlet in autumn
up to 115 ft (35 m)
up to 87 ft (27 m)
long, bright green seed pods turn brown and coil on opening
shiny red seeds of uniform size
feathery pinnate foliage
fragrant cream flowers
grayish bark

Habitat Deciduous forest; E. North America	Parts used

Family LEGUMINOSAE	Species *Adenanthera pavonina*	Local name Circassian Tree

BEAD TREE

This ornamental tree boasts brilliant red seeds that drop from coiled brown seed pods.

• **USES** The seeds can be roasted and eaten and are strung as necklaces and used in children's games. Their even weight was once used as a measure by jewelers and apothecaries. The hard red wood yields a red dye, and the saponin-rich bark extract has detergent properties. A leaf decoction is used in India for rheumatism and gout.

• **REMARK** This fast-growing tree provides shade for coffee and nutmeg crops.

Habitat Low altitude tropical forest; S.E. Asia	Parts used

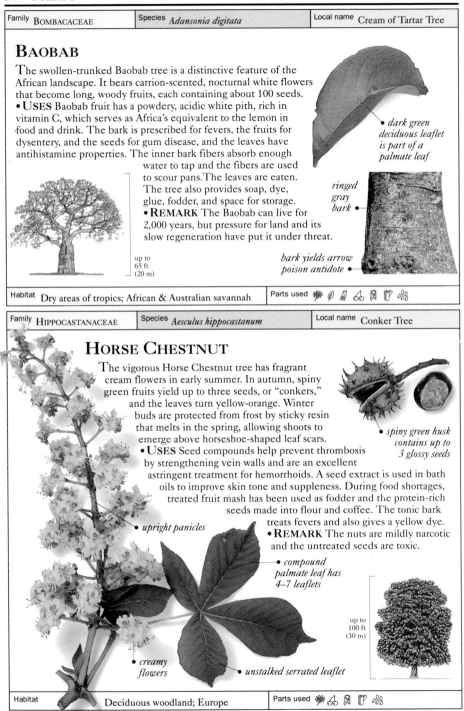

Family BOMBACACEAE | Species *Adansonia digitata* | Local name Cream of Tartar Tree

BAOBAB

The swollen-trunked Baobab tree is a distinctive feature of the African landscape. It bears carrion-scented, nocturnal white flowers that become long, woody fruits, each containing about 100 seeds. • **USES** Baobab fruit has a powdery, acidic white pith, rich in vitamin C, which serves as Africa's equivalent to the lemon in food and drink. The bark is prescribed for fevers, the fruits for dysentery, and the seeds for gum disease, and the leaves have antihistamine properties. The inner bark fibers absorb enough water to tap and the fibers are used to scour pans.The leaves are eaten. The tree also provides soap, dye, glue, fodder, and space for storage. • **REMARK** The Baobab can live for 2,000 years, but pressure for land and its slow regeneration have put it under threat.

• *dark green deciduous leaflet is part of a palmate leaf*

ringed gray bark •

bark yields arrow poison antidote •

up to 65 ft (20 m)

Habitat Dry areas of tropics; African & Australian savannah | Parts used

Family HIPPOCASTANACEAE | Species *Aesculus hippocastanum* | Local name Conker Tree

HORSE CHESTNUT

The vigorous Horse Chestnut tree has fragrant cream flowers in early summer. In autumn, spiny green fruits yield up to three seeds, or "conkers," and the leaves turn yellow-orange. Winter buds are protected from frost by sticky resin that melts in the spring, allowing shoots to emerge above horseshoe-shaped leaf scars. • **USES** Seed compounds help prevent thrombosis by strengthening vein walls and are an excellent astringent treatment for hemorrhoids. A seed extract is used in bath oils to improve skin tone and suppleness. During food shortages, treated fruit mash has been used as fodder and the protein-rich seeds made into flour and coffee. The tonic bark treats fevers and also gives a yellow dye. • **REMARK** The nuts are mildly narcotic and the untreated seeds are toxic.

• *spiny green husk contains up to 3 glossy seeds*

• *upright panicles*

• *compound palmate leaf has 4–7 leaflets*

up to 100 ft (30 m)

• *creamy flowers*

• *unstalked serrated leaflet*

Habitat Deciduous woodland; Europe | Parts used

Family EUPHORBIACEAE | Species *Aleurites moluccana* | Local name Kemiri / Buah Keras

CANDLENUT TREE

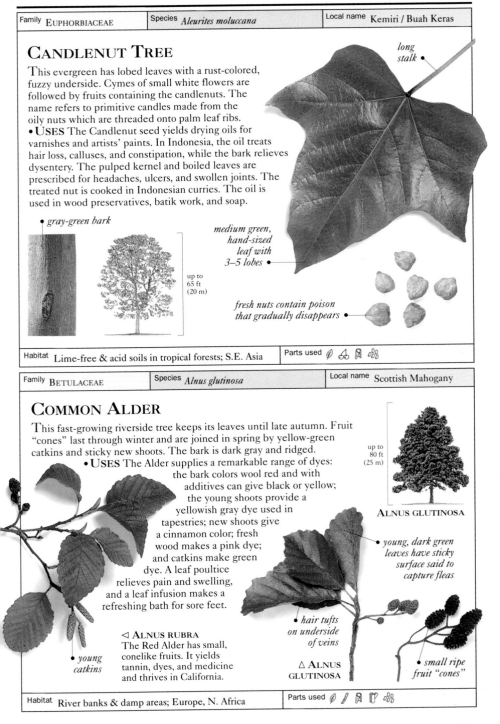

This evergreen has lobed leaves with a rust-colored, fuzzy underside. Cymes of small white flowers are followed by fruits containing the candlenuts. The name refers to primitive candles made from the oily nuts which are threaded onto palm leaf ribs.

• **USES** The Candlenut seed yields drying oils for varnishes and artists' paints. In Indonesia, the oil treats hair loss, calluses, and constipation, while the bark relieves dysentery. The pulped kernel and boiled leaves are prescribed for headaches, ulcers, and swollen joints. The treated nut is cooked in Indonesian curries. The oil is used in wood preservatives, batik work, and soap.

long stalk

medium green, hand-sized leaf with 3–5 lobes

gray-green bark

up to 65 ft (20 m)

fresh nuts contain poison that gradually disappears

Habitat Lime-free & acid soils in tropical forests; S.E. Asia | Parts used

Family BETULACEAE | Species *Alnus glutinosa* | Local name Scottish Mahogany

COMMON ALDER

This fast-growing riverside tree keeps its leaves until late autumn. Fruit "cones" last through winter and are joined in spring by yellow-green catkins and sticky new shoots. The bark is dark gray and ridged.

• **USES** The Alder supplies a remarkable range of dyes: the bark colors wool red and with additives can give black or yellow; the young shoots provide a yellowish gray dye used in tapestries; new shoots give a cinnamon color; fresh wood makes a pink dye; and catkins make green dye. A leaf poultice relieves pain and swelling, and a leaf infusion makes a refreshing bath for sore feet.

up to 80 ft (25 m)

ALNUS GLUTINOSA

young, dark green leaves have sticky surface said to capture fleas

young catkins

◁ ALNUS RUBRA
The Red Alder has small, conelike fruits. It yields tannin, dyes, and medicine and thrives in California.

hair tufts on underside of veins

△ ALNUS GLUTINOSA

small ripe fruit "cones"

Habitat River banks & damp areas; Europe, N. Africa | Parts used

Family ANACARDIACEAE | Species *Anacardium occidentale* | Local name Cajugaha

CASHEW

This evergreen shade tree sports continuous panicles of scented, pale green-striped, rose-pink flowers followed by fleshy, swollen stems or "apples," with a protruding, kidney-shaped fruit containing the nut.
• **USES** The nutritious nuts are used in Asian cookery, and young shoots, leaves, and buds are eaten raw. The brewed "apple" makes alcoholic *cajuado*. The leaf, flower, bark, and oil from the poisonous nut shell are used medicinally. The oil is caustic and causes dermatitis but is used (with risk) to remove old skin, corns, and ringworm. The fruit juice yields indelible ink and tribal paints.

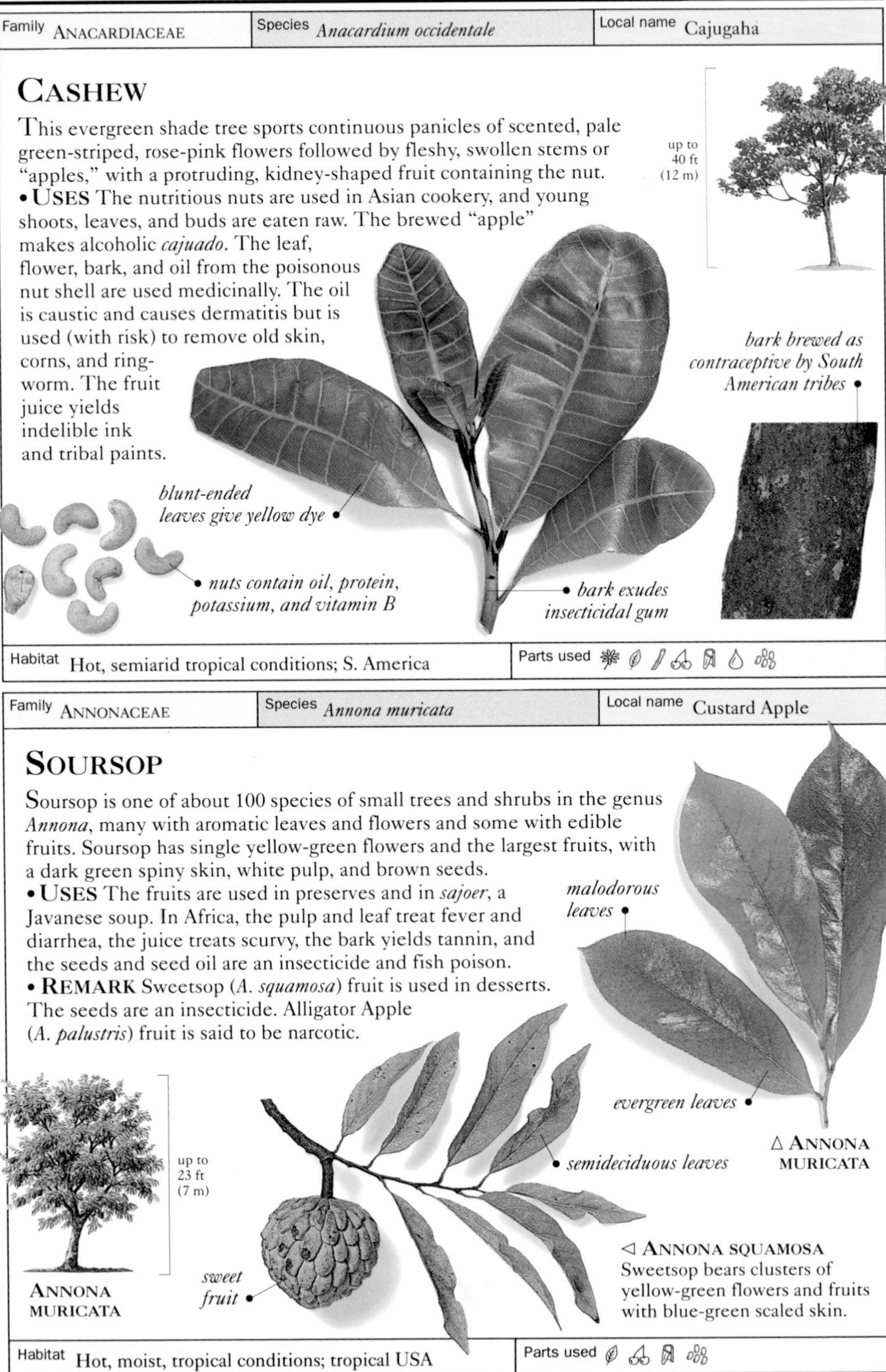
up to
40 ft
(12 m)
bark brewed as contraceptive by South American tribes
blunt-ended leaves give yellow dye
nuts contain oil, protein, potassium, and vitamin B
bark exudes insecticidal gum
malodorous leaves
evergreen leaves
semideciduous leaves
up to
23 ft
(7 m)
sweet fruit

Habitat Hot, semiarid tropical conditions; S. America | Parts used

Family ANNONACEAE | Species *Annona muricata* | Local name Custard Apple

SOURSOP

Soursop is one of about 100 species of small trees and shrubs in the genus *Annona*, many with aromatic leaves and flowers and some with edible fruits. Soursop has single yellow-green flowers and the largest fruits, with a dark green spiny skin, white pulp, and brown seeds.
• **USES** The fruits are used in preserves and in *sajoer*, a Javanese soup. In Africa, the pulp and leaf treat fever and diarrhea, the juice treats scurvy, the bark yields tannin, and the seeds and seed oil are an insecticide and fish poison.
• **REMARK** Sweetsop (*A. squamosa*) fruit is used in desserts. The seeds are an insecticide. Alligator Apple (*A. palustris*) fruit is said to be narcotic.

△ ANNONA MURICATA

ANNONA MURICATA

◁ ANNONA SQUAMOSA Sweetsop bears clusters of yellow-green flowers and fruits with blue-green scaled skin.

Habitat Hot, moist, tropical conditions; tropical USA | Parts used

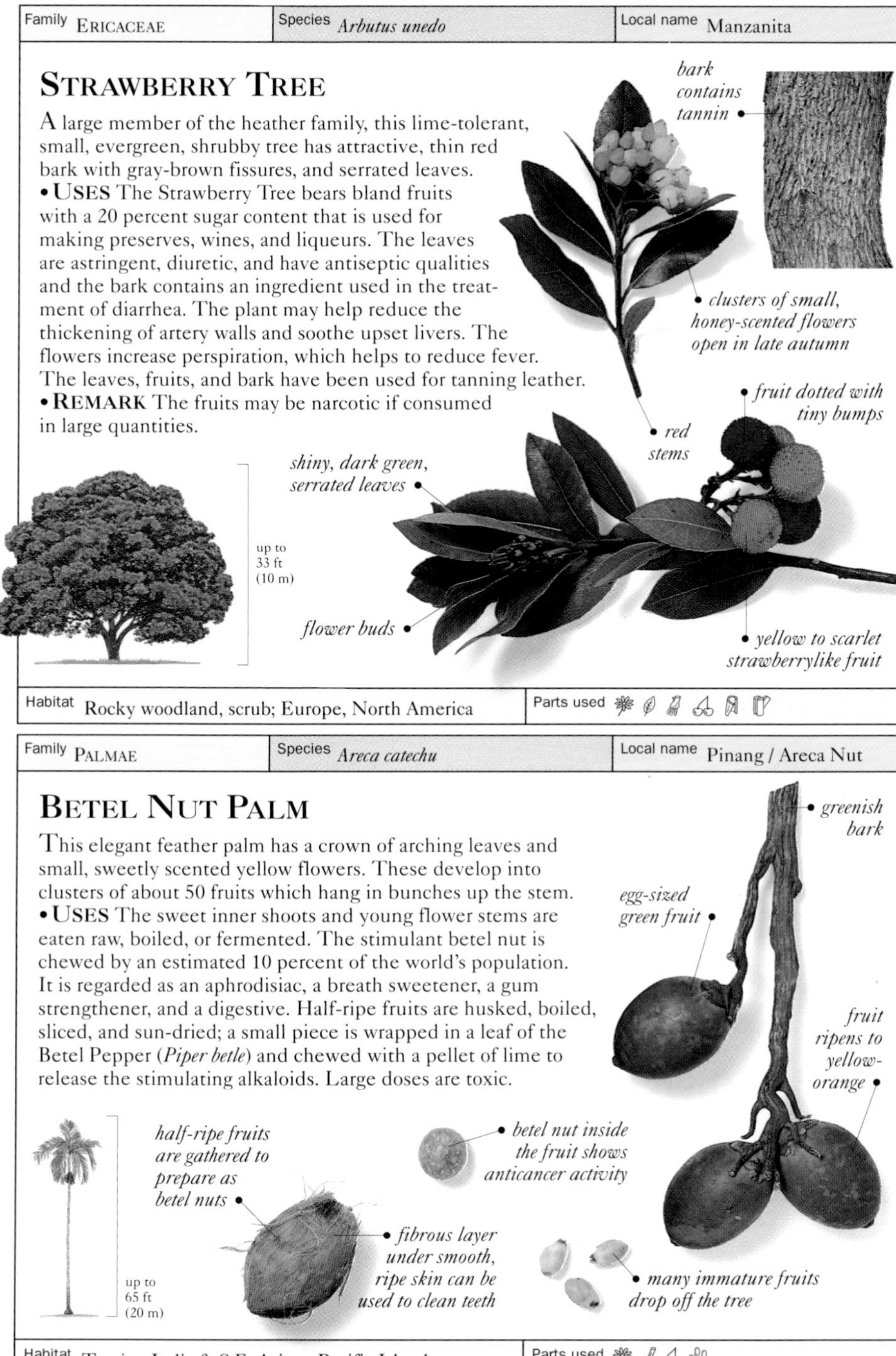
bark contains tannin
clusters of small, honey-scented flowers open in late autumn
fruit dotted with tiny bumps
red stems
shiny, dark green, serrated leaves
up to 33 ft (10 m)
flower buds
yellow to scarlet strawberrylike fruit
greenish bark
egg-sized green fruit
fruit ripens to yellow-orange
half-ripe fruits are gathered to prepare as betel nuts
betel nut inside the fruit shows anticancer activity
fibrous layer under smooth, ripe skin can be used to clean teeth
many immature fruits drop off the tree
up to 65 ft (20 m)

Family ERICACEAE	Species *Arbutus unedo*	Local name Manzanita

STRAWBERRY TREE

A large member of the heather family, this lime-tolerant, small, evergreen, shrubby tree has attractive, thin red bark with gray-brown fissures, and serrated leaves.

• **USES** The Strawberry Tree bears bland fruits with a 20 percent sugar content that is used for making preserves, wines, and liqueurs. The leaves are astringent, diuretic, and have antiseptic qualities and the bark contains an ingredient used in the treatment of diarrhea. The plant may help reduce the thickening of artery walls and soothe upset livers. The flowers increase perspiration, which helps to reduce fever. The leaves, fruits, and bark have been used for tanning leather.

• **REMARK** The fruits may be narcotic if consumed in large quantities.

Habitat Rocky woodland, scrub; Europe, North America	Parts used

Family PALMAE	Species *Areca catechu*	Local name Pinang / Areca Nut

BETEL NUT PALM

This elegant feather palm has a crown of arching leaves and small, sweetly scented yellow flowers. These develop into clusters of about 50 fruits which hang in bunches up the stem.

• **USES** The sweet inner shoots and young flower stems are eaten raw, boiled, or fermented. The stimulant betel nut is chewed by an estimated 10 percent of the world's population. It is regarded as an aphrodisiac, a breath sweetener, a gum strengthener, and a digestive. Half-ripe fruits are husked, boiled, sliced, and sun-dried; a small piece is wrapped in a leaf of the Betel Pepper (*Piper betle*) and chewed with a pellet of lime to release the stimulating alkaloids. Large doses are toxic.

Habitat Tropics; India & S.E. Asia to Pacific Islands	Parts used

Family PALMAE	Species *Arenga pinnata*	Local name Gomuti Palm

SUGAR PALM

The Sugar Palm is crowned with a spray of feathery leaves. The ringed trunk is clothed with the fibrous black sheaths of old leaves.

• **USES** Palm sugar is produced by tapping the tree's sap. The sap is collected and evaporated to a thick syrup that cools to a toffeelike sugar. The stem pith is used as a starchy food thickener. Juice from the developing flower is fermented into palm wine, or "toddy," which is used medicinally to treat menstrual disorders and vertigo, or distilled to make the liqueur *arrack*. The root is used in local medicine to treat kidney stones. The young leaf sheaths produce useful fibers and the trunks are made into water pipes.

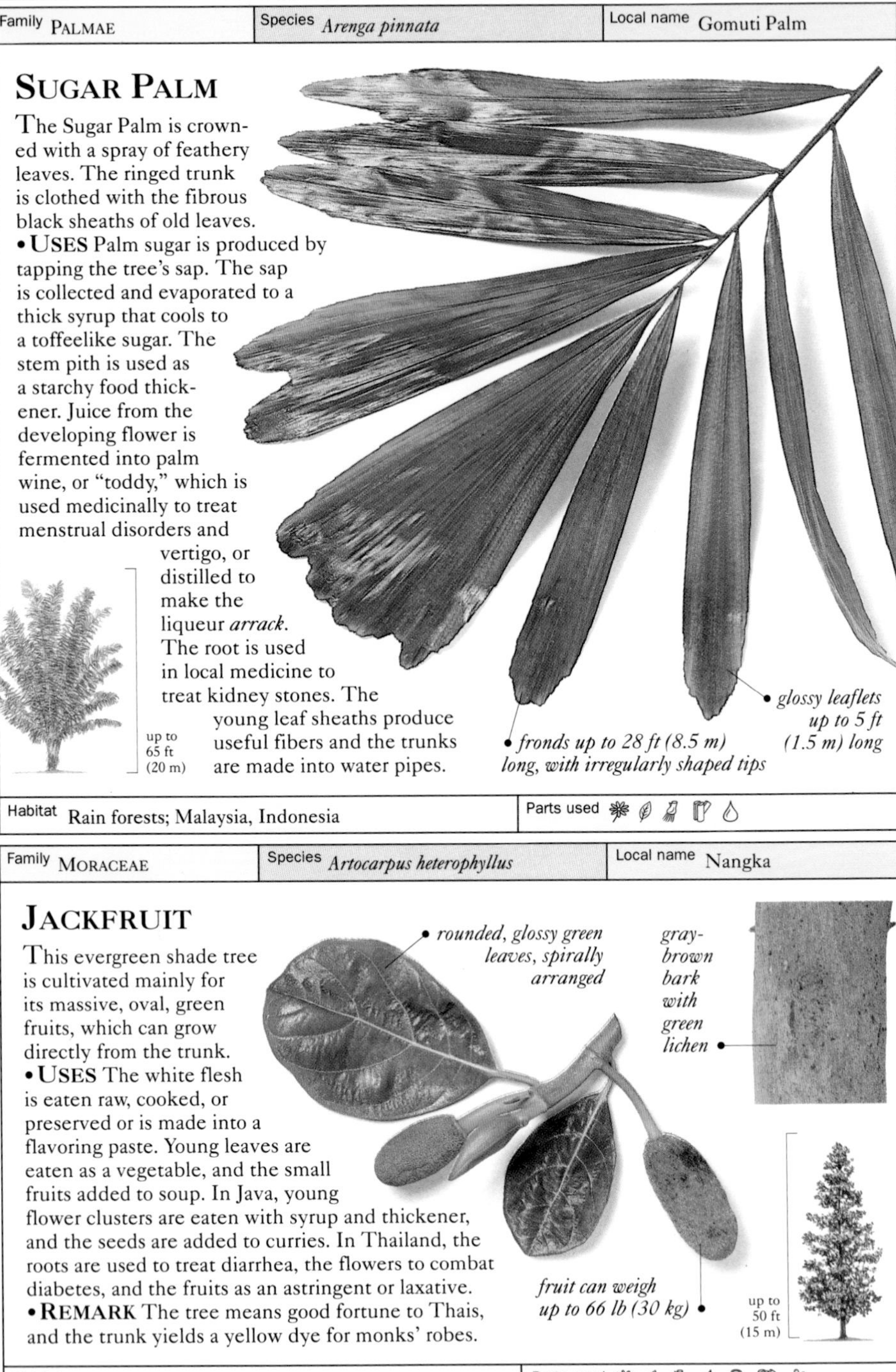

up to 65 ft (20 m)
fronds up to 28 ft (8.5 m) long, with irregularly shaped tips
glossy leaflets up to 5 ft (1.5 m) long
rounded, glossy green leaves, spirally arranged
gray-brown bark with green lichen
fruit can weigh up to 66 lb (30 kg)
up to 50 ft (15 m)

Habitat Rain forests; Malaysia, Indonesia	Parts used

Family MORACEAE	Species *Artocarpus heterophyllus*	Local name Nangka

JACKFRUIT

This evergreen shade tree is cultivated mainly for its massive, oval, green fruits, which can grow directly from the trunk.

• **USES** The white flesh is eaten raw, cooked, or preserved or is made into a flavoring paste. Young leaves are eaten as a vegetable, and the small fruits added to soup. In Java, young flower clusters are eaten with syrup and thickener, and the seeds are added to curries. In Thailand, the roots are used to treat diarrhea, the flowers to combat diabetes, and the fruits as an astringent or laxative.

• **REMARK** The tree means good fortune to Thais, and the trunk yields a yellow dye for monks' robes.

Habitat Tropical forests & river banks; S.E. Asia	Parts used

Family OXALIDACEAE	Species *Averrhoa carambola*	Local name Carambola

STAR FRUIT

This dense, symmetrical tree is widely cultivated in the tropics for its attractive, edible fruits.

• **USES** The fruits have a spicy, quincelike aroma and are efficient thirst quenchers. They are enjoyed raw, and in Asia, are often eaten with salt, served in salads, or used to flavor jam, drinks, and candies. In Thailand, they are given to reduce blood sugar levels in diabetics, and in Indonesia, for hypertension, gingivitis, and acne. The flowers are used locally for coughs, and the leaves are prescribed for rheumatism.

• **REMARK** *Averrhoa bilimbi*, the Bilimbi or Cucumber Tree, has yellow acidic fruits about 2¼ in (7 cm) long, popular in pickles, jams, and drinks.

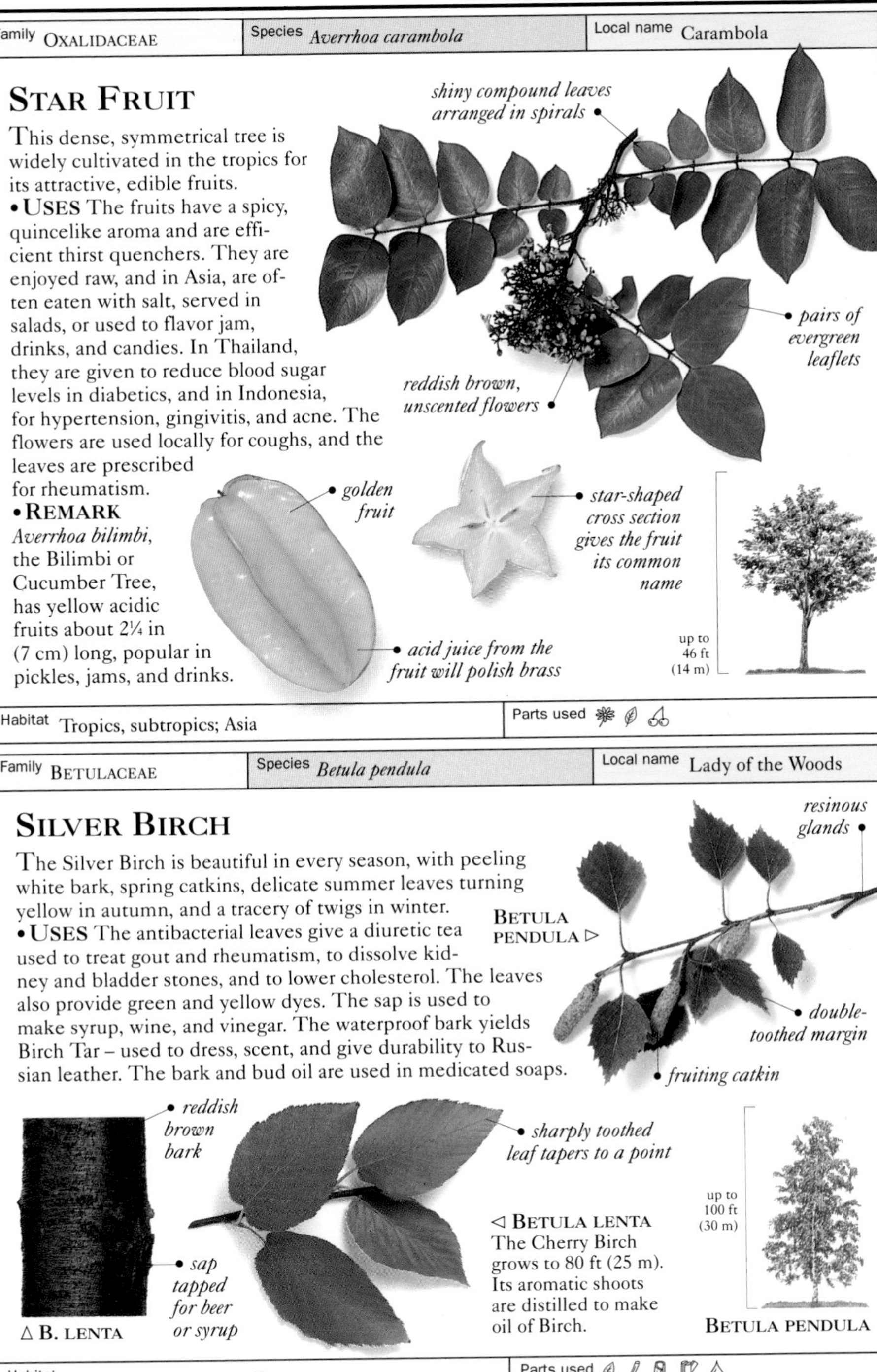
shiny compound leaves arranged in spirals
pairs of evergreen leaflets
reddish brown, unscented flowers
golden fruit
star-shaped cross section gives the fruit its common name
acid juice from the fruit will polish brass
up to 46 ft (14 m)
resinous glands
BETULA PENDULA ▷
double-toothed margin
fruiting catkin
reddish brown bark
sharply toothed leaf tapers to a point
sap tapped for beer or syrup
up to 100 ft (30 m)

Habitat Tropics, subtropics; Asia	Parts used

Family BETULACEAE	Species *Betula pendula*	Local name Lady of the Woods

SILVER BIRCH

The Silver Birch is beautiful in every season, with peeling white bark, spring catkins, delicate summer leaves turning yellow in autumn, and a tracery of twigs in winter.

• **USES** The antibacterial leaves give a diuretic tea used to treat gout and rheumatism, to dissolve kidney and bladder stones, and to lower cholesterol. The leaves also provide green and yellow dyes. The sap is used to make syrup, wine, and vinegar. The waterproof bark yields Birch Tar – used to dress, scent, and give durability to Russian leather. The bark and bud oil are used in medicated soaps.

△ B. LENTA

◁ BETULA LENTA The Cherry Birch grows to 80 ft (25 m). Its aromatic shoots are distilled to make oil of Birch.

BETULA PENDULA

Habitat Young woods; N. Asia, Europe	Parts used

Family BIXACAE	Species *Bixa orellana*	Local name Annatto or Urucú

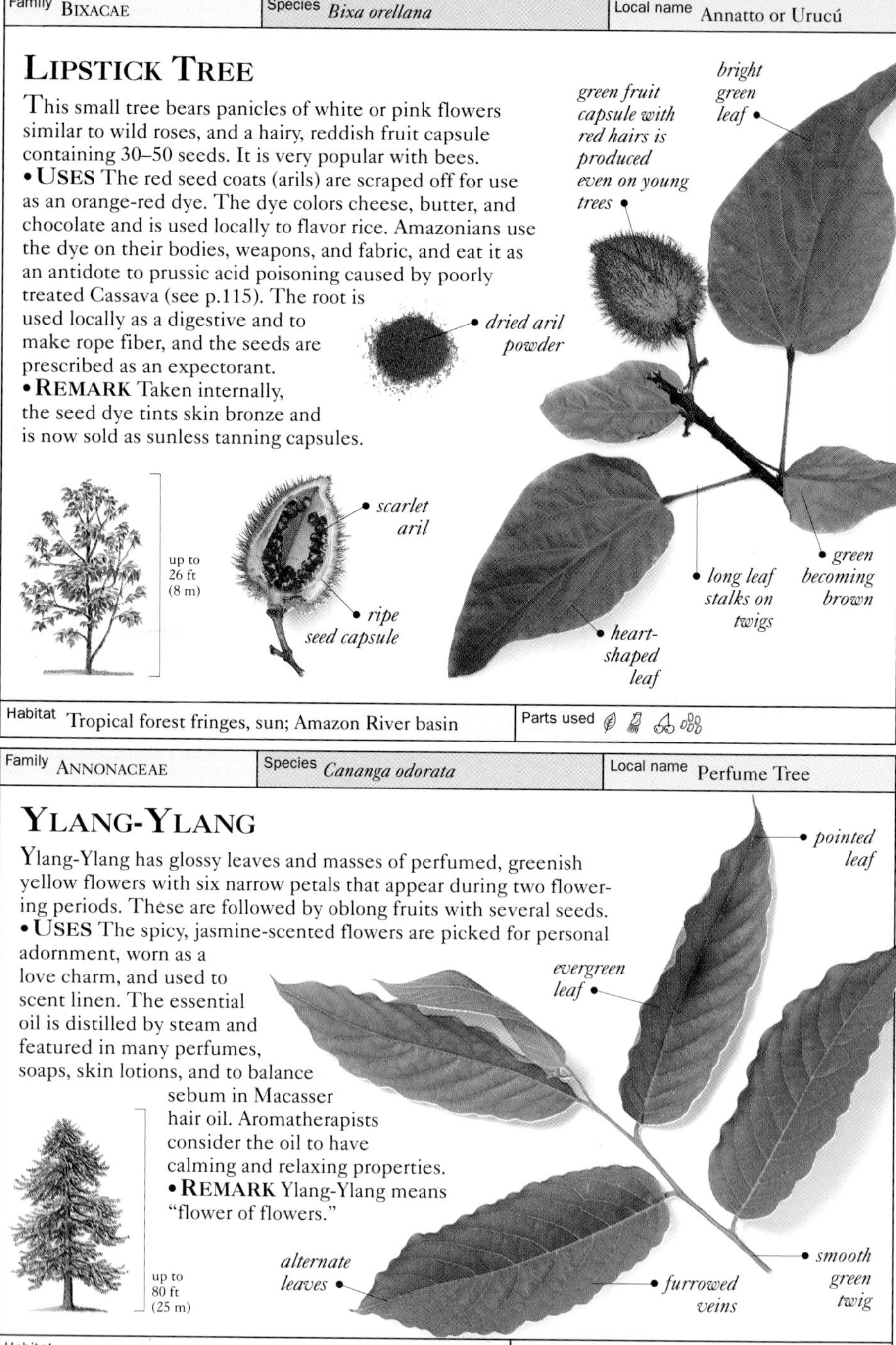
green fruit capsule with red hairs is produced even on young trees
bright green leaf
dried aril powder
scarlet aril
ripe seed capsule
up to 26 ft (8 m)
long leaf stalks on twigs
green becoming brown
heart-shaped leaf
pointed leaf
evergreen leaf
alternate leaves
furrowed veins
smooth green twig
up to 80 ft (25 m)

LIPSTICK TREE

This small tree bears panicles of white or pink flowers similar to wild roses, and a hairy, reddish fruit capsule containing 30–50 seeds. It is very popular with bees.

• **USES** The red seed coats (arils) are scraped off for use as an orange-red dye. The dye colors cheese, butter, and chocolate and is used locally to flavor rice. Amazonians use the dye on their bodies, weapons, and fabric, and eat it as an antidote to prussic acid poisoning caused by poorly treated Cassava (see p.115). The root is used locally as a digestive and to make rope fiber, and the seeds are prescribed as an expectorant.

• **REMARK** Taken internally, the seed dye tints skin bronze and is now sold as sunless tanning capsules.

Habitat Tropical forest fringes, sun; Amazon River basin	Parts used

Family ANNONACEAE	Species *Cananga odorata*	Local name Perfume Tree

YLANG-YLANG

Ylang-Ylang has glossy leaves and masses of perfumed, greenish yellow flowers with six narrow petals that appear during two flowering periods. These are followed by oblong fruits with several seeds.

• **USES** The spicy, jasmine-scented flowers are picked for personal adornment, worn as a love charm, and used to scent linen. The essential oil is distilled by steam and featured in many perfumes, soaps, skin lotions, and to balance sebum in Macasser hair oil. Aromatherapists consider the oil to have calming and relaxing properties.

• **REMARK** Ylang-Ylang means "flower of flowers."

Habitat Moist or seasonal forests; India, Indonesia, Myanmar	Parts used

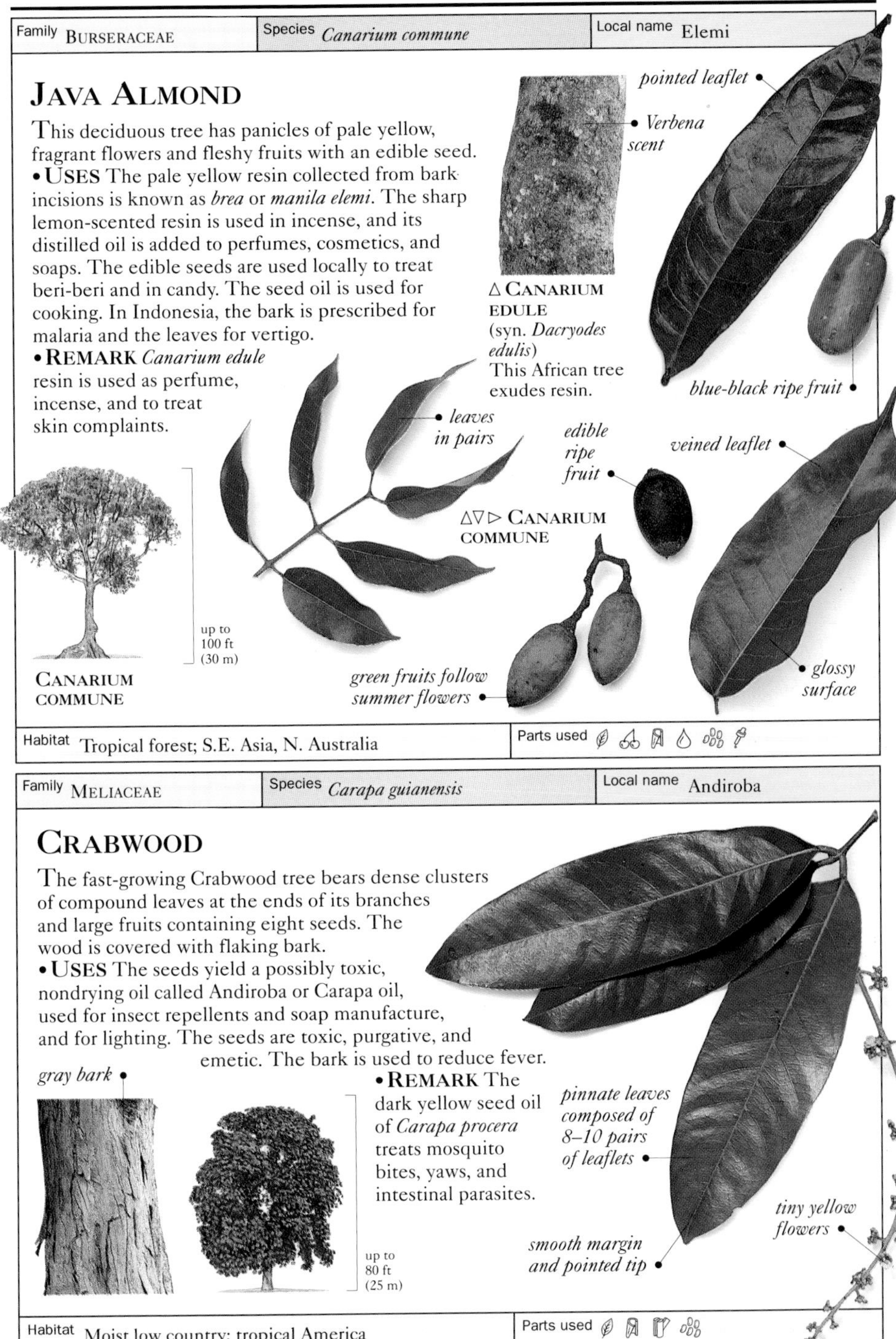

Family BURSERACEAE	Species *Canarium commune*	Local name Elemi

JAVA ALMOND

This deciduous tree has panicles of pale yellow, fragrant flowers and fleshy fruits with an edible seed.

• **USES** The pale yellow resin collected from bark incisions is known as *brea* or *manila elemi*. The sharp lemon-scented resin is used in incense, and its distilled oil is added to perfumes, cosmetics, and soaps. The edible seeds are used locally to treat beri-beri and in candy. The seed oil is used for cooking. In Indonesia, the bark is prescribed for malaria and the leaves for vertigo.

• **REMARK** *Canarium edule* resin is used as perfume, incense, and to treat skin complaints.

pointed leaflet
Verbena scent
blue-black ripe fruit
leaves in pairs
edible ripe fruit
veined leaflet
glossy surface
green fruits follow summer flowers
up to 100 ft (30 m)

△ CANARIUM EDULE (syn. *Dacryodes edulis*) This African tree exudes resin.

△▽▷ CANARIUM COMMUNE

CANARIUM COMMUNE

Habitat Tropical forest; S.E. Asia, N. Australia	Parts used

Family MELIACEAE	Species *Carapa guianensis*	Local name Andiroba

CRABWOOD

The fast-growing Crabwood tree bears dense clusters of compound leaves at the ends of its branches and large fruits containing eight seeds. The wood is covered with flaking bark.

• **USES** The seeds yield a possibly toxic, nondrying oil called Andiroba or Carapa oil, used for insect repellents and soap manufacture, and for lighting. The seeds are toxic, purgative, and emetic. The bark is used to reduce fever.

• **REMARK** The dark yellow seed oil of *Carapa procera* treats mosquito bites, yaws, and intestinal parasites.

gray bark
pinnate leaves composed of 8–10 pairs of leaflets
tiny yellow flowers
smooth margin and pointed tip
up to 80 ft (25 m)

Habitat Moist low country; tropical America	Parts used

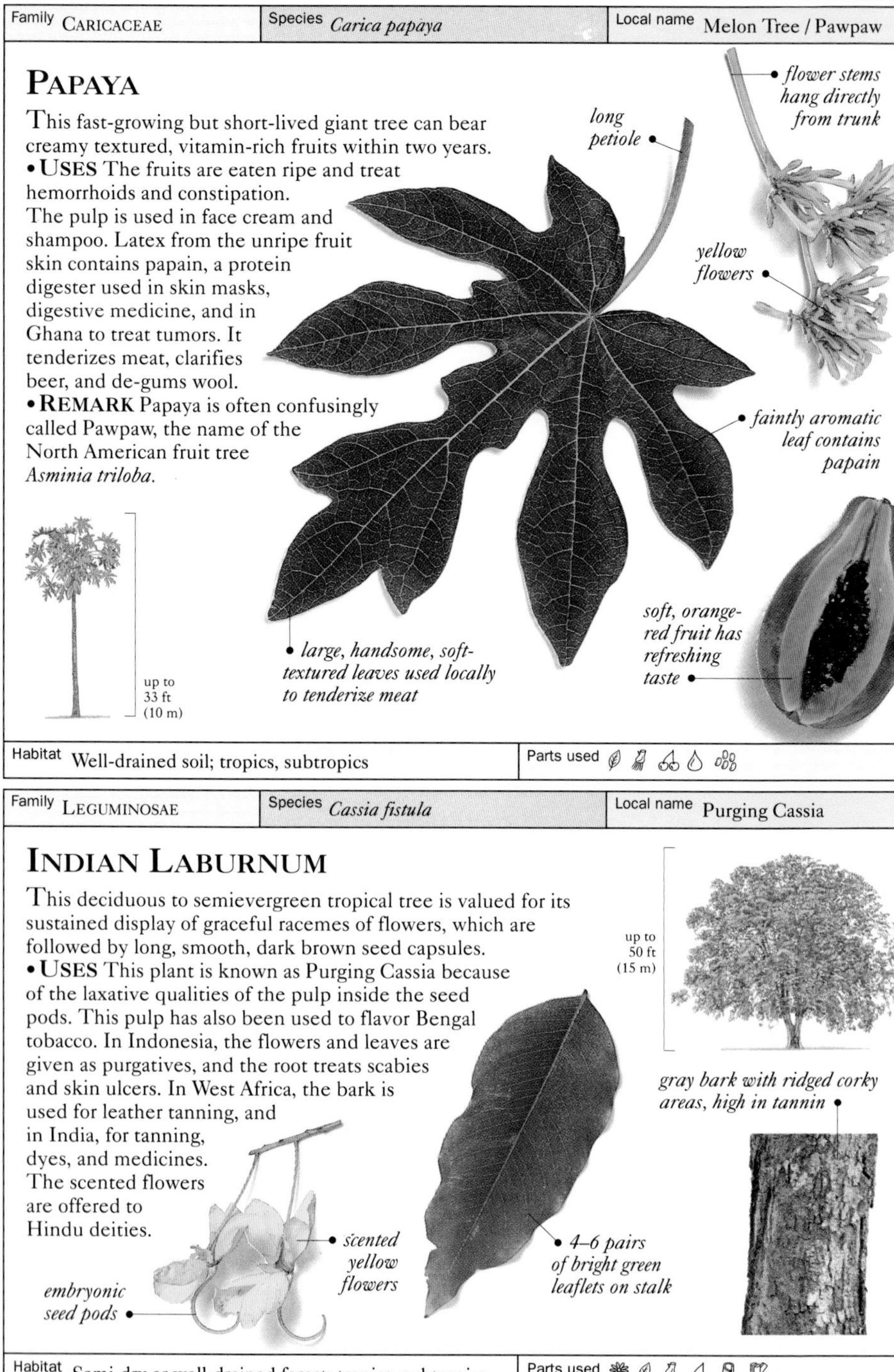
long petiole
flower stems hang directly from trunk
yellow flowers
faintly aromatic leaf contains papain
soft, orange-red fruit has refreshing taste
large, handsome, soft-textured leaves used locally to tenderize meat
up to 33 ft (10 m)
up to 50 ft (15 m)
gray bark with ridged corky areas, high in tannin
scented yellow flowers
embryonic seed pods
4–6 pairs of bright green leaflets on stalk

Family CARICACEAE	Species *Carica papaya*	Local name Melon Tree / Pawpaw

PAPAYA

This fast-growing but short-lived giant tree can bear creamy textured, vitamin-rich fruits within two years.

• **USES** The fruits are eaten ripe and treat hemorrhoids and constipation. The pulp is used in face cream and shampoo. Latex from the unripe fruit skin contains papain, a protein digester used in skin masks, digestive medicine, and in Ghana to treat tumors. It tenderizes meat, clarifies beer, and de-gums wool.

• **REMARK** Papaya is often confusingly called Pawpaw, the name of the North American fruit tree *Asminia triloba*.

Habitat Well-drained soil; tropics, subtropics	Parts used

Family LEGUMINOSAE	Species *Cassia fistula*	Local name Purging Cassia

INDIAN LABURNUM

This deciduous to semievergreen tropical tree is valued for its sustained display of graceful racemes of flowers, which are followed by long, smooth, dark brown seed capsules.

• **USES** This plant is known as Purging Cassia because of the laxative qualities of the pulp inside the seed pods. This pulp has also been used to flavor Bengal tobacco. In Indonesia, the flowers and leaves are given as purgatives, and the root treats scabies and skin ulcers. In West Africa, the bark is used for leather tanning, and in India, for tanning, dyes, and medicines. The scented flowers are offered to Hindu deities.

Habitat Semi-dry or well-drained forest; tropics, subtropics	Parts used

Family	Species	Local name
FAGACEAE	*Castanea sativa*	Spanish Chestnut

SWEET CHESTNUT

Cultivated for 3,000 years, this drought-resistant tree has smooth gray bark that develops brown spiral ridges with age. Creamy yellow summer flowers are followed by autumn fruit husks containing glossy brown nuts.

• **USES** Sweet Chestnut yields young timber poles valued for hop-growing and nuts that can be roasted, boiled, or ground into a nutritious flour. The nuts flavor sweetmeats such as Marron Glacé. Nut meal whitens linen and forms starch. The astringent leaves are a witch hazel substitute and are infused to treat convulsive coughs. Shampoo made from the leaves and nut skins gives golden highlights to hair.

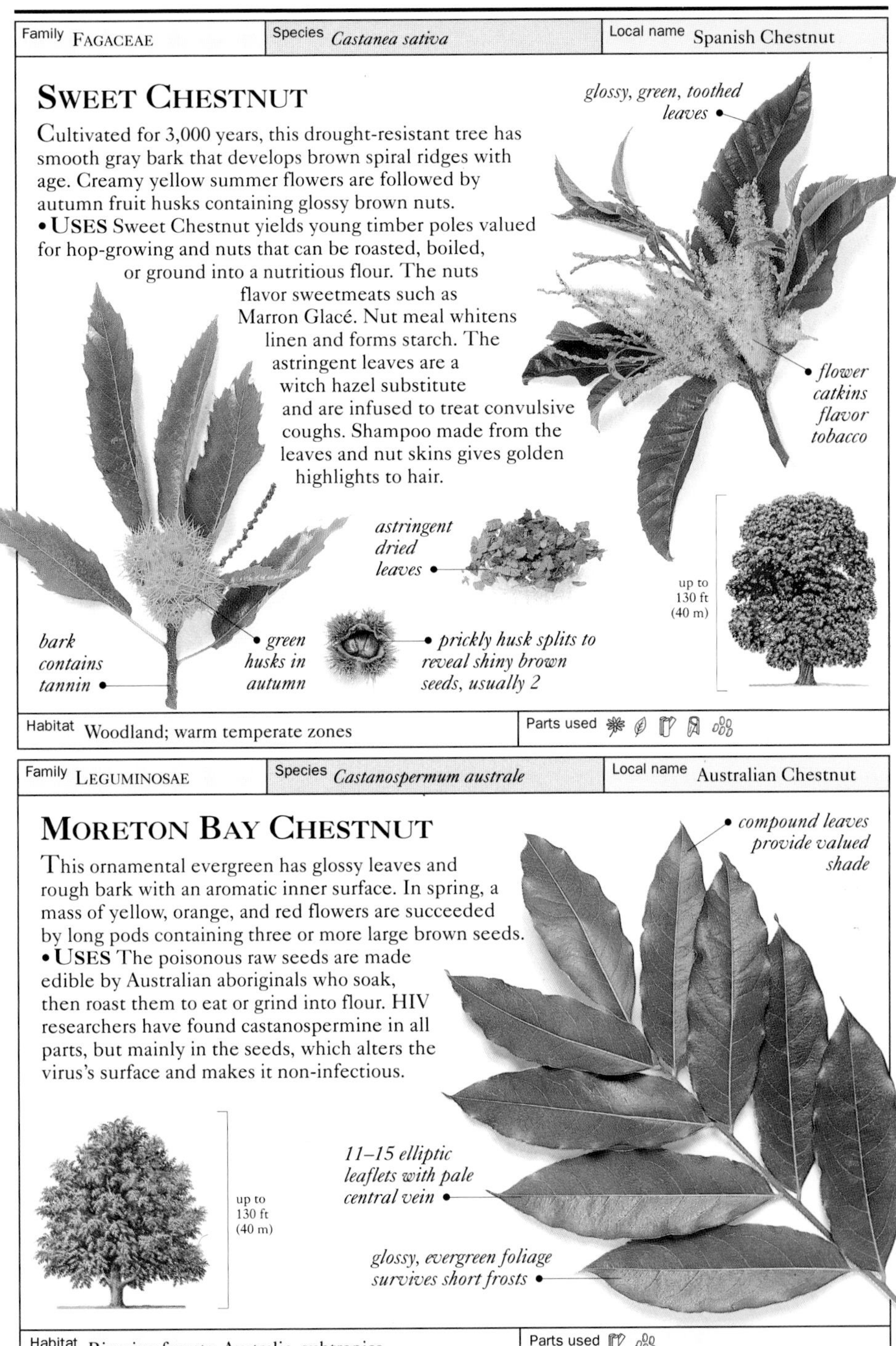
glossy, green, toothed leaves
flower catkins flavor tobacco
astringent dried leaves
up to 130 ft (40 m)
bark contains tannin
green husks in autumn
prickly husk splits to reveal shiny brown seeds, usually 2
compound leaves provide valued shade
11–15 elliptic leaflets with pale central vein
glossy, evergreen foliage survives short frosts
up to 130 ft (40 m)

Habitat	Parts used
Woodland; warm temperate zones	

Family	Species	Local name
LEGUMINOSAE	*Castanospermum australe*	Australian Chestnut

MORETON BAY CHESTNUT

This ornamental evergreen has glossy leaves and rough bark with an aromatic inner surface. In spring, a mass of yellow, orange, and red flowers are succeeded by long pods containing three or more large brown seeds.

• **USES** The poisonous raw seeds are made edible by Australian aboriginals who soak, then roast them to eat or grind into flour. HIV researchers have found castanospermine in all parts, but mainly in the seeds, which alters the virus's surface and makes it non-infectious.

Habitat	Parts used
Riverine forests; Australia, subtropics	

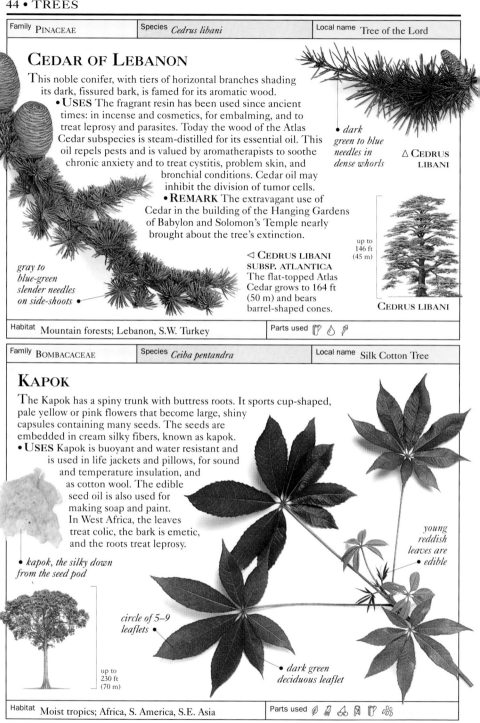

Family PINACEAE	Species *Cedrus libani*	Local name Tree of the Lord

CEDAR OF LEBANON

This noble conifer, with tiers of horizontal branches shading its dark, fissured bark, is famed for its aromatic wood.

• **USES** The fragrant resin has been used since ancient times: in incense and cosmetics, for embalming, and to treat leprosy and parasites. Today the wood of the Atlas Cedar subspecies is steam-distilled for its essential oil. This oil repels pests and is valued by aromatherapists to soothe chronic anxiety and to treat cystitis, problem skin, and bronchial conditions. Cedar oil may inhibit the division of tumor cells.

• **REMARK** The extravagant use of Cedar in the building of the Hanging Gardens of Babylon and Solomon's Temple nearly brought about the tree's extinction.

• dark green to blue needles in dense whorls

△ CEDRUS LIBANI

up to 146 ft (45 m)

CEDRUS LIBANI

gray to blue-green slender needles on side-shoots •

◁ CEDRUS LIBANI SUBSP. ATLANTICA
The flat-topped Atlas Cedar grows to 164 ft (50 m) and bears barrel-shaped cones.

Habitat Mountain forests; Lebanon, S.W. Turkey	Parts used

Family BOMBACACEAE	Species *Ceiba pentandra*	Local name Silk Cotton Tree

KAPOK

The Kapok has a spiny trunk with buttress roots. It sports cup-shaped, pale yellow or pink flowers that become large, shiny capsules containing many seeds. The seeds are embedded in cream silky fibers, known as kapok.

• **USES** Kapok is buoyant and water resistant and is used in life jackets and pillows, for sound and temperature insulation, and as cotton wool. The edible seed oil is also used for making soap and paint. In West Africa, the leaves treat colic, the bark is emetic, and the roots treat leprosy.

• kapok, the silky down from the seed pod

young reddish leaves are • edible

circle of 5–9 leaflets •

• dark green deciduous leaflet

up to 230 ft (70 m)

Habitat Moist tropics; Africa, S. America, S.E. Asia	Parts used

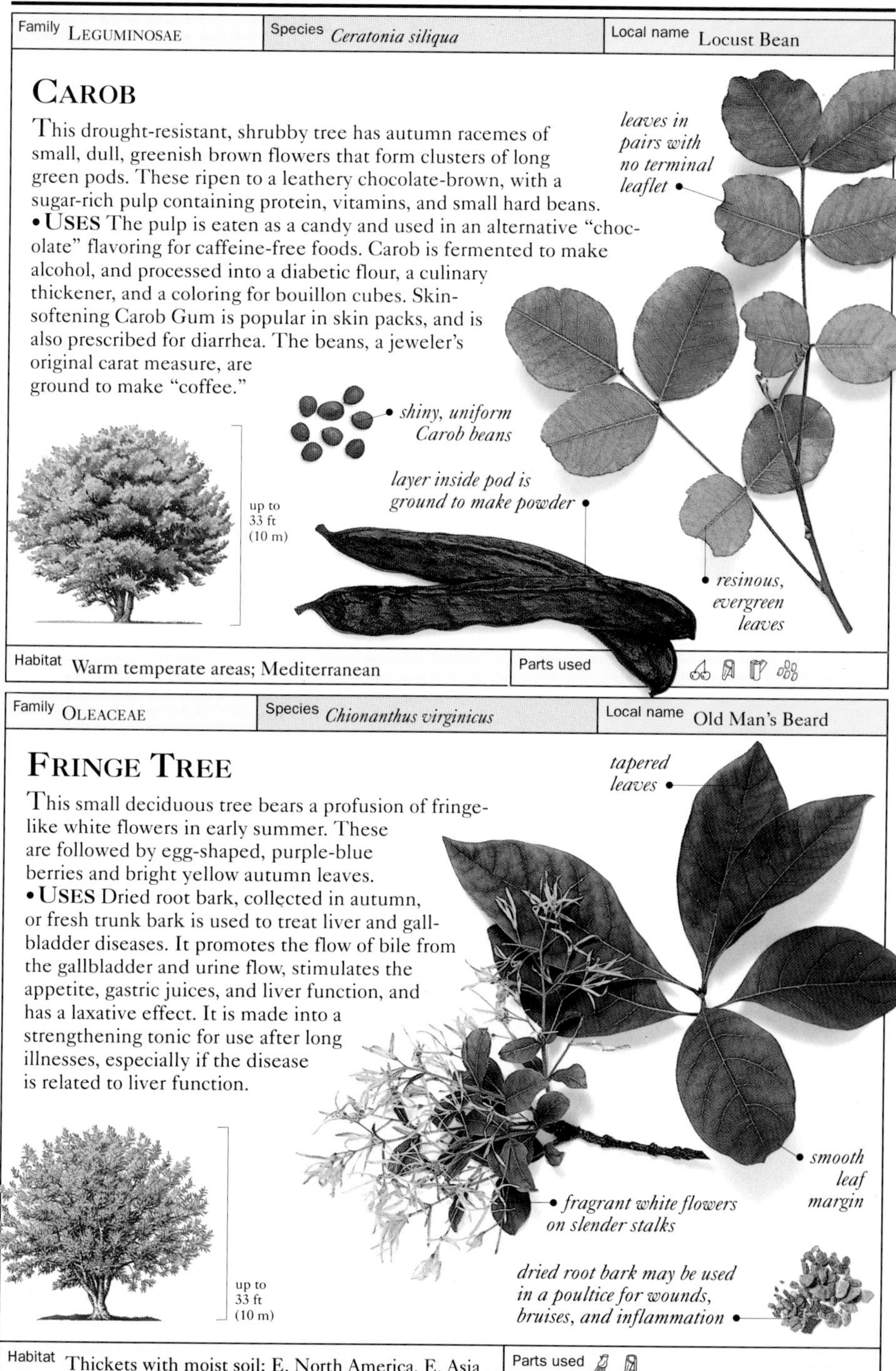
leaves in pairs with no terminal leaflet
shiny, uniform Carob beans
layer inside pod is ground to make powder
resinous, evergreen leaves
up to 33 ft (10 m)
tapered leaves
smooth leaf margin
fragrant white flowers on slender stalks
dried root bark may be used in a poultice for wounds, bruises, and inflammation
up to 33 ft (10 m)

Family LEGUMINOSAE	Species *Ceratonia siliqua*	Local name Locust Bean

CAROB

This drought-resistant, shrubby tree has autumn racemes of small, dull, greenish brown flowers that form clusters of long green pods. These ripen to a leathery chocolate-brown, with a sugar-rich pulp containing protein, vitamins, and small hard beans. • **USES** The pulp is eaten as a candy and used in an alternative "chocolate" flavoring for caffeine-free foods. Carob is fermented to make alcohol, and processed into a diabetic flour, a culinary thickener, and a coloring for bouillon cubes. Skin-softening Carob Gum is popular in skin packs, and is also prescribed for diarrhea. The beans, a jeweler's original carat measure, are ground to make "coffee."

Habitat Warm temperate areas; Mediterranean	Parts used

Family OLEACEAE	Species *Chionanthus virginicus*	Local name Old Man's Beard

FRINGE TREE

This small deciduous tree bears a profusion of fringe-like white flowers in early summer. These are followed by egg-shaped, purple-blue berries and bright yellow autumn leaves. • **USES** Dried root bark, collected in autumn, or fresh trunk bark is used to treat liver and gallbladder diseases. It promotes the flow of bile from the gallbladder and urine flow, stimulates the appetite, gastric juices, and liver function, and has a laxative effect. It is made into a strengthening tonic for use after long illnesses, especially if the disease is related to liver function.

Habitat Thickets with moist soil; E. North America, E. Asia	Parts used

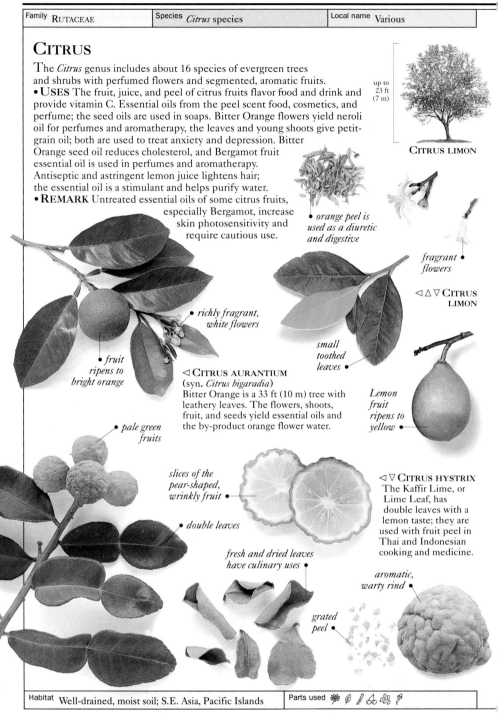

Family RUTACEAE	Species *Citrus* species	Local name Various

CITRUS

The *Citrus* genus includes about 16 species of evergreen trees and shrubs with perfumed flowers and segmented, aromatic fruits.

• **USES** The fruit, juice, and peel of citrus fruits flavor food and drink and provide vitamin C. Essential oils from the peel scent food, cosmetics, and perfume; the seed oils are used in soaps. Bitter Orange flowers yield neroli oil for perfumes and aromatherapy, the leaves and young shoots give petitgrain oil; both are used to treat anxiety and depression. Bitter Orange seed oil reduces cholesterol, and Bergamot fruit essential oil is used in perfumes and aromatherapy. Antiseptic and astringent lemon juice lightens hair; the essential oil is a stimulant and helps purify water.

• **REMARK** Untreated essential oils of some citrus fruits, especially Bergamot, increase skin photosensitivity and require cautious use.

up to 23 ft (7 m)

CITRUS LIMON

orange peel is used as a diuretic and digestive

fragrant flowers

◁ △ ▽ CITRUS LIMON

small toothed leaves

Lemon fruit ripens to yellow

richly fragrant, white flowers

fruit ripens to bright orange

◁ CITRUS AURANTIUM
(syn. *Citrus bigaradia*)
Bitter Orange is a 33 ft (10 m) tree with leathery leaves. The flowers, shoots, fruit, and seeds yield essential oils and the by-product orange flower water.

pale green fruits

slices of the pear-shaped, wrinkly fruit

double leaves

◁ ▽ CITRUS HYSTRIX
The Kaffir Lime, or Lime Leaf, has double leaves with a lemon taste; they are used with fruit peel in Thai and Indonesian cooking and medicine.

fresh and dried leaves have culinary uses

aromatic, warty rind

grated peel

Habitat Well-drained, moist soil; S.E. Asia, Pacific Islands	Parts used

CITRUS AURANTIFOLIA ▷
Lime is a spiny, untidy tree with small white flowers and greeny yellow fruits, popular in tropical cuisine.

▽ X CITROFORTUNELLA MICROCARPA
(syn. *Citrus microcarpa*)
Musk Lemon is a small, dense, almost spineless tree with sour fruits used as flavoring. It is a popular house plant.

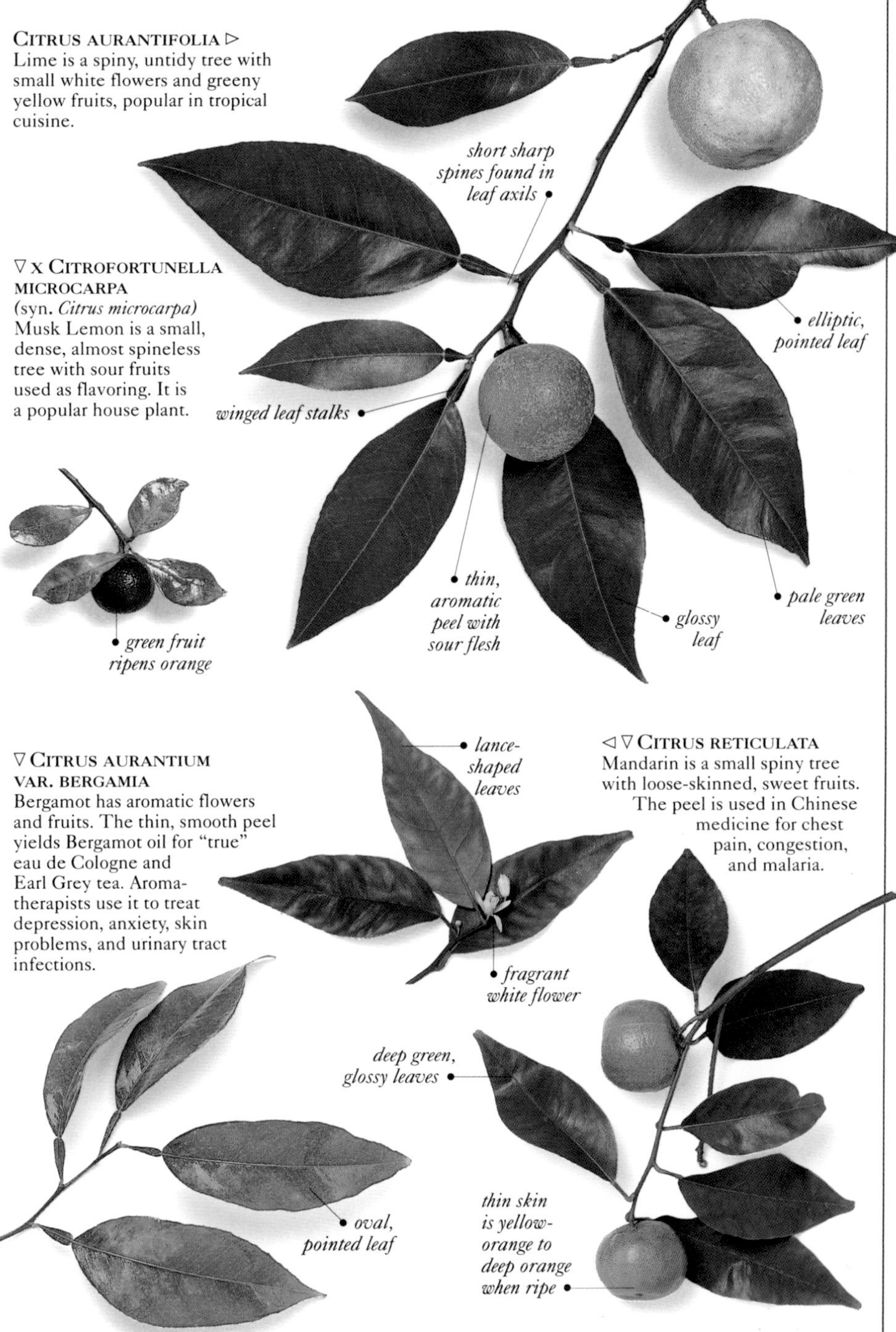
short sharp spines found in leaf axils
elliptic, pointed leaf
winged leaf stalks
thin, aromatic peel with sour flesh
glossy leaf
pale green leaves
green fruit ripens orange
lance-shaped leaves
fragrant white flower
deep green, glossy leaves
oval, pointed leaf
thin skin is yellow-orange to deep orange when ripe

▽ CITRUS AURANTIUM VAR. BERGAMIA
Bergamot has aromatic flowers and fruits. The thin, smooth peel yields Bergamot oil for "true" eau de Cologne and Earl Grey tea. Aromatherapists use it to treat depression, anxiety, skin problems, and urinary tract infections.

◁ ▽ CITRUS RETICULATA
Mandarin is a small spiny tree with loose-skinned, sweet fruits. The peel is used in Chinese medicine for chest pain, congestion, and malaria.

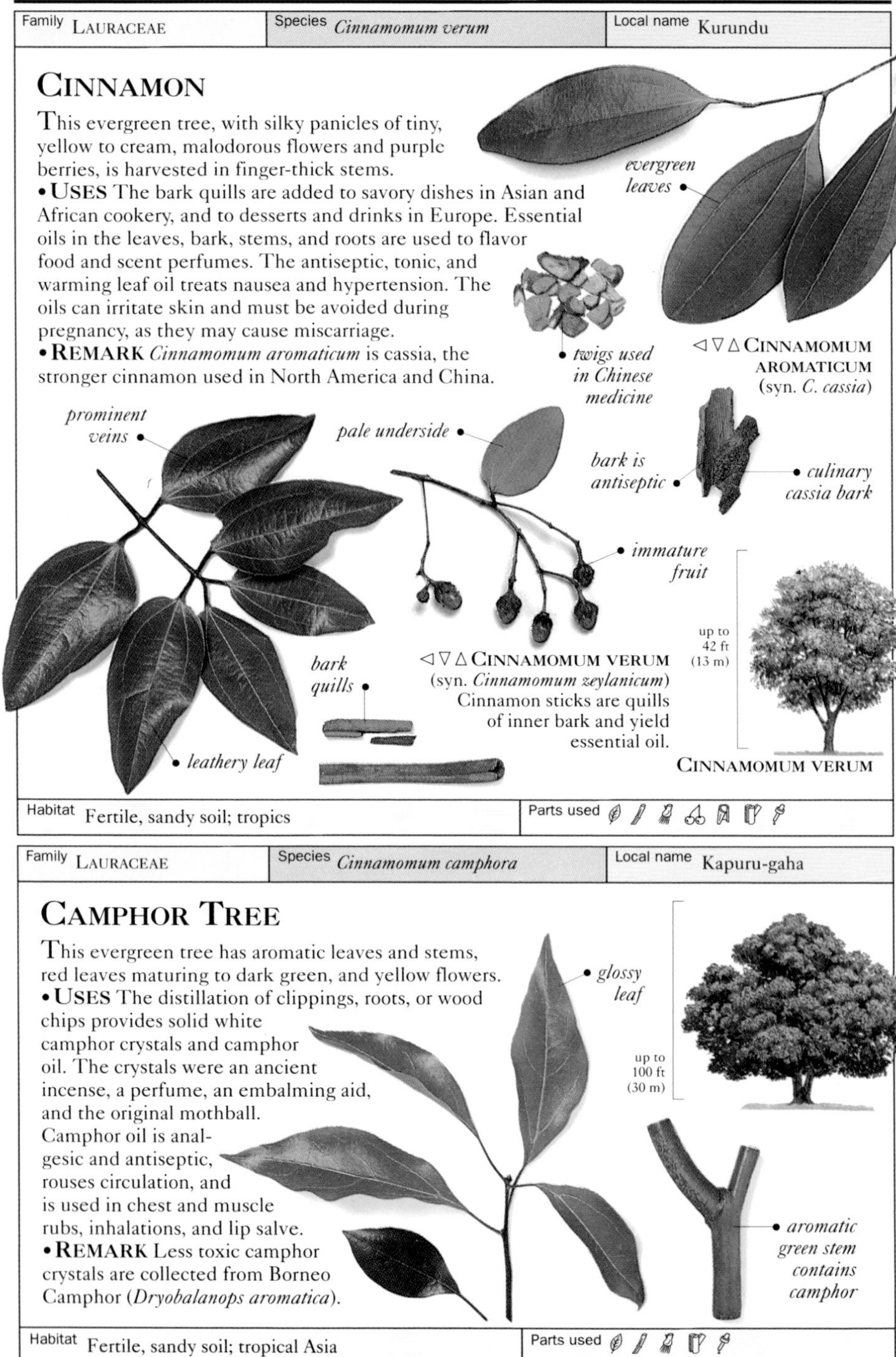
evergreen leaves
twigs used in Chinese medicine
prominent veins
pale underside
bark is antiseptic
culinary cassia bark
immature fruit
up to 42 ft (13 m)
bark quills
leathery leaf
glossy leaf
up to 100 ft (30 m)
aromatic green stem contains camphor

Family LAURACEAE	Species *Cinnamomum verum*	Local name Kurundu

CINNAMON

This evergreen tree, with silky panicles of tiny, yellow to cream, malodorous flowers and purple berries, is harvested in finger-thick stems.

• **USES** The bark quills are added to savory dishes in Asian and African cookery, and to desserts and drinks in Europe. Essential oils in the leaves, bark, stems, and roots are used to flavor food and scent perfumes. The antiseptic, tonic, and warming leaf oil treats nausea and hypertension. The oils can irritate skin and must be avoided during pregnancy, as they may cause miscarriage.

• **REMARK** *Cinnamomum aromaticum* is cassia, the stronger cinnamon used in North America and China.

◁ ▽ △ CINNAMOMUM AROMATICUM (syn. *C. cassia*)

◁ ▽ △ CINNAMOMUM VERUM (syn. *Cinnamomum zeylanicum*) Cinnamon sticks are quills of inner bark and yield essential oil.

CINNAMOMUM VERUM

Habitat Fertile, sandy soil; tropics	Parts used

Family LAURACEAE	Species *Cinnamomum camphora*	Local name Kapuru-gaha

CAMPHOR TREE

This evergreen tree has aromatic leaves and stems, red leaves maturing to dark green, and yellow flowers.

• **USES** The distillation of clippings, roots, or wood chips provides solid white camphor crystals and camphor oil. The crystals were an ancient incense, a perfume, an embalming aid, and the original mothball. Camphor oil is analgesic and antiseptic, rouses circulation, and is used in chest and muscle rubs, inhalations, and lip salve.

• **REMARK** Less toxic camphor crystals are collected from Borneo Camphor (*Dryobalanops aromatica*).

Habitat Fertile, sandy soil; tropical Asia	Parts used

Family PALMAE	Species *Cocos nucifera*	Local name Tennai or Thenga

COCONUT PALM

This graceful, leaning palm is topped by a spray of pinnate leaves 20 ft (6 m) long, an inflorescence of cream flowers, and large, single-seeded fruits. The husk under the ripe skin houses the hard-shelled coconut.

• **USES** The most valuable of all the palms. The trunk is used as building material, the leaves for thatch and weaving, and the palm heart (stem tip) is cooked. The sap is tapped for palm sugar, fermented for toddy, or distilled to make the spirit *arrack*. The coconut shell contains the white meat layer of edible coconut, and refreshing coconut "milk." The milk is gradually absorbed by the ripening meat, which when dried is called "copra" and yields coconut oil for soap, synthetic rubber, glycerine, cosmetics, and special diets for disorders where other fats are not absorbed.

• **REMARK** The word "coco," Spanish for a grinning face, refers to the eyes on the coconut base.

fruits range from green to orange and pale yellow, and hang in clusters at top of trunk

shells provide utensils, fuel, and charcoal to absorb poisons

outer layer matures to fibrous husk, sold as coir and compost

very small, unripe fruit cooked in curries

nutritious, milky coconut juice taken for fever and urinary disorders

up to 100 ft (30 m)

"King Coconut" yields aromatic hair, skin, and sun oils

the edible-husked young coconut is called "Nawasi"

when dried, meat is called "copra," and yields coconut oil

gray trunk with crescent scars

ripe white meat is shredded to make dried coconut or macerated to make milk

Habitat Salty, sandy soil; tropics, subtropics	Parts used

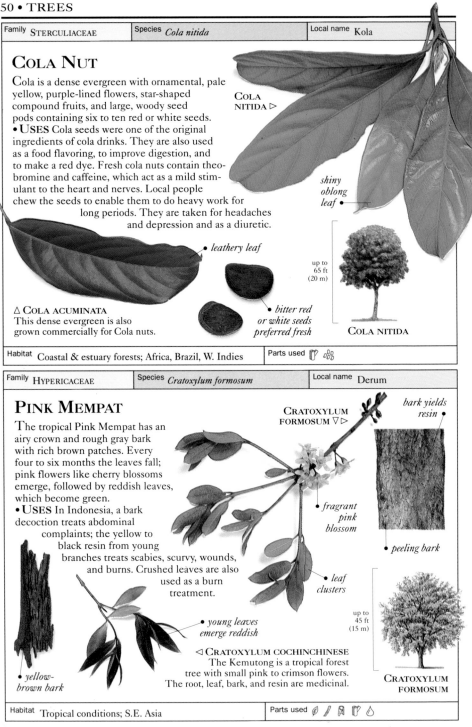

Family STERCULIACEAE	Species *Cola nitida*	Local name Kola

COLA NUT

Cola is a dense evergreen with ornamental, pale yellow, purple-lined flowers, star-shaped compound fruits, and large, woody seed pods containing six to ten red or white seeds.
• USES Cola seeds were one of the original ingredients of cola drinks. They are also used as a food flavoring, to improve digestion, and to make a red dye. Fresh cola nuts contain theobromine and caffeine, which act as a mild stimulant to the heart and nerves. Local people chew the seeds to enable them to do heavy work for long periods. They are taken for headaches and depression and as a diuretic.

COLA NITIDA ▷

shiny oblong leaf

leathery leaf

up to 65 ft (20 m)

△ COLA ACUMINATA
This dense evergreen is also grown commercially for Cola nuts.

bitter red or white seeds preferred fresh

COLA NITIDA

Habitat Coastal & estuary forests; Africa, Brazil, W. Indies	Parts used

Family HYPERICACEAE	Species *Cratoxylum formosum*	Local name Derum

PINK MEMPAT

The tropical Pink Mempat has an airy crown and rough gray bark with rich brown patches. Every four to six months the leaves fall; pink flowers like cherry blossoms emerge, followed by reddish leaves, which become green.
• USES In Indonesia, a bark decoction treats abdominal complaints; the yellow to black resin from young branches treats scabies, scurvy, wounds, and burns. Crushed leaves are also used as a burn treatment.

CRATOXYLUM FORMOSUM ▽▷

bark yields resin

fragrant pink blossom

peeling bark

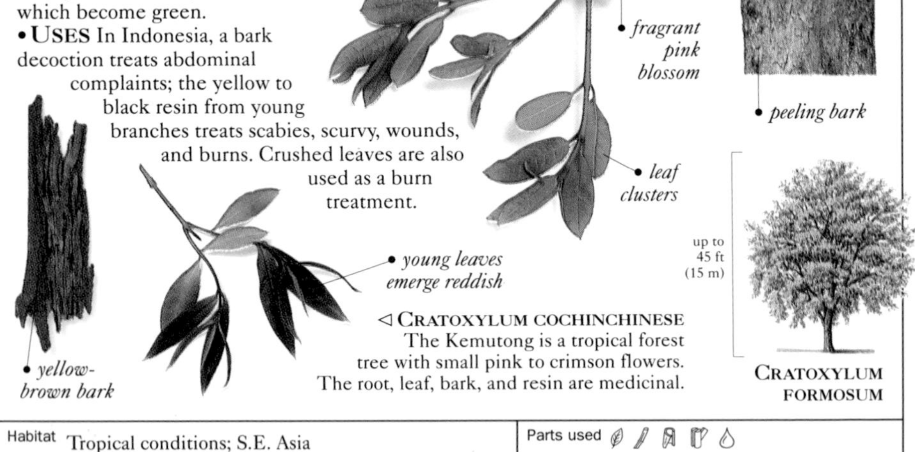
leaf clusters
up to 45 ft (15 m)
young leaves emerge reddish
yellow-brown bark

◁ CRATOXYLUM COCHINCHINESE
The Kemutong is a tropical forest tree with small pink to crimson flowers. The root, leaf, bark, and resin are medicinal.

CRATOXYLUM FORMOSUM

Habitat Tropical conditions; S.E. Asia	Parts used

Family CUPRESSACEAE	Species *Cupressus sempervirens*	Local name Cemetery Cypress

ITALIAN CYPRESS

This tall evergreen has gray-brown bark, and tiny, dark green leaves. It bears yellowish male cones and green female cones, which ripen to brown. • **USES** Cypress Oil, distilled from the leaves, branches, and cones, has a refreshing, camphor-resinous scent, popular in perfumes, aftershaves, and soaps. Aromatherapists use its astringency and vein-constricting properties to treat broken capillaries and excess fluid conditions, such as cellulite and heavy menstruation; as a circulation tonic for varicose veins and hemorrhoids; and as an antispasmodic to reduce cough spasms.

'SWANE'S GOLDEN' ▽
This is a small, slow-growing, compact cultivar with gold-tipped foliage.

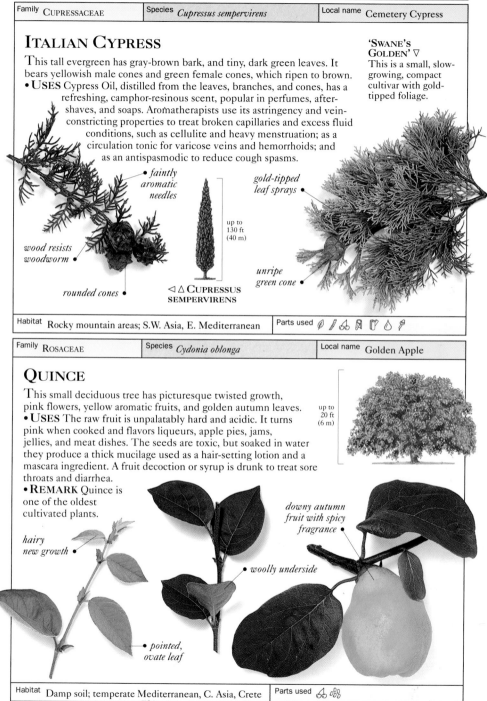

faintly aromatic needles

wood resists woodworm

rounded cones

up to 130 ft (40 m)

◁ △ CUPRESSUS SEMPERVIRENS

gold-tipped leaf sprays

unripe green cone

Habitat Rocky mountain areas; S.W. Asia, E. Mediterranean	Parts used

Family ROSACEAE	Species *Cydonia oblonga*	Local name Golden Apple

QUINCE

This small deciduous tree has picturesque twisted growth, pink flowers, yellow aromatic fruits, and golden autumn leaves. • **USES** The raw fruit is unpalatably hard and acidic. It turns pink when cooked and flavors liqueurs, apple pies, jams, jellies, and meat dishes. The seeds are toxic, but soaked in water they produce a thick mucilage used as a hair-setting lotion and a mascara ingredient. A fruit decoction or syrup is drunk to treat sore throats and diarrhea.
• **REMARK** Quince is one of the oldest cultivated plants.

up to 20 ft (6 m)

hairy new growth

woolly underside

downy autumn fruit with spicy fragrance

pointed, ovate leaf

Habitat Damp soil; temperate Mediterranean, C. Asia, Crete	Parts used

Family DILLENIACEAE	Species *Dillenia indica*	Local name Chulta

ELEPHANT APPLE

This evergreen with 12-in- (30-cm-) long serrated leaves is prized for its large, white, scented flowers and round, fleshy fruits.

• **USES** In India, the juicy acid sepals around the fruits are eaten as vegetables and made into cooling drinks, preserves, and jellies. The fruit is used in Malaysian curry and the pulp in a hair wash. The wood ash of *Dillenia aurea* is added to clay bricks to increase fire resistance. The bark treats thrush; leaf juice is applied to prevent baldness.

• **REMARK** The leaves are used to polish ivory.

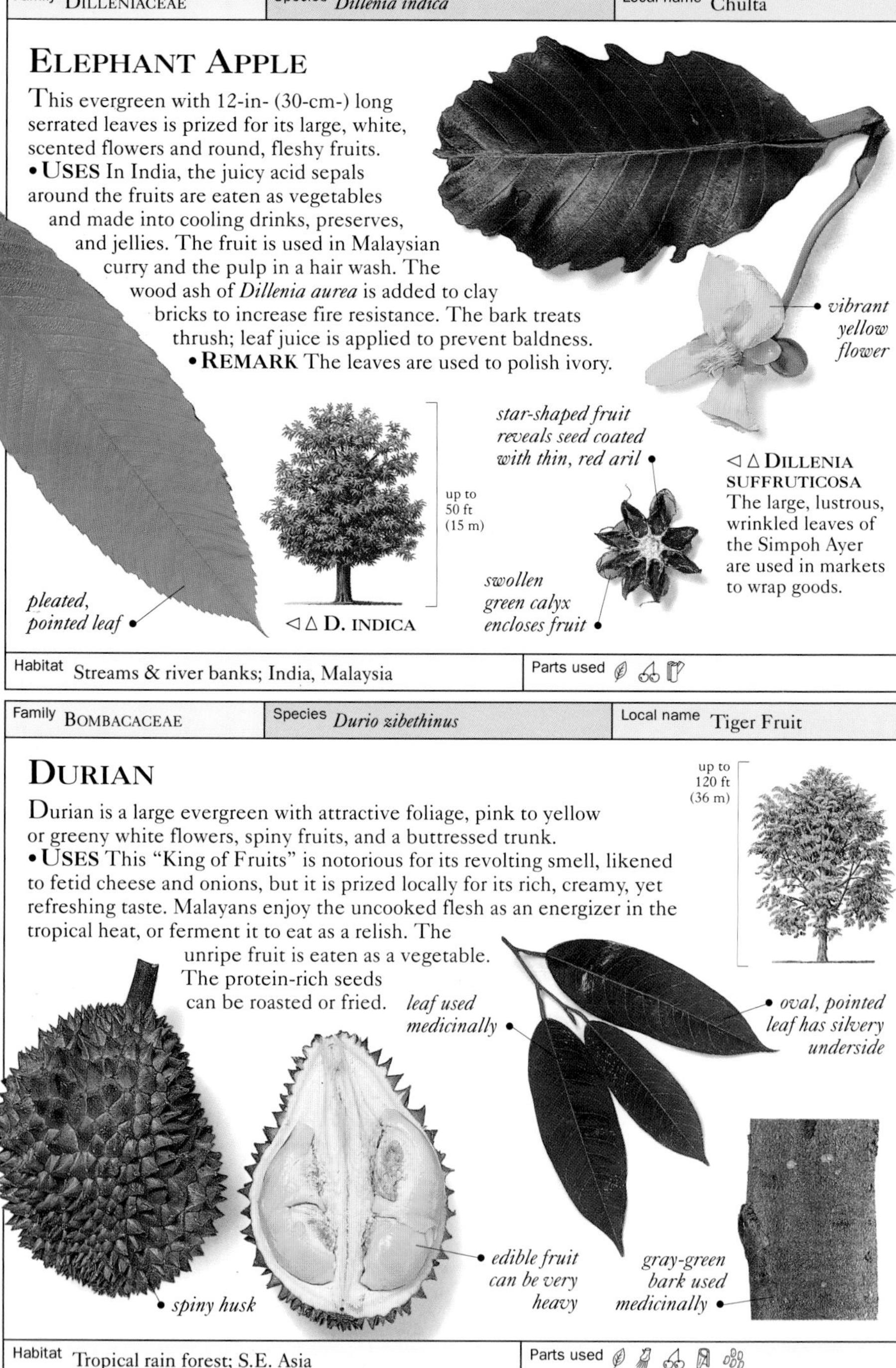
vibrant yellow flower
star-shaped fruit reveals seed coated with thin, red aril
up to 50 ft (15 m)
swollen green calyx encloses fruit
pleated, pointed leaf
up to 120 ft (36 m)
leaf used medicinally
oval, pointed leaf has silvery underside
edible fruit can be very heavy
gray-green bark used medicinally
spiny husk

◁ △ **D. INDICA**

◁ △ **DILLENIA SUFFRUTICOSA** The large, lustrous, wrinkled leaves of the Simpoh Ayer are used in markets to wrap goods.

Habitat Streams & river banks; India, Malaysia	Parts used

Family BOMBACACEAE	Species *Durio zibethinus*	Local name Tiger Fruit

DURIAN

Durian is a large evergreen with attractive foliage, pink to yellow or greeny white flowers, spiny fruits, and a buttressed trunk.

• **USES** This "King of Fruits" is notorious for its revolting smell, likened to fetid cheese and onions, but it is prized locally for its rich, creamy, yet refreshing taste. Malayans enjoy the uncooked flesh as an energizer in the tropical heat, or ferment it to eat as a relish. The unripe fruit is eaten as a vegetable. The protein-rich seeds can be roasted or fried.

Habitat Tropical rain forest; S.E. Asia	Parts used

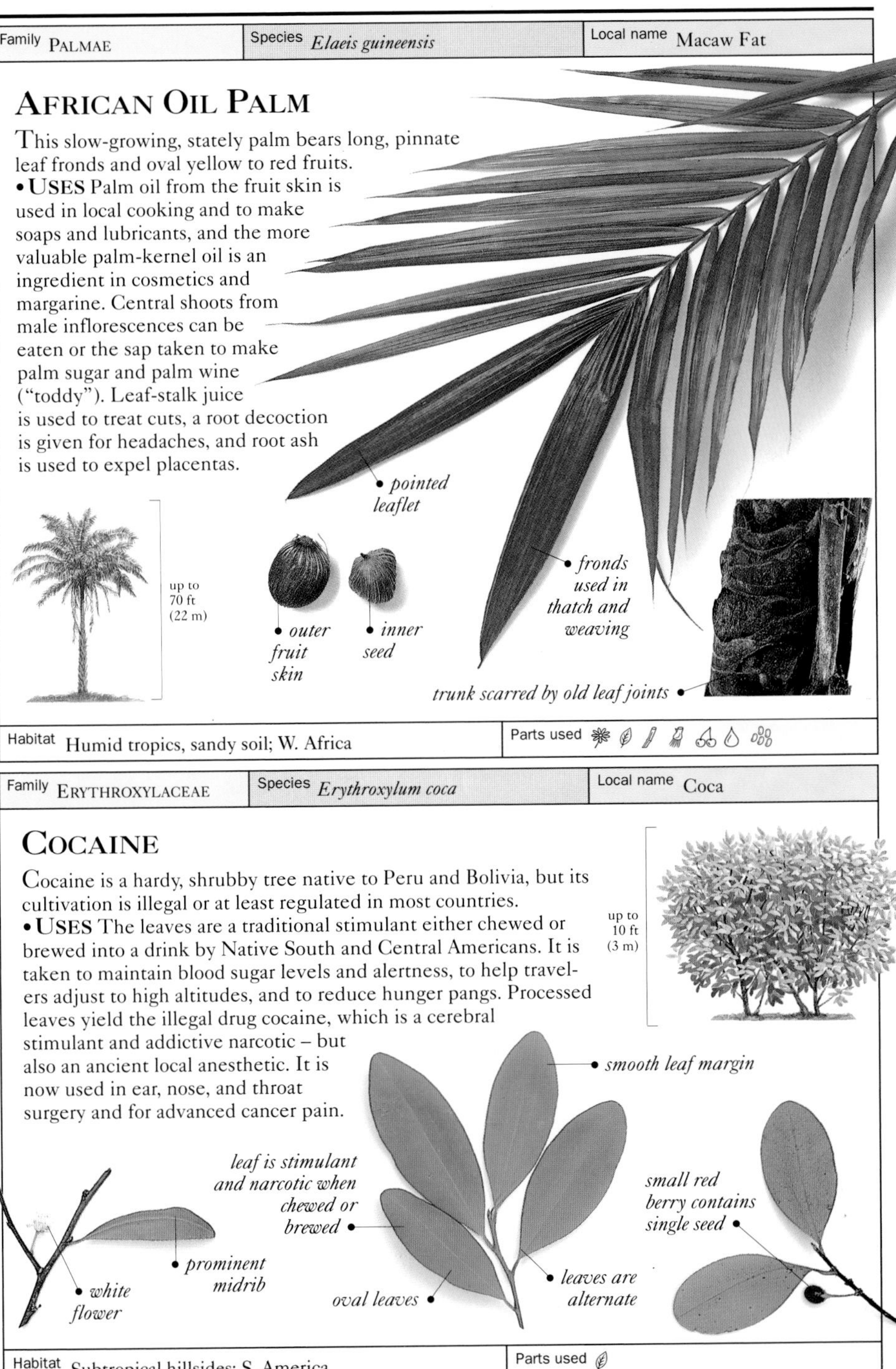

Family PALMAE	Species *Elaeis guineensis*	Local name Macaw Fat

AFRICAN OIL PALM

This slow-growing, stately palm bears long, pinnate leaf fronds and oval yellow to red fruits.

• **USES** Palm oil from the fruit skin is used in local cooking and to make soaps and lubricants, and the more valuable palm-kernel oil is an ingredient in cosmetics and margarine. Central shoots from male inflorescences can be eaten or the sap taken to make palm sugar and palm wine ("toddy"). Leaf-stalk juice is used to treat cuts, a root decoction is given for headaches, and root ash is used to expel placentas.

pointed leaflet
up to 70 ft (22 m)
outer fruit skin
inner seed
fronds used in thatch and weaving
trunk scarred by old leaf joints

Habitat Humid tropics, sandy soil; W. Africa	Parts used

Family ERYTHROXYLACEAE	Species *Erythroxylum coca*	Local name Coca

COCAINE

Cocaine is a hardy, shrubby tree native to Peru and Bolivia, but its cultivation is illegal or at least regulated in most countries.

• **USES** The leaves are a traditional stimulant either chewed or brewed into a drink by Native South and Central Americans. It is taken to maintain blood sugar levels and alertness, to help travelers adjust to high altitudes, and to reduce hunger pangs. Processed leaves yield the illegal drug cocaine, which is a cerebral stimulant and addictive narcotic – but also an ancient local anesthetic. It is now used in ear, nose, and throat surgery and for advanced cancer pain.

up to 10 ft (3 m)
smooth leaf margin
leaf is stimulant and narcotic when chewed or brewed
small red berry contains single seed
prominent midrib
white flower
oval leaves
leaves are alternate

Habitat Subtropical hillsides; S. America	Parts used

Family MYRTACEAE	Species *Eucalyptus* species	Local name Gum Tree

EUCALYPTUS

The *Eucalyptus* genus comprises over 500 species of aromatic trees and shrubs with deciduous bark. The most common species, Tasmanian Blue Gum (*Eucalyptus globulus*), has a blue-gray trunk, blue-green juvenile leaves, green adult leaves, and white flower stamens.
• **USES** Eucalyptus leaves, scented of balsamic camphor, are used by aboriginals to bind wounds; the flower nectar gives honey; and the oil, distilled from the leaves and twigs, is used in medicines, aromatherapy, and perfumes. Eucalyptus oil is antiseptic, expectorant, and antiviral, treats pulmonary tuberculosis, lowers blood sugar levels, and is useful for burns, catarrh, and flu.
• **REMARK** The roots of *Eucalyptus* trees secrete a poisonous chemical, inhibiting the growth of nearby plants.

camphor scent

△ EUCALYPTUS GLOBULUS

up to 230 ft (70 m)

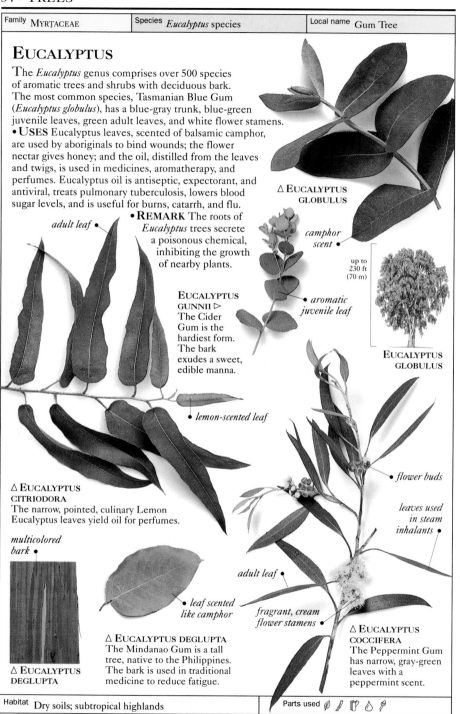

EUCALYPTUS GLOBULUS

adult leaf

aromatic juvenile leaf

EUCALYPTUS GUNNII ▷ The Cider Gum is the hardiest form. The bark exudes a sweet, edible manna.

lemon-scented leaf

△ EUCALYPTUS CITRIODORA
The narrow, pointed, culinary Lemon Eucalyptus leaves yield oil for perfumes.

flower buds

leaves used in steam inhalants

multicolored bark

△ EUCALYPTUS DEGLUPTA

leaf scented like camphor

△ EUCALYPTUS DEGLUPTA
The Mindanao Gum is a tall tree, native to the Philippines. The bark is used in traditional medicine to reduce fatigue.

adult leaf

fragrant, cream flower stamens

△ EUCALYPTUS COCCIFERA
The Peppermint Gum has narrow, gray-green leaves with a peppermint scent.

Habitat Dry soils; subtropical highlands	Parts used

Family EUCOMMIACEAE	Species *Eucommia ulmoides*	Local name Du zhong

GUTTA-PERCHA TREE

The leaves, seeds, roots, and bark of this vigorous tree contain a useful gum, or gutta-percha. The Gutta-percha Tree can be identified by slowly tearing a leaf, revealing the connecting strings of latex.

• **USES** The bark has a pleasant taste and is ascribed warming properties in traditional Chinese medicine. It is used as a tonic for the liver and kidneys, and it lowers blood pressure and decreases absorption of cholesterol. It is given to build up muscles and bones weakened by joint injury, or back strain during pregnancy. The bark is also prescribed for emotional problems.

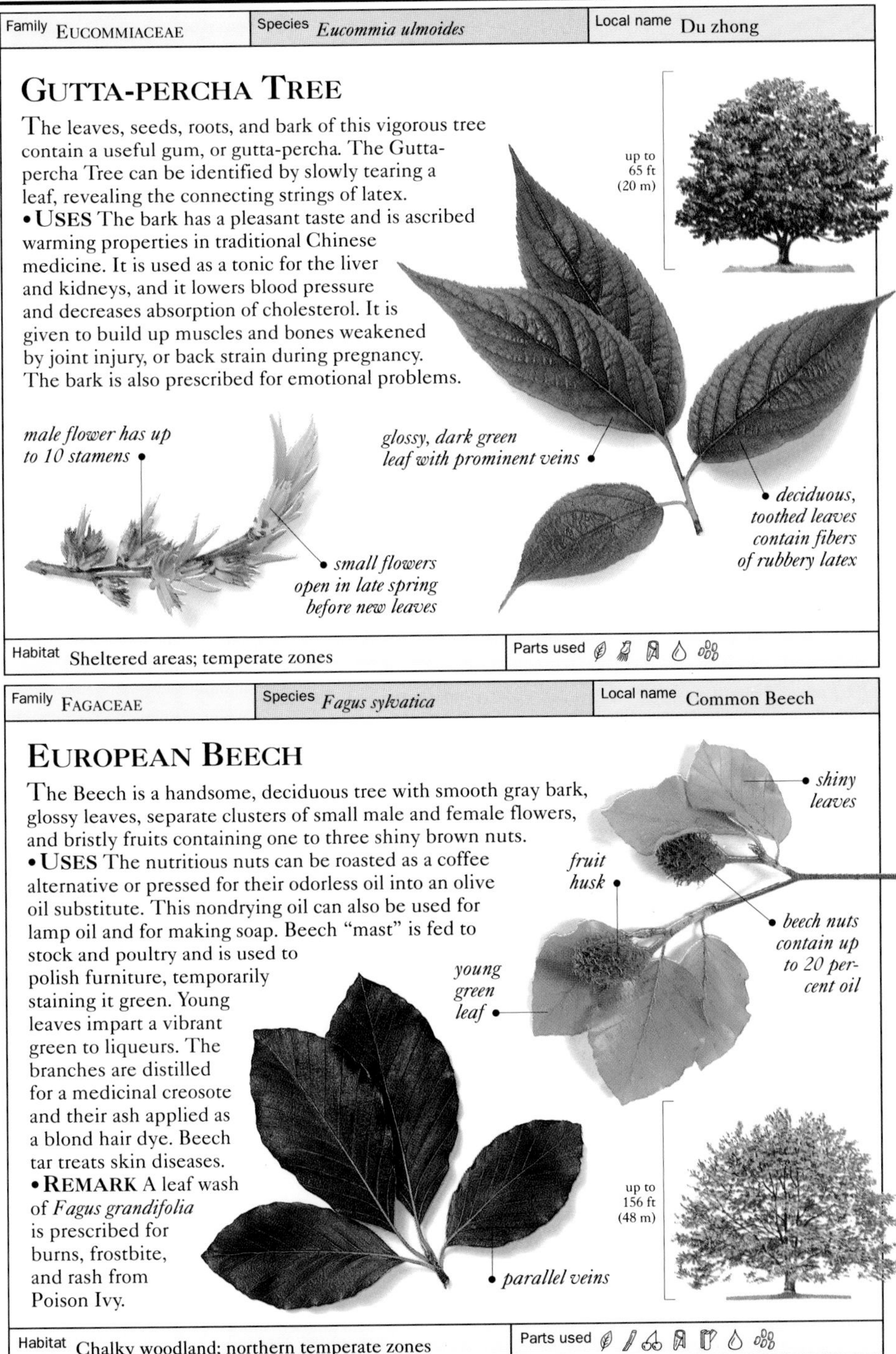
up to
65 ft
(20 m)
male flower has up to 10 stamens
glossy, dark green leaf with prominent veins
deciduous, toothed leaves contain fibers of rubbery latex
small flowers open in late spring before new leaves
shiny leaves
fruit husk
beech nuts contain up to 20 percent oil
young green leaf
parallel veins
up to
156 ft
(48 m)

Habitat Sheltered areas; temperate zones	Parts used

Family FAGACEAE	Species *Fagus sylvatica*	Local name Common Beech

EUROPEAN BEECH

The Beech is a handsome, deciduous tree with smooth gray bark, glossy leaves, separate clusters of small male and female flowers, and bristly fruits containing one to three shiny brown nuts.

• **USES** The nutritious nuts can be roasted as a coffee alternative or pressed for their odorless oil into an olive oil substitute. This nondrying oil can also be used for lamp oil and for making soap. Beech "mast" is fed to stock and poultry and is used to polish furniture, temporarily staining it green. Young leaves impart a vibrant green to liqueurs. The branches are distilled for a medicinal creosote and their ash applied as a blond hair dye. Beech tar treats skin diseases.

• **REMARK** A leaf wash of *Fagus grandifolia* is prescribed for burns, frostbite, and rash from Poison Ivy.

Habitat Chalky woodland; northern temperate zones	Parts used

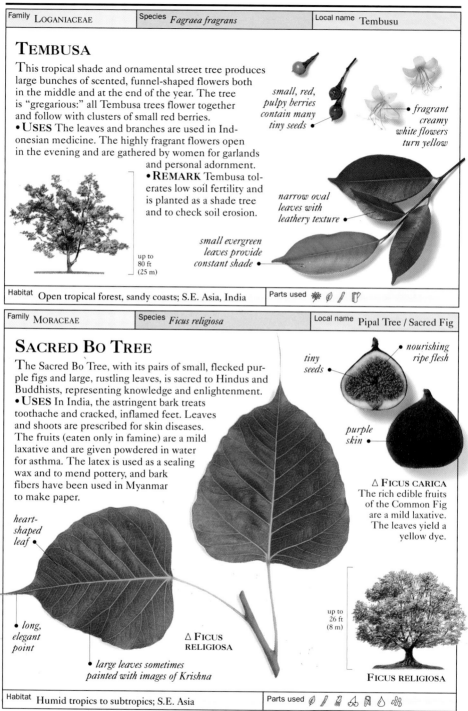

Family LOGANIACEAE	Species *Fagraea fragrans*	Local name Tembusu

TEMBUSA

This tropical shade and ornamental street tree produces large bunches of scented, funnel-shaped flowers both in the middle and at the end of the year. The tree is "gregarious:" all Tembusa trees flower together and follow with clusters of small red berries.

• **USES** The leaves and branches are used in Indonesian medicine. The highly fragrant flowers open in the evening and are gathered by women for garlands and personal adornment.

• **REMARK** Tembusa tolerates low soil fertility and is planted as a shade tree and to check soil erosion.

up to 80 ft (25 m)

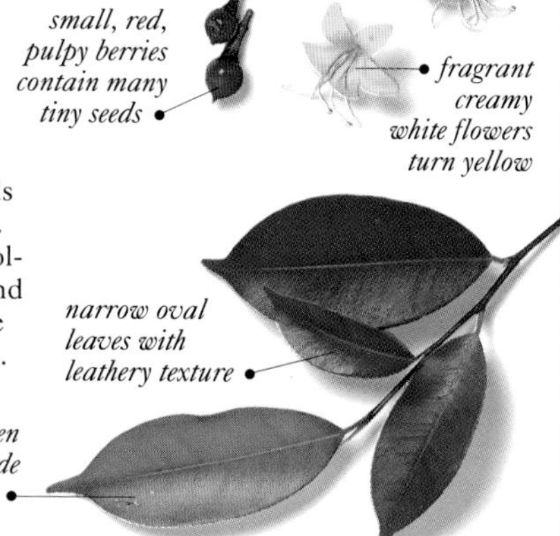
small, red, pulpy berries contain many tiny seeds
fragrant creamy white flowers turn yellow
narrow oval leaves with leathery texture
small evergreen leaves provide constant shade

Habitat Open tropical forest, sandy coasts; S.E. Asia, India	Parts used

Family MORACEAE	Species *Ficus religiosa*	Local name Pipal Tree / Sacred Fig

SACRED BO TREE

The Sacred Bo Tree, with its pairs of small, flecked purple figs and large, rustling leaves, is sacred to Hindus and Buddhists, representing knowledge and enlightenment.

• **USES** In India, the astringent bark treats toothache and cracked, inflamed feet. Leaves and shoots are prescribed for skin diseases. The fruits (eaten only in famine) are a mild laxative and are given powdered in water for asthma. The latex is used as a sealing wax and to mend pottery, and bark fibers have been used in Myanmar to make paper.

tiny seeds

nourishing ripe flesh

purple skin

△ FICUS CARICA
The rich edible fruits of the Common Fig are a mild laxative. The leaves yield a yellow dye.

heart-shaped leaf
long, elegant point
large leaves sometimes painted with images of Krishna

△ FICUS RELIGIOSA

up to 26 ft (8 m)

FICUS RELIGIOSA

Habitat Humid tropics to subtropics; S.E. Asia	Parts used

Family OLEACEAE	Species *Fraxinus ornus*	Local name Flowering Ash

MANNA ASH

This spring-flowering deciduous tree has smooth gray bark and showy, scented flowers, although the scent is unpleasant to some. • **USES** During the flowering season, bark excisions yield a sweet sap called manna (although this name is applied to the product of several plants). It makes a nutritious and gentle tonic for convalescence and is used to disguise other medicines, but it is mainly prescribed as a mild laxative for children and pregnant women.

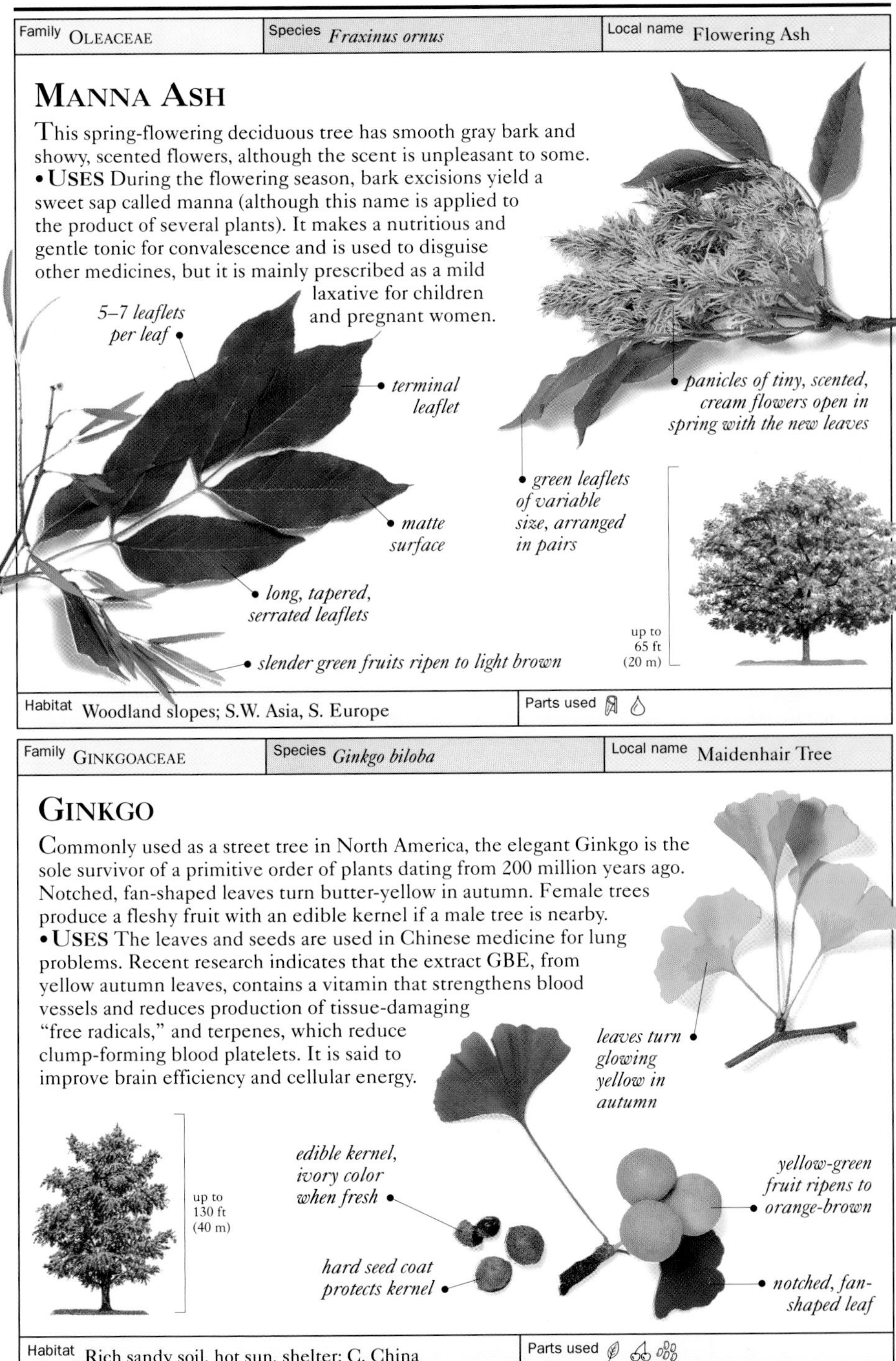
5–7 leaflets per leaf
terminal leaflet
matte surface
long, tapered, serrated leaflets
slender green fruits ripen to light brown
panicles of tiny, scented, cream flowers open in spring with the new leaves
green leaflets of variable size, arranged in pairs
up to 65 ft (20 m)
edible kernel, ivory color when fresh
hard seed coat protects kernel
leaves turn glowing yellow in autumn
yellow-green fruit ripens to orange-brown
notched, fan-shaped leaf
up to 130 ft (40 m)

Habitat Woodland slopes; S.W. Asia, S. Europe	Parts used

Family GINKGOACEAE	Species *Ginkgo biloba*	Local name Maidenhair Tree

GINKGO

Commonly used as a street tree in North America, the elegant Ginkgo is the sole survivor of a primitive order of plants dating from 200 million years ago. Notched, fan-shaped leaves turn butter-yellow in autumn. Female trees produce a fleshy fruit with an edible kernel if a male tree is nearby. • **USES** The leaves and seeds are used in Chinese medicine for lung problems. Recent research indicates that the extract GBE, from yellow autumn leaves, contains a vitamin that strengthens blood vessels and reduces production of tissue-damaging "free radicals," and terpenes, which reduce clump-forming blood platelets. It is said to improve brain efficiency and cellular energy.

Habitat Rich sandy soil, hot sun, shelter; C. China	Parts used

Family GNETACEAE	Species *Gnetum gnemon*	Local name Spinach Joint Fir

GNEMON TREE

The Gnemon Tree is a tropical evergreen with short, drooping branches and a gray trunk with rings created by the scars of old leaf joints. Small "flowers" yield yellow "fruits" that ripen to orange-red and contain a large kernel.

• **USES** Edible young leaves, shoots, and inflorescences are steamed and served hot with coconut milk, or in vegetable soup. The seeds are ground into a flour and made into frying crackers called "emping." In Indonesia, the leaves and seeds are given for anemia and fluid retention, and the root as an antidote for poison and a treatment for malaria.

• **REMARK** The *Gnetum* genus is thought to be a botanical link between conifers and flowering plants.

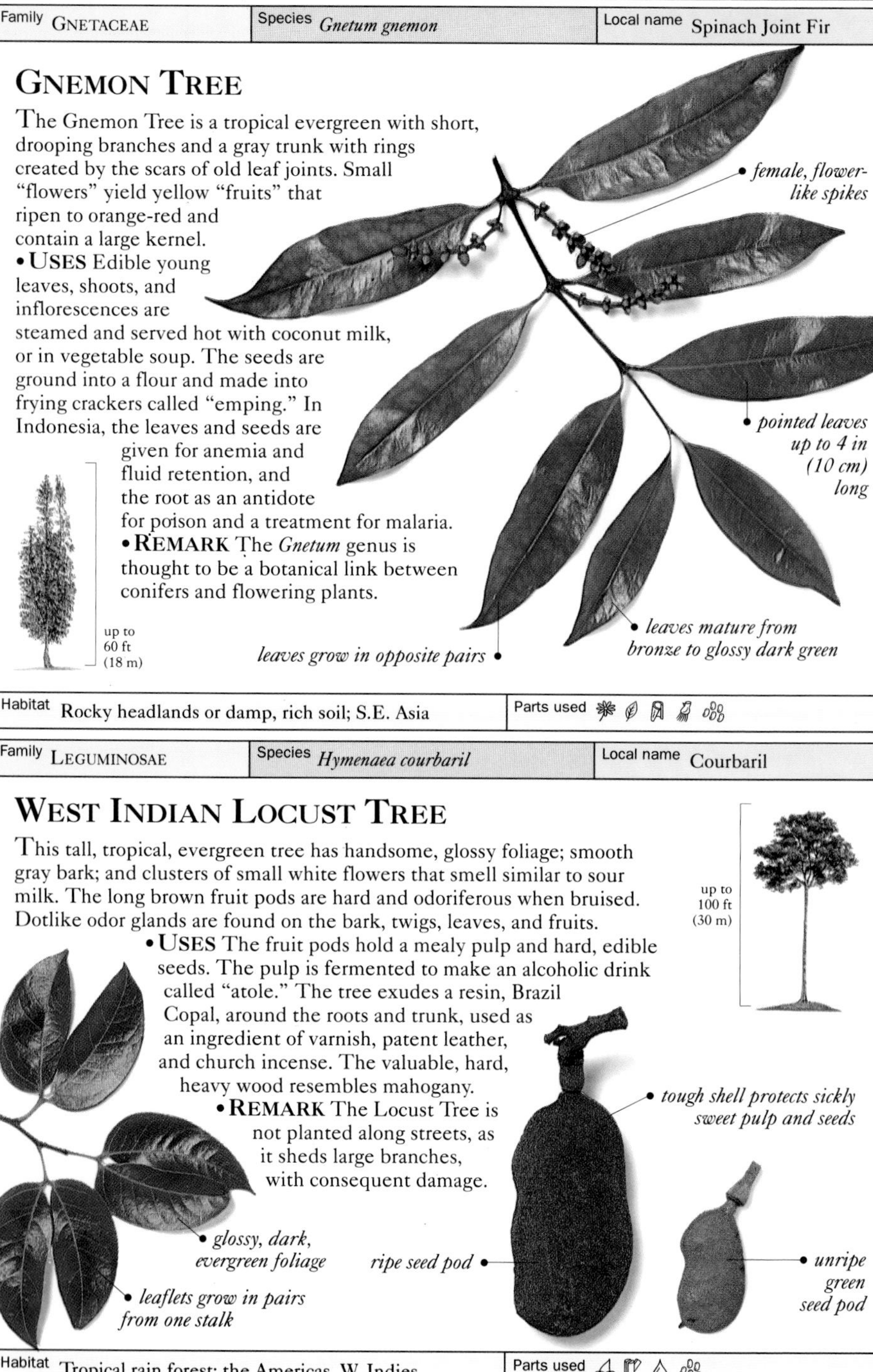
female, flower-like spikes
pointed leaves up to 4 in (10 cm) long
up to 60 ft (18 m)
leaves grow in opposite pairs
leaves mature from bronze to glossy dark green
up to 100 ft (30 m)
tough shell protects sickly sweet pulp and seeds
glossy, dark, evergreen foliage
ripe seed pod
unripe green seed pod
leaflets grow in pairs from one stalk

Habitat Rocky headlands or damp, rich soil; S.E. Asia	Parts used

Family LEGUMINOSAE	Species *Hymenaea courbaril*	Local name Courbaril

WEST INDIAN LOCUST TREE

This tall, tropical, evergreen tree has handsome, glossy foliage; smooth gray bark; and clusters of small white flowers that smell similar to sour milk. The long brown fruit pods are hard and odoriferous when bruised. Dotlike odor glands are found on the bark, twigs, leaves, and fruits.

• **USES** The fruit pods hold a mealy pulp and hard, edible seeds. The pulp is fermented to make an alcoholic drink called "atole." The tree exudes a resin, Brazil Copal, around the roots and trunk, used as an ingredient of varnish, patent leather, and church incense. The valuable, hard, heavy wood resembles mahogany.

• **REMARK** The Locust Tree is not planted along streets, as it sheds large branches, with consequent damage.

Habitat Tropical rain forest; the Americas, W. Indies	Parts used

Family ILLICIACEAE	Species *Illicium verum*	Local name Chinese Anise

STAR ANISE

All parts of this small, evergreen tree are aromatic: the smooth, gray-white bark; narrow to elliptic, shiny green leaves; solitary yellow flowers; and glossy brown seeds.
• **USES** The distinctive seeds and pods are used as a spice in Asian cookery, notably as an ingredient of Chinese five-spice powder. The fruits and foliage yield essential oil, used as a substitute anise seed flavoring, or, medicinally, to promote appetite and digestion and to relieve chest complaints, rheumatism, and flatulence. The oil appears in soaps, hair oils, and Asian perfumes.
• **REMARK** Japanese Star Anise (*Illicium anisatum*) has cardamom-scented, poisonous fruits, used externally in Asian medicine. Its flowers lack scent and the leaves are a poison. This Star Anise is revered in Japan and planted near Buddhist temples, where the bark is burned as incense.

◁ ILLICIUM VERUM

each point of the star-shaped seed pod contains a seed

ILLICIUM ANISATUM ▽

smooth, aromatic, evergreen leaves are poisonous

up to 60 ft (18 m)

ILLICIUM VERUM

Habitat Lime-free soils, light tropics; China, Vietnam	Parts used

Family JUGLANDACEAE	Species *Juglans regia*	Local name Persian Walnut

ENGLISH WALNUT

The deciduous English Walnut has smooth silver bark that fissures with age, dark green leaves, and male catkins in spring or early summer. The autumn fruits appear singly, in pairs, or in threes.
• **USES** English Walnut consumption reduces cholesterol. The nuts are enjoyed fresh in salads and sweets, or are pickled before their shells harden. They give edible walnut oil which is a nondrying oil also used in soap production. In China, the nuts treat wheezing, back and leg pain, and constipation. The bark, leaves, and husks yield a brown dye. Crushed leaves treat skin eruptions and repel insects.
• **REMARK** In India, the Walnut and Chestnut trees are symbols of longevity.

5–9 pointed leaflets on leaf stalk

edible kernel

hard-shelled walnut develops inside fruit

up to 100 ft (30 m)

smooth, dark green leaflets, aromatic when bruised

green leaf stalk

green fruit on sturdy, short stalk

Habitat Open woodland; S.E. Europe, Himalayas, China	Parts used

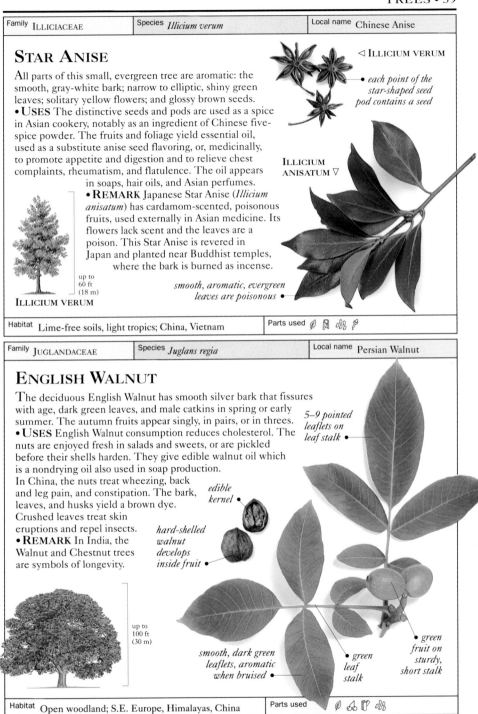

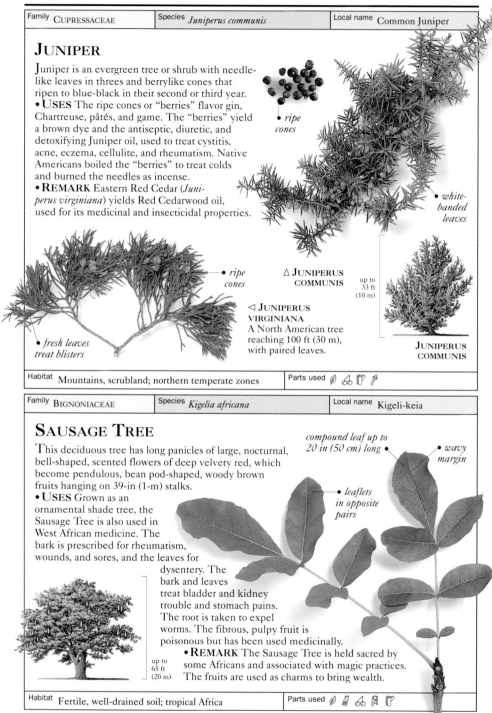

Family CUPRESSACEAE	Species *Juniperus communis*	Local name Common Juniper

JUNIPER

Juniper is an evergreen tree or shrub with needle-like leaves in threes and berrylike cones that ripen to blue-black in their second or third year.

• **USES** The ripe cones or "berries" flavor gin, Chartreuse, pâtés, and game. The "berries" yield a brown dye and the antiseptic, diuretic, and detoxifying Juniper oil, used to treat cystitis, acne, eczema, cellulite, and rheumatism. Native Americans boiled the "berries" to treat colds and burned the needles as incense.

• **REMARK** Eastern Red Cedar (*Juniperus virginiana*) yields Red Cedarwood oil, used for its medicinal and insecticidal properties.

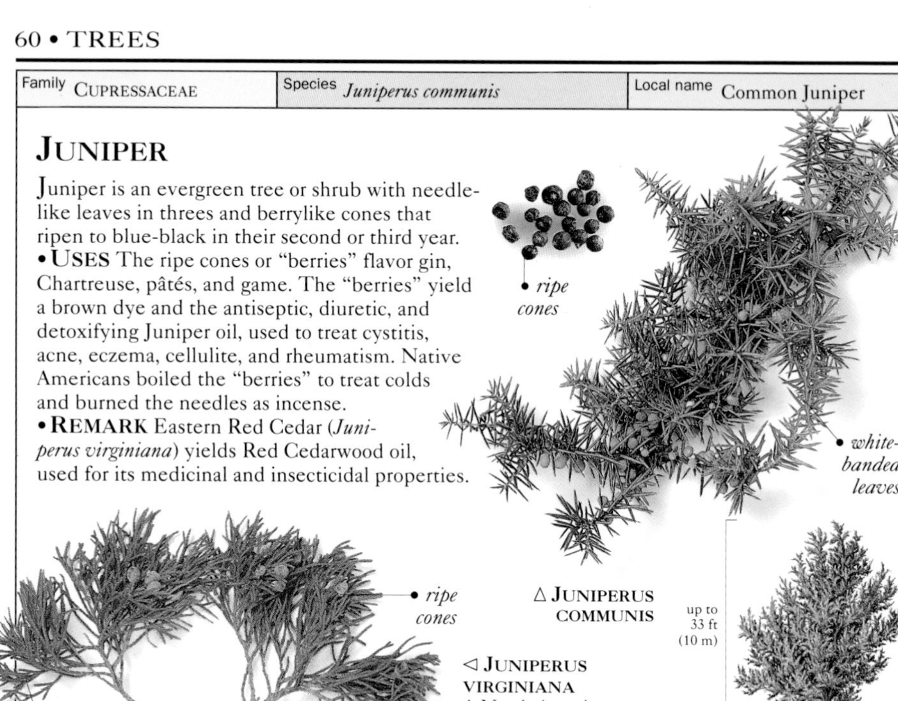
ripe cones
white-banded leaves
ripe cones
fresh leaves treat blisters
up to 33 ft (10 m)

△ JUNIPERUS COMMUNIS

◁ JUNIPERUS VIRGINIANA
A North American tree reaching 100 ft (30 m), with paired leaves.

JUNIPERUS COMMUNIS

Habitat Mountains, scrubland; northern temperate zones	Parts used

Family BIGNONIACEAE	Species *Kigelia africana*	Local name Kigeli-keia

SAUSAGE TREE

This deciduous tree has long panicles of large, nocturnal, bell-shaped, scented flowers of deep velvety red, which become pendulous, bean pod-shaped, woody brown fruits hanging on 39-in (1-m) stalks.

• **USES** Grown as an ornamental shade tree, the Sausage Tree is also used in West African medicine. The bark is prescribed for rheumatism, wounds, and sores, and the leaves for dysentery. The bark and leaves treat bladder and kidney trouble and stomach pains. The root is taken to expel worms. The fibrous, pulpy fruit is poisonous but has been used medicinally.

• **REMARK** The Sausage Tree is held sacred by some Africans and associated with magic practices. The fruits are used as charms to bring wealth.

compound leaf up to 20 in (50 cm) long

wavy margin

leaflets in opposite pairs

up to 65 ft (20 m)

Habitat Fertile, well-drained soil; tropical Africa	Parts used

Family PINACEAE	Species *Larix laricina*	Local name American Larch

TAMARACK

This deciduous conifer has elegant, horizontal branches with slender, drooping branchlets and gray bark that turns brown and scaly with age. • **USES** A medicinal tree of the Canadian native peoples, the inner bark hastens tissue renewal, and the Cree used it to stop bleeding, for earache and eye inflammation, and as a wash for running sores, gangrene, and itchy skin. The bark extract is a laxative and a diuretic, treating jaundice and colic. It is drunk as a weak tea to treat melancholy, and the resin is chewed for sore throats. • **REMARK** The inner bark of the European Larch (*Larix decidua*) is astringent and diuretic, used to treat bronchitis and urinary inflammation.

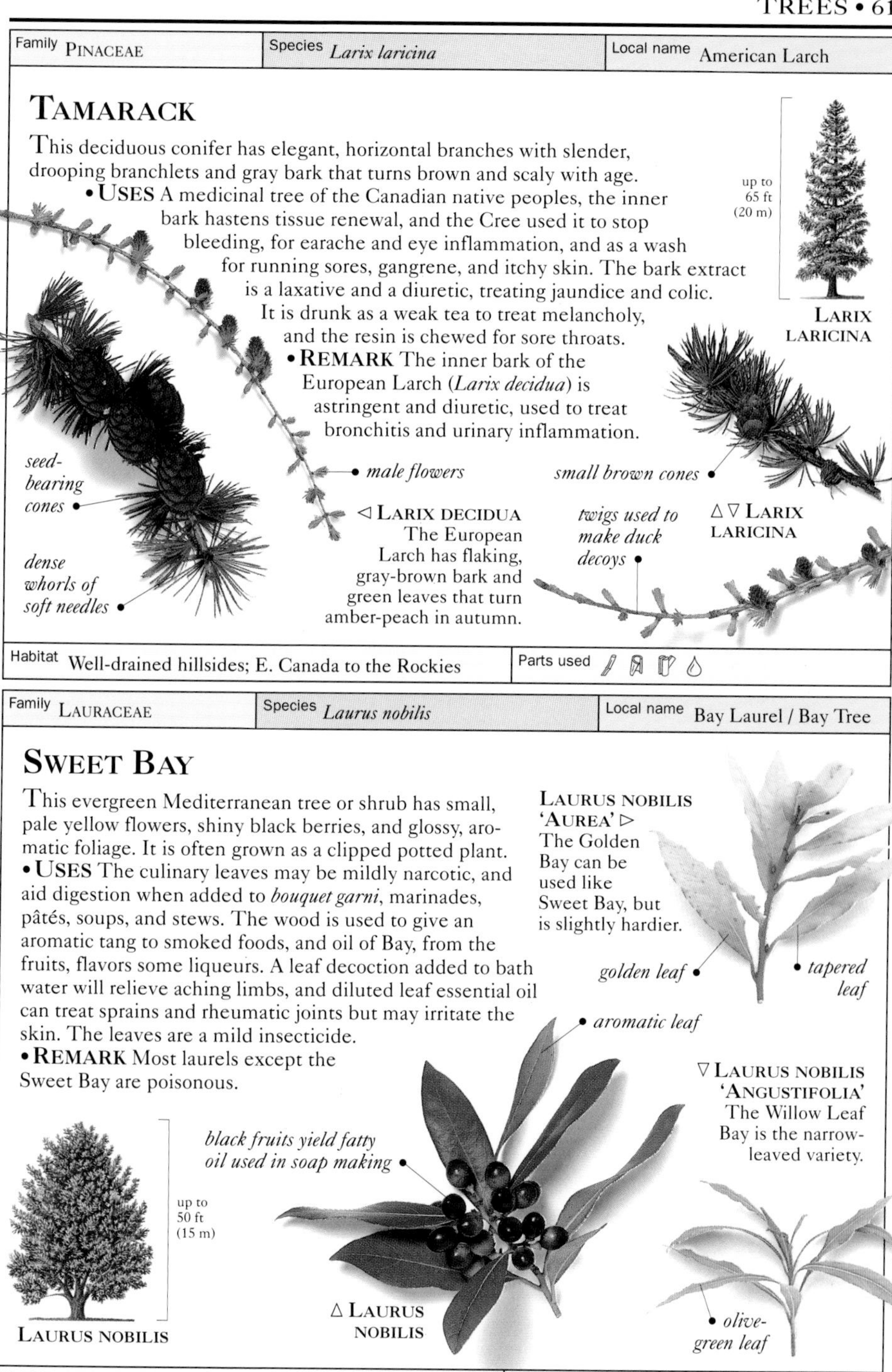
up to
65 ft
(20 m)
LARIX LARICINA
seed-bearing cones
dense whorls of soft needles
male flowers
small brown cones
twigs used to make duck decoys
up to
50 ft
(15 m)
LAURUS NOBILIS
golden leaf
tapered leaf
aromatic leaf
black fruits yield fatty oil used in soap making
olive-green leaf

◁ LARIX DECIDUA The European Larch has flaking, gray-brown bark and green leaves that turn amber-peach in autumn.

△▽ LARIX LARICINA

Habitat Well-drained hillsides; E. Canada to the Rockies	Parts used

Family LAURACEAE	Species *Laurus nobilis*	Local name Bay Laurel / Bay Tree

SWEET BAY

This evergreen Mediterranean tree or shrub has small, pale yellow flowers, shiny black berries, and glossy, aromatic foliage. It is often grown as a clipped potted plant. • **USES** The culinary leaves may be mildly narcotic, and aid digestion when added to *bouquet garni*, marinades, pâtés, soups, and stews. The wood is used to give an aromatic tang to smoked foods, and oil of Bay, from the fruits, flavors some liqueurs. A leaf decoction added to bath water will relieve aching limbs, and diluted leaf essential oil can treat sprains and rheumatic joints but may irritate the skin. The leaves are a mild insecticide.
• **REMARK** Most laurels except the Sweet Bay are poisonous.

LAURUS NOBILIS 'AUREA' ▷ The Golden Bay can be used like Sweet Bay, but is slightly hardier.

▽ LAURUS NOBILIS 'ANGUSTIFOLIA' The Willow Leaf Bay is the narrow-leaved variety.

△ LAURUS NOBILIS

Habitat Moist rocky valleys; Mediterranean	Parts used

Family OLEACEAE | Species *Ligustrum lucidum* | Local name White Wax Tree

CHINESE GLOSSY PRIVET

This evergreen tree or shrub bears bronze leaves that mature to green, cream flowers, and black berries.

• **USES** Glossy Privet is a Chinese yin nourishment. The fruit is said to aid kidney function and strengthen muscles and bones and is prescribed for rheumatic pain, back and knee weakness, palpitations, and insomnia, and to aid clear vision and hearing. The fruit is also prescribed for premature graying, dryness, and loss of hair. The leaves and young shoots give a strong yellow fabric dye, and ripe berries produce a gray-green dye. The flowers of Common Privet (*Ligustrum vulgare*) yield a mild perfume, and an oil infusion to reduce wind- and sunburn. The bark gives a yellow dye.

• **REMARK** The local name "White Wax Tree" is from an industrial wax, produced when insects feed on the stems.

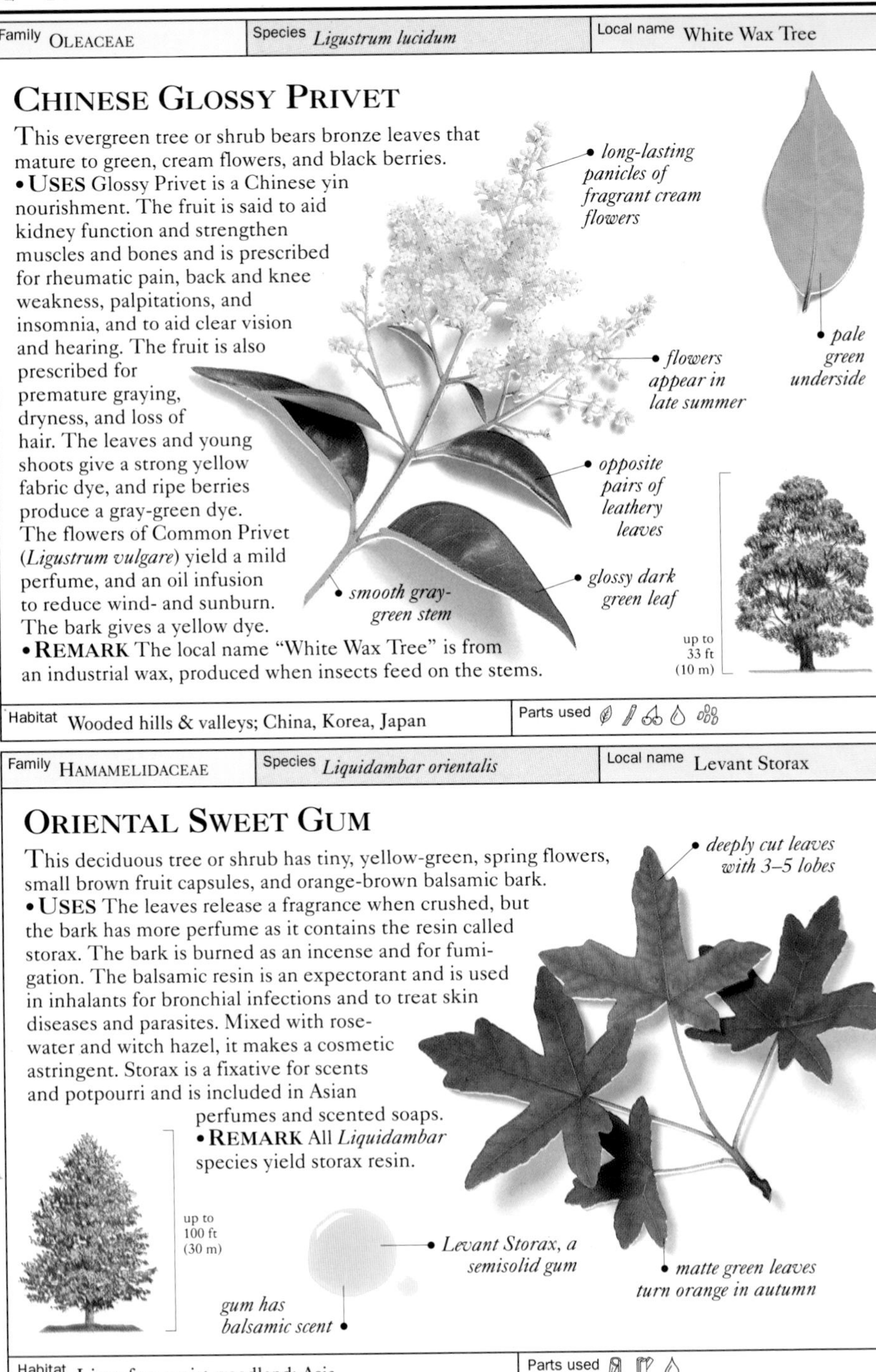
long-lasting panicles of fragrant cream flowers
pale green underside
flowers appear in late summer
opposite pairs of leathery leaves
glossy dark green leaf
smooth gray-green stem
up to 33 ft (10 m)
deeply cut leaves with 3–5 lobes
Levant Storax, a semisolid gum
gum has balsamic scent
matte green leaves turn orange in autumn
up to 100 ft (30 m)

Habitat Wooded hills & valleys; China, Korea, Japan | Parts used

Family HAMAMELIDACEAE | Species *Liquidambar orientalis* | Local name Levant Storax

ORIENTAL SWEET GUM

This deciduous tree or shrub has tiny, yellow-green, spring flowers, small brown fruit capsules, and orange-brown balsamic bark.

• **USES** The leaves release a fragrance when crushed, but the bark has more perfume as it contains the resin called storax. The bark is burned as an incense and for fumigation. The balsamic resin is an expectorant and is used in inhalants for bronchial infections and to treat skin diseases and parasites. Mixed with rose-water and witch hazel, it makes a cosmetic astringent. Storax is a fixative for scents and potpourri and is included in Asian perfumes and scented soaps.

• **REMARK** All *Liquidambar* species yield storax resin.

Habitat Lime-free moist woodland; Asia | Parts used

Family MAGNOLIACEAE | Species *Magnolia officinalis* | Local name Chuan how-pow

MAGNOLIA

The deciduous Magnolia has purplish gray bark, long, wavy-edged, light green leaves, and large, fragrant, solitary, cream-white flowers.

• **USES** Magnolia species are used for their aromatic, stimulant, and tonic properties. The bark contains an essential oil and a muscle relaxant, and is used to treat stomach spasms, peptic ulcers, diarrhea, vomiting, coughs, and asthma. It is an antiseptic treatment for typhoid, malaria, and salmonella.

• **REMARK** The shape of Magnolia flowers indicates that this native Chinese tree has stayed almost unchanged for 100 million years.

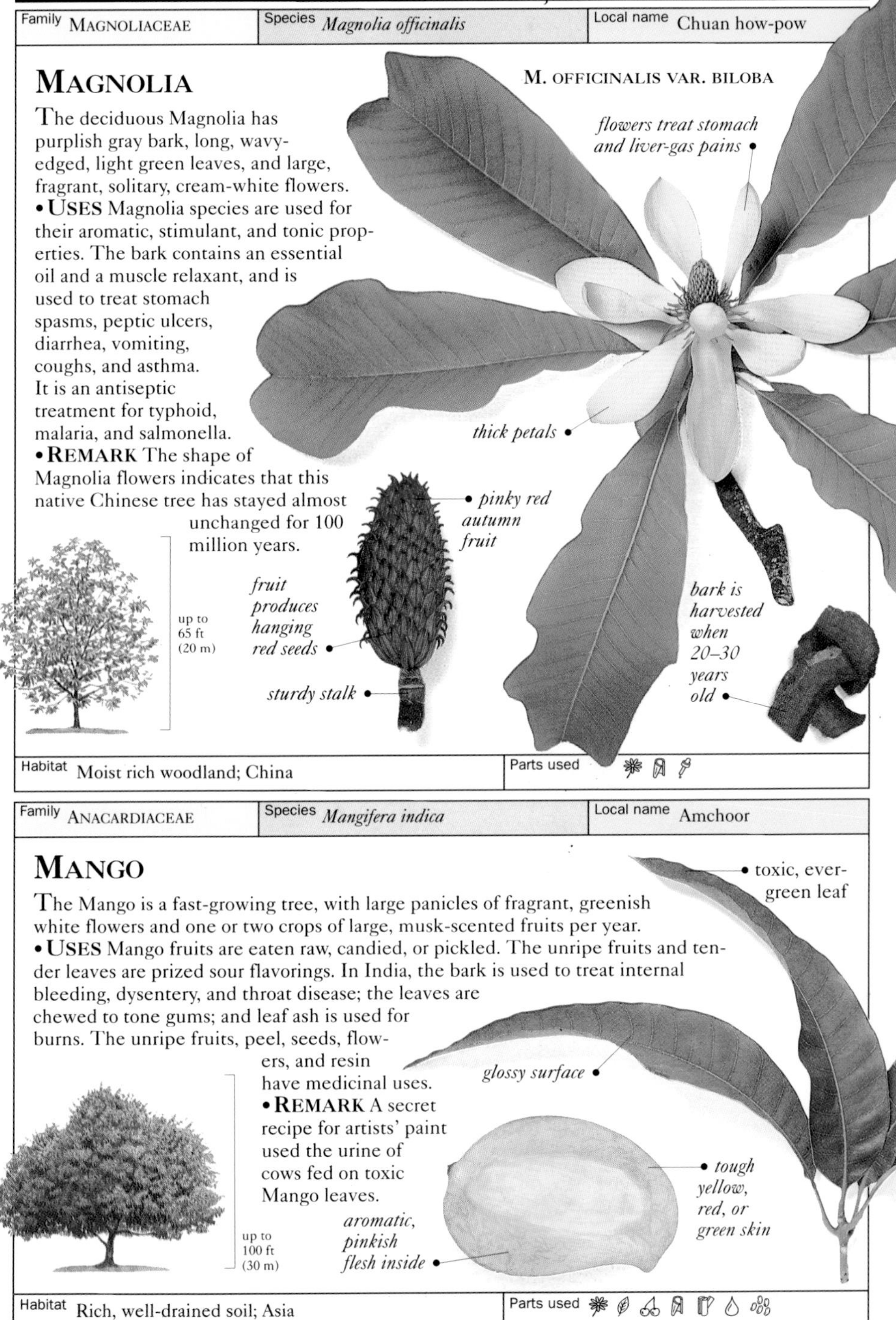
M. OFFICINALIS VAR. BILOBA
flowers treat stomach and liver-gas pains
thick petals
pinky red autumn fruit
fruit produces hanging red seeds
sturdy stalk
bark is harvested when 20–30 years old
up to 65 ft (20 m)
toxic, evergreen leaf
glossy surface
tough yellow, red, or green skin
aromatic, pinkish flesh inside
up to 100 ft (30 m)

Habitat Moist rich woodland; China | Parts used

Family ANACARDIACEAE | Species *Mangifera indica* | Local name Amchoor

MANGO

The Mango is a fast-growing tree, with large panicles of fragrant, greenish white flowers and one or two crops of large, musk-scented fruits per year.

• **USES** Mango fruits are eaten raw, candied, or pickled. The unripe fruits and tender leaves are prized sour flavorings. In India, the bark is used to treat internal bleeding, dysentery, and throat disease; the leaves are chewed to tone gums; and leaf ash is used for burns. The unripe fruits, peel, seeds, flowers, and resin have medicinal uses.

• **REMARK** A secret recipe for artists' paint used the urine of cows fed on toxic Mango leaves.

Habitat Rich, well-drained soil; Asia | Parts used

Family MYRTACEAE	Species *Melaleuca bracteata*	Local name Feathery Ti Tree

BLACK TEA TREE

The Black Tea Tree is an elegant small tree or shrub with gnarled, twisting branches; feathery, light and dark green foliage; and small flowers with conspicuous stamens and woody seed pods. The *Melaleuca* genus includes over 150 species of evergreen trees and shrubs, many of which yield important essential oils.

• **USES** Although the essential oil from this species is not known to have the powerful medicinal applications of its more famous cousins, the light oil, extracted mainly from the aromatic leaves, is a mild stimulant with insect-repellent properties and a clean, refreshing, sweet fragrance used in perfumes. This oil's potential awaits further investigation by scientists.

• **REMARK** Many species are called Tea Tree because their growing tips resemble the tea plant, although they are not related.

up to 6½ ft (2 m)

• aromatic leaves

Habitat Coastal soils; Australia to Malaysia	Parts used

Family MYRTACEAE	Species *Melaleuca cajuputi*	Local name Paper Bark Tree

CAJUPUT

This evergreen has a dense, gray-green crown on a stout, often twisted, trunk covered with pink, papery, fibrous bark.

• **USES** Antiseptic Cajuput oil is extracted from the leaves and twigs. Most commercial Cajuput oil comes from the leaves and twigs of *Melaleuca leucadendron*, almost identical to *M. cajuputi* and said to be the same species by some authorities. The oil is an insecticide, a stimulant, a gastrointestinal antiseptic, and a painkiller, and combats airborne infections. Tea Tree oil from *M. alternifolia* is the most important product of the genus and has huge healing potential. It is a powerful antiseptic and immunostimulant, active against bacteria, viruses, and fungi such as athlete's foot and thrush. It helps treat colds, flu, lesions, warts, and acne. Niaouli oil is distilled from the leaves and shoots of *M. viridiflora*. It strengthens the immune system, and is an antiseptic for chest infections, and a tissue stimulant for wounds and acne. A layer applied before cobalt radiation therapy reduces burns.

MELALEUCA LEUCADENDRON ▷
MELALEUCA CAJUPUTI ▽
• pale, papery bark peels easily
• pink-fawn fibrous bark in layers

△ MELALEUCA LEUCADENDRON Woody fruit capsules appear after flowers.

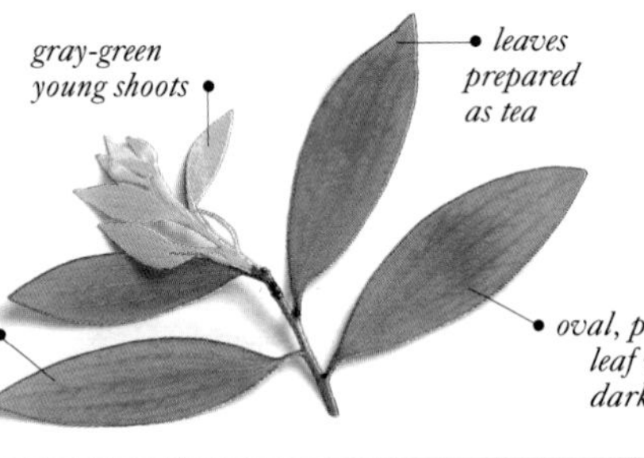
gray-green young shoots
• leaves prepared as tea
crushed leaf applied as painkiller and inhaled for headaches
• oval, pointed leaf with 3 dark veins

up to 80 ft (25 m)

◁ △ M. CAJUPUTI

Habitat Coastal swampland; Australia to Malaysia	Parts used

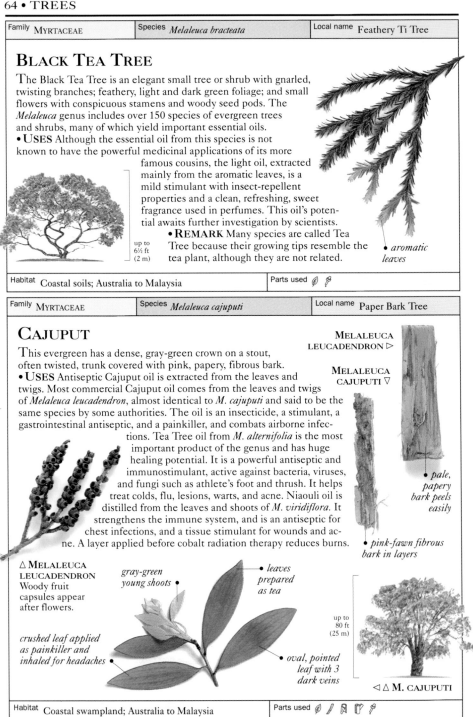

Family MELIACEAE	Species *Melia azadirachta*	Local name Margosa

NEEM TREE

This deep-rooted shade tree with small white flowers remains evergreen except during drought. Fast-growing and tolerant of poor sites, it is valued as the village pharmacy.

• **USES** The seed oil treats leprosy and other skin diseases, shows carcinogen-reducing properties, and is antifungal and antiviral. The bark, leaves, and roots are tonic and reduce fever. The leaves are antiseptic and expel worms. As a nontoxic pesticide the seed oil compounds destroy bacteria and over 200 insect species, including locusts and mites. The spermicidal seeds may result in a safe male contraceptive pill.

• **REMARK** The Neem Tree is valuable for reforestation programs on marginal land.

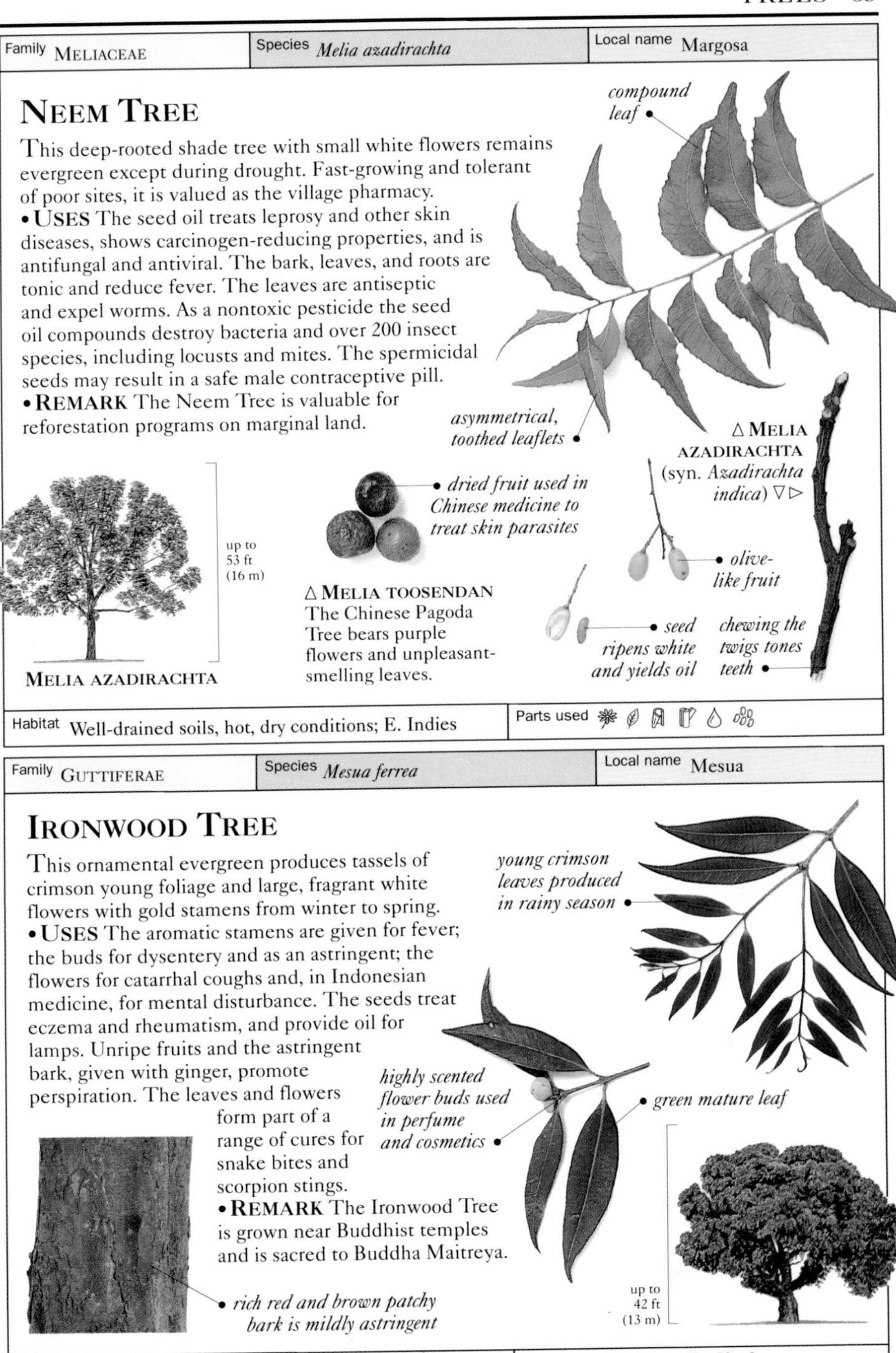
compound leaf
asymmetrical, toothed leaflets
dried fruit used in Chinese medicine to treat skin parasites
olive-like fruit
seed ripens white and yields oil
chewing the twigs tones teeth
up to 53 ft (16 m)
young crimson leaves produced in rainy season
highly scented flower buds used in perfume and cosmetics
green mature leaf
rich red and brown patchy bark is mildly astringent
up to 42 ft (13 m)

△ MELIA AZADIRACHTA (syn. *Azadirachta indica*) ▽ ▷

MELIA AZADIRACHTA

△ MELIA TOOSENDAN The Chinese Pagoda Tree bears purple flowers and unpleasant-smelling leaves.

Habitat Well-drained soils, hot, dry conditions; E. Indies	Parts used

Family GUTTIFERAE	Species *Mesua ferrea*	Local name Mesua

IRONWOOD TREE

This ornamental evergreen produces tassels of crimson young foliage and large, fragrant white flowers with gold stamens from winter to spring.

• **USES** The aromatic stamens are given for fever; the buds for dysentery and as an astringent; the flowers for catarrhal coughs and, in Indonesian medicine, for mental disturbance. The seeds treat eczema and rheumatism, and provide oil for lamps. Unripe fruits and the astringent bark, given with ginger, promote perspiration. The leaves and flowers form part of a range of cures for snake bites and scorpion stings.

• **REMARK** The Ironwood Tree is grown near Buddhist temples and is sacred to Buddha Maitreya.

Habitat Fertile loam; E. Himalayas to Malaysia	Parts used

Family MAGNOLIACEAE	Species *Michelia champaca*	Local name Chêmpaka

CHAMPACA

Champaca is a fast-growing evergreen valued for its small, waxy, perfumed, white or golden flowers.

• **USES** The tree is planted in Malay graveyards and Indian temple grounds to supply flowers for religious offerings. The decorative blossoms yield the celebrated champac perfume, used to scent clothes and hair oils. In India, the leaves are fed to silkworms, the bark reduces fevers, the purgative root treats abscesses, the flowers treat kidney disease, and the flower oil helps inflamed eyes.

• **REMARK** The flowers of the Banana Shrub (*Michelia figo*) yield a banana-scented hair oil.

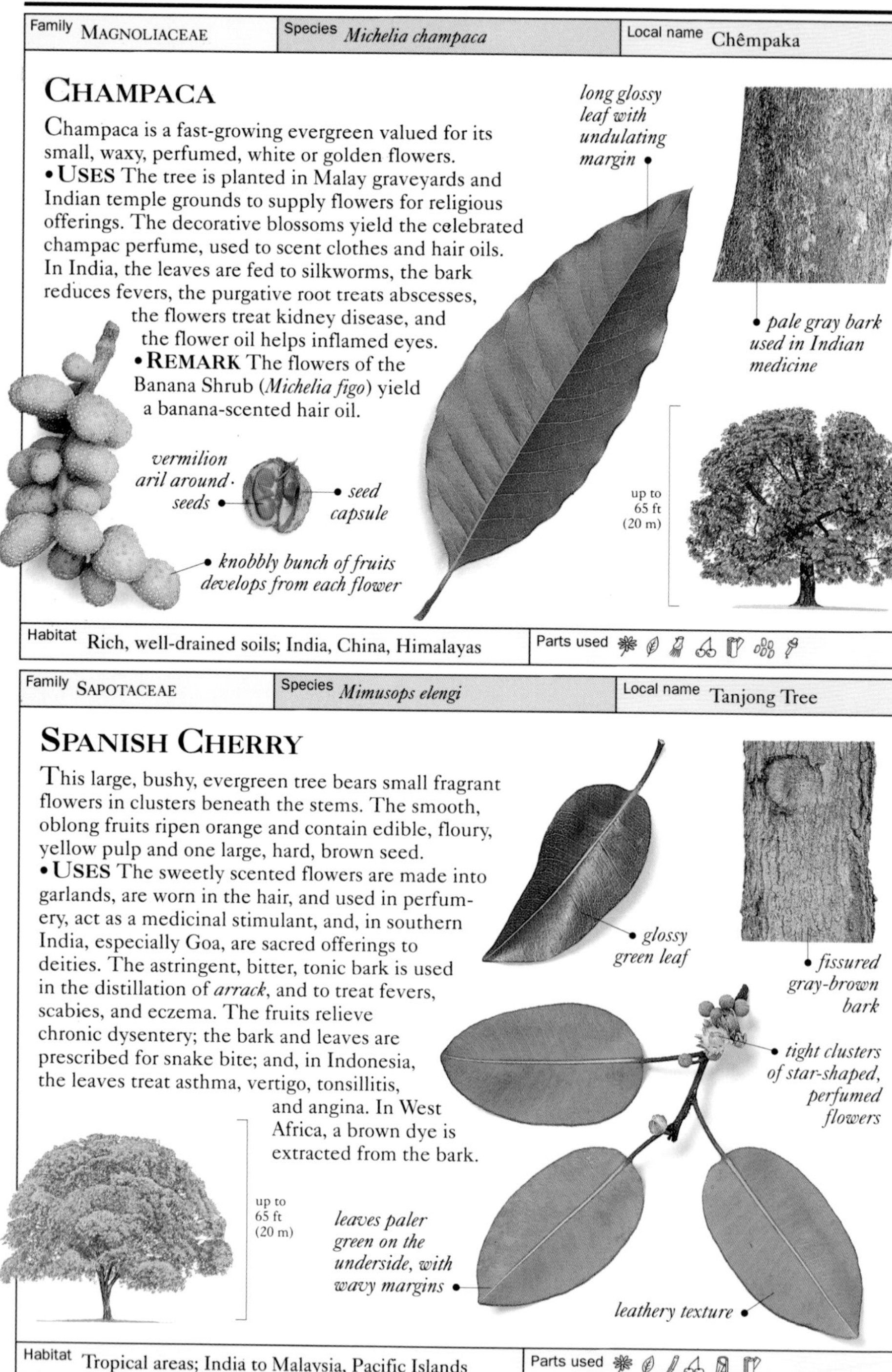
long glossy leaf with undulating margin
pale gray bark used in Indian medicine
up to 65 ft (20 m)
vermilion aril around seeds
seed capsule
knobbly bunch of fruits develops from each flower
glossy green leaf
fissured gray-brown bark
tight clusters of star-shaped, perfumed flowers
up to 65 ft (20 m)
leaves paler green on the underside, with wavy margins
leathery texture

Habitat Rich, well-drained soils; India, China, Himalayas	Parts used

Family SAPOTACEAE	Species *Mimusops elengi*	Local name Tanjong Tree

SPANISH CHERRY

This large, bushy, evergreen tree bears small fragrant flowers in clusters beneath the stems. The smooth, oblong fruits ripen orange and contain edible, floury, yellow pulp and one large, hard, brown seed.

• **USES** The sweetly scented flowers are made into garlands, are worn in the hair, and used in perfumery, act as a medicinal stimulant, and, in southern India, especially Goa, are sacred offerings to deities. The astringent, bitter, tonic bark is used in the distillation of *arrack*, and to treat fevers, scabies, and eczema. The fruits relieve chronic dysentery; the bark and leaves are prescribed for snake bite; and, in Indonesia, the leaves treat asthma, vertigo, tonsillitis, and angina. In West Africa, a brown dye is extracted from the bark.

Habitat Tropical areas; India to Malaysia, Pacific Islands	Parts used

Family ANNONACEAE	Species *Monodora myristica*	Local name Jamaica Nutmeg

Calabash Nutmeg

This ornamental evergreen has fragrant, orchid-like, yellow-spotted crimson flowers and large globular fruits with many seeds.

• **USES** The seeds contain a nutmeg-flavored oil used in local cooking. The seeds are roasted, ground, and applied to wounds or are chewed and rubbed on the forehead to relieve headaches. They are also made into decorative beadwork and crushed to yield an insecticide. The root is chewed for toothache.

• **REMARK** The Orchid Flower Tree (*Monodora tenuifolia*) yields edible, aromatic seeds used for seasoning and eaten by children.

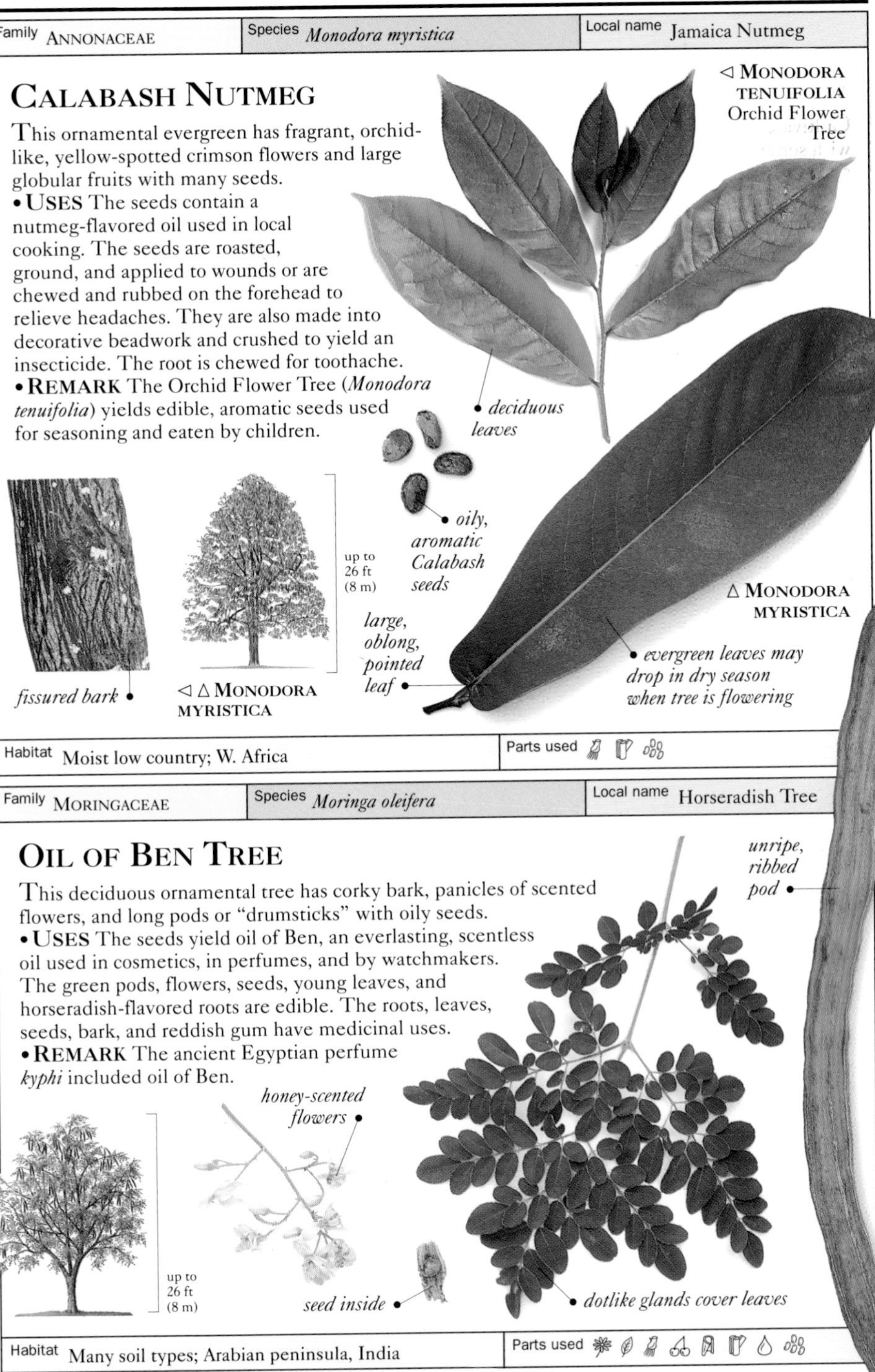
◁ MONODORA TENUIFOLIA Orchid Flower Tree
• deciduous leaves
• oily, aromatic Calabash seeds
△ MONODORA MYRISTICA
large, oblong, pointed leaf •
• evergreen leaves may drop in dry season when tree is flowering
up to 26 ft (8 m)
fissured bark •
◁ △ MONODORA MYRISTICA
unripe, ribbed pod •
honey-scented flowers •
up to 26 ft (8 m)
seed inside •
• dotlike glands cover leaves

Habitat Moist low country; W. Africa	Parts used

Family MORINGACEAE	Species *Moringa oleifera*	Local name Horseradish Tree

Oil of Ben Tree

This deciduous ornamental tree has corky bark, panicles of scented flowers, and long pods or "drumsticks" with oily seeds.

• **USES** The seeds yield oil of Ben, an everlasting, scentless oil used in cosmetics, in perfumes, and by watchmakers. The green pods, flowers, seeds, young leaves, and horseradish-flavored roots are edible. The roots, leaves, seeds, bark, and reddish gum have medicinal uses.

• **REMARK** The ancient Egyptian perfume *kyphi* included oil of Ben.

Habitat Many soil types; Arabian peninsula, India	Parts used

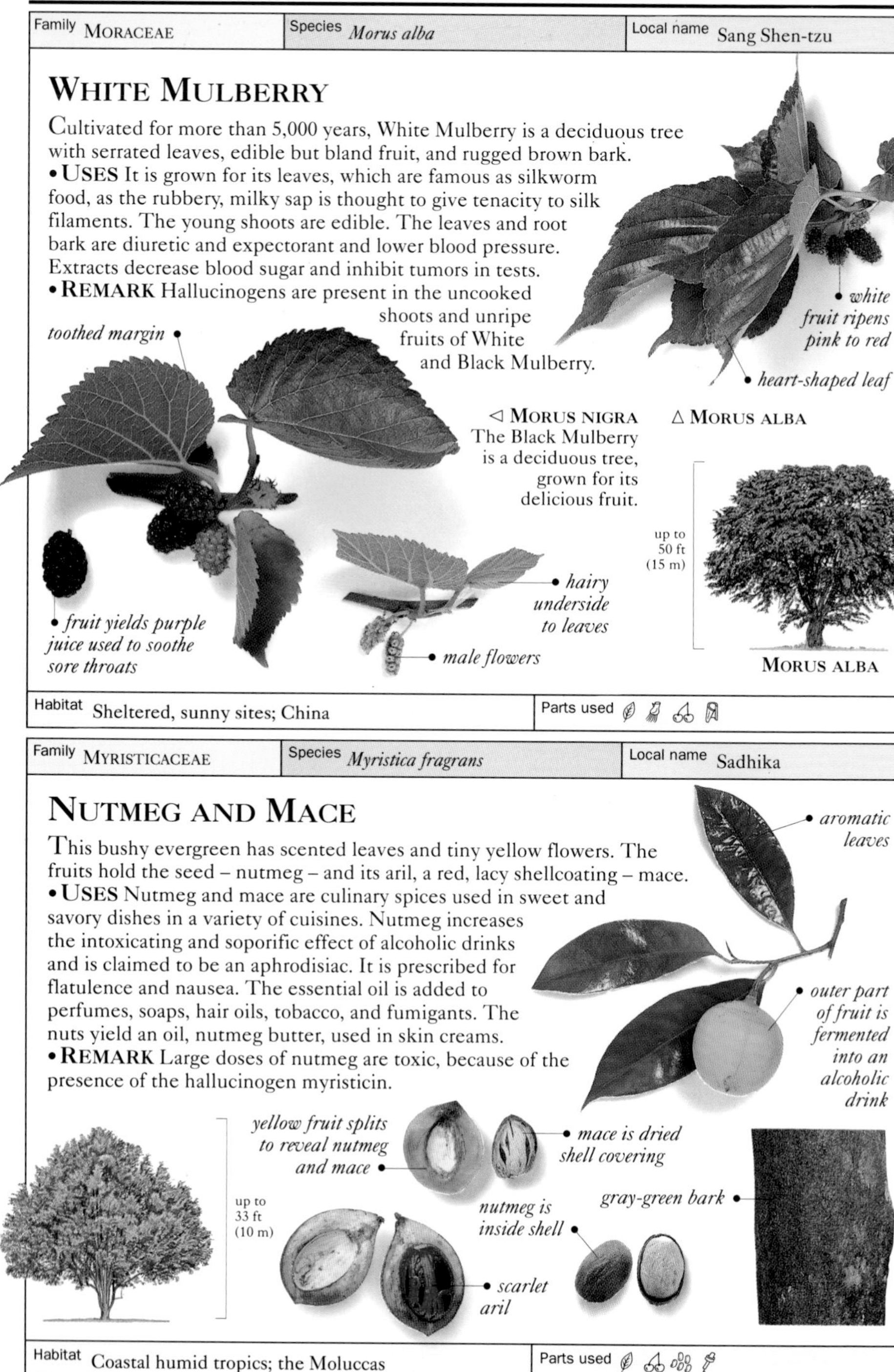
white fruit ripens pink to red
heart-shaped leaf
toothed margin
fruit yields purple juice used to soothe sore throats
hairy underside to leaves
male flowers
aromatic leaves
outer part of fruit is fermented into an alcoholic drink
yellow fruit splits to reveal nutmeg and mace
mace is dried shell covering
gray-green bark
nutmeg is inside shell
scarlet aril

Family MORACEAE	Species *Morus alba*	Local name Sang Shen-tzu

WHITE MULBERRY

Cultivated for more than 5,000 years, White Mulberry is a deciduous tree with serrated leaves, edible but bland fruit, and rugged brown bark.

• **USES** It is grown for its leaves, which are famous as silkworm food, as the rubbery, milky sap is thought to give tenacity to silk filaments. The young shoots are edible. The leaves and root bark are diuretic and expectorant and lower blood pressure. Extracts decrease blood sugar and inhibit tumors in tests.

• **REMARK** Hallucinogens are present in the uncooked shoots and unripe fruits of White and Black Mulberry.

◁ MORUS NIGRA The Black Mulberry is a deciduous tree, grown for its delicious fruit.

△ MORUS ALBA

up to 50 ft (15 m)

MORUS ALBA

Habitat Sheltered, sunny sites; China	Parts used

Family MYRISTICACEAE	Species *Myristica fragrans*	Local name Sadhika

NUTMEG AND MACE

This bushy evergreen has scented leaves and tiny yellow flowers. The fruits hold the seed – nutmeg – and its aril, a red, lacy shellcoating – mace.

• **USES** Nutmeg and mace are culinary spices used in sweet and savory dishes in a variety of cuisines. Nutmeg increases the intoxicating and soporific effect of alcoholic drinks and is claimed to be an aphrodisiac. It is prescribed for flatulence and nausea. The essential oil is added to perfumes, soaps, hair oils, tobacco, and fumigants. The nuts yield an oil, nutmeg butter, used in skin creams.

• **REMARK** Large doses of nutmeg are toxic, because of the presence of the hallucinogen myristicin.

up to 33 ft (10 m)

Habitat Coastal humid tropics; the Moluccas	Parts used

Family LEGUMINOSAE	Species *Myroxylon balsamum*	Local name Balsam Tree

BALSAM OF TOLU

All parts of this straight-trunked tree are aromatic: the resinous bark, gland-dotted leaves, small white flowers, winged fruits, and the beans.
• **USES** Bark incisions yield balsam of Tolu, a balsamic resin with a cinnamon-vanilla scent and sweet citrus taste, used as a flavoring, antiseptic, and expectorant in cold and cough medicines, including "friar's balsam." It is also a perfume fixative used in soap and hair tonics. The finest scent is extracted from the flower calces and a less active "white balsam" from the fruits.
• **REMARK** A gum resin from Balsam of Peru (*Myroxylon balsamum* var. *pereirae*) treats skin diseases.

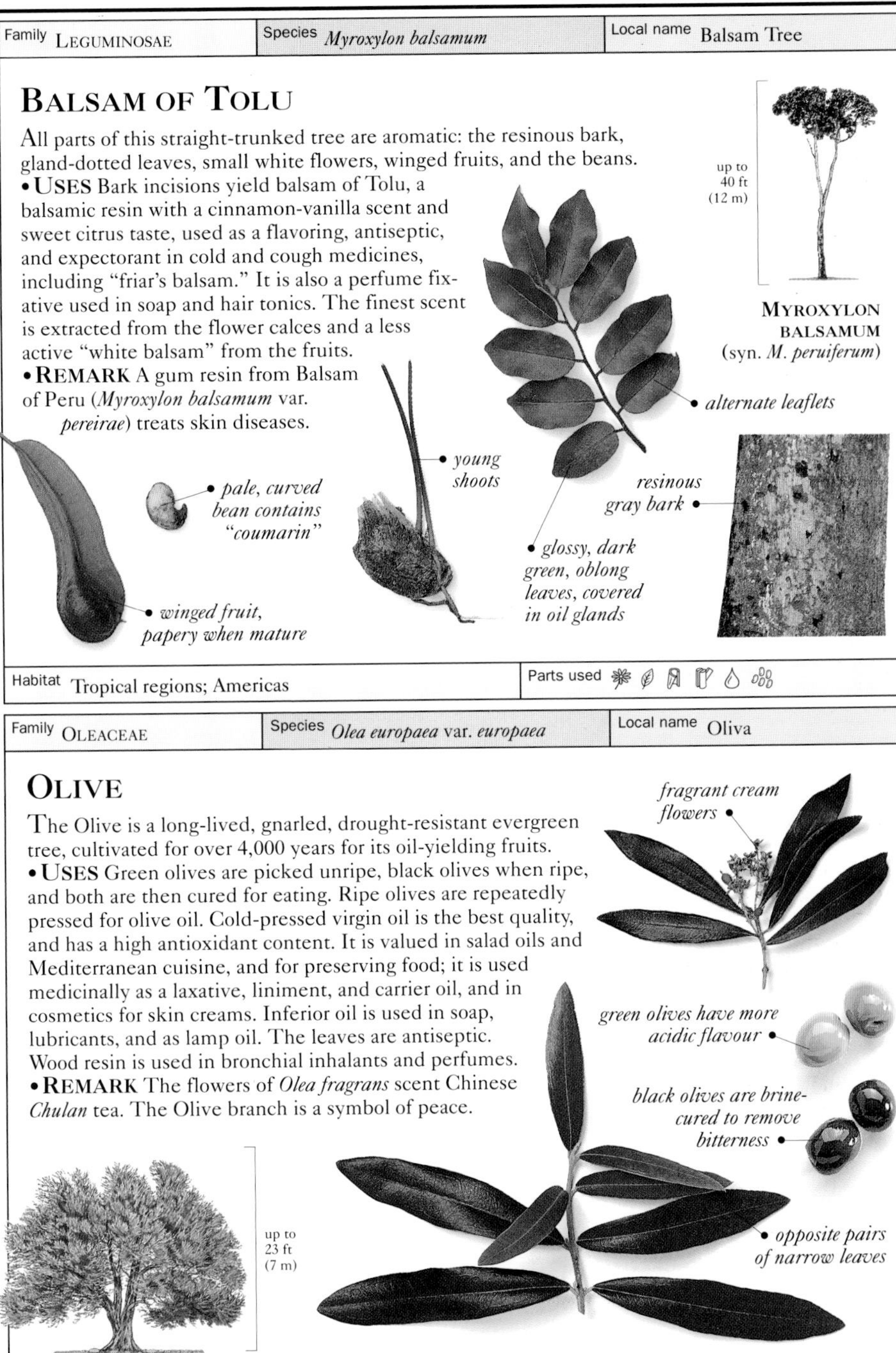
up to
40 ft
(12 m)
MYROXYLON BALSAMUM
(syn. *M. peruiferum*)
alternate leaflets
young shoots
pale, curved bean contains "coumarin"
resinous gray bark
glossy, dark green, oblong leaves, covered in oil glands
winged fruit, papery when mature
fragrant cream flowers
green olives have more acidic flavour
black olives are brine-cured to remove bitterness
opposite pairs of narrow leaves
up to
23 ft
(7 m)

Habitat Tropical regions; Americas	Parts used

Family OLEACEAE	Species *Olea europaea* var. *europaea*	Local name Oliva

OLIVE

The Olive is a long-lived, gnarled, drought-resistant evergreen tree, cultivated for over 4,000 years for its oil-yielding fruits.
• **USES** Green olives are picked unripe, black olives when ripe, and both are then cured for eating. Ripe olives are repeatedly pressed for olive oil. Cold-pressed virgin oil is the best quality, and has a high antioxidant content. It is valued in salad oils and Mediterranean cuisine, and for preserving food; it is used medicinally as a laxative, liniment, and carrier oil, and in cosmetics for skin creams. Inferior oil is used in soap, lubricants, and as lamp oil. The leaves are antiseptic. Wood resin is used in bronchial inhalants and perfumes.
• **REMARK** The flowers of *Olea fragrans* scent Chinese *Chulan* tea. The Olive branch is a symbol of peace.

Habitat Frost-free hillsides; Mediterranean	Parts used

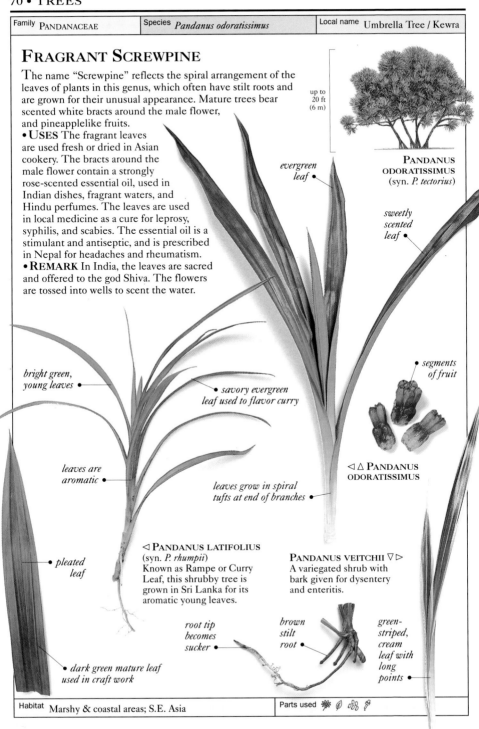

Family PANDANACEAE	Species *Pandanus odoratissimus*	Local name Umbrella Tree / Kewra

FRAGRANT SCREWPINE

The name "Screwpine" reflects the spiral arrangement of the leaves of plants in this genus, which often have stilt roots and are grown for their unusual appearance. Mature trees bear scented white bracts around the male flower, and pineapplelike fruits.

• **USES** The fragrant leaves are used fresh or dried in Asian cookery. The bracts around the male flower contain a strongly rose-scented essential oil, used in Indian dishes, fragrant waters, and Hindu perfumes. The leaves are used in local medicine as a cure for leprosy, syphilis, and scabies. The essential oil is a stimulant and antiseptic, and is prescribed in Nepal for headaches and rheumatism.

• **REMARK** In India, the leaves are sacred and offered to the god Shiva. The flowers are tossed into wells to scent the water.

up to 20 ft (6 m)

PANDANUS ODORATISSIMUS (syn. *P. tectorius*)

evergreen leaf

sweetly scented leaf

segments of fruit

◁ △ PANDANUS ODORATISSIMUS

leaves grow in spiral tufts at end of branches

bright green, young leaves

savory evergreen leaf used to flavor curry

leaves are aromatic

pleated leaf

dark green mature leaf used in craft work

◁ PANDANUS LATIFOLIUS (syn. *P. rhumpii*)
Known as Rampe or Curry Leaf, this shrubby tree is grown in Sri Lanka for its aromatic young leaves.

PANDANUS VEITCHII ▽ ▷
A variegated shrub with bark given for dysentery and enteritis.

root tip becomes sucker

brown stilt root

green-striped, cream leaf with long points

Habitat Marshy & coastal areas; S.E. Asia	Parts used

Family FLACOURTIACEAE	Species *Pangium edule*	Local name Pokok keluak

PANGIUM

Pangium has blue-green flowers, brown fruits up to 6 in (15 cm), and seeds in aromatic, edible pulp.

• **USES** The leaves are used to wrap and preserve meat, and the leaves, bark, and raw seeds are used when fishing and to kill lice. A leaf wash is disinfectant and is applied to wounds and scabies. The root oil soothes rheumatism; the seeds yield a lamp oil.

• **REMARK** Pangium parts, especially the seeds, contain poisonous prussic acid, but this is removed by cooking.

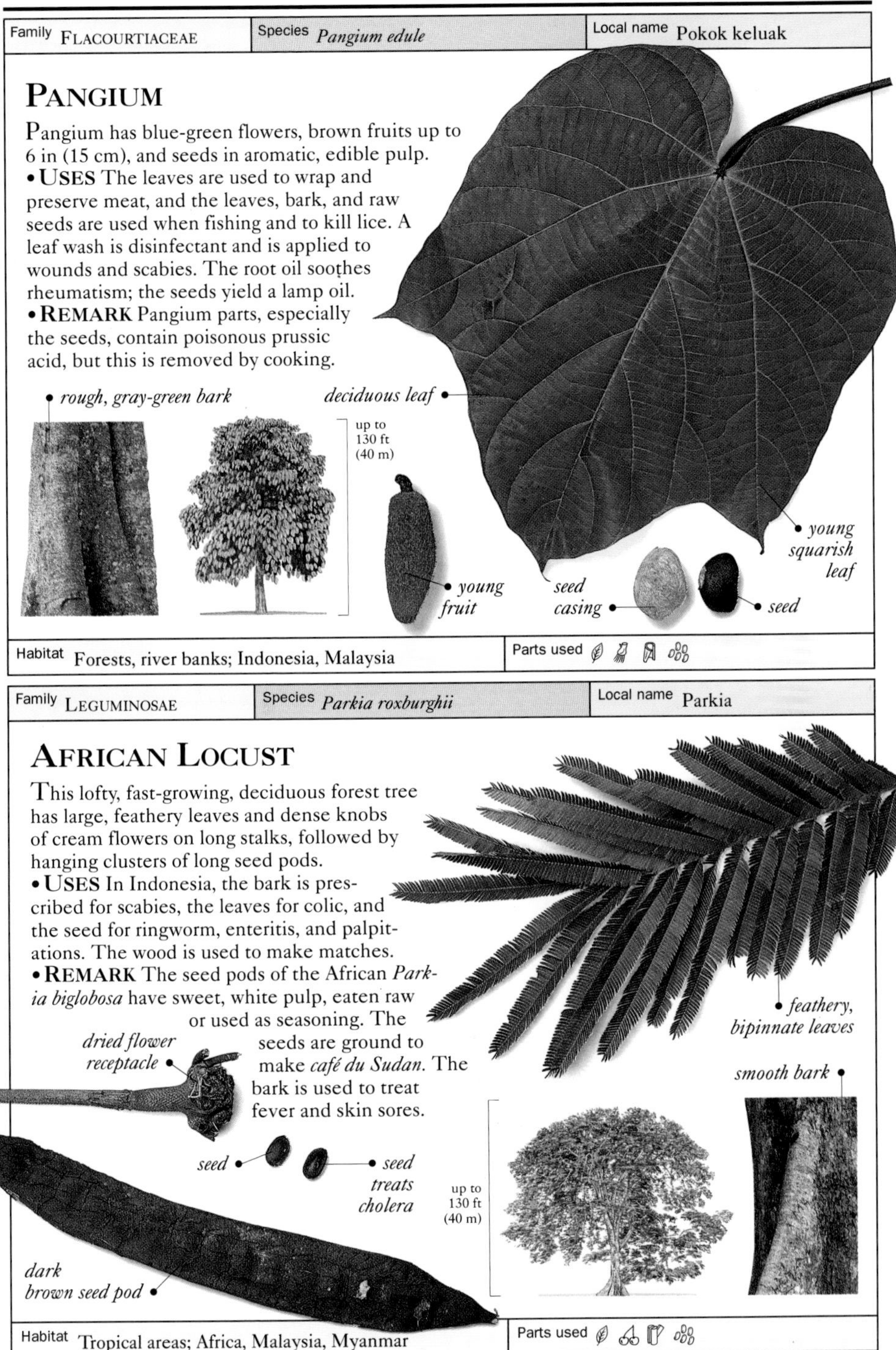
rough, gray-green bark
deciduous leaf
up to 130 ft (40 m)
young fruit
seed casing
seed
young squarish leaf
dried flower receptacle
seed
seed treats cholera
dark brown seed pod
feathery, bipinnate leaves
smooth bark
up to 130 ft (40 m)

Habitat Forests, river banks; Indonesia, Malaysia	Parts used

Family LEGUMINOSAE	Species *Parkia roxburghii*	Local name Parkia

AFRICAN LOCUST

This lofty, fast-growing, deciduous forest tree has large, feathery leaves and dense knobs of cream flowers on long stalks, followed by hanging clusters of long seed pods.

• **USES** In Indonesia, the bark is prescribed for scabies, the leaves for colic, and the seed for ringworm, enteritis, and palpitations. The wood is used to make matches.

• **REMARK** The seed pods of the African *Parkia biglobosa* have sweet, white pulp, eaten raw or used as seasoning. The seeds are ground to make *café du Sudan*. The bark is used to treat fever and skin sores.

Habitat Tropical areas; Africa, Malaysia, Myanmar	Parts used

Family LAURACEAE	Species *Persea americana*	Local name Alligator Pear

AVOCADO TREE

This evergreen tree or shrub has panicles of tiny greenish flowers and pear-shaped green fruits. The Mexican varieties of this plant have anise seed-scented leaves.
• **USES** The delicious edible avocado pulp has the highest protein content of any fruit. Extracted oil from the fruit is used in skin creams and massage oils for its penetrative powers, which improve dull and lifeless skin. The infused diuretic leaves are drunk to cleanse the liver and reduce high blood pressure. The bark and leaves are used to treat stomach and chest ailments and control menstruation. The seeds help treat dysentery.

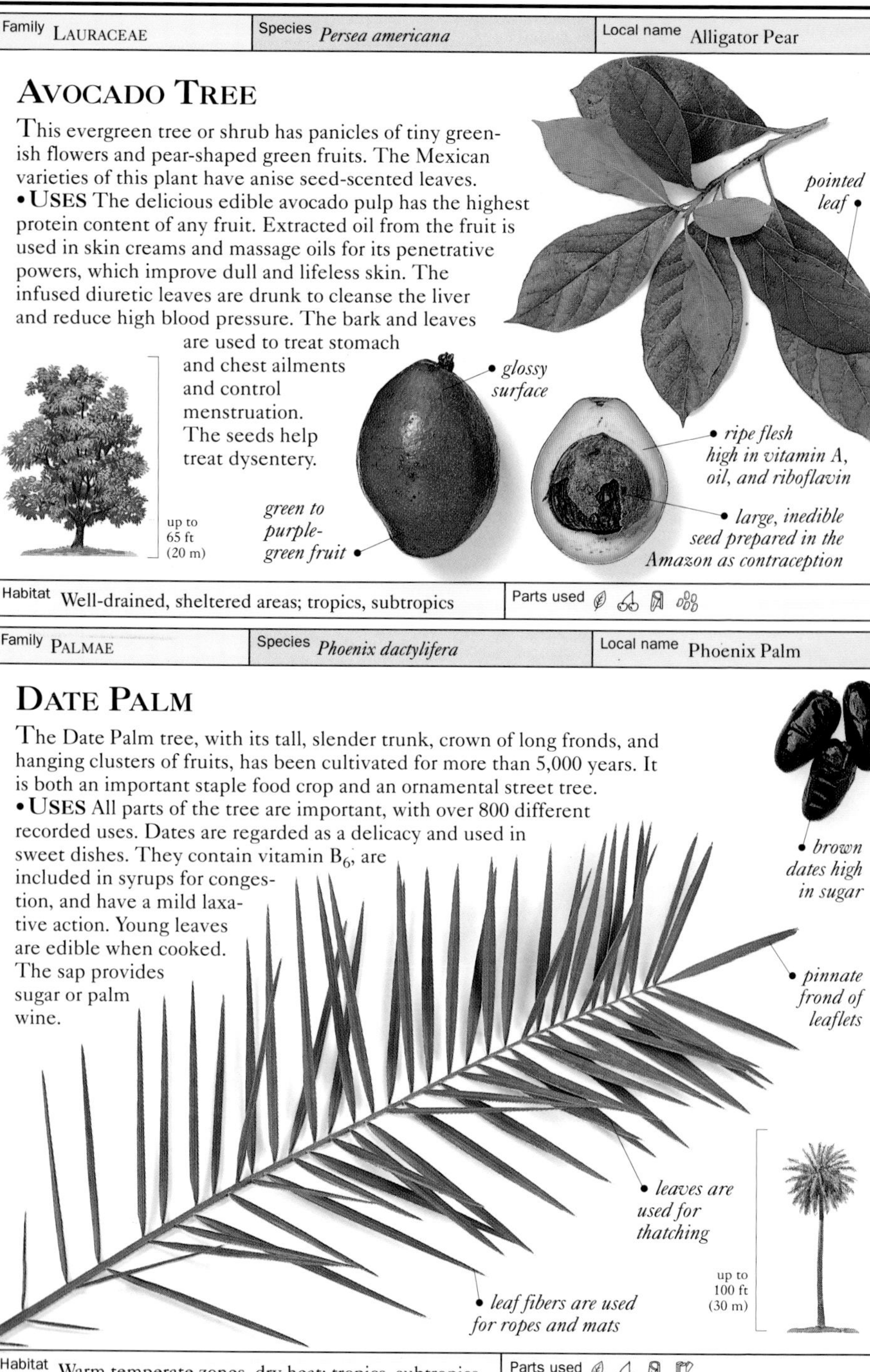
pointed leaf
glossy surface
up to 65 ft (20 m)
green to purple-green fruit
ripe flesh high in vitamin A, oil, and riboflavin
large, inedible seed prepared in the Amazon as contraception
brown dates high in sugar
pinnate frond of leaflets
leaves are used for thatching
up to 100 ft (30 m)
leaf fibers are used for ropes and mats

Habitat Well-drained, sheltered areas; tropics, subtropics	Parts used

Family PALMAE	Species *Phoenix dactylifera*	Local name Phoenix Palm

DATE PALM

The Date Palm tree, with its tall, slender trunk, crown of long fronds, and hanging clusters of fruits, has been cultivated for more than 5,000 years. It is both an important staple food crop and an ornamental street tree.
• **USES** All parts of the tree are important, with over 800 different recorded uses. Dates are regarded as a delicacy and used in sweet dishes. They contain vitamin B_6, are included in syrups for congestion, and have a mild laxative action. Young leaves are edible when cooked. The sap provides sugar or palm wine.

Habitat Warm temperate zones, dry heat; tropics, subtropics	Parts used

Family PINACEAE	Species *Pinus pinea*	Local name Umbrella Pine

STONE PINE

The Stone Pine has deeply grooved, scaly, orange-brown bark, long, gray-green, needlelike leaves, yellow male "flowers," green female "flowers," and heavy, egg-shaped cones.

• **USES** Planted for its umbrella-shaped head, the Stone Pine is also cultivated for its edible kernels or pine nuts. Mature cones are collected during the winter and sun-dried the following summer to open the scales and release the kernels, which are usually sold with their shells removed. Famous in pesto sauce and used extensively in ancient Roman cookery, pine nuts can be eaten raw, roasted, or salted. Their taste enhances vegetarian and meat dishes. Stone Pine kernels are the most commonly processed, but kernels from other pines and the Monkey Puzzle Tree are eaten.

• **REMARK** In China, the evergreen pines are symbols of long life and consistency.

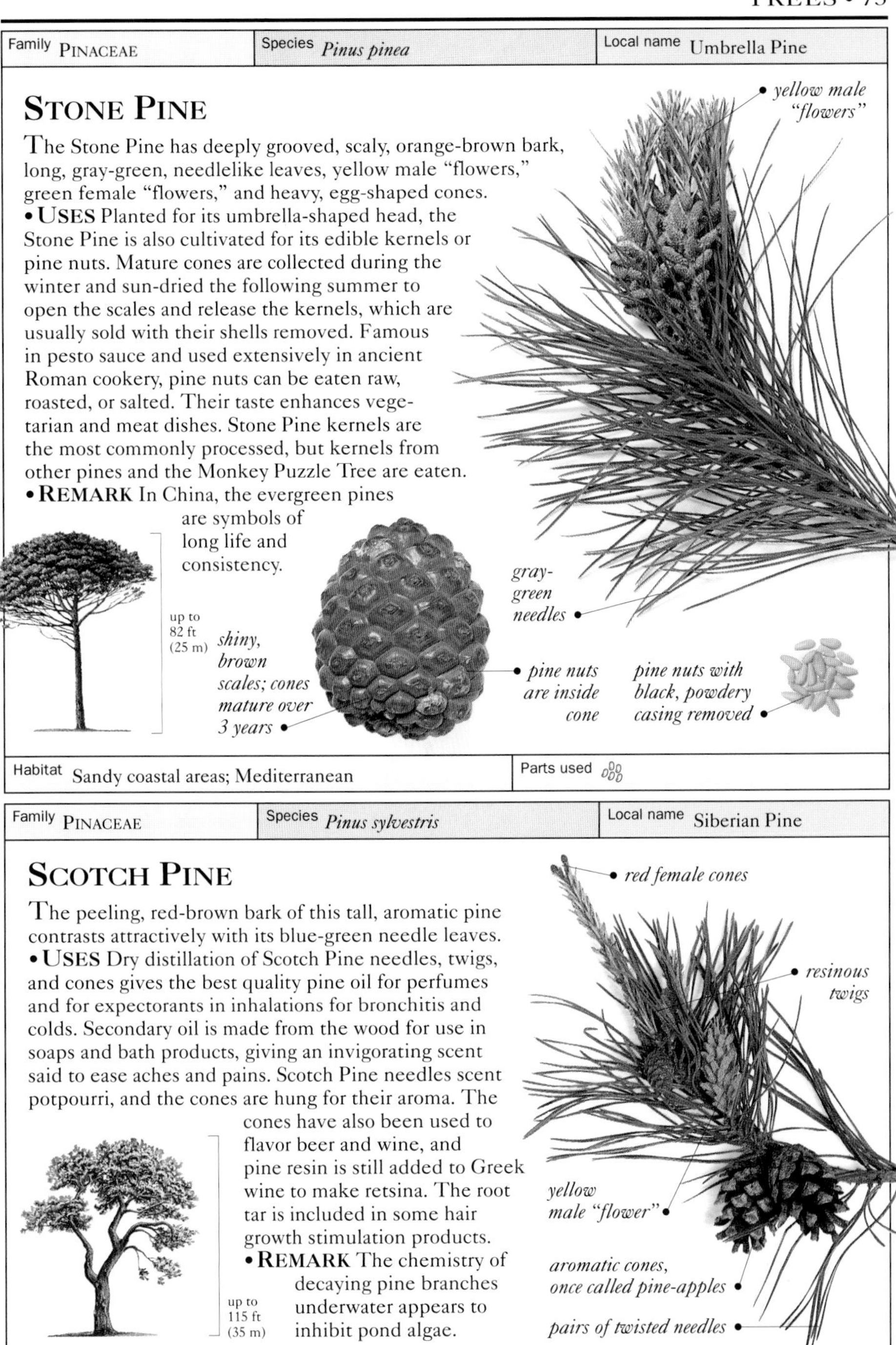
yellow male "flowers"
gray-green needles
up to 82 ft (25 m)
shiny, brown scales; cones mature over 3 years
pine nuts are inside cone
pine nuts with black, powdery casing removed
red female cones
resinous twigs
yellow male "flower"
aromatic cones, once called pine-apples
pairs of twisted needles
up to 115 ft (35 m)

Habitat Sandy coastal areas; Mediterranean	Parts used

Family PINACEAE	Species *Pinus sylvestris*	Local name Siberian Pine

SCOTCH PINE

The peeling, red-brown bark of this tall, aromatic pine contrasts attractively with its blue-green needle leaves.

• **USES** Dry distillation of Scotch Pine needles, twigs, and cones gives the best quality pine oil for perfumes and for expectorants in inhalations for bronchitis and colds. Secondary oil is made from the wood for use in soaps and bath products, giving an invigorating scent said to ease aches and pains. Scotch Pine needles scent potpourri, and the cones are hung for their aroma. The cones have also been used to flavor beer and wine, and pine resin is still added to Greek wine to make retsina. The root tar is included in some hair growth stimulation products.

• **REMARK** The chemistry of decaying pine branches underwater appears to inhibit pond algae.

Habitat Mountain areas; northern temperate regions	Parts used

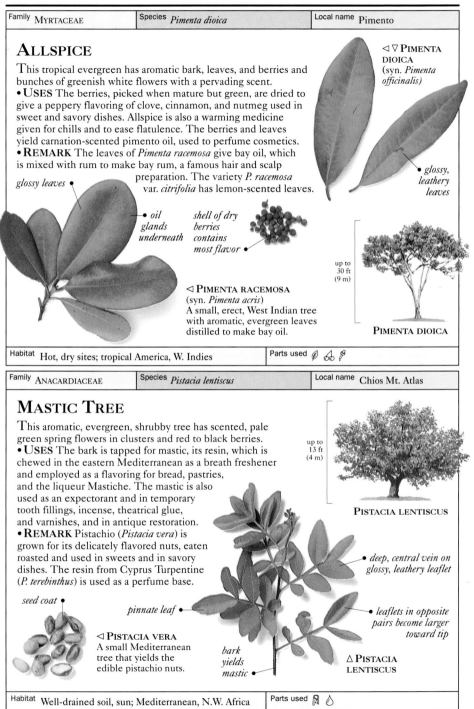

Family MYRTACEAE	Species *Pimenta dioica*	Local name Pimento

ALLSPICE

This tropical evergreen has aromatic bark, leaves, and berries and bunches of greenish white flowers with a pervading scent.

• **USES** The berries, picked when mature but green, are dried to give a peppery flavoring of clove, cinnamon, and nutmeg used in sweet and savory dishes. Allspice is also a warming medicine given for chills and to ease flatulence. The berries and leaves yield carnation-scented pimento oil, used to perfume cosmetics.

• **REMARK** The leaves of *Pimenta racemosa* give bay oil, which is mixed with rum to make bay rum, a famous hair and scalp preparation. The variety *P. racemosa* var. *citrifolia* has lemon-scented leaves.

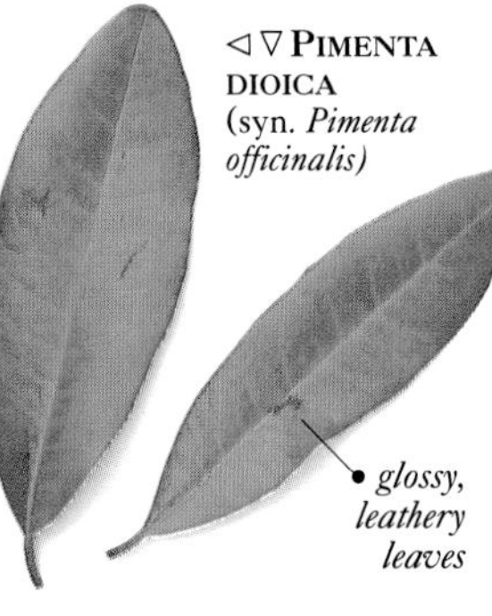
glossy, leathery leaves

◁ ▽ **PIMENTA DIOICA** (syn. *Pimenta officinalis*)

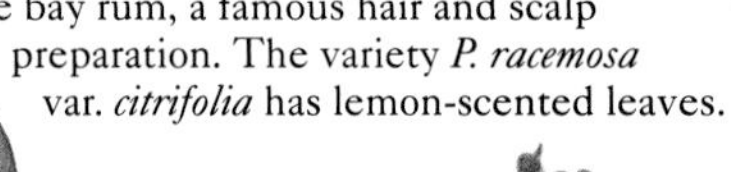

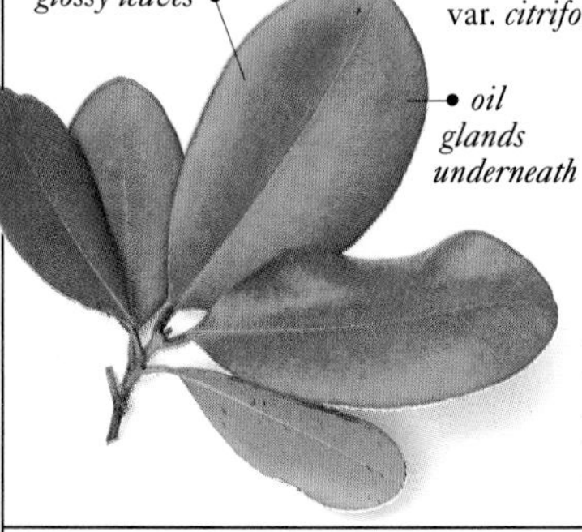
glossy leaves
oil glands underneath
shell of dry berries contains most flavor

◁ **PIMENTA RACEMOSA** (syn. *Pimenta acris*)
A small, erect, West Indian tree with aromatic, evergreen leaves distilled to make bay oil.

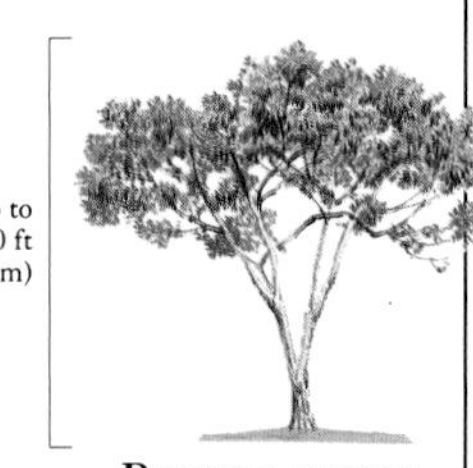
up to 30 ft (9 m)

PIMENTA DIOICA

Habitat Hot, dry sites; tropical America, W. Indies	Parts used

Family ANACARDIACEAE	Species *Pistacia lentiscus*	Local name Chios Mt. Atlas

MASTIC TREE

This aromatic, evergreen, shrubby tree has scented, pale green spring flowers in clusters and red to black berries.

• **USES** The bark is tapped for mastic, its resin, which is chewed in the eastern Mediterranean as a breath freshener and employed as a flavoring for bread, pastries, and the liqueur Mastiche. The mastic is also used as an expectorant and in temporary tooth fillings, incense, theatrical glue, and varnishes, and in antique restoration.

• **REMARK** Pistachio (*Pistacia vera*) is grown for its delicately flavored nuts, eaten roasted and used in sweets and in savory dishes. The resin from Cyprus Turpentine (*P. terebinthus*) is used as a perfume base.

up to 13 ft (4 m)

PISTACIA LENTISCUS

seed coat

◁ **PISTACIA VERA**
A small Mediterranean tree that yields the edible pistachio nuts.

pinnate leaf • *deep, central vein on glossy, leathery leaflet* • *leaflets in opposite pairs become larger toward tip* • *bark yields mastic*

△ **PISTACIA LENTISCUS**

Habitat Well-drained soil, sun; Mediterranean, N.W. Africa	Parts used

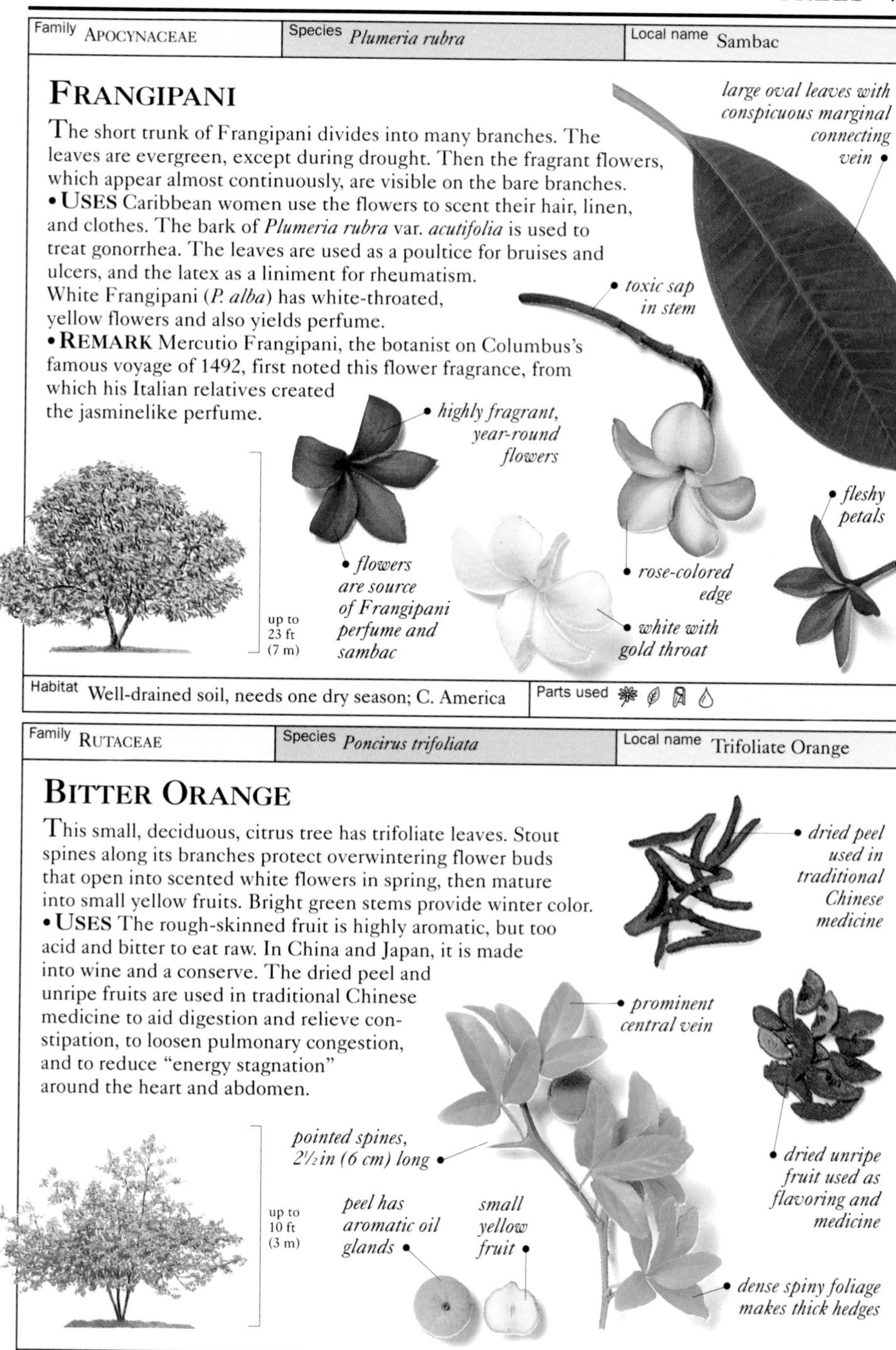
large oval leaves with conspicuous marginal connecting vein
toxic sap in stem
highly fragrant, year-round flowers
fleshy petals
flowers are source of Frangipani perfume and sambac
rose-colored edge
white with gold throat
up to 23 ft (7 m)
dried peel used in traditional Chinese medicine
prominent central vein
dried unripe fruit used as flavoring and medicine
pointed spines, 2½ in (6 cm) long
peel has aromatic oil glands
small yellow fruit
dense spiny foliage makes thick hedges
up to 10 ft (3 m)

Family Apocynaceae	Species *Plumeria rubra*	Local name Sambac

Frangipani

The short trunk of Frangipani divides into many branches. The leaves are evergreen, except during drought. Then the fragrant flowers, which appear almost continuously, are visible on the bare branches.
• **Uses** Caribbean women use the flowers to scent their hair, linen, and clothes. The bark of *Plumeria rubra* var. *acutifolia* is used to treat gonorrhea. The leaves are used as a poultice for bruises and ulcers, and the latex as a liniment for rheumatism. White Frangipani (*P. alba*) has white-throated, yellow flowers and also yields perfume.
• **Remark** Mercutio Frangipani, the botanist on Columbus's famous voyage of 1492, first noted this flower fragrance, from which his Italian relatives created the jasminelike perfume.

Habitat Well-drained soil, needs one dry season; C. America	Parts used

Family Rutaceae	Species *Poncirus trifoliata*	Local name Trifoliate Orange

Bitter Orange

This small, deciduous, citrus tree has trifoliate leaves. Stout spines along its branches protect overwintering flower buds that open into scented white flowers in spring, then mature into small yellow fruits. Bright green stems provide winter color.
• **Uses** The rough-skinned fruit is highly aromatic, but too acid and bitter to eat raw. In China and Japan, it is made into wine and a conserve. The dried peel and unripe fruits are used in traditional Chinese medicine to aid digestion and relieve constipation, to loosen pulmonary congestion, and to reduce "energy stagnation" around the heart and abdomen.

Habitat Chalky soil; China, Japan	Parts used

Family ROSACEAE	Species *Prunus* species	Local name Various

PRUNUS

Trees of this genus have attractive flowers and bark, and bear finely toothed, deciduous leaves and various single-stoned fruits.

• **USES** The sweet fruits of Peach, Plum, and Apricot are eaten fresh, dried, or as jam. With the bitter fruits of Sloe, Bullace, Black Cherry, and Chokecherry, they flavor alcoholic drinks and preserves. Almonds (whole and ground) flavor many dishes. Almond essence is a flavoring distilled from the seeds of Bitter Almond (*Prunus dulcis* var. *amara*); Almond oil is a fixed oil, pressed from Sweet Almond seeds and, like Peach and Apricot seed oils, used in cosmetics, massage oils, and medicines. Peach and Apricot fruits are used in facial skin masks. Chokecherry bark tea is used to clear the throats of singers and public speakers.

• **REMARK** The seed, bark, and leaves of Black Cherry, Bullace, Chokecherry, and Bitter Almond contain prunasin, which converts into toxic hydrocyanic acid during digestion or on contact with water. Most need treatment before they are safe to use.

seed inhibits tumors and yields a flavoring essential oil

sweet edible fruit

◁ △ **PRUNUS ARMENIACA**
The 33-ft (10-m) Apricot is a drought-resistant tree with red shoots, finely toothed, roundish leaves, mainly white flowers in spring, and edible golden fruit said to promote longevity.

pink flowers

dark bark

downy green fruit

fixed oil from kernel used in cosmetics and aromatherapy

◁ △ ▽ **PRUNUS DULCIS**
The 30-ft (9-m) Sweet Almond tree has dark-colored bark, rose to white flowers in early spring, and dry-fleshed fruit with a pitted stone containing a nutritious seed.

narrow, pointed leaf

smooth, green, finely toothed leaves used to treat whooping cough

△ **PRUNUS PERSICA** ▽
The Peach Tree bears solitary, pink spring flowers used to expel intestinal parasites. The sweet fruit, with a furrowed stone, encases a seed that is pressed for Peach oil, used in cosmetics and aromatherapy.

juicy flesh

narrow, tapered, finely toothed, dark green leaf

up to 20 ft (6 m)

PRUNUS PERSICA

seeds pressed for Peach oil

ripe seeds treat digestive disturbances in Chinese medicine

aromatic, yellow-red fruit used in skin masks

Habitat Temperate mountainous woodland; China	Parts used

flat stone
contains
white seed
matte green
leaves
fruit ripens
to purple
young leaves
bluntly toothed
when mature
yellow,
purple,
red, or
blue fruit
2 plums
fused
prunes are
the dried
fruit
shiny
green
leaves
white, early
spring flowers
leaves
turn yellow
in autumn
aromatic
bark
small, serrated, oval
leaves on dark,
thorny branches
purple-bloomed,
black fruit
"bottle-brush"
racemes of cream
flowers appear in
late spring
leaves yield
a mouthwash
shiny, dark
green leaf
with paler
underside
serrated
leaf
leaves turn
orange-yellow
in autumn
astringent,
sedative bark is
used in cough
medicines
brown bark has
unpleasant scent

PRUNUS DOMESTICA SUBSP. INSTITIA ▽ ▷
The 23-ft (7-m) Bullace Tree has mildly purgative flowers, and styptic roots and branch bark, used to reduce bleeding and fevers.

PRUNUS DOMESTICA △ ▷
The 40-ft (12-m) Plum Tree has white, five-petaled spring flowers and sweet, juicy autumn fruits. The seeds are ground and added to facial masks. The dried fruits are given for their laxative effect.

◁ PRUNUS SEROTINA △
The astringent, bitter black berries of the 80-ft (25-m) Black Cherry flavor wine and jam. The inner bark is a digestive and a sedative expectorant for coughs.

PRUNUS SPINOSA ▷
The 13-ft (4-m) Sloe or Blackthorn has white flowers. The astringent fruits make Sloe gin. Traditionally, the wood was used to make clubs.

◁ PRUNUS VIRGINIANA △ ▷
The 11½-ft (3.5-m) shrubby Chokecherry has white flowers and red berries, edible when cooked but with a poisonous stone. Powdered berries were once used to improve the appetite.

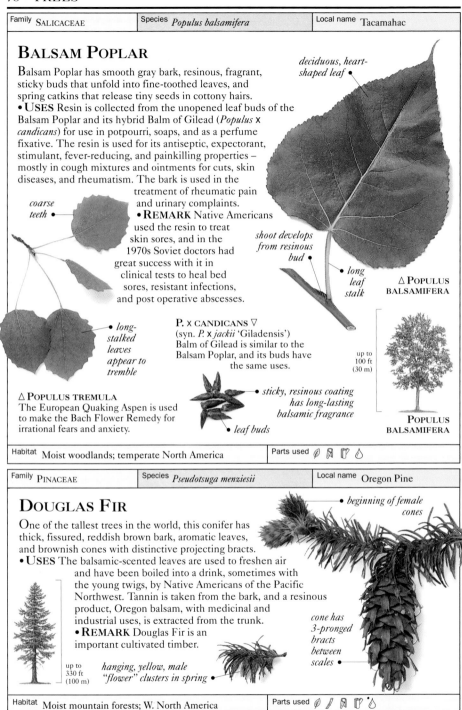

Family SALICACEAE	Species *Populus balsamifera*	Local name Tacamahac

BALSAM POPLAR

Balsam Poplar has smooth gray bark, resinous, fragrant, sticky buds that unfold into fine-toothed leaves, and spring catkins that release tiny seeds in cottony hairs.

• **USES** Resin is collected from the unopened leaf buds of the Balsam Poplar and its hybrid Balm of Gilead (*Populus* x *candicans*) for use in potpourri, soaps, and as a perfume fixative. The resin is used for its antiseptic, expectorant, stimulant, fever-reducing, and painkilling properties – mostly in cough mixtures and ointments for cuts, skin diseases, and rheumatism. The bark is used in the treatment of rheumatic pain and urinary complaints.

• **REMARK** Native Americans used the resin to treat skin sores, and in the 1970s Soviet doctors had great success with it in clinical tests to heal bed sores, resistant infections, and post operative abscesses.

deciduous, heart-shaped leaf

shoot develops from resinous bud

long leaf stalk

△ POPULUS BALSAMIFERA

coarse teeth

long-stalked leaves appear to tremble

△ POPULUS TREMULA
The European Quaking Aspen is used to make the Bach Flower Remedy for irrational fears and anxiety.

P. X CANDICANS ▽
(syn. *P.* x *jackii* 'Giladensis')
Balm of Gilead is similar to the Balsam Poplar, and its buds have the same uses.

sticky, resinous coating has long-lasting balsamic fragrance

leaf buds

up to 100 ft (30 m)

POPULUS BALSAMIFERA

Habitat Moist woodlands; temperate North America	Parts used

Family PINACEAE	Species *Pseudotsuga menziesii*	Local name Oregon Pine

DOUGLAS FIR

One of the tallest trees in the world, this conifer has thick, fissured, reddish brown bark, aromatic leaves, and brownish cones with distinctive projecting bracts.

• **USES** The balsamic-scented leaves are used to freshen air and have been boiled into a drink, sometimes with the young twigs, by Native Americans of the Pacific Northwest. Tannin is taken from the bark, and a resinous product, Oregon balsam, with medicinal and industrial uses, is extracted from the trunk.

• **REMARK** Douglas Fir is an important cultivated timber.

beginning of female cones

cone has 3-pronged bracts between scales

up to 330 ft (100 m)

hanging, yellow, male "flower" clusters in spring

Habitat Moist mountain forests; W. North America	Parts used 

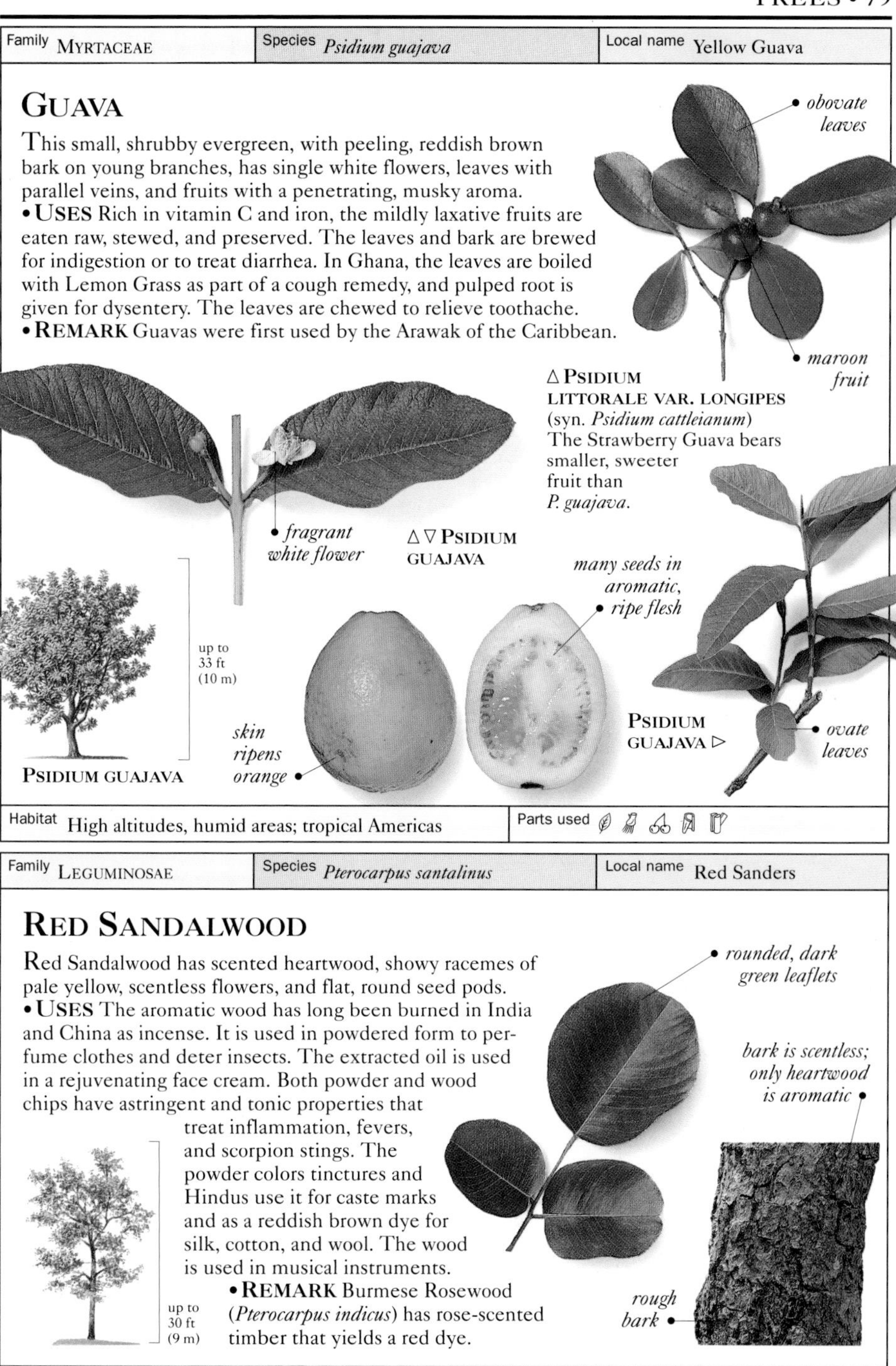
obovate leaves
maroon fruit
fragrant white flower
many seeds in aromatic, ripe flesh
up to 33 ft (10 m)
skin ripens orange
ovate leaves
rounded, dark green leaflets
bark is scentless; only heartwood is aromatic
rough bark
up to 30 ft (9 m)

Family MYRTACEAE	Species *Psidium guajava*	Local name Yellow Guava

GUAVA

This small, shrubby evergreen, with peeling, reddish brown bark on young branches, has single white flowers, leaves with parallel veins, and fruits with a penetrating, musky aroma.

• **USES** Rich in vitamin C and iron, the mildly laxative fruits are eaten raw, stewed, and preserved. The leaves and bark are brewed for indigestion or to treat diarrhea. In Ghana, the leaves are boiled with Lemon Grass as part of a cough remedy, and pulped root is given for dysentery. The leaves are chewed to relieve toothache.

• **REMARK** Guavas were first used by the Arawak of the Caribbean.

△ **PSIDIUM LITTORALE VAR. LONGIPES** (syn. *Psidium cattleianum*) The Strawberry Guava bears smaller, sweeter fruit than *P. guajava*.

△ ▽ **PSIDIUM GUAJAVA**

PSIDIUM GUAJAVA

PSIDIUM GUAJAVA ▷

Habitat High altitudes, humid areas; tropical Americas	Parts used

Family LEGUMINOSAE	Species *Pterocarpus santalinus*	Local name Red Sanders

RED SANDALWOOD

Red Sandalwood has scented heartwood, showy racemes of pale yellow, scentless flowers, and flat, round seed pods.

• **USES** The aromatic wood has long been burned in India and China as incense. It is used in powdered form to perfume clothes and deter insects. The extracted oil is used in a rejuvenating face cream. Both powder and wood chips have astringent and tonic properties that treat inflammation, fevers, and scorpion stings. The powder colors tinctures and Hindus use it for caste marks and as a reddish brown dye for silk, cotton, and wool. The wood is used in musical instruments.

• **REMARK** Burmese Rosewood (*Pterocarpus indicus*) has rose-scented timber that yields a red dye.

Habitat Forested hills; S. India	Parts used

Family PUNICACEAE	Species *Punica granatum*	Local name Apple of Carthage

POMEGRANATE

This small, deciduous tree, occasionally with spiny branches, has beautifully colored foliage in spring and autumn, showy, fragrant, scarlet summer flowers, and shiny, apple-sized fruits.
• **USES** The sweet juice is used to make grenadine, a flavoring for cocktails, sherbet, and pickles. The sour pulp is boiled to make pomegranate syrup, which gives perfume and sourness to Middle Eastern cuisine. Seeds dried with their aril give the sour Indian condiment *anardana*. The rind is used to treat dysentery, and the root bark to combat tapeworm. The fruits, rind, and bark yield fabric dyes.
• **REMARK** The Pomegranate is an ancient symbol of fertility.

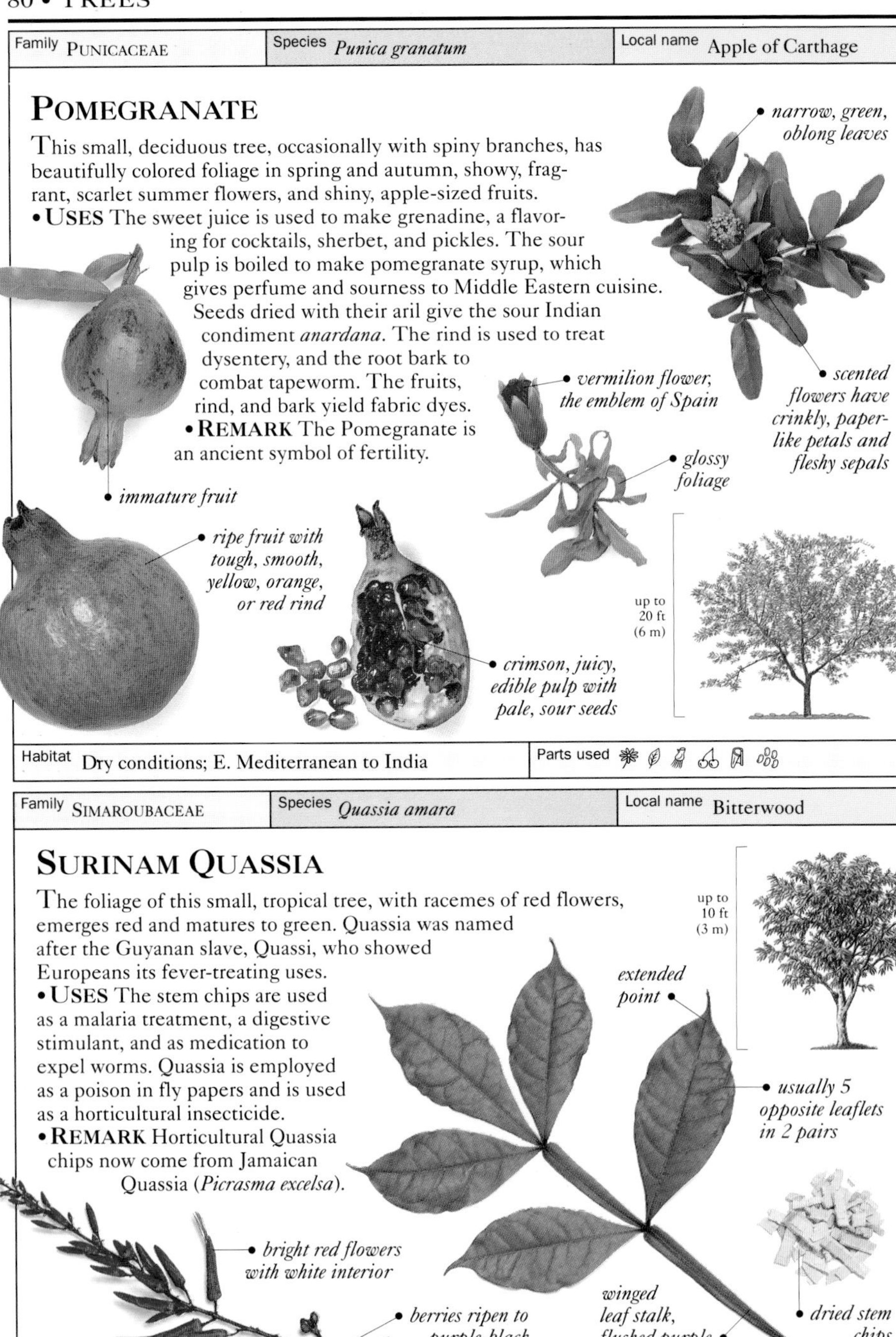
narrow, green, oblong leaves
scented flowers have crinkly, paper-like petals and fleshy sepals
vermilion flower, the emblem of Spain
glossy foliage
immature fruit
ripe fruit with tough, smooth, yellow, orange, or red rind
crimson, juicy, edible pulp with pale, sour seeds
up to 20 ft (6 m)

Habitat Dry conditions; E. Mediterranean to India	Parts used

Family SIMAROUBACEAE	Species *Quassia amara*	Local name Bitterwood

SURINAM QUASSIA

The foliage of this small, tropical tree, with racemes of red flowers, emerges red and matures to green. Quassia was named after the Guyanan slave, Quassi, who showed Europeans its fever-treating uses.
• **USES** The stem chips are used as a malaria treatment, a digestive stimulant, and as medication to expel worms. Quassia is employed as a poison in fly papers and is used as a horticultural insecticide.
• **REMARK** Horticultural Quassia chips now come from Jamaican Quassia (*Picrasma excelsa*).

up to 10 ft (3 m)
extended point
usually 5 opposite leaflets in 2 pairs
bright red flowers with white interior
berries ripen to purple-black
winged leaf stalk, flushed purple
dried stem chips

Habitat Marshy river sides or ridge forests; S. America	Parts used

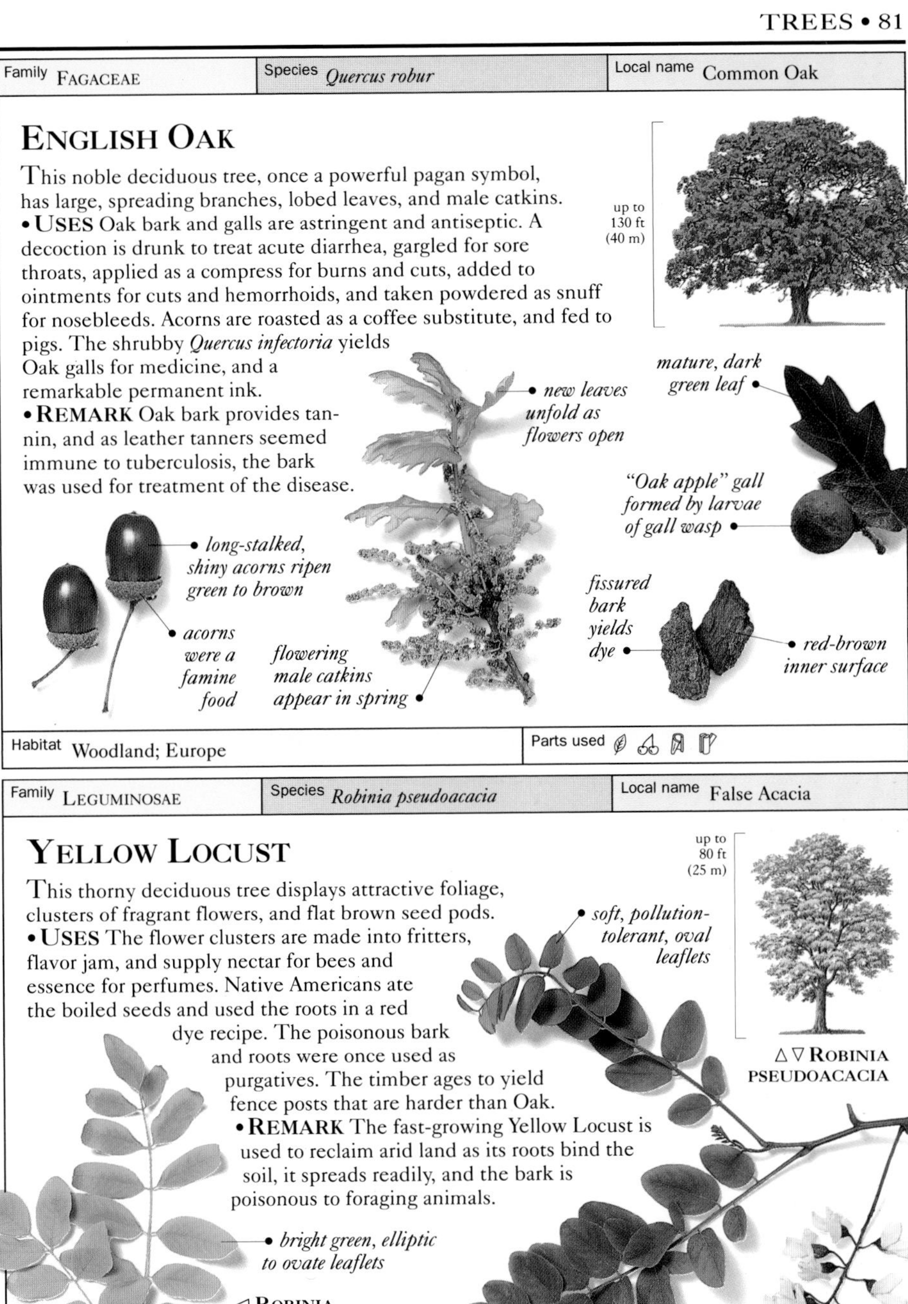
up to
130 ft
(40 m)
new leaves
unfold as
flowers open
mature, dark
green leaf
"Oak apple" gall
formed by larvae
of gall wasp
long-stalked,
shiny acorns ripen
green to brown
acorns
were a
famine
food
flowering
male catkins
appear in spring
fissured
bark
yields
dye
red-brown
inner surface
up to
80 ft
(25 m)
soft, pollution-
tolerant, oval
leaflets
bright green, elliptic
to ovate leaflets
pealike flowers

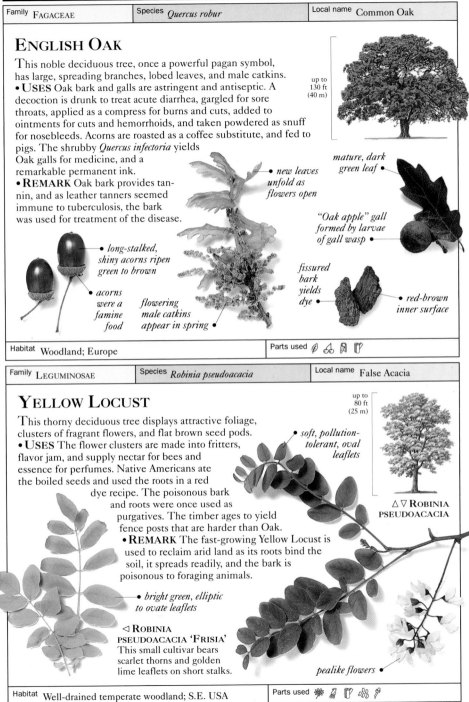

Family FAGACEAE | Species *Quercus robur* | Local name Common Oak

ENGLISH OAK

This noble deciduous tree, once a powerful pagan symbol, has large, spreading branches, lobed leaves, and male catkins.

• **USES** Oak bark and galls are astringent and antiseptic. A decoction is drunk to treat acute diarrhea, gargled for sore throats, applied as a compress for burns and cuts, added to ointments for cuts and hemorrhoids, and taken powdered as snuff for nosebleeds. Acorns are roasted as a coffee substitute, and fed to pigs. The shrubby *Quercus infectoria* yields Oak galls for medicine, and a remarkable permanent ink.

• **REMARK** Oak bark provides tannin, and as leather tanners seemed immune to tuberculosis, the bark was used for treatment of the disease.

Habitat Woodland; Europe | Parts used

Family LEGUMINOSAE | Species *Robinia pseudoacacia* | Local name False Acacia

YELLOW LOCUST

This thorny deciduous tree displays attractive foliage, clusters of fragrant flowers, and flat brown seed pods.

• **USES** The flower clusters are made into fritters, flavor jam, and supply nectar for bees and essence for perfumes. Native Americans ate the boiled seeds and used the roots in a red dye recipe. The poisonous bark and roots were once used as purgatives. The timber ages to yield fence posts that are harder than Oak.

• **REMARK** The fast-growing Yellow Locust is used to reclaim arid land as its roots bind the soil, it spreads readily, and the bark is poisonous to foraging animals.

△▽ ROBINIA PSEUDOACACIA

◁ ROBINIA PSEUDOACACIA 'FRISIA'
This small cultivar bears scarlet thorns and golden lime leaflets on short stalks.

Habitat Well-drained temperate woodland; S.E. USA | Parts used

Family SALICACEAE	Species *Salix alba*	Local name European Willow

WHITE WILLOW

Deeply fissured, dark gray bark, elegant branches, and spring catkins mark this deciduous waterside tree. • **USES** The stem bark is a painkiller, a fever-reducer, and an original source of salicylic acid for aspirin. Various bark extracts are used as a sore throat gargle; for heartburn; stomach problems, and food poisoning; to relieve arthritic pain; and to remove corns. Infused leaves make a tea for nervous insomnia and are added to baths to ease rheumatism. Pussy Willow (*Salix caprea*) has similar medicinal uses. *S. babylonica* root bark treats leukemia and restores bone marrow function after chemotherapy. The *Salix* species provide the best-quality artists' charcoal, branches are used for weaving, and the White Willow var. *caerulea* is the source of wood for cricket bats. • **REMARK** The genus name *Salix* comes from the Celtic *sal-lis*, "near water."

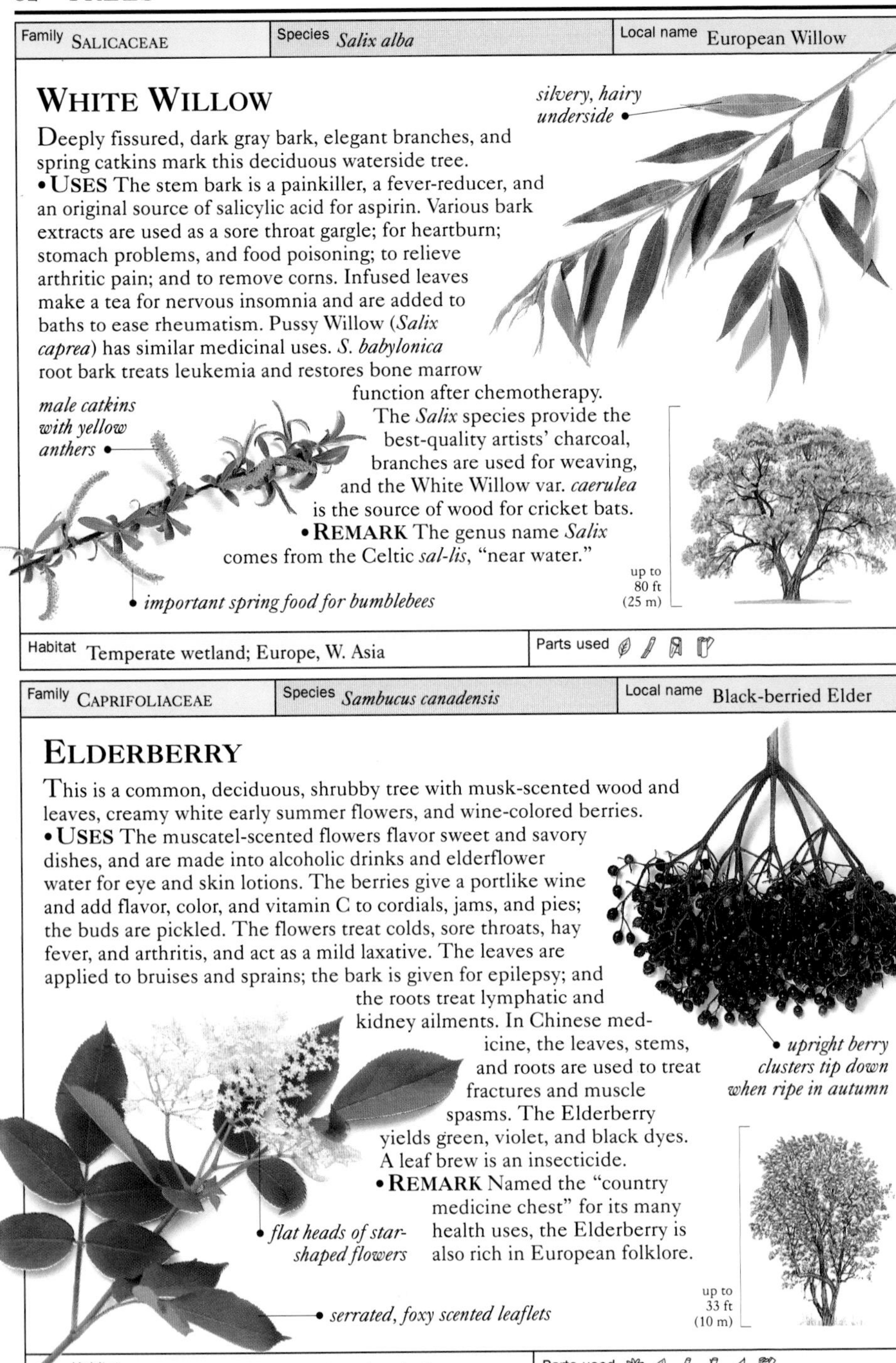

silvery, hairy underside
male catkins with yellow anthers
important spring food for bumblebees
up to 80 ft (25 m)

Habitat Temperate wetland; Europe, W. Asia	Parts used

Family CAPRIFOLIACEAE	Species *Sambucus canadensis*	Local name Black-berried Elder

ELDERBERRY

This is a common, deciduous, shrubby tree with musk-scented wood and leaves, creamy white early summer flowers, and wine-colored berries. • **USES** The muscatel-scented flowers flavor sweet and savory dishes, and are made into alcoholic drinks and elderflower water for eye and skin lotions. The berries give a portlike wine and add flavor, color, and vitamin C to cordials, jams, and pies; the buds are pickled. The flowers treat colds, sore throats, hay fever, and arthritis, and act as a mild laxative. The leaves are applied to bruises and sprains; the bark is given for epilepsy; and the roots treat lymphatic and kidney ailments. In Chinese medicine, the leaves, stems, and roots are used to treat fractures and muscle spasms. The Elderberry yields green, violet, and black dyes. A leaf brew is an insecticide. • **REMARK** Named the "country medicine chest" for its many health uses, the Elderberry is also rich in European folklore.

upright berry clusters tip down when ripe in autumn
flat heads of star-shaped flowers
serrated, foxy scented leaflets
up to 33 ft (10 m)

Habitat Temperate regions; northern hemisphere	Parts used

Family SANTALACEAE	Species *Santalum album*	Local name Indian Sandalwood

SANDALWOOD

Processed for its fragrant reddish heartwood, the Sandalwood is a slow-growing, semiparasitic evergreen, with slender, drooping branches, panicles of small pale yellow to purple flowers, and pea-sized fruits containing one seed.

• **USES** All parts yield Sandalwood oil, particularly the heartwood and the roots which yield about 61 percent essential oil. The distilled oil is used in many perfumes, in aftershaves to soothe shaving rash, and in cosmetics – where it is of special benefit to mature skins. Recorded in Ayurvedic medicine and Egyptian embalming, the oil is now used as an inhalant for its expectorant and sedative effect on coughs and as a powerful antiseptic for lung and urinary tract infections. The essential oil is distilled from the wood and used in aromatherapy for tension, anxiety, and as an aphrodisiac.

• **REMARK** Sandalwood gives a popular incense, as its calming effect aids meditation. It is commonly used for funeral pyres in India, where devotees believe the scent protects places from evil spirits.

gray-brown bark yields 2 percent Sandalwood oil

oval, tapering, evergreen leaves

leaves in opposite pairs

leaves and shoots yield 4 percent Sandalwood oil

up to 60 ft (18 m)

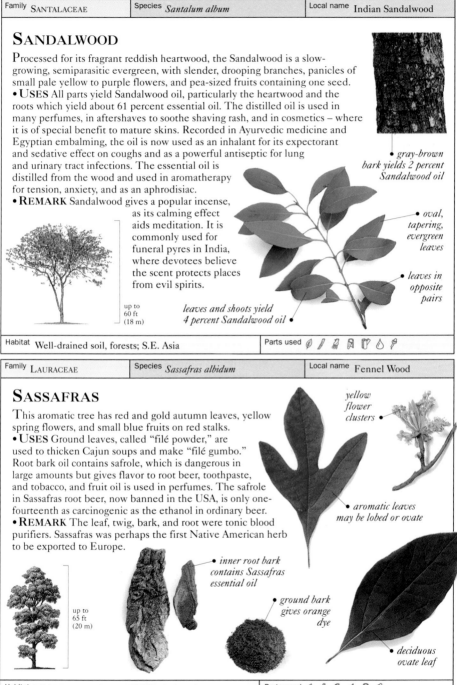

Habitat Well-drained soil, forests; S.E. Asia	Parts used

Family LAURACEAE	Species *Sassafras albidum*	Local name Fennel Wood

SASSAFRAS

This aromatic tree has red and gold autumn leaves, yellow spring flowers, and small blue fruits on red stalks.

• **USES** Ground leaves, called "filé powder," are used to thicken Cajun soups and make "filé gumbo." Root bark oil contains safrole, which is dangerous in large amounts but gives flavor to root beer, toothpaste, and tobacco, and fruit oil is used in perfumes. The safrole in Sassafras root beer, now banned in the USA, is only one-fourteenth as carcinogenic as the ethanol in ordinary beer.

• **REMARK** The leaf, twig, bark, and root were tonic blood purifiers. Sassafras was perhaps the first Native American herb to be exported to Europe.

yellow flower clusters

aromatic leaves may be lobed or ovate

inner root bark contains Sassafras essential oil

ground bark gives orange dye

deciduous ovate leaf

up to 65 ft (20 m)

Habitat Thickly wooded areas; E. North America	Parts used

Family LEGUMINOSAE	Species *Sophora japonica*	Local name Chinese Scholar Tree

PAGODA TREE

When mature, this attractive legume has panicles of fragrant, cream, pealike, summer flowers and fruit pods which are pinched between the seeds.

• **USES** In China, the buds, flowers, and fruit pods are used to reduce fevers, stop bleeding, and control nerves and dizziness; the flowers are also used to treat high blood pressure. The pods yield a yellow fabric dye.

• **REMARK** Beans from the Mescal Bean Tree (*Sophora secundiflora*) contain cytisine, which can cause intoxication and death. Once used by Native American tribes to induce visions, the beans were superseded by the safer Peyote.

up to 80 ft (25 m)

SOPHORA JAPONICA

deciduous foliage may remain green until it falls

pointed ovate leaflet

notched at tip

obovate leaflets

△ SOPHORA SECUNDIFLORA
Mescal Bean Tree is a small evergreen with fragrant, violet-blue flowers and a long, woody fruit pod with up to eight bright red beans.

leaflets in opposite pairs

glossy green stem

△ SOPHORA JAPONICA

Habitat Tolerates drought & poor soils; China, Korea	Parts used

Family ROSACEAE	Species *Sorbus aucuparia*	Local name Rowan

EUROPEAN MOUNTAIN ASH

The European Mountain Ash bears clusters of spring flowers and bright red berries in autumn, when the leaves may turn red.

• **USES** The berries, rich in vitamin C, can be made into a tart jelly, ground into flour, fermented into wine, or distilled into spirit. The seeds should be removed as they can contain hydrocyanic acid. The berries are also made into a skin mask or a sore throat gargle. The bark and leaves are used in a gargle for thrush.

• **REMARK** It is a traditional country charm against witchcraft.

dense clusters of berries

cream flowers

deciduous serrated leaflets have asymmetrical base

opposite pairs

up to 50 ft (15 m)

Habitat Woodland, upland; northern hemisphere	Parts used

Family STYRACACEAE	Species *Styrax benzoin*	Local name Gum Benjamin

BENZOIN

Benzoin is a shrubby tree with gray bark, simple leaves, and short racemes of small, fragrant, bell-shaped white flowers. The scented yellowish resin is thought to be created in response to injury, so it is tapped by making hatchet incisions in the trunk. • **USES** The resin, called benzoin or gum benjamin, is used as incense, a fixative in perfumes, and is added to cosmetics to prevent fats turning rancid. It is an antiseptic treatment for cracked and chapped skin, and an expectorant for severe bronchitis. As part of friar's balsam, it soothes coughs and sore throats. Benzoin is used in aromatherapy, but may cause allergies. • **REMARK** *Styrax officinale* produces storax, the fragrant resin that is burned as incense.

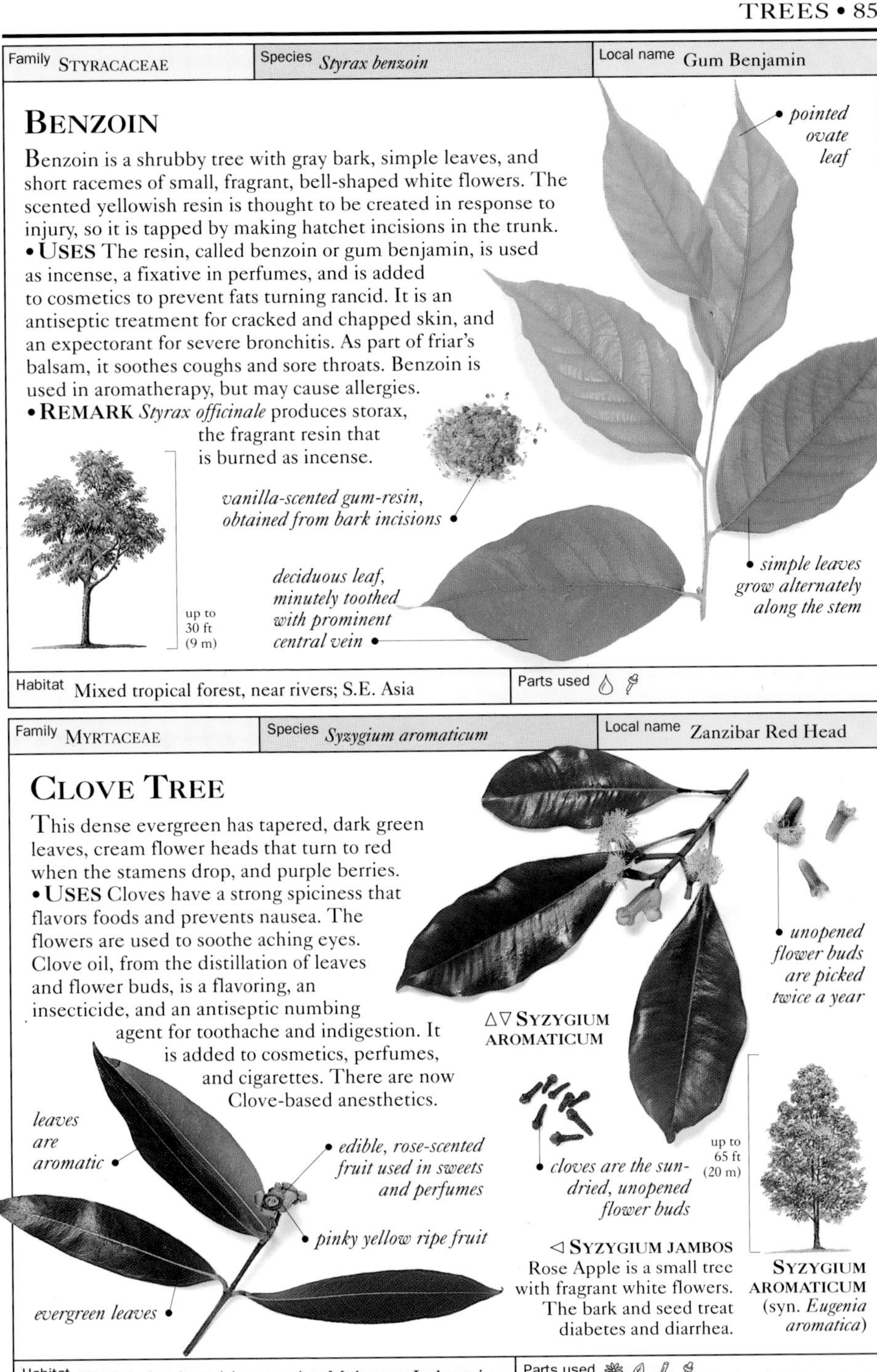

pointed ovate leaf
vanilla-scented gum-resin, obtained from bark incisions
up to 30 ft (9 m)
deciduous leaf, minutely toothed with prominent central vein
simple leaves grow alternately along the stem
leaves are aromatic
edible, rose-scented fruit used in sweets and perfumes
pinky yellow ripe fruit
evergreen leaves
unopened flower buds are picked twice a year
cloves are the sun-dried, unopened flower buds
up to 65 ft (20 m)

Habitat Mixed tropical forest, near rivers; S.E. Asia	Parts used

Family MYRTACEAE	Species *Syzygium aromaticum*	Local name Zanzibar Red Head

CLOVE TREE

This dense evergreen has tapered, dark green leaves, cream flower heads that turn to red when the stamens drop, and purple berries. • **USES** Cloves have a strong spiciness that flavors foods and prevents nausea. The flowers are used to soothe aching eyes. Clove oil, from the distillation of leaves and flower buds, is a flavoring, an insecticide, and an antiseptic numbing agent for toothache and indigestion. It is added to cosmetics, perfumes, and cigarettes. There are now Clove-based anesthetics.

△▽ SYZYGIUM AROMATICUM

◁ SYZYGIUM JAMBOS
Rose Apple is a small tree with fragrant white flowers. The bark and seed treat diabetes and diarrhea.

SYZYGIUM AROMATICUM (syn. *Eugenia aromatica*)

Habitat Well-drained maritime tropics; Moluccas, Indonesia	Parts used

Family LEGUMINOSAE	Species *Tamarindus indica*	Local name Indian Date

TAMARIND

The Tamarind is a long-lived evergreen, with elegant foliage on arching branches and hanging racemes of fragrant, rose-veined cream flowers.

• **USES** The ripe fruit pods contain a pleasantly sour pulp used to flavor Indian curries and chutneys, Malay satays, Caribbean sweets, and a refreshing drink for Ramadan. In Thailand, the flowers and leaves are used as flavorings, and in India, the seed pectin is used in jam-making. The aerial parts have laxative, astringent, and fever-reducing properties; the bark treats asthma; a seed- or leaf-paste reduces boils; the seeds help diarrhea; and the flowers reduce blood pressure. The vitamin- and mineral-rich pulp is used in Chinese medicine.

• **REMARK** Tamarind is used in many commercial products, including Worcestershire sauce and Angostura bitters.

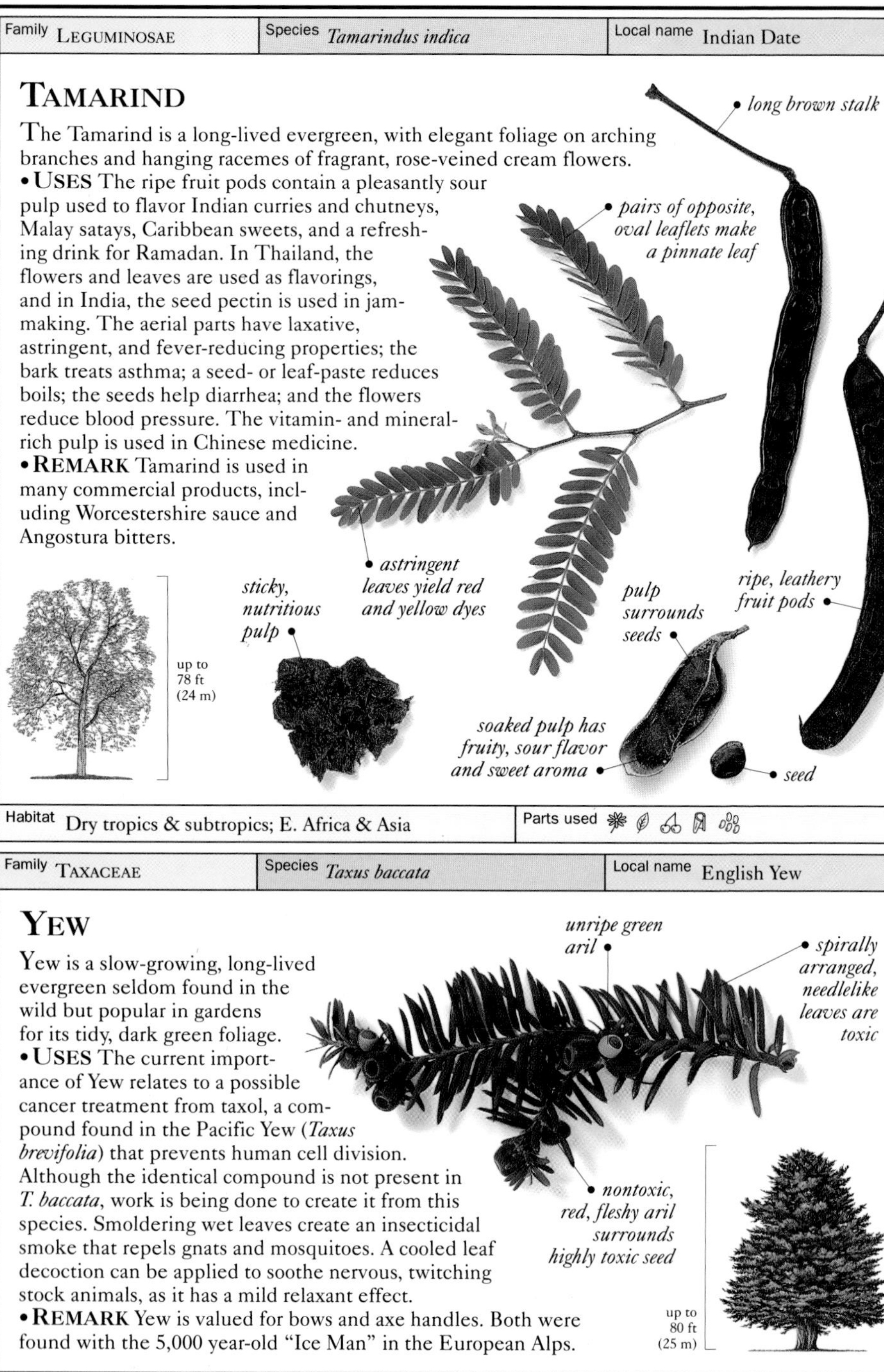
long brown stalk
pairs of opposite, oval leaflets make a pinnate leaf
astringent leaves yield red and yellow dyes
sticky, nutritious pulp
pulp surrounds seeds
ripe, leathery fruit pods
up to 78 ft (24 m)
soaked pulp has fruity, sour flavor and sweet aroma
seed
unripe green aril
spirally arranged, needlelike leaves are toxic
nontoxic, red, fleshy aril surrounds highly toxic seed
up to 80 ft (25 m)

Habitat Dry tropics & subtropics; E. Africa & Asia	Parts used

Family TAXACEAE	Species *Taxus baccata*	Local name English Yew

YEW

Yew is a slow-growing, long-lived evergreen seldom found in the wild but popular in gardens for its tidy, dark green foliage.

• **USES** The current importance of Yew relates to a possible cancer treatment from taxol, a compound found in the Pacific Yew (*Taxus brevifolia*) that prevents human cell division. Although the identical compound is not present in *T. baccata*, work is being done to create it from this species. Smoldering wet leaves create an insecticidal smoke that repels gnats and mosquitoes. A cooled leaf decoction can be applied to soothe nervous, twitching stock animals, as it has a mild relaxant effect.

• **REMARK** Yew is valued for bows and axe handles. Both were found with the 5,000 year-old "Ice Man" in the European Alps.

Habitat Limey woodland; temperate northern hemisphere	Parts used

Family STERCULIACEAE	Species *Theobroma cacao*	Local name Chocolate Nut Tree

COCOA TREE

The Cocoa Tree has evergreen leaves, scented flowers, and fruits growing directly from the trunk. The fruits contains pink pulp and pale pink beans. • **USES** Cocoa beans are fermented and roasted to develop the chocolate flavor and color, and then made into block chocolate or powder to flavor food and drinks. Cocoa contains caffeine and theobromine. It is mildly diuretic and stimulant, and was given for angina pains. The leaf is used as a heart tonic in Colombia. Cocoa butter is a popular cosmetic emollient as it protects the skin and is slow to go rancid. • **REMARK** "Chocolatl" is an Aztec word; it was the Aztecs who developed cocoa into a chocolate drink.

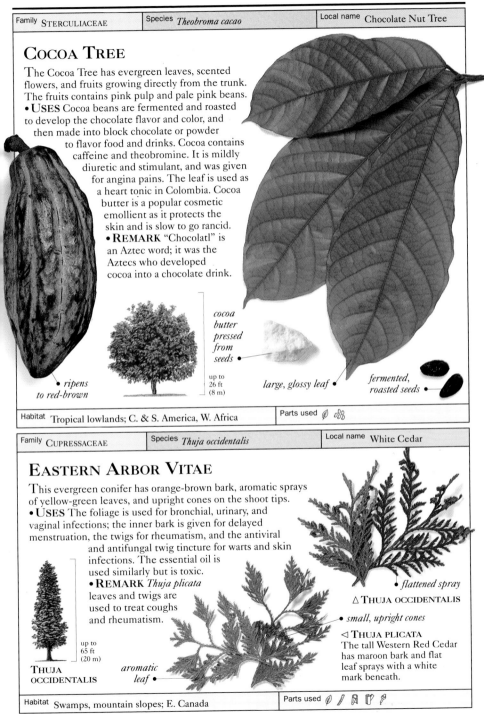

cocoa butter pressed from seeds

ripens to red-brown

up to 26 ft (8 m)

large, glossy leaf

fermented, roasted seeds

Habitat Tropical lowlands; C. & S. America, W. Africa	Parts used

Family CUPRESSACEAE	Species *Thuja occidentalis*	Local name White Cedar

EASTERN ARBOR VITAE

This evergreen conifer has orange-brown bark, aromatic sprays of yellow-green leaves, and upright cones on the shoot tips. • **USES** The foliage is used for bronchial, urinary, and vaginal infections; the inner bark is given for delayed menstruation, the twigs for rheumatism, and the antiviral and antifungal twig tincture for warts and skin infections. The essential oil is used similarly but is toxic. • **REMARK** *Thuja plicata* leaves and twigs are used to treat coughs and rheumatism.

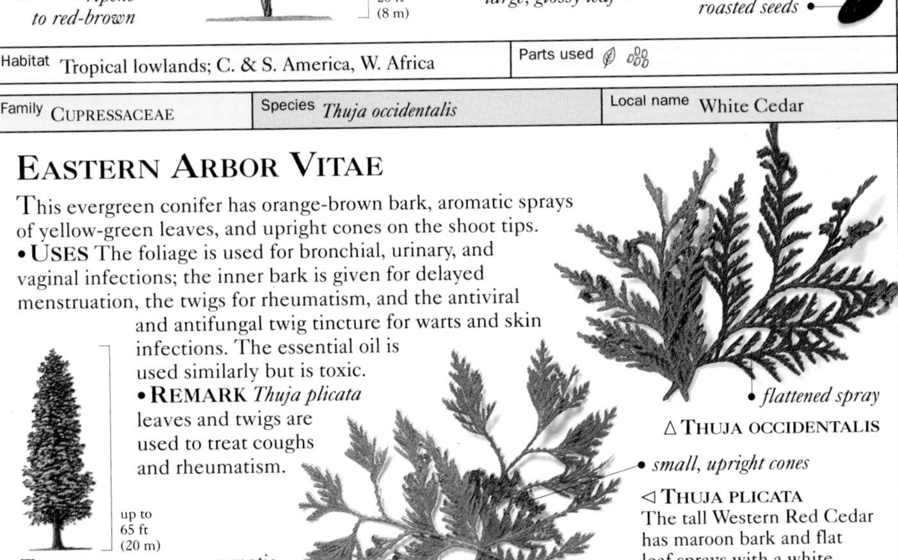

flattened spray
small, upright cones
aromatic leaf
up to 65 ft (20 m)

△ THUJA OCCIDENTALIS

◁ THUJA PLICATA
The tall Western Red Cedar has maroon bark and flat leaf sprays with a white mark beneath.

THUJA OCCIDENTALIS

Habitat Swamps, mountain slopes; E. Canada	Parts used

Family TILIACEAE	Species *Tilia* species	Local name Lime / Basswood

LINDEN

Linden have very small fragrant flowers, but species can be difficult to identify, as they hybridize freely.

• **USES** The flowers of the Common, Large-leaved, and Littleleaf Linden are brewed to make a tea, the classic digestive end to a continental meal, and a treatment for insomnia, nervous tension, and overwrought children. It induces sweating which reduces colds, headaches, and flu, and may lower blood pressure and help arteriosclerosis. Linden water is a skin tonic and is used in bath preparations to soothe rheumatic aches. The world's most valued honey is made from Linden blossom and is used in liqueurs and medicines. The inner bark treats kidney stones, gout, and coronary disease.

• **REMARK** The names "Linden," "Lime," and "Basswood" refer to the linenlike bast fibers below the bark, once used as rope.

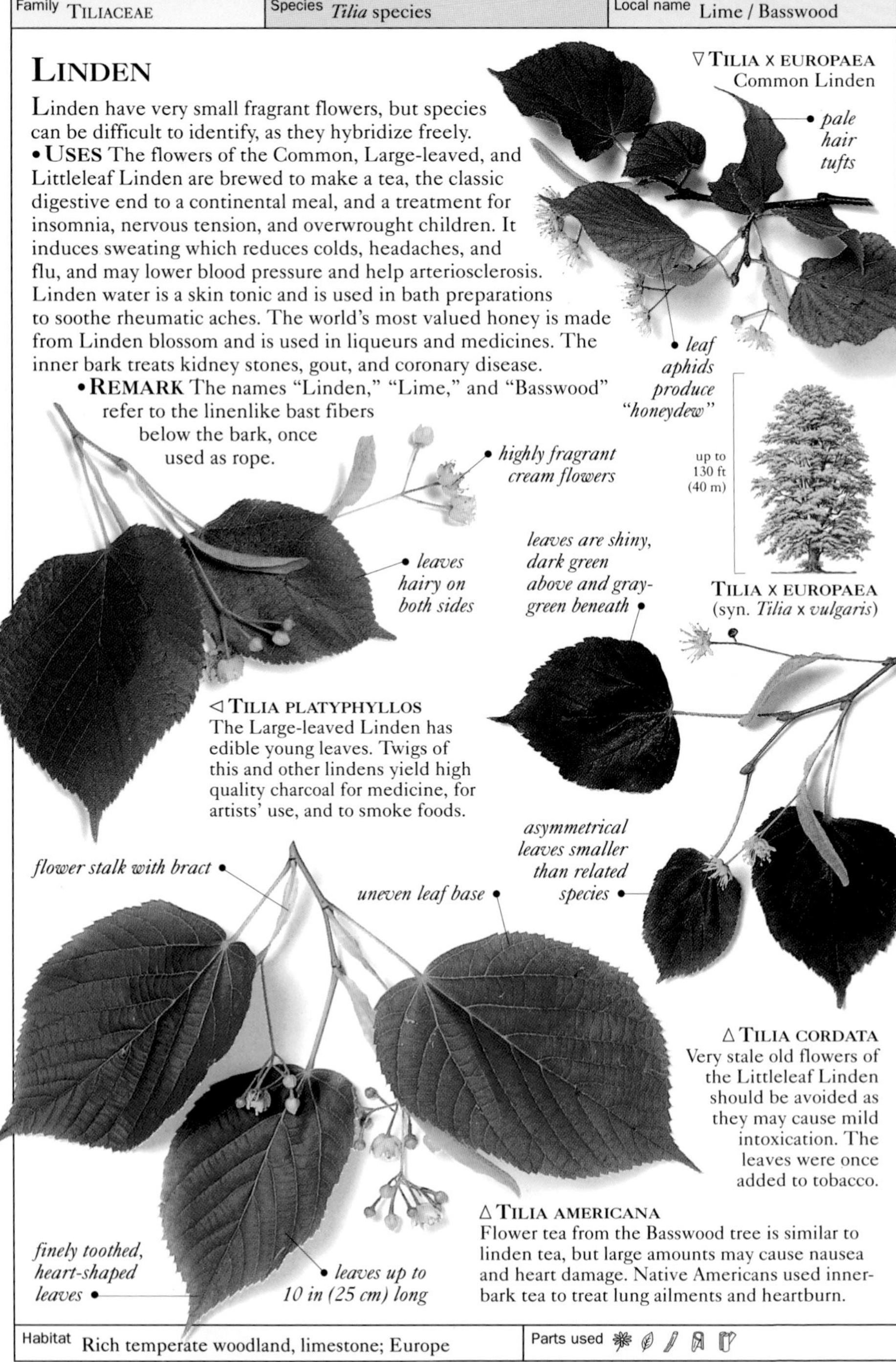
pale hair tufts
leaf aphids produce "honeydew"
up to 130 ft (40 m)
highly fragrant cream flowers
leaves hairy on both sides
leaves are shiny, dark green above and gray-green beneath
flower stalk with bract
uneven leaf base
asymmetrical leaves smaller than related species
finely toothed, heart-shaped leaves
leaves up to 10 in (25 cm) long

▽ TILIA X EUROPAEA
Common Linden

TILIA X EUROPAEA
(syn. *Tilia x vulgaris*)

◁ TILIA PLATYPHYLLOS
The Large-leaved Linden has edible young leaves. Twigs of this and other lindens yield high quality charcoal for medicine, for artists' use, and to smoke foods.

△ TILIA CORDATA
Very stale old flowers of the Littleleaf Linden should be avoided as they may cause mild intoxication. The leaves were once added to tobacco.

△ TILIA AMERICANA
Flower tea from the Basswood tree is similar to linden tea, but large amounts may cause nausea and heart damage. Native Americans used inner-bark tea to treat lung ailments and heartburn.

Habitat Rich temperate woodland, limestone; Europe	Parts used

Family LAURACEAE	Species *Ulmus procera*	Local name Vanishing Elm

Family ULMACEAE	Species *Ulmus procera*	Local name Vanishing Elm

ENGLISH ELM

The Elm is a tall, deciduous tree with fissured bark, serrated leaves, red flower stamens, and flat-winged fruits with a central seed. Its unique silhouette is vanishing from Europe and North America – due to the ravages of Dutch elm disease.

• **USES** Elm leaves are used in hemorrhoid ointments and in a decoction for red, inflamed skin. The branch sap has served as a lotion to combat baldness, while the diuretic inner bark is made into a homeopathic astringent tincture. English Elm is used as a Bach Flower Remedy.

• **REMARK** The sticky, aromatic inner bark of Slippery Elm (*Ulmus rubra*) is used in commercial convalescent drinks and as a laxative. Many Native American tribes used this bark in the treatment of tumors.

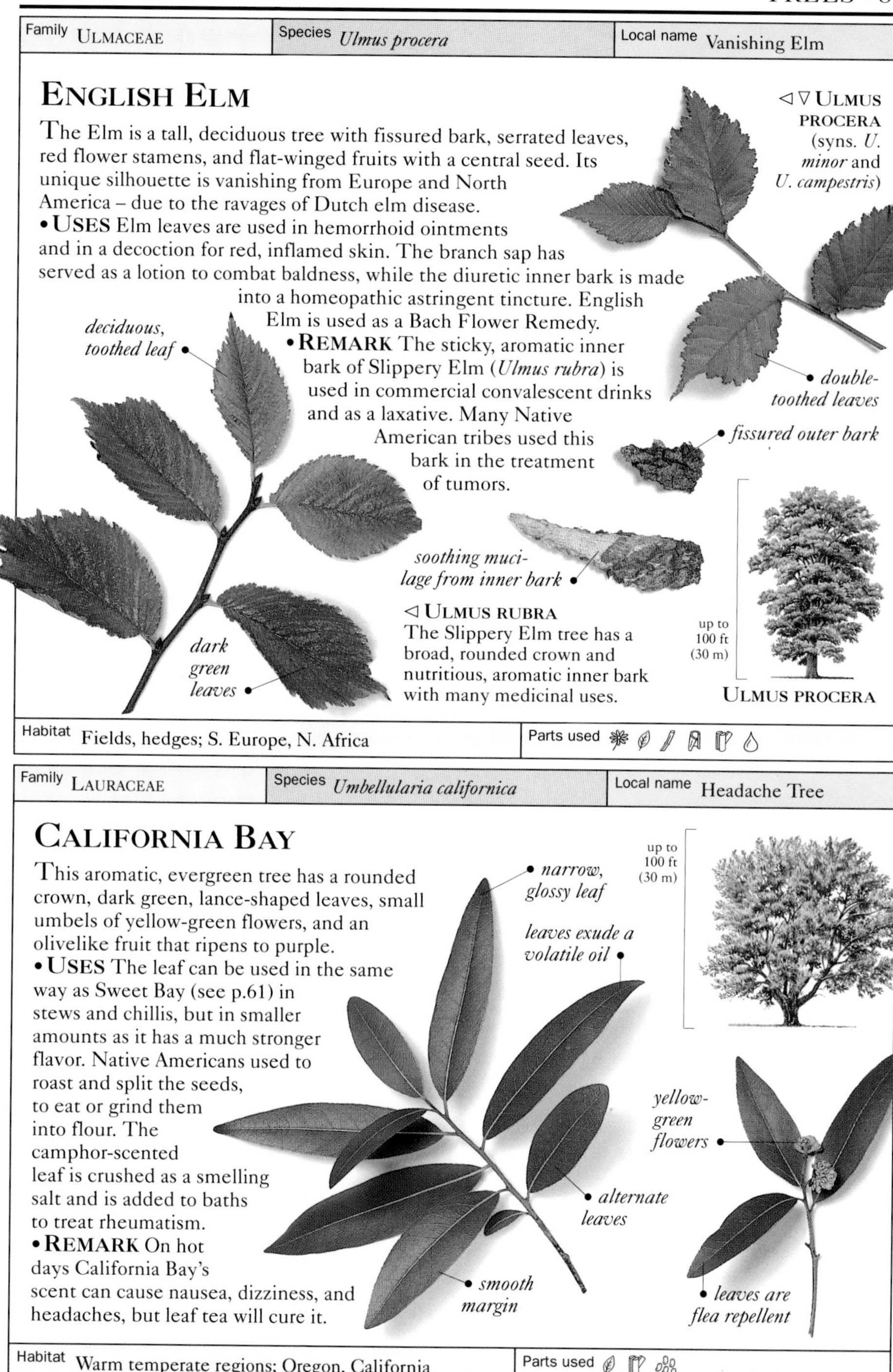
◁ ▽ ULMUS PROCERA (syns. *U. minor* and *U. campestris*)
deciduous, toothed leaf
double-toothed leaves
fissured outer bark
soothing mucilage from inner bark
dark green leaves
up to 100 ft (30 m)
ULMUS PROCERA

◁ ULMUS RUBRA
The Slippery Elm tree has a broad, rounded crown and nutritious, aromatic inner bark with many medicinal uses.

Habitat Fields, hedges; S. Europe, N. Africa	Parts used

Family LAURACEAE	Species *Umbellularia californica*	Local name Headache Tree

CALIFORNIA BAY

This aromatic, evergreen tree has a rounded crown, dark green, lance-shaped leaves, small umbels of yellow-green flowers, and an olivelike fruit that ripens to purple.

• **USES** The leaf can be used in the same way as Sweet Bay (see p.61) in stews and chillis, but in smaller amounts as it has a much stronger flavor. Native Americans used to roast and split the seeds, to eat or grind them into flour. The camphor-scented leaf is crushed as a smelling salt and is added to baths to treat rheumatism.

• **REMARK** On hot days California Bay's scent can cause nausea, dizziness, and headaches, but leaf tea will cure it.

narrow, glossy leaf
leaves exude a volatile oil
up to 100 ft (30 m)
yellow-green flowers
alternate leaves
smooth margin
leaves are flea repellent

Habitat Warm temperate regions; Oregon, California	Parts used

Family VERBENACEAE	Species *Vitex negundo*	Local name Chinese Vitex

CHASTE TREE

This shrubby, deciduous tree has elegant, aromatic, compound leaves, fragrant lilac flowers, and small scented berries.

• **USES** In traditional Chinese medicine, the root, leaves, and fruits are used to prevent malaria and treat wheezing, colds, coughs, and bacterial dysentery. In Indonesia, the leaves treat abscesses and ulcers, while in Nepal they are smoked for headaches, the leaf juice is given for rheumatic joints, the flower buds for pneumonia, the dried fruits as a dewormer, and the roots are prescribed as an expectorant and a tonic.

• **REMARK** The dried fruit of *Vitex agnus-castus* contain hormonelike substances that reduce sexual desire in men and help regulate periods and treat symptoms of premenstrual syndrome.

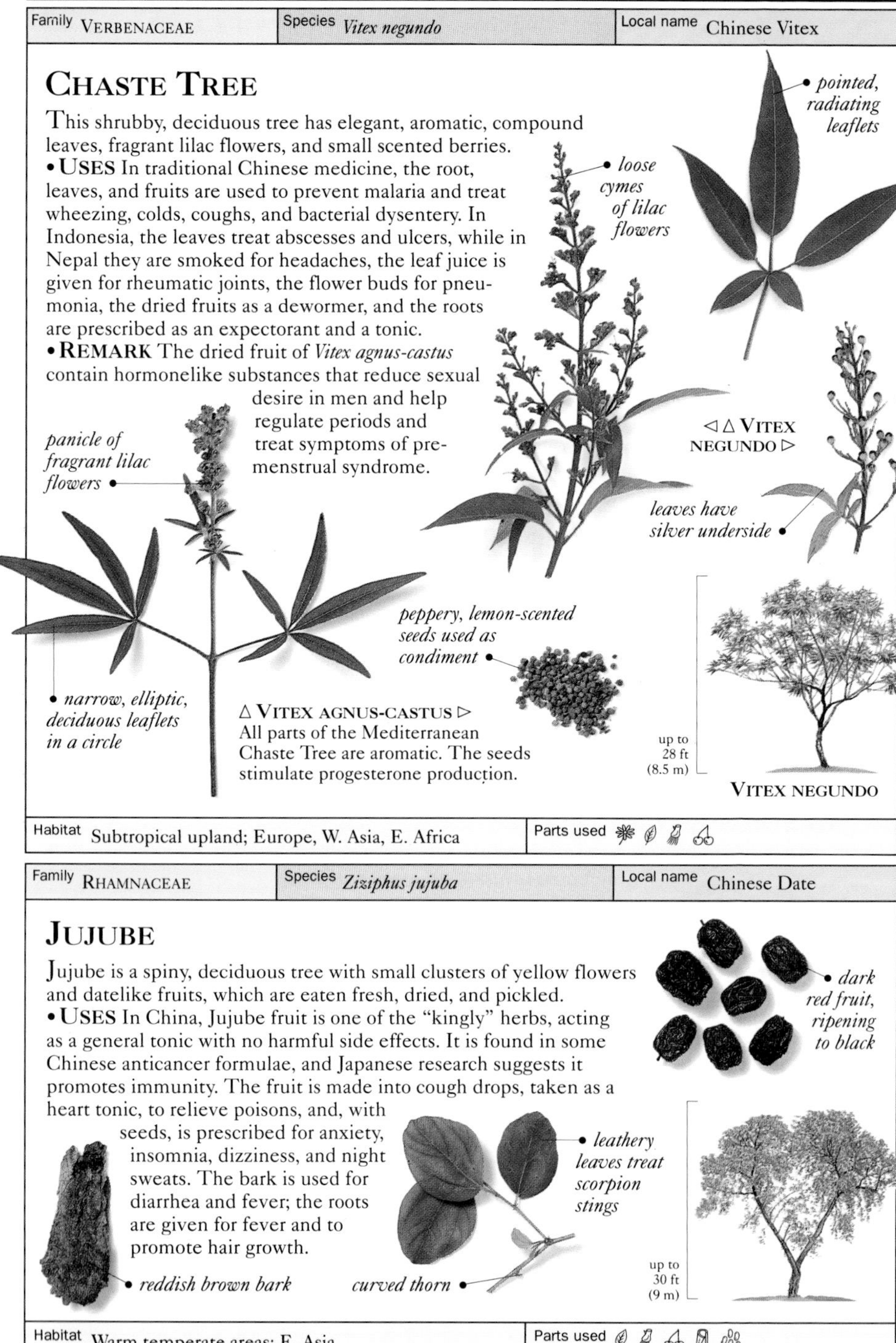

pointed, radiating leaflets
loose cymes of lilac flowers
◁ △ VITEX NEGUNDO ▷
leaves have silver underside
panicle of fragrant lilac flowers
peppery, lemon-scented seeds used as condiment
narrow, elliptic, deciduous leaflets in a circle
up to 28 ft (8.5 m)
VITEX NEGUNDO
dark red fruit, ripening to black
leathery leaves treat scorpion stings
reddish brown bark
curved thorn
up to 30 ft (9 m)

△ VITEX AGNUS-CASTUS ▷
All parts of the Mediterranean Chaste Tree are aromatic. The seeds stimulate progesterone production.

Habitat Subtropical upland; Europe, W. Asia, E. Africa	Parts used

Family RHAMNACEAE	Species *Ziziphus jujuba*	Local name Chinese Date

JUJUBE

Jujube is a spiny, deciduous tree with small clusters of yellow flowers and datelike fruits, which are eaten fresh, dried, and pickled.

• **USES** In China, Jujube fruit is one of the "kingly" herbs, acting as a general tonic with no harmful side effects. It is found in some Chinese anticancer formulae, and Japanese research suggests it promotes immunity. The fruit is made into cough drops, taken as a heart tonic, to relieve poisons, and, with seeds, is prescribed for anxiety, insomnia, dizziness, and night sweats. The bark is used for diarrhea and fever; the roots are given for fever and to promote hair growth.

Habitat Warm temperate areas; E. Asia	Parts used

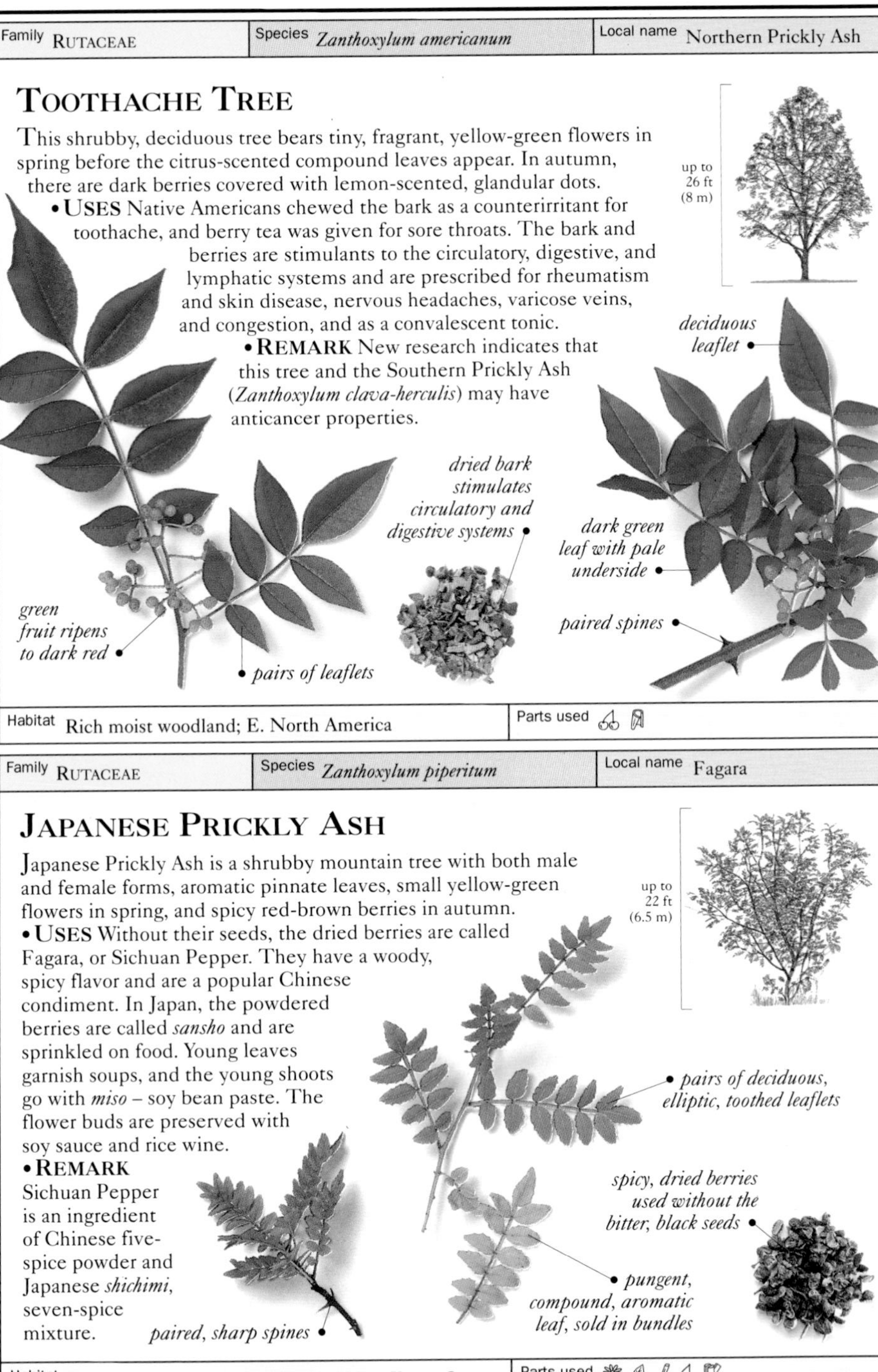

up to
26 ft
(8 m)
deciduous
leaflet
dried bark
stimulates
circulatory and
digestive systems
dark green
leaf with pale
underside
green
fruit ripens
to dark red
pairs of leaflets
paired spines
up to
22 ft
(6.5 m)
pairs of deciduous,
elliptic, toothed leaflets
spicy, dried berries
used without the
bitter, black seeds
pungent,
compound, aromatic
leaf, sold in bundles
paired, sharp spines

Family RUTACEAE	Species *Zanthoxylum americanum*	Local name Northern Prickly Ash

TOOTHACHE TREE

This shrubby, deciduous tree bears tiny, fragrant, yellow-green flowers in spring before the citrus-scented compound leaves appear. In autumn, there are dark berries covered with lemon-scented, glandular dots.

• **USES** Native Americans chewed the bark as a counterirritant for toothache, and berry tea was given for sore throats. The bark and berries are stimulants to the circulatory, digestive, and lymphatic systems and are prescribed for rheumatism and skin disease, nervous headaches, varicose veins, and congestion, and as a convalescent tonic.

• **REMARK** New research indicates that this tree and the Southern Prickly Ash (*Zanthoxylum clava-herculis*) may have anticancer properties.

Habitat Rich moist woodland; E. North America	Parts used

Family RUTACEAE	Species *Zanthoxylum piperitum*	Local name Fagara

JAPANESE PRICKLY ASH

Japanese Prickly Ash is a shrubby mountain tree with both male and female forms, aromatic pinnate leaves, small yellow-green flowers in spring, and spicy red-brown berries in autumn.

• **USES** Without their seeds, the dried berries are called Fagara, or Sichuan Pepper. They have a woody, spicy flavor and are a popular Chinese condiment. In Japan, the powdered berries are called *sansho* and are sprinkled on food. Young leaves garnish soups, and the young shoots go with *miso* – soy bean paste. The flower buds are preserved with soy sauce and rice wine.

• **REMARK** Sichuan Pepper is an ingredient of Chinese five-spice powder and Japanese *shichimi*, seven-spice mixture.

Habitat Warm temperate mountains; N. China, Korea, Japan	Parts used

SHRUBS

Family LEGUMINOSAE	Species *Acacia dealbata*	Local name Silver Wattle

MIMOSA

This deciduous evergreen shrub has blue-green to medium green leaves, with fine, gray-white hairs and fragrant yellow inflorescences. Trees and shrubs in the genus *Acacia* tolerate dry conditions, where they help restore fertility to the soil.
• **USES** Boiled leaves, shoots, and seeds are edible, and the roots can be tapped for water. Mimosa is sold in florists and grown in South Africa for its bark-tannin and gum. Mimosa or Cassie essential oil, used in perfumes, is distilled from the flowers of *A. farnesiana* and *A. baileyana*. The thorns of *A. cornigera* treat asthma, the root delays snake bite effects, and the bark is given for skin problems. *A. catechu* wood yields dye and catechu, an extract chewed with betel nuts and used to treat sore throats. *A. senegal* is the main source of gum arabic, used in sweets, inks, fabric printing, artists' paints, and to add shine to silk and crepes.
• **REMARK** *Acacia* pods growing on trees in the African savannah are irresistible food for elephants. Biting ants inhabit the thorns of *A. cornigera* and protect it against herbivores.

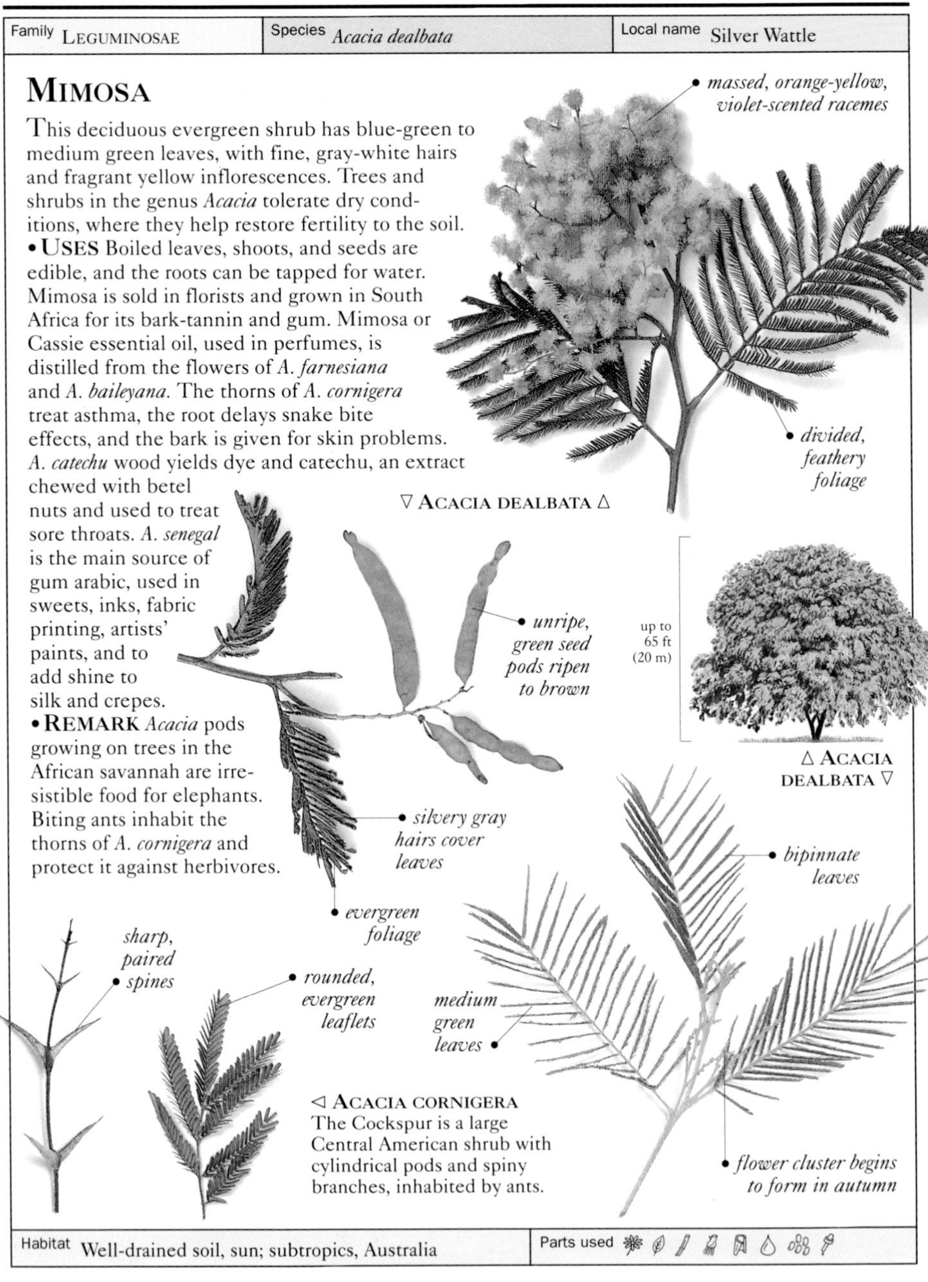

massed, orange-yellow, violet-scented racemes
divided, feathery foliage
▽ ACACIA DEALBATA △
unripe, green seed pods ripen to brown
up to 65 ft (20 m)
△ ACACIA DEALBATA ▽
silvery gray hairs cover leaves
evergreen foliage
bipinnate leaves
sharp, paired spines
rounded, evergreen leaflets
medium green leaves
flower cluster begins to form in autumn

◁ ACACIA CORNIGERA
The Cockspur is a large Central American shrub with cylindrical pods and spiny branches, inhabited by ants.

Habitat Well-drained soil, sun; subtropics, Australia	Parts used

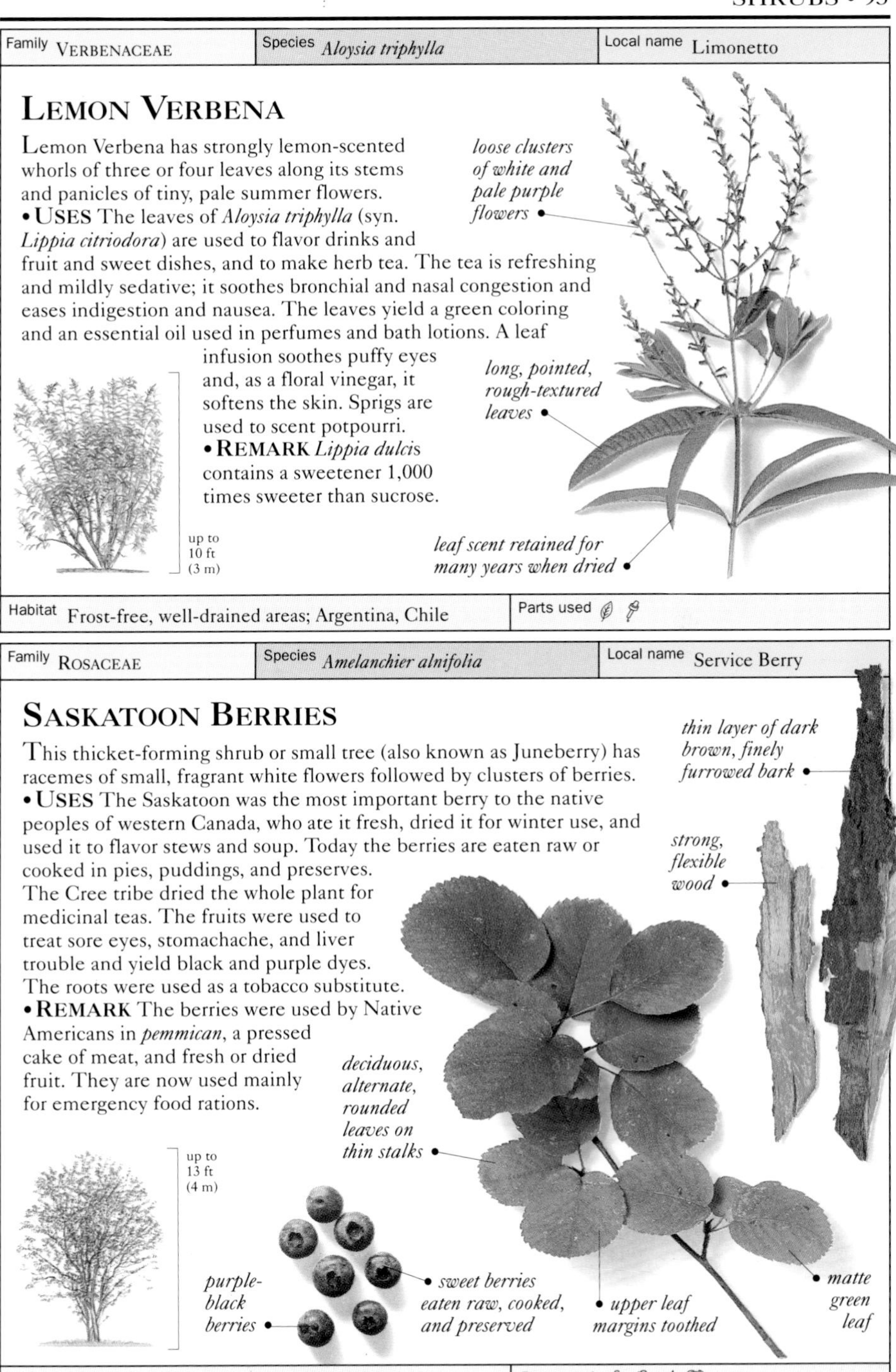
loose clusters of white and pale purple flowers
long, pointed, rough-textured leaves
leaf scent retained for many years when dried
up to 10 ft (3 m)
thin layer of dark brown, finely furrowed bark
strong, flexible wood
deciduous, alternate, rounded leaves on thin stalks
up to 13 ft (4 m)
purple-black berries
sweet berries eaten raw, cooked, and preserved
upper leaf margins toothed
matte green leaf

Family VERBENACEAE | Species *Aloysia triphylla* | Local name Limonetto

LEMON VERBENA

Lemon Verbena has strongly lemon-scented whorls of three or four leaves along its stems and panicles of tiny, pale summer flowers.

• **USES** The leaves of *Aloysia triphylla* (syn. *Lippia citriodora*) are used to flavor drinks and fruit and sweet dishes, and to make herb tea. The tea is refreshing and mildly sedative; it soothes bronchial and nasal congestion and eases indigestion and nausea. The leaves yield a green coloring and an essential oil used in perfumes and bath lotions. A leaf infusion soothes puffy eyes and, as a floral vinegar, it softens the skin. Sprigs are used to scent potpourri.

• **REMARK** *Lippia dulcis* contains a sweetener 1,000 times sweeter than sucrose.

Habitat Frost-free, well-drained areas; Argentina, Chile | Parts used

Family ROSACEAE | Species *Amelanchier alnifolia* | Local name Service Berry

SASKATOON BERRIES

This thicket-forming shrub or small tree (also known as Juneberry) has racemes of small, fragrant white flowers followed by clusters of berries.

• **USES** The Saskatoon was the most important berry to the native peoples of western Canada, who ate it fresh, dried it for winter use, and used it to flavor stews and soup. Today the berries are eaten raw or cooked in pies, puddings, and preserves. The Cree tribe dried the whole plant for medicinal teas. The fruits were used to treat sore eyes, stomachache, and liver trouble and yield black and purple dyes. The roots were used as a tobacco substitute.

• **REMARK** The berries were used by Native Americans in *pemmican*, a pressed cake of meat, and fresh or dried fruit. They are now used mainly for emergency food rations.

Habitat Wet woodland; W. Canada | Parts used

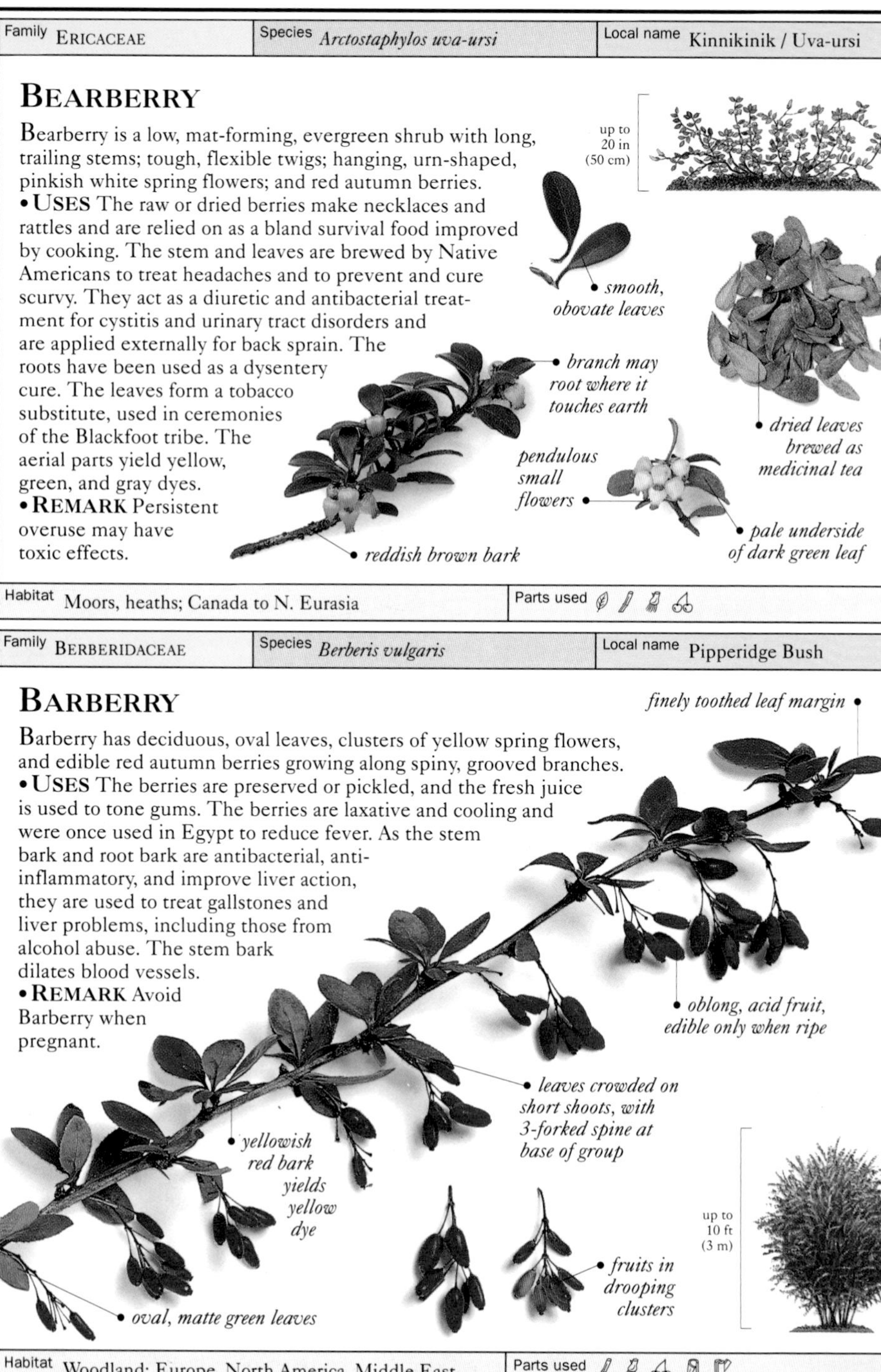
up to
20 in
(50 cm)
smooth,
obovate leaves
branch may
root where it
touches earth
dried leaves
brewed as
medicinal tea
pendulous
small
flowers
pale underside
of dark green leaf
reddish brown bark
finely toothed leaf margin
oblong, acid fruit,
edible only when ripe
leaves crowded on
short shoots, with
3-forked spine at
base of group
yellowish
red bark
yields
yellow
dye
up to
10 ft
(3 m)
fruits in
drooping
clusters
oval, matte green leaves

Family ERICACEAE	Species *Arctostaphylos uva-ursi*	Local name Kinnikinik / Uva-ursi

BEARBERRY

Bearberry is a low, mat-forming, evergreen shrub with long, trailing stems; tough, flexible twigs; hanging, urn-shaped, pinkish white spring flowers; and red autumn berries.

• **USES** The raw or dried berries make necklaces and rattles and are relied on as a bland survival food improved by cooking. The stem and leaves are brewed by Native Americans to treat headaches and to prevent and cure scurvy. They act as a diuretic and antibacterial treatment for cystitis and urinary tract disorders and are applied externally for back sprain. The roots have been used as a dysentery cure. The leaves form a tobacco substitute, used in ceremonies of the Blackfoot tribe. The aerial parts yield yellow, green, and gray dyes.

• **REMARK** Persistent overuse may have toxic effects.

Habitat Moors, heaths; Canada to N. Eurasia	Parts used

Family BERBERIDACEAE	Species *Berberis vulgaris*	Local name Pipperidge Bush

BARBERRY

Barberry has deciduous, oval leaves, clusters of yellow spring flowers, and edible red autumn berries growing along spiny, grooved branches.

• **USES** The berries are preserved or pickled, and the fresh juice is used to tone gums. The berries are laxative and cooling and were once used in Egypt to reduce fever. As the stem bark and root bark are antibacterial, anti-inflammatory, and improve liver action, they are used to treat gallstones and liver problems, including those from alcohol abuse. The stem bark dilates blood vessels.

• **REMARK** Avoid Barberry when pregnant.

Habitat Woodland; Europe, North America, Middle East	Parts used

Family	Species	Local name
BUXACEAE	*Buxus sempervirens*	American Boxwood

BOXWOOD

Boxwood is an evergreen shrub or small tree of variable form with small, yellow-green flowers in spring, berries with black seeds, and leafy stems with a distinctive scent.

• **USES** The leaves contain buxine and were once used to purify blood, improve hair growth and horses' coats, and, with bark, were given to treat rheumatism and expel worms. They are now considered too toxic, except in homeopathic doses. The wood is narcotic and sedative, and its distilled oil treated toothache and hemorrhoids. Leached leaves and wood yield an auburn hair dye, and the bark is used in perfumes.

• **REMARK** Animals can die from eating Boxwood leaves. The hard wood is used to make some scientific instruments, flutes, and combs.

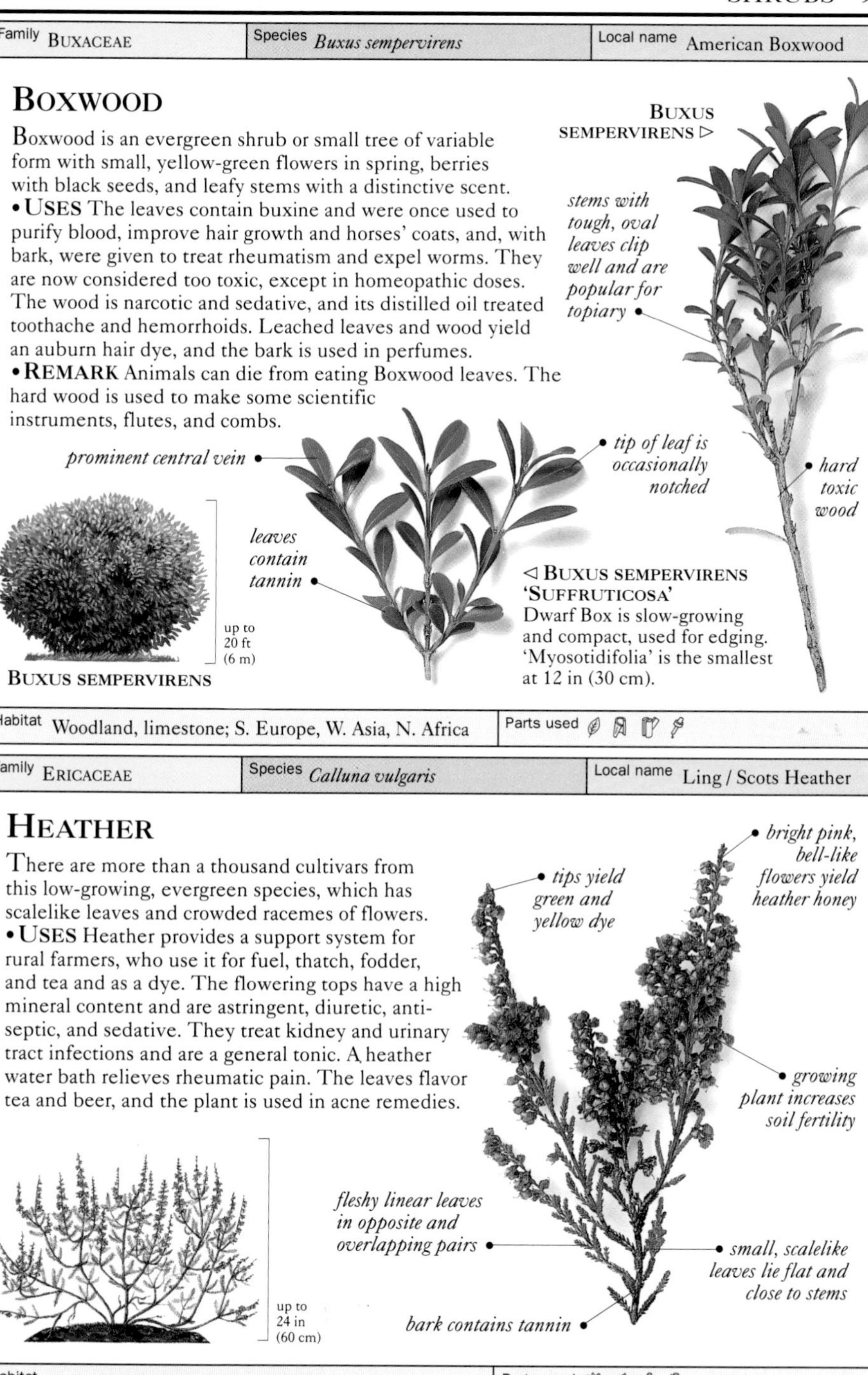
BUXUS SEMPERVIRENS ▷
stems with tough, oval leaves clip well and are popular for topiary
prominent central vein
tip of leaf is occasionally notched
hard toxic wood
leaves contain tannin
up to 20 ft (6 m)
BUXUS SEMPERVIRENS
tips yield green and yellow dye
bright pink, bell-like flowers yield heather honey
growing plant increases soil fertility
fleshy linear leaves in opposite and overlapping pairs
small, scalelike leaves lie flat and close to stems
bark contains tannin
up to 24 in (60 cm)

◁ **BUXUS SEMPERVIRENS 'SUFFRUTICOSA'**
Dwarf Box is slow-growing and compact, used for edging. 'Myosotidifolia' is the smallest at 12 in (30 cm).

Habitat	Parts used
Woodland, limestone; S. Europe, W. Asia, N. Africa	

Family	Species	Local name
ERICACEAE	*Calluna vulgaris*	Ling / Scots Heather

HEATHER

There are more than a thousand cultivars from this low-growing, evergreen species, which has scalelike leaves and crowded racemes of flowers.

• **USES** Heather provides a support system for rural farmers, who use it for fuel, thatch, fodder, and tea and as a dye. The flowering tops have a high mineral content and are astringent, diuretic, antiseptic, and sedative. They treat kidney and urinary tract infections and are a general tonic. A heather water bath relieves rheumatic pain. The leaves flavor tea and beer, and the plant is used in acne remedies.

Habitat	Parts used
Acid soils, moorland; Europe, North America	

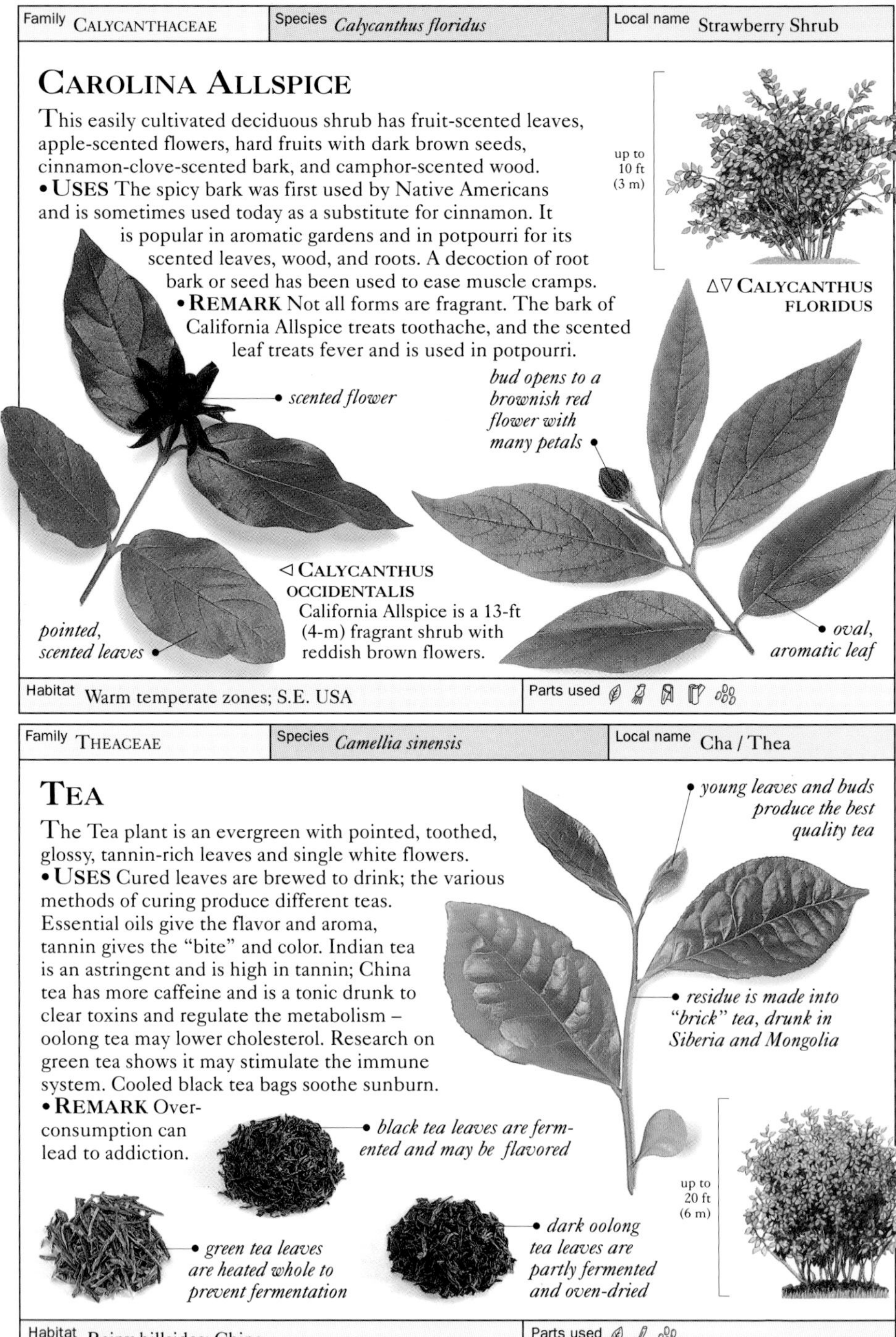
up to
10 ft
(3 m)
scented flower
bud opens to a
brownish red
flower with
many petals
pointed,
scented leaves
oval,
aromatic leaf
young leaves and buds
produce the best
quality tea
residue is made into
"brick" tea, drunk in
Siberia and Mongolia
black tea leaves are fermented and may be flavored
up to
20 ft
(6 m)
green tea leaves
are heated whole to
prevent fermentation
dark oolong
tea leaves are
partly fermented
and oven-dried

Family CALYCANTHACEAE	Species *Calycanthus floridus*	Local name Strawberry Shrub

CAROLINA ALLSPICE

This easily cultivated deciduous shrub has fruit-scented leaves, apple-scented flowers, hard fruits with dark brown seeds, cinnamon-clove-scented bark, and camphor-scented wood. • **USES** The spicy bark was first used by Native Americans and is sometimes used today as a substitute for cinnamon. It is popular in aromatic gardens and in potpourri for its scented leaves, wood, and roots. A decoction of root bark or seed has been used to ease muscle cramps. • **REMARK** Not all forms are fragrant. The bark of California Allspice treats toothache, and the scented leaf treats fever and is used in potpourri.

△▽ CALYCANTHUS FLORIDUS

◁ CALYCANTHUS OCCIDENTALIS
California Allspice is a 13-ft (4-m) fragrant shrub with reddish brown flowers.

Habitat Warm temperate zones; S.E. USA	Parts used

Family THEACEAE	Species *Camellia sinensis*	Local name Cha / Thea

TEA

The Tea plant is an evergreen with pointed, toothed, glossy, tannin-rich leaves and single white flowers. • **USES** Cured leaves are brewed to drink; the various methods of curing produce different teas. Essential oils give the flavor and aroma, tannin gives the "bite" and color. Indian tea is an astringent and is high in tannin; China tea has more caffeine and is a tonic drunk to clear toxins and regulate the metabolism – oolong tea may lower cholesterol. Research on green tea shows it may stimulate the immune system. Cooled black tea bags soothe sunburn. • **REMARK** Over-consumption can lead to addiction.

Habitat Rainy hillsides; China	Parts used

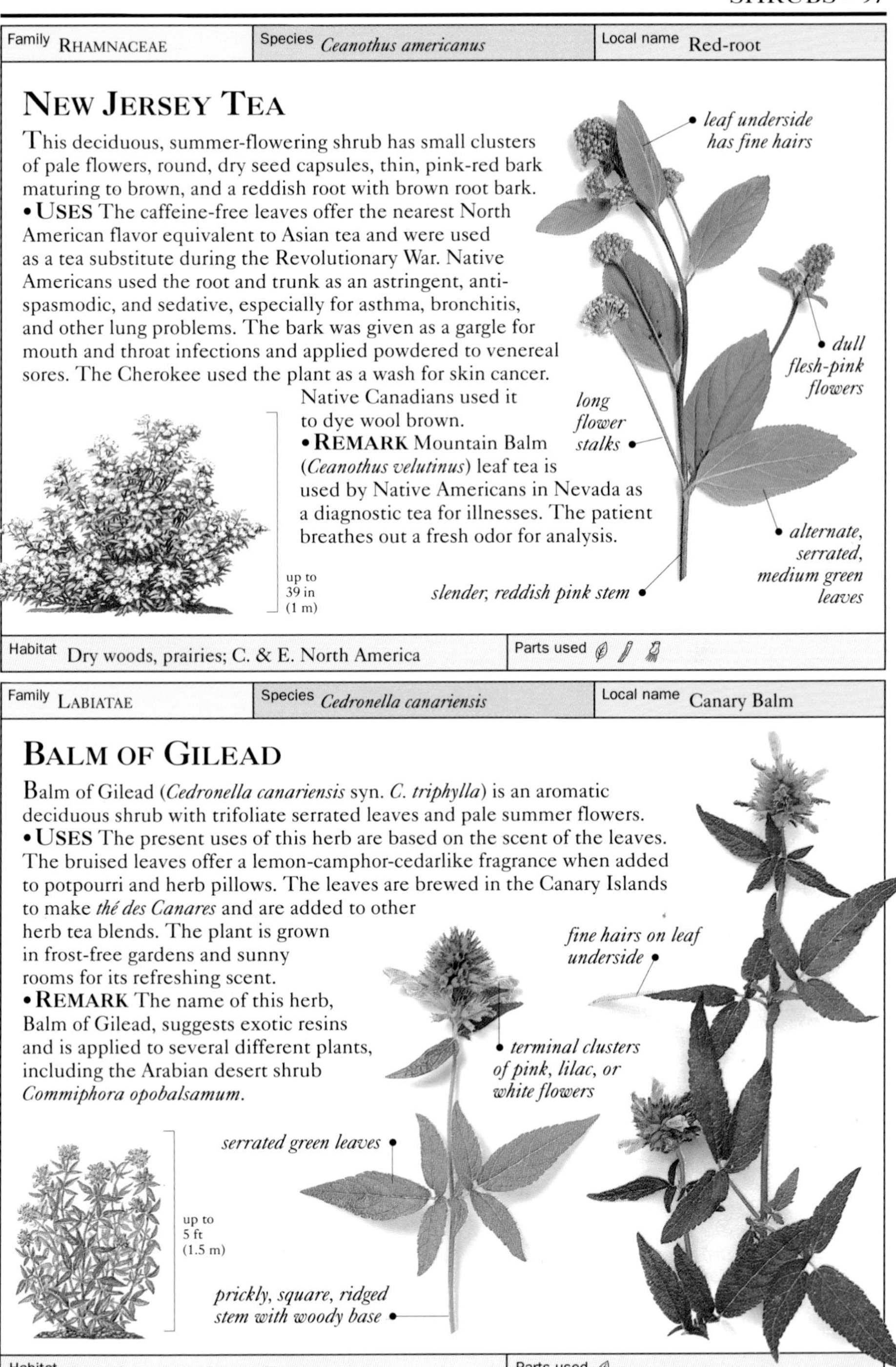
leaf underside has fine hairs
dull flesh-pink flowers
long flower stalks
alternate, serrated, medium green leaves
slender, reddish pink stem
up to 39 in (1 m)
fine hairs on leaf underside
terminal clusters of pink, lilac, or white flowers
serrated green leaves
prickly, square, ridged stem with woody base
up to 5 ft (1.5 m)

Family RHAMNACEAE	Species *Ceanothus americanus*	Local name Red-root

NEW JERSEY TEA

This deciduous, summer-flowering shrub has small clusters of pale flowers, round, dry seed capsules, thin, pink-red bark maturing to brown, and a reddish root with brown root bark. • **USES** The caffeine-free leaves offer the nearest North American flavor equivalent to Asian tea and were used as a tea substitute during the Revolutionary War. Native Americans used the root and trunk as an astringent, antispasmodic, and sedative, especially for asthma, bronchitis, and other lung problems. The bark was given as a gargle for mouth and throat infections and applied powdered to venereal sores. The Cherokee used the plant as a wash for skin cancer. Native Canadians used it to dye wool brown. • **REMARK** Mountain Balm (*Ceanothus velutinus*) leaf tea is used by Native Americans in Nevada as a diagnostic tea for illnesses. The patient breathes out a fresh odor for analysis.

Habitat Dry woods, prairies; C. & E. North America	Parts used

Family LABIATAE	Species *Cedronella canariensis*	Local name Canary Balm

BALM OF GILEAD

Balm of Gilead (*Cedronella canariensis* syn. *C. triphylla*) is an aromatic deciduous shrub with trifoliate serrated leaves and pale summer flowers. • **USES** The present uses of this herb are based on the scent of the leaves. The bruised leaves offer a lemon-camphor-cedarlike fragrance when added to potpourri and herb pillows. The leaves are brewed in the Canary Islands to make *thé des Canares* and are added to other herb tea blends. The plant is grown in frost-free gardens and sunny rooms for its refreshing scent. • **REMARK** The name of this herb, Balm of Gilead, suggests exotic resins and is applied to several different plants, including the Arabian desert shrub *Commiphora opobalsamum*.

Habitat Frost-free areas; Canary Islands	Parts used

Family COMPOSITAE | Species *Chrysothamnus nauseosus* | Local name Gray Rabbitbrush

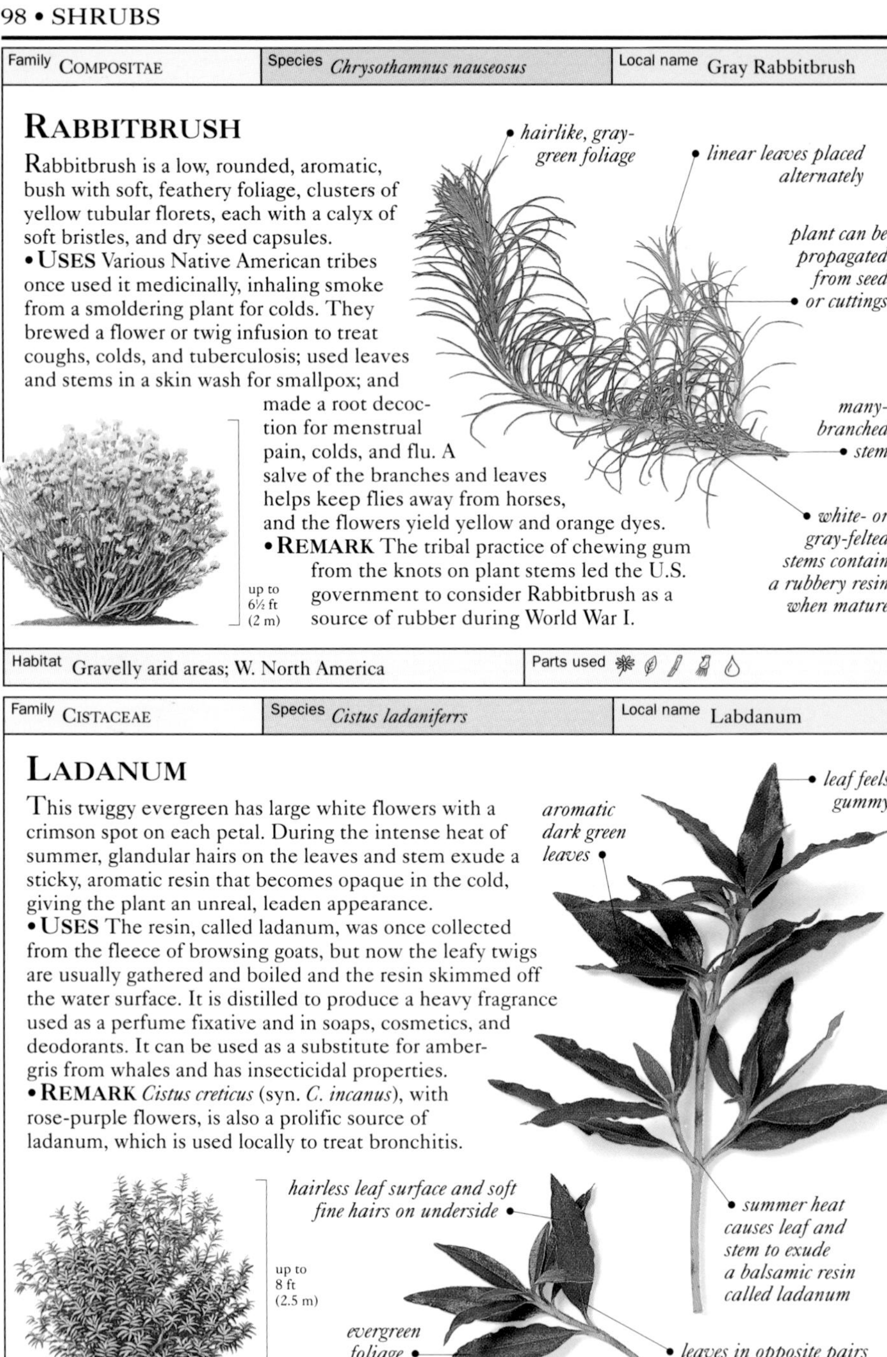
hairlike, gray-green foliage
linear leaves placed alternately
plant can be propagated from seed or cuttings
many-branched stem
white- or gray-felted stems contain a rubbery resin when mature
up to 6½ ft (2 m)
aromatic dark green leaves
leaf feels gummy
hairless leaf surface and soft fine hairs on underside
summer heat causes leaf and stem to exude a balsamic resin called ladanum
up to 8 ft (2.5 m)
evergreen foliage
leaves in opposite pairs

RABBITBRUSH

Rabbitbrush is a low, rounded, aromatic, bush with soft, feathery foliage, clusters of yellow tubular florets, each with a calyx of soft bristles, and dry seed capsules.

• **USES** Various Native American tribes once used it medicinally, inhaling smoke from a smoldering plant for colds. They brewed a flower or twig infusion to treat coughs, colds, and tuberculosis; used leaves and stems in a skin wash for smallpox; and made a root decoction for menstrual pain, colds, and flu. A salve of the branches and leaves helps keep flies away from horses, and the flowers yield yellow and orange dyes.

• **REMARK** The tribal practice of chewing gum from the knots on plant stems led the U.S. government to consider Rabbitbrush as a source of rubber during World War I.

Habitat Gravelly arid areas; W. North America | Parts used

Family CISTACEAE | Species *Cistus ladaniferrs* | Local name Labdanum

LADANUM

This twiggy evergreen has large white flowers with a crimson spot on each petal. During the intense heat of summer, glandular hairs on the leaves and stem exude a sticky, aromatic resin that becomes opaque in the cold, giving the plant an unreal, leaden appearance.

• **USES** The resin, called ladanum, was once collected from the fleece of browsing goats, but now the leafy twigs are usually gathered and boiled and the resin skimmed off the water surface. It is distilled to produce a heavy fragrance used as a perfume fixative and in soaps, cosmetics, and deodorants. It can be used as a substitute for ambergris from whales and has insecticidal properties.

• **REMARK** *Cistus creticus* (syn. *C. incanus*), with rose-purple flowers, is also a prolific source of ladanum, which is used locally to treat bronchitis.

Habitat Rocky scrubland; Mediterranean | Parts used

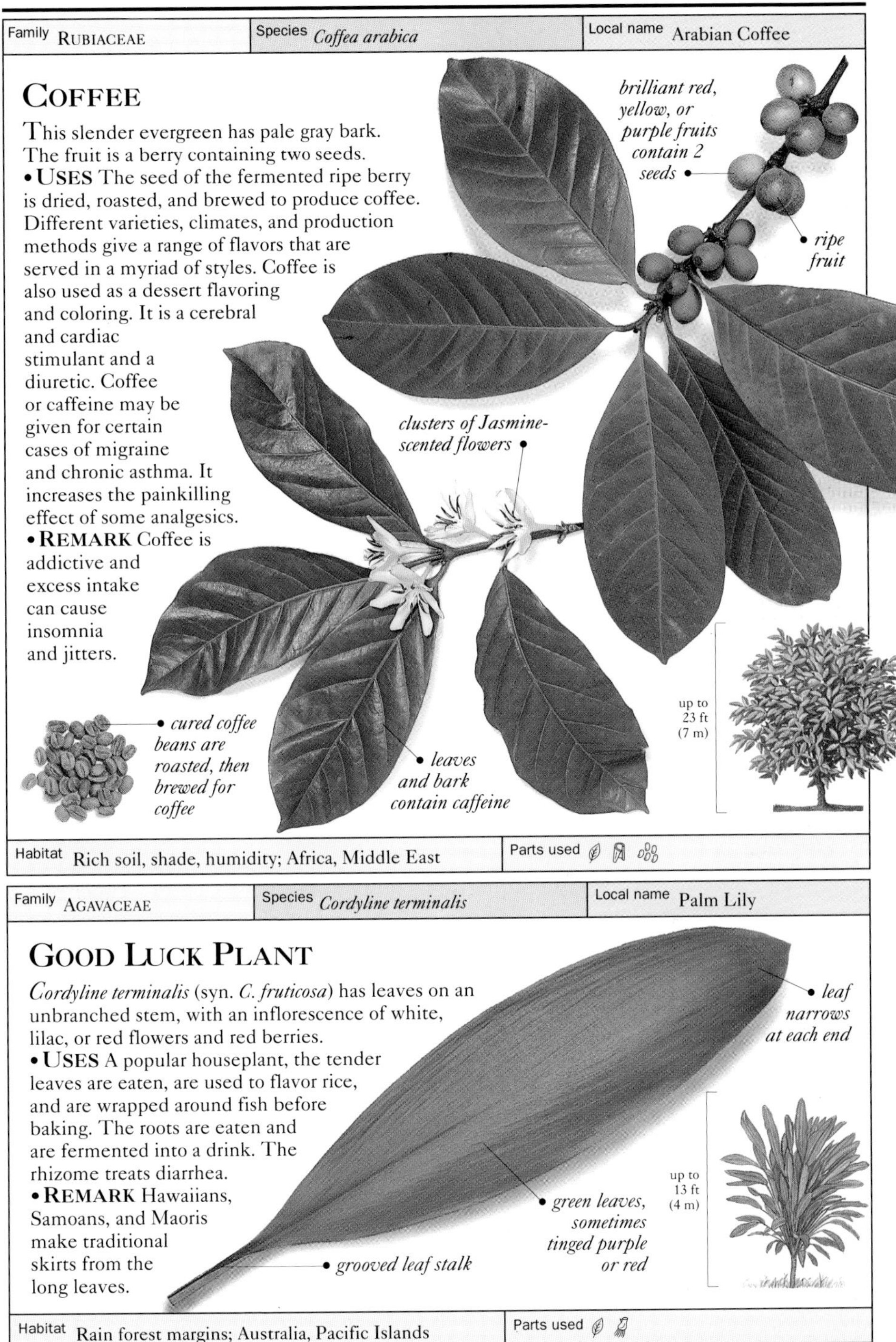
brilliant red, yellow, or purple fruits contain 2 seeds
ripe fruit
clusters of Jasmine-scented flowers
cured coffee beans are roasted, then brewed for coffee
leaves and bark contain caffeine
up to 23 ft (7 m)
leaf narrows at each end
green leaves, sometimes tinged purple or red
grooved leaf stalk
up to 13 ft (4 m)

Family RUBIACEAE | Species *Coffea arabica* | Local name Arabian Coffee

COFFEE

This slender evergreen has pale gray bark. The fruit is a berry containing two seeds.

• **USES** The seed of the fermented ripe berry is dried, roasted, and brewed to produce coffee. Different varieties, climates, and production methods give a range of flavors that are served in a myriad of styles. Coffee is also used as a dessert flavoring and coloring. It is a cerebral and cardiac stimulant and a diuretic. Coffee or caffeine may be given for certain cases of migraine and chronic asthma. It increases the painkilling effect of some analgesics.

• **REMARK** Coffee is addictive and excess intake can cause insomnia and jitters.

Habitat Rich soil, shade, humidity; Africa, Middle East | Parts used

Family AGAVACEAE | Species *Cordyline terminalis* | Local name Palm Lily

GOOD LUCK PLANT

Cordyline terminalis (syn. *C. fruticosa*) has leaves on an unbranched stem, with an inflorescence of white, lilac, or red flowers and red berries.

• **USES** A popular houseplant, the tender leaves are eaten, are used to flavor rice, and are wrapped around fish before baking. The roots are eaten and are fermented into a drink. The rhizome treats diarrhea.

• **REMARK** Hawaiians, Samoans, and Maoris make traditional skirts from the long leaves.

Habitat Rain forest margins; Australia, Pacific Islands | Parts used

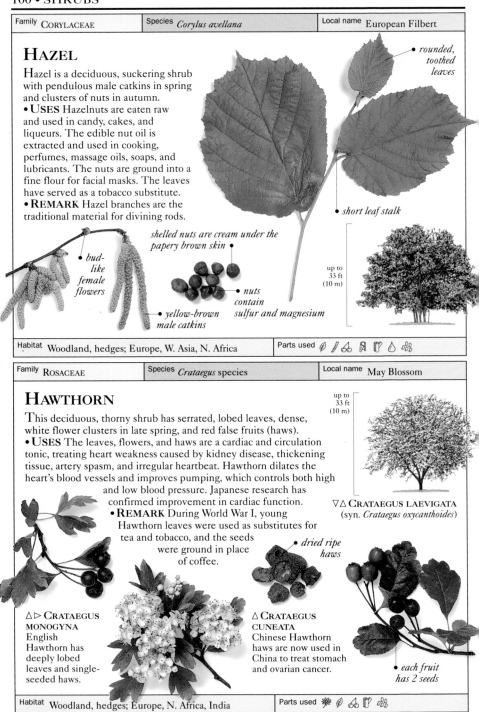

Family CORYLACEAE	Species *Corylus avellana*	Local name European Filbert

HAZEL

Hazel is a deciduous, suckering shrub with pendulous male catkins in spring and clusters of nuts in autumn.

• **USES** Hazelnuts are eaten raw and used in candy, cakes, and liqueurs. The edible nut oil is extracted and used in cooking, perfumes, massage oils, soaps, and lubricants. The nuts are ground into a fine flour for facial masks. The leaves have served as a tobacco substitute.

• **REMARK** Hazel branches are the traditional material for divining rods.

rounded, toothed leaves

short leaf stalk

shelled nuts are cream under the papery brown skin

bud-like female flowers

nuts contain sulfur and magnesium

yellow-brown male catkins

up to 33 ft (10 m)

Habitat Woodland, hedges; Europe, W. Asia, N. Africa	Parts used

Family ROSACEAE	Species *Crataegus* species	Local name May Blossom

HAWTHORN

This deciduous, thorny shrub has serrated, lobed leaves, dense, white flower clusters in late spring, and red false fruits (haws).

• **USES** The leaves, flowers, and haws are a cardiac and circulation tonic, treating heart weakness caused by kidney disease, thickening tissue, artery spasm, and irregular heartbeat. Hawthorn dilates the heart's blood vessels and improves pumping, which controls both high and low blood pressure. Japanese research has confirmed improvement in cardiac function.

• **REMARK** During World War I, young Hawthorn leaves were used as substitutes for tea and tobacco, and the seeds were ground in place of coffee.

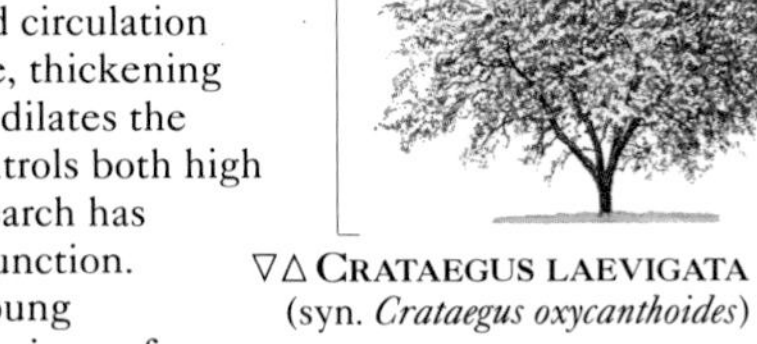

up to 33 ft (10 m)

▽△ CRATAEGUS LAEVIGATA (syn. *Crataegus oxycanthoides*)

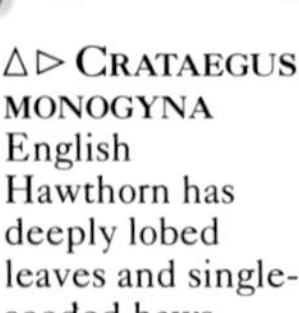

△▷ CRATAEGUS MONOGYNA English Hawthorn has deeply lobed leaves and single-seeded haws.

dried ripe haws

△ CRATAEGUS CUNEATA Chinese Hawthorn haws are now used in China to treat stomach and ovarian cancer.

each fruit has 2 seeds

Habitat Woodland, hedges; Europe, N. Africa, India	Parts used

Family EUPHORBIACEAE	Species *Croton tiglium*	Local name Purging Croton

CROTON

Croton has malodorous, dark green leaves, inconspicuous flower racemes, and a brown seed capsule with three hard black seeds.

• **USES** The seed oil is a dangerous, violent purgative now used only for extreme blockages or externally as a counterirritant. In China, tiny amounts of processed seed are used to treat epilepsy, malaria, and chest congestion. In Malaysia, whole seeds are used to stun fish. The tumor-promoting properties of the oil are being used to investigate how cancerous cells develop from normal ones.

• **REMARK** Sweetbark (*Croton eluteria*) is a decorative shrub with a metallic appearance, fragrant white flowers, and aromatic tonic bark that burns with a musky scent. It has mild narcotic properties and is given for malaria, nausea, and headaches.

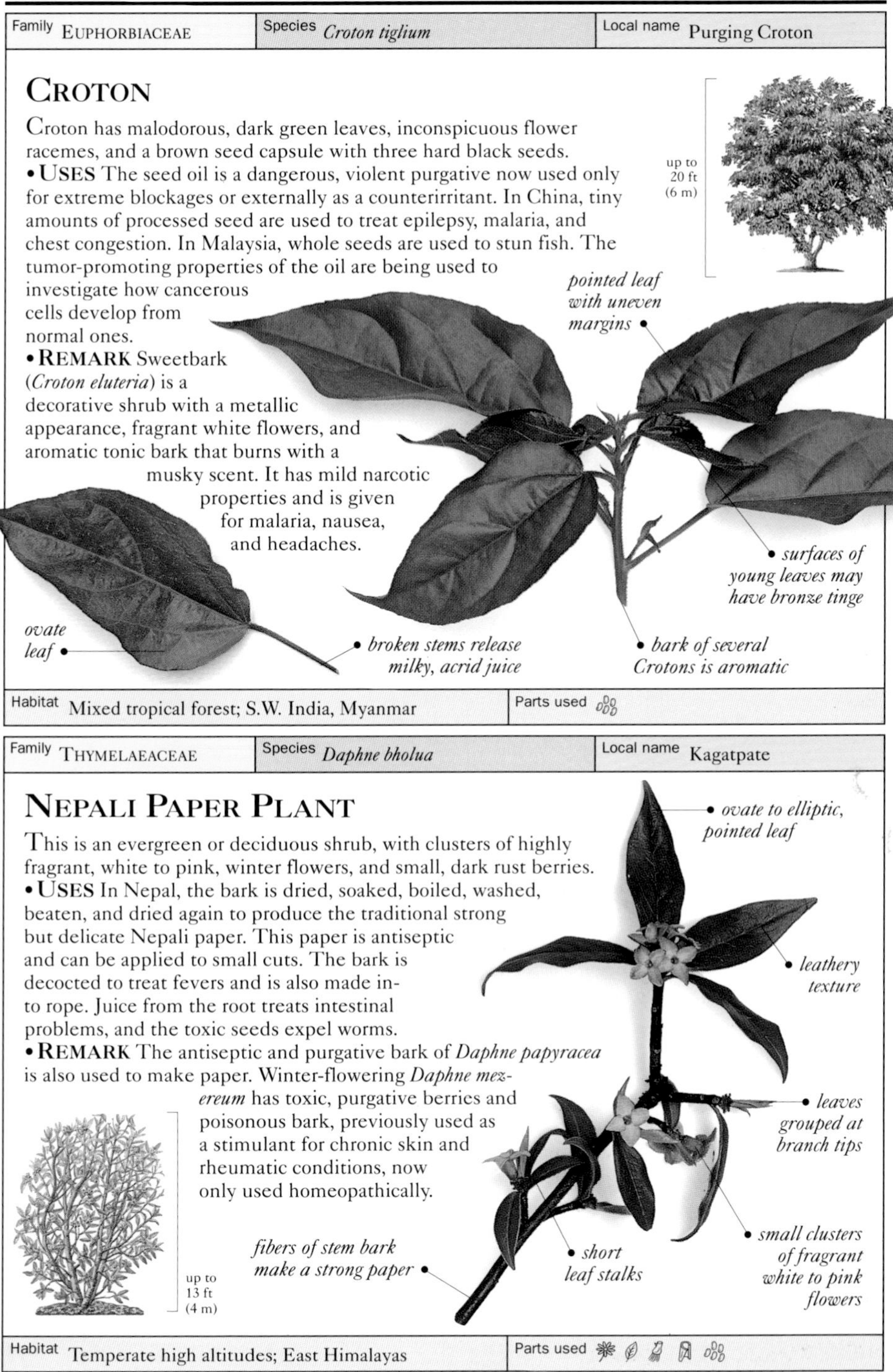
up to
20 ft
(6 m)
pointed leaf with uneven margins
surfaces of young leaves may have bronze tinge
ovate leaf
broken stems release milky, acrid juice
bark of several Crotons is aromatic
ovate to elliptic, pointed leaf
leathery texture
leaves grouped at branch tips
small clusters of fragrant white to pink flowers
short leaf stalks
fibers of stem bark make a strong paper
up to
13 ft
(4 m)

Habitat Mixed tropical forest; S.W. India, Myanmar	Parts used

Family THYMELAEACEAE	Species *Daphne bholua*	Local name Kagatpate

NEPALI PAPER PLANT

This is an evergreen or deciduous shrub, with clusters of highly fragrant, white to pink, winter flowers, and small, dark rust berries.

• **USES** In Nepal, the bark is dried, soaked, boiled, washed, beaten, and dried again to produce the traditional strong but delicate Nepali paper. This paper is antiseptic and can be applied to small cuts. The bark is decocted to treat fevers and is also made into rope. Juice from the root treats intestinal problems, and the toxic seeds expel worms.

• **REMARK** The antiseptic and purgative bark of *Daphne papyracea* is also used to make paper. Winter-flowering *Daphne mezereum* has toxic, purgative berries and poisonous bark, previously used as a stimulant for chronic skin and rheumatic conditions, now only used homeopathically.

Habitat Temperate high altitudes; East Himalayas	Parts used

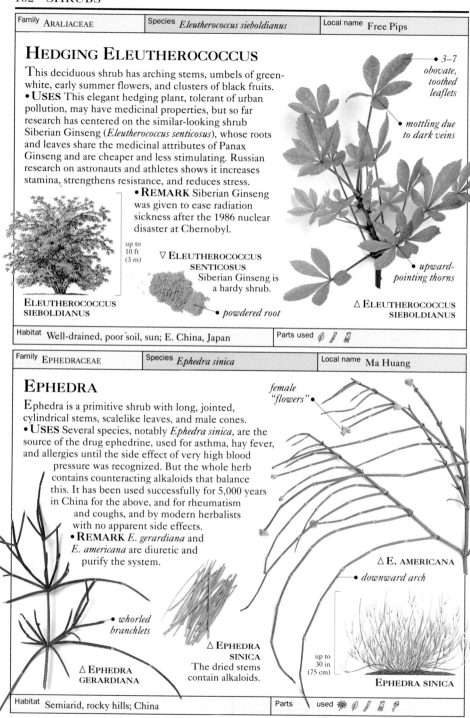

Family ARALIACEAE	Species *Eleutherococcus sieboldianus*	Local name Free Pips

HEDGING ELEUTHEROCOCCUS

This deciduous shrub has arching stems, umbels of green-white, early summer flowers, and clusters of black fruits.
• **USES** This elegant hedging plant, tolerant of urban pollution, may have medicinal properties, but so far research has centered on the similar-looking shrub Siberian Ginseng (*Eleutherococcus senticosus*), whose roots and leaves share the medicinal attributes of Panax Ginseng and are cheaper and less stimulating. Russian research on astronauts and athletes shows it increases stamina, strengthens resistance, and reduces stress.
• **REMARK** Siberian Ginseng was given to ease radiation sickness after the 1986 nuclear disaster at Chernobyl.

up to 10 ft (3 m)

ELEUTHEROCOCCUS SIEBOLDIANUS

▽ ELEUTHEROCOCCUS SENTICOSUS
Siberian Ginseng is a hardy shrub.

powdered root

3–7 obovate, toothed leaflets

mottling due to dark veins

upward-pointing thorns

△ ELEUTHEROCOCCUS SIEBOLDIANUS

Habitat Well-drained, poor soil, sun; E. China, Japan	Parts used

Family EPHEDRACEAE	Species *Ephedra sinica*	Local name Ma Huang

EPHEDRA

Ephedra is a primitive shrub with long, jointed, cylindrical stems, scalelike leaves, and male cones.
• **USES** Several species, notably *Ephedra sinica*, are the source of the drug ephedrine, used for asthma, hay fever, and allergies until the side effect of very high blood pressure was recognized. But the whole herb contains counteracting alkaloids that balance this. It has been used successfully for 5,000 years in China for the above, and for rheumatism and coughs, and by modern herbalists with no apparent side effects.
• **REMARK** *E. gerardiana* and *E. americana* are diuretic and purify the system.

female "flowers"

△ E. AMERICANA

downward arch

whorled branchlets

△ EPHEDRA GERARDIANA

△ EPHEDRA SINICA
The dried stems contain alkaloids.

up to 30 in (75 cm)

EPHEDRA SINICA

Habitat Semiarid, rocky hills; China	Parts used

Family OLEACEAE	Species *Forsythia suspensa*	Local name Lian Qiao

FORSYTHIA

Forsythia is a deciduous shrub; in spring, it bears golden yellow flowers at nodes before the leaves and seed capsules appear.

• **USES** In China, the seed capsule is a cooling antibacterial, used to detoxify, reduce swelling, promote drainage, and treat flu, colds, fever, measles, chicken pox, sore throats, and boils, and help to control strokes. The leaf treats skin problems and the root is prescribed for fever. In China, a leaf and twig decoction is given for breast cancer, where tests have confirmed antitumor action.

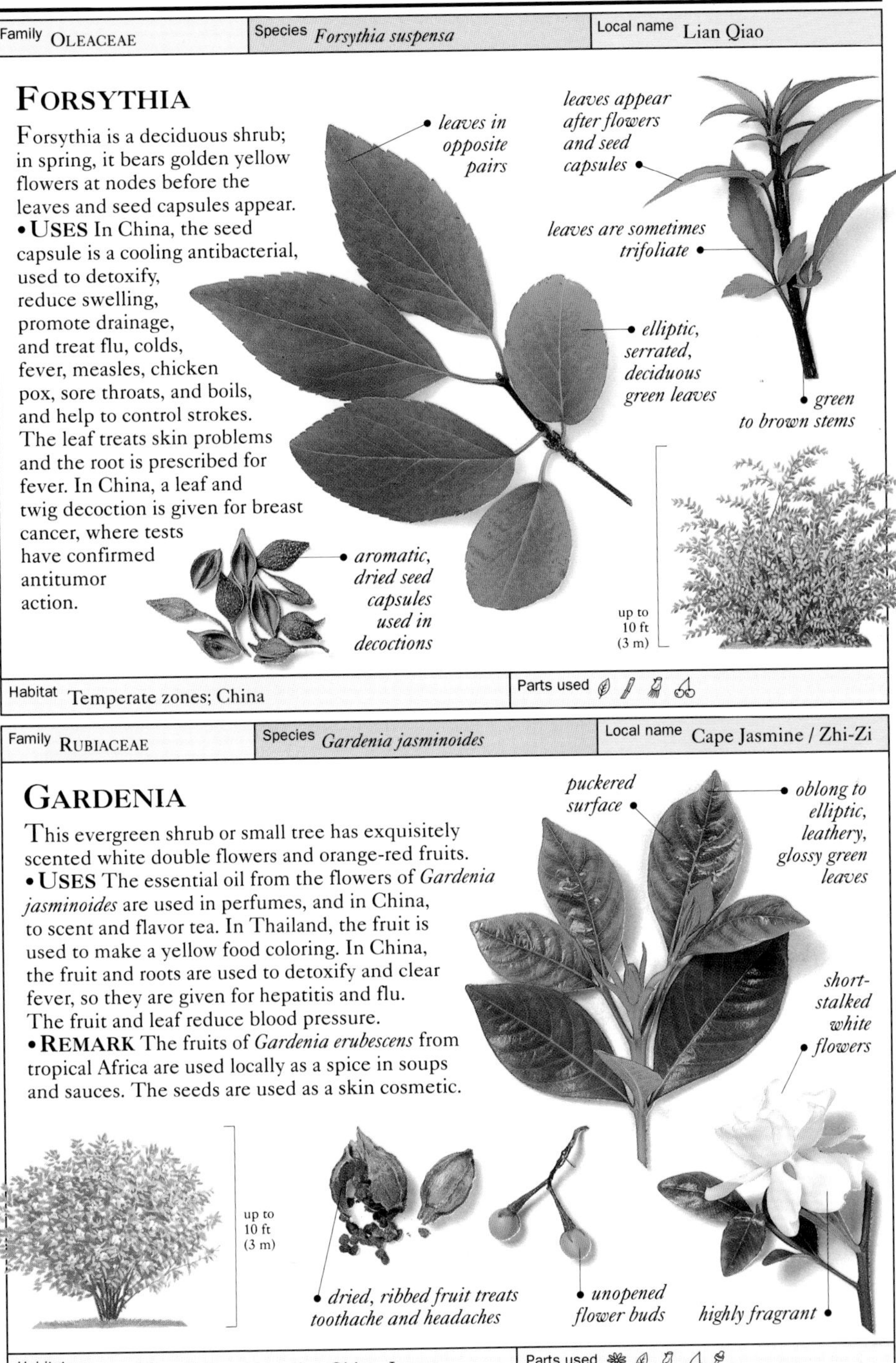
leaves in opposite pairs
leaves appear after flowers and seed capsules
leaves are sometimes trifoliate
elliptic, serrated, deciduous green leaves
green to brown stems
aromatic, dried seed capsules used in decoctions
up to 10 ft (3 m)
puckered surface
oblong to elliptic, leathery, glossy green leaves
short-stalked white flowers
up to 10 ft (3 m)
dried, ribbed fruit treats toothache and headaches
unopened flower buds
highly fragrant

Habitat Temperate zones; China	Parts used

Family RUBIACEAE	Species *Gardenia jasminoides*	Local name Cape Jasmine / Zhi-Zi

GARDENIA

This evergreen shrub or small tree has exquisitely scented white double flowers and orange-red fruits.

• **USES** The essential oil from the flowers of *Gardenia jasminoides* are used in perfumes, and in China, to scent and flavor tea. In Thailand, the fruit is used to make a yellow food coloring. In China, the fruit and roots are used to detoxify and clear fever, so they are given for hepatitis and flu. The fruit and leaf reduce blood pressure.

• **REMARK** The fruits of *Gardenia erubescens* from tropical Africa are used locally as a spice in soups and sauces. The seeds are used as a skin cosmetic.

Habitat Rich acidic soil, humid tropics; China, Japan	Parts used

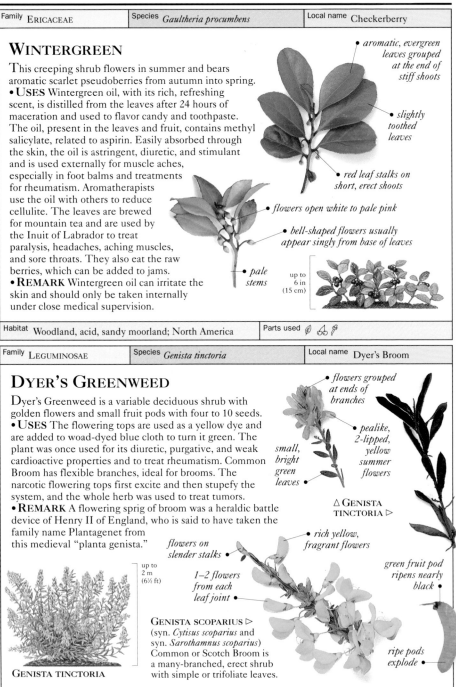

Family ERICACEAE	Species *Gaultheria procumbens*	Local name Checkerberry

WINTERGREEN

This creeping shrub flowers in summer and bears aromatic scarlet pseudoberries from autumn into spring.
• **USES** Wintergreen oil, with its rich, refreshing scent, is distilled from the leaves after 24 hours of maceration and used to flavor candy and toothpaste. The oil, present in the leaves and fruit, contains methyl salicylate, related to aspirin. Easily absorbed through the skin, the oil is astringent, diuretic, and stimulant and is used externally for muscle aches, especially in foot balms and treatments for rheumatism. Aromatherapists use the oil with others to reduce cellulite. The leaves are brewed for mountain tea and are used by the Inuit of Labrador to treat paralysis, headaches, aching muscles, and sore throats. They also eat the raw berries, which can be added to jams.
• **REMARK** Wintergreen oil can irritate the skin and should only be taken internally under close medical supervision.

• *aromatic, evergreen leaves grouped at the end of stiff shoots*

• *slightly toothed leaves*

• *red leaf stalks on short, erect shoots*

• *flowers open white to pale pink*

• *bell-shaped flowers usually appear singly from base of leaves*

• *pale stems*

up to 6 in (15 cm)

Habitat Woodland, acid, sandy moorland; North America	Parts used

Family LEGUMINOSAE	Species *Genista tinctoria*	Local name Dyer's Broom

DYER'S GREENWEED

Dyer's Greenweed is a variable deciduous shrub with golden flowers and small fruit pods with four to 10 seeds.
• **USES** The flowering tops are used as a yellow dye and are added to woad-dyed blue cloth to turn it green. The plant was once used for its diuretic, purgative, and weak cardioactive properties and to treat rheumatism. Common Broom has flexible branches, ideal for brooms. The narcotic flowering tops first excite and then stupefy the system, and the whole herb was used to treat tumors.
• **REMARK** A flowering sprig of broom was a heraldic battle device of Henry II of England, who is said to have taken the family name Plantagenet from this medieval "planta genista."

• *flowers grouped at ends of branches*

• *pealike, 2-lipped, yellow summer flowers*

small, bright green leaves •

△ GENISTA TINCTORIA ▷

• *rich yellow, fragrant flowers*

flowers on slender stalks •

green fruit pod ripens nearly black •

1–2 flowers from each leaf joint •

up to 2 m (6½ ft)

GENISTA SCOPARIUS ▷ (syn. *Cytisus scoparius* and syn. *Sarothamnus scoparius*) Common or Scotch Broom is a many-branched, erect shrub with simple or trifoliate leaves.

ripe pods explode •

GENISTA TINCTORIA

Habitat Northern temperate areas; Europe to S.W. Siberia	Parts used

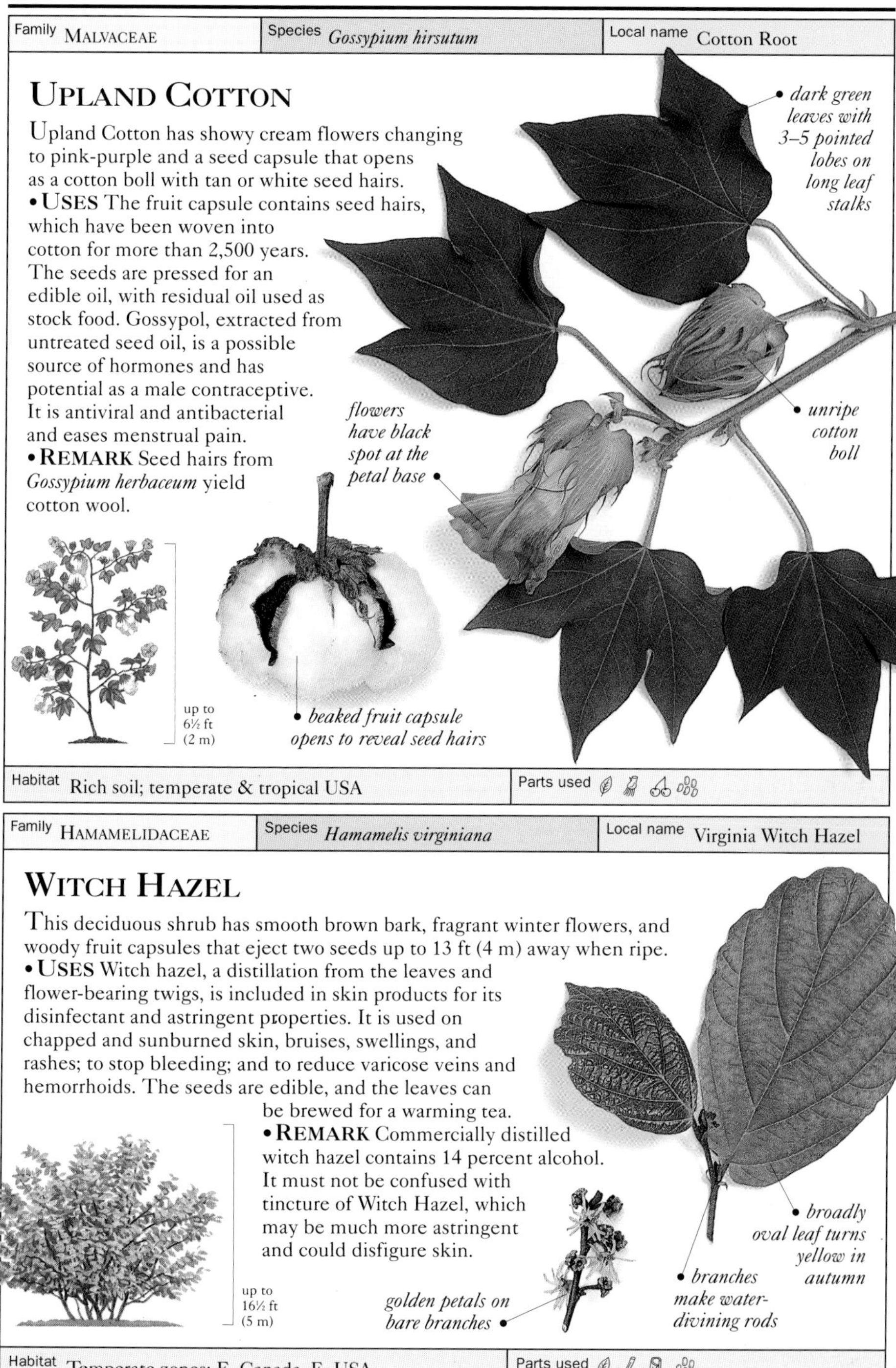
dark green leaves with 3–5 pointed lobes on long leaf stalks
unripe cotton boll
flowers have black spot at the petal base
beaked fruit capsule opens to reveal seed hairs
up to 6½ ft (2 m)
broadly oval leaf turns yellow in autumn
branches make water-divining rods
golden petals on bare branches
up to 16½ ft (5 m)

Family MALVACEAE	Species *Gossypium hirsutum*	Local name Cotton Root

UPLAND COTTON

Upland Cotton has showy cream flowers changing to pink-purple and a seed capsule that opens as a cotton boll with tan or white seed hairs.

• **USES** The fruit capsule contains seed hairs, which have been woven into cotton for more than 2,500 years. The seeds are pressed for an edible oil, with residual oil used as stock food. Gossypol, extracted from untreated seed oil, is a possible source of hormones and has potential as a male contraceptive. It is antiviral and antibacterial and eases menstrual pain.

• **REMARK** Seed hairs from *Gossypium herbaceum* yield cotton wool.

Habitat Rich soil; temperate & tropical USA	Parts used

Family HAMAMELIDACEAE	Species *Hamamelis virginiana*	Local name Virginia Witch Hazel

WITCH HAZEL

This deciduous shrub has smooth brown bark, fragrant winter flowers, and woody fruit capsules that eject two seeds up to 13 ft (4 m) away when ripe.

• **USES** Witch hazel, a distillation from the leaves and flower-bearing twigs, is included in skin products for its disinfectant and astringent properties. It is used on chapped and sunburned skin, bruises, swellings, and rashes; to stop bleeding; and to reduce varicose veins and hemorrhoids. The seeds are edible, and the leaves can be brewed for a warming tea.

• **REMARK** Commercially distilled witch hazel contains 14 percent alcohol. It must not be confused with tincture of Witch Hazel, which may be much more astringent and could disfigure skin.

Habitat Temperate zones; E. Canada, E. USA	Parts used

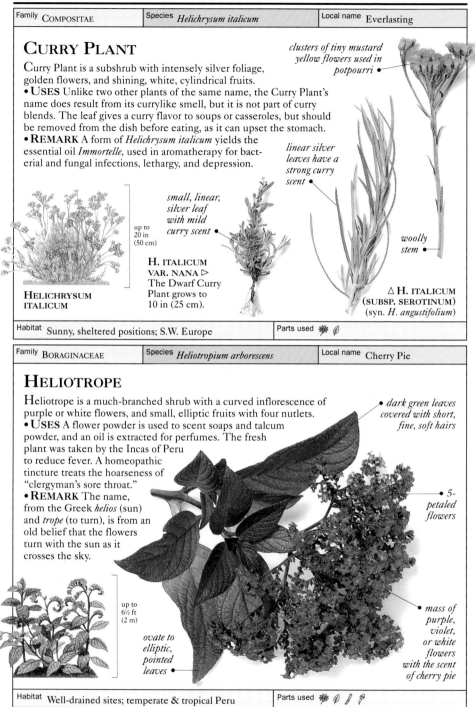

Family COMPOSITAE	Species *Helichrysum italicum*	Local name Everlasting

CURRY PLANT

Curry Plant is a subshrub with intensely silver foliage, golden flowers, and shining, white, cylindrical fruits.

• **USES** Unlike two other plants of the same name, the Curry Plant's name does result from its currylike smell, but it is not part of curry blends. The leaf gives a curry flavor to soups or casseroles, but should be removed from the dish before eating, as it can upset the stomach.

• **REMARK** A form of *Helichrysum italicum* yields the essential oil *Immortelle*, used in aromatherapy for bacterial and fungal infections, lethargy, and depression.

clusters of tiny mustard yellow flowers used in potpourri

linear silver leaves have a strong curry scent

woolly stem

small, linear, silver leaf with mild curry scent

up to 20 in (50 cm)

HELICHRYSUM ITALICUM

H. ITALICUM VAR. NANA ▷ The Dwarf Curry Plant grows to 10 in (25 cm).

△ **H. ITALICUM (SUBSP. SEROTINUM)** (syn. *H. angustifolium*)

Habitat Sunny, sheltered positions; S.W. Europe	Parts used

Family BORAGINACEAE	Species *Heliotropium arborescens*	Local name Cherry Pie

HELIOTROPE

Heliotrope is a much-branched shrub with a curved inflorescence of purple or white flowers, and small, elliptic fruits with four nutlets.

• **USES** A flower powder is used to scent soaps and talcum powder, and an oil is extracted for perfumes. The fresh plant was taken by the Incas of Peru to reduce fever. A homeopathic tincture treats the hoarseness of "clergyman's sore throat."

• **REMARK** The name, from the Greek *helios* (sun) and *trope* (to turn), is from an old belief that the flowers turn with the sun as it crosses the sky.

dark green leaves covered with short, fine, soft hairs
5-petaled flowers
mass of purple, violet, or white flowers with the scent of cherry pie
ovate to elliptic, pointed leaves
up to 6½ ft (2 m)

Habitat Well-drained sites; temperate & tropical Peru	Parts used

Family MALVACEAE	Species *Hibiscus sabdariffa*	Local name Jamaica Sorrel

ROSELLE

This annual shrub has yellow-petaled flowers that drop off, leaving protective sepals; these swell into a succulent "fruit." • **USES** The "fruit" give a burgundy color and acid flavor to jellies, sauces, wines, and herb teas. The young leaves are cooked, the fermented juice of young "fruit" is added to rum, and the ripe "fruit" is made into jam. The "fruit" is astringent and is used to dress wounds and treat coughs. The dried petals treat fever and tapeworm. The inner stem bark yields a strong, jutelike fiber. • **REMARK** The flowers of Choublac (*Hibiscus rosa-sinensis*) yield a red food coloring, a tea, and a black shoe polish. Chinese women used the petal juice to blacken eyebrows. In Southeast Asia the bark, root, leaf, and flowers have medicinal uses.

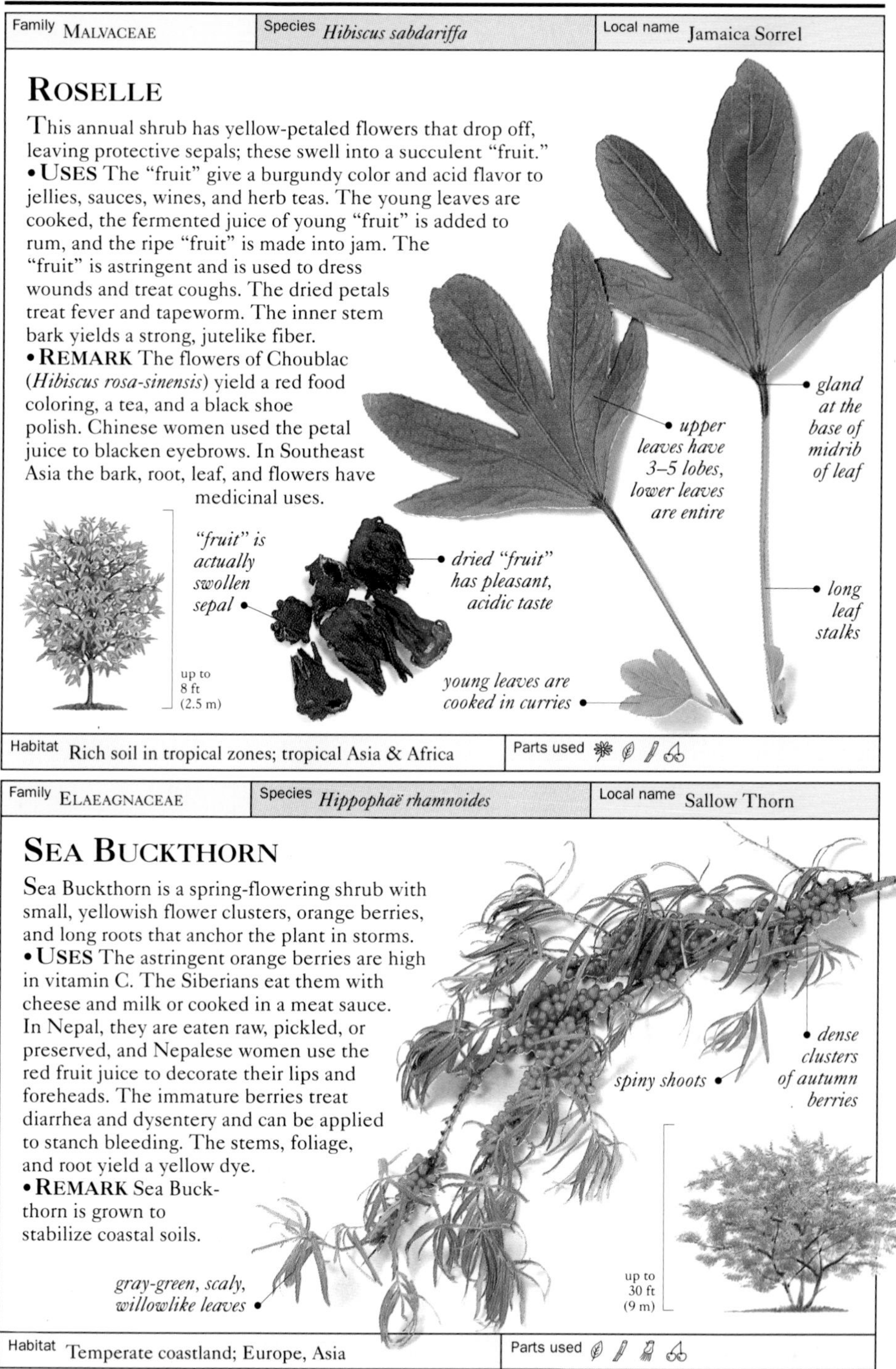
upper leaves have 3–5 lobes, lower leaves are entire
gland at the base of midrib of leaf
"fruit" is actually swollen sepal
dried "fruit" has pleasant, acidic taste
long leaf stalks
up to 8 ft (2.5 m)
young leaves are cooked in curries
dense clusters of autumn berries
spiny shoots
up to 30 ft (9 m)
gray-green, scaly, willowlike leaves

Habitat Rich soil in tropical zones; tropical Asia & Africa	Parts used

Family ELAEAGNACEAE	Species *Hippophaë rhamnoides*	Local name Sallow Thorn

SEA BUCKTHORN

Sea Buckthorn is a spring-flowering shrub with small, yellowish flower clusters, orange berries, and long roots that anchor the plant in storms. • **USES** The astringent orange berries are high in vitamin C. The Siberians eat them with cheese and milk or cooked in a meat sauce. In Nepal, they are eaten raw, pickled, or preserved, and Nepalese women use the red fruit juice to decorate their lips and foreheads. The immature berries treat diarrhea and dysentery and can be applied to stanch bleeding. The stems, foliage, and root yield a yellow dye. • **REMARK** Sea Buckthorn is grown to stabilize coastal soils.

Habitat Temperate coastland; Europe, Asia	Parts used

Family LABIATAE	Species *Hyssopus officinalis*	Local name Issopo Celestino

HYSSOP

Hyssop is a semievergreen shrub or subshrub with aromatic leaves and spikes of blue, two-lipped, late-summer flowers.
• **USES** The sharp-flavored leaf is added to liqueurs, adds bite to sweet and savory dishes, and aids in the digestion of fatty meat. Once used for purifying temples and cleansing lepers, the leaves contain an antiseptic, antiviral oil. A mold that produces penicillin grows on the leaves. An infusion is taken as a sedative expectorant for flu, bronchitis, and phlegm. A leaf poultice treats bruises and wounds. The essential oil is used to treat cold sores, disperse bruises, and heal scars. This oil can be hazardous and should be avoided when epilepsy, high blood pressure, or pregnancy are indicated. Hyssop is added to potpourri and laundry rinses.
• **REMARK** Hyssop is used in companion planting to distract cabbage butterflies and planted near vines to increase their yield.

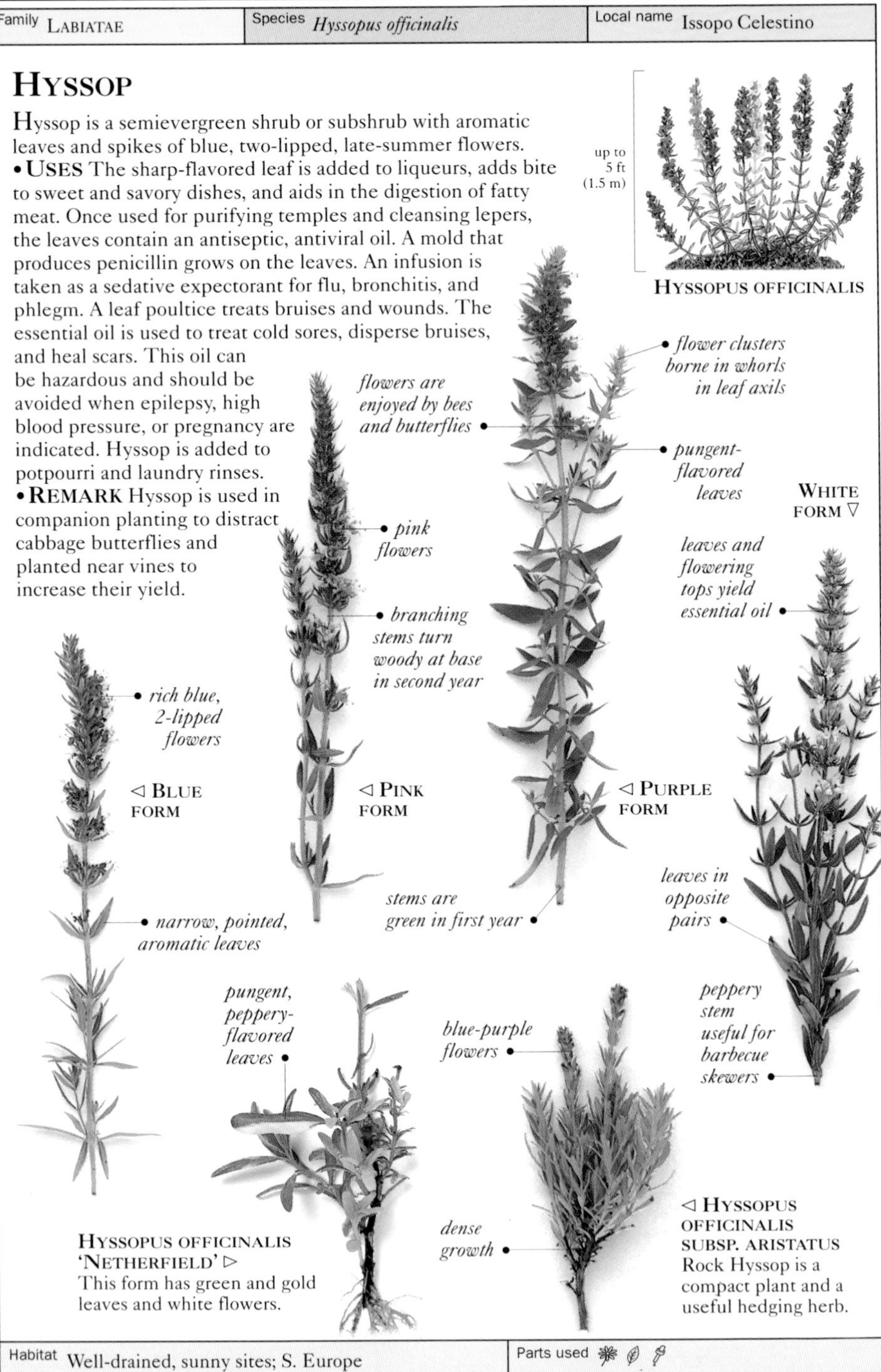
up to 5 ft (1.5 m)
HYSSOPUS OFFICINALIS
flower clusters borne in whorls in leaf axils
flowers are enjoyed by bees and butterflies
pungent-flavored leaves
WHITE FORM ▽
pink flowers
leaves and flowering tops yield essential oil
branching stems turn woody at base in second year
rich blue, 2-lipped flowers
◁ BLUE FORM
◁ PINK FORM
◁ PURPLE FORM
leaves in opposite pairs
stems are green in first year
narrow, pointed, aromatic leaves
pungent, peppery-flavored leaves
peppery stem useful for barbecue skewers
blue-purple flowers
dense growth

HYSSOPUS OFFICINALIS 'NETHERFIELD' ▷
This form has green and gold leaves and white flowers.

◁ HYSSOPUS OFFICINALIS SUBSP. ARISTATUS
Rock Hyssop is a compact plant and a useful hedging herb.

Habitat Well-drained, sunny sites; S. Europe	Parts used

Family AQUIFOLIACEAE	Species *Ilex vomitoria*	Local name Yaupon / Emetic Holly

BLACK DRINK PLANT

This evergreen shrub has white flowers and scarlet fruits. • **USES** The narcotic leaves are used ceremonially by Native Americans. They are brewed for a stimulant emetic called black drink, taken by warriors for purification before war councils. The berries also cause vomiting and have been used as emergency treatment for poisoning. The leaves of several *Ilex* species yield caffeine drinks used locally as tea. *Ilex guayusa* is the source of *guayusa*, an Amazon stimulant tea. *I. paraguariensis* gives *Yerba Maté*, popular in South America, and a tonic, laxative, diuretic, and muscle relaxant that reduces appetite and is said to increase intellectual vigor. • **REMARK** English Holly (*I. aquifolium*) does not yield a stimulant tea. Infused leaves treat colds and coughs.

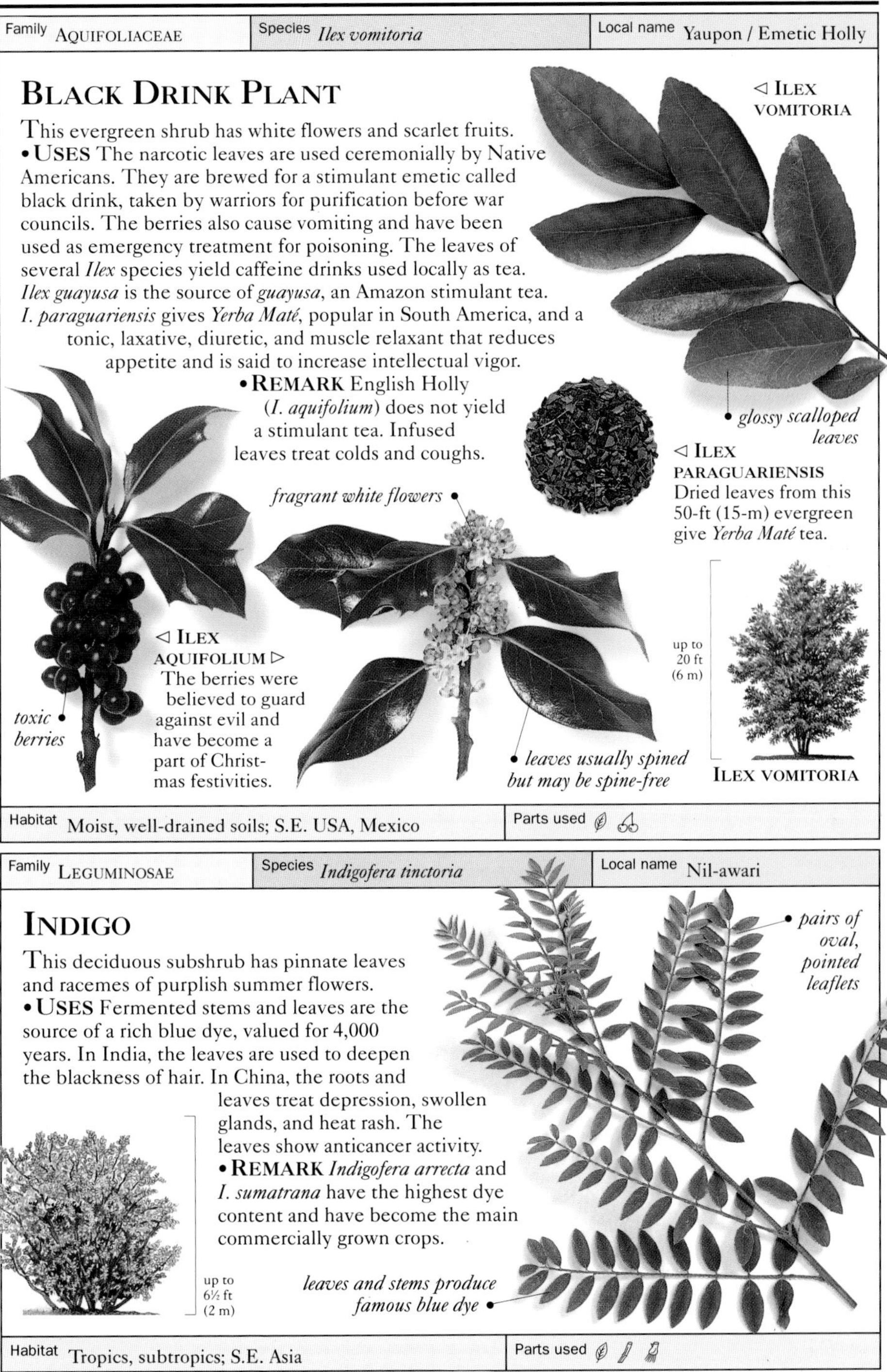
◁ ILEX VOMITORIA
glossy scalloped leaves
fragrant white flowers
toxic berries
leaves usually spined but may be spine-free
up to 20 ft (6 m)
ILEX VOMITORIA
pairs of oval, pointed leaflets
leaves and stems produce famous blue dye
up to 6½ ft (2 m)

◁ ILEX PARAGUARIENSIS Dried leaves from this 50-ft (15-m) evergreen give *Yerba Maté* tea.

◁ ILEX AQUIFOLIUM ▷ The berries were believed to guard against evil and have become a part of Christmas festivities.

Habitat Moist, well-drained soils; S.E. USA, Mexico	Parts used

Family LEGUMINOSAE	Species *Indigofera tinctoria*	Local name Nil-awari

INDIGO

This deciduous subshrub has pinnate leaves and racemes of purplish summer flowers. • **USES** Fermented stems and leaves are the source of a rich blue dye, valued for 4,000 years. In India, the leaves are used to deepen the blackness of hair. In China, the roots and leaves treat depression, swollen glands, and heat rash. The leaves show anticancer activity. • **REMARK** *Indigofera arrecta* and *I. sumatrana* have the highest dye content and have become the main commercially grown crops.

Habitat Tropics, subtropics; S.E. Asia	Parts used

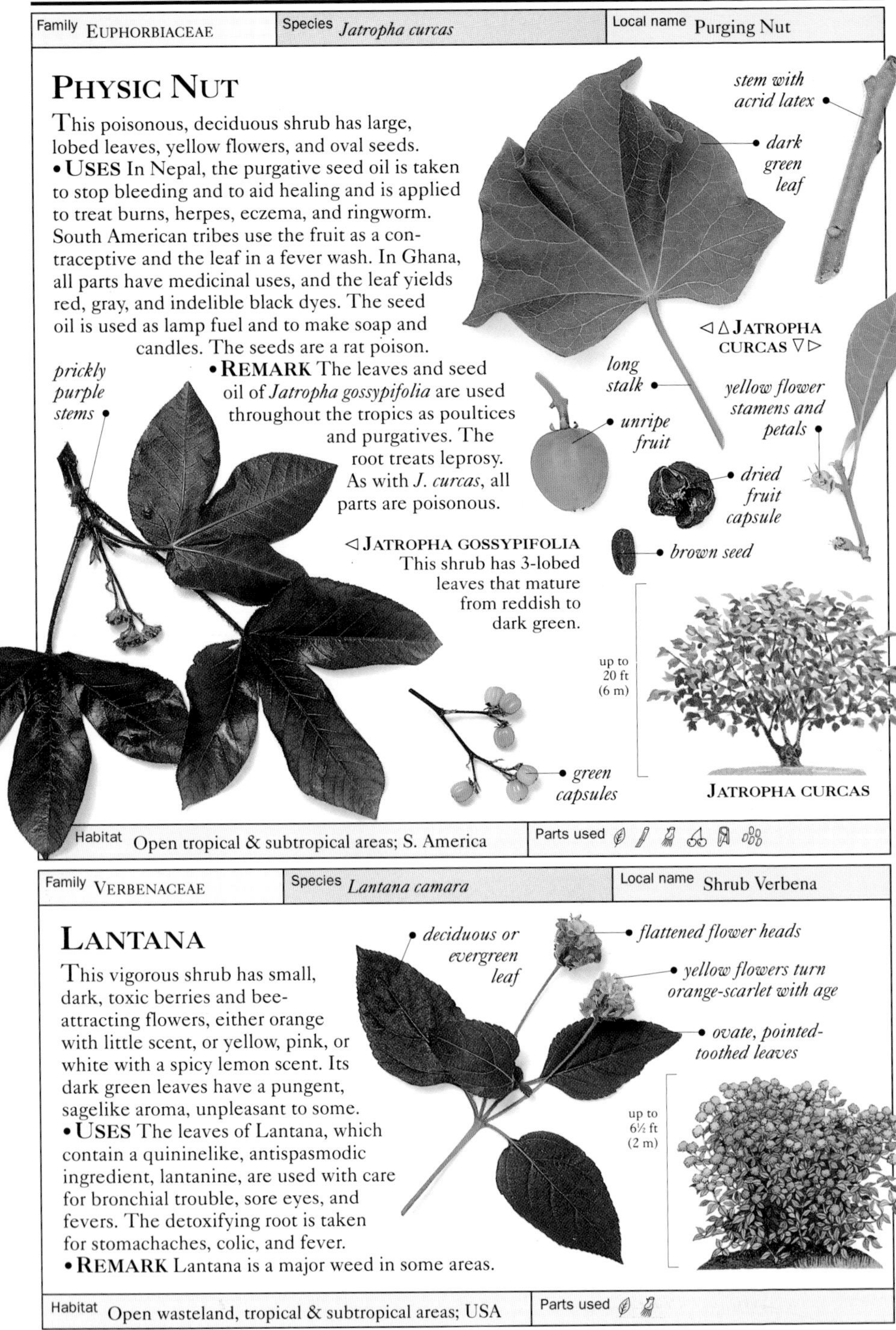
stem with acrid latex
dark green leaf
◁ △ JATROPHA CURCAS ▽ ▷
long stalk
unripe fruit
yellow flower stamens and petals
dried fruit capsule
brown seed
prickly purple stems
green capsules
up to 20 ft (6 m)
JATROPHA CURCAS
deciduous or evergreen leaf
flattened flower heads
yellow flowers turn orange-scarlet with age
ovate, pointed-toothed leaves
up to 6½ ft (2 m)

Family	Species	Local name
EUPHORBIACEAE	*Jatropha curcas*	Purging Nut

PHYSIC NUT

This poisonous, deciduous shrub has large, lobed leaves, yellow flowers, and oval seeds.

• **USES** In Nepal, the purgative seed oil is taken to stop bleeding and to aid healing and is applied to treat burns, herpes, eczema, and ringworm. South American tribes use the fruit as a contraceptive and the leaf in a fever wash. In Ghana, all parts have medicinal uses, and the leaf yields red, gray, and indelible black dyes. The seed oil is used as lamp fuel and to make soap and candles. The seeds are a rat poison.

• **REMARK** The leaves and seed oil of *Jatropha gossypifolia* are used throughout the tropics as poultices and purgatives. The root treats leprosy. As with *J. curcas*, all parts are poisonous.

◁ JATROPHA GOSSYPIFOLIA This shrub has 3-lobed leaves that mature from reddish to dark green.

Habitat: Open tropical & subtropical areas; S. America

Parts used:

Family	Species	Local name
VERBENACEAE	*Lantana camara*	Shrub Verbena

LANTANA

This vigorous shrub has small, dark, toxic berries and bee-attracting flowers, either orange with little scent, or yellow, pink, or white with a spicy lemon scent. Its dark green leaves have a pungent, sagelike aroma, unpleasant to some.

• **USES** The leaves of Lantana, which contain a quininelike, antispasmodic ingredient, lantanine, are used with care for bronchial trouble, sore eyes, and fevers. The detoxifying root is taken for stomachaches, colic, and fever.

• **REMARK** Lantana is a major weed in some areas.

Habitat: Open wasteland, tropical & subtropical areas; USA

Parts used:

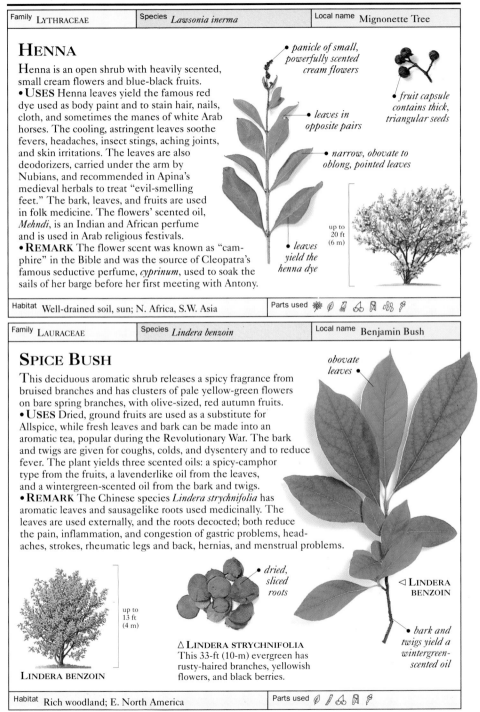

Family LYTHRACEAE	Species *Lawsonia inerma*	Local name Mignonette Tree

HENNA

Henna is an open shrub with heavily scented, small cream flowers and blue-black fruits.

• **USES** Henna leaves yield the famous red dye used as body paint and to stain hair, nails, cloth, and sometimes the manes of white Arab horses. The cooling, astringent leaves soothe fevers, headaches, insect stings, aching joints, and skin irritations. The leaves are also deodorizers, carried under the arm by Nubians, and recommended in Apina's medieval herbals to treat "evil-smelling feet." The bark, leaves, and fruits are used in folk medicine. The flowers' scented oil, *Mehndi*, is an Indian and African perfume and is used in Arab religious festivals.

• **REMARK** The flower scent was known as "camphire" in the Bible and was the source of Cleopatra's famous seductive perfume, *cyprinum*, used to soak the sails of her barge before her first meeting with Antony.

• panicle of small, powerfully scented cream flowers

• fruit capsule contains thick, triangular seeds

• leaves in opposite pairs

• narrow, obovate to oblong, pointed leaves

• leaves yield the henna dye

up to 20 ft (6 m)

Habitat Well-drained soil, sun; N. Africa, S.W. Asia	Parts used

Family LAURACEAE	Species *Lindera benzoin*	Local name Benjamin Bush

SPICE BUSH

This deciduous aromatic shrub releases a spicy fragrance from bruised branches and has clusters of pale yellow-green flowers on bare spring branches, with olive-sized, red autumn fruits.

• **USES** Dried, ground fruits are used as a substitute for Allspice, while fresh leaves and bark can be made into an aromatic tea, popular during the Revolutionary War. The bark and twigs are given for coughs, colds, and dysentery and to reduce fever. The plant yields three scented oils: a spicy-camphor type from the fruits, a lavenderlike oil from the leaves, and a wintergreen-scented oil from the bark and twigs.

• **REMARK** The Chinese species *Lindera strychnifolia* has aromatic leaves and sausagelike roots used medicinally. The leaves are used externally, and the roots decocted; both reduce the pain, inflammation, and congestion of gastric problems, headaches, strokes, rheumatic legs and back, hernias, and menstrual problems.

obovate leaves •

◁ LINDERA BENZOIN

• bark and twigs yield a wintergreen-scented oil

up to 13 ft (4 m)

LINDERA BENZOIN

• dried, sliced roots

△ LINDERA STRYCHNIFOLIA
This 33-ft (10-m) evergreen has rusty-haired branches, yellowish flowers, and black berries.

Habitat Rich woodland; E. North America	Parts used

Family LABIATAE	Species *Lavandula* species	Local name Various

LAVENDER

There are 28 species of these aromatic, evergreen, shrubby perennials, all with small, linear leaves and spikes of fragrant, usually purple or blue, two-lipped flowers.

• **USES** Aromatic oil glands cover all aerial parts but are most concentrated in the flowers. The flowers flavor jams, vinegar, sweets, cream, and Provençal stews, and are crystallized for decoration. Dried flowers add long-lasting fragrance to sachets and potpourri. Flower water is a skin toner useful for speeding cell renewal and is an antiseptic for acne. Flower tea treats anxiety, headaches, flatulence, nausea, dizziness, and halitosis. Flower sprigs of Spike Lavender (*Lavandula latifolia*) are a fly repellent. The essential oil is a highly valued perfume and healer. It is antiseptic, mildly sedative, and pain-killing. It is applied to insect bites and treats burns, sore throats, and headaches. It treats rheumatic aches, high blood pressure, insomnia, depression, lymphatic congestion, menstrual problems, and poor digestion. Perillyl alcohol distilled from Lavender is an anti-cancer compound.

• **REMARK** The best-quality essential oil is from *L. stoechas* and *L. angustifolia*.

spikes of purplish blue, scented flowers in summer

narrow, gray-green, fragrant leaves

LAVANDULA ANGUSTIFOLIA ▷
English Lavender may grow to 30 in (75 cm) tall.

up to 39 in (1 m)

LAVANDULA ANGUSTIFOLIA

soft pink flowers

△ LAVANDULA ANGUSTIFOLIA 'LODDEN PINK'
This cultivar grows to 17½ in (45 cm).

silver-gray leaves

△ LAVANDULA ANGUSTIFOLIA 'HIDCOTE'
A slow-growing cultivar that may reach 16 in (40 cm).

purple flowers

LAVANDULA △ ANGUSTIFOLIA 'VERA'
The leaves of Dutch Lavender are more silver and compact than *L. angustifolia*.

rich, purple-blue flowers

LAVANDULA △ ANGUSTIFOLIA 'FOLGATE'
This 18-in (45-cm) compact Lavender has narrow, gray-green leaves.

long flower spikes

LAVANDULA △ ANGUSTIFOLIA 'TWICKEL PURPLE'
A bushy and compact cultivar with green leaves, sometimes flushed purple.

Habitat Sunny sites, warm temperate regions; Mediterranean	Parts used

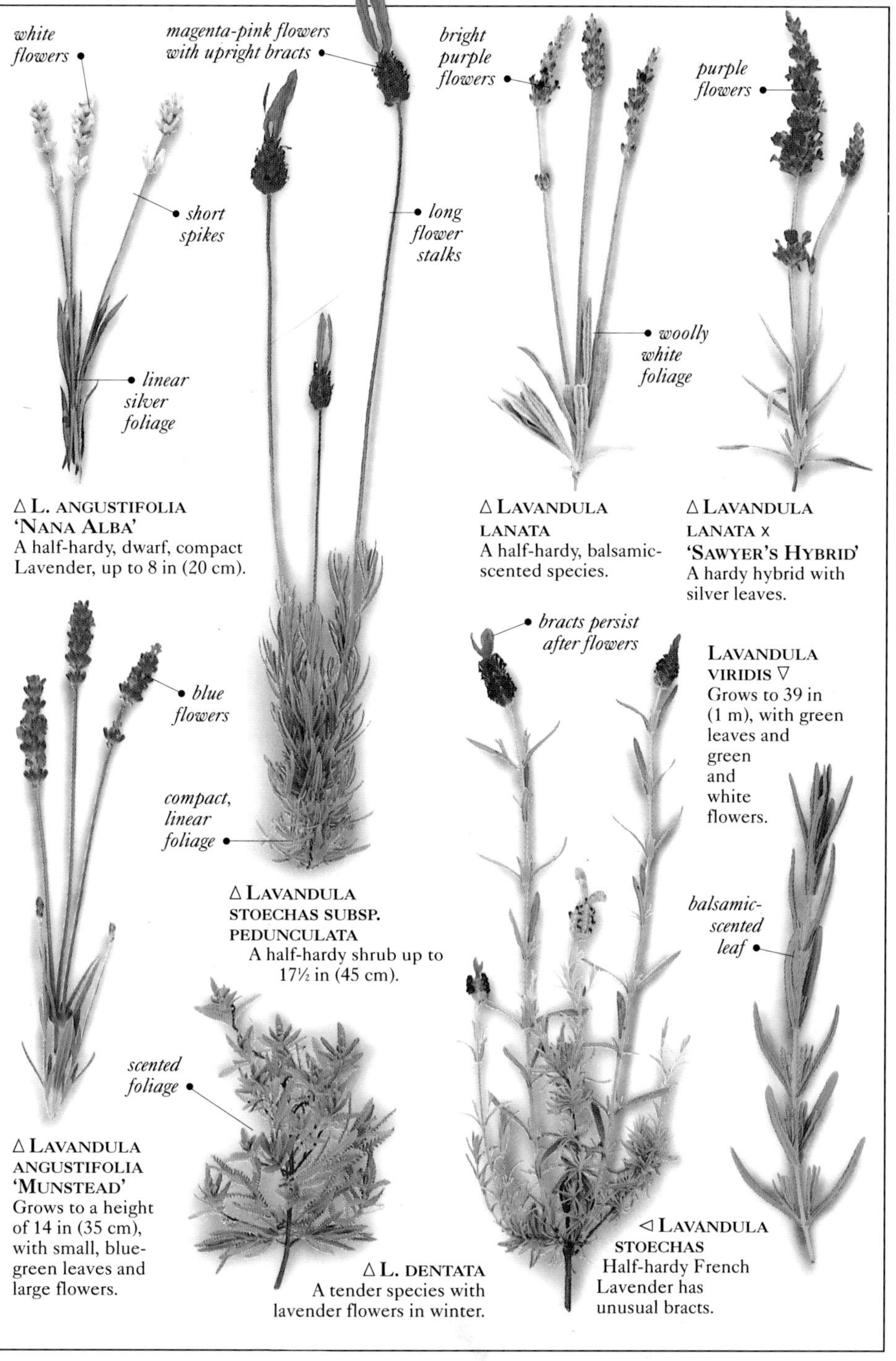
white flowers
magenta-pink flowers with upright bracts
bright purple flowers
purple flowers
short spikes
long flower stalks
woolly white foliage
linear silver foliage
blue flowers
compact, linear foliage
bracts persist after flowers
balsamic-scented leaf
scented foliage

△ L. ANGUSTIFOLIA 'NANA ALBA'
A half-hardy, dwarf, compact Lavender, up to 8 in (20 cm).

△ LAVANDULA LANATA
A half-hardy, balsamic-scented species.

△ LAVANDULA LANATA x 'SAWYER'S HYBRID'
A hardy hybrid with silver leaves.

△ LAVANDULA STOECHAS SUBSP. PEDUNCULATA
A half-hardy shrub up to 17½ in (45 cm).

LAVANDULA VIRIDIS ▽
Grows to 39 in (1 m), with green leaves and green and white flowers.

△ LAVANDULA ANGUSTIFOLIA 'MUNSTEAD'
Grows to a height of 14 in (35 cm), with small, blue-green leaves and large flowers.

△ L. DENTATA
A tender species with lavender flowers in winter.

◁ LAVANDULA STOECHAS
Half-hardy French Lavender has unusual bracts.

Family SOLANACEAE	Species *Lycium chinense*	Local name Matrimony Vine

WOLFBERRY

This is a deciduous, summer-flowering shrub with bright green leaves on arching stems, purple flowers, and long-lasting, vermilion to scarlet berries that appear in autumn and early winter.

• **USES** The berries, root bark, and, occasionally, leaves are used in Chinese medicine to lift the spirits and tone the liver, kidneys, and blood. Wolfberry is used to treat pneumonia in children, diabetes, tuberculosis, and dimmed vision as a result of malnutrition. It is taken with other herbs to slow the aging process by improving muscle growth and preventing premature gray hair, facial skin roughness, and pigmentation.

• **REMARK** Wolfberries are often included in Chinese medicinal meals, in a recipe for tonic soup, *congee* (rice porridge), and a spirit drink.

ripening orange-red fruit
dried scarlet wolfberries are a Chinese tonic, Ji Zi
alternate leaves
long, narrow leaves, slightly wider below the middle
flowers with pointed, light purple, sometimes yellow, petals
up to 13 ft (4 m)

Habitat Temperate zones; E. Asia	Parts used

Family BERBERIDACEAE	Species *Mahonia aquifolium*	Local name Mountain Grape

OREGON GRAPE

The evergreen *Mahonia aquifolium* (syn. *Berberis aquifolium*) has gray-brown bark, dark green leaves that turn purple-red in autumn, fragrant flowers, and mauve-black berries.

• **USES** The root and underground suckers are used by herbalists for their blood-cleansing properties to treat skin disorders such as eczema, acne, psoriasis, and cold sores. They act as a digestive and liver tonic and are given to improve the appetite, suppress nausea, and reduce rheumatic inflammation. The root yields a yellow dye. Avoid during pregnancy.

• **REMARK** *M. japonica* leaves have shown anticancer activity in tests.

spiny-toothed leaves
tight clusters of golden flowers
smooth bark
underground suckers are used to cleanse blood
up to 6½ ft (2 m)

Habitat Open temperate areas; N.W. America, W. Canada	Parts used

Family EUPHORBIACEAE	Species *Manihot esculenta*	Local name Manioc / Tapioca

CASSAVA

Cassava has large, fleshy roots, woody stems with milky juice, leaves on long stalks, large flower racemes, and winged fruit capsules.

• **USES** The tubers are eaten as a vegetable, ground into flour, processed for tapioca, and fermented into alcohol. They contain poisonous prussic acid, which must be removed by soaking, pressing, or cooking. The boiled, bitter, antiseptic juice is used in "pepper-pot" sauce. The leaves are applied for fever and headaches.

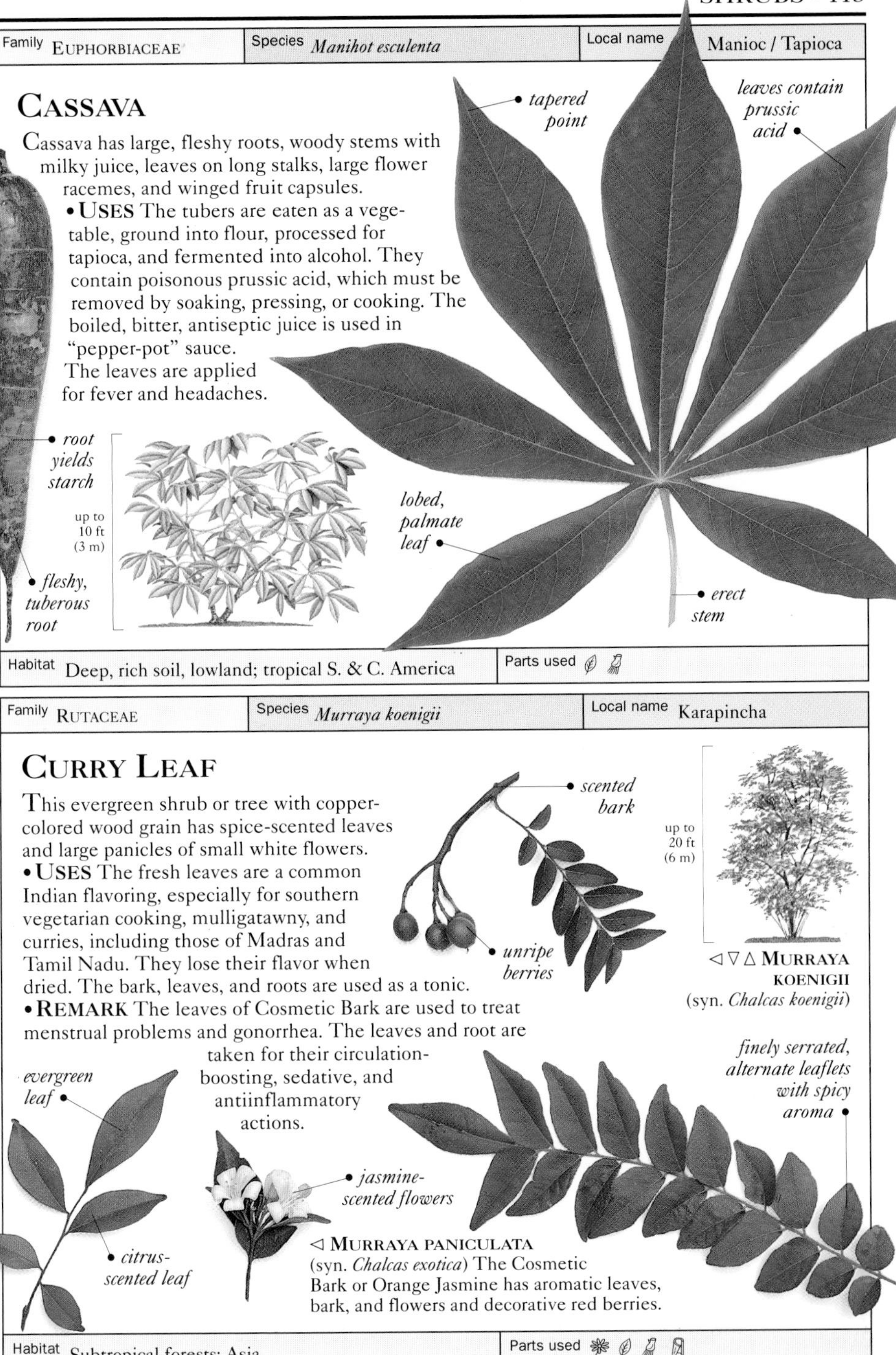
tapered point
leaves contain prussic acid
root yields starch
up to 10 ft (3 m)
lobed, palmate leaf
fleshy, tuberous root
erect stem
scented bark
up to 20 ft (6 m)
unripe berries
evergreen leaf
finely serrated, alternate leaflets with spicy aroma
jasmine-scented flowers
citrus-scented leaf

Habitat Deep, rich soil, lowland; tropical S. & C. America	Parts used

Family RUTACEAE	Species *Murraya koenigii*	Local name Karapincha

CURRY LEAF

This evergreen shrub or tree with copper-colored wood grain has spice-scented leaves and large panicles of small white flowers.

• **USES** The fresh leaves are a common Indian flavoring, especially for southern vegetarian cooking, mulligatawny, and curries, including those of Madras and Tamil Nadu. They lose their flavor when dried. The bark, leaves, and roots are used as a tonic.

• **REMARK** The leaves of Cosmetic Bark are used to treat menstrual problems and gonorrhea. The leaves and root are taken for their circulation-boosting, sedative, and antiinflammatory actions.

◁ ▽ △ **MURRAYA KOENIGII** (syn. *Chalcas koenigii*)

◁ **MURRAYA PANICULATA** (syn. *Chalcas exotica*) The Cosmetic Bark or Orange Jasmine has aromatic leaves, bark, and flowers and decorative red berries.

Habitat Subtropical forests; Asia	Parts used

Family MYRICACEAE	Species *Myrica cerifera*	Local name Candleberry

WAX MYRTLE

Wax Myrtle is a spring-flowering evergreen with male and female catkins on separate bushes, and wax-covered, pale green berries. • **USES** Wax Myrtle and California Wax Myrtle berries season meat and yield balsamic-scented wax used in candles, shaving soap, and cosmetics. Both have tonic root bark that is astringent and antibacterial, stimulates blood circulation and lymph drainage, and treats intestinal and stomach infections. The leaves of all three illustrated species yield a tea for fevers. • **REMARK** The fragrant leaves of Sweet Gale repel insects and moths.

up to 40 ft (12 m)
MYRICA CERIFERA
forward-pointing teeth
◁ MYRICA CALIFORNICA
The aromatic California Wax Myrtle has green catkins, and purple berries.
MYRICA CERIFERA ▽
gland-dotted, aromatic leaves
MYRICA CALIFORNICA ▷
reddish, aromatic twigs
MYRICA GALE ▷
Sweet Gale or Bog Myrtle is a deciduous, aromatic shrub with resinous nuts.
rounded tip
yellowish catkins
shiny dark green leaves with deeply embedded oil glands
scented flowers
up to 16½ ft (5 m)
'Tarentina,' a narrow-leaved, compact form

Habitat Damp thickets; E. North America	Parts used

Family MYRTACEAE	Species *Myrtus communis*	Local name Myrtle

SWEET MYRTLE

This dense, evergreen shrub has aromatic leaves and flower buds, creamy white flowers, and blue-black berries. • **USES** The flowers are made into toilet water called *eau d'ange*, added with the leaves to acne ointment, and dried for potpourri. Dried leaves are used for herb pillows. The flower buds and berries give an orange-blossom scent to sweet dishes, and the leaves add flavor and aroma to roasting meat. The leaves are antiseptic and astringent and are used in decoction, on bruises and hemorrhoids. Leaf essential oil is the source of myrtol, given for gingivitis. • **REMARK** Sweet Myrtle is used in bridal wreaths as a symbol of beauty and chastity.

Habitat Sun, well-drained soil; Mediterranean, N. Africa	Parts used

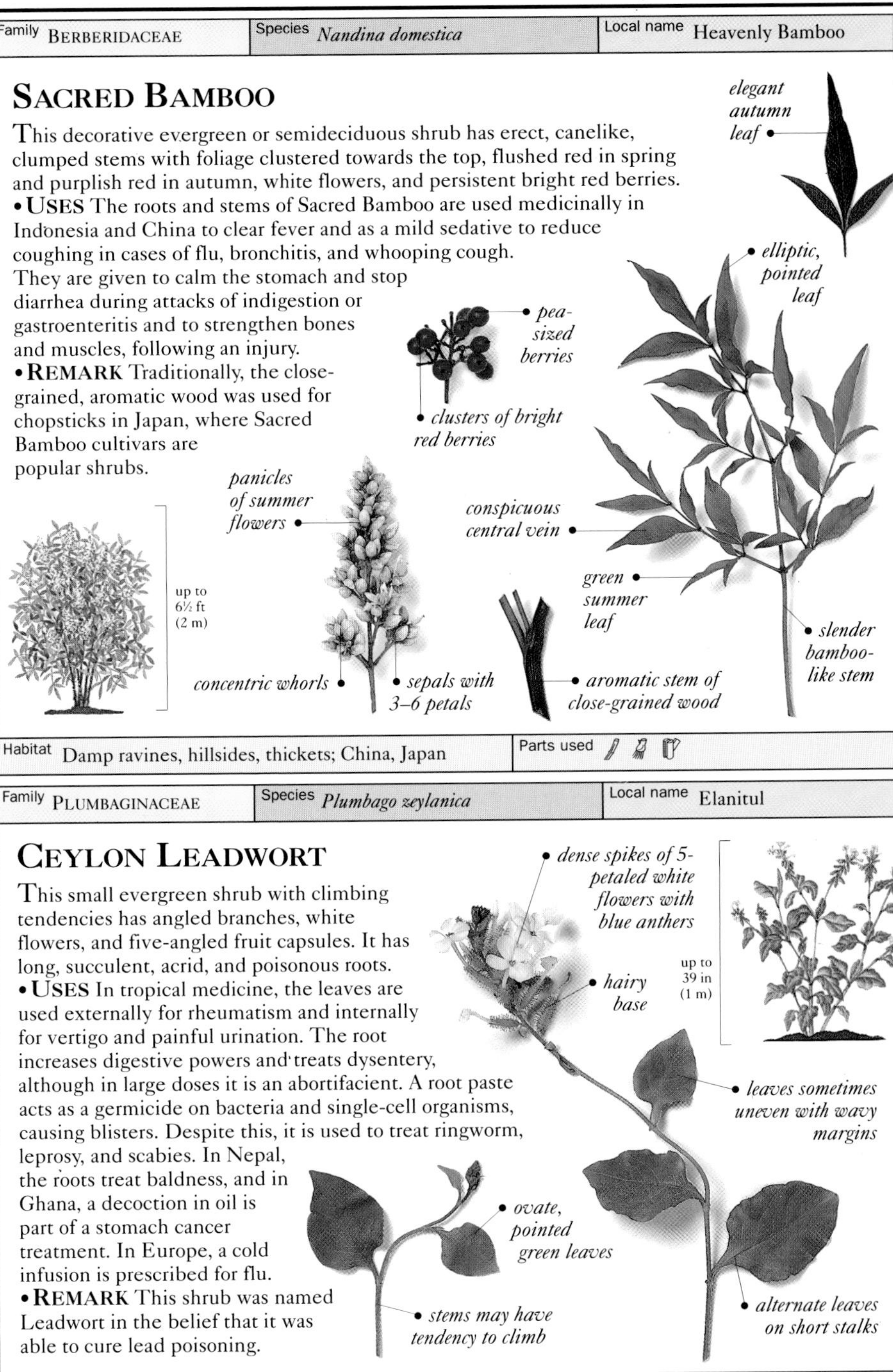
elegant autumn leaf
elliptic, pointed leaf
pea-sized berries
clusters of bright red berries
panicles of summer flowers
conspicuous central vein
up to 6½ ft (2 m)
green summer leaf
slender bamboo-like stem
concentric whorls
sepals with 3–6 petals
aromatic stem of close-grained wood
dense spikes of 5-petaled white flowers with blue anthers
hairy base
up to 39 in (1 m)
leaves sometimes uneven with wavy margins
ovate, pointed green leaves
stems may have tendency to climb
alternate leaves on short stalks

Family BERBERIDACEAE	Species *Nandina domestica*	Local name Heavenly Bamboo

SACRED BAMBOO

This decorative evergreen or semideciduous shrub has erect, canelike, clumped stems with foliage clustered towards the top, flushed red in spring and purplish red in autumn, white flowers, and persistent bright red berries.

• **USES** The roots and stems of Sacred Bamboo are used medicinally in Indonesia and China to clear fever and as a mild sedative to reduce coughing in cases of flu, bronchitis, and whooping cough. They are given to calm the stomach and stop diarrhea during attacks of indigestion or gastroenteritis and to strengthen bones and muscles, following an injury.

• **REMARK** Traditionally, the close-grained, aromatic wood was used for chopsticks in Japan, where Sacred Bamboo cultivars are popular shrubs.

Habitat Damp ravines, hillsides, thickets; China, Japan	Parts used

Family PLUMBAGINACEAE	Species *Plumbago zeylanica*	Local name Elanitul

CEYLON LEADWORT

This small evergreen shrub with climbing tendencies has angled branches, white flowers, and five-angled fruit capsules. It has long, succulent, acrid, and poisonous roots.

• **USES** In tropical medicine, the leaves are used externally for rheumatism and internally for vertigo and painful urination. The root increases digestive powers and treats dysentery, although in large doses it is an abortifacient. A root paste acts as a germicide on bacteria and single-cell organisms, causing blisters. Despite this, it is used to treat ringworm, leprosy, and scabies. In Nepal, the roots treat baldness, and in Ghana, a decoction in oil is part of a stomach cancer treatment. In Europe, a cold infusion is prescribed for flu.

• **REMARK** This shrub was named Leadwort in the belief that it was able to cure lead poisoning.

Habitat Tropical regions, open areas; S.E. Asia to Australia	Parts used

Family Apocynaceae	Species *Rauvolfia serpentina*	Local name Indian Snake Root

Rauvolfia

This evergreen, with leaves in whorls along the stem, has red flowers and small fruits that, unusually, appear together.

• **USES** The root has been used for 3,000 years in Ayurvedic medicine to treat high blood pressure, insomnia, and some forms of insanity. Western medicine isolated the active alkaloid, reserpine, used in tranquilizers and to treat hypertension, but manic depression was a side effect, and the extract is now seldom used. As the whole plant contains 50 additional alkaloids that balance reserpine, Rauvolfia's use continues.

• **REMARK** The calming tea was endorsed by Mahatma Gandhi.

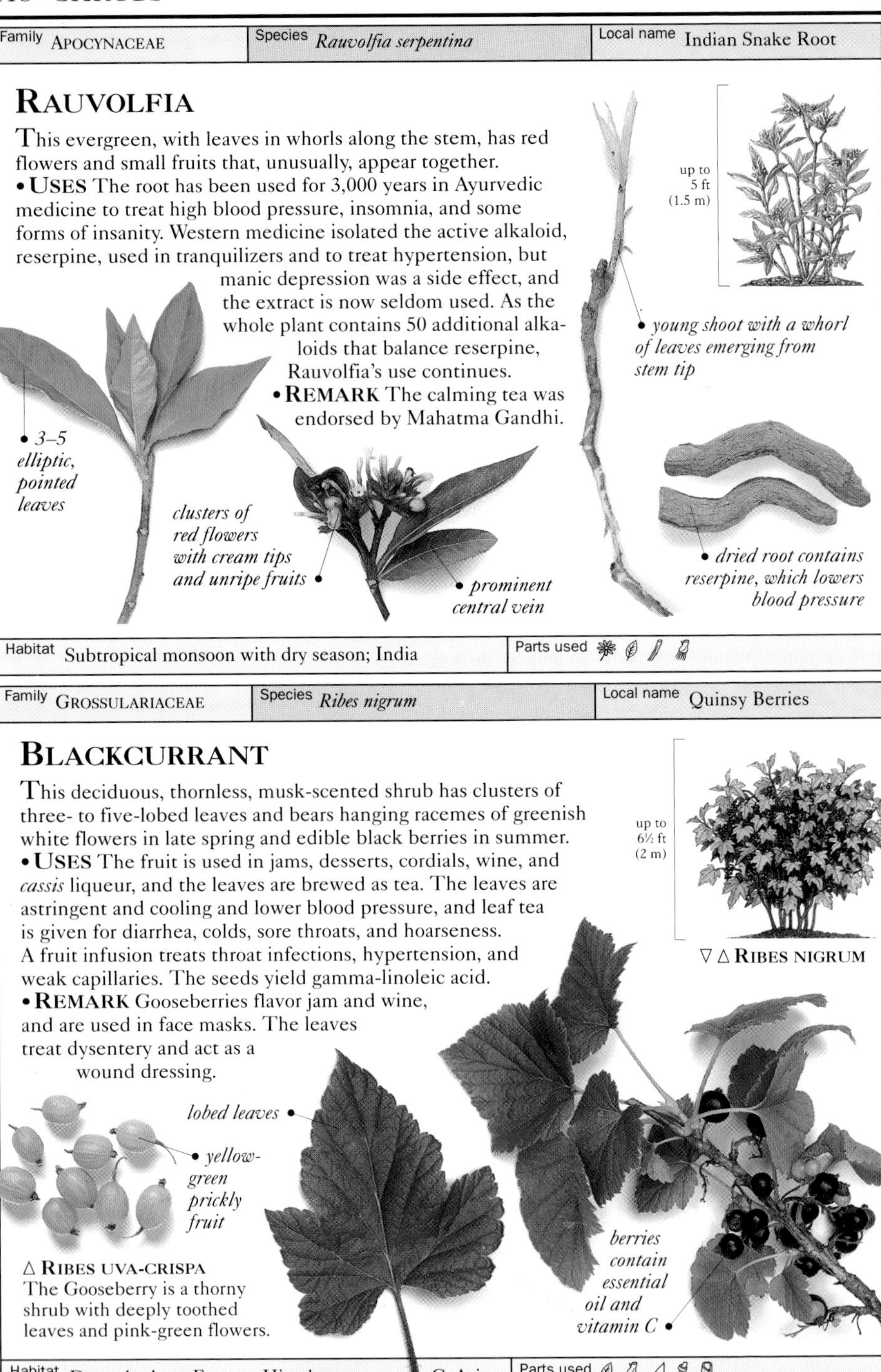
up to
5 ft
(1.5 m)
• young shoot with a whorl of leaves emerging from stem tip
• 3–5 elliptic, pointed leaves
clusters of red flowers with cream tips and unripe fruits •
• prominent central vein
• dried root contains reserpine, which lowers blood pressure

Habitat Subtropical monsoon with dry season; India	Parts used

Family Grossulariaceae	Species *Ribes nigrum*	Local name Quinsy Berries

Blackcurrant

This deciduous, thornless, musk-scented shrub has clusters of three- to five-lobed leaves and bears hanging racemes of greenish white flowers in late spring and edible black berries in summer.

• **USES** The fruit is used in jams, desserts, cordials, wine, and *cassis* liqueur, and the leaves are brewed as tea. The leaves are astringent and cooling and lower blood pressure, and leaf tea is given for diarrhea, colds, sore throats, and hoarseness. A fruit infusion treats throat infections, hypertension, and weak capillaries. The seeds yield gamma-linoleic acid.

• **REMARK** Gooseberries flavor jam and wine, and are used in face masks. The leaves treat dysentery and act as a wound dressing.

up to
6½ ft
(2 m)
lobed leaves •
• yellow-green prickly fruit
berries contain essential oil and vitamin C •

▽ △ Ribes nigrum

△ **Ribes uva-crispa**
The Gooseberry is a thorny shrub with deeply toothed leaves and pink-green flowers.

Habitat Damp hedges; Europe, Himalayas, C. Asia	Parts used

Family ANACARDIACEAE	Species *Rhus typhina*	Local name Indian Lemonade

STAG HORN SUMACH

The narrow leaflets of this deciduous shrub turn vermilion in autumn, and dense flower panicles produce acid-flavored berries. • **USES** Romans in Britain used the flowers to color rice. The sour berries feature extensively in Middle Eastern cooking, although Sicilian Sumach berries are preferred. Juice from the soaked seeds or dried berries are used in salad dressings, yogurt, sauces, and marinades. The powdered berries flavor fish and meat.

• **REMARK** Plants of the *Toxicodendron* genus, such as Poison Ivy, also called Sumachs, are highly poisonous.

up to
33 ft
(10 m)
RHUS TYPHINA
cluster of brick-red berries used to make "Indian Lemonade" in the USA
dried berries soaked to make a drink
△ RHUS TYPHINA
ripe red berries
pinnate leaves
unripe berries
cracked, seedless berries
brown seeds from center of berries
dried berries
red autumn leaves used for tanning and dyeing
red-tinged twigs

◁ ▽ RHUS GLABRA
Smooth Sumach or the Vinegar Tree is a 10-ft (3-m) North American tree or shrub with sour culinary berries.

RHUS COPALLINA ▽
The fruits of the deciduous Winged Sumach flavor drinks, and the roots treat dysentery.

◁ △ RHUS CORIORIA
The Sicilian Sumach produces the best-flavored berries, which are soaked for a fruity-sour, culinary juice.

Habitat Dry, open scrubland; E. North America	Parts used

Family ROSACEAE	Species *Rosa* species	Local name Various

ROSE

Roses are mainly deciduous with prickly stems, compound leaves of up to nine leaflets, fragrant flowers, and autumn hips.

• **USES** The Rose has aromatic, cosmetic, medicinal, culinary, and craft uses. Fresh petals and rosewater flavor sweet and savory dishes and are crystallized for decoration. Rosewater revives tired skin and eyes. Dried petals retain their scent and are the basis of potpourri. Dog Rose (*Rosa canina*, left) is the major source of hips for jam, syrup, tea, and wine. Leaf tea has a mild laxative effect and is applied as a wound poultice. Rose oil from Damask, Bourbon, and other Rose species is used in most good perfumes. Associated with pure love and femininity, it is valued by aromatherapists for its rejuvenating qualities.

• **REMARK** Oil from the variety 'Rosa Mosqueta, the Amazon' (*Rosa rubirinova*), is used in surgery to speed healing and is noteworthy in the growing Amazon cosmetic industry.

• scented flower

up to 18 ft (5.5 m)

ROSA CANINA

white or pink flowers with 5 petals •

• solitary or grouped flowers with green sepals

medium green toothed leaflets •

△ ▽ ROSA CANINA

• vigorous arching or climbing stems with strong, downward-hooked prickles

• dried petals add scent and color to potpourri and sachets

• fragrant petals feature in Turkish delight and Arab and Indian dishes

5–7 elliptic, serrated leaflets •

vermilion hips •

smooth, pointed leaves •

• fragrant petals with bitter base removed are used for flavoring

stiff bristles •

◁ ROSA DAMASCENA 'TRIGINTIPETALA'
Damask Rose oil contains anti-viral compounds with moderate anti-HIV activity.

dried hips •

△▽ ROSA CANINA

• when fresh, hips are rich in vitamins, C, B, E, and K

• normally 5–7 serrated leaflets

• deciduous gray-green leaves

• flower bud can be pickled or dried whole for potpourri

hips contain irritant hairs that must be strained from hip tea •

Habitat Temperate & subtropical zones; China	Parts used

deep pink, lightly scented, single flower
flowers yield Rose oil through distillation or enfleurage
fragrant flowers can be used in cooking and cosmetics
fragrant "old rose" petals
5–9 small toothed leaflets with apple fragrance
fragrant bud
sepals
large green bracts
scented, striped petals
narrow stipule
deep pink petals
crimson petals
wrinkled, serrated leaflets
perfumed flowers

ROSA RUBIGINOSA △ ▷
(syn. *Rosa eglanteria*)
The dense growth of the Sweet Brier, Shakespeare's Eglantine, with apple-scented leaves is good as an aromatic hedge plant.

PICKED FLOWERS △
'Charles de Mills' Rose with petals of 'Maiden's Blush,' 'Mme Isaac,' 'Pereire,' 'Alba Maxima,' and 'Old Blush.'

ROSA GALLICA 'VERSICOLOR' ▷
Rosa Mundi is a 6½ ft (2 m) shrub with prickly stems, and fragrant, semidouble flowers with red-, pink-, and white-striped petals. It is named after Henry II's fair Rosamond.

ROSA GALLICA 'OFFICINALIS' ▽ ▷
Apothecary's Rose has semidouble, deep pink flowers whose fragrance increases when dried. It is the approved Rose for medicinal use as rose-water and was popular in medieval England.

◁ △ **ROSA RUGOSA**
The Japanese Rose is an erect shrub with densely prickled stems, fragrant single flowers, and large red hips – a rich source of vitamin C. The root is used medicinally in China.

Family LABIATAE	Species *Rosmarinus officinalis*	Local name Sea Dew

ROSEMARY

Rosemary is a dense, evergreen, aromatic shrub with resinous, needlelike leaves, and soft, blue, pollen-rich spring flowers loved by bees.

• **USES** Rosemary leaves are an ancient savory herb, especially popular in Italian dishes, and with shellfish, pork, and lamb. The antiseptic, antioxidant leaves help preserve food, aid digestion of fat, and are included in several slimming compounds. The flowers can be used fresh as a garnish or crystallized as decoration. Distilled flower water makes a soothing eyewash. The leaves are used in *eau-de-Cologne*, dark hair conditioning rinses, and dandruff shampoos. Rosemary stimulates circulation and eases aching joints by increasing blood supply.

• **REMARK** The distilled oil of the flowering tops is invigorating, antibacterial, and antifungal. It stimulates the central nervous system and blood circulation, relieving muscular pain.

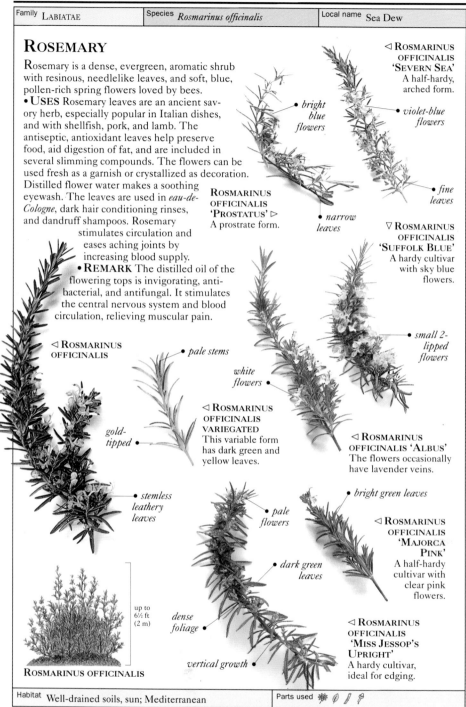

◁ **ROSMARINUS OFFICINALIS 'SEVERN SEA'**
A half-hardy, arched form.

violet-blue flowers

fine leaves

bright blue flowers

ROSMARINUS OFFICINALIS 'PROSTATUS' ▷
A prostrate form.

narrow leaves

▽ **ROSMARINUS OFFICINALIS 'SUFFOLK BLUE'**
A hardy cultivar with sky blue flowers.

small 2-lipped flowers

◁ **ROSMARINUS OFFICINALIS**

stemless leathery leaves

pale stems

gold-tipped

◁ **ROSMARINUS OFFICINALIS VARIEGATED**
This variable form has dark green and yellow leaves.

white flowers

◁ **ROSMARINUS OFFICINALIS 'ALBUS'**
The flowers occasionally have lavender veins.

bright green leaves

◁ **ROSMARINUS OFFICINALIS 'MAJORCA PINK'**
A half-hardy cultivar with clear pink flowers.

pale flowers

dark green leaves

dense foliage

vertical growth

◁ **ROSMARINUS OFFICINALIS 'MISS JESSOP'S UPRIGHT'**
A hardy cultivar, ideal for edging.

up to 6½ ft (2 m)

ROSMARINUS OFFICINALIS

Habitat Well-drained soils, sun; Mediterranean	Parts used

Family ROSACEAE	Species *Rubus idaeus*	Local name Framboise

RASPBERRY

Raspberry has bristly, biennial stems with many prickles, pinnate leaves, small white flowers, and delicious red fruits. • **USES** Raspberries are a food and flavoring, yield a red dye, and give a facial mask for reddened skin. They reduce anemia and in China are prescribed for kidney problems and bedwetting. The leaves (properly dried to avoid toxins), contain tannin. Leaf tea is taken during late pregnancy to tone uterine and pelvic muscles. The tea reduces menstrual pain. • **REMARK** A Blackberry leaf decoction is a blood and skin tonic, and a poultice treats eczema.

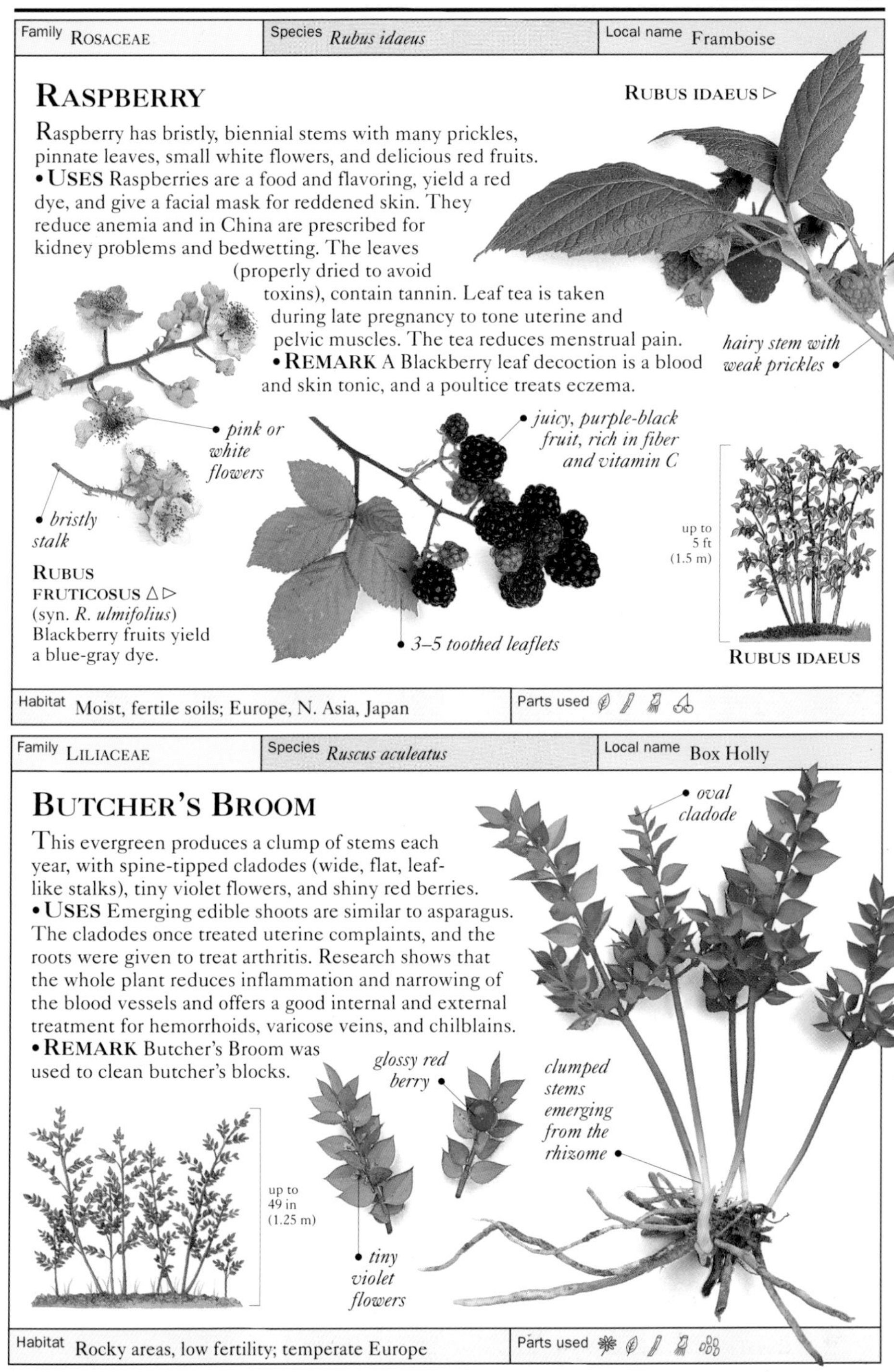
RUBUS IDAEUS ▷
hairy stem with weak prickles
pink or white flowers
bristly stalk
juicy, purple-black fruit, rich in fiber and vitamin C
3–5 toothed leaflets
up to 5 ft (1.5 m)
RUBUS IDAEUS
oval cladode
glossy red berry
clumped stems emerging from the rhizome
tiny violet flowers
up to 49 in (1.25 m)

RUBUS FRUTICOSUS △ ▷ (syn. *R. ulmifolius*) Blackberry fruits yield a blue-gray dye.

Habitat Moist, fertile soils; Europe, N. Asia, Japan	Parts used

Family LILIACEAE	Species *Ruscus aculeatus*	Local name Box Holly

BUTCHER'S BROOM

This evergreen produces a clump of stems each year, with spine-tipped cladodes (wide, flat, leaf-like stalks), tiny violet flowers, and shiny red berries. • **USES** Emerging edible shoots are similar to asparagus. The cladodes once treated uterine complaints, and the roots were given to treat arthritis. Research shows that the whole plant reduces inflammation and narrowing of the blood vessels and offers a good internal and external treatment for hemorrhoids, varicose veins, and chilblains. • **REMARK** Butcher's Broom was used to clean butcher's blocks.

Habitat Rocky areas, low fertility; temperate Europe	Parts used

Family RUTACEAE	Species *Ruta graveolens*	Local name Herb of Grace

RUE

This evergreen subshrub has yellow summer flowers and deeply divided, bluish, aromatic leaves.
• **USES** The bitter leaves, rich in iron and other minerals, when used sparingly add a musky tang to food and to grappa and other alcoholic drinks. Rue is stimulant and abortifacient and strengthens capillaries. Its antispasmodic action treats high blood pressure, epilepsy, and colic. A leaf wash treats tired eyes and was used by da Vinci and Michelangelo. The dried leaf is a powerful insecticide and a germicide for wounds. The oil is used in the perfume industry.
• **REMARK** Rue's round-lobed leaves inspired the symbol for the suit of clubs. The stem sap may cause a skin rash.

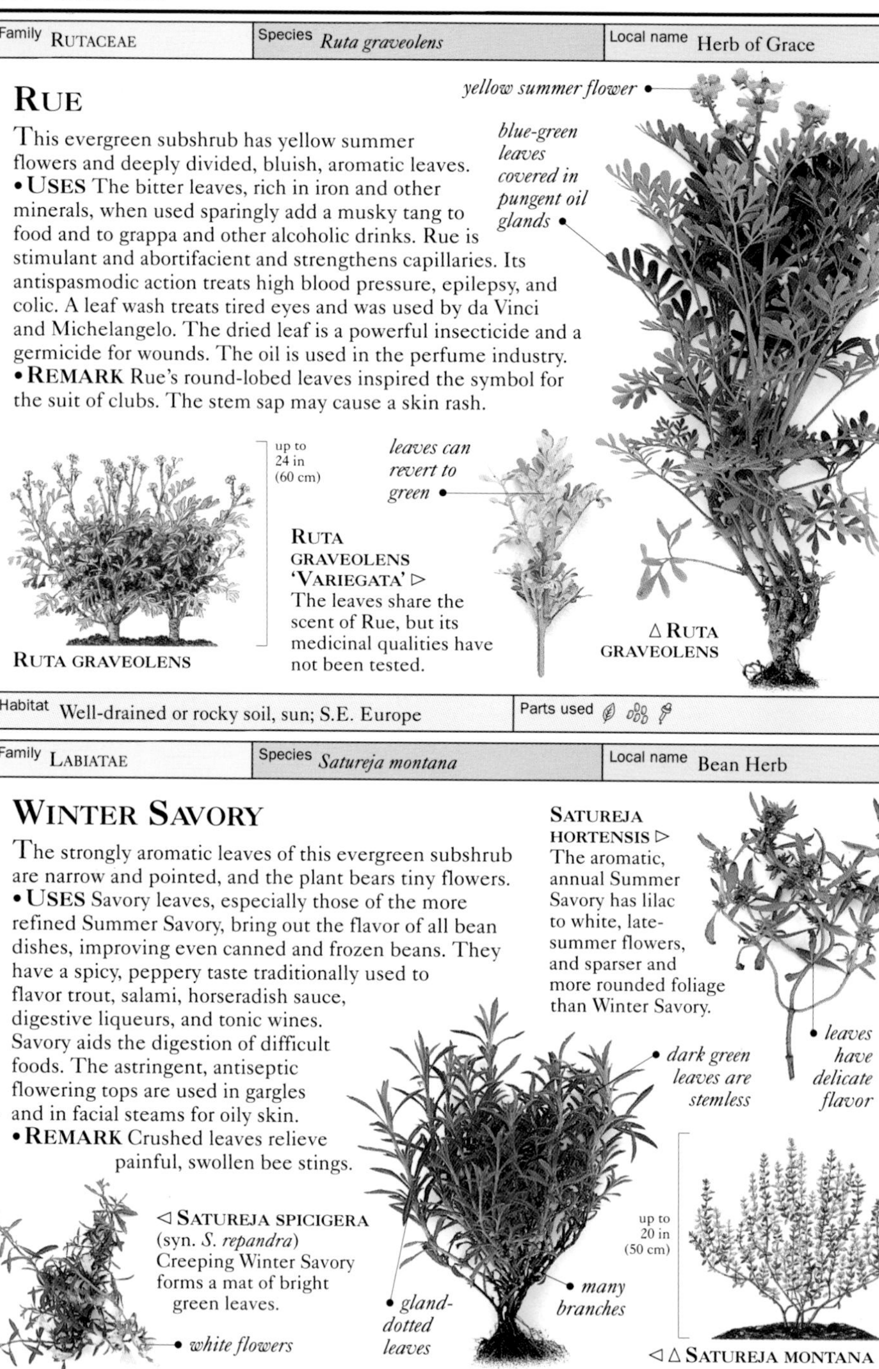

yellow summer flower
blue-green leaves covered in pungent oil glands
up to 24 in (60 cm)
leaves can revert to green
dark green leaves are stemless
leaves have delicate flavor
up to 20 in (50 cm)
many branches
gland-dotted leaves
white flowers

RUTA GRAVEOLENS

RUTA GRAVEOLENS 'VARIEGATA' ▷ The leaves share the scent of Rue, but its medicinal qualities have not been tested.

△ RUTA GRAVEOLENS

Habitat Well-drained or rocky soil, sun; S.E. Europe	Parts used

Family LABIATAE	Species *Satureja montana*	Local name Bean Herb

WINTER SAVORY

The strongly aromatic leaves of this evergreen subshrub are narrow and pointed, and the plant bears tiny flowers.
• **USES** Savory leaves, especially those of the more refined Summer Savory, bring out the flavor of all bean dishes, improving even canned and frozen beans. They have a spicy, peppery taste traditionally used to flavor trout, salami, horseradish sauce, digestive liqueurs, and tonic wines. Savory aids the digestion of difficult foods. The astringent, antiseptic flowering tops are used in gargles and in facial steams for oily skin.
• **REMARK** Crushed leaves relieve painful, swollen bee stings.

SATUREJA HORTENSIS ▷ The aromatic, annual Summer Savory has lilac to white, late-summer flowers, and sparser and more rounded foliage than Winter Savory.

◁ SATUREJA SPICIGERA (syn. *S. repandra*) Creeping Winter Savory forms a mat of bright green leaves.

◁ △ SATUREJA MONTANA

Habitat Well-drained soil, sun, temperate zones; S. Europe	Parts used

Family COMPOSITAE	Species *Santolina chamaecyparissus*	Local name Lavender Cotton

SANTOLINA

This dense evergreen has finely divided, pungently aromatic foliage with a lemony undertone, mustard yellow flowers in late summer, and a dry, oblong seed capsule.

• **USES** The leaves are added to potpourri, and sprigs are placed among clothes, linen, carpets, and books to deter moths. The leaf is mixed with Chamomile and Coltsfoot for herbal tobacco, the flower is dried for decorations, and the whole plant is used in borders and herb gardens. It was valued in medieval times to kill intestinal worms, cleanse kidneys, stimulate menstruation, and help cure jaundice. A flower and leaf wash heals ringworm and skin scabs.

• **REMARK** Although Santolina is known as Lavender Cotton and French Lavender, it is not a true Lavender but a member of the Daisy family.

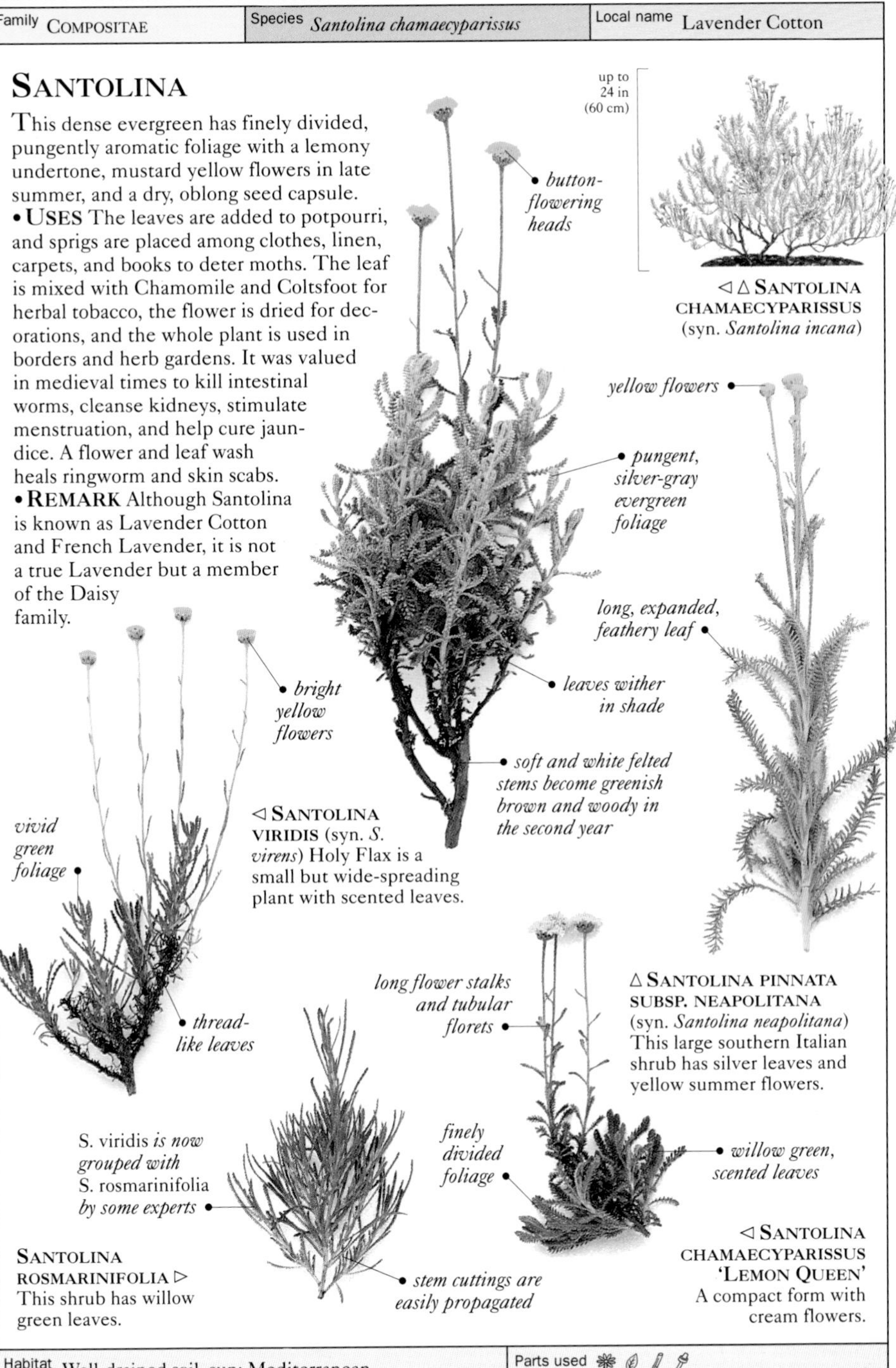
up to
24 in
(60 cm)
button-flowering heads
yellow flowers
pungent, silver-gray evergreen foliage
long, expanded, feathery leaf
leaves wither in shade
bright yellow flowers
soft and white felted stems become greenish brown and woody in the second year
vivid green foliage
thread-like leaves
long flower stalks and tubular florets
finely divided foliage
willow green, scented leaves
S. viridis *is now grouped with* S. rosmarinifolia *by some experts*
stem cuttings are easily propagated

◁ △ **SANTOLINA CHAMAECYPARISSUS** (syn. *Santolina incana*)

◁ **SANTOLINA VIRIDIS** (syn. *S. virens*) Holy Flax is a small but wide-spreading plant with scented leaves.

△ **SANTOLINA PINNATA SUBSP. NEAPOLITANA** (syn. *Santolina neapolitana*) This large southern Italian shrub has silver leaves and yellow summer flowers.

SANTOLINA ROSMARINIFOLIA ▷ This shrub has willow green leaves.

◁ **SANTOLINA CHAMAECYPARISSUS 'LEMON QUEEN'** A compact form with cream flowers.

Habitat Well-drained soil, sun; Mediterranean	Parts used

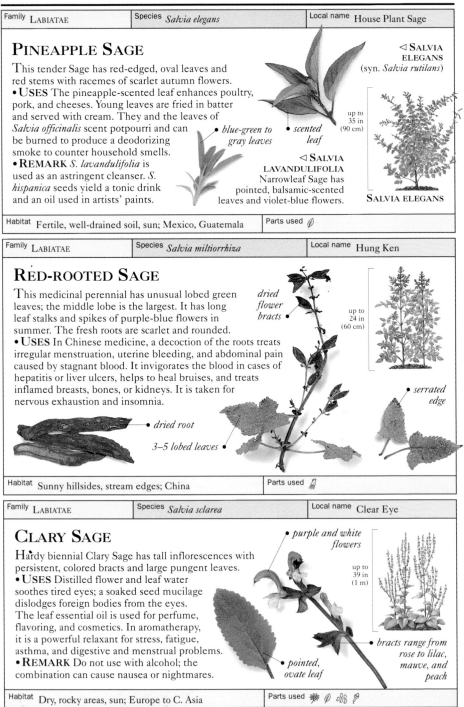

Family LABIATAE | Species *Salvia elegans* | Local name House Plant Sage

PINEAPPLE SAGE

This tender Sage has red-edged, oval leaves and red stems with racemes of scarlet autumn flowers.

• **USES** The pineapple-scented leaf enhances poultry, pork, and cheeses. Young leaves are fried in batter and served with cream. They and the leaves of *Salvia officinalis* scent potpourri and can be burned to produce a deodorizing smoke to counter household smells.

• **REMARK** *S. lavandulifolia* is used as an astringent cleanser. *S. hispanica* seeds yield a tonic drink and an oil used in artists' paints.

◁ SALVIA ELEGANS (syn. *Salvia rutilans*)

scented leaf

blue-green to gray leaves

◁ SALVIA LAVANDULIFOLIA Narrowleaf Sage has pointed, balsamic-scented leaves and violet-blue flowers.

up to 35 in (90 cm)

SALVIA ELEGANS

Habitat Fertile, well-drained soil, sun; Mexico, Guatemala | Parts used

Family LABIATAE | Species *Salvia miltiorrhiza* | Local name Hung Ken

RED-ROOTED SAGE

This medicinal perennial has unusual lobed green leaves; the middle lobe is the largest. It has long leaf stalks and spikes of purple-blue flowers in summer. The fresh roots are scarlet and rounded.

• **USES** In Chinese medicine, a decoction of the roots treats irregular menstruation, uterine bleeding, and abdominal pain caused by stagnant blood. It invigorates the blood in cases of hepatitis or liver ulcers, helps to heal bruises, and treats inflamed breasts, bones, or kidneys. It is taken for nervous exhaustion and insomnia.

dried flower bracts

up to 24 in (60 cm)

serrated edge

dried root

3–5 lobed leaves

Habitat Sunny hillsides, stream edges; China | Parts used

Family LABIATAE | Species *Salvia sclarea* | Local name Clear Eye

CLARY SAGE

Hardy biennial Clary Sage has tall inflorescences with persistent, colored bracts and large pungent leaves.

• **USES** Distilled flower and leaf water soothes tired eyes; a soaked seed mucilage dislodges foreign bodies from the eyes. The leaf essential oil is used for perfume, flavoring, and cosmetics. In aromatherapy, it is a powerful relaxant for stress, fatigue, asthma, and digestive and menstrual problems.

• **REMARK** Do not use with alcohol; the combination can cause nausea or nightmares.

purple and white flowers

up to 39 in (1 m)

bracts range from rose to lilac, mauve, and peach

pointed, ovate leaf

Habitat Dry, rocky areas, sun; Europe to C. Asia | Parts used

Family LABIATAE	Species *Salvia officinalis*	Local name Garden Sage

SAGE

Sage is an aromatic evergreen with gray-green, textured leaves, and mauve-blue flowers in summer.

• **USES** Sage leaf has a strong taste that increases when dried. Used sparingly to flavor and aid the digestion of fatty meats, it is popular in poultry stuffing and combines well with strongly flavored foods. The flowers are tossed in salads and are brewed for a light, balsamic tea, while the leaf tea is an antiseptic nerve and blood tonic. Sage contains hormone precursors that help irregular menstruation and menopause symptoms.

• **REMARK** Avoid large doses during pregnancy.

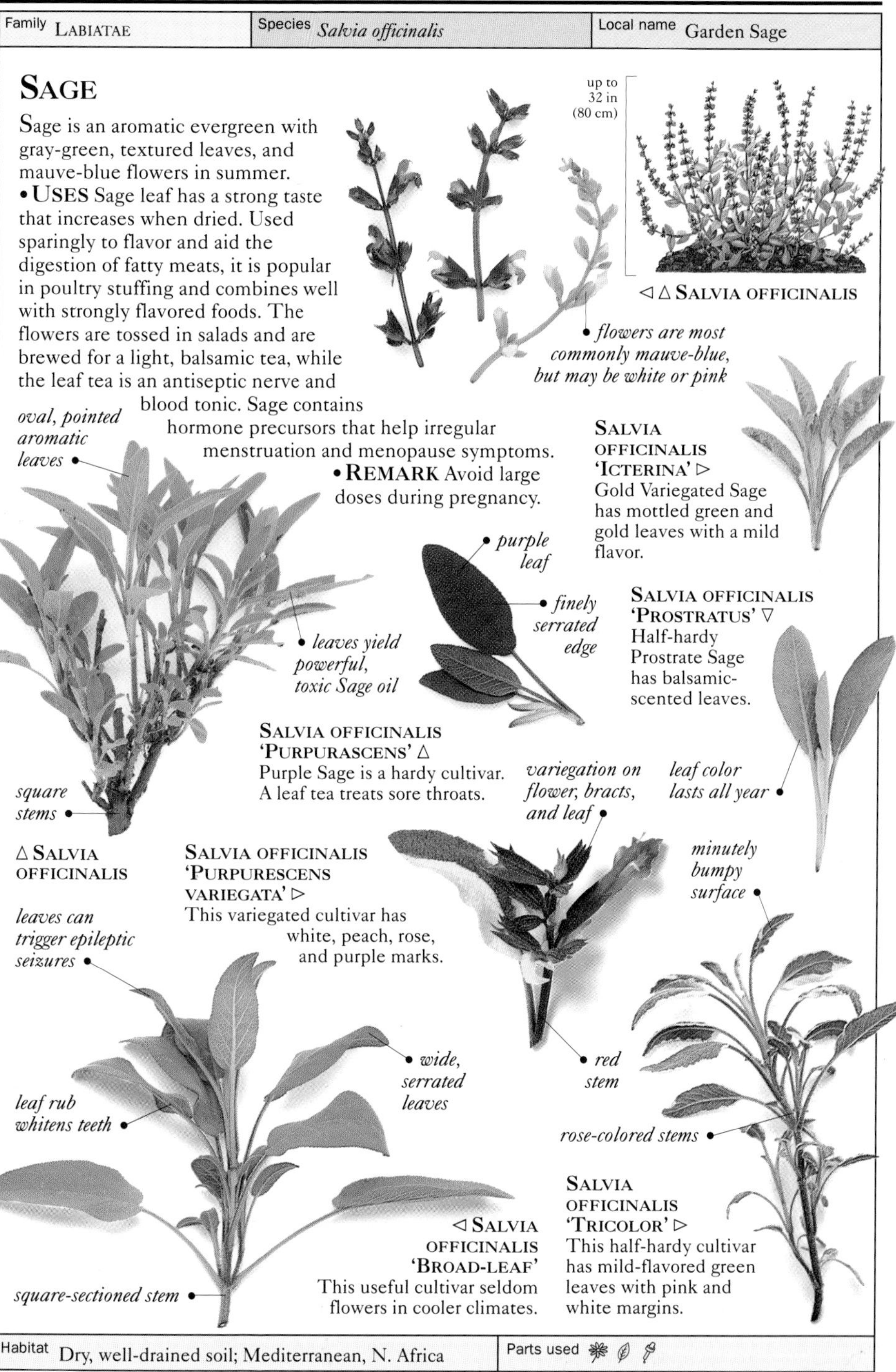

up to 32 in (80 cm)
◁ △ SALVIA OFFICINALIS
flowers are most commonly mauve-blue, but may be white or pink
oval, pointed aromatic leaves
leaves yield powerful, toxic Sage oil
square stems
△ SALVIA OFFICINALIS
purple leaf
finely serrated edge
SALVIA OFFICINALIS 'PURPURASCENS' △
Purple Sage is a hardy cultivar. A leaf tea treats sore throats.
SALVIA OFFICINALIS 'ICTERINA' ▷
Gold Variegated Sage has mottled green and gold leaves with a mild flavor.
SALVIA OFFICINALIS 'PROSTRATUS' ▽
Half-hardy Prostrate Sage has balsamic-scented leaves.
leaf color lasts all year
variegation on flower, bracts, and leaf
SALVIA OFFICINALIS 'PURPURESCENS VARIEGATA' ▷
This variegated cultivar has white, peach, rose, and purple marks.
red stem
minutely bumpy surface
leaves can trigger epileptic seizures
wide, serrated leaves
leaf rub whitens teeth
square-sectioned stem
◁ SALVIA OFFICINALIS 'BROAD-LEAF'
This useful cultivar seldom flowers in cooler climates.
rose-colored stems
SALVIA OFFICINALIS 'TRICOLOR' ▷
This half-hardy cultivar has mild-flavored green leaves with pink and white margins.

Habitat Dry, well-drained soil; Mediterranean, N. Africa	Parts used

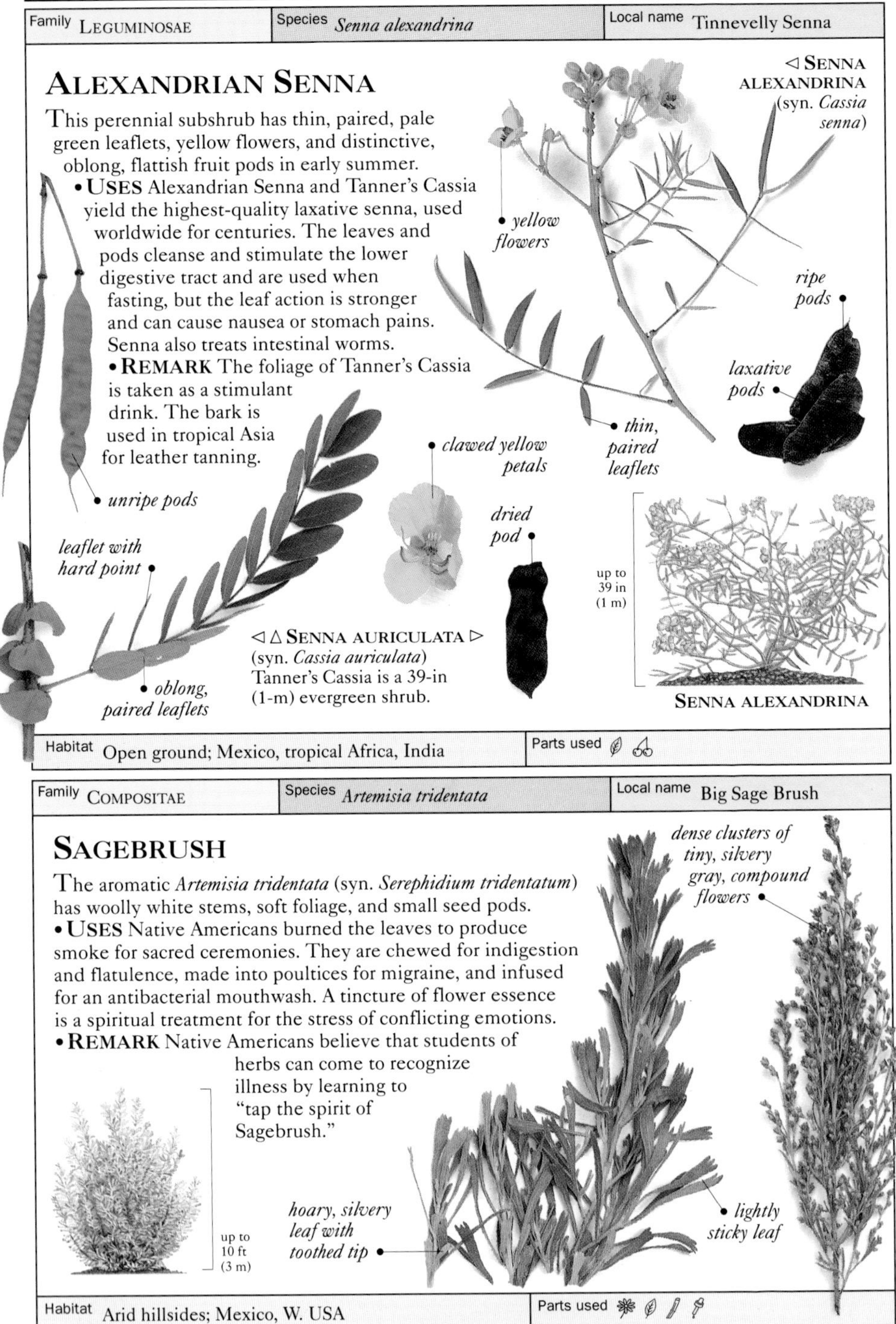
◁ SENNA ALEXANDRINA (syn. *Cassia senna*)
yellow flowers
ripe pods
laxative pods
thin, paired leaflets
clawed yellow petals
unripe pods
leaflet with hard point
dried pod
up to 39 in (1 m)
oblong, paired leaflets
SENNA ALEXANDRINA
dense clusters of tiny, silvery gray, compound flowers
hoary, silvery leaf with toothed tip
lightly sticky leaf
up to 10 ft (3 m)

Family LEGUMINOSAE | Species *Senna alexandrina* | Local name Tinnevelly Senna

ALEXANDRIAN SENNA

This perennial subshrub has thin, paired, pale green leaflets, yellow flowers, and distinctive, oblong, flattish fruit pods in early summer.

• **USES** Alexandrian Senna and Tanner's Cassia yield the highest-quality laxative senna, used worldwide for centuries. The leaves and pods cleanse and stimulate the lower digestive tract and are used when fasting, but the leaf action is stronger and can cause nausea or stomach pains. Senna also treats intestinal worms.

• **REMARK** The foliage of Tanner's Cassia is taken as a stimulant drink. The bark is used in tropical Asia for leather tanning.

◁ △ SENNA AURICULATA ▷ (syn. *Cassia auriculata*) Tanner's Cassia is a 39-in (1-m) evergreen shrub.

Habitat Open ground; Mexico, tropical Africa, India | Parts used

Family COMPOSITAE | Species *Artemisia tridentata* | Local name Big Sage Brush

SAGEBRUSH

The aromatic *Artemisia tridentata* (syn. *Serephidium tridentatum*) has woolly white stems, soft foliage, and small seed pods.

• **USES** Native Americans burned the leaves to produce smoke for sacred ceremonies. They are chewed for indigestion and flatulence, made into poultices for migraine, and infused for an antibacterial mouthwash. A tincture of flower essence is a spiritual treatment for the stress of conflicting emotions.

• **REMARK** Native Americans believe that students of herbs can come to recognize illness by learning to "tap the spirit of Sagebrush."

Habitat Arid hillsides; Mexico, W. USA | Parts used

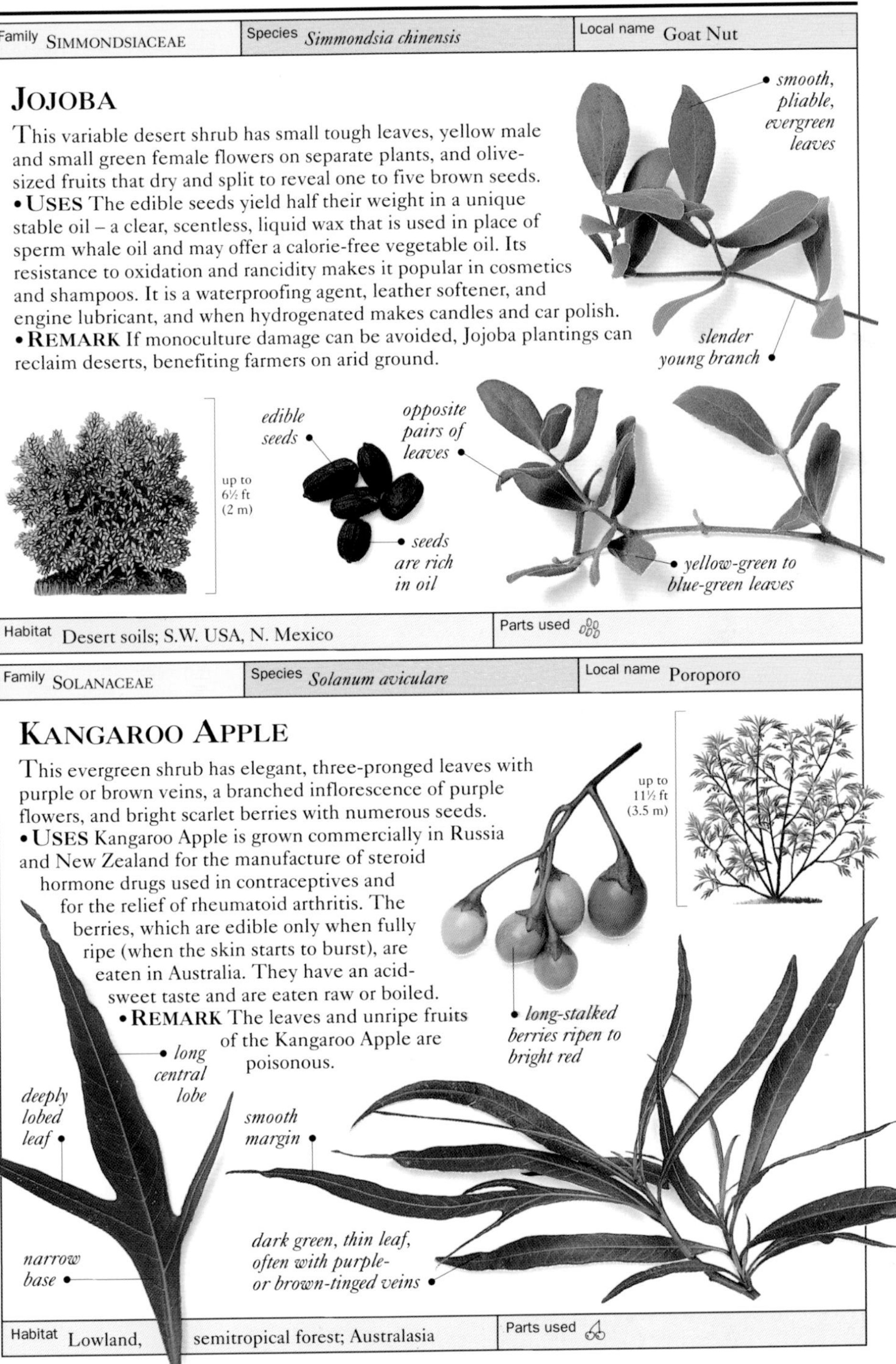
smooth, pliable, evergreen leaves
slender young branch
edible seeds
opposite pairs of leaves
up to 6½ ft (2 m)
seeds are rich in oil
yellow-green to blue-green leaves
up to 11½ ft (3.5 m)
long-stalked berries ripen to bright red
long central lobe
deeply lobed leaf
smooth margin
narrow base
dark green, thin leaf, often with purple- or brown-tinged veins

Family SIMMONDSIACEAE	Species *Simmondsia chinensis*	Local name Goat Nut

JOJOBA

This variable desert shrub has small tough leaves, yellow male and small green female flowers on separate plants, and olive-sized fruits that dry and split to reveal one to five brown seeds.
• **USES** The edible seeds yield half their weight in a unique stable oil – a clear, scentless, liquid wax that is used in place of sperm whale oil and may offer a calorie-free vegetable oil. Its resistance to oxidation and rancidity makes it popular in cosmetics and shampoos. It is a waterproofing agent, leather softener, and engine lubricant, and when hydrogenated makes candles and car polish.
• **REMARK** If monoculture damage can be avoided, Jojoba plantings can reclaim deserts, benefiting farmers on arid ground.

Habitat Desert soils; S.W. USA, N. Mexico	Parts used

Family SOLANACEAE	Species *Solanum aviculare*	Local name Poroporo

KANGAROO APPLE

This evergreen shrub has elegant, three-pronged leaves with purple or brown veins, a branched inflorescence of purple flowers, and bright scarlet berries with numerous seeds.
• **USES** Kangaroo Apple is grown commercially in Russia and New Zealand for the manufacture of steroid hormone drugs used in contraceptives and for the relief of rheumatoid arthritis. The berries, which are edible only when fully ripe (when the skin starts to burst), are eaten in Australia. They have an acid-sweet taste and are eaten raw or boiled.
• **REMARK** The leaves and unripe fruits of the Kangaroo Apple are poisonous.

Habitat Lowland, semitropical forest; Australasia	Parts used

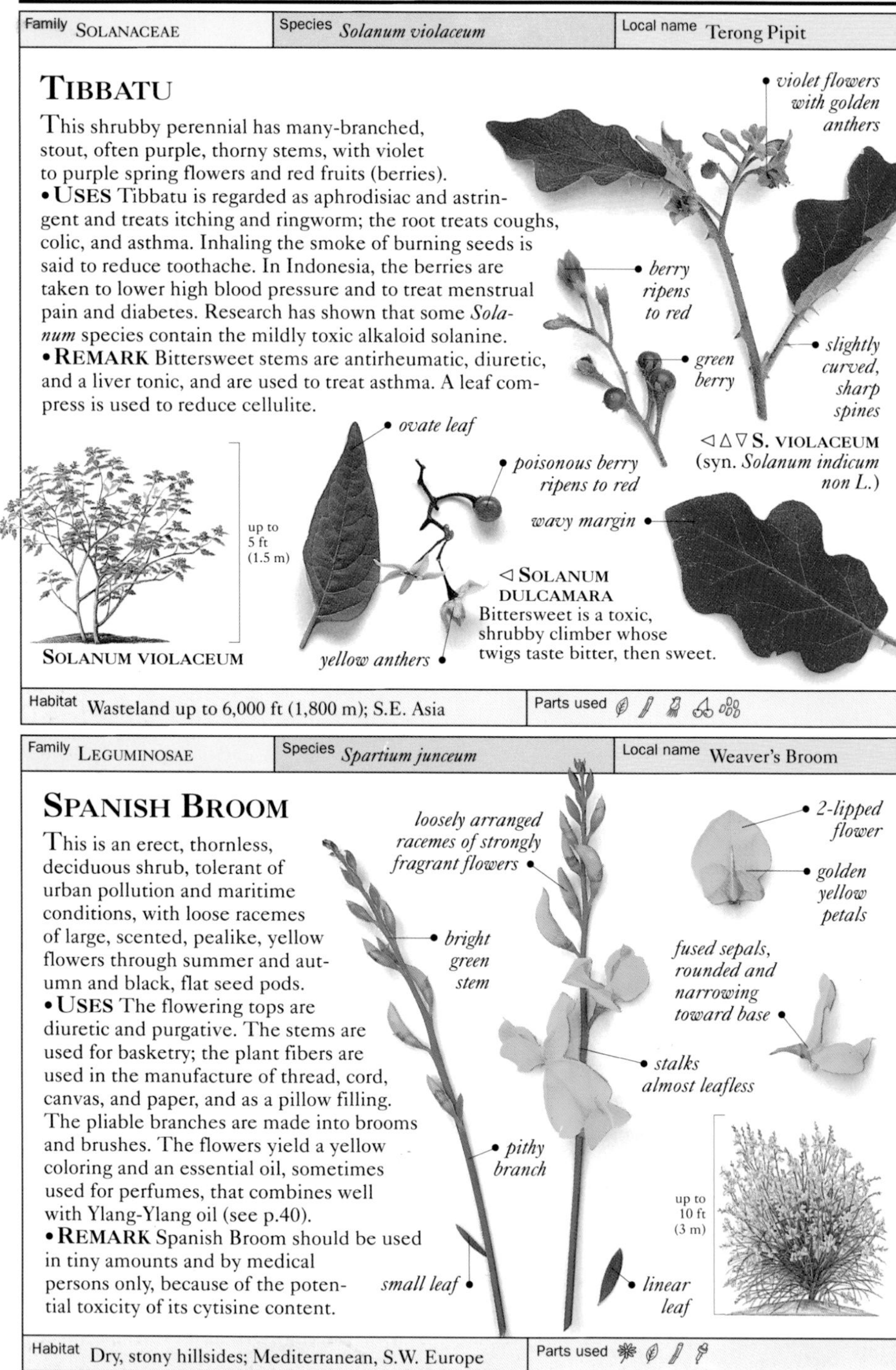
violet flowers with golden anthers
berry ripens to red
green berry
slightly curved, sharp spines
ovate leaf
poisonous berry ripens to red
wavy margin
yellow anthers
up to 5 ft (1.5 m)
loosely arranged racemes of strongly fragrant flowers
2-lipped flower
golden yellow petals
bright green stem
fused sepals, rounded and narrowing toward base
stalks almost leafless
pithy branch
small leaf
linear leaf
up to 10 ft (3 m)

Family SOLANACEAE	Species *Solanum violaceum*	Local name Terong Pipit

TIBBATU

This shrubby perennial has many-branched, stout, often purple, thorny stems, with violet to purple spring flowers and red fruits (berries).

• **USES** Tibbatu is regarded as aphrodisiac and astringent and treats itching and ringworm; the root treats coughs, colic, and asthma. Inhaling the smoke of burning seeds is said to reduce toothache. In Indonesia, the berries are taken to lower high blood pressure and to treat menstrual pain and diabetes. Research has shown that some *Solanum* species contain the mildly toxic alkaloid solanine.

• **REMARK** Bittersweet stems are antirheumatic, diuretic, and a liver tonic, and are used to treat asthma. A leaf compress is used to reduce cellulite.

◁ △ ▽ S. VIOLACEUM (syn. *Solanum indicum* non L.)

◁ SOLANUM DULCAMARA Bittersweet is a toxic, shrubby climber whose twigs taste bitter, then sweet.

SOLANUM VIOLACEUM

Habitat Wasteland up to 6,000 ft (1,800 m); S.E. Asia	Parts used

Family LEGUMINOSAE	Species *Spartium junceum*	Local name Weaver's Broom

SPANISH BROOM

This is an erect, thornless, deciduous shrub, tolerant of urban pollution and maritime conditions, with loose racemes of large, scented, pealike, yellow flowers through summer and autumn and black, flat seed pods.

• **USES** The flowering tops are diuretic and purgative. The stems are used for basketry; the plant fibers are used in the manufacture of thread, cord, canvas, and paper, and as a pillow filling. The pliable branches are made into brooms and brushes. The flowers yield a yellow coloring and an essential oil, sometimes used for perfumes, that combines well with Ylang-Ylang oil (see p.40).

• **REMARK** Spanish Broom should be used in tiny amounts and by medical persons only, because of the potential toxicity of its cytisine content.

Habitat Dry, stony hillsides; Mediterranean, S.W. Europe	Parts used

Family LOGANIACEAE | Species *Strychnos nux-vomica* | Local name Nux-vomica

STRYCHNINE

This shrub or tree has oval leaves and green-white flowers, followed by yellow, tennis-ball sized fruits with grayish disk-shaped seeds.

• **USES** The bark, root, and seed coat contain poisonous strychnine and brucine, once used to stimulate nerves but now used only in tiny doses in homeopathy. In Nepal, the treated seeds are given as a digestive tonic and for rabies, menstrual problems, and paralysis.

• **REMARK** In India, the Clearing Nut (*Strychnos potatorum*) is put in water jars, causing any impurities in the water to sink to the bottom. The Amazon climber *S. toxifera* was part of the curare arrow poison and is now a life-saving muscle relaxant used during surgery.

smooth shiny leaves in opposite pairs
bark treats cholera in India
up to 65 ft (20 m)
fine hairs give satin sheen
ash-gray seed
leaves used as poultice
waxy flowers
up to 23 ft (7 m)
heart-shaped, deciduous leaves
slight creasing along center

Habitat Sandy soil, dry forests; India, Myanmar | Parts used

Family OLEACEAE | Species *Syringa vulgaris* | Local name Syringa

LILAC

Lilac is a deciduous, twiggy shrub or small tree with a mass of leaves and showy panicles of small, waxy, spring flowers that exude a sweet, wafting perfume. Lilacs are available in white, pink, blue, and purple cultivars. The flower stalks have minute glands.

• **USES** The perfume is extracted from the flowers and used commercially. The flowers were once used to treat fever. In the language of flowers, Lilac symbolized the first emotions of love.

• **REMARK** If inhaled too deeply, the strong flower fragrance can cause nausea.

Habitat Mountainous woodland; S.E. Europe | Parts used

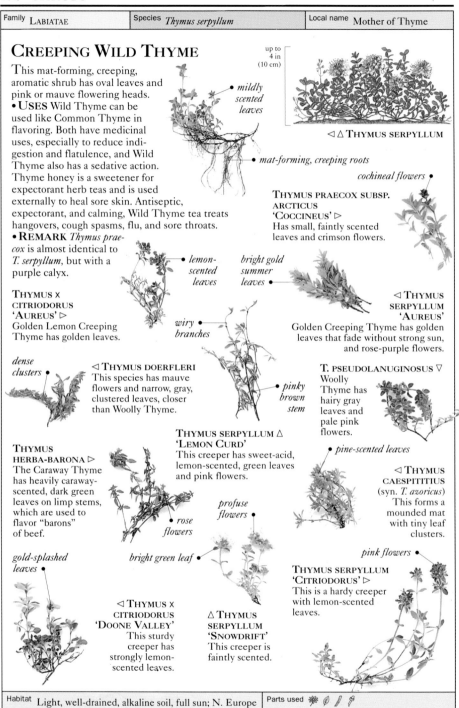

Family LABIATAE	Species *Thymus serpyllum*	Local name Mother of Thyme

CREEPING WILD THYME

This mat-forming, creeping, aromatic shrub has oval leaves and pink or mauve flowering heads.
• **USES** Wild Thyme can be used like Common Thyme in flavoring. Both have medicinal uses, especially to reduce indigestion and flatulence, and Wild Thyme also has a sedative action. Thyme honey is a sweetener for expectorant herb teas and is used externally to heal sore skin. Antiseptic, expectorant, and calming, Wild Thyme tea treats hangovers, cough spasms, flu, and sore throats.
• **REMARK** *Thymus praecox* is almost identical to *T. serpyllum,* but with a purple calyx.

mildly scented leaves

mat-forming, creeping roots

up to 4 in (10 cm)

◁ △ THYMUS SERPYLLUM

cochineal flowers

THYMUS PRAECOX SUBSP. ARCTICUS 'COCCINEUS' ▷
Has small, faintly scented leaves and crimson flowers.

lemon-scented leaves

THYMUS X CITRIODORUS 'AUREUS' ▷
Golden Lemon Creeping Thyme has golden leaves.

bright gold summer leaves

◁ THYMUS SERPYLLUM 'AUREUS'
Golden Creeping Thyme has golden leaves that fade without strong sun, and rose-purple flowers.

wiry branches

dense clusters

◁ THYMUS DOERFLERI
This species has mauve flowers and narrow, gray, clustered leaves, closer than Woolly Thyme.

pinky brown stem

T. PSEUDOLANUGINOSUS ▽
Woolly Thyme has hairy gray leaves and pale pink flowers.

THYMUS SERPYLLUM △ 'LEMON CURD'
This creeper has sweet-acid, lemon-scented, green leaves and pink flowers.

THYMUS HERBA-BARONA ▷
The Caraway Thyme has heavily caraway-scented, dark green leaves on limp stems, which are used to flavor "barons" of beef.

rose flowers

pine-scented leaves

◁ THYMUS CAESPITITIUS (syn. *T. azoricus*)
This forms a mounded mat with tiny leaf clusters.

profuse flowers

bright green leaf

gold-splashed leaves

pink flowers

THYMUS SERPYLLUM 'CITRIODORUS' ▷
This is a hardy creeper with lemon-scented leaves.

◁ THYMUS X CITRIODORUS 'DOONE VALLEY'
This sturdy creeper has strongly lemon-scented leaves.

△ THYMUS SERPYLLUM 'SNOWDRIFT'
This creeper is faintly scented.

Habitat Light, well-drained, alkaline soil, full sun; N. Europe	Parts used

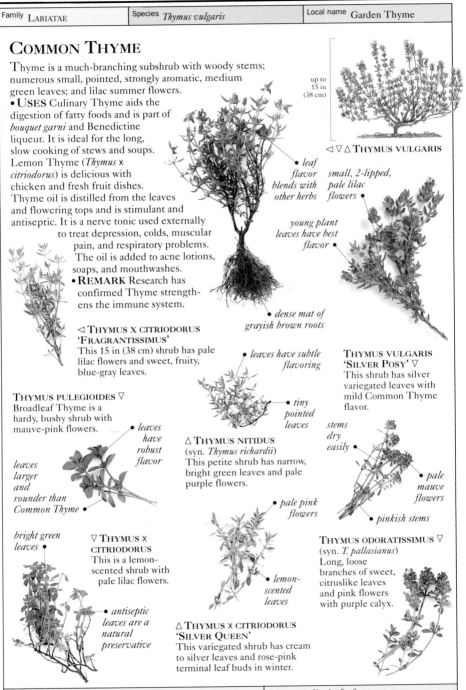

Family LABIATAE	Species *Thymus vulgaris*	Local name Garden Thyme

COMMON THYME

Thyme is a much-branching subshrub with woody stems; numerous small, pointed, strongly aromatic, medium green leaves; and lilac summer flowers.

• **USES** Culinary Thyme aids the digestion of fatty foods and is part of *bouquet garni* and Benedictine liqueur. It is ideal for the long, slow cooking of stews and soups. Lemon Thyme (*Thymus* x *citriodorus*) is delicious with chicken and fresh fruit dishes. Thyme oil is distilled from the leaves and flowering tops and is stimulant and antiseptic. It is a nerve tonic used externally to treat depression, colds, muscular pain, and respiratory problems. The oil is added to acne lotions, soaps, and mouthwashes.

• **REMARK** Research has confirmed Thyme strengthens the immune system.

up to 15 in (38 cm)

◁ ▽ △ THYMUS VULGARIS

leaf flavor blends with other herbs

dense mat of grayish brown roots

small, 2-lipped, pale lilac flowers

young plant leaves have best flavor

◁ THYMUS X CITRIODORUS 'FRAGRANTISSIMUS'
This 15 in (38 cm) shrub has pale lilac flowers and sweet, fruity, blue-gray leaves.

THYMUS VULGARIS 'SILVER POSY' ▽
This shrub has silver variegated leaves with mild Common Thyme flavor.

leaves have subtle flavoring

tiny pointed leaves

△ THYMUS NITIDUS
(syn. *Thymus richardii*)
This petite shrub has narrow, bright green leaves and pale purple flowers.

THYMUS PULEGIOIDES ▽
Broadleaf Thyme is a hardy, bushy shrub with mauve-pink flowers.

leaves have robust flavor

leaves larger and rounder than Common Thyme

stems dry easily

pale mauve flowers

pinkish stems

pale pink flowers

lemon-scented leaves

bright green leaves

▽ THYMUS X CITRIODORUS
This is a lemon-scented shrub with pale lilac flowers.

antiseptic leaves are a natural preservative

△ THYMUS X CITRIODORUS 'SILVER QUEEN'
This variegated shrub has cream to silver leaves and rose-pink terminal leaf buds in winter.

THYMUS ODORATISSIMUS ▽
(syn. *T. pallasianus*)
Long, loose branches of sweet, citruslike leaves and pink flowers with purple calyx.

Habitat Light, well-drained soil, sun; W. Mediterranean	Parts used

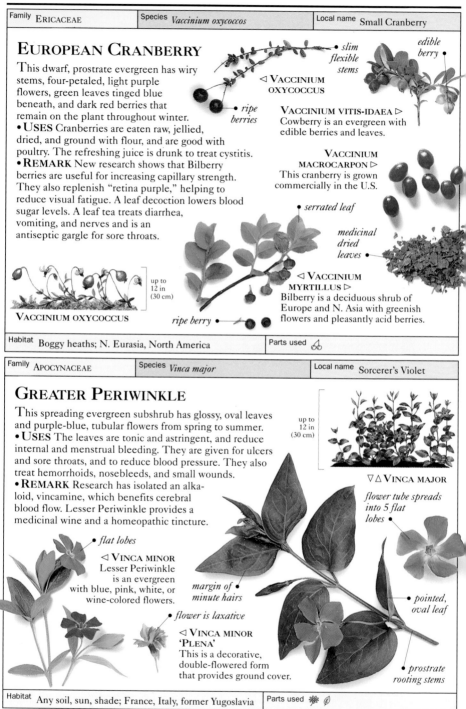

Family ERICACEAE	Species *Vaccinium oxycoccos*	Local name Small Cranberry

European Cranberry

This dwarf, prostrate evergreen has wiry stems, four-petaled, light purple flowers, green leaves tinged blue beneath, and dark red berries that remain on the plant throughout winter.

• **USES** Cranberries are eaten raw, jellied, dried, and ground with flour, and are good with poultry. The refreshing juice is drunk to treat cystitis.

• **REMARK** New research shows that Bilberry berries are useful for increasing capillary strength. They also replenish "retina purple," helping to reduce visual fatigue. A leaf decoction lowers blood sugar levels. A leaf tea treats diarrhea, vomiting, and nerves and is an antiseptic gargle for sore throats.

slim flexible stems

ripe berries

◁ VACCINIUM OXYCOCCUS

edible berry

VACCINIUM VITIS-IDAEA ▷
Cowberry is an evergreen with edible berries and leaves.

VACCINIUM MACROCARPON ▷
This cranberry is grown commercially in the U.S.

serrated leaf

medicinal dried leaves

up to 12 in (30 cm)

VACCINIUM OXYCOCCUS

ripe berry

◁ VACCINIUM MYRTILLUS ▷
Bilberry is a deciduous shrub of Europe and N. Asia with greenish flowers and pleasantly acid berries.

Habitat Boggy heaths; N. Eurasia, North America	Parts used

Family APOCYNACEAE	Species *Vinca major*	Local name Sorcerer's Violet

Greater Periwinkle

This spreading evergreen subshrub has glossy, oval leaves and purple-blue, tubular flowers from spring to summer.

• **USES** The leaves are tonic and astringent, and reduce internal and menstrual bleeding. They are given for ulcers and sore throats, and to reduce blood pressure. They also treat hemorrhoids, nosebleeds, and small wounds.

• **REMARK** Research has isolated an alkaloid, vincamine, which benefits cerebral blood flow. Lesser Periwinkle provides a medicinal wine and a homeopathic tincture.

up to 12 in (30 cm)

▽△ VINCA MAJOR

flower tube spreads into 5 flat lobes

flat lobes

◁ VINCA MINOR
Lesser Periwinkle is an evergreen with blue, pink, white, or wine-colored flowers.

margin of minute hairs

pointed, oval leaf

flower is laxative

◁ VINCA MINOR 'PLENA'
This is a decorative, double-flowered form that provides ground cover.

prostrate rooting stems

Habitat Any soil, sun, shade; France, Italy, former Yugoslavia	Parts used

Family CAPRIFOLIACEAE	Species *Viburnum opulus*	Local name Guelder Rose

CRAMPBARK

This deciduous, thicket-forming shrub has attractive, cream flower heads, maplelike leaves that turn burgundy in autumn, and bright red berries.

• **USES** The poisonous fresh berries are edible when cooked and are used in a tart jelly or a distilled spirit. The stem bark is sedative and antispasmodic, reducing muscle cramps and intestinal spasms. Native Americans used stem bark to treat mumps. The berries yield a dye.

• **REMARK** *Viburnum prunifolium* bark is used similarly. The leaf, stem, and bark of *V. edule* and *V. trilobum* are given by the Alberta Cree tribe for many illnesses, especially high fever and pain relief.

leaves with 3 or 5 lobes
dark green leaves, smooth above, downy beneath
dried bark is given for muscle and menstrual cramps
berry clusters on long stalks
up to 13½ ft (4.5 m)
stiff sword-shaped leaf with spine tip
white anthers
whitish green flowers open in the evening
up to 13½ ft (4.5 m)
deep green leaf edged with twisted threads
panicles of pendulous flowers

Habitat Woodland clearings, wet soil; Europe, N. Africa, Asia	Parts used

Family AGAVACEAE	Species *Yucca filamentosa*	Local name Needle Palm

YUCCA

This evergreen, clump-forming plant behaves seasonally in desert areas, flowering with the rains, which can be years apart. The tall spikes of scented, tuliplike flowers yield dry fruits.

• **USES** Often found in barren landscapes, Yuccas are a food and resource plant of Native Americans. The flower stalks are eaten when fully grown but before buds open. The flower buds and petals are cooked, and the fruit is eaten raw. The leaves are woven into baskets and leaf fibers used for rope. A root poultice or salve treats skin sores and sprains and, decocted as tea, may ease arthritic pain.

• **REMARK** Yucca and Soapweed (*Yucca glauca*) contain astringent saponin used in cosmetics, soap, and a shampoo used in the cleansing ceremony of Hopi tribal weddings.

Habitat Dry, sandy areas; S.E. USA	Parts used

HERBACEOUS PERENNIALS

Family COMPOSITAE	Species *Achillea millefolium*	Local name Milfoil

YARROW

Yarrow has a creeping rhizome; erect, downy stems; soft, pungent, finely divided leaves; and dense, flat, white or pink-tinged flower heads from summer to autumn.

• **USES** The peppery leaf is finely chopped into salads and, with the flowers, used to flavor liqueurs. The flowering tops are a digestive and cleansing tonic and a diuretic and are used to reduce high blood pressure. Fresh leaves arrest bleeding and are applied as a poultice to wounds or are placed on shaving cuts. Flowers treat eczema and catarrh from allergies. Flower essential oil treats colds, flu, and inflamed joints. Native Americans used a root decoction to strengthen muscles.

• **REMARK** Overuse can make the skin sensitive to sunlight, and it should be taken in small doses. Avoid during pregnancy.

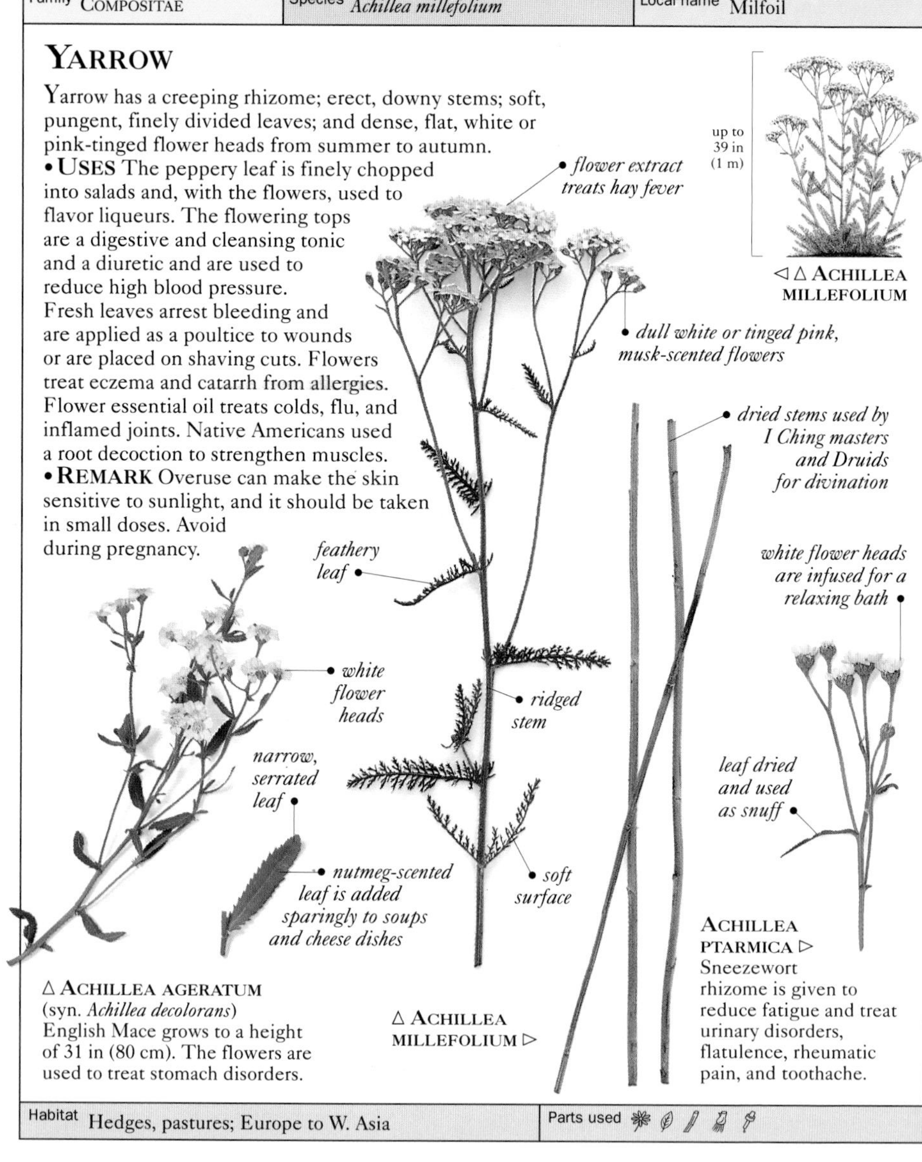
up to
39 in
(1 m)
◁ △ ACHILLEA MILLEFOLIUM
flower extract treats hay fever
dull white or tinged pink, musk-scented flowers
dried stems used by I Ching masters and Druids for divination
feathery leaf
white flower heads are infused for a relaxing bath
white flower heads
ridged stem
narrow, serrated leaf
leaf dried and used as snuff
nutmeg-scented leaf is added sparingly to soups and cheese dishes
soft surface

△ ACHILLEA AGERATUM (syn. *Achillea decolorans*) English Mace grows to a height of 31 in (80 cm). The flowers are used to treat stomach disorders.

△ ACHILLEA MILLEFOLIUM ▷

ACHILLEA PTARMICA ▷ Sneezewort rhizome is given to reduce fatigue and treat urinary disorders, flatulence, rheumatic pain, and toothache.

Habitat Hedges, pastures; Europe to W. Asia	Parts used

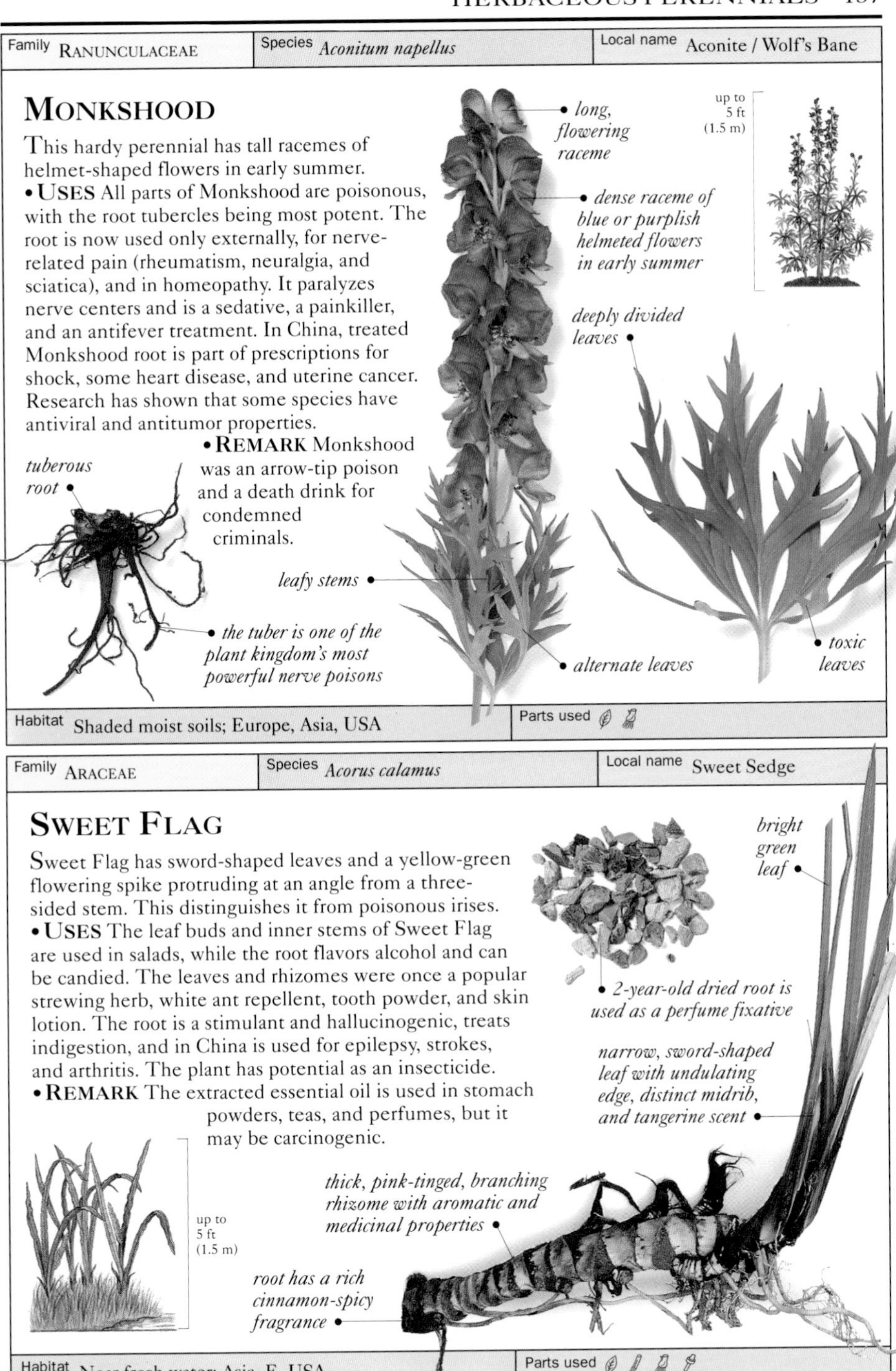
long, flowering raceme
dense raceme of blue or purplish helmeted flowers in early summer
up to 5 ft (1.5 m)
deeply divided leaves
tuberous root
leafy stems
the tuber is one of the plant kingdom's most powerful nerve poisons
alternate leaves
toxic leaves
bright green leaf
2-year-old dried root is used as a perfume fixative
narrow, sword-shaped leaf with undulating edge, distinct midrib, and tangerine scent
thick, pink-tinged, branching rhizome with aromatic and medicinal properties
up to 5 ft (1.5 m)
root has a rich cinnamon-spicy fragrance

Family RANUNCULACEAE	Species *Aconitum napellus*	Local name Aconite / Wolf's Bane

MONKSHOOD

This hardy perennial has tall racemes of helmet-shaped flowers in early summer.

• **USES** All parts of Monkshood are poisonous, with the root tubercles being most potent. The root is now used only externally, for nerve-related pain (rheumatism, neuralgia, and sciatica), and in homeopathy. It paralyzes nerve centers and is a sedative, a painkiller, and an antifever treatment. In China, treated Monkshood root is part of prescriptions for shock, some heart disease, and uterine cancer. Research has shown that some species have antiviral and antitumor properties.

• **REMARK** Monkshood was an arrow-tip poison and a death drink for condemned criminals.

Habitat Shaded moist soils; Europe, Asia, USA	Parts used

Family ARACEAE	Species *Acorus calamus*	Local name Sweet Sedge

SWEET FLAG

Sweet Flag has sword-shaped leaves and a yellow-green flowering spike protruding at an angle from a three-sided stem. This distinguishes it from poisonous irises.

• **USES** The leaf buds and inner stems of Sweet Flag are used in salads, while the root flavors alcohol and can be candied. The leaves and rhizomes were once a popular strewing herb, white ant repellent, tooth powder, and skin lotion. The root is a stimulant and hallucinogenic, treats indigestion, and in China is used for epilepsy, strokes, and arthritis. The plant has potential as an insecticide.

• **REMARK** The extracted essential oil is used in stomach powders, teas, and perfumes, but it may be carcinogenic.

Habitat Near fresh water; Asia, E. USA	Parts used

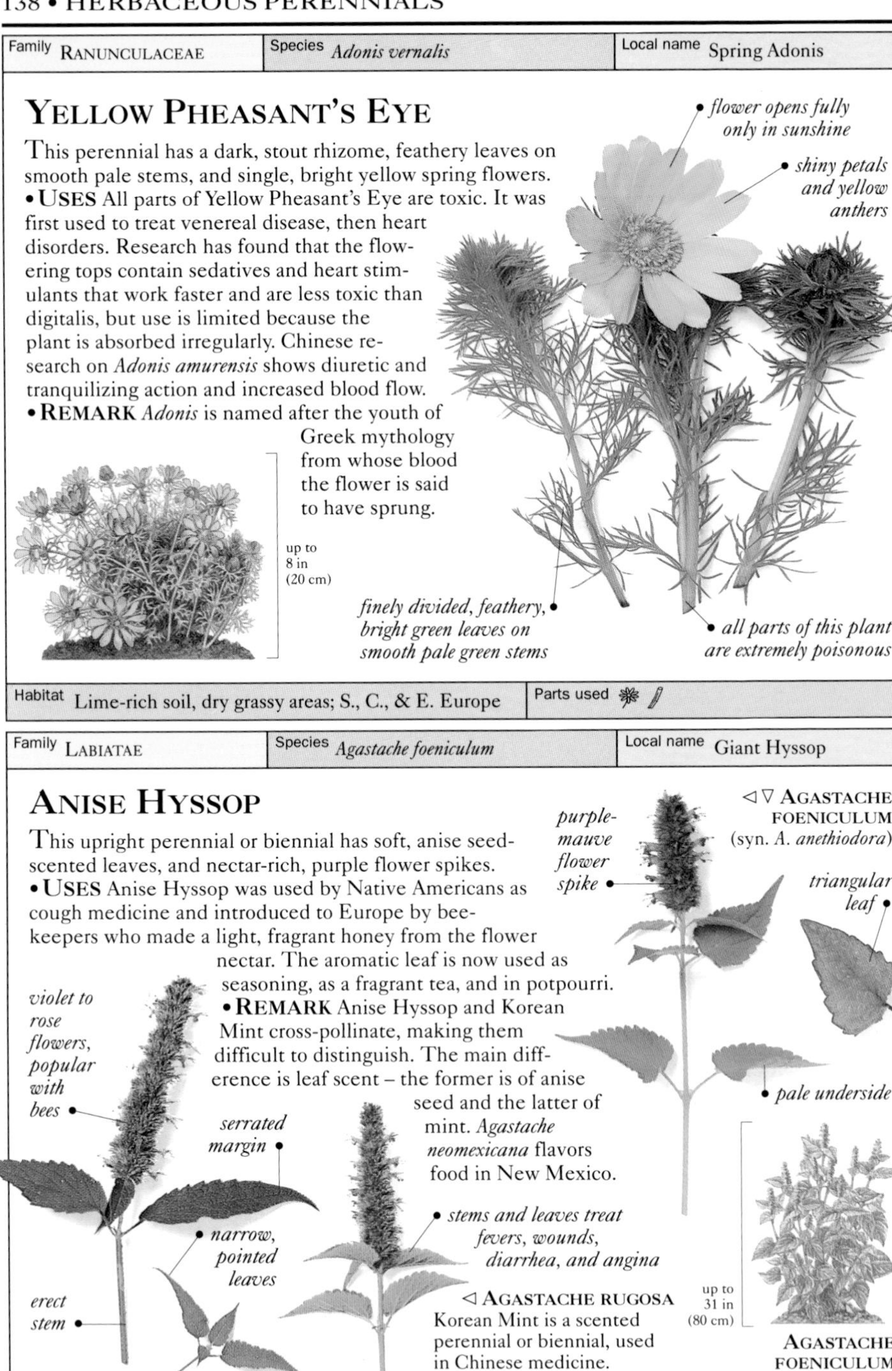
flower opens fully only in sunshine
shiny petals and yellow anthers
up to 8 in (20 cm)
finely divided, feathery, bright green leaves on smooth pale green stems
all parts of this plant are extremely poisonous
purple-mauve flower spike
◁ ▽ AGASTACHE FOENICULUM (syn. A. anethiodora)
triangular leaf
pale underside
violet to rose flowers, popular with bees
serrated margin
narrow, pointed leaves
erect stem
stems and leaves treat fevers, wounds, diarrhea, and angina
up to 31 in (80 cm)
AGASTACHE FOENICULUM

Family RANUNCULACEAE | Species *Adonis vernalis* | Local name Spring Adonis

YELLOW PHEASANT'S EYE

This perennial has a dark, stout rhizome, feathery leaves on smooth pale stems, and single, bright yellow spring flowers.
• **USES** All parts of Yellow Pheasant's Eye are toxic. It was first used to treat venereal disease, then heart disorders. Research has found that the flowering tops contain sedatives and heart stimulants that work faster and are less toxic than digitalis, but use is limited because the plant is absorbed irregularly. Chinese research on *Adonis amurensis* shows diuretic and tranquilizing action and increased blood flow.
• **REMARK** *Adonis* is named after the youth of Greek mythology from whose blood the flower is said to have sprung.

Habitat Lime-rich soil, dry grassy areas; S., C., & E. Europe | Parts used

Family LABIATAE | Species *Agastache foeniculum* | Local name Giant Hyssop

ANISE HYSSOP

This upright perennial or biennial has soft, anise seed-scented leaves, and nectar-rich, purple flower spikes.
• **USES** Anise Hyssop was used by Native Americans as cough medicine and introduced to Europe by beekeepers who made a light, fragrant honey from the flower nectar. The aromatic leaf is now used as seasoning, as a fragrant tea, and in potpourri.
• **REMARK** Anise Hyssop and Korean Mint cross-pollinate, making them difficult to distinguish. The main difference is leaf scent – the former is of anise seed and the latter of mint. *Agastache neomexicana* flavors food in New Mexico.

◁ AGASTACHE RUGOSA
Korean Mint is a scented perennial or biennial, used in Chinese medicine.

Habitat Moist woodland, high plains; North America | Parts used

Family AGAVACEAE	Species *Agave americana*	Local name Century Plant

AGAVE

This half-hardy succulent has a rosette of sword-shaped leaves, and a tall flowering panicle with pale yellow, tubular, bell-like flowers on small side branches. These and the spiny leaf margins distinguish it from a Yucca.

• **USES** Sap collected when the flower stalk is removed is fermented into the drink *pulque*, and the large bud at the stem base can be roasted. Flower stalk tops yield a ceremonial black body paint, and pulped leaves and roots give a soapy lather. The leaf sap is laxative and treats burns. Leaves are made into papyruslike paper, and the fibers into twine.

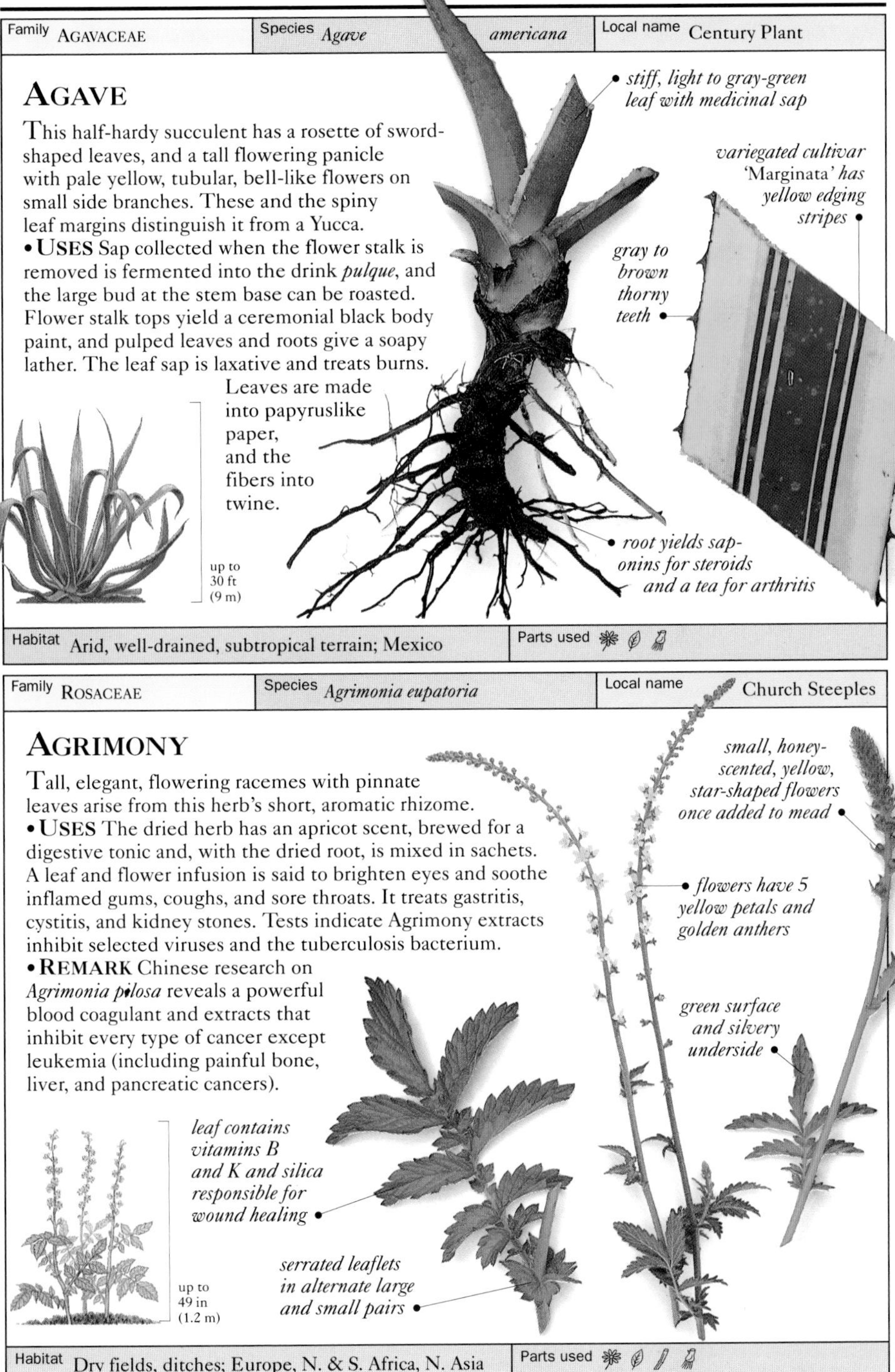

stiff, light to gray-green leaf with medicinal sap
variegated cultivar 'Marginata' has yellow edging stripes
gray to brown thorny teeth
root yields saponins for steroids and a tea for arthritis
up to 30 ft (9 m)
leaf contains vitamins B and K and silica responsible for wound healing
small, honey-scented, yellow, star-shaped flowers once added to mead
flowers have 5 yellow petals and golden anthers
green surface and silvery underside
serrated leaflets in alternate large and small pairs
up to 49 in (1.2 m)

Habitat Arid, well-drained, subtropical terrain; Mexico	Parts used

Family ROSACEAE	Species *Agrimonia eupatoria*	Local name Church Steeples

AGRIMONY

Tall, elegant, flowering racemes with pinnate leaves arise from this herb's short, aromatic rhizome.

• **USES** The dried herb has an apricot scent, brewed for a digestive tonic and, with the dried root, is mixed in sachets. A leaf and flower infusion is said to brighten eyes and soothe inflamed gums, coughs, and sore throats. It treats gastritis, cystitis, and kidney stones. Tests indicate Agrimony extracts inhibit selected viruses and the tuberculosis bacterium.

• **REMARK** Chinese research on *Agrimonia pilosa* reveals a powerful blood coagulant and extracts that inhibit every type of cancer except leukemia (including painful bone, liver, and pancreatic cancers).

Habitat Dry fields, ditches; Europe, N. & S. Africa, N. Asia	Parts used

Family LABIATAE	Species *Ajuga reptans*	Local name Carpet Bugle

BUGLE

Bugle is a low-growing, creeping, rhizomatous ground-cover, with many stems that bear decorative foliage and spikes of blue tubular flowers.

• **USES** The shoots can be used in salads. The plant is an analgesic for bruises and small wounds and is a mild laxative. An infusion has been used to stop internal bleeding and may lower blood pressure. Historically, Bugle was given for jaundice and for obstructions of the liver and spleen and as a mild narcotic. In homeopathy, it is used for throat irritation and mouth ulcers.

• **REMARK** *Ajuga chamaepitys* is used to treat gout and rheumatism and to promote menstrual flow.

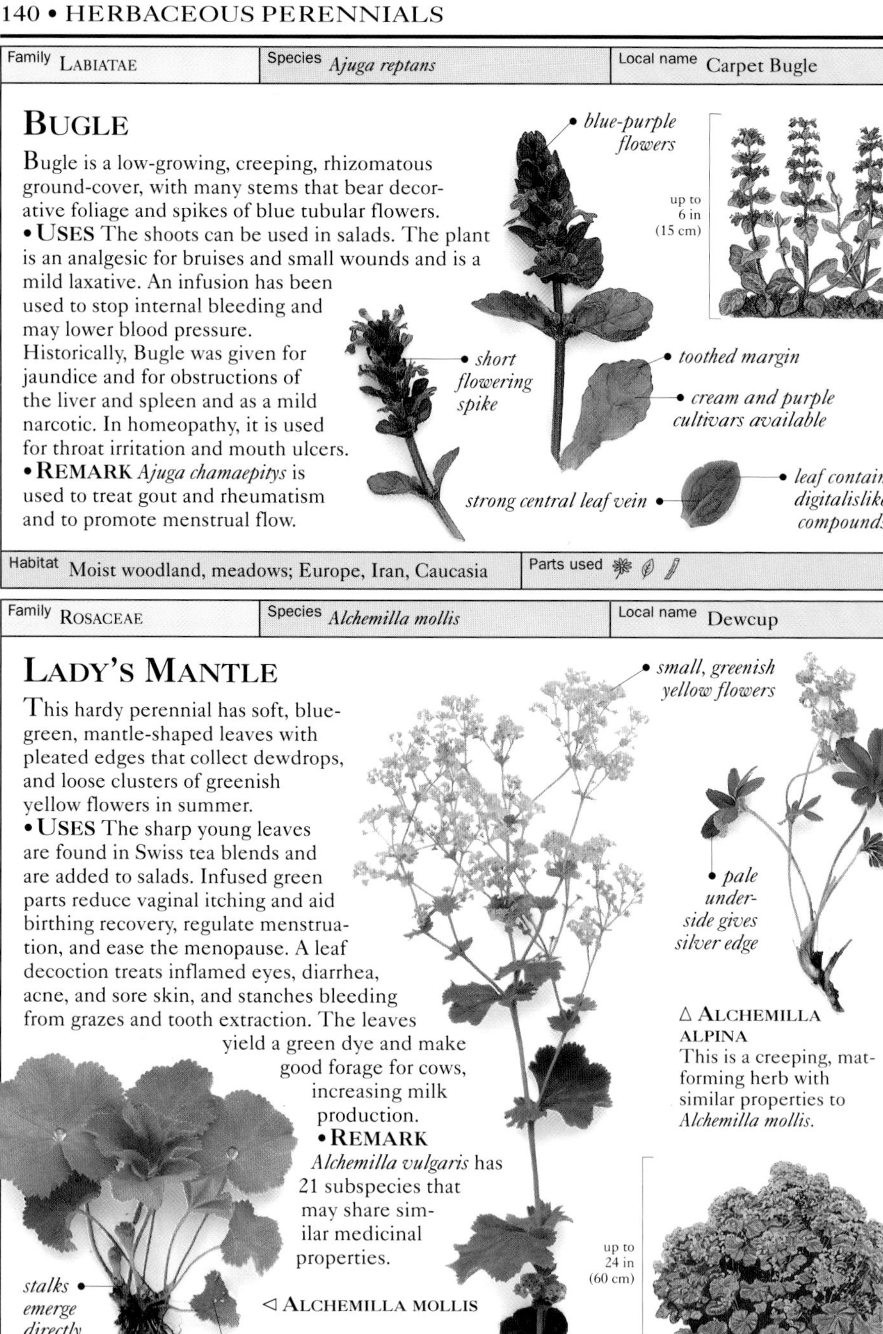

blue-purple flowers
up to 6 in (15 cm)
short flowering spike
toothed margin
cream and purple cultivars available
strong central leaf vein
leaf contain digitalislike compounds
small, greenish yellow flowers
pale underside gives silver edge
up to 24 in (60 cm)
stalks emerge directly from base
serrated leaves with up to 11 lobes

Habitat Moist woodland, meadows; Europe, Iran, Caucasia	Parts used

Family ROSACEAE	Species *Alchemilla mollis*	Local name Dewcup

LADY'S MANTLE

This hardy perennial has soft, blue-green, mantle-shaped leaves with pleated edges that collect dewdrops, and loose clusters of greenish yellow flowers in summer.

• **USES** The sharp young leaves are found in Swiss tea blends and are added to salads. Infused green parts reduce vaginal itching and aid birthing recovery, regulate menstruation, and ease the menopause. A leaf decoction treats inflamed eyes, diarrhea, acne, and sore skin, and stanches bleeding from grazes and tooth extraction. The leaves yield a green dye and make good forage for cows, increasing milk production.

• **REMARK** *Alchemilla vulgaris* has 21 subspecies that may share similar medicinal properties.

△ ALCHEMILLA ALPINA
This is a creeping, mat-forming herb with similar properties to *Alchemilla mollis*.

◁ ALCHEMILLA MOLLIS

◁ △ ALCHEMILLA MOLLIS

Habitat Meadows, temperate climates; E. Europe	Parts used

Family LILIACEAE	Species *Aloe vera*	Local name Barbados Aloe

ALOE VERA

This evergreen, stemless perennial forms a dense rosette of leaves with irregular white marks and a spike of yellow flowers.

• **USES** The plant has remarkable qualities. Two parts are used: the clear, gel-like central leaf pulp, and the yellow-green juice from the green part of the leaf. The gel is used in creams to soothe, heal, and moisturize the skin, and in shampoos for dry, itchy scalps. It cools the skin, protects it from airborne infections and fungi, and reduces scarring. It speeds cell regeneration, and so treats radiation burns, coral wounds, and dermatitis. It can be scraped from split leaves for first-aid treatment of small burns, cuts, chapped skin, sunburn, eczema, and Poison Ivy rash. Compounds in the leaf juice are added to sun screens for protection against UV rays and have shown anticancer activity.

• **REMARK** *Aloe perryi* was famed for its rich violet dye.

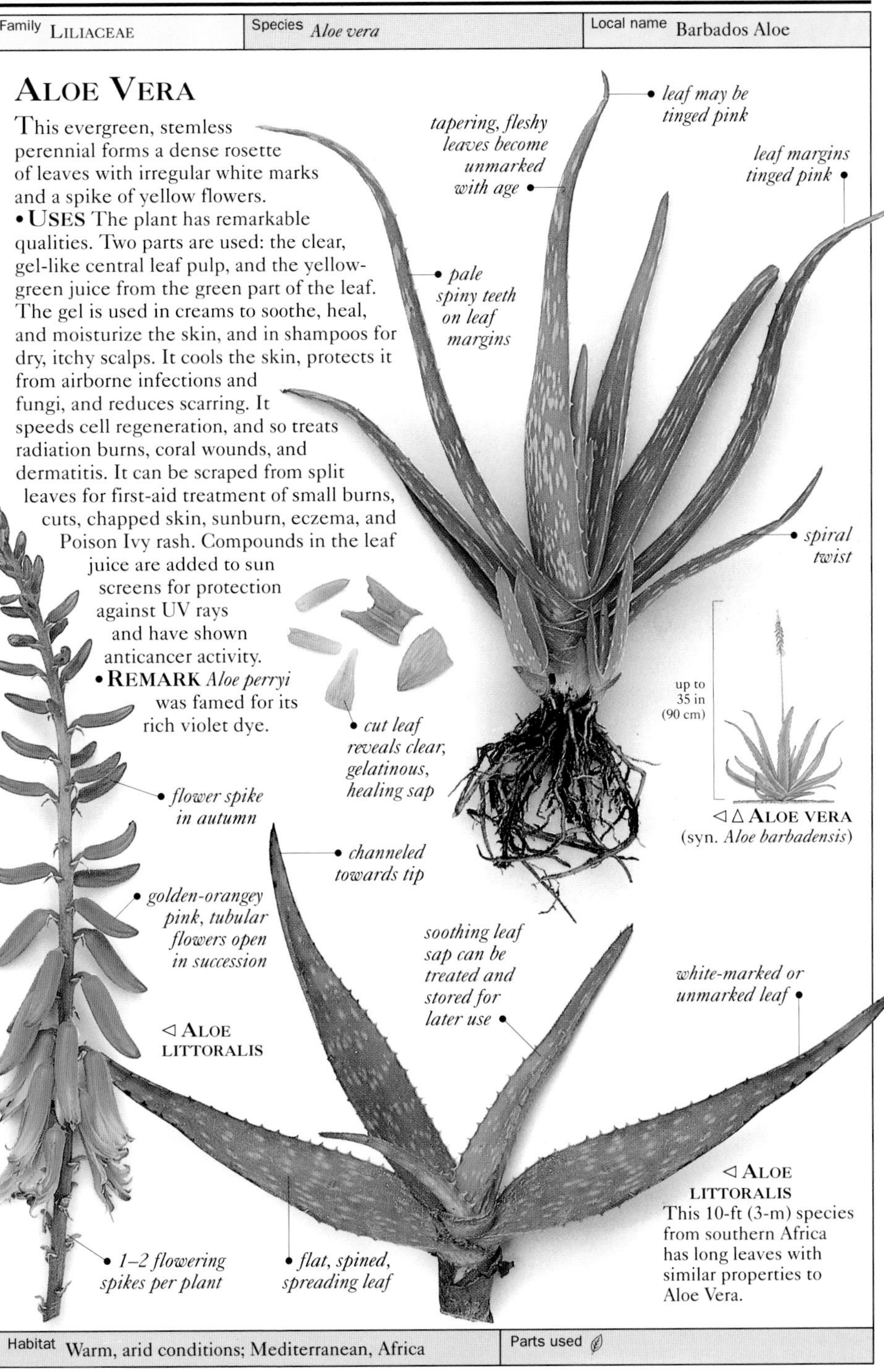
leaf may be tinged pink
tapering, fleshy leaves become unmarked with age
leaf margins tinged pink
pale spiny teeth on leaf margins
spiral twist
up to 35 in (90 cm)
cut leaf reveals clear, gelatinous, healing sap
flower spike in autumn
channeled towards tip
golden-orangey pink, tubular flowers open in succession
soothing leaf sap can be treated and stored for later use
white-marked or unmarked leaf
1–2 flowering spikes per plant
flat, spined, spreading leaf

◁ △ ALOE VERA (syn. *Aloe barbadensis*)

◁ ALOE LITTORALIS

◁ ALOE LITTORALIS This 10-ft (3-m) species from southern Africa has long leaves with similar properties to Aloe Vera.

Habitat Warm, arid conditions; Mediterranean, Africa	Parts used

Family LILIACEAE	Species *Allium sativum*	Local name Various

GARLIC

Garlic has a clustered bulb made up of several bulblets (cloves) enclosed in a papery tunic. It has a single stem with long, thin leaves and an umbel of edible flowers, some of which are replaced by sterile bulbils.

• **USES** The cloves add flavor to savory dishes, especially in hot countries where the plants develop the best flavor. Garlic purifies the blood, helps control acne, and reduces blood pressure, cholesterol, and clotting. Tests confirm antibiotic activity against samples of candida, cholera, staphylococcus, salmonella, dysentery, and typhus; and a mild antifungal action. Garlic clears phlegm, thus providing treatment for colds, bronchitis, pulmonary tuberculosis, and whooping cough. New tests suggest it has a role in treating lead poisoning, some carcinomas, and diabetes.

• **REMARK** The *Allium* species form one of the most popular and widely used flavoring groups. All *Alliums* contain iron and vitamins and are mildly antibiotic.

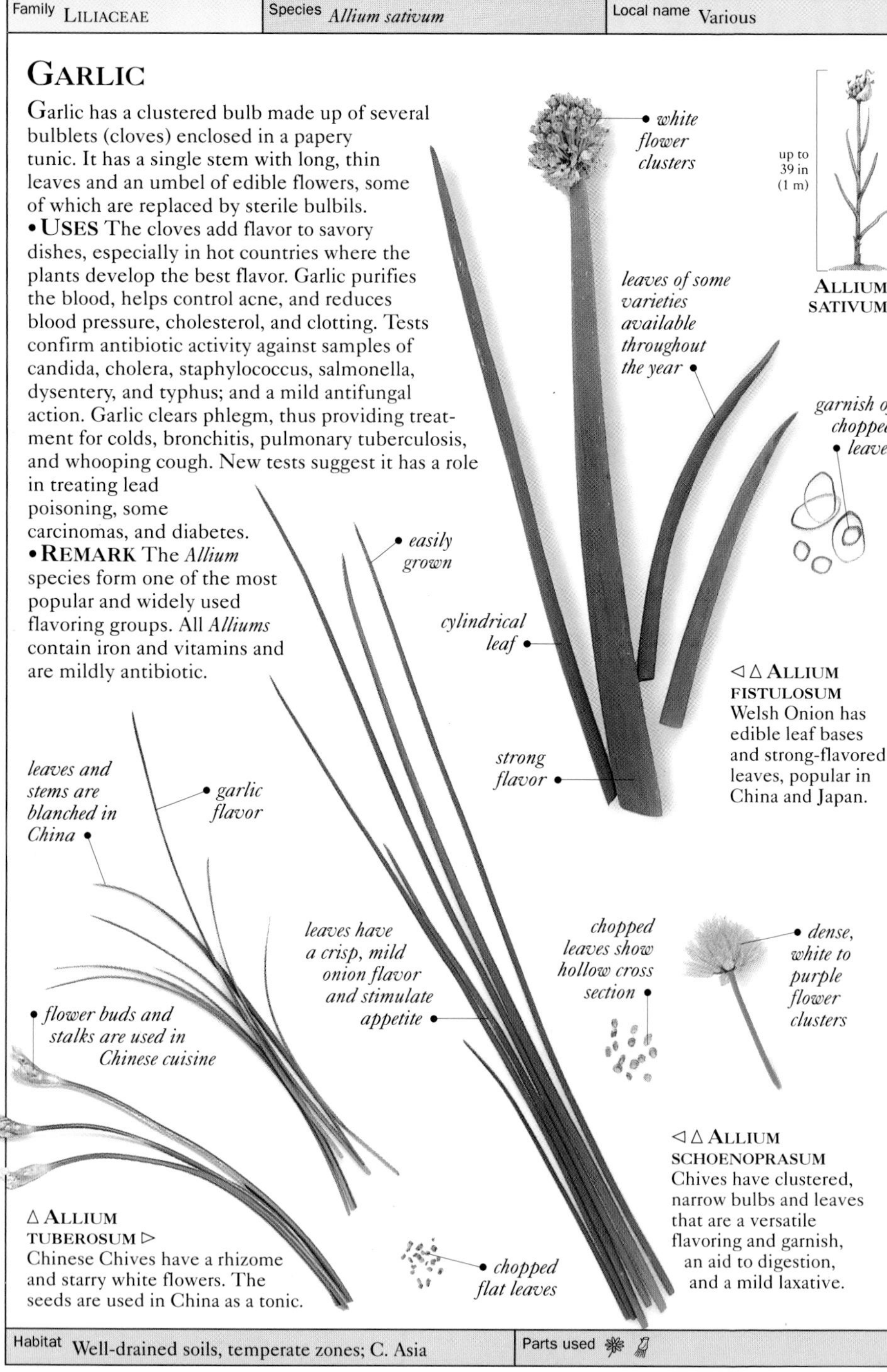
white flower clusters
up to 39 in (1 m)
ALLIUM SATIVUM
leaves of some varieties available throughout the year
garnish of chopped leaves
easily grown
cylindrical leaf
strong flavor
leaves and stems are blanched in China
garlic flavor
leaves have a crisp, mild onion flavor and stimulate appetite
chopped leaves show hollow cross section
dense, white to purple flower clusters
flower buds and stalks are used in Chinese cuisine
chopped flat leaves

◁ △ **ALLIUM FISTULOSUM** Welsh Onion has edible leaf bases and strong-flavored leaves, popular in China and Japan.

◁ △ **ALLIUM SCHOENOPRASUM** Chives have clustered, narrow bulbs and leaves that are a versatile flavoring and garnish, an aid to digestion, and a mild laxative.

△ **ALLIUM TUBEROSUM** ▷ Chinese Chives have a rhizome and starry white flowers. The seeds are used in China as a tonic.

Habitat Well-drained soils, temperate zones; C. Asia	Parts used

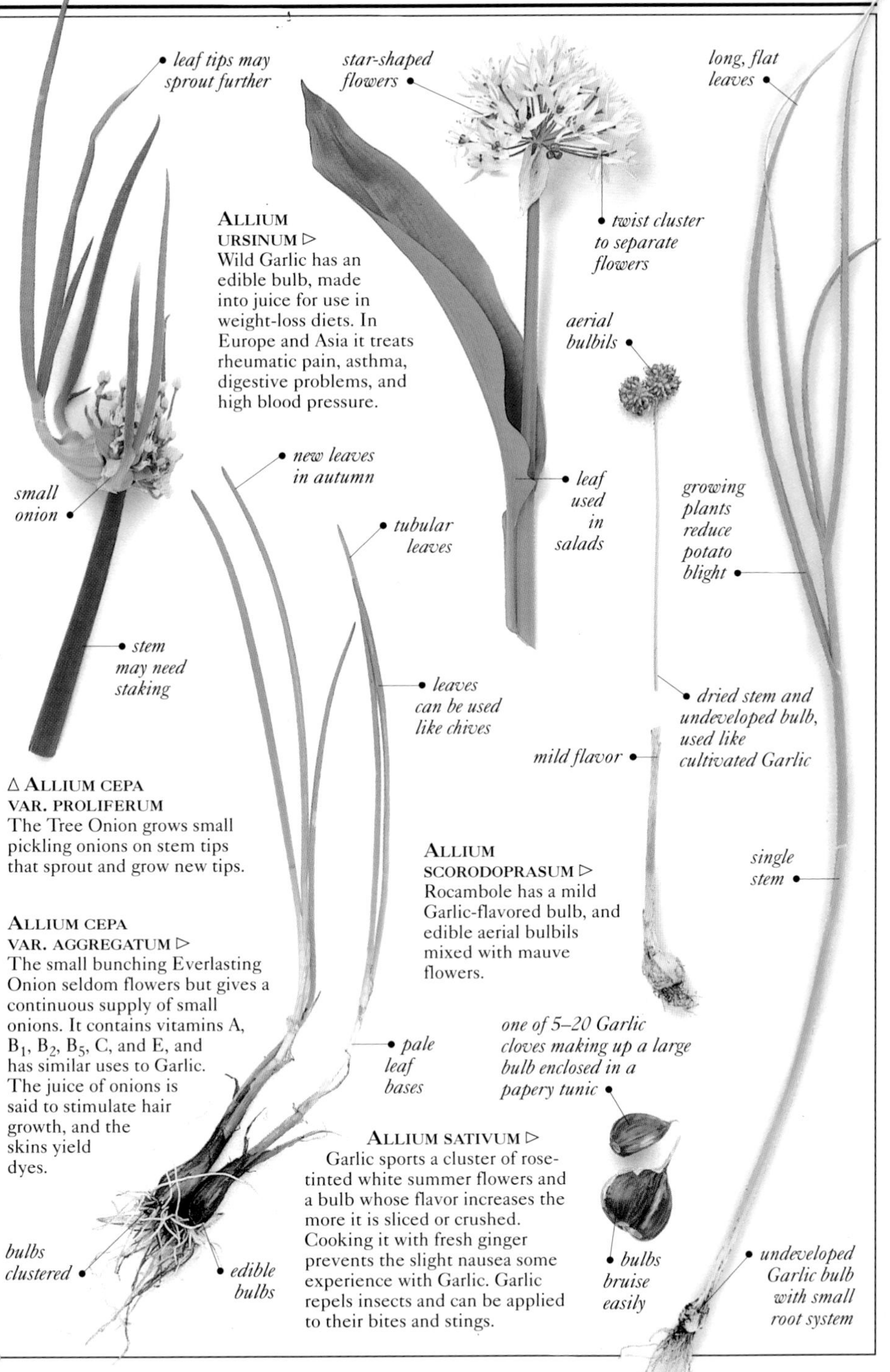
leaf tips may sprout further
small onion
stem may need staking
star-shaped flowers
twist cluster to separate flowers
leaf used in salads
new leaves in autumn
tubular leaves
leaves can be used like chives
pale leaf bases
bulbs clustered
edible bulbs
long, flat leaves
aerial bulbils
growing plants reduce potato blight
dried stem and undeveloped bulb, used like cultivated Garlic
mild flavor
single stem
one of 5–20 Garlic cloves making up a large bulb enclosed in a papery tunic
bulbs bruise easily
undeveloped Garlic bulb with small root system

ALLIUM URSINUM ▷
Wild Garlic has an edible bulb, made into juice for use in weight-loss diets. In Europe and Asia it treats rheumatic pain, asthma, digestive problems, and high blood pressure.

△ ALLIUM CEPA VAR. PROLIFERUM
The Tree Onion grows small pickling onions on stem tips that sprout and grow new tips.

ALLIUM CEPA VAR. AGGREGATUM ▷
The small bunching Everlasting Onion seldom flowers but gives a continuous supply of small onions. It contains vitamins A, B_1, B_2, B_5, C, and E, and has similar uses to Garlic. The juice of onions is said to stimulate hair growth, and the skins yield dyes.

ALLIUM SCORODOPRASUM ▷
Rocambole has a mild Garlic-flavored bulb, and edible aerial bulbils mixed with mauve flowers.

ALLIUM SATIVUM ▷
Garlic sports a cluster of rose-tinted white summer flowers and a bulb whose flavor increases the more it is sliced or crushed. Cooking it with fresh ginger prevents the slight nausea some experience with Garlic. Garlic repels insects and can be applied to their bites and stings.

Family ZINGIBERACEAE	Species *Alpinia galanga*	Local name Siamese Ginger

GREATER GALANGAL

Galangal has dark green, sword-shaped leaves, white flowers with pink veins, round red seed capsules, and an aromatic rhizome.

• **USES** The rhizome has a spicy, gingerlike flavor used in Southeast Asian soups and curries. The young shoots and flowers are eaten raw, and the flowers can be boiled or pickled. In Asia, the fresh rhizome is used to treat bronchitis, measles, gastritis, cholera, and scaly skin diseases and is used in a snuff for colds. The seed is given for digestive problems. The rhizome yields an essential oil, *essence d'Amali*, used in perfumes.

• **REMARK** Lesser Galangal (*Alpinia officinarum)* rhizome flavors tea, curries, pickles, and *Chartreuse* and *Nastoika* liqueurs. It treats indigestion and ulcers.

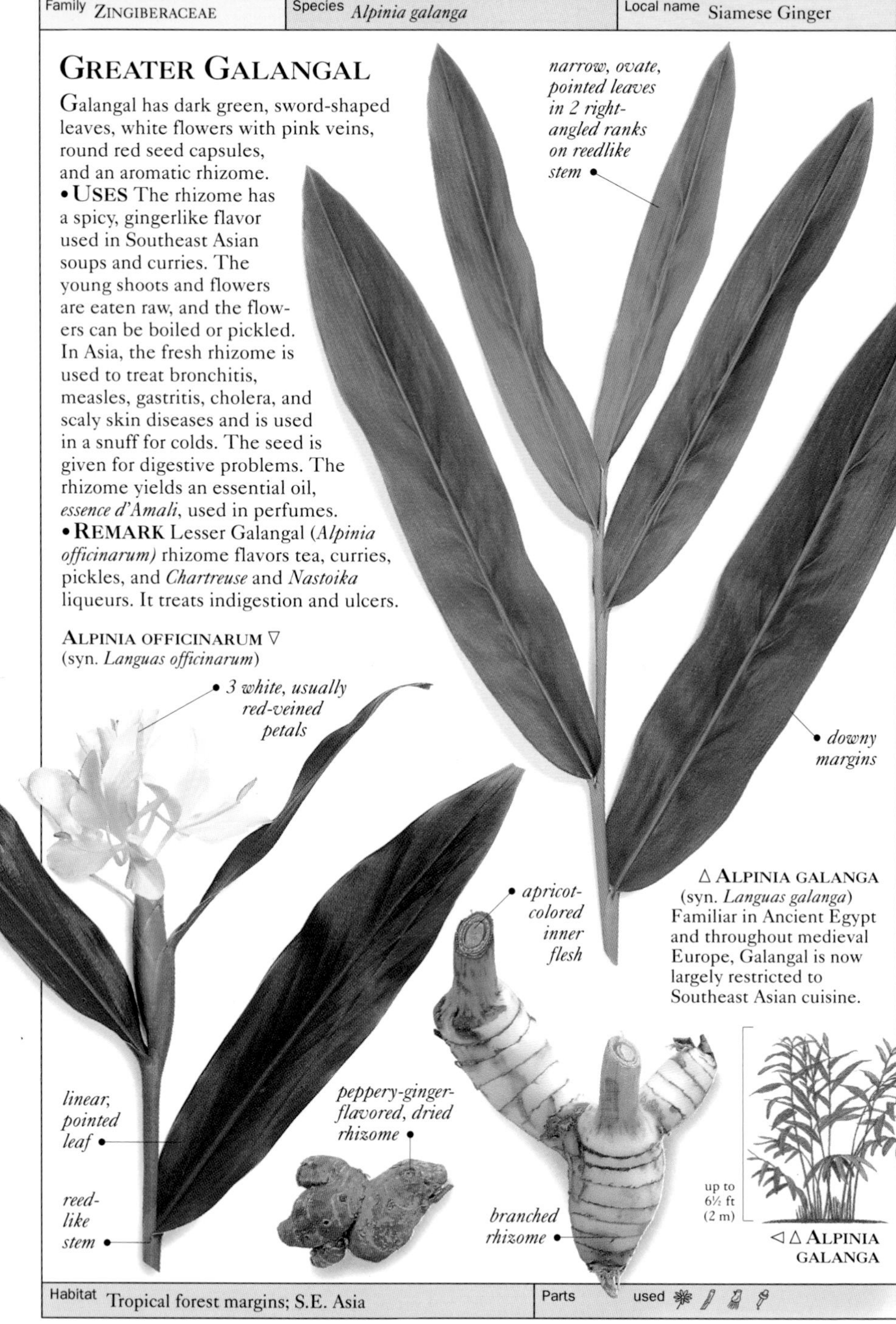
narrow, ovate, pointed leaves in 2 right-angled ranks on reedlike stem
downy margins
3 white, usually red-veined petals
apricot-colored inner flesh
linear, pointed leaf
reed-like stem
peppery-ginger-flavored, dried rhizome
branched rhizome
up to 6½ ft (2 m)

ALPINIA OFFICINARUM ▽
(syn. *Languas officinarum*)

△ ALPINIA GALANGA
(syn. *Languas galanga*)
Familiar in Ancient Egypt and throughout medieval Europe, Galangal is now largely restricted to Southeast Asian cuisine.

◁ △ ALPINIA GALANGA

Habitat Tropical forest margins; S.E. Asia	Parts used

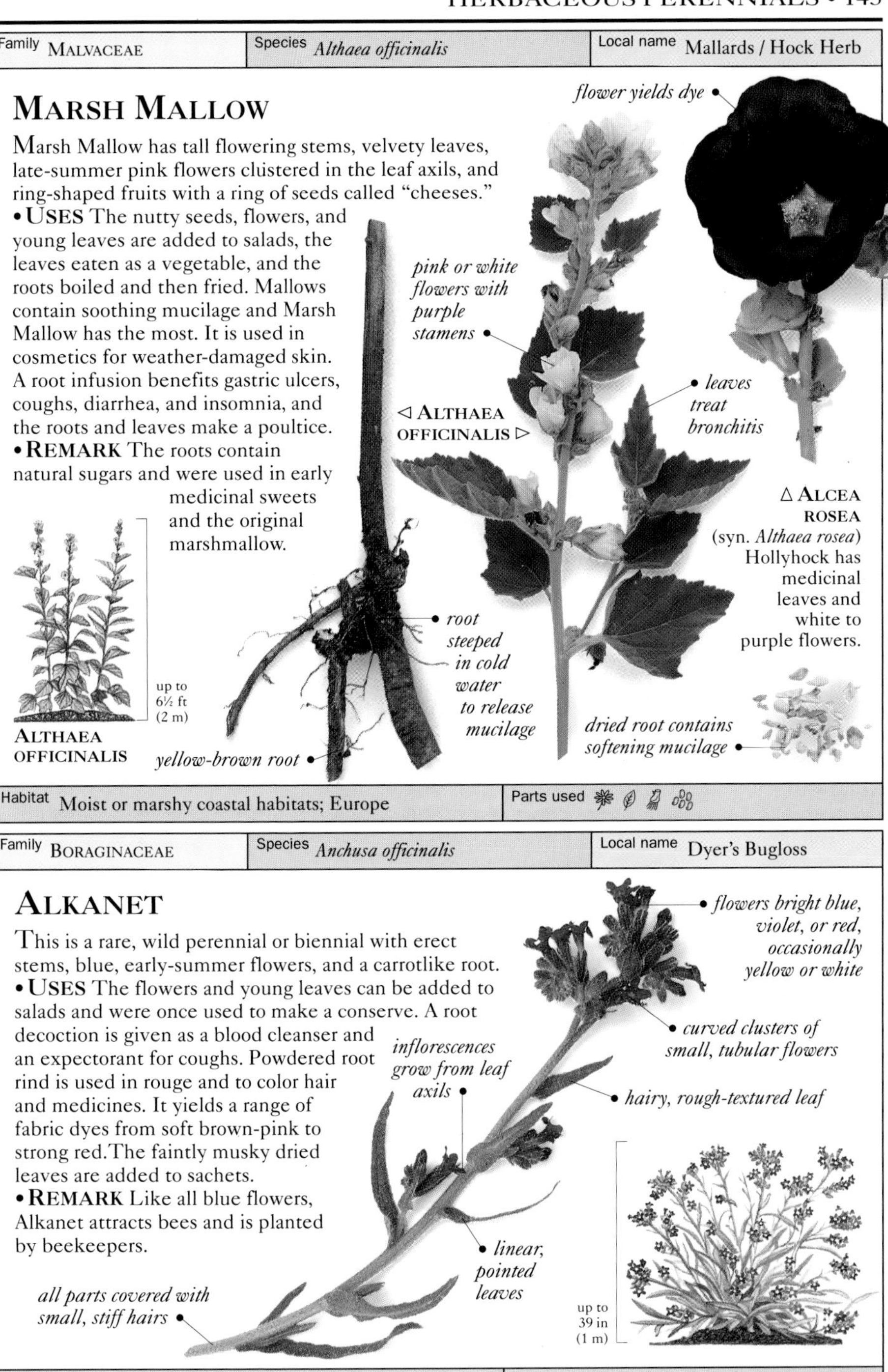
flower yields dye
pink or white flowers with purple stamens
◁ ALTHAEA OFFICINALIS ▷
leaves treat bronchitis
△ ALCEA ROSEA (syn. Althaea rosea) Hollyhock has medicinal leaves and white to purple flowers.
root steeped in cold water to release mucilage
dried root contains softening mucilage
yellow-brown root
up to 6½ ft (2 m)
ALTHAEA OFFICINALIS
flowers bright blue, violet, or red, occasionally yellow or white
curved clusters of small, tubular flowers
inflorescences grow from leaf axils
hairy, rough-textured leaf
linear, pointed leaves
all parts covered with small, stiff hairs
up to 39 in (1 m)

Family MALVACEAE	Species *Althaea officinalis*	Local name Mallards / Hock Herb

MARSH MALLOW

Marsh Mallow has tall flowering stems, velvety leaves, late-summer pink flowers clustered in the leaf axils, and ring-shaped fruits with a ring of seeds called "cheeses."

• **USES** The nutty seeds, flowers, and young leaves are added to salads, the leaves eaten as a vegetable, and the roots boiled and then fried. Mallows contain soothing mucilage and Marsh Mallow has the most. It is used in cosmetics for weather-damaged skin. A root infusion benefits gastric ulcers, coughs, diarrhea, and insomnia, and the roots and leaves make a poultice.

• **REMARK** The roots contain natural sugars and were used in early medicinal sweets and the original marshmallow.

Habitat Moist or marshy coastal habitats; Europe	Parts used

Family BORAGINACEAE	Species *Anchusa officinalis*	Local name Dyer's Bugloss

ALKANET

This is a rare, wild perennial or biennial with erect stems, blue, early-summer flowers, and a carrotlike root.

• **USES** The flowers and young leaves can be added to salads and were once used to make a conserve. A root decoction is given as a blood cleanser and an expectorant for coughs. Powdered root rind is used in rouge and to color hair and medicines. It yields a range of fabric dyes from soft brown-pink to strong red.The faintly musky dried leaves are added to sachets.

• **REMARK** Like all blue flowers, Alkanet attracts bees and is planted by beekeepers.

Habitat Wasteland, rocky habitats; Europe, Asia	Parts used

Family BROMELIACEAE	Species *Ananas comosus*	Local name Annasi / Anay'nus

PINEAPPLE

Unlike tree-perching bromeliads, Pineapple is planted in the ground. It has a dense rosette of leaves, allowing it to make maximum use of rainwater, and a conical spike of violet-red flowers with yellow bracts.

• **USES** A popular tropical fruit, it has a high sugar content and is rich in vitamins A, B, and C. The flesh is eaten raw, cooked, battered, jellied, candied, juiced, or made into alcohol, including *Vin d'Ananas*. New shoots are added to curries, waste is made into vinegar or fed to livestock, and the flesh is used in facial masks as the enzymes digest dead skin. The fruit helps menstrual, urinary, and digestive problems, beri-beri, worms, and nervous exhaustion. Plant enzymes reduce swelling, intensify antibiotics, and break down the fibrin protein that causes heart attacks and strokes.

• **REMARK** In Sri Lanka, the fruit is eaten by smokers to clear the lungs. It can aggravate skin rashes.

up to 39 in (1 m)
large, juicy, seedless fruit
compound fruit made up of more than 100 fused, small fruitlets
terminal crown, or coma, of 20–30 leaves
spiny margins
long, channeled leaf
leaf of some varieties is source of piña fiber for embroidery thread
spiny fruit skin is infused in water for a refreshing drink in Haiti
the coma can be rooted for Pineapple propagation
paler reverse side
long fruit not fully ripe
rigid, linear leaf
short-stalked fruit stem
warm leaf infusion given for spider bites

Habitat Lowland tropics; Brazil	Parts used

Family COMPOSITAE	Species *Anthemis tinctoria*	Yellow Chamomile

DYER'S CHAMOMILE

Dyer's Chamomile is a short-lived, upright perennial. It has segmented foliage which contrasts attractively with the abundant, long-stemmed, daisylike, golden summer flowers and small, ribbed fruits.

• **USES** With different fixatives the flowers yield a range of fabric dyes from bright yellow to khaki and olive. In North America the seed oil was used to treat earache and deafness. The plant has similar antispasmodic and menstrual-stimulating properties to Mayweed (*Anthemis cotula*). The flowers are popularly used preserved with glycerine.

• **REMARK** The green parts of Mayweed have been used to prevent spasms and promote menstrual flow. Mayweed contains a potent allergen which may account for mistaken reports of allergy to Chamomile (*Chamaemelum nobile*), which it closely resembles.

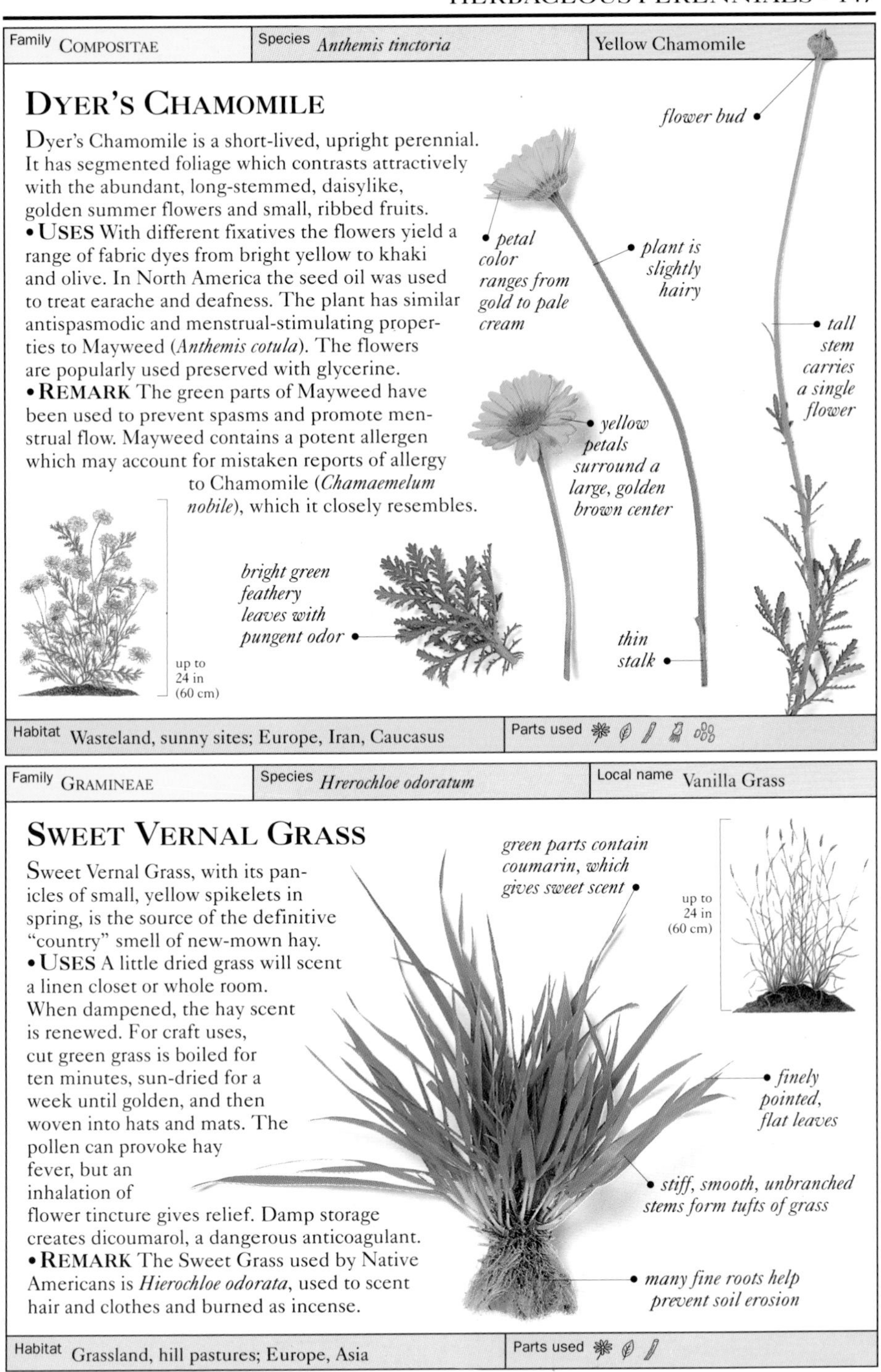
flower bud
petal color ranges from gold to pale cream
plant is slightly hairy
tall stem carries a single flower
yellow petals surround a large, golden brown center
bright green feathery leaves with pungent odor
thin stalk
up to 24 in (60 cm)
green parts contain coumarin, which gives sweet scent
up to 24 in (60 cm)
finely pointed, flat leaves
stiff, smooth, unbranched stems form tufts of grass
many fine roots help prevent soil erosion

Habitat Wasteland, sunny sites; Europe, Iran, Caucasus	Parts used

Family GRAMINEAE	Species *Hrerochloe odoratum*	Local name Vanilla Grass

SWEET VERNAL GRASS

Sweet Vernal Grass, with its panicles of small, yellow spikelets in spring, is the source of the definitive "country" smell of new-mown hay.

• **USES** A little dried grass will scent a linen closet or whole room. When dampened, the hay scent is renewed. For craft uses, cut green grass is boiled for ten minutes, sun-dried for a week until golden, and then woven into hats and mats. The pollen can provoke hay fever, but an inhalation of flower tincture gives relief. Damp storage creates dicoumarol, a dangerous anticoagulant.

• **REMARK** The Sweet Grass used by Native Americans is *Hierochloe odorata*, used to scent hair and clothes and burned as incense.

Habitat Grassland, hill pastures; Europe, Asia	Parts used

Family RANUNCULACEAE	Species *Aquilegia vulgaris*	Local name Granny's Bonnet

COLUMBINE

Columbine hybridizes freely with other *Aquilegias*. It has slender, erect stems, leaflets, and an erect rootstock. The flowers are usually blue or purple and may be fragrant.

• **USES** The root has been used under medical supervision for the external treatment of common skin diseases. The flowers and leaves are now considered too poisonous to use as diuretics. Columbine is employed in homeopathy to treat problems of the nervous system.

• **REMARK** The seeds contain poisonous hydrocyanic acid, which can be fatal for children.

nodding, 5-petaled flower with gold stamens
round-toothed leaflet
up to 28 in (70 cm)
segmented leaf
medicinal roots
short, orange-brown rootstock
large leaf, pungent when bruised
wavy toothed margin
root releases oil when grated
root contains calcium, sodium, magnesium, and vitamins B and C
long, ridged stalk
outer part of root core is most pungent
up to 39 in (1 m)
pungent root increases disease resistance of potatoes growing nearby
cream flesh

Habitat Light woods, wet areas; W., C., & S. Europe	Parts used

Family CRUCIFERAE	Species *Armoracia rusticana*	Local name Red Cole

HORSERADISH

Horseradish (syn. *Cochlearia armoracia*) has long, fleshy roots, large rough leaves, and a panicle of small white four-petaled flowers.

• **USES** Young leaves are added to salads. The freshly grated root is a condiment served in a cream sauce. A pungent oil from the grated root clears sinuses. The root has antibiotic properties, stimulates digestion and circulation, treats inflamed gums, and eliminates mucus and waste fluids. It is given for lung and urinary infections and used in a poultice for rheumatism and bronchitis. Dried leaves yield a yellow dye.

Habitat Fertile fields, waste areas near streams; S.E. Europe	Parts used

Family COMPOSITAE	Species *Arnica montana*	Local name Leopard's Bane

ARNICA

Arnica has creeping rhizomes and erect stems with yellow, daisylike flowers in summer.

• **USES** The toxic flowers contain compounds that stimulate circulation and reduce inflammation. An ointment or tincture is applied externally (never on broken skin) for bruises, sprains, and muscular and rheumatic pain. Recent research shows that Arnica stimulates the immune system.

• **REMARK** It is toxic; use only for medical and homeopathic application, for epilepsy, wounds, and seasickness.

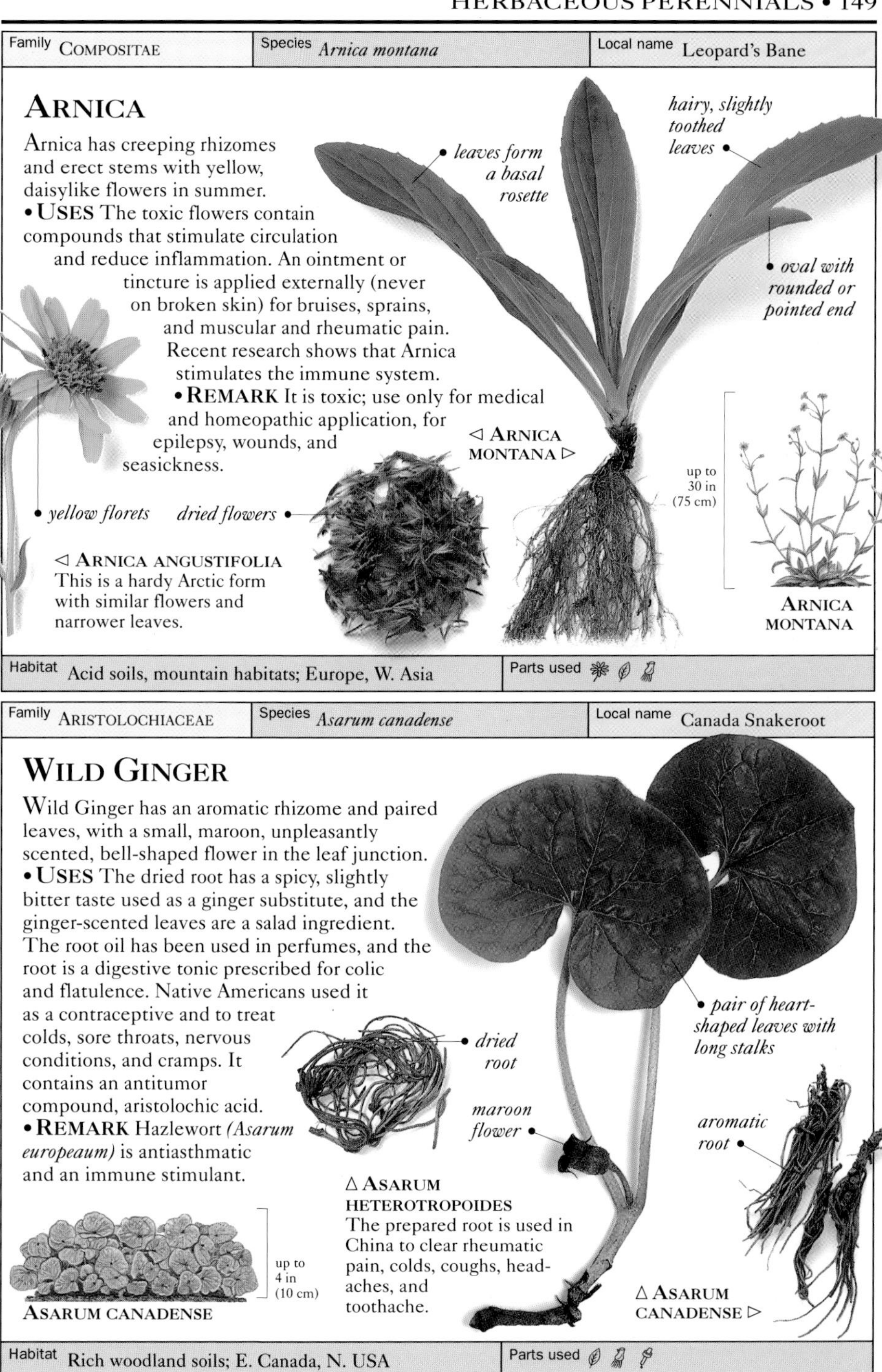

leaves form a basal rosette
hairy, slightly toothed leaves
oval with rounded or pointed end
yellow florets
dried flowers
up to 30 in (75 cm)
pair of heart-shaped leaves with long stalks
dried root
maroon flower
aromatic root
up to 4 in (10 cm)

◁ ARNICA MONTANA ▷

ARNICA MONTANA

◁ ARNICA ANGUSTIFOLIA This is a hardy Arctic form with similar flowers and narrower leaves.

Habitat Acid soils, mountain habitats; Europe, W. Asia	Parts used

Family ARISTOLOCHIACEAE	Species *Asarum canadense*	Local name Canada Snakeroot

WILD GINGER

Wild Ginger has an aromatic rhizome and paired leaves, with a small, maroon, unpleasantly scented, bell-shaped flower in the leaf junction.

• **USES** The dried root has a spicy, slightly bitter taste used as a ginger substitute, and the ginger-scented leaves are a salad ingredient. The root oil has been used in perfumes, and the root is a digestive tonic prescribed for colic and flatulence. Native Americans used it as a contraceptive and to treat colds, sore throats, nervous conditions, and cramps. It contains an antitumor compound, aristolochic acid.

• **REMARK** Hazlewort *(Asarum europeaum)* is antiasthmatic and an immune stimulant.

△ ASARUM HETEROTROPOIDES The prepared root is used in China to clear rheumatic pain, colds, coughs, headaches, and toothache.

ASARUM CANADENSE

△ ASARUM CANADENSE ▷

Habitat Rich woodland soils; E. Canada, N. USA	Parts used

Family COMPOSITAE	Species *Artemisia abrotanum*	Local name Lad's Love

SOUTHERNWOOD

This strongly aromatic, shrubby perennial has semievergreen, threadlike leaves and small, dense heads of yellow florets appearing in summer.

• **USES** The foliage has a sweet, strong fragrance with a hint of lemon, used in aromatic vinegars, floral waters, and potpourri. It is rubbed on the skin to deter flies and placed among clothes to repel moths. The leaf tea is a tonic and is given to children to dispel parasitic worms. The leaf is added to baths and poultices to treat skin conditions and put into herb pillows to ease insomnia.

• **REMARK** Several *Artemisias* are planted for their silver foliage and for herb posies.

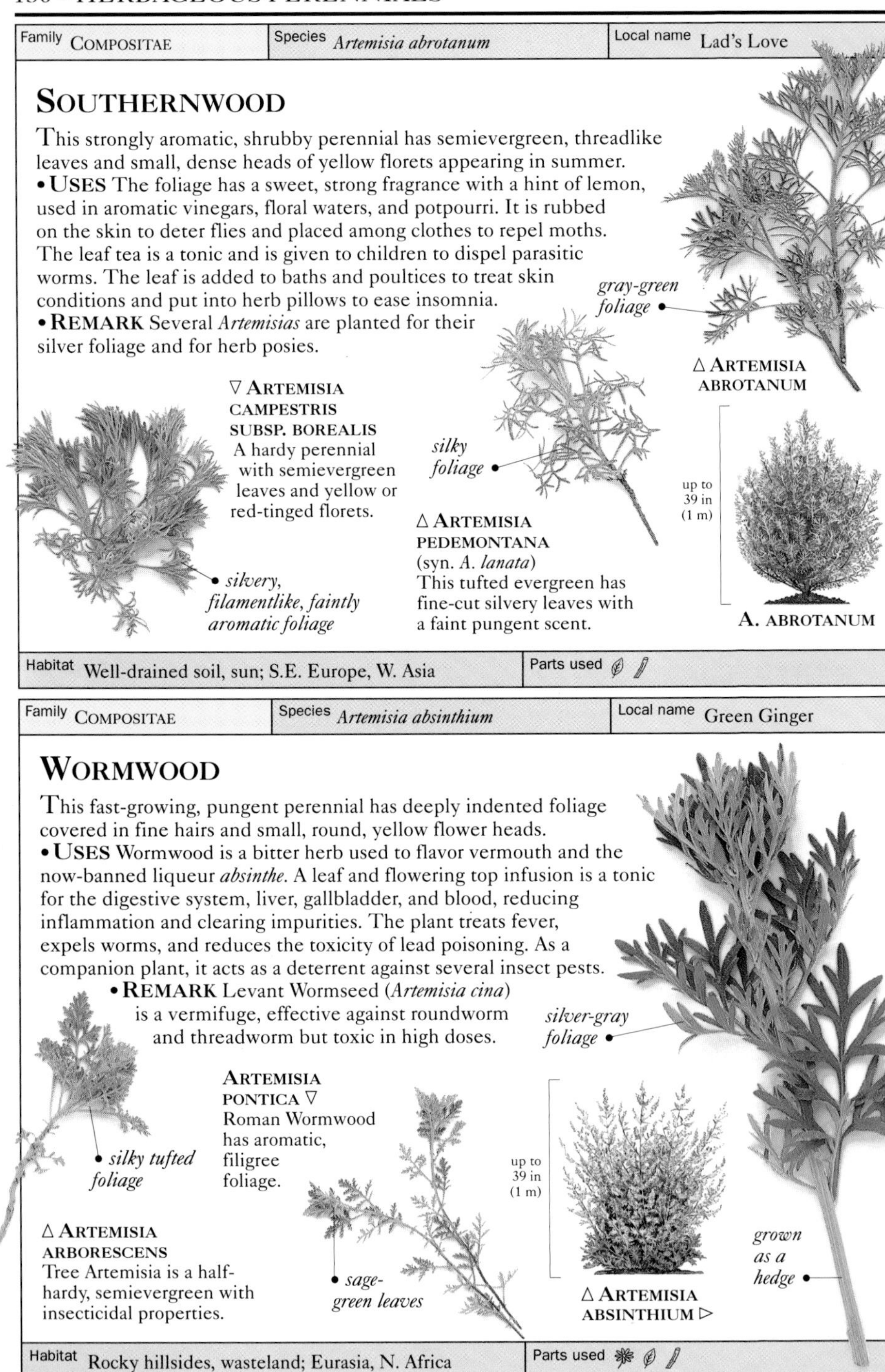

gray-green foliage
silky foliage
silvery, filamentlike, faintly aromatic foliage
up to 39 in (1 m)
silky tufted foliage
silver-gray foliage
up to 39 in (1 m)
sage-green leaves
grown as a hedge

△ ARTEMISIA ABROTANUM

▽ ARTEMISIA CAMPESTRIS SUBSP. BOREALIS
A hardy perennial with semievergreen leaves and yellow or red-tinged florets.

△ ARTEMISIA PEDEMONTANA (syn. *A. lanata*)
This tufted evergreen has fine-cut silvery leaves with a faint pungent scent.

A. ABROTANUM

Habitat Well-drained soil, sun; S.E. Europe, W. Asia	Parts used

Family COMPOSITAE	Species *Artemisia absinthium*	Local name Green Ginger

WORMWOOD

This fast-growing, pungent perennial has deeply indented foliage covered in fine hairs and small, round, yellow flower heads.

• **USES** Wormwood is a bitter herb used to flavor vermouth and the now-banned liqueur *absinthe*. A leaf and flowering top infusion is a tonic for the digestive system, liver, gallbladder, and blood, reducing inflammation and clearing impurities. The plant treats fever, expels worms, and reduces the toxicity of lead poisoning. As a companion plant, it acts as a deterrent against several insect pests.

• **REMARK** Levant Wormseed (*Artemisia cina*) is a vermifuge, effective against roundworm and threadworm but toxic in high doses.

ARTEMISIA PONTICA ▽
Roman Wormwood has aromatic, filigree foliage.

△ ARTEMISIA ARBORESCENS
Tree Artemisia is a half-hardy, semievergreen with insecticidal properties.

△ ARTEMISIA ABSINTHIUM ▷

Habitat Rocky hillsides, wasteland; Eurasia, N. Africa	Parts used

Family COMPOSITAE	Species *Artemisia dracunculus*	Local name Estragon

FRENCH TARRAGON

This many-branched perennial has greenish flowers and narrow leaves whose bittersweet, peppery taste has anise undertones. • **USES** Essential to French cuisine, it flavors savory foods and is part of the *fines herbes* mix. The leaves contain iodine, mineral salts, and vitamins A and C. Leaf tea stimulates the appetite, is a digestive, and a general tonic. Chewing leaves numbs the taste buds before taking bitter medicine. The root reduces toothache. • **REMARK** French and Russian Tarragons both originated in Russia, but Russian Tarragon is hardier and seeds more readily.

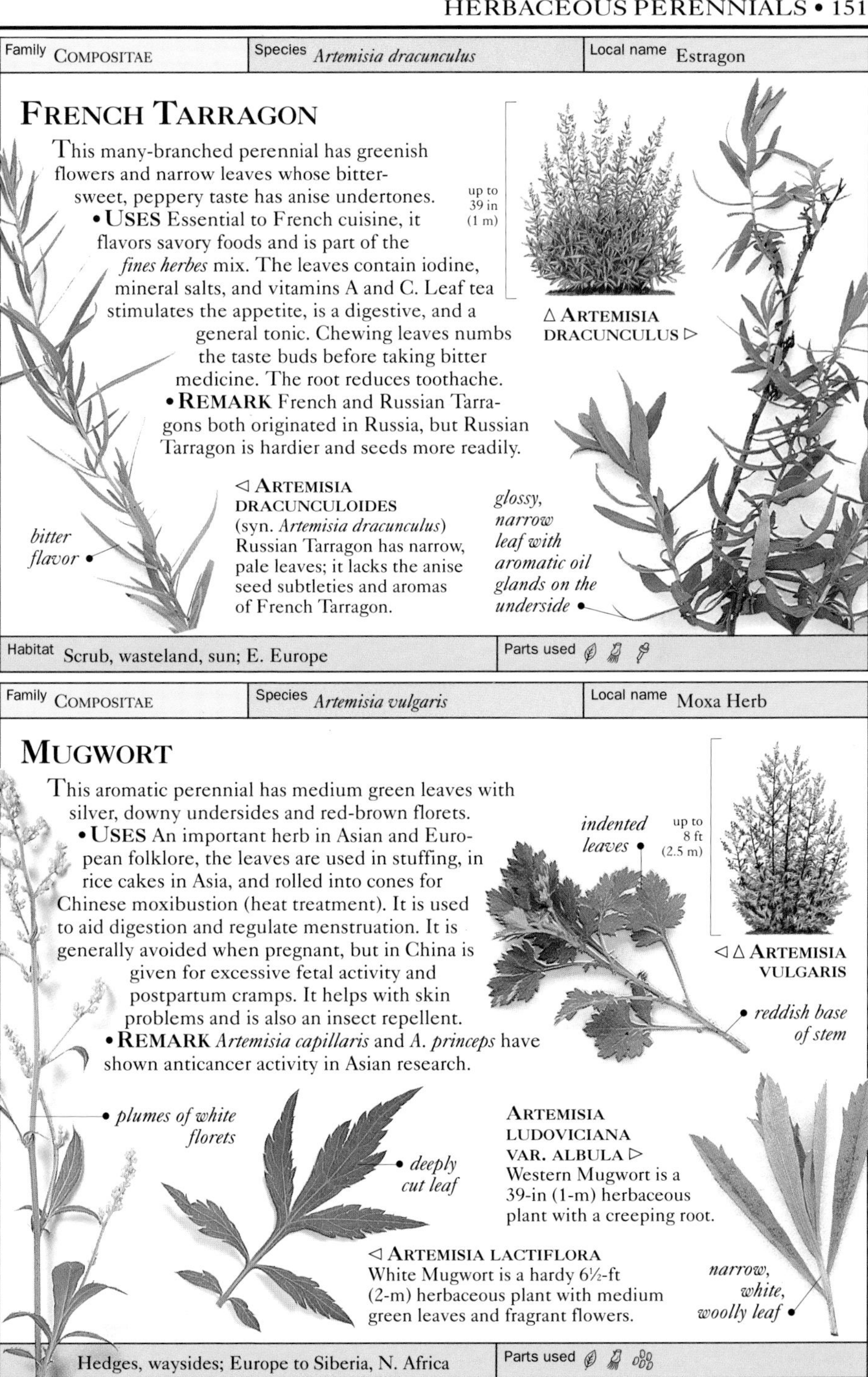
up to
39 in
(1 m)
bitter
flavor
glossy,
narrow
leaf with
aromatic oil
glands on the
underside
indented
leaves
up to
8 ft
(2.5 m)
reddish base
of stem
plumes of white
florets
deeply
cut leaf
narrow,
white,
woolly leaf

△ ARTEMISIA DRACUNCULUS ▷

◁ ARTEMISIA DRACUNCULOIDES (syn. *Artemisia dracunculus*) Russian Tarragon has narrow, pale leaves; it lacks the anise seed subtleties and aromas of French Tarragon.

Habitat Scrub, wasteland, sun; E. Europe	Parts used

Family COMPOSITAE	Species *Artemisia vulgaris*	Local name Moxa Herb

MUGWORT

This aromatic perennial has medium green leaves with silver, downy undersides and red-brown florets. • **USES** An important herb in Asian and European folklore, the leaves are used in stuffing, in rice cakes in Asia, and rolled into cones for Chinese moxibustion (heat treatment). It is used to aid digestion and regulate menstruation. It is generally avoided when pregnant, but in China is given for excessive fetal activity and postpartum cramps. It helps with skin problems and is also an insect repellent. • **REMARK** *Artemisia capillaris* and *A. princeps* have shown anticancer activity in Asian research.

◁ △ ARTEMISIA VULGARIS

ARTEMISIA LUDOVICIANA VAR. ALBULA ▷ Western Mugwort is a 39-in (1-m) herbaceous plant with a creeping root.

◁ ARTEMISIA LACTIFLORA White Mugwort is a hardy 6½-ft (2-m) herbaceous plant with medium green leaves and fragrant flowers.

Hedges, waysides; Europe to Siberia, N. Africa	Parts used

Family ASCLEPIADACEAE	Species *Asclepias tuberosa*	Local name Butterfly Weed

PLEURISY ROOT

Pleurisy Root has robust stems with narrow leaves and terminal cymes of nectar-rich orange flowers. Unlike other milkweeds, which have white sap, it has clear or green juice.

• USES Tender shoots, roots, and young seed pods are cooked as vegetables, and the flowers are a crude sweetener. The root increases bronchial dilation and lymphatic drainage and is a specific treatment for pleurisy and bronchitis. It is given for some uterine problems, and tests have confirmed estrogenic activity. Large doses and the fresh leaf tea cause vomiting. The sap contains the enzyme asclepain which helps to remove warts. *Asclepias syraca* root has been used to cause temporary sterility. *A. speciosa* helps chronically weak kidneys. All milkweeds are potentially dangerous.

• REMARK Many Native Americans used Pleurisy Root; it was one of the most important medicines of the Menomini tribe.

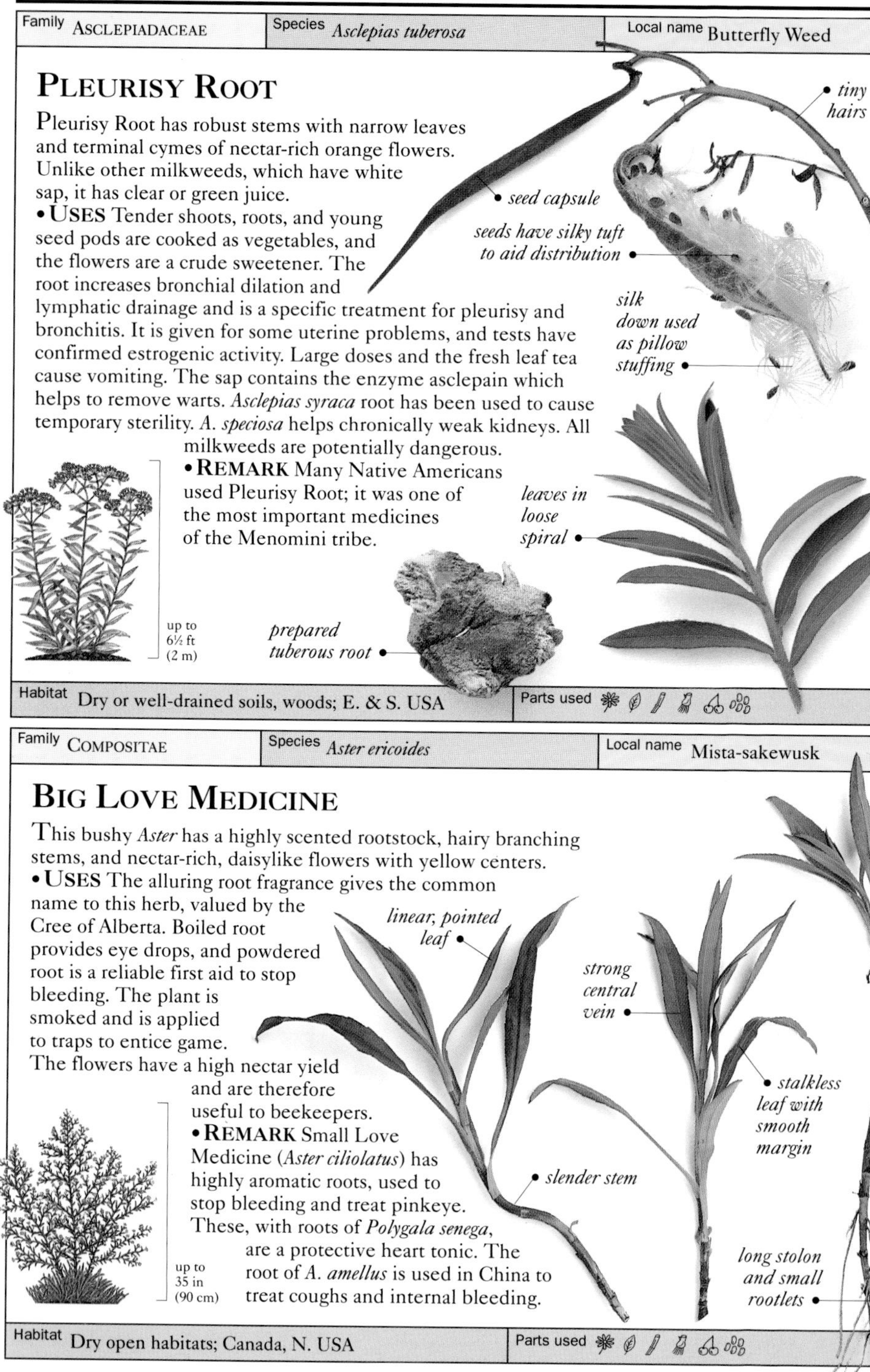

tiny hairs
seed capsule
seeds have silky tuft to aid distribution
silk down used as pillow stuffing
leaves in loose spiral
up to 6½ ft (2 m)
prepared tuberous root
linear, pointed leaf
strong central vein
stalkless leaf with smooth margin
slender stem
up to 35 in (90 cm)
long stolon and small rootlets

Habitat Dry or well-drained soils, woods; E. & S. USA | Parts used

Family COMPOSITAE	Species *Aster ericoides*	Local name Mista-sakewusk

BIG LOVE MEDICINE

This bushy *Aster* has a highly scented rootstock, hairy branching stems, and nectar-rich, daisylike flowers with yellow centers.

• USES The alluring root fragrance gives the common name to this herb, valued by the Cree of Alberta. Boiled root provides eye drops, and powdered root is a reliable first aid to stop bleeding. The plant is smoked and is applied to traps to entice game. The flowers have a high nectar yield and are therefore useful to beekeepers.

• REMARK Small Love Medicine (*Aster ciliolatus*) has highly aromatic roots, used to stop bleeding and treat pinkeye. These, with roots of *Polygala senega*, are a protective heart tonic. The root of *A. amellus* is used in China to treat coughs and internal bleeding.

Habitat Dry open habitats; Canada, N. USA | Parts used

Family SOLANACEAE	Species *Atropa belladonna*	Local name Belladonna

DEADLY NIGHTSHADE

This poisonous, short-lived perennial has red stem sap and solitary, tubular, purple-brown to green flowers from midsummer to early autumn. These are followed by glossy black berries.

• **USES** The leaves and root are narcotic and sedative. An extract dilates the eye pupils, an effect once thought by Italian women to look seductive, but now used for surgical examination. The leaves and root first stimulate and then depress the central nervous system. They are used as an antispasmodic for respiratory problems and for rheumatic and muscular pain, and as a stomach sedative. They reduce nasal secretions.

• **REMARK** All parts are very poisonous and should be used only under medical supervision.

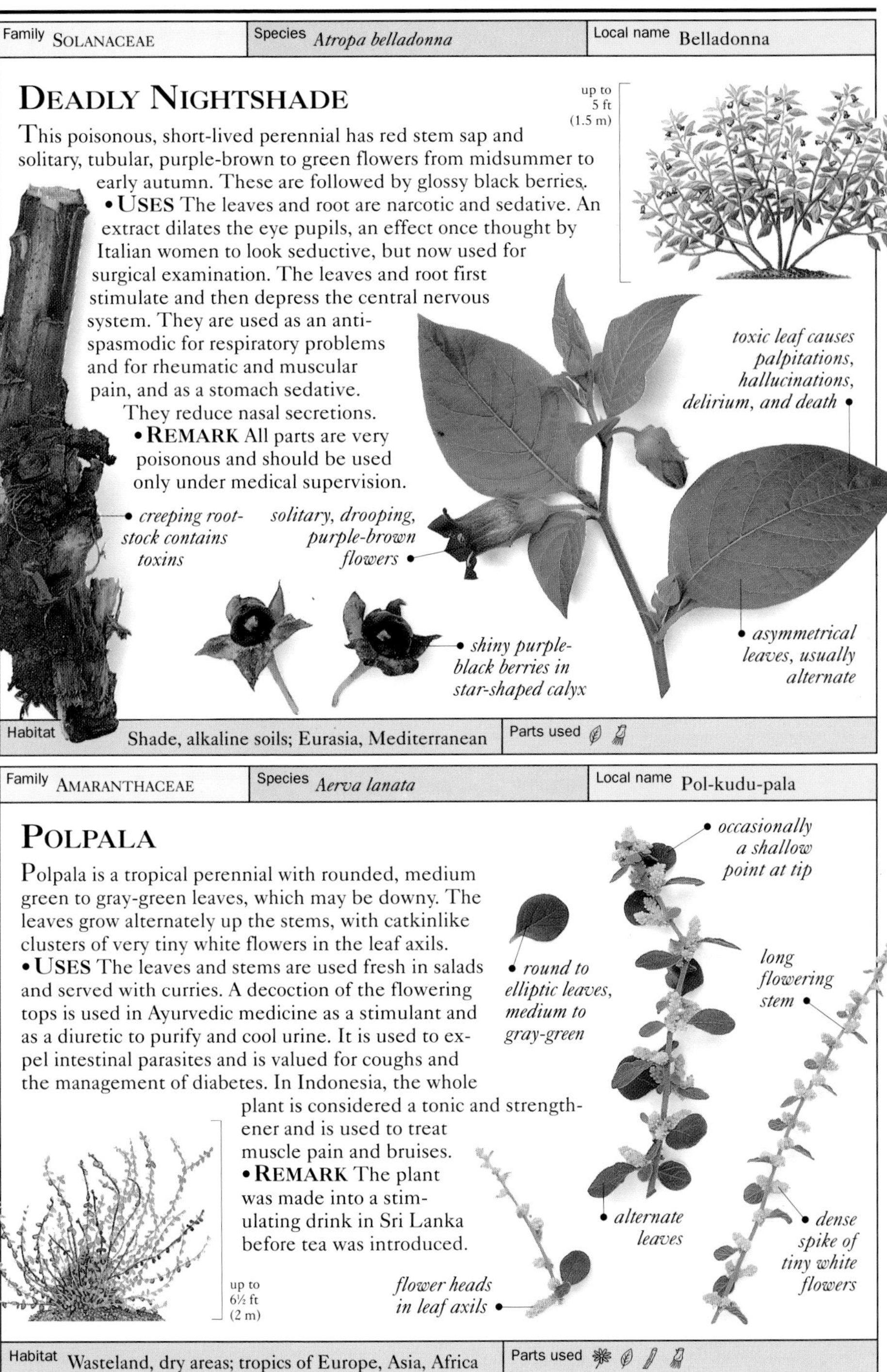
up to 5 ft (1.5 m)
toxic leaf causes palpitations, hallucinations, delirium, and death
creeping rootstock contains toxins
solitary, drooping, purple-brown flowers
shiny purple-black berries in star-shaped calyx
asymmetrical leaves, usually alternate
round to elliptic leaves, medium to gray-green
occasionally a shallow point at tip
long flowering stem
alternate leaves
dense spike of tiny white flowers
flower heads in leaf axils
up to 6½ ft (2 m)

Habitat Shade, alkaline soils; Eurasia, Mediterranean	Parts used

Family AMARANTHACEAE	Species *Aerva lanata*	Local name Pol-kudu-pala

POLPALA

Polpala is a tropical perennial with rounded, medium green to gray-green leaves, which may be downy. The leaves grow alternately up the stems, with catkinlike clusters of very tiny white flowers in the leaf axils.

• **USES** The leaves and stems are used fresh in salads and served with curries. A decoction of the flowering tops is used in Ayurvedic medicine as a stimulant and as a diuretic to purify and cool urine. It is used to expel intestinal parasites and is valued for coughs and the management of diabetes. In Indonesia, the whole plant is considered a tonic and strengthener and is used to treat muscle pain and bruises.

• **REMARK** The plant was made into a stimulating drink in Sri Lanka before tea was introduced.

Habitat Wasteland, dry areas; tropics of Europe, Asia, Africa	Parts used

Family SCROPHULARIACEAE	Species *Bacopa monnieri*	Local name Water Hyssop

BACOPA

This perennial forms dense mats of foliage on waterside mud and bears axial clusters of small, bell-shaped, white or pale blue flowers in summer.

• **USES** The succulent leaves and stems of Bacopa have a slightly biting taste, enjoyed as a salad herb, and taken to improve the memory. Hindus use an infusion as a nerve tonic, particularly for epilepsy. In Indonesia, Bacopa is taken for the tropical disease filariasis. In China, the plant is credited with warming the kidneys and stimulating yang energy. It is prescribed for impotence, premature ejaculation, kidney-related backache, uterine fertility problems, irregular menstruation, and rheumatism.

• **REMARK** New research has shown that Bacopa has great potential as a nourishing brain tonic.

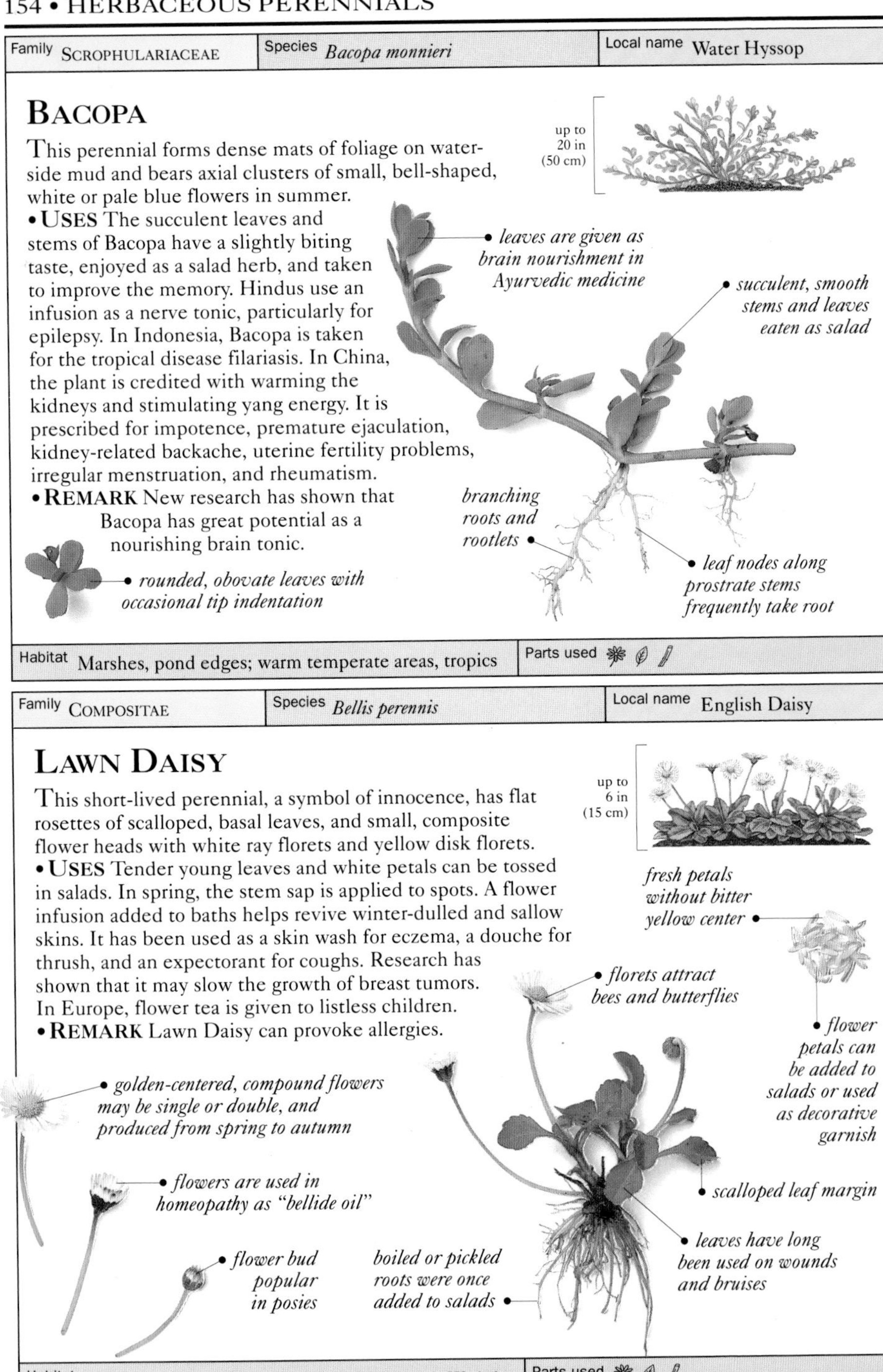

up to 20 in (50 cm)
leaves are given as brain nourishment in Ayurvedic medicine
succulent, smooth stems and leaves eaten as salad
branching roots and rootlets
leaf nodes along prostrate stems frequently take root
rounded, obovate leaves with occasional tip indentation
up to 6 in (15 cm)
fresh petals without bitter yellow center
florets attract bees and butterflies
flower petals can be added to salads or used as decorative garnish
golden-centered, compound flowers may be single or double, and produced from spring to autumn
flowers are used in homeopathy as "bellide oil"
scalloped leaf margin
leaves have long been used on wounds and bruises
flower bud popular in posies
boiled or pickled roots were once added to salads

Habitat Marshes, pond edges; warm temperate areas, tropics	Parts used

Family COMPOSITAE	Species *Bellis perennis*	Local name English Daisy

LAWN DAISY

This short-lived perennial, a symbol of innocence, has flat rosettes of scalloped, basal leaves, and small, composite flower heads with white ray florets and yellow disk florets.

• **USES** Tender young leaves and white petals can be tossed in salads. In spring, the stem sap is applied to spots. A flower infusion added to baths helps revive winter-dulled and sallow skins. It has been used as a skin wash for eczema, a douche for thrush, and an expectorant for coughs. Research has shown that it may slow the growth of breast tumors. In Europe, flower tea is given to listless children.

• **REMARK** Lawn Daisy can provoke allergies.

Habitat Grassy areas, meadows; S., W., & C. Europe, W. Asia	Parts used

Family ZINGIBERACEAE	Species *Boesenbergia rotunda*	Local name Kachai

KRA CHAAI

Boesenbergia rotunda (syn. *Kaempferia pandurata*) has fingerlike rhizomes, shoots with up to four, short-stemmed leaves, and a spike of white or pink flowers with a pink-spotted white lip.

• **USES** The aromatic roots are widely cultivated in Thailand and Indonesia for the spicy flavor they give to savory dishes, including vegetable soups, fish dishes, and curries. They are also used to reduce flatulence and to treat diarrhea, dysentery, and worms.

• **REMARK** In Thailand, the leaves are regarded as an antidote to certain poisons.

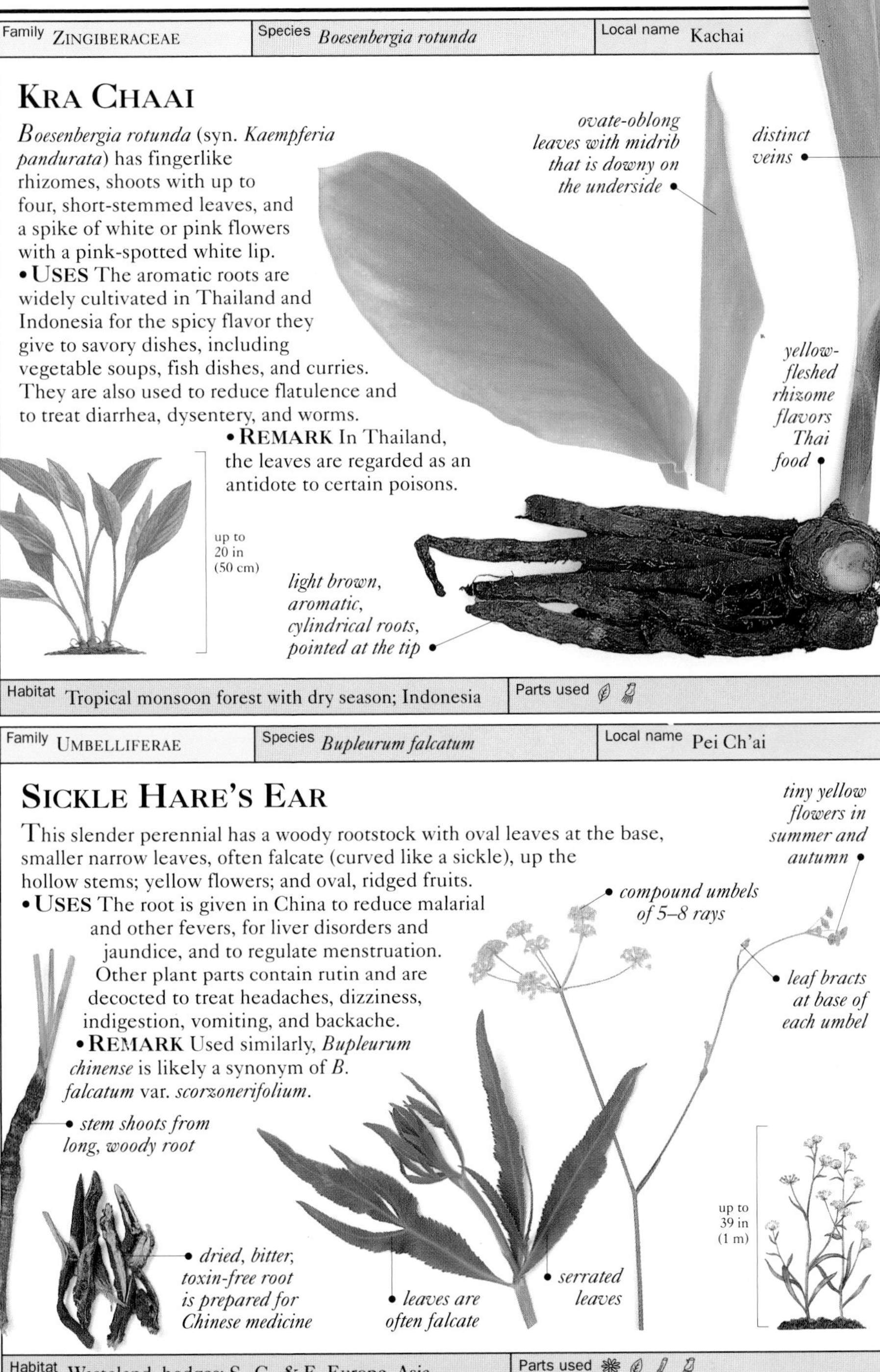
ovate-oblong leaves with midrib that is downy on the underside
distinct veins
yellow-fleshed rhizome flavors Thai food
up to 20 in (50 cm)
light brown, aromatic, cylindrical roots, pointed at the tip
tiny yellow flowers in summer and autumn
compound umbels of 5–8 rays
leaf bracts at base of each umbel
stem shoots from long, woody root
dried, bitter, toxin-free root is prepared for Chinese medicine
leaves are often falcate
serrated leaves
up to 39 in (1 m)

Habitat Tropical monsoon forest with dry season; Indonesia	Parts used

Family UMBELLIFERAE	Species *Bupleurum falcatum*	Local name Pei Ch'ai

SICKLE HARE'S EAR

This slender perennial has a woody rootstock with oval leaves at the base, smaller narrow leaves, often falcate (curved like a sickle), up the hollow stems; yellow flowers; and oval, ridged fruits.

• **USES** The root is given in China to reduce malarial and other fevers, for liver disorders and jaundice, and to regulate menstruation. Other plant parts contain rutin and are decocted to treat headaches, dizziness, indigestion, vomiting, and backache.

• **REMARK** Used similarly, *Bupleurum chinense* is likely a synonym of *B. falcatum* var. *scorzonerifolium*.

Habitat Wasteland, hedges; S., C., & E. Europe, Asia	Parts used

Family LABIATAE	Species *Calamintha grandiflora*	Local name Mountain Balm

LARGE-FLOWERED CALAMINT

This aromatic perennial has a thin, creeping rhizome, deep green, slightly hairy leaves with six teeth on each side, and a flowering spike bearing inflorescences of up to five tubular pink flowers in summer.

• **USES** Calamint contains camphorlike essential oils. A leaf infusion yields a peppermint flavor and is made into a syrup to ease coughs. Fresh leaves make a poultice for bruises. The tea is drunk for flatulent colic and as an invigorating tonic recommended by 17th-century English herbalist Nicholas Culpeper for "all afflictions of the brain."

• **REMARK** The leaves of *Calamintha sylvatica* and *C. nepeta* are used as an expectorant and diaphoretic to promote perspiration.

leaf with unusual brown fringe

pointed-toothed, dark green leaf

up to 24 in (60 cm)

◁ △ CALAMINTHA GRANDIFLORA

◁ ▽ CALAMINTHA SYLVATICA (syn. *C. ascendens*) Common Calamint has mint-scented leaves, and late-summer flowers.

◁ CALAMINTHA GRANDIFLORA 'VARIEGATA' Has dark green markings.

green-splashed gold leaves with 6 teeth on each side

oval, blunt-ended leaf

pink-spotted purple flower

Habitat Mountainous woods; S.E. Europe, Anatolia, N. Iran	Parts used

Family LILIACEAE	Species *Camassia quamash*	Local name Quamash

CAMAS

This bulbous, shade-tolerant perennial with grasslike leaf blades has showy blue flowering spikes in late spring.

• **USES** The bulb was an important Native American food source that caused intertribal war over possession of its habitat. Camas is high in sugar but low in starch. It is eaten raw or boiled or is slowly baked in special pits to enhance its sweetness. The baked bulbs thicken and flavor gravy; any surplus was sun-dried whole or mashed into cakes with berries for winter use. The water in which the bulbs were boiled provided a sweetish drink.

• **REMARK** The bulbs of Eastern Camas (*Camassia scilloides* syn. *C. esculenta*) can also be eaten. The cream-flowered Death Camas (*Zigadenus venenosus*) looks similar but is fatally poisonous.

tapered point

lance-shaped leaves emerge from the bulb

green, unripe seed capsule

dark green, grasslike blades

edible rounded bulb with black outer skin and pale flesh

bulbs should be picked when blue flowers appear

up to 32 in (80 cm)

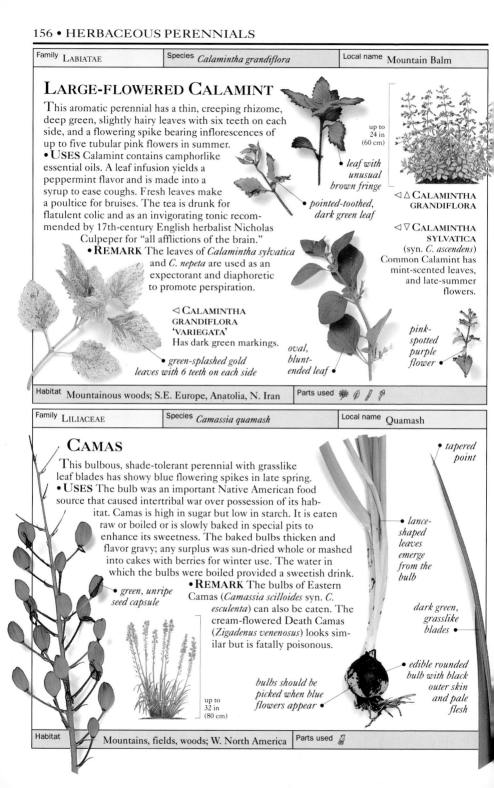

Habitat Mountains, fields, woods; W. North America	Parts used

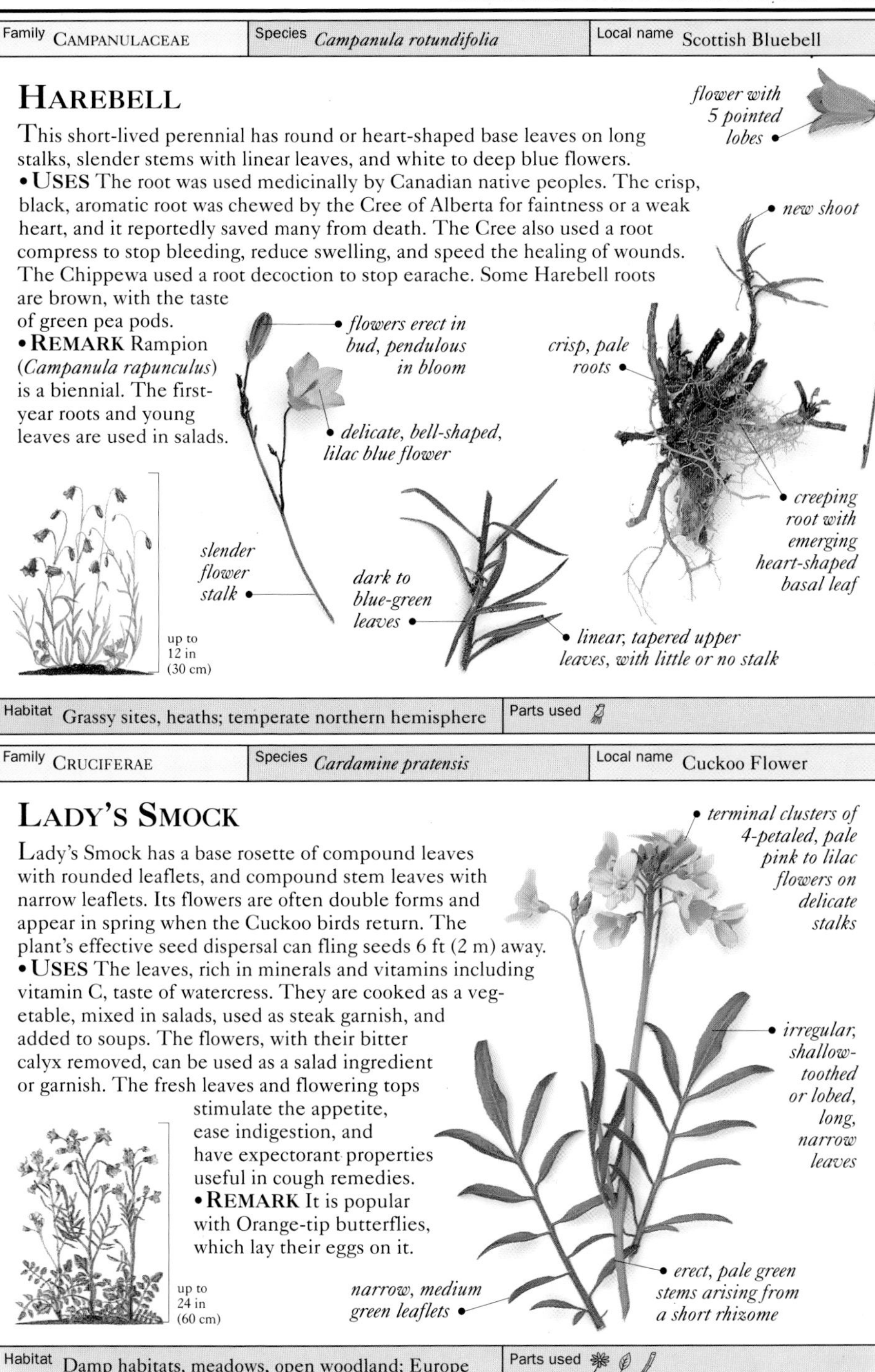
flower with 5 pointed lobes
new shoot
flowers erect in bud, pendulous in bloom
crisp, pale roots
delicate, bell-shaped, lilac blue flower
creeping root with emerging heart-shaped basal leaf
slender flower stalk
dark to blue-green leaves
linear, tapered upper leaves, with little or no stalk
up to 12 in (30 cm)
terminal clusters of 4-petaled, pale pink to lilac flowers on delicate stalks
irregular, shallow-toothed or lobed, long, narrow leaves
erect, pale green stems arising from a short rhizome
narrow, medium green leaflets
up to 24 in (60 cm)

Family CAMPANULACEAE	Species *Campanula rotundifolia*	Local name Scottish Bluebell

HAREBELL

This short-lived perennial has round or heart-shaped base leaves on long stalks, slender stems with linear leaves, and white to deep blue flowers.

• **USES** The root was used medicinally by Canadian native peoples. The crisp, black, aromatic root was chewed by the Cree of Alberta for faintness or a weak heart, and it reportedly saved many from death. The Cree also used a root compress to stop bleeding, reduce swelling, and speed the healing of wounds. The Chippewa used a root decoction to stop earache. Some Harebell roots are brown, with the taste of green pea pods.

• **REMARK** Rampion (*Campanula rapunculus*) is a biennial. The first-year roots and young leaves are used in salads.

Habitat Grassy sites, heaths; temperate northern hemisphere	Parts used

Family CRUCIFERAE	Species *Cardamine pratensis*	Local name Cuckoo Flower

LADY'S SMOCK

Lady's Smock has a base rosette of compound leaves with rounded leaflets, and compound stem leaves with narrow leaflets. Its flowers are often double forms and appear in spring when the Cuckoo birds return. The plant's effective seed dispersal can fling seeds 6 ft (2 m) away.

• **USES** The leaves, rich in minerals and vitamins including vitamin C, taste of watercress. They are cooked as a vegetable, mixed in salads, used as steak garnish, and added to soups. The flowers, with their bitter calyx removed, can be used as a salad ingredient or garnish. The fresh leaves and flowering tops stimulate the appetite, ease indigestion, and have expectorant properties useful in cough remedies.

• **REMARK** It is popular with Orange-tip butterflies, which lay their eggs on it.

Habitat Damp habitats, meadows, open woodland; Europe	Parts used

Family COMPOSITAE	Species *Carlina acaulis*	Dwarf Thistle

STEMLESS CARLINE THISTLE

This stemless thistle has a rosette of spiny leaves and a lilac-brown or white flower head surrounded by silvery, papery bracts.

• **USES** The flower receptacle is eaten like Artichoke, and the leaves used to curdle milk. The roots, macerated in wine, give a digestive stomach tonic, beneficial for eczema and skin rashes. A root infusion is diuretic, mildly laxative, an antiseptic gargle and wound wash, a liver tonic, and a worm expellant, and is used by vets to stimulate cattle appetites. A country humidity gauge, the flower bracts close as rain approaches.

• **REMARK** Named *Carlina* after the Emperor Charlemagne who dreamed of it as a plague cure, it became popular in poison and snake bite remedies and protective charms.

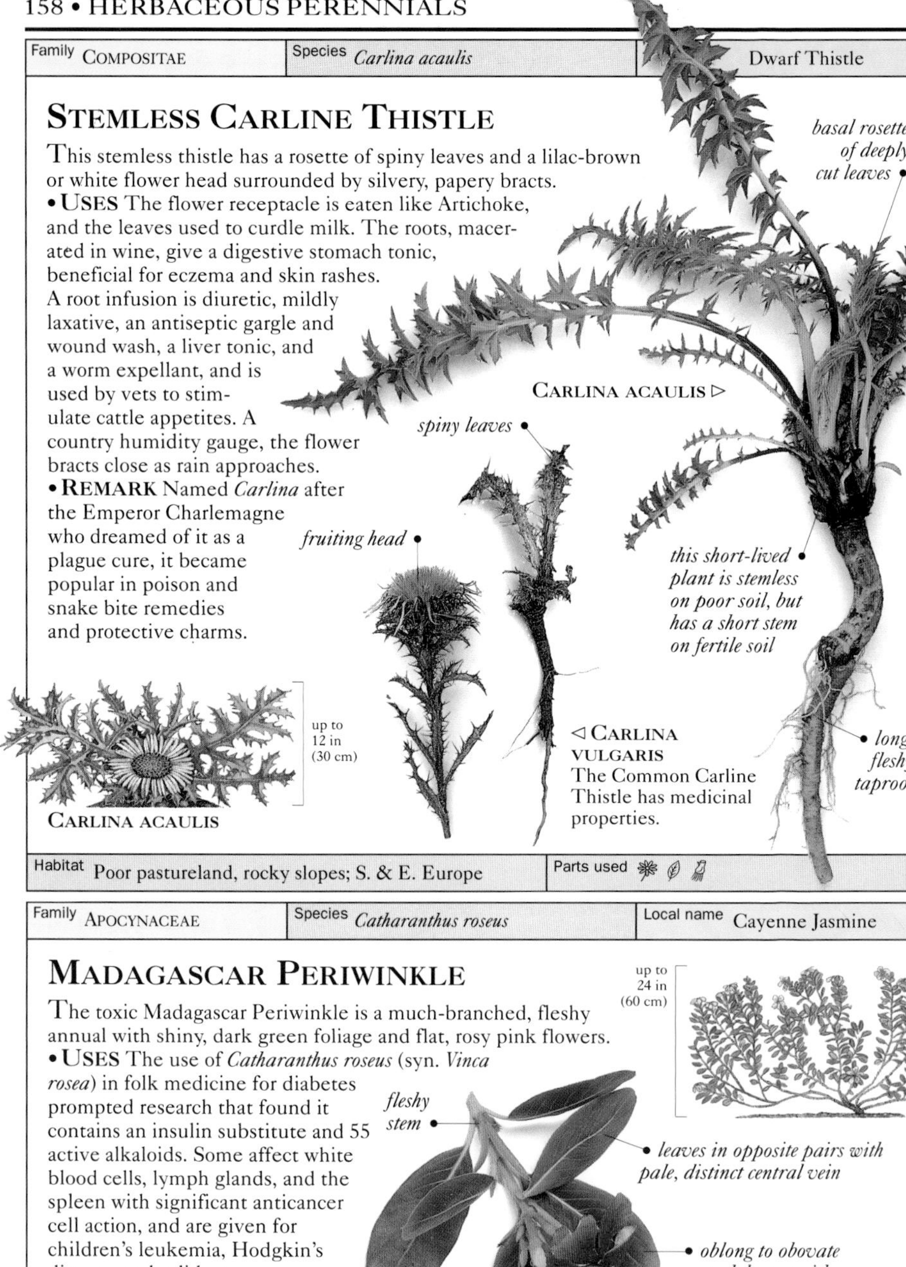
basal rosette of deeply cut leaves
spiny leaves
fruiting head
this short-lived plant is stemless on poor soil, but has a short stem on fertile soil
long, fleshy taproot
up to 12 in (30 cm)
fleshy stem
leaves in opposite pairs with pale, distinct central vein
oblong to obovate smooth leaves with smooth margins
5-petaled rosy pink, white, or crimson flowers with darker centers
up to 24 in (60 cm)

CARLINA ACAULIS ▷

◁ CARLINA VULGARIS
The Common Carline Thistle has medicinal properties.

CARLINA ACAULIS

Habitat Poor pastureland, rocky slopes; S. & E. Europe	Parts used

Family APOCYNACEAE	Species *Catharanthus roseus*	Local name Cayenne Jasmine

MADAGASCAR PERIWINKLE

The toxic Madagascar Periwinkle is a much-branched, fleshy annual with shiny, dark green foliage and flat, rosy pink flowers.

• **USES** The use of *Catharanthus roseus* (syn. *Vinca rosea*) in folk medicine for diabetes prompted research that found it contains an insulin substitute and 55 active alkaloids. Some affect white blood cells, lymph glands, and the spleen with significant anticancer cell action, and are given for children's leukemia, Hodgkin's disease, and solid tumors. Unfortunately, healthy cells are also affected, causing short-term side effects.

• **REMARK** The Madagascar Periwinkle plant is poisonous to humans and livestock.

Habitat Sunny, humid tropics; Madagascar	Parts used

Family UMBELLIFERAE	Species *Centella asiatica*	Local name Gotu-kola

CENTELLA

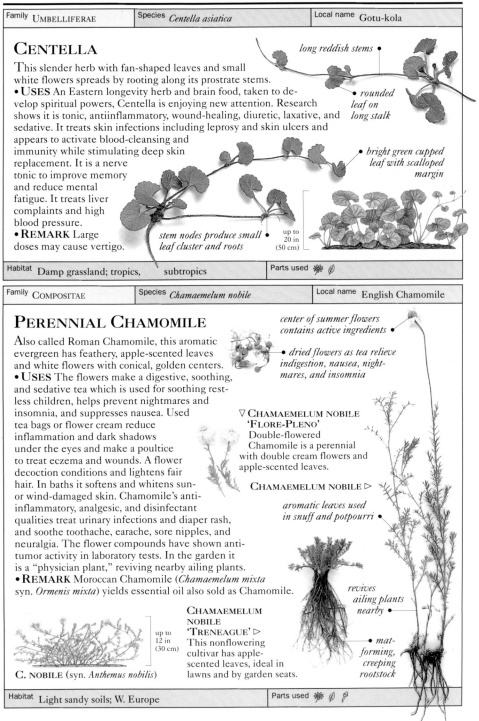

This slender herb with fan-shaped leaves and small white flowers spreads by rooting along its prostrate stems.

• **USES** An Eastern longevity herb and brain food, taken to develop spiritual powers, Centella is enjoying new attention. Research shows it is tonic, antiinflammatory, wound-healing, diuretic, laxative, and sedative. It treats skin infections including leprosy and skin ulcers and appears to activate blood-cleansing and immunity while stimulating deep skin replacement. It is a nerve tonic to improve memory and reduce mental fatigue. It treats liver complaints and high blood pressure.

• **REMARK** Large doses may cause vertigo.

long reddish stems

rounded leaf on long stalk

bright green cupped leaf with scalloped margin

stem nodes produce small leaf cluster and roots

up to 20 in (50 cm)

Habitat Damp grassland; tropics, subtropics	Parts used

Family COMPOSITAE	Species *Chamaemelum nobile*	Local name English Chamomile

PERENNIAL CHAMOMILE

Also called Roman Chamomile, this aromatic evergreen has feathery, apple-scented leaves and white flowers with conical, golden centers.

• **USES** The flowers make a digestive, soothing, and sedative tea which is used for soothing restless children, helps prevent nightmares and insomnia, and suppresses nausea. Used tea bags or flower cream reduce inflammation and dark shadows under the eyes and make a poultice to treat eczema and wounds. A flower decoction conditions and lightens fair hair. In baths it softens and whitens sun- or wind-damaged skin. Chamomile's anti-inflammatory, analgesic, and disinfectant qualities treat urinary infections and diaper rash, and soothe toothache, earache, sore nipples, and neuralgia. The flower compounds have shown anti-tumor activity in laboratory tests. In the garden it is a "physician plant," reviving nearby ailing plants.

• **REMARK** Moroccan Chamomile (*Chamaemelum mixta* syn. *Ormenis mixta*) yields essential oil also sold as Chamomile.

center of summer flowers contains active ingredients

dried flowers as tea relieve indigestion, nausea, nightmares, and insomnia

▽ CHAMAEMELUM NOBILE 'FLORE-PLENO' Double-flowered Chamomile is a perennial with double cream flowers and apple-scented leaves.

CHAMAEMELUM NOBILE ▷

aromatic leaves used in snuff and potpourri

revives ailing plants nearby

mat-forming, creeping rootstock

up to
12 in
(30 cm)
C. NOBILE (syn. *Anthemus nobilis*)

CHAMAEMELUM NOBILE 'TRENEAGUE' ▷ This nonflowering cultivar has apple-scented leaves, ideal in lawns and by garden seats.

Habitat Light sandy soils; W. Europe	Parts used

Family CHENOPODIACEAE	Species *Chenopodium bonus-henricus*	Local name Allgood

GOOD KING HENRY

This historical, arrow-leaved, upright perennial has dense spikes of tiny summer flowers that form fruits containing tan seeds.
• **USES** The leaves contain vitamins, minerals, and iron and are added to salads, cooked like spinach, or used in casseroles, stuffings, and soups. Young asparaguslike shoots are eaten as vegetables. The plant should be avoided in cases of kidney complaint. A leaf poultice soothes sore skin, the root is used in a cough remedy for sheep, and the seeds in the manufacture of shagreen (artificially grained leather).
• **REMARK** The name relates to similar looking Bad Henry which is poisonous; this one is not. It was a popular English vegetable in the 1500s. The California Soap Plant (*Chenopodium californicum*) yields saponins for soapmaking. *C. vulneraria* yields dye.

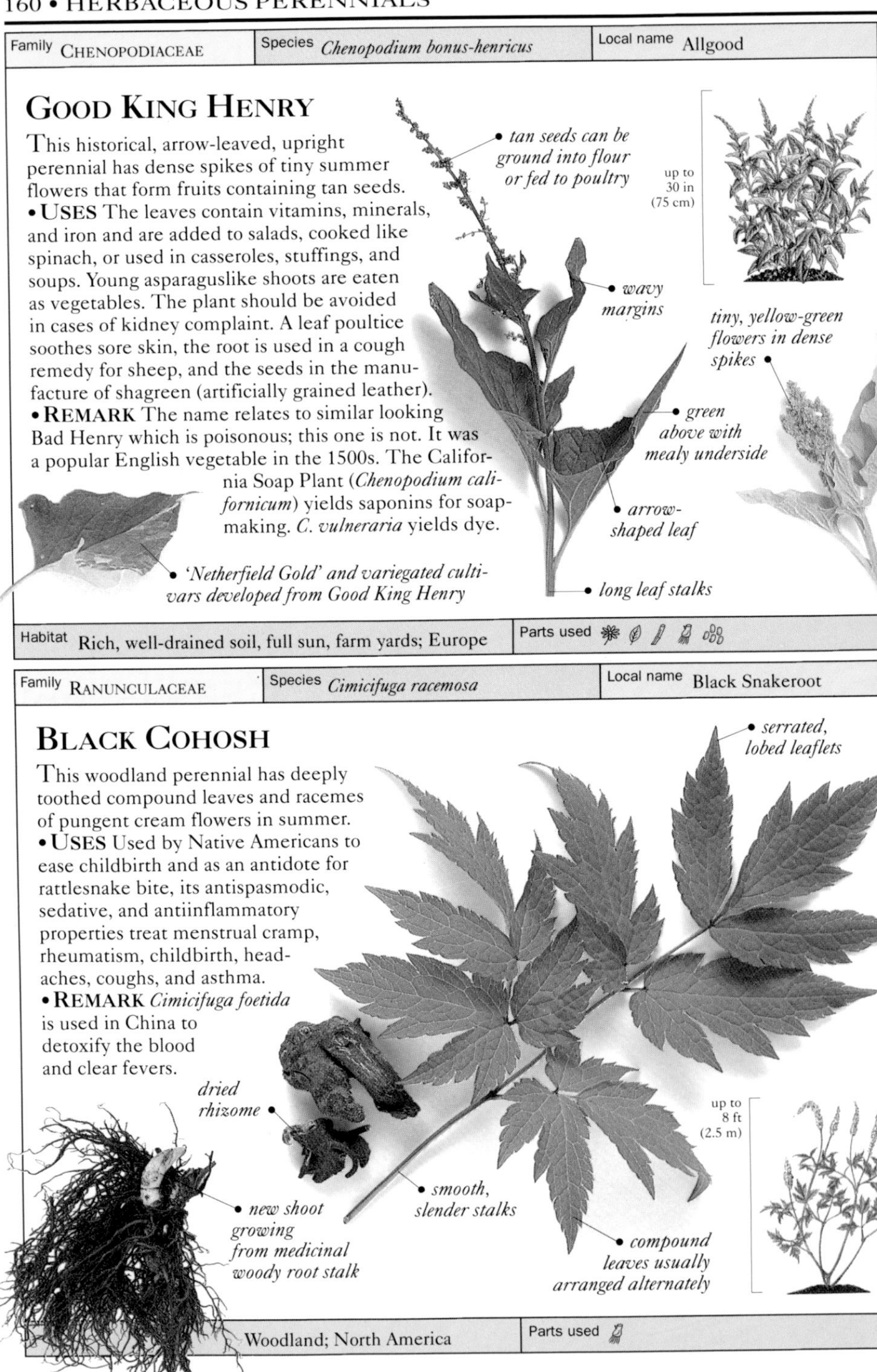
tan seeds can be ground into flour or fed to poultry
up to 30 in (75 cm)
wavy margins
tiny, yellow-green flowers in dense spikes
green above with mealy underside
arrow-shaped leaf
'Netherfield Gold' and variegated cultivars developed from Good King Henry
long leaf stalks
serrated, lobed leaflets
dried rhizome
up to 8 ft (2.5 m)
smooth, slender stalks
new shoot growing from medicinal woody root stalk
compound leaves usually arranged alternately

Habitat Rich, well-drained soil, full sun, farm yards; Europe	Parts used

Family RANUNCULACEAE	Species *Cimicifuga racemosa*	Local name Black Snakeroot

BLACK COHOSH

This woodland perennial has deeply toothed compound leaves and racemes of pungent cream flowers in summer.
• **USES** Used by Native Americans to ease childbirth and as an antidote for rattlesnake bite, its antispasmodic, sedative, and antiinflammatory properties treat menstrual cramp, rheumatism, childbirth, headaches, coughs, and asthma.
• **REMARK** *Cimicifuga foetida* is used in China to detoxify the blood and clear fevers.

Woodland; North America	Parts used

Family LILIACEAE	Species *Convallaria majalis*	Local name May Lily

LILY OF THE VALLEY

This hardy perennial has a spice-scented creeping rhizome and fragrant white flowers in late spring, followed by scarlet berries.

• **USES** The essential oil of this bridal flower is used in perfumes but is so difficult to extract that most products use a chemical substitute. Distilled flower water is an astringent and whitening skin wash called *aqua aurea*. It also reduces fluid retention caused by heart problems and in China is given as a tonic. The leaves yield a green dye. The plant was believed to treat gout, to "comfort the heart," and to restore speech and memory (from the head-clearing effect of inhaling the snuff of the roots and flowers). The flowering tops and roots are used to regulate heartbeat in the same way as *Digitalis* species (see p.247) but are less toxic.

• **REMARK** Lily of the Valley is a potentially poisonous plant and should be given by medical personnel only.

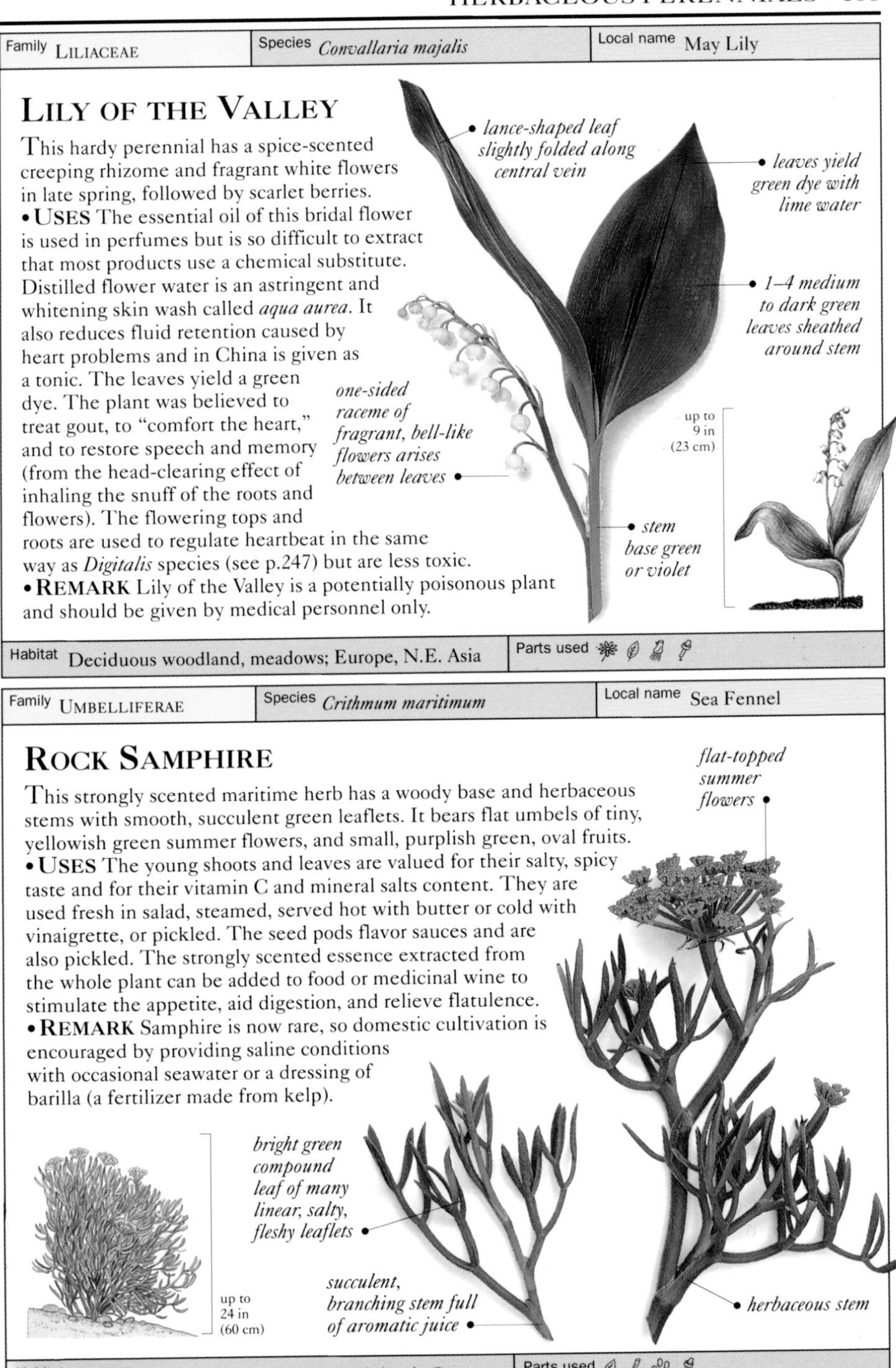
lance-shaped leaf slightly folded along central vein
leaves yield green dye with lime water
1–4 medium to dark green leaves sheathed around stem
one-sided raceme of fragrant, bell-like flowers arises between leaves
up to 9 in (23 cm)
stem base green or violet
flat-topped summer flowers
bright green compound leaf of many linear, salty, fleshy leaflets
succulent, branching stem full of aromatic juice
herbaceous stem
up to 24 in (60 cm)

Habitat Deciduous woodland, meadows; Europe, N.E. Asia	Parts used

Family UMBELLIFERAE	Species *Crithmum maritimum*	Local name Sea Fennel

ROCK SAMPHIRE

This strongly scented maritime herb has a woody base and herbaceous stems with smooth, succulent green leaflets. It bears flat umbels of tiny, yellowish green summer flowers, and small, purplish green, oval fruits.

• **USES** The young shoots and leaves are valued for their salty, spicy taste and for their vitamin C and mineral salts content. They are used fresh in salad, steamed, served hot with butter or cold with vinaigrette, or pickled. The seed pods flavor sauces and are also pickled. The strongly scented essence extracted from the whole plant can be added to food or medicinal wine to stimulate the appetite, aid digestion, and relieve flatulence.

• **REMARK** Samphire is now rare, so domestic cultivation is encouraged by providing saline conditions with occasional seawater or a dressing of barilla (a fertilizer made from kelp).

Habitat Moist maritime habitats; European Atlantic Coast	Parts used

Family IRIDACEAE	Species *Crocus sativus*	Local name Karcom

SAFFRON CROCUS

Saffron Crocus is a corm with grasslike leaves. It has a mauve flower with three protruding, vermilion stigmas, in autumn after a long, hot summer.

• **USES** The stigmas and style tops flavor and color liqueurs and many dishes, especially rice. Saffron is considered an aphrodisiac, but too much may be narcotic. It is given to reduce fevers, cramps, and enlarged livers, and to calm nerves, and is applied externally for bruises, rheumatism, and neuralgia. In India, saffron is used ceremonially. Although water soluble, it is used cosmetically and as a sacred dye.

• **REMARK** Turmeric is often mistakenly called saffron in Asia.

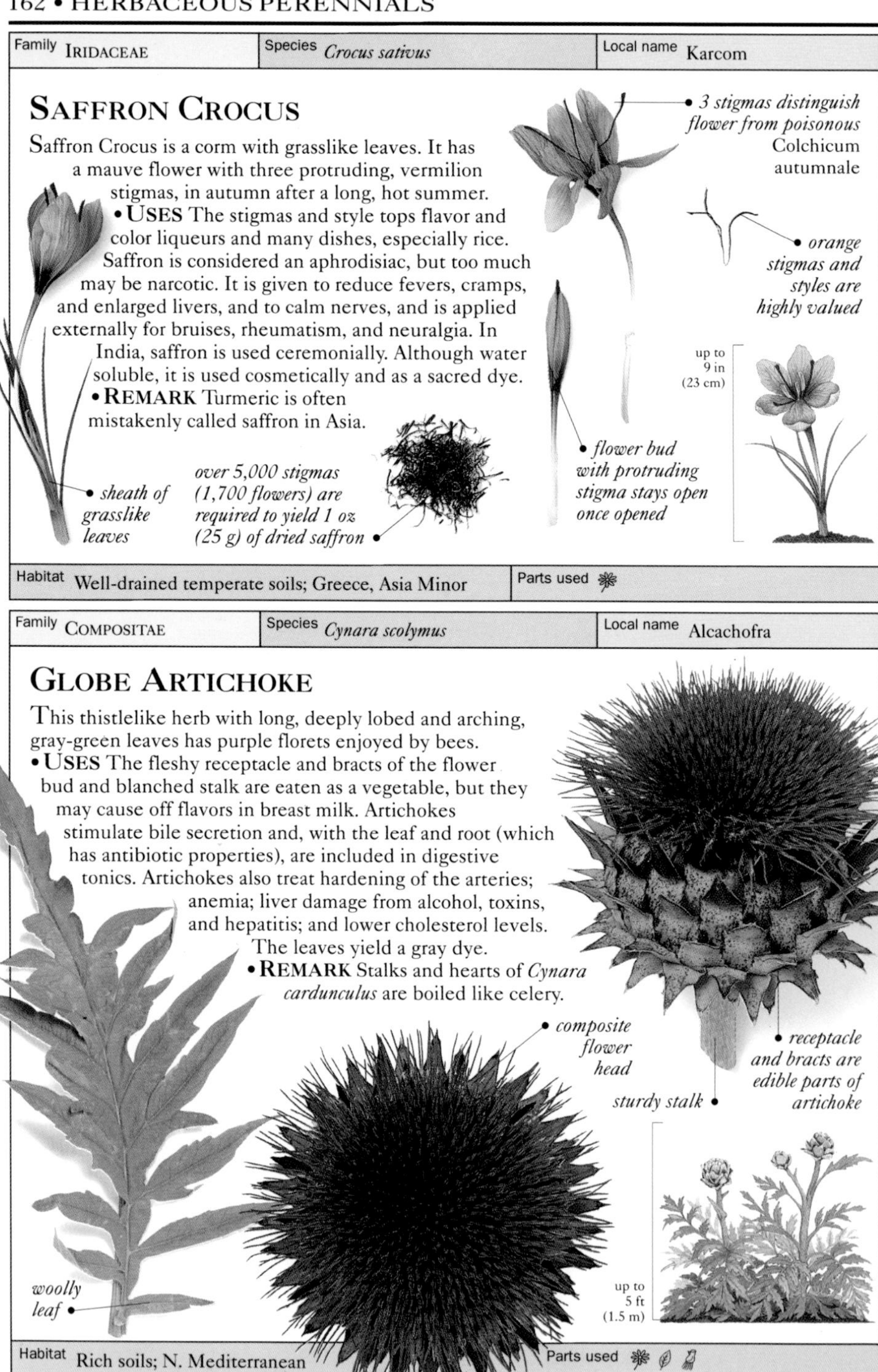

3 stigmas distinguish flower from poisonous Colchicum autumnale
orange stigmas and styles are highly valued
up to 9 in (23 cm)
flower bud with protruding stigma stays open once opened
over 5,000 stigmas (1,700 flowers) are required to yield 1 oz (25 g) of dried saffron
sheath of grasslike leaves
composite flower head
receptacle and bracts are edible parts of artichoke
sturdy stalk
woolly leaf
up to 5 ft (1.5 m)

Habitat Well-drained temperate soils; Greece, Asia Minor	Parts used

Family COMPOSITAE	Species *Cynara scolymus*	Local name Alcachofra

GLOBE ARTICHOKE

This thistlelike herb with long, deeply lobed and arching, gray-green leaves has purple florets enjoyed by bees.

• **USES** The fleshy receptacle and bracts of the flower bud and blanched stalk are eaten as a vegetable, but they may cause off flavors in breast milk. Artichokes stimulate bile secretion and, with the leaf and root (which has antibiotic properties), are included in digestive tonics. Artichokes also treat hardening of the arteries; anemia; liver damage from alcohol, toxins, and hepatitis; and lower cholesterol levels. The leaves yield a gray dye.

• **REMARK** Stalks and hearts of *Cynara cardunculus* are boiled like celery.

Habitat Rich soils; N. Mediterranean	Parts used

Family	Species	Local name
ZINGIBERACEAE	*Curcuma longa*	Yu-chin / Besar

TURMERIC

Turmeric has an aromatic rhizome, large leaves, and yellow flowers with pink bracts.

• **USES** The dried root gives flavor and color to curry powders, many Indian dishes, and piccalilli and is sometimes sold as saffron. The inflorescences and shoots are Thai vegetables. In Chinese medicine, the root stimulates circulation and resolves clots and bruises. It is a Thai treatment for cobra venom. Research shows that Turmeric strengthens the gallbladder, inhibits dangerous blood clotting, reduces liver toxins and helps it metabolize fats (possibly assisting weight loss), and has an antiinflammatory, nonsteroidal action. Turmeric gives a golden fabric dye and features in Indian ceremonies.

• **REMARK** Zeodary has reduced cervical cancer in trials and has increased the effectiveness of radiotherapy and chemotherapy.

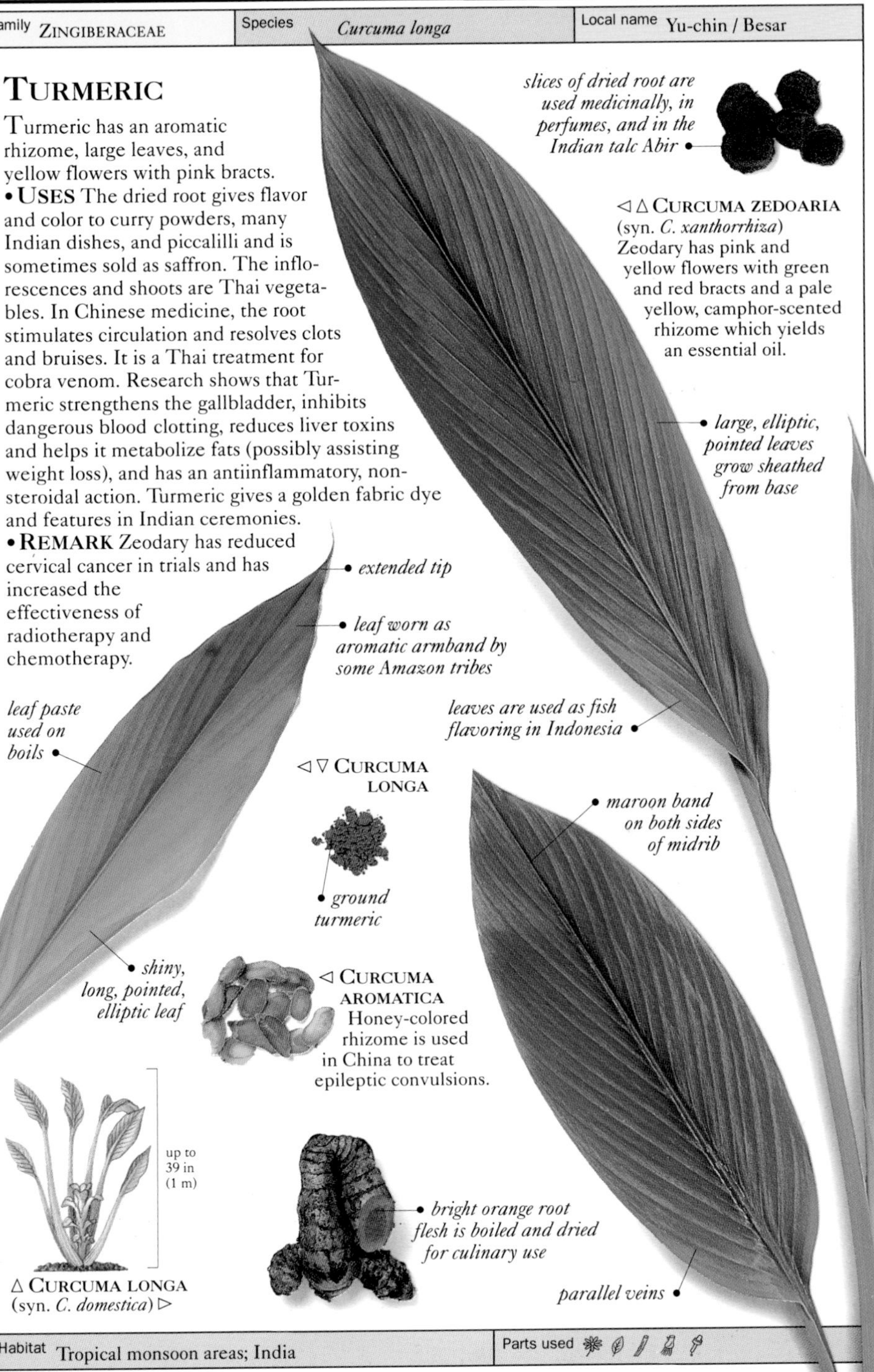

slices of dried root are used medicinally, in perfumes, and in the Indian talc Abir
large, elliptic, pointed leaves grow sheathed from base
leaves are used as fish flavoring in Indonesia
extended tip
leaf worn as aromatic armband by some Amazon tribes
leaf paste used on boils
ground turmeric
shiny, long, pointed, elliptic leaf
maroon band on both sides of midrib
bright orange root flesh is boiled and dried for culinary use
parallel veins
up to 39 in (1 m)

◁ △ CURCUMA ZEDOARIA (syn. *C. xanthorrhiza*) Zeodary has pink and yellow flowers with green and red bracts and a pale yellow, camphor-scented rhizome which yields an essential oil.

◁ ▽ CURCUMA LONGA

◁ CURCUMA AROMATICA Honey-colored rhizome is used in China to treat epileptic convulsions.

△ CURCUMA LONGA (syn. *C. domestica*) ▷

Habitat	Parts used
Tropical monsoon areas; India	

Family GRAMINEAE	Species *Cymbopogon citratus*	Local name Melissa Grass / Sereh

LEMON GRASS

This aromatic grass has clumped, bulbous stems becoming leaf blades and a branched panicle of flowers. • **USES** The stem and leaf, used widely in Thai cuisine, have a distinct lemon flavor. Leaf tea treats diarrhea, stomachache, headaches, fevers, and flu, and is antiseptic. The essential oil is used in cosmetics and food and in aromatherapy to improve circulation and muscle tone. The antiseptic oil treats athlete's foot and acne, and a spray reduces air-borne bacteria. • **REMARK** *Cymbopogon flexuosus* yields a slightly different Lemon Grass oil *Vervaines des Indes. C. martini* leaves yield palmarosa oil with a gingery-floral scent, said to aid skin cell renewal.

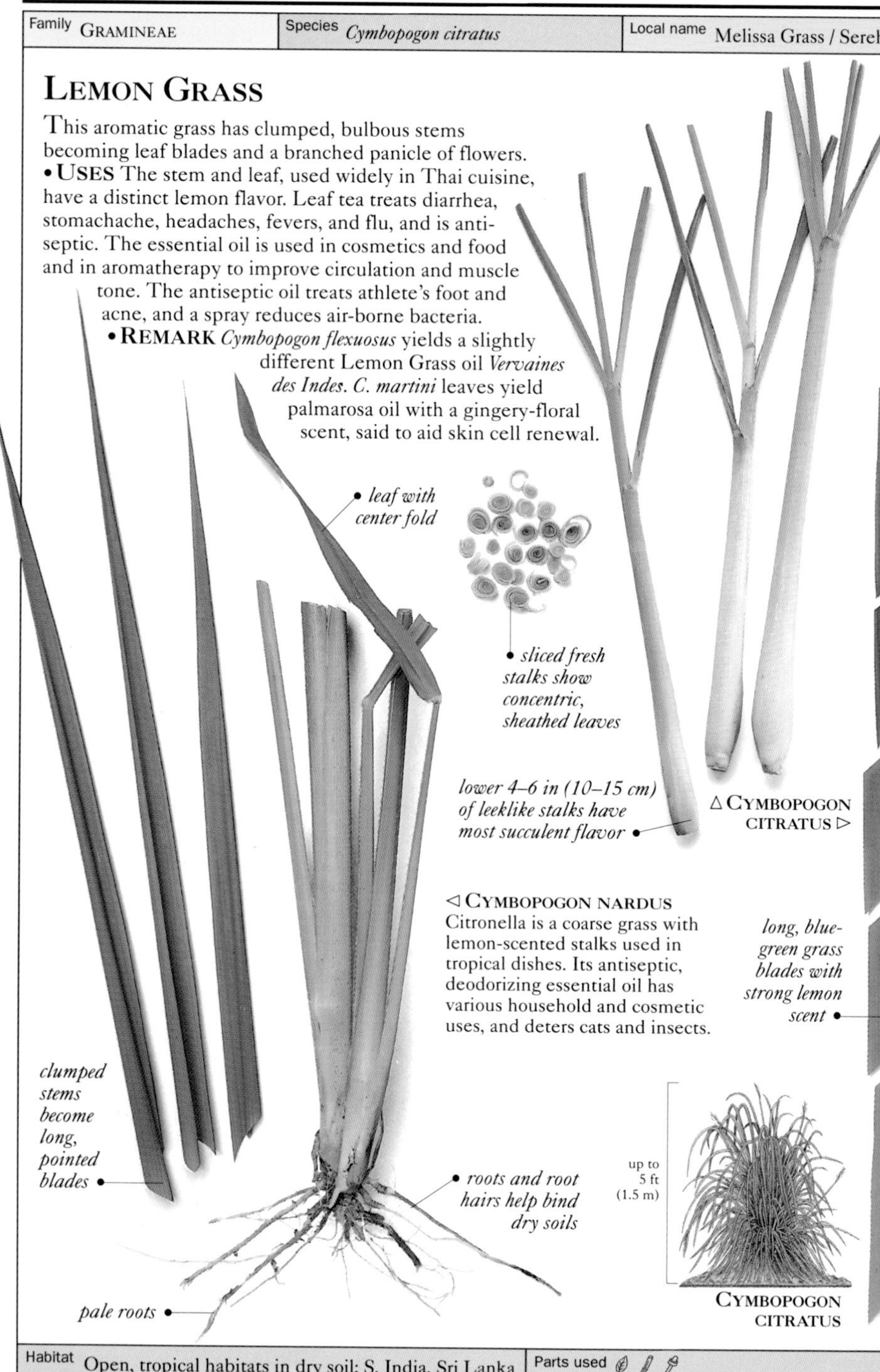
leaf with center fold
sliced fresh stalks show concentric, sheathed leaves
lower 4–6 in (10–15 cm) of leeklike stalks have most succulent flavor
long, blue-green grass blades with strong lemon scent
clumped stems become long, pointed blades
roots and root hairs help bind dry soils
pale roots
up to 5 ft (1.5 m)

△ CYMBOPOGON CITRATUS ▷

◁ CYMBOPOGON NARDUS
Citronella is a coarse grass with lemon-scented stalks used in tropical dishes. Its antiseptic, deodorizing essential oil has various household and cosmetic uses, and deters cats and insects.

CYMBOPOGON CITRATUS

Habitat Open, tropical habitats in dry soil; S. India, Sri Lanka	Parts used

Family CYPERACEAE	Species *Cyperus papyrus*	Local name Egyptian Paper Reed

PAPYRUS

This leafless sedge, the bulrush associated with the baby Moses, grows an umbel of blade-like bracts, with rays of tiny flower spikelets springing from the stem tops.

• **USES** The stem pith was used to make the first form of paper in 3,000–2,500 BC; its Greek name *biblos* or *byblos* is the origin of the word bible. The Egyptians ate the rhizomes, used them medicinally, wove the fibers into sail cloth, and decorated temples and tombs with bouquets. Today stems make fuel, matting, baskets, and buoyant bundles bound together to make local sailing craft.

• **REMARK** The rhizome of the hardy water plant Sweet Galingale (*Cyperus longus*) has a violet perfume used in old recipes. *C. odoratus* with aromatic stems and roots is the voodoo perfume *priprioca*. Rhizomes of *C. scariosus* yield the Bombay perfume *surat*.

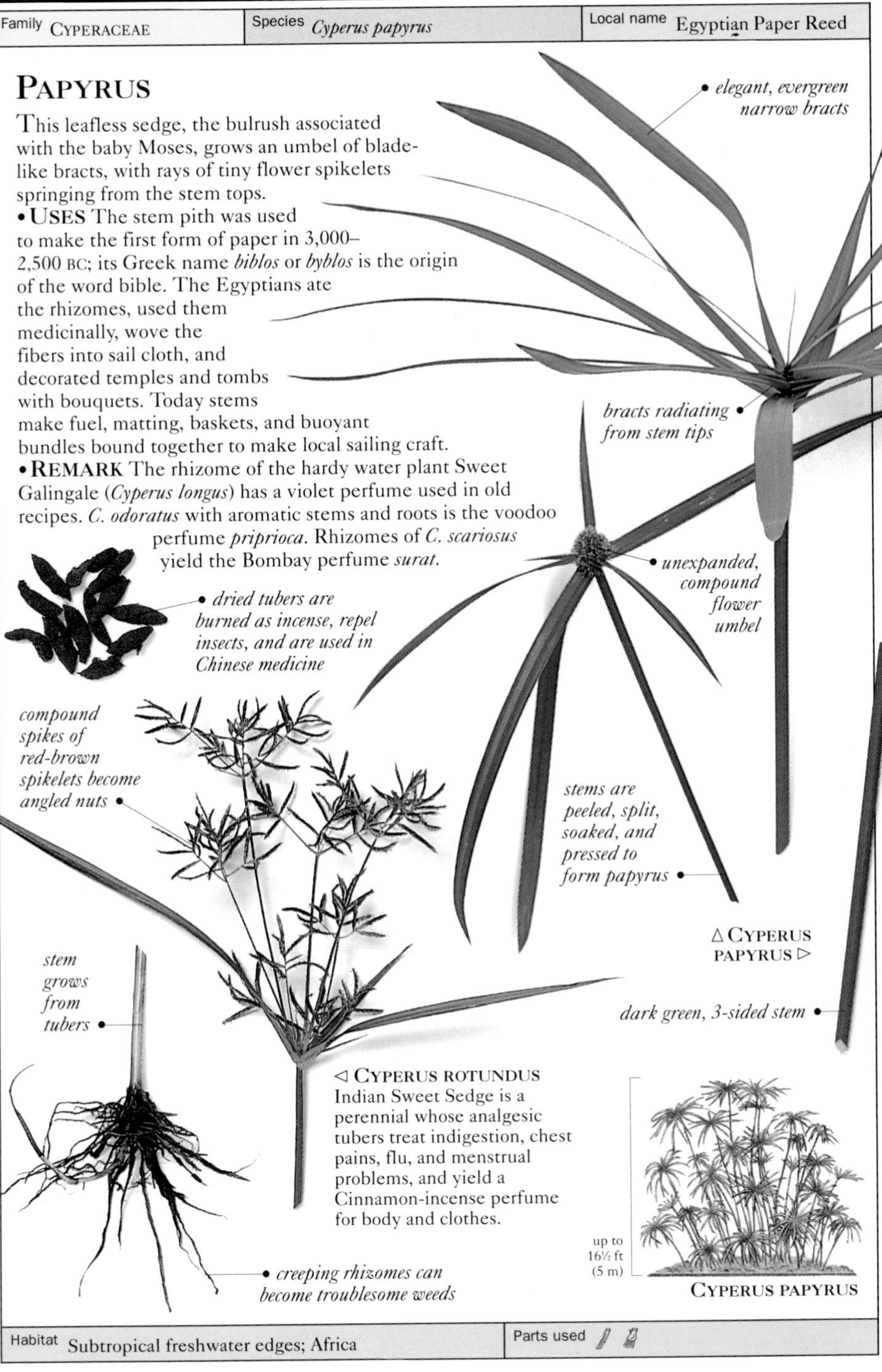
elegant, evergreen narrow bracts
bracts radiating from stem tips
unexpanded, compound flower umbel
dried tubers are burned as incense, repel insects, and are used in Chinese medicine
compound spikes of red-brown spikelets become angled nuts
stems are peeled, split, soaked, and pressed to form papyrus
△ CYPERUS PAPYRUS ▷
dark green, 3-sided stem
stem grows from tubers
creeping rhizomes can become troublesome weeds
up to 16½ ft (5 m)
CYPERUS PAPYRUS

◁ CYPERUS ROTUNDUS
Indian Sweet Sedge is a perennial whose analgesic tubers treat indigestion, chest pains, flu, and menstrual problems, and yield a Cinnamon-incense perfume for body and clothes.

Habitat Subtropical freshwater edges; Africa	Parts used

Family CARYOPHYLLACEAE	Species *Dianthus caryophyllus*	Local name Gillyflower

CLOVE PINK

This short-lived perennial has blue-green, grasslike foliage and spicy, fragrant, long-lasting summer flowers in white, pink, or purple.

• **USES** This "flower of divinity" and symbol of betrothal, woven into garlands, is the parent of cultivated carnations, although it is now seldom available in its true form. Fortunately, the petals of any clove-scented Pink, with the bitter white heel removed, can be added to fruit dishes, sandwiches, soups, and sauces, or used to make floral syrup, vinegar, liqueur, or wine. This was Chaucer's "sops in wine" and is still enjoyed as a nerve tonic today. The petals are crystallized for culinary decoration and were believed to give unlimited energy. The strong, sweet-spicy scent is used in soaps and perfumes.

• **REMARK** *Dianthus plumarius* is the parent of many old-fashioned pinks. The root and plant of *D. chinensis* and other species inhibit test tumors.

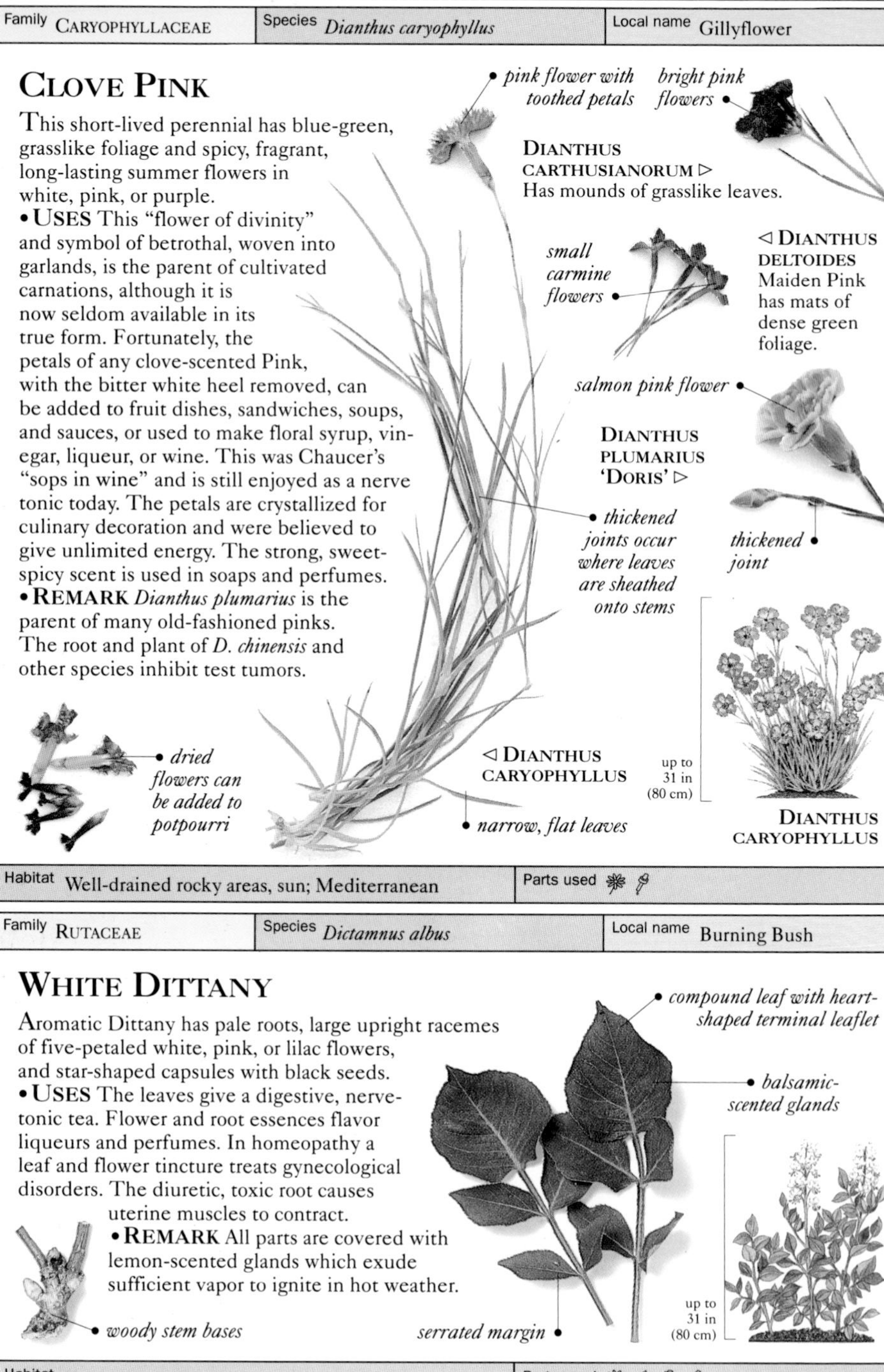

pink flower with toothed petals
bright pink flowers
DIANTHUS CARTHUSIANORUM ▷
Has mounds of grasslike leaves.
small carmine flowers
◁ DIANTHUS DELTOIDES
Maiden Pink has mats of dense green foliage.
salmon pink flower
DIANTHUS PLUMARIUS 'DORIS' ▷
thickened joints occur where leaves are sheathed onto stems
thickened joint
up to 31 in (80 cm)
DIANTHUS CARYOPHYLLUS
◁ DIANTHUS CARYOPHYLLUS
narrow, flat leaves
dried flowers can be added to potpourri

Habitat Well-drained rocky areas, sun; Mediterranean	Parts used

Family RUTACEAE	Species *Dictamnus albus*	Local name Burning Bush

WHITE DITTANY

Aromatic Dittany has pale roots, large upright racemes of five-petaled white, pink, or lilac flowers, and star-shaped capsules with black seeds.

• **USES** The leaves give a digestive, nerve-tonic tea. Flower and root essences flavor liqueurs and perfumes. In homeopathy a leaf and flower tincture treats gynecological disorders. The diuretic, toxic root causes uterine muscles to contract.

• **REMARK** All parts are covered with lemon-scented glands which exude sufficient vapor to ignite in hot weather.

compound leaf with heart-shaped terminal leaflet
balsamic-scented glands
woody stem bases
serrated margin
up to 31 in (80 cm)

Habitat High altitudes; S.W. Europe, S. & C. Asia	Parts used

Family COMPOSITAE	Species *Echinacea angustifolia*	Local name Purple Cone Flower

ECHINACEA

Rhizomatous Echinacea has long stems bearing summer flower heads, with rose-pink to purple florets around the central cone.

• **USES** The rhizome is the most significant proven herbal immune system stimulant and is under investigation by AIDS researchers. Without toxicity, it stimulates the body's defenses against disease. It is also antibiotic, antiviral, and restores inflamed connective tissue. It treats fevers and infections and may reduce allergies.

• **REMARK** There are many hybrids between *Echinacea purpurea* and *E. angustifolia.*

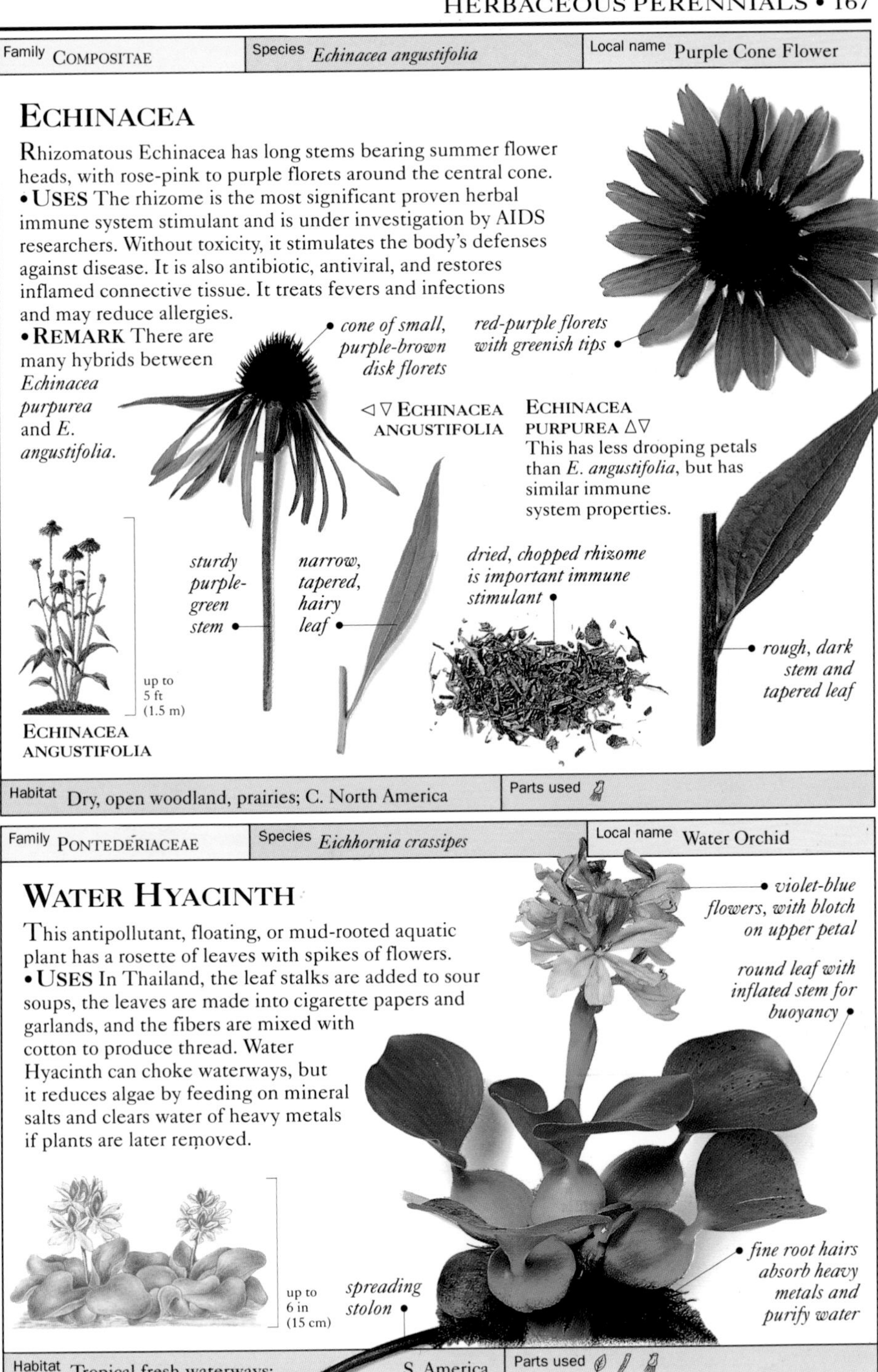
cone of small, purple-brown disk florets
red-purple florets with greenish tips
sturdy purple-green stem
narrow, tapered, hairy leaf
dried, chopped rhizome is important immune stimulant
rough, dark stem and tapered leaf
up to 5 ft (1.5 m)
violet-blue flowers, with blotch on upper petal
round leaf with inflated stem for buoyancy
fine root hairs absorb heavy metals and purify water
spreading stolon
up to 6 in (15 cm)

◁ ▽ ECHINACEA ANGUSTIFOLIA

ECHINACEA PURPUREA △▽
This has less drooping petals than *E. angustifolia*, but has similar immune system properties.

ECHINACEA ANGUSTIFOLIA

Habitat Dry, open woodland, prairies; C. North America	Parts used

Family PONTEDERIACEAE	Species *Eichhornia crassipes*	Local name Water Orchid

WATER HYACINTH

This antipollutant, floating, or mud-rooted aquatic plant has a rosette of leaves with spikes of flowers.

• **USES** In Thailand, the leaf stalks are added to sour soups, the leaves are made into cigarette papers and garlands, and the fibers are mixed with cotton to produce thread. Water Hyacinth can choke waterways, but it reduces algae by feeding on mineral salts and clears water of heavy metals if plants are later removed.

Habitat Tropical fresh waterways; S. America	Parts used

Family COMPOSITAE	Species *Eupatorium purpureum*	Local name Joe-Pye Weed

SWEET JOE PYE

This stately herb has whorls of three to six leaves that have a faint scent of vanilla or apple peel, and pink flowers in late summer.
• **USES** Named after the Native American who cured New Englanders of typhus, the rhizome is still used to induce fever-breaking sweats. It tones the reproductive system, eases menstrual cramps, and helps gout, rheumatism, and kidney and urinary problems. The seeds yield a pink textile dye, used by Native Americans.
• **REMARK** Compounds of *Eupatorium perfoliatum*, *E. cannabinum*, and possibly *E. purpureum* have exhibited antitumor properties. The green parts of *E. odoratum* are used in China to destroy parasitic worms and to stop bleeding.

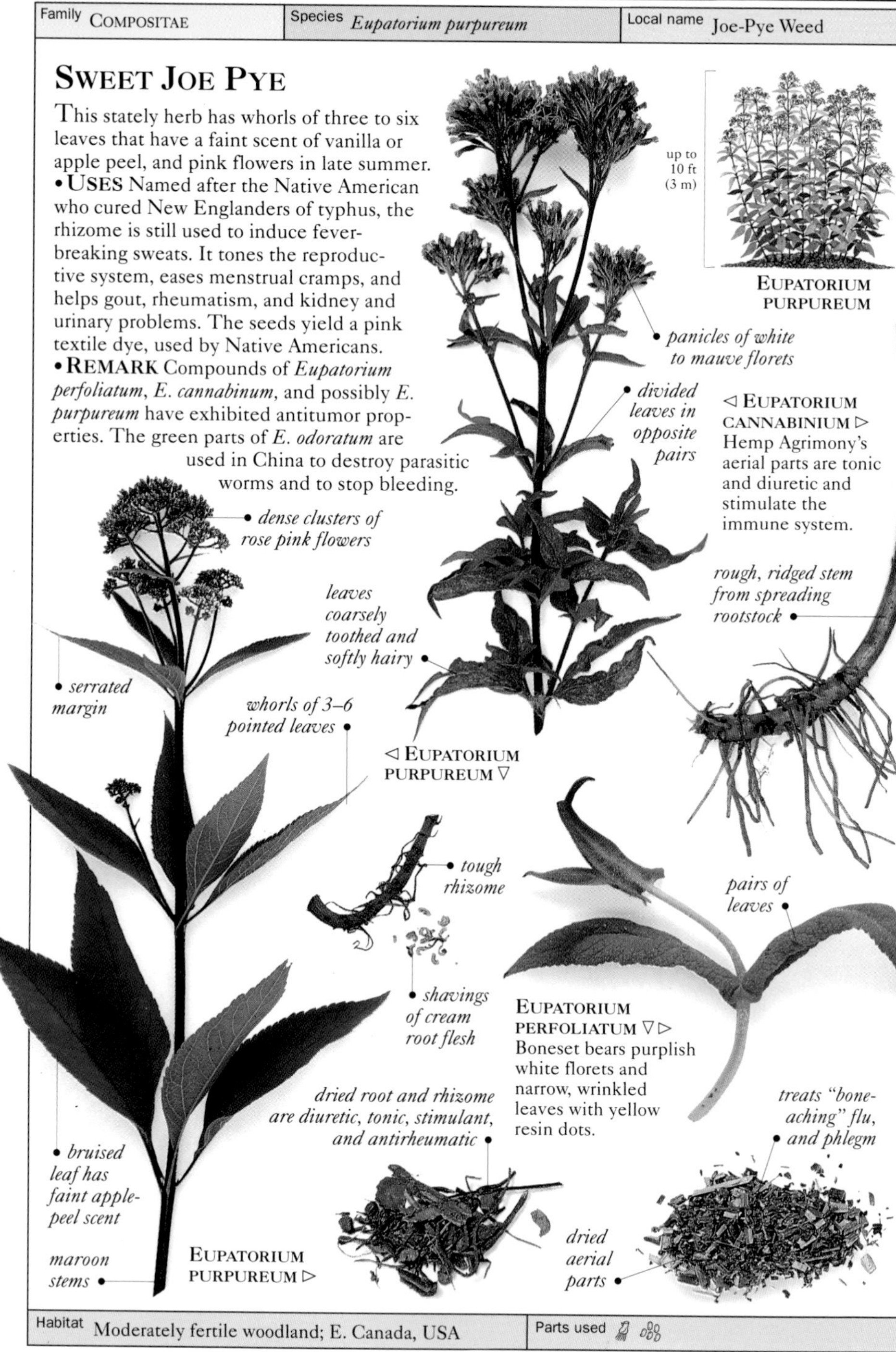
up to 10 ft (3 m)
EUPATORIUM PURPUREUM
panicles of white to mauve florets
divided leaves in opposite pairs
◁ EUPATORIUM CANNABINIUM ▷
Hemp Agrimony's aerial parts are tonic and diuretic and stimulate the immune system.
rough, ridged stem from spreading rootstock
dense clusters of rose pink flowers
leaves coarsely toothed and softly hairy
serrated margin
whorls of 3–6 pointed leaves
◁ EUPATORIUM PURPUREUM ▽
tough rhizome
pairs of leaves
shavings of cream root flesh
EUPATORIUM PERFOLIATUM ▽ ▷
Boneset bears purplish white florets and narrow, wrinkled leaves with yellow resin dots.
dried root and rhizome are diuretic, tonic, stimulant, and antirheumatic
treats "bone-aching" flu, and phlegm
bruised leaf has faint apple-peel scent
maroon stems
EUPATORIUM PURPUREUM ▷
dried aerial parts

Habitat Moderately fertile woodland; E. Canada, USA	Parts used

Family ZINGIBERACEAE	Species *Elettaria cardamomum*	Local name Cardamon

CARDAMOM

This perennial bears violet-striped, white flowers and aromatic green fruits on erect or trailing racemes.

• **USES** The seed pods are an expensive spice, sold as whole green, bleached, or sun-dried cardamom. The seeds are an important ingredient of Indian garam masala, Arab baharat, Ethiopian berbere, curry powders, pilaus, and many sweet dishes. They are also valued by Bedouins to flavor coffee and by Danes for fancy breads and are chewed to sweeten the breath. The seeds are digestive, stimulant, and antispasmodic, and the rhizome is given for fatigue and fever. The essential oil from almost-ripe fruits is used in liqueurs and perfumes.

• **REMARK** Cardamom seeds are a symbol of hospitality.

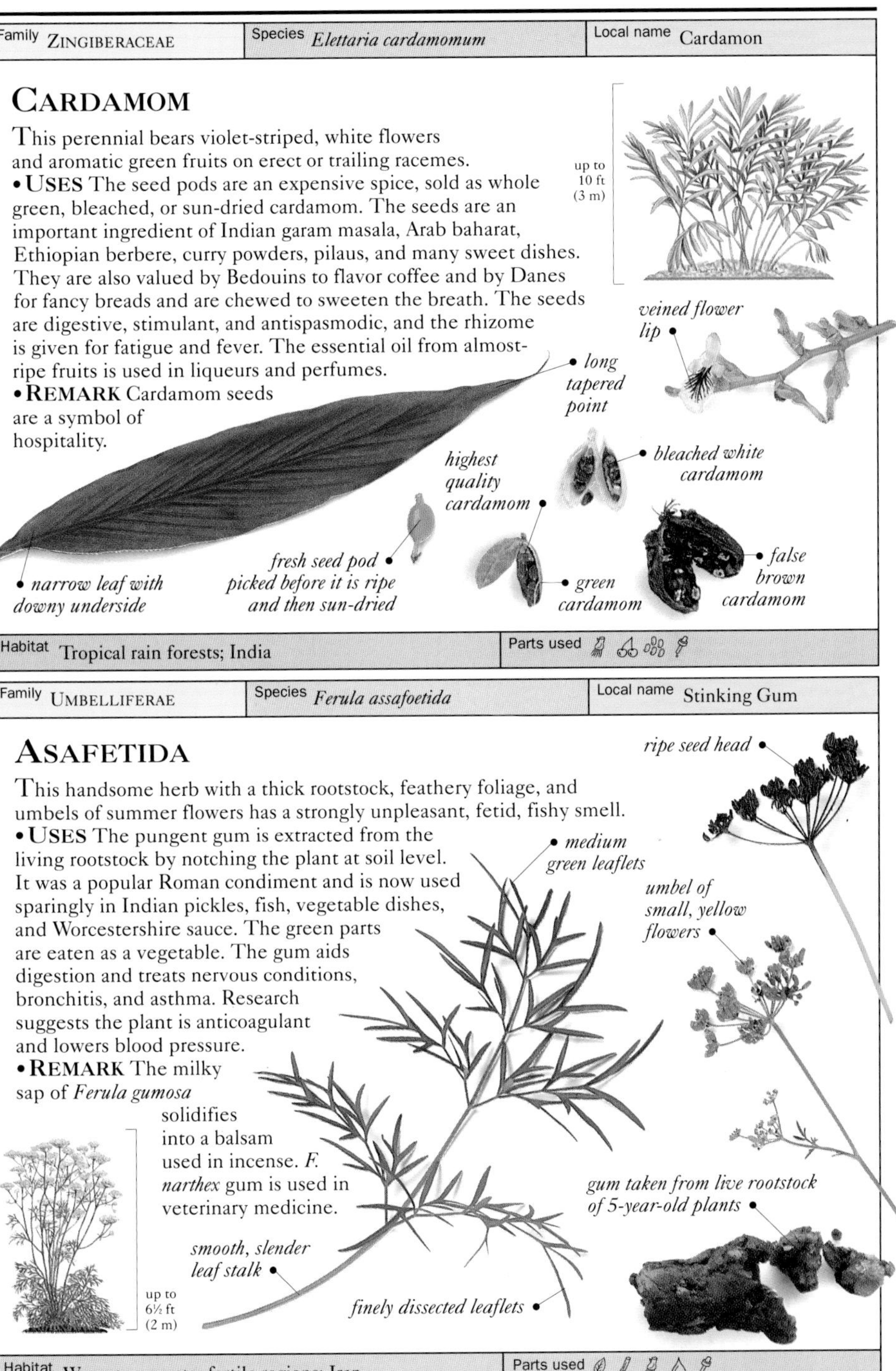
up to
10 ft
(3 m)
veined flower lip
long tapered point
highest quality cardamom
bleached white cardamom
narrow leaf with downy underside
fresh seed pod picked before it is ripe and then sun-dried
green cardamom
false brown cardamom
ripe seed head
medium green leaflets
umbel of small, yellow flowers
gum taken from live rootstock of 5-year-old plants
smooth, slender leaf stalk
finely dissected leaflets
up to
6½ ft
(2 m)

Habitat Tropical rain forests; India	Parts used

Family UMBELLIFERAE	Species *Ferula assafoetida*	Local name Stinking Gum

ASAFETIDA

This handsome herb with a thick rootstock, feathery foliage, and umbels of summer flowers has a strongly unpleasant, fetid, fishy smell.

• **USES** The pungent gum is extracted from the living rootstock by notching the plant at soil level. It was a popular Roman condiment and is now used sparingly in Indian pickles, fish, vegetable dishes, and Worcestershire sauce. The green parts are eaten as a vegetable. The gum aids digestion and treats nervous conditions, bronchitis, and asthma. Research suggests the plant is anticoagulant and lowers blood pressure.

• **REMARK** The milky sap of *Ferula gumosa* solidifies into a balsam used in incense. *F. narthex* gum is used in veterinary medicine.

Habitat Warm temperate, fertile regions; Iran	Parts used

Family ROSACEAE	Species *Filipendula ulmaria*	Local name Queen of the Meadow

MEADOWSWEET

This herb has upright stems of wintergreen-scented, divided leaves, topped by frothy corymbs of almond-scented cream flowers. • **USES** The flowers give an almond flavor to mead, herb wines, jam, and stewed fruit. Dried flowers scent linen and yield an astringent skin tonic. Flower buds contain salicylic acid, from which aspirin was synthesized, but the herb as a whole is gentler on the stomach. Herbalists use flower tea for stomach ulcers and headaches, as an antiseptic diuretic, and for feverish colds, diarrhea, and heartburn; its mild painkilling, antiinflammatory action treats rheumatism. The flowering tops yield a greenish yellow dye, the leaf and stem a blue dye, and the root a black dye. • **REMARK** Meadowsweet was sacred to the Druids and the favored strewing herb of Elizabeth I.

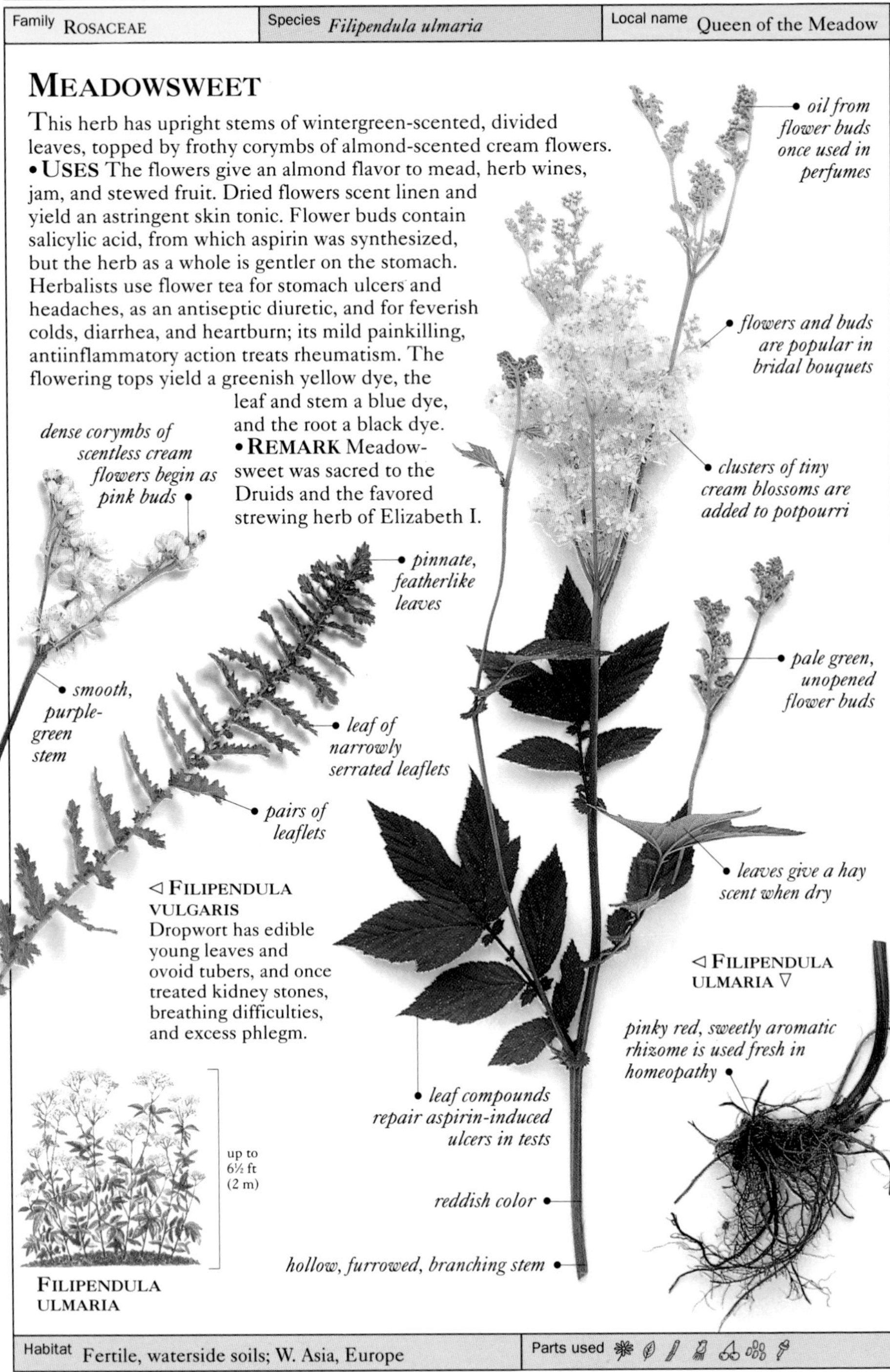

oil from flower buds once used in perfumes
flowers and buds are popular in bridal bouquets
clusters of tiny cream blossoms are added to potpourri
dense corymbs of scentless cream flowers begin as pink buds
pinnate, featherlike leaves
smooth, purple-green stem
leaf of narrowly serrated leaflets
pairs of leaflets
pale green, unopened flower buds
leaves give a hay scent when dry
pinky red, sweetly aromatic rhizome is used fresh in homeopathy
leaf compounds repair aspirin-induced ulcers in tests
reddish color
hollow, furrowed, branching stem
up to 6½ ft (2 m)

◁ **FILIPENDULA VULGARIS**
Dropwort has edible young leaves and ovoid tubers, and once treated kidney stones, breathing difficulties, and excess phlegm.

◁ **FILIPENDULA ULMARIA** ▽

FILIPENDULA ULMARIA

Habitat Fertile, waterside soils; W. Asia, Europe	Parts used

Family UMBELLIFERAE	Species *Foeniculum vulgare*	Local name Finocchio / Fenouil

FENNEL

This herb has finely cut feathery foliage, umbels of midsummer flowers, curved, ribbed seeds, and a thick root, all with a fresh anise seed flavor.

• **USES** The seeds flavor breads, curries, apple pie, and fish sauces and are sprouted as a salad herb. Their essence flavors liqueurs and toothpaste. The seeds are chewed to allay hunger and ease indigestion. They are brewed for constipation, to increase breast milk and regulate menstruation; with root extract, they are detoxifying and diuretic. Research indicates Fennel helps repair the liver after alcohol damage. Seed and leaf steam aids deep skin cleansing, and the essential oil (used conservatively) is used in a muscle-toning massage.

• **REMARK** Fennel oil should not be used by epileptics or young children.

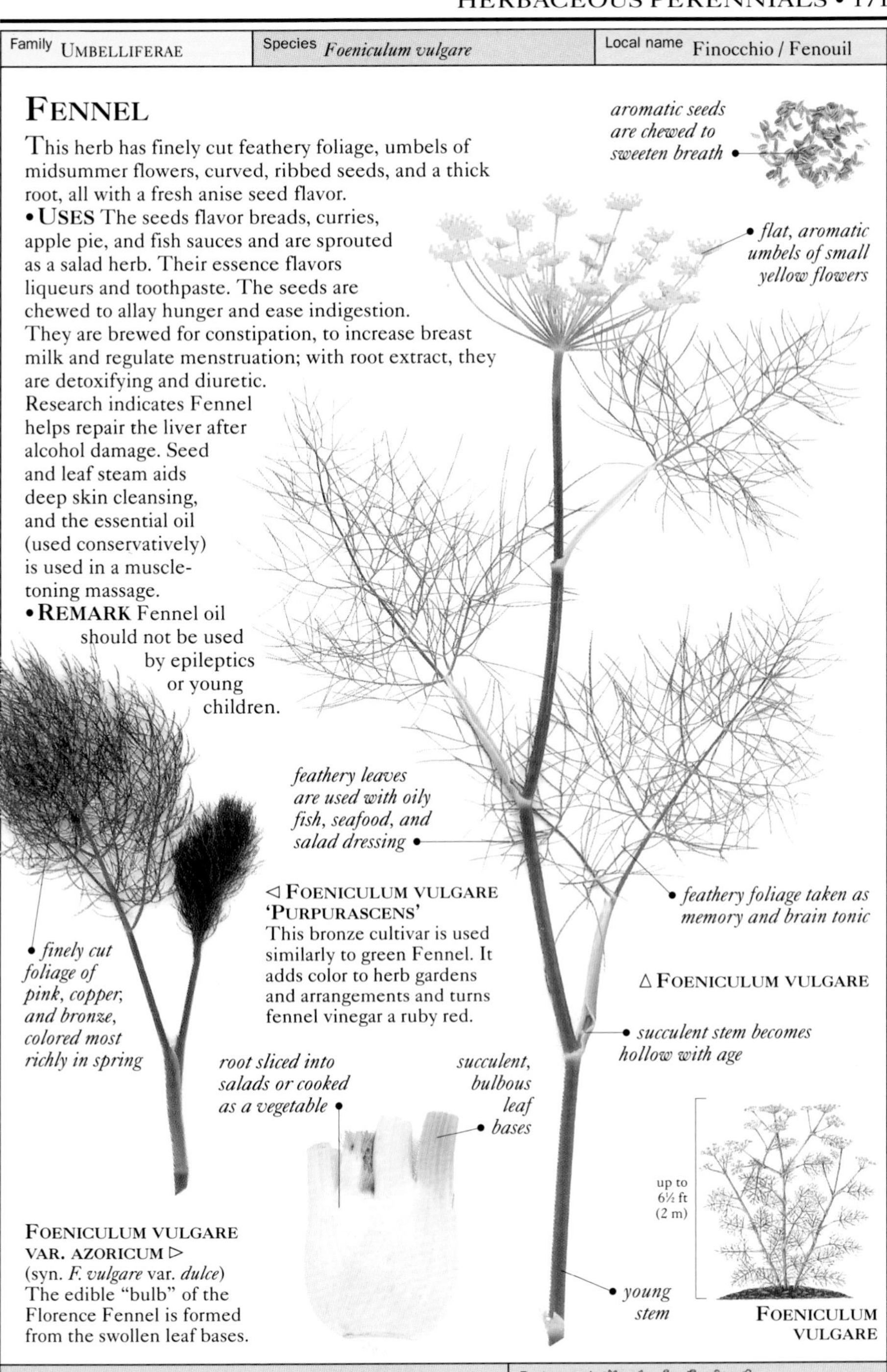
aromatic seeds are chewed to sweeten breath
flat, aromatic umbels of small yellow flowers
feathery leaves are used with oily fish, seafood, and salad dressing
feathery foliage taken as memory and brain tonic
finely cut foliage of pink, copper, and bronze, colored most richly in spring
succulent stem becomes hollow with age
root sliced into salads or cooked as a vegetable
succulent, bulbous leaf bases
young stem
up to 6½ ft (2 m)

◁ FOENICULUM VULGARE 'PURPURASCENS'
This bronze cultivar is used similarly to green Fennel. It adds color to herb gardens and arrangements and turns fennel vinegar a ruby red.

△ FOENICULUM VULGARE

FOENICULUM VULGARE

FOENICULUM VULGARE VAR. AZORICUM ▷
(syn. *F. vulgare* var. *dulce*)
The edible "bulb" of the Florence Fennel is formed from the swollen leaf bases.

Habitat Well-drained loam; Europe, Mediterranean	Parts used

flowers from spring to first frosts
leaf with 3 toothed leaflets
fruit contains iron and vitamin C
often evergreen, leaves turn red and scented in autumn
root is tonic and diuretic
leaves for internal use must be dried thoroughly to avoid toxins
short woody rootstock with numerous rootlets
up to 12 in (30 cm)
medium green leaflet with pale underside
upright, hollow, branching stem
smooth margins
lavender, pink, or white flowers
leaf stems carry leaflets that end in a tiny spur
up to 5 ft (1.5 m)

Family Rosaceae | Species *Fragaria vesca* | Local name Woodland Strawberry

Wild Strawberry

Wild Strawberry has a basal rosette of bright green, three-part leaves, fruits from summer to autumn, and runners producing young plants. • **Uses** The popular fruit is rich in iron and potassium; flavors liqueurs and preserves; is valuable for anemia, diabetes, rheumatic gout, and kidney and liver complaints; and makes a drink to cool fevers. Fresh Strawberry removes tartar and teeth stains, soothes sunburn, and lightens freckles.

Dried leaves are added to potpourri. The astringent leaf makes a calming herbal tea and is an oily skin toner. With the root, it treats diarrhea and urinary disorders.

◁ **Fragaria vesca 'Variegata'**
Dark and gray-green leaves have cream edging, but no fruits.

Fragaria vesca

Habitat Cool, open woodland; Europe | Parts used

Family Leguminosae | Species *Galega officinalis* | Local name French Lilac

Goat's Rue

Smooth, hollow, branched stems bear compound leaves of paired leaflets, loose racemes of pealike flowers in late summer, and long, cylindrical, red-brown pods with two to six kidney-shaped seeds.
• **Uses** Fresh juice pressed from the green parts clots milk and is used in cheese-making. A tea made from flowering tops strengthens the antibiotic activity of other agents and stimulates milk production in humans and livestock by up to 50 percent. The plant is diuretic, reduces fevers, expels parasitic worms, and helps reduce fatigue.
• **Remark** The aerial parts reduce blood sugar, which, when supervised, may help diabetics.

Habitat Ditches, river banks; C. & S. Europe, Asia Minor | Parts used

Family RUBIACEAE	Species *Galium odoratum*	Local name Waldmeister

SWEET WOODRUFF

This woodland herb has a red-brown, creeping rootstock, attractive "ruffs" of six to nine elliptic leaves at intervals on the stem, and small clusters of brilliant white flowers in late spring.

• **USES** The sweet, new-mown-hay scent of coumarin in the leaves develops only as the leaves dry out, so they must be picked several hours before use. They are added to liqueurs, white wines, and German May Bowl punch. They also flavor sorbets, fruit salads, and aromatic snuff. The refreshing leaf tea is a diuretic liver tonic, gives antispasmodic relief for stomach pains, and is a gentle sedative for children and elderly people. Bruised fresh leaves are an anticoagulant for wounds. Dried leaves deter insects, act as a fixative in potpourri, and scent linen.

• **REMARK** All *Galium* rhizomes yield the red dye characteristic of the Rubiaceae family. The powdered herb of *Galium verum* soothes red, inflamed skin.

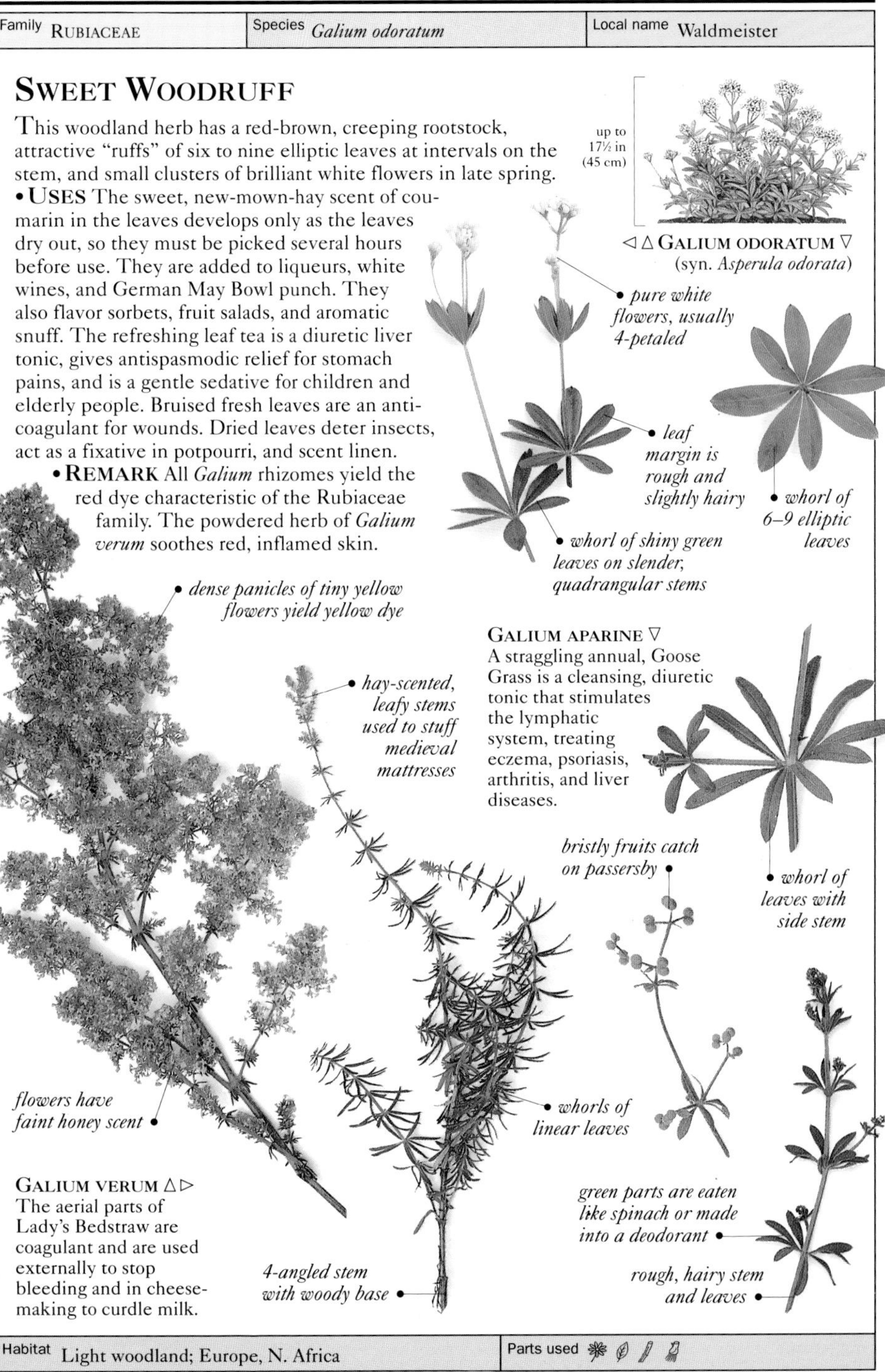
up to
17½ in
(45 cm)
pure white flowers, usually 4-petaled
leaf margin is rough and slightly hairy
whorl of 6–9 elliptic leaves
whorl of shiny green leaves on slender, quadrangular stems
dense panicles of tiny yellow flowers yield yellow dye
hay-scented, leafy stems used to stuff medieval mattresses
bristly fruits catch on passersby
whorl of leaves with side stem
flowers have faint honey scent
whorls of linear leaves
green parts are eaten like spinach or made into a deodorant
4-angled stem with woody base
rough, hairy stem and leaves

◁ △ GALIUM ODORATUM ▽
(syn. *Asperula odorata*)

GALIUM APARINE ▽
A straggling annual, Goose Grass is a cleansing, diuretic tonic that stimulates the lymphatic system, treating eczema, psoriasis, arthritis, and liver diseases.

GALIUM VERUM △ ▷
The aerial parts of Lady's Bedstraw are coagulant and are used externally to stop bleeding and in cheese-making to curdle milk.

Habitat Light woodland; Europe, N. Africa	Parts used

Family GERANIACEAE | Species *Geranium macrorrhizum* | Local name Bigroot Geranium

GERANIUM ROOT

This sticky, aromatic perennial has hairy, toothed leaves that turn red-gold in autumn, red to purple flowers, and explosive seed dispersal.

• **USES** The spicy leaves and root are added to potpourri and considered aphrodisiac in Bulgaria.

• **REMARK** A root infusion of *Geranium maculatum* is used as a mouthwash for ulcers and throat infections. It is used internally for diarrhea, stomach ulcers, internal bleeding, and externally for hemorrhoids. *G. robertianum* lowers blood sugar and may help diabetics. It is used like the valuable, rare Goldenseal.

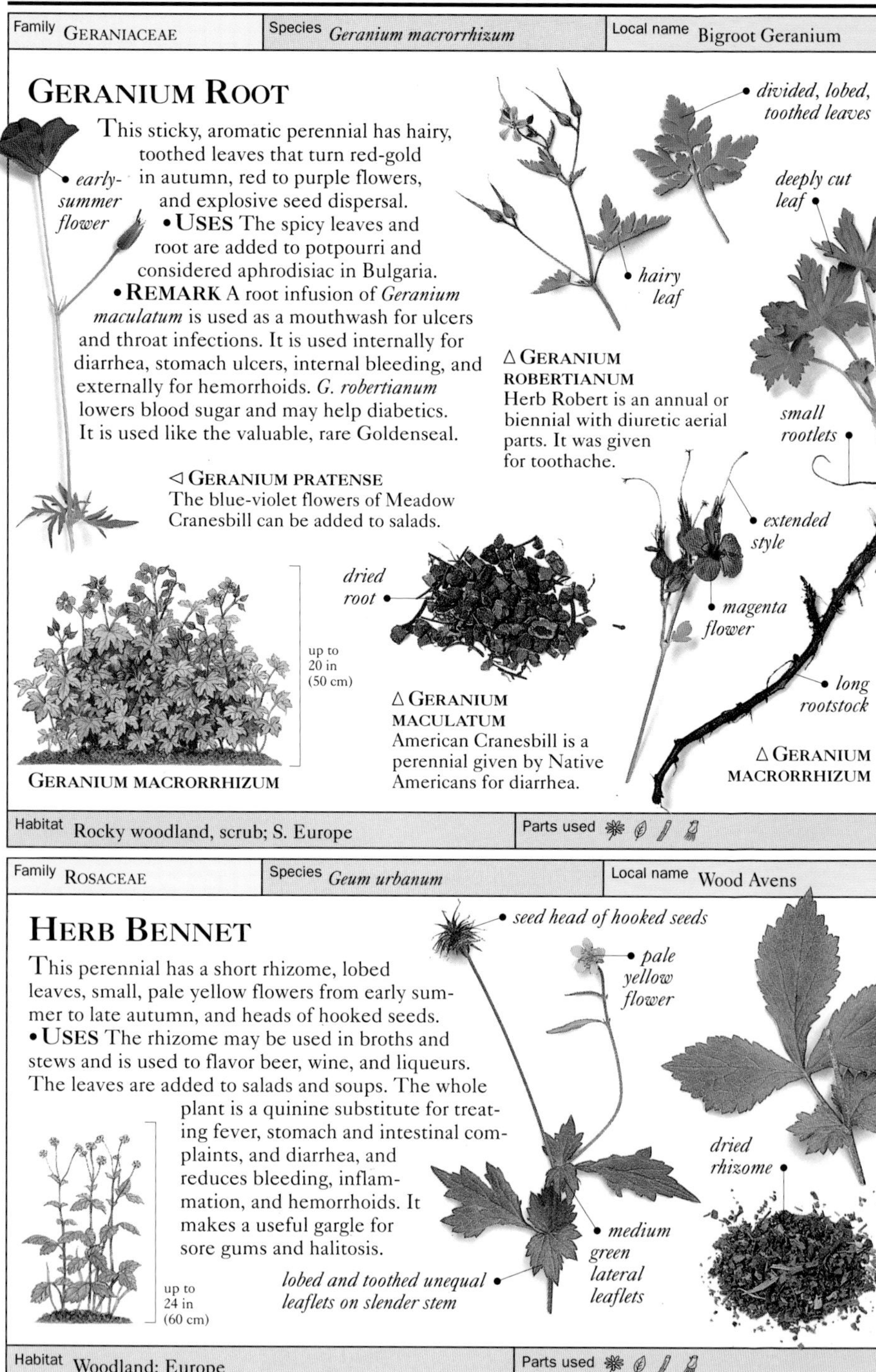

early-summer flower
divided, lobed, toothed leaves
deeply cut leaf
hairy leaf
small rootlets
extended style
dried root
magenta flower
long rootstock
up to 20 in (50 cm)
seed head of hooked seeds
pale yellow flower
dried rhizome
medium green lateral leaflets
lobed and toothed unequal leaflets on slender stem
up to 24 in (60 cm)

◁ GERANIUM PRATENSE
The blue-violet flowers of Meadow Cranesbill can be added to salads.

△ GERANIUM ROBERTIANUM
Herb Robert is an annual or biennial with diuretic aerial parts. It was given for toothache.

GERANIUM MACRORRHIZUM

△ GERANIUM MACULATUM
American Cranesbill is a perennial given by Native Americans for diarrhea.

△ GERANIUM MACRORRHIZUM

Habitat Rocky woodland, scrub; S. Europe | Parts used

Family ROSACEAE | Species *Geum urbanum* | Local name Wood Avens

HERB BENNET

This perennial has a short rhizome, lobed leaves, small, pale yellow flowers from early summer to late autumn, and heads of hooked seeds.

• **USES** The rhizome may be used in broths and stews and is used to flavor beer, wine, and liqueurs. The leaves are added to salads and soups. The whole plant is a quinine substitute for treating fever, stomach and intestinal complaints, and diarrhea, and reduces bleeding, inflammation, and hemorrhoids. It makes a useful gargle for sore gums and halitosis.

Habitat Woodland; Europe | Parts used

Family LABIATAE	Species *Glechoma hederacea*	Local name Gill-over-the-ground

GROUND IVY

Ground Ivy has non-flowering creeping stems and flowering erect stems with pink-white to blue-purple flowers.

• **USES** The young leaves are eaten in salads and brewed into aromatic "gill" tea. This traditional blood cleanser, tonic, and diuretic is given for gastritis, kidney stones, cystitis, and tinnitus and as an expectorant for phlegm. The leaves reduce bruises and inflammation.

• **REMARK** The variegated form is a popular container plant.

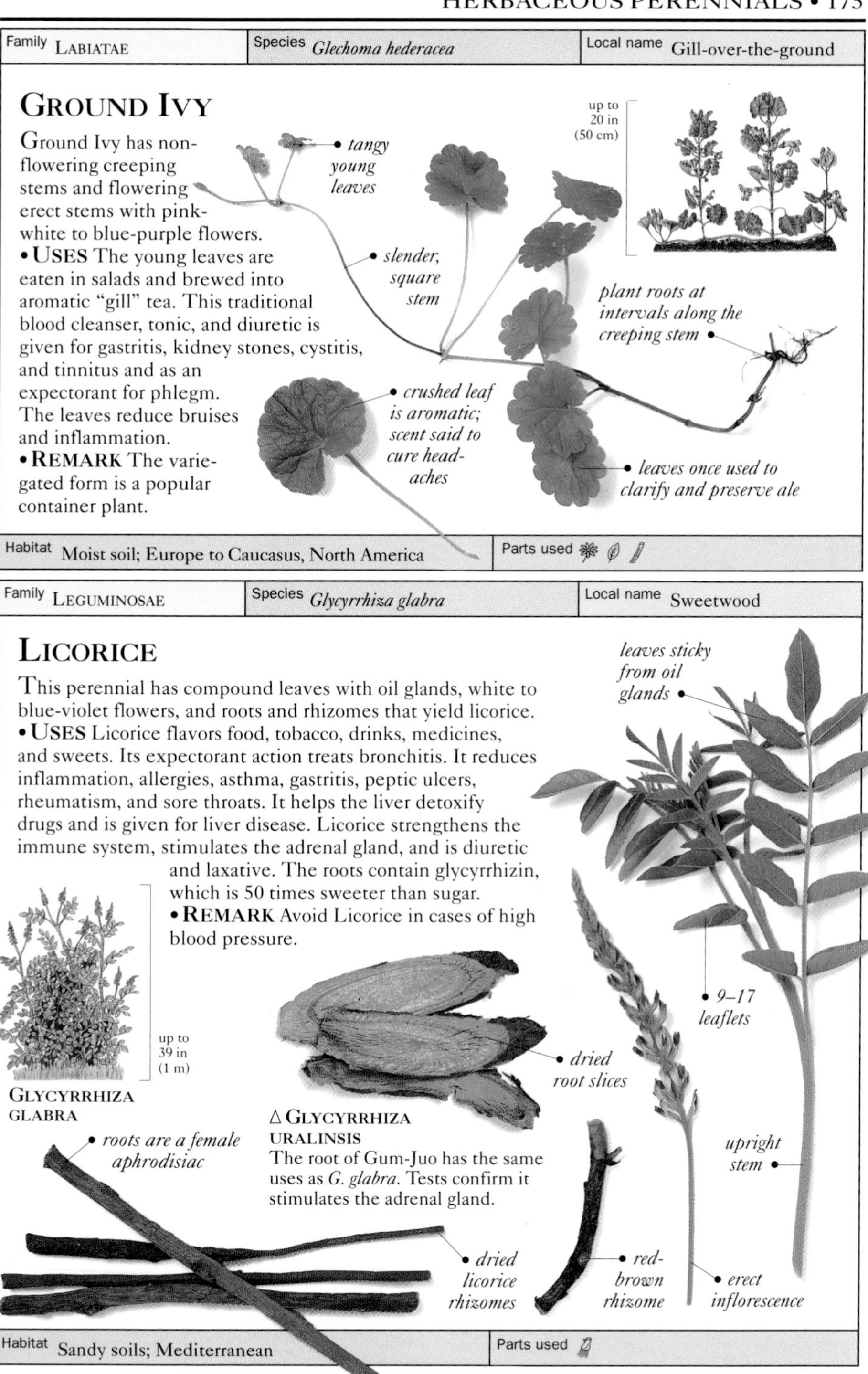
up to 20 in (50 cm)
tangy young leaves
slender, square stem
plant roots at intervals along the creeping stem
crushed leaf is aromatic; scent said to cure headaches
leaves once used to clarify and preserve ale
leaves sticky from oil glands
9–17 leaflets
up to 39 in (1 m)
dried root slices
roots are a female aphrodisiac
upright stem
dried licorice rhizomes
red-brown rhizome
erect inflorescence

Habitat Moist soil; Europe to Caucasus, North America	Parts used

Family LEGUMINOSAE	Species *Glycyrrhiza glabra*	Local name Sweetwood

LICORICE

This perennial has compound leaves with oil glands, white to blue-violet flowers, and roots and rhizomes that yield licorice.

• **USES** Licorice flavors food, tobacco, drinks, medicines, and sweets. Its expectorant action treats bronchitis. It reduces inflammation, allergies, asthma, gastritis, peptic ulcers, rheumatism, and sore throats. It helps the liver detoxify drugs and is given for liver disease. Licorice strengthens the immune system, stimulates the adrenal gland, and is diuretic and laxative. The roots contain glycyrrhizin, which is 50 times sweeter than sugar.

• **REMARK** Avoid Licorice in cases of high blood pressure.

GLYCYRRHIZA GLABRA

△ GLYCYRRHIZA URALINSIS
The root of Gum-Juo has the same uses as *G. glabra*. Tests confirm it stimulates the adrenal gland.

Habitat Sandy soils; Mediterranean	Parts used

Family COMPOSITAE	Species *Gynura* species	Local name Purple Gynura

GYNURA

This erect or spreading perennial has furry leaves with green or purple undersides and malodorous, yellow-orange flower heads.

• **USES** Young shoots of *Gynura bicolor* and *G. procumbens* are eaten, and the leaves are used to treat fevers, dysentery, and kidney complaints. In China, the plant and root of *G. segetum* and *G. divaricata* stimulate circulation, detoxify, and arrest bleeding.

• **REMARK** *G. bicolor* is grown as a houseplant.

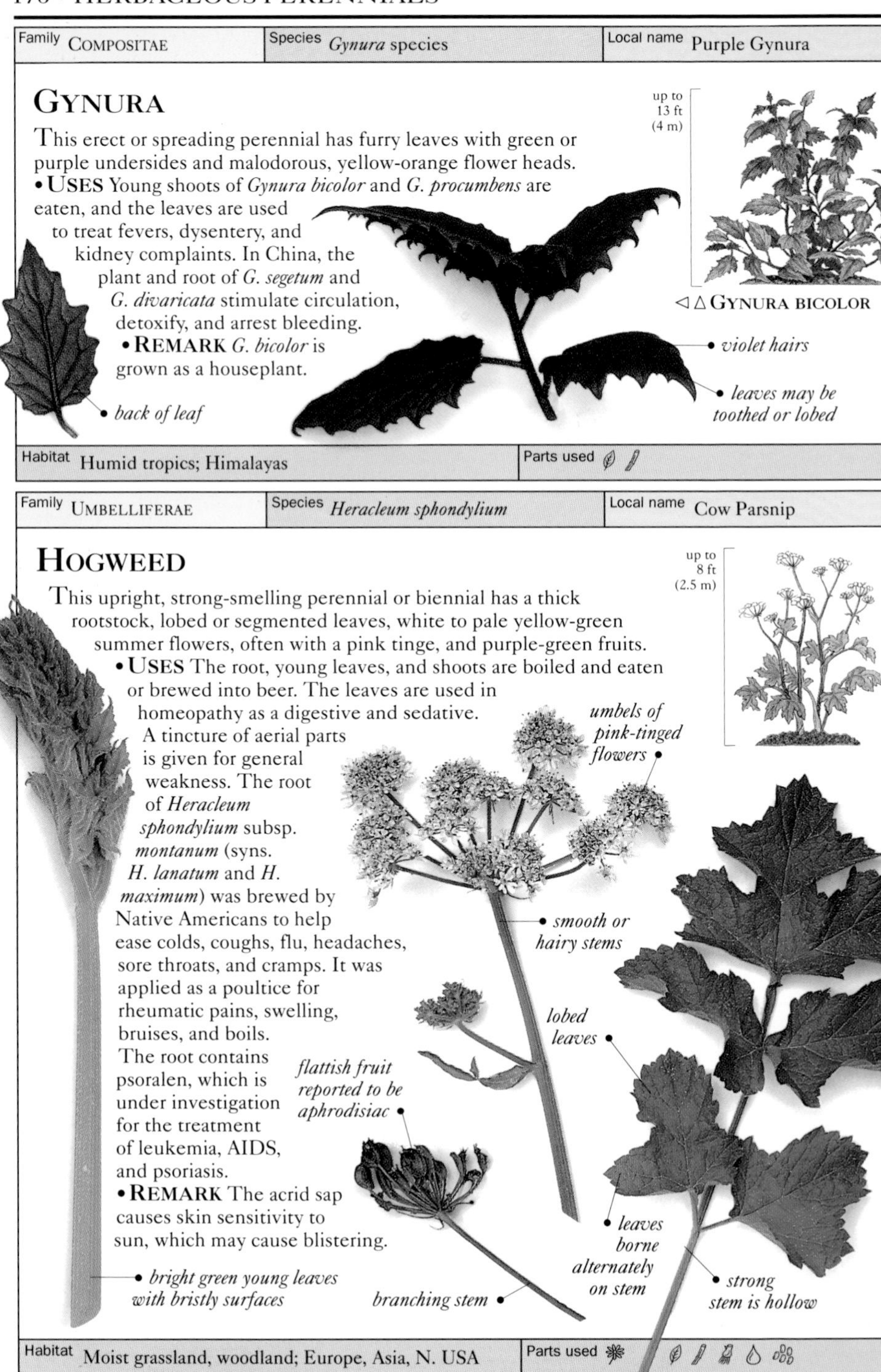
up to
13 ft
(4 m)
◁ △ GYNURA BICOLOR
violet hairs
leaves may be toothed or lobed
back of leaf
up to
8 ft
(2.5 m)
umbels of pink-tinged flowers
smooth or hairy stems
lobed leaves
flattish fruit reported to be aphrodisiac
leaves borne alternately on stem
strong stem is hollow
bright green young leaves with bristly surfaces
branching stem

Habitat Humid tropics; Himalayas	Parts used

Family UMBELLIFERAE	Species *Heracleum sphondylium*	Local name Cow Parsnip

HOGWEED

This upright, strong-smelling perennial or biennial has a thick rootstock, lobed or segmented leaves, white to pale yellow-green summer flowers, often with a pink tinge, and purple-green fruits.

• **USES** The root, young leaves, and shoots are boiled and eaten or brewed into beer. The leaves are used in homeopathy as a digestive and sedative. A tincture of aerial parts is given for general weakness. The root of *Heracleum sphondylium* subsp. *montanum* (syns. *H. lanatum* and *H. maximum*) was brewed by Native Americans to help ease colds, coughs, flu, headaches, sore throats, and cramps. It was applied as a poultice for rheumatic pains, swelling, bruises, and boils. The root contains psoralen, which is under investigation for the treatment of leukemia, AIDS, and psoriasis.

• **REMARK** The acrid sap causes skin sensitivity to sun, which may cause blistering.

Habitat Moist grassland, woodland; Europe, Asia, N. USA	Parts used

Family LILIACEAE	Species *Endymion non-scripta*	Local name Wild Hyacinth

BLUEBELL

Bluebell is a bulb with glossy, sword-shaped leaves and a sturdy flower stalk of drooping, violet-blue bells with a fresh fragrance. The petals lack the markings of other ancient hyacinth flowers, which look like the letters AL, hence the species name *non-scripta*.

• **USES** The bulb is rich in starch, historically used to stiffen collars and ruffs. The bulb and stem contain gum that makes a strong glue once used for bookbinding and to set feathers on arrows. The poet Tennyson wrote of its juice being used to cure snake bite. The bulb, poisonous when fresh, has diuretic and styptic qualities, although it is seldom used today.

• **REMARK** It was once the national flower of England.

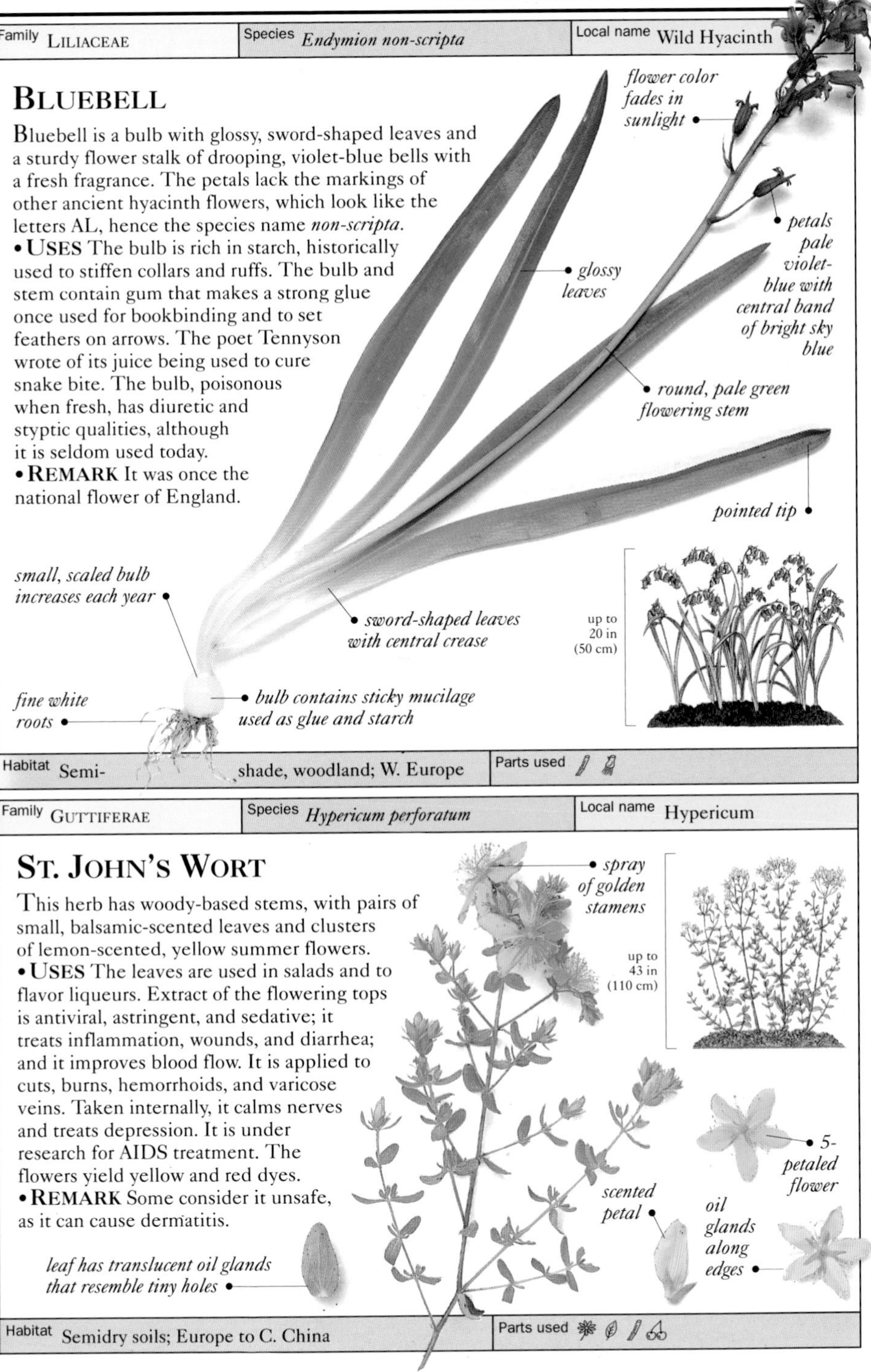
flower color fades in sunlight
petals pale violet-blue with central band of bright sky blue
glossy leaves
round, pale green flowering stem
pointed tip
small, scaled bulb increases each year
sword-shaped leaves with central crease
up to 20 in (50 cm)
fine white roots
bulb contains sticky mucilage used as glue and starch
spray of golden stamens
up to 43 in (110 cm)
5-petaled flower
scented petal
oil glands along edges
leaf has translucent oil glands that resemble tiny holes

Habitat Semi-shade, woodland; W. Europe	Parts used

Family GUTTIFERAE	Species *Hypericum perforatum*	Local name Hypericum

ST. JOHN'S WORT

This herb has woody-based stems, with pairs of small, balsamic-scented leaves and clusters of lemon-scented, yellow summer flowers.

• **USES** The leaves are used in salads and to flavor liqueurs. Extract of the flowering tops is antiviral, astringent, and sedative; it treats inflammation, wounds, and diarrhea; and it improves blood flow. It is applied to cuts, burns, hemorrhoids, and varicose veins. Taken internally, it calms nerves and treats depression. It is under research for AIDS treatment. The flowers yield yellow and red dyes.

• **REMARK** Some consider it unsafe, as it can cause dermatitis.

Habitat Semidry soils; Europe to C. China	Parts used

Family GRAMINEAE	Species *Imperata cylindrica*	Local name Pai Mao-ken

WOOLLY GRASS

This perennial grass has horizontal rhizomes covered in scales and tall stems with long, narrow leaf blades. It has a plumelike, panicle inflorescence with a dense covering of silky, silvery hairs in summer.

• **USES** In China, the antiviral roots, flowers, and slender stems are considered to have cooling properties and are brewed either together or singly. The rhizome is prescribed to reduce fevers, to stop bleeding, for coughs with phlegm, and as a diuretic for urinary tract infections. It also treats flu, internal bleeding, jaundice, and kidney problems. The flowers are given for nosebleeds and lung problems, and to quench fever thirst. The herb treats hypertension and has displayed anticancer properties in tests.

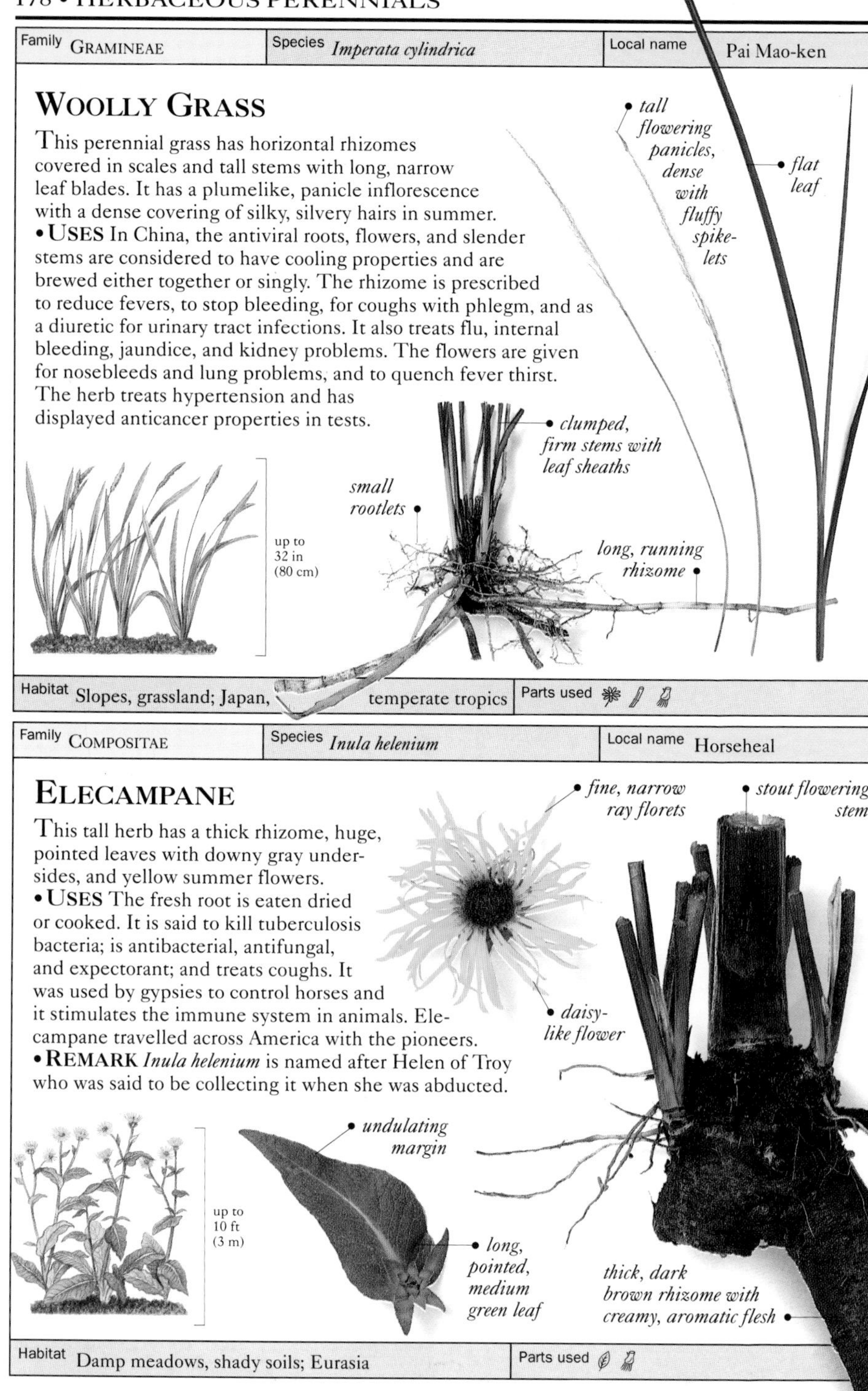
tall flowering panicles, dense with fluffy spikelets
flat leaf
clumped, firm stems with leaf sheaths
small rootlets
up to 32 in (80 cm)
long, running rhizome
fine, narrow ray florets
stout flowering stem
daisy-like flower
undulating margin
up to 10 ft (3 m)
long, pointed, medium green leaf
thick, dark brown rhizome with creamy, aromatic flesh

Habitat Slopes, grassland; Japan, temperate tropics	Parts used

Family COMPOSITAE	Species *Inula helenium*	Local name Horseheal

ELECAMPANE

This tall herb has a thick rhizome, huge, pointed leaves with downy gray undersides, and yellow summer flowers.

• **USES** The fresh root is eaten dried or cooked. It is said to kill tuberculosis bacteria; is antibacterial, antifungal, and expectorant; and treats coughs. It was used by gypsies to control horses and it stimulates the immune system in animals. Elecampane travelled across America with the pioneers.

• **REMARK** *Inula helenium* is named after Helen of Troy who was said to be collecting it when she was abducted.

Habitat Damp meadows, shady soils; Eurasia	Parts used

Family IRIDACEAE	Species *Iris germanica* var. *florentina*	Local name Fleur-de-lis

ORRIS ROOT

Orris Root has a stout rhizome, swordlike leaves, and large, scented flowers in early summer that range in color from pale blue to white.

• **USES** The violet-scented rhizome has a bitter flavor used in liqueurs; pieces are made into rosary beads; and powdered, it forms a base for tooth powders and cosmetics, acts as a fixative in potpourri, and scents linen. Oil from the roots is used as a violet substitute in perfumes. Irises are grown along the ridge of thatched roofs in France to bind and protect the straw.

• **REMARK** The fresh leaves and roots of all irises are highly poisonous. The seeds of *Iris lactae* var. *chinensis* inhibit DNA synthesis of cancer cells and promote cell immunity.

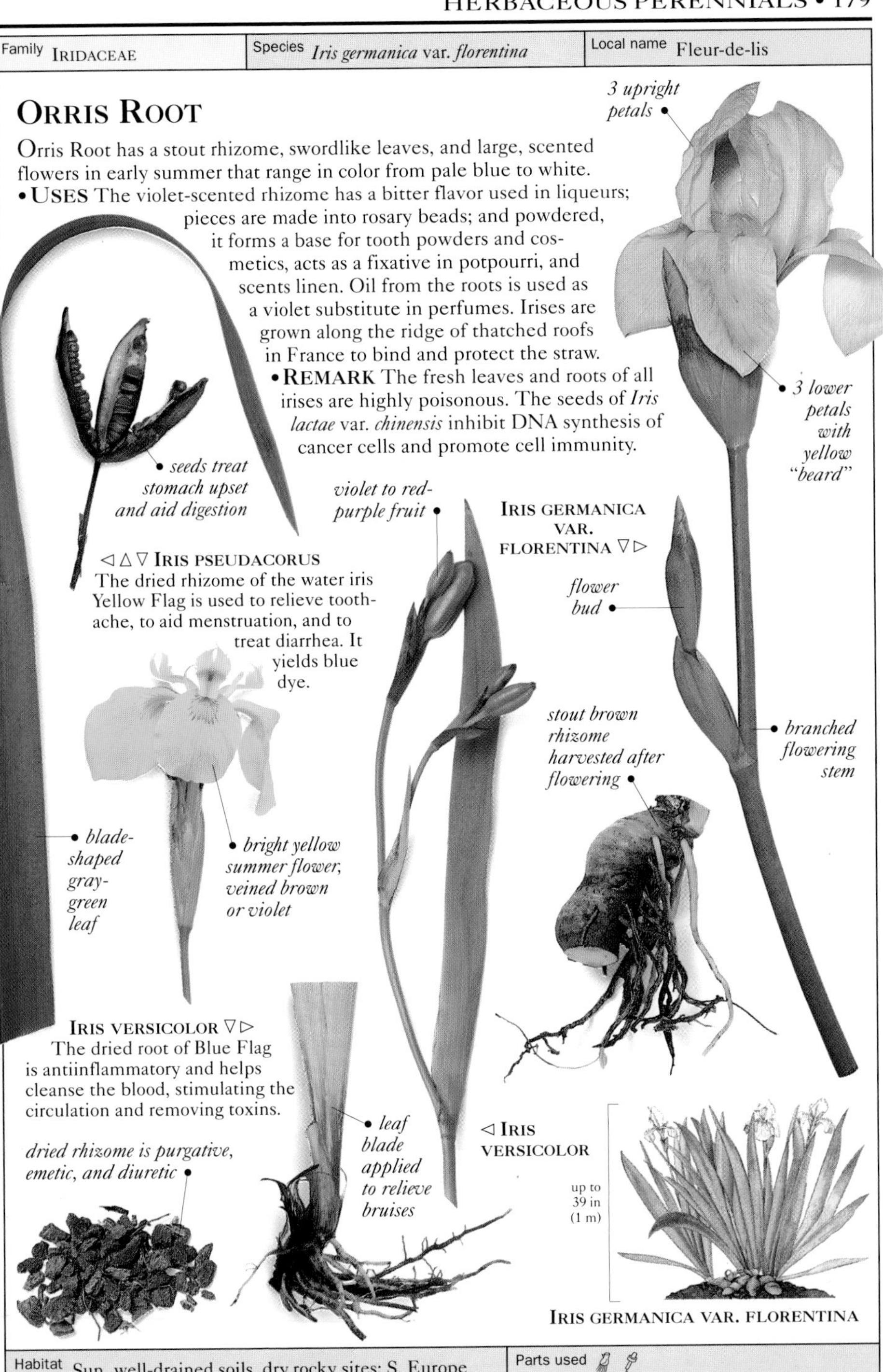
3 upright petals
3 lower petals with yellow "beard"
seeds treat stomach upset and aid digestion
violet to red-purple fruit
flower bud
branched flowering stem
stout brown rhizome harvested after flowering
blade-shaped gray-green leaf
bright yellow summer flower, veined brown or violet
dried rhizome is purgative, emetic, and diuretic
leaf blade applied to relieve bruises
up to 39 in (1 m)

IRIS GERMANICA VAR. FLORENTINA ▽ ▷

◁ △ ▽ IRIS PSEUDACORUS
The dried rhizome of the water iris Yellow Flag is used to relieve toothache, to aid menstruation, and to treat diarrhea. It yields blue dye.

IRIS VERSICOLOR ▽ ▷
The dried root of Blue Flag is antiinflammatory and helps cleanse the blood, stimulating the circulation and removing toxins.

◁ IRIS VERSICOLOR

IRIS GERMANICA VAR. FLORENTINA

Habitat Sun, well-drained soils, dry rocky sites; S. Europe	Parts used

Family ZINGIBERACEAE	Species *Kaempferia angustifolia*	Himalayan Ginger Lily

RESURRECTION LILY

This stemless, rhizomatous herb has clusters of leaves and sparse spikes of fragrant white and lilac flowers.

• **USES** The aromatic rhizome is chewed for pleasure in Asia and powdered as snuff to reduce the nasal congestion of colds. It treats high fevers, diarrhea, dysentery, and obesity. The essential oils are used commercially.

• **REMARK** The leaf and rhizome of *Kaempferia rotunda* is a condiment. The rhizome also treats stomachache and wounds.

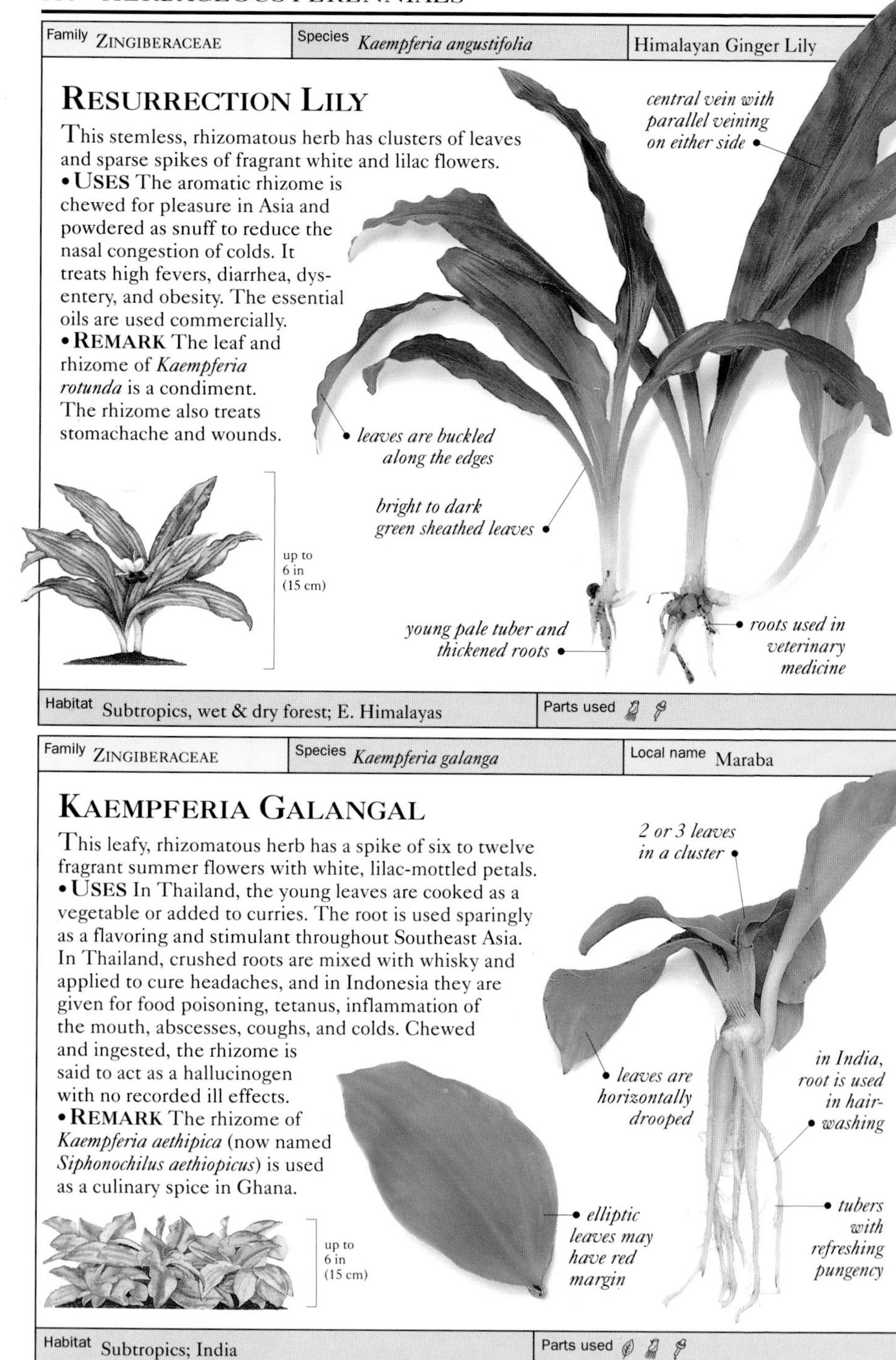
central vein with parallel veining on either side
leaves are buckled along the edges
bright to dark green sheathed leaves
up to 6 in (15 cm)
young pale tuber and thickened roots
roots used in veterinary medicine
2 or 3 leaves in a cluster
leaves are horizontally drooped
in India, root is used in hair-washing
elliptic leaves may have red margin
tubers with refreshing pungency
up to 6 in (15 cm)

Habitat Subtropics, wet & dry forest; E. Himalayas	Parts used

Family ZINGIBERACEAE	Species *Kaempferia galanga*	Local name Maraba

KAEMPFERIA GALANGAL

This leafy, rhizomatous herb has a spike of six to twelve fragrant summer flowers with white, lilac-mottled petals.

• **USES** In Thailand, the young leaves are cooked as a vegetable or added to curries. The root is used sparingly as a flavoring and stimulant throughout Southeast Asia. In Thailand, crushed roots are mixed with whisky and applied to cure headaches, and in Indonesia they are given for food poisoning, tetanus, inflammation of the mouth, abscesses, coughs, and colds. Chewed and ingested, the rhizome is said to act as a hallucinogen with no recorded ill effects.

• **REMARK** The rhizome of *Kaempferia aethipica* (now named *Siphonochilus aethiopicus*) is used as a culinary spice in Ghana.

Habitat Subtropics; India	Parts used

Family LABIATAE	Species *Lamium album*	Local name Archangel

WHITE DEAD NETTLE

This nonstinging Dead Nettle's long rhizome bears erect stems that are square and hollow, with opposite pairs of bright green leaves and clusters of tubular white flowers.

• **USES** The young leaves can be boiled as vegetables or added to soups. The flowering plant is decocted as a blood tonic. It constricts blood vessels, treating excessive menstruation, vaginal discharge, cystitis, hemorrhoids, burns, and some eye conditions. An infusion is made into an astringent wash for eczema, to stop wounds from bleeding, and is drunk as a tonic for the reproductive organs.

• **REMARK** It is not related to the Stinging Nettle.

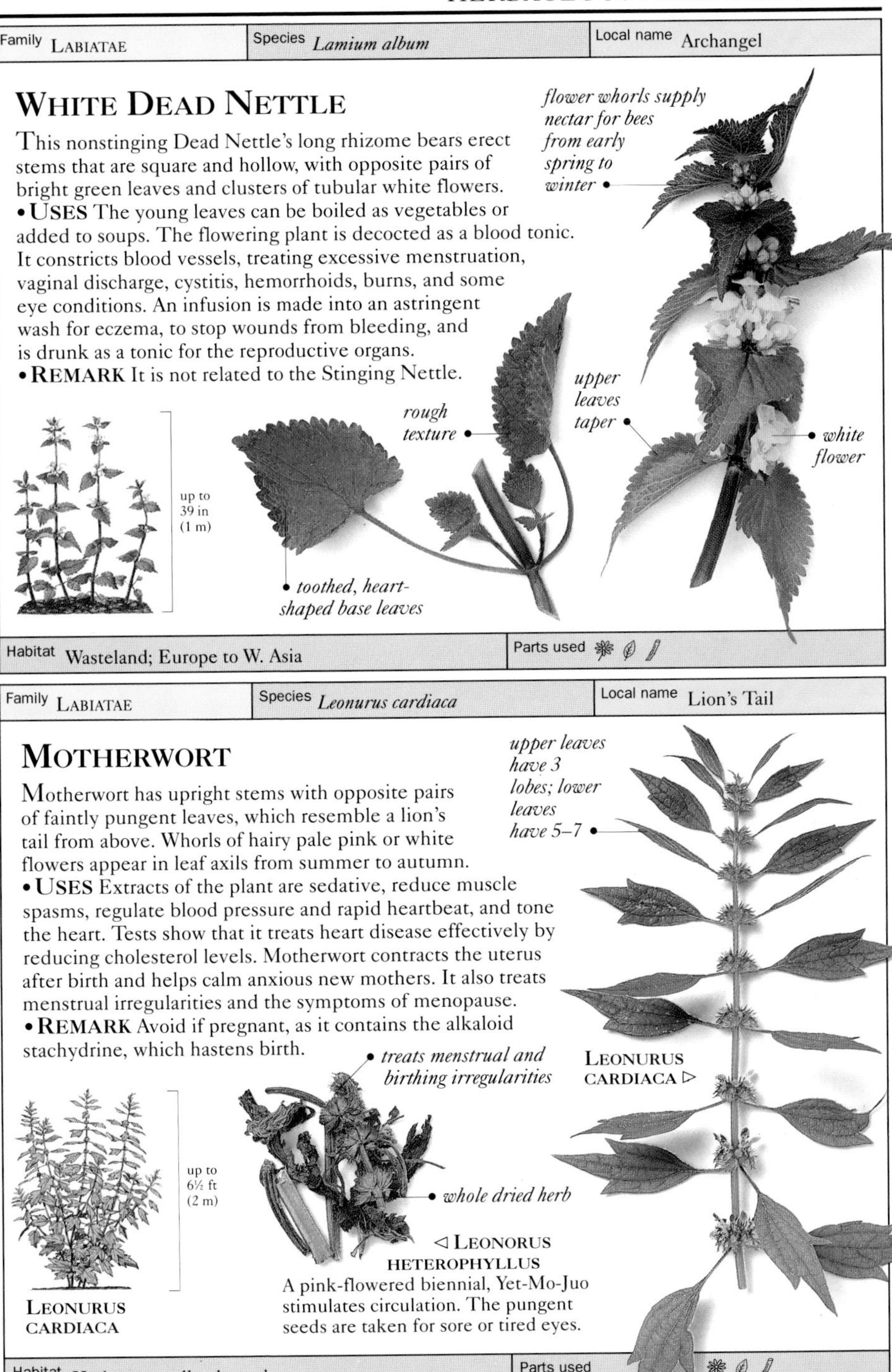
flower whorls supply nectar for bees from early spring to winter
upper leaves taper
white flower
rough texture
toothed, heart-shaped base leaves
up to 39 in (1 m)
upper leaves have 3 lobes; lower leaves have 5–7
LEONURUS CARDIACA ▷
treats menstrual and birthing irregularities
whole dried herb
up to 6½ ft (2 m)
LEONURUS CARDIACA

Habitat Wasteland; Europe to W. Asia	Parts used

Family LABIATAE	Species *Leonurus cardiaca*	Local name Lion's Tail

MOTHERWORT

Motherwort has upright stems with opposite pairs of faintly pungent leaves, which resemble a lion's tail from above. Whorls of hairy pale pink or white flowers appear in leaf axils from summer to autumn.

• **USES** Extracts of the plant are sedative, reduce muscle spasms, regulate blood pressure and rapid heartbeat, and tone the heart. Tests show that it treats heart disease effectively by reducing cholesterol levels. Motherwort contracts the uterus after birth and helps calm anxious new mothers. It also treats menstrual irregularities and the symptoms of menopause.

• **REMARK** Avoid if pregnant, as it contains the alkaloid stachydrine, which hastens birth.

◁ **LEONORUS HETEROPHYLLUS**
A pink-flowered biennial, Yet-Mo-Juo stimulates circulation. The pungent seeds are taken for sore or tired eyes.

Habitat Hedges, woodland; northern temperate zones	Parts used

Family COMPOSITAE | Species *Chrysanthemum leucanthemum* | Local name Moon Daisy

OX-EYE DAISY

This herb has scalloped, spoon-shaped lower leaves, narrow upper leaves, and daisylike flowers.

• **USES** Tender shoots are added to salads; roots and leaves are sometimes cooked. The green parts and balsamic flowers are a tonic and antispasmodic treatment for chest complaints. Distilled water of the whole plant soothes conjunctivitis and the leaf and flower are applied to wounds and bruises. The root is prescribed for sweating caused by tuberculosis.

• **REMARK** Dedicated to Artemis, goddess of women, this is considered a woman's herb.

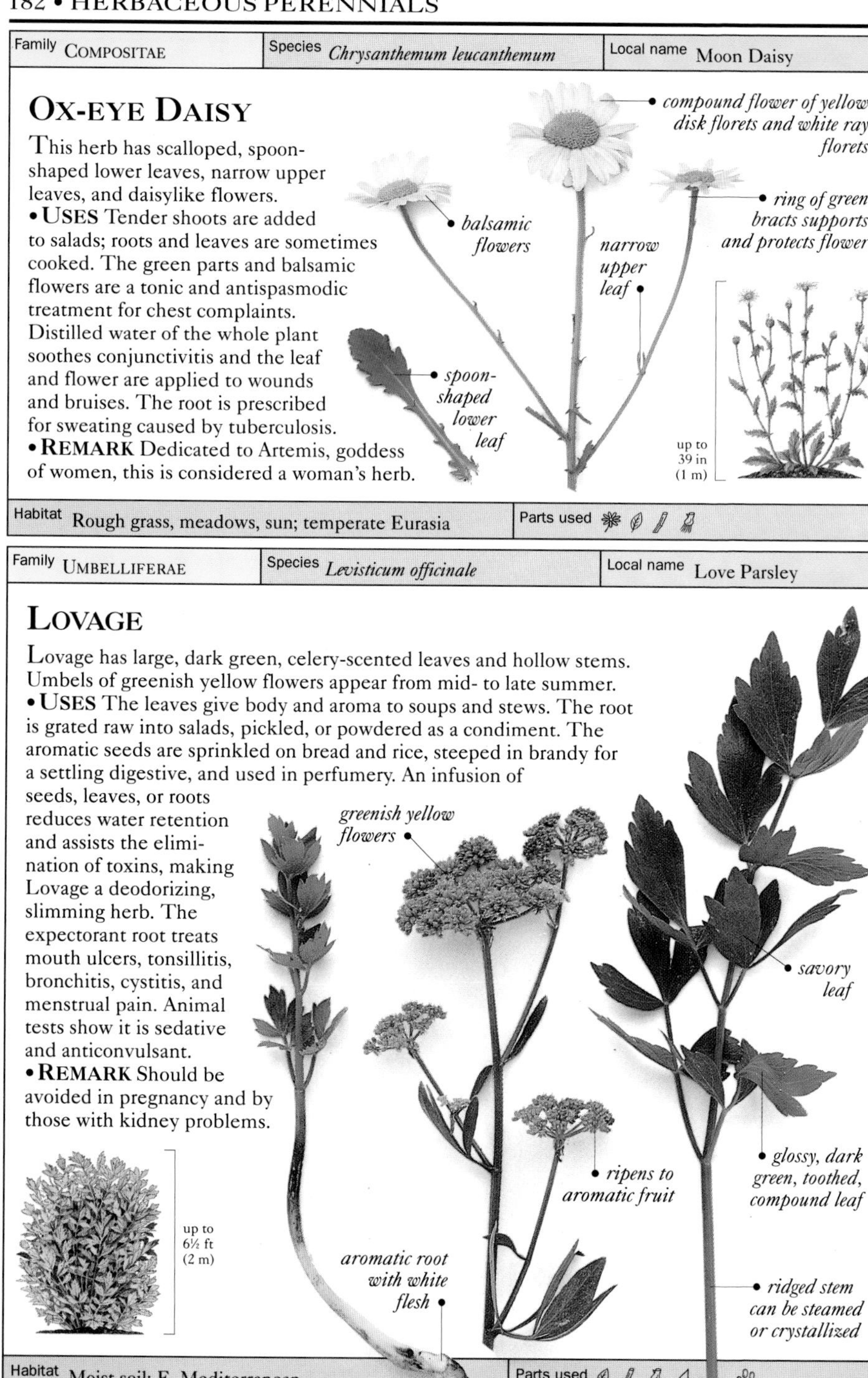

compound flower of yellow disk florets and white ray florets
balsamic flowers
narrow upper leaf
ring of green bracts supports and protects flower
spoon-shaped lower leaf
up to 39 in (1 m)

Habitat Rough grass, meadows, sun; temperate Eurasia | Parts used

Family UMBELLIFERAE | Species *Levisticum officinale* | Local name Love Parsley

LOVAGE

Lovage has large, dark green, celery-scented leaves and hollow stems. Umbels of greenish yellow flowers appear from mid- to late summer.

• **USES** The leaves give body and aroma to soups and stews. The root is grated raw into salads, pickled, or powdered as a condiment. The aromatic seeds are sprinkled on bread and rice, steeped in brandy for a settling digestive, and used in perfumery. An infusion of seeds, leaves, or roots reduces water retention and assists the elimination of toxins, making Lovage a deodorizing, slimming herb. The expectorant root treats mouth ulcers, tonsillitis, bronchitis, cystitis, and menstrual pain. Animal tests show it is sedative and anticonvulsant.

• **REMARK** Should be avoided in pregnancy and by those with kidney problems.

greenish yellow flowers
savory leaf
ripens to aromatic fruit
glossy, dark green, toothed, compound leaf
up to 6½ ft (2 m)
aromatic root with white flesh
ridged stem can be steamed or crystallized

Habitat Moist soil; E. Mediterranean | Parts used

Family COMPOSITAE | Species *Liatris spicata* | Local name Button Snakewort

GAY FEATHER

This striking rhizomatous herb has long stems with many thin, radiating leaves, and feathery, compound flowers.

• **USES** The leaves and turpentine-scented root are powdered to repel insects and flavor tobacco. The diuretic, sweat-inducing, and antibacterial root is decocted for use as a sore throat gargle and once treated gonorrhea.

• **REMARK** *Liatris chapmannii* contains liatrin, which has anticancer properties. Vanilla Plant (*L. odoratissima*) leaves contain coumarin, which repels moths; they are soothing and reduce fevers. The root is a strong diuretic.

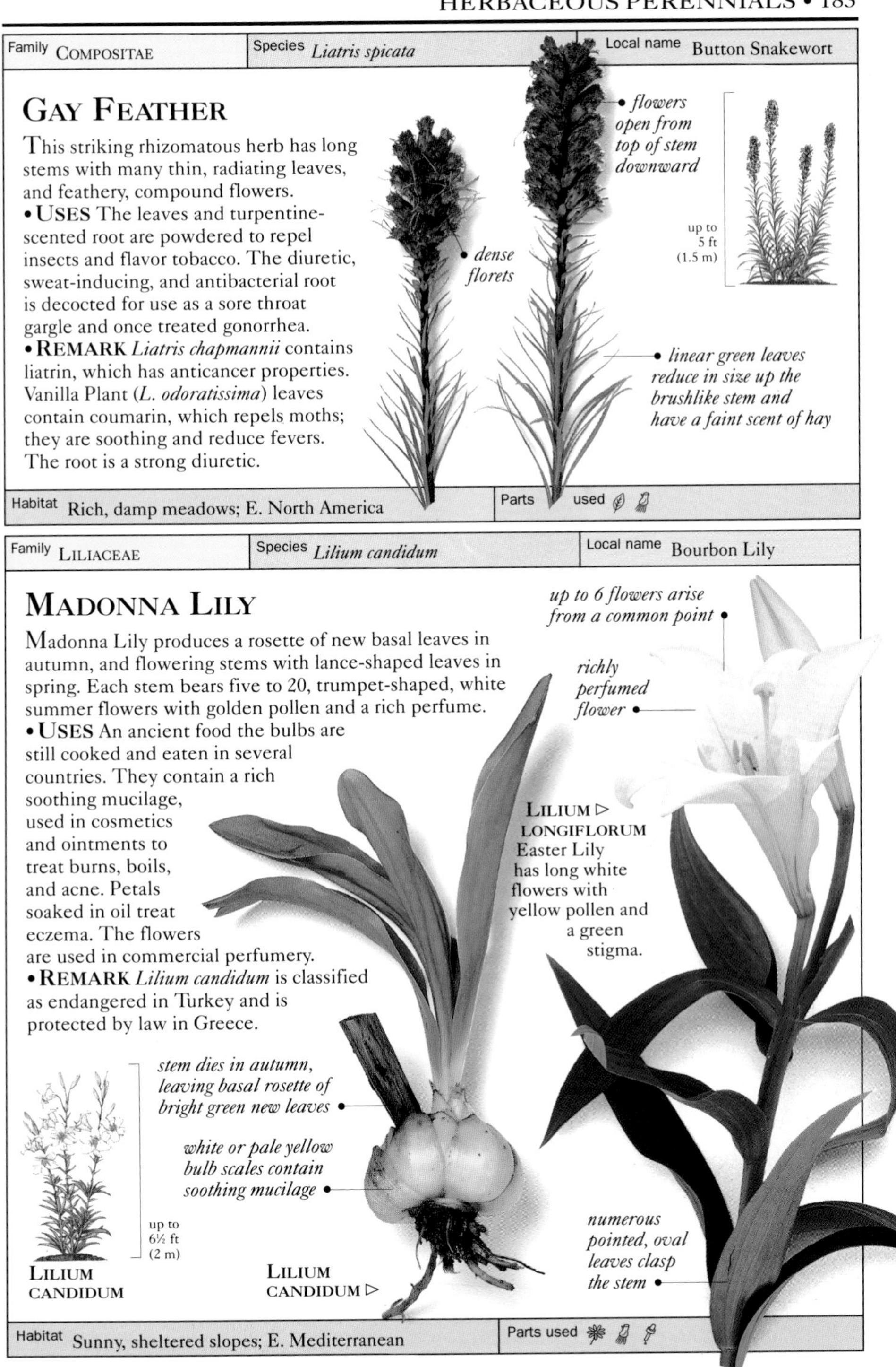

flowers open from top of stem downward
dense florets
up to 5 ft (1.5 m)
linear green leaves reduce in size up the brushlike stem and have a faint scent of hay
up to 6 flowers arise from a common point
richly perfumed flower
LILIUM ▷ LONGIFLORUM
Easter Lily has long white flowers with yellow pollen and a green stigma.
stem dies in autumn, leaving basal rosette of bright green new leaves
white or pale yellow bulb scales contain soothing mucilage
up to 6½ ft (2 m)
LILIUM CANDIDUM
LILIUM CANDIDUM ▷
numerous pointed, oval leaves clasp the stem

Habitat Rich, damp meadows; E. North America | Parts used

Family LILIACEAE | Species *Lilium candidum* | Local name Bourbon Lily

MADONNA LILY

Madonna Lily produces a rosette of new basal leaves in autumn, and flowering stems with lance-shaped leaves in spring. Each stem bears five to 20, trumpet-shaped, white summer flowers with golden pollen and a rich perfume.

• **USES** An ancient food the bulbs are still cooked and eaten in several countries. They contain a rich soothing mucilage, used in cosmetics and ointments to treat burns, boils, and acne. Petals soaked in oil treat eczema. The flowers are used in commercial perfumery.

• **REMARK** *Lilium candidum* is classified as endangered in Turkey and is protected by law in Greece.

Habitat Sunny, sheltered slopes; E. Mediterranean | Parts used

Family CAMPANULACEAE	Species *Lobelia siphilitica*	Local name Blue Cardinal Flower

GIANT LOBELIA

This erect, leafy perennial with lance-shaped leaves has tubular blue flowers from summer to autumn.

• **USES** Decocted root was used by the Iroquois to treat syphilis. It is given for fluid retention and is used in homeopathy for diarrhea. Powdered root was put in the bed of arguing Iroquois couples to rekindle love.

• **REMARK** The leaves and shoots of Cardinal Flower (*Lobelia cardinalis*) and Indian Tobacco (*L. inflata*) contain alkaloids that are expectorant and cause vomiting. Cardinal Flower is milder and is used to treat bronchial spasms. Indian Tobacco is more poisonous, with side effects, but as it stimulates respiration, it is smoked to treat asthma and bronchitis and to improve mental clarity. It is added to smoking-cessation mixtures as a nicotine substitute. Both should be taken in small doses and given by qualified medical personnel only.

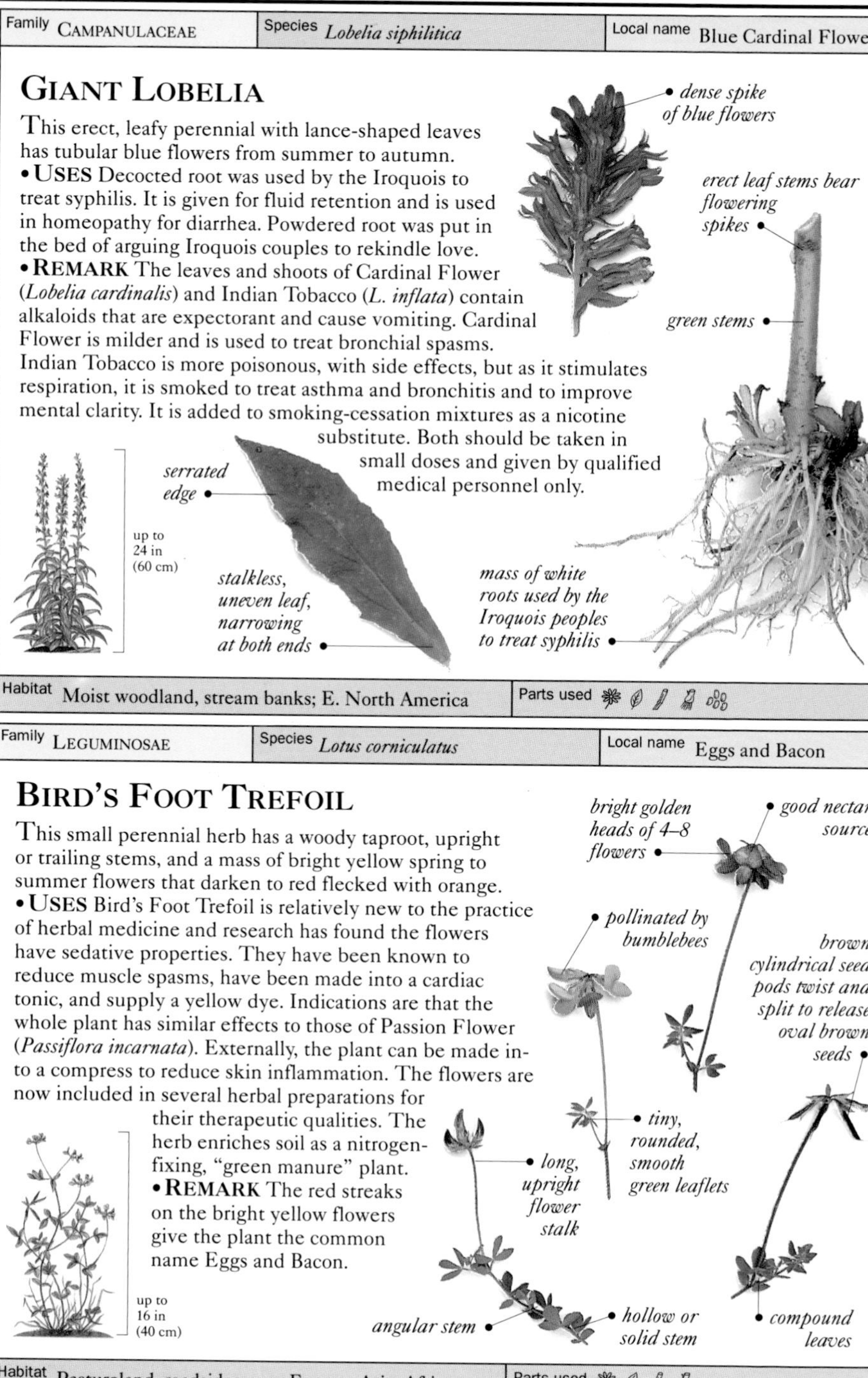

dense spike of blue flowers
erect leaf stems bear flowering spikes
green stems
serrated edge
up to 24 in (60 cm)
stalkless, uneven leaf, narrowing at both ends
mass of white roots used by the Iroquois peoples to treat syphilis
bright golden heads of 4–8 flowers
good nectar source
pollinated by bumblebees
brown cylindrical seed pods twist and split to release oval brown seeds
tiny, rounded, smooth green leaflets
long, upright flower stalk
up to 16 in (40 cm)
angular stem
hollow or solid stem
compound leaves

Habitat Moist woodland, stream banks; E. North America	Parts used

Family LEGUMINOSAE	Species *Lotus corniculatus*	Local name Eggs and Bacon

BIRD'S FOOT TREFOIL

This small perennial herb has a woody taproot, upright or trailing stems, and a mass of bright yellow spring to summer flowers that darken to red flecked with orange.

• **USES** Bird's Foot Trefoil is relatively new to the practice of herbal medicine and research has found the flowers have sedative properties. They have been known to reduce muscle spasms, have been made into a cardiac tonic, and supply a yellow dye. Indications are that the whole plant has similar effects to those of Passion Flower (*Passiflora incarnata*). Externally, the plant can be made into a compress to reduce skin inflammation. The flowers are now included in several herbal preparations for their therapeutic qualities. The herb enriches soil as a nitrogen-fixing, "green manure" plant.

• **REMARK** The red streaks on the bright yellow flowers give the plant the common name Eggs and Bacon.

Habitat Pastureland, roadsides, sun; Europe, Asia, Africa	Parts used

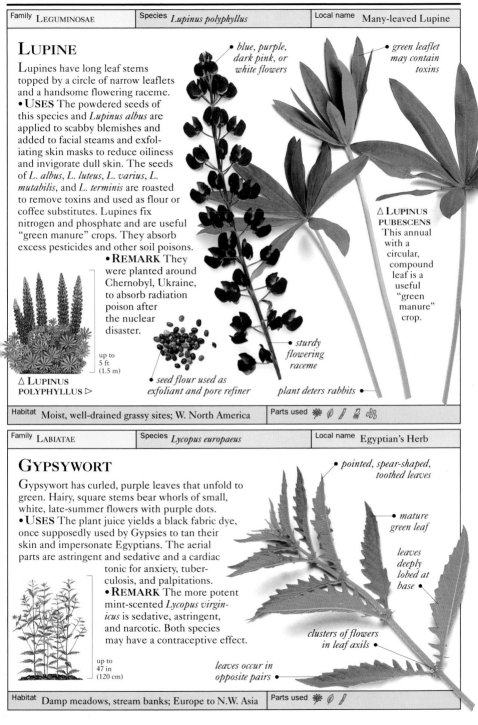

Family LEGUMINOSAE	Species *Lupinus polyphyllus*	Local name Many-leaved Lupine

LUPINE

Lupines have long leaf stems topped by a circle of narrow leaflets and a handsome flowering raceme.
• **USES** The powdered seeds of this species and *Lupinus albus* are applied to scabby blemishes and added to facial steams and exfoliating skin masks to reduce oiliness and invigorate dull skin. The seeds of *L. albus*, *L. luteus*, *L. varius*, *L. mutabilis*, and *L. terminis* are roasted to remove toxins and used as flour or coffee substitutes. Lupines fix nitrogen and phosphate and are useful "green manure" crops. They absorb excess pesticides and other soil poisons.
• **REMARK** They were planted around Chernobyl, Ukraine, to absorb radiation poison after the nuclear disaster.

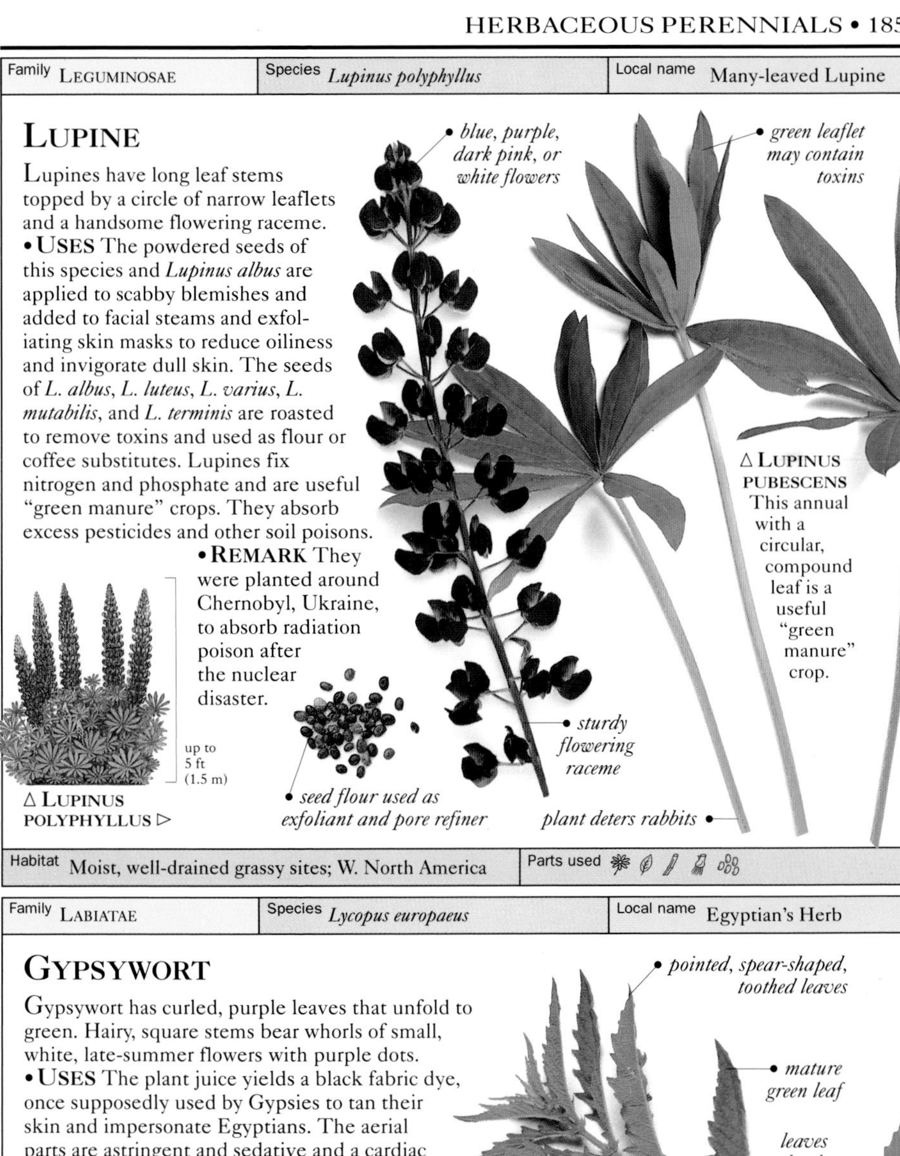

blue, purple, dark pink, or white flowers
green leaflet may contain toxins
sturdy flowering raceme
seed flour used as exfoliant and pore refiner
plant deters rabbits
up to 5 ft (1.5 m)

△ LUPINUS PUBESCENS This annual with a circular, compound leaf is a useful "green manure" crop.

△ LUPINUS POLYPHYLLUS ▷

Habitat Moist, well-drained grassy sites; W. North America	Parts used

Family LABIATAE	Species *Lycopus europaeus*	Local name Egyptian's Herb

GYPSYWORT

Gypsywort has curled, purple leaves that unfold to green. Hairy, square stems bear whorls of small, white, late-summer flowers with purple dots.
• **USES** The plant juice yields a black fabric dye, once supposedly used by Gypsies to tan their skin and impersonate Egyptians. The aerial parts are astringent and sedative and a cardiac tonic for anxiety, tuberculosis, and palpitations.
• **REMARK** The more potent mint-scented *Lycopus virginicus* is sedative, astringent, and narcotic. Both species may have a contraceptive effect.

pointed, spear-shaped, toothed leaves

mature green leaf

leaves deeply lobed at base

clusters of flowers in leaf axils

leaves occur in opposite pairs

up to 47 in (120 cm)

Habitat Damp meadows, stream banks; Europe to N.W. Asia	Parts used

Family LYTHRACEAE	Species *Lythrum salicaria*	Local name Spiked Loosestrife

PURPLE LOOSESTRIFE

Purple Loosestrife has a creeping rootstock, angled stems with lance-shaped leaves, and spikes of purple-red flowers. • **USES** The leaves are eaten as an emergency vegetable and fermented into a mild alcohol. The astringent leaves tighten skin, counter wrinkles, and add sheen to blond hair. The herb brightens eyes and reduces puffiness. It shrinks blood capillaries, reducing over-reddened skin and curbing nosebleeds. The flowering plant is an intestinal disinfectant, treating diarrhea and food poisoning. It acts as a typhus antibiotic, a sore throat gargle, and is given for fever and liver problems, to cleanse sores, and to stanch bleeding wounds. • **REMARK** *Lythrum verticillatum* has similar uses, and is planted in pastures to prevent abortion in cows and mares.

up to 47 in (120 cm)

• *spike of long-lasting, late-summer flowers*

• *clustered whorls of purple-red flowers in bract axils*

• *angled stem covered in soft, fine hairs*

• *opposite leaves with smooth margin*

narrow, pointed leaves •

Habitat Water-retentive land; temperate Europe, Asia, Africa	Parts used

Family MALVACEAE	Species *Malva moschata*	Local name Cutleaf Mallow

MUSK MALLOW

Musk Mallow has faintly musky, elegantly cut leaves on branching stems and rounded, shallow-lobed basal leaves with large, white or pink flowers throughout summer. • **USES** The flowers are used in salads, and the leaves and young shoots which contain vitamins A, B, and C, are boiled as a vegetable. The leaves and roots are added to soothing skin ointments and cough syrups. • **REMARK** Common Mallow is used like Musk Mallow, but is more potent. The leaves, flowers, and roots soothe membranes, reduce inflammation, and are given for bronchitis and gastrointestinal irritations.

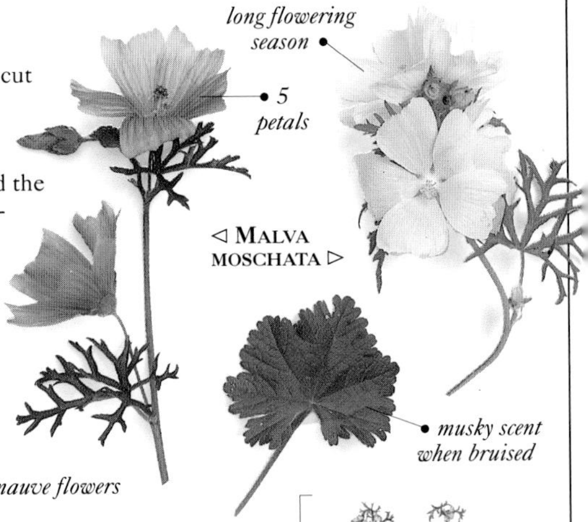

long flowering season •

• *5 petals*

◁ MALVA MOSCHATA ▷

• *musky scent when bruised*

• *veined mauve flowers*

◁ MALVA SYLVESTRIS
Common Mallow is a perennial with a pulpy taproot and emollient, expectorant, vitamin-rich leaves.

up to 24 in (60 cm)

• *toothed leaf with soft hairs*

• *a leaf poultice soothes insect bites*

MALVA MOSCHATA

Habitat Wasteland, sun; Europe, N.W. Africa	Parts used

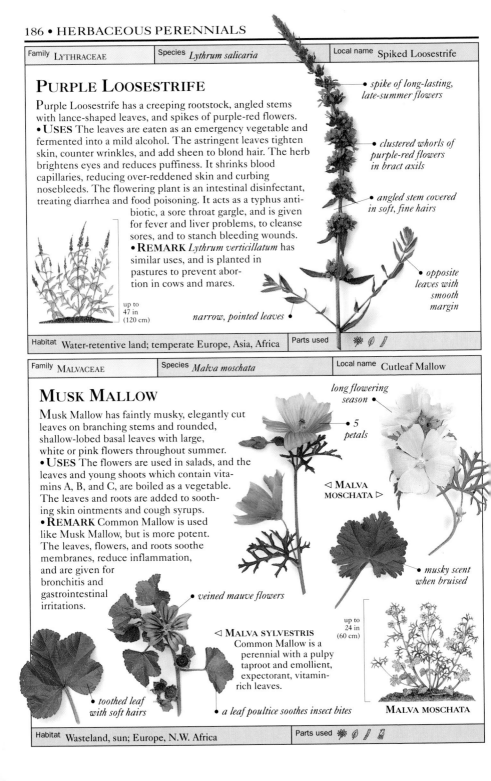

Family SOLANACEAE	Species *Mandragora officinarum*	Devil's Apple

MANDRAKE

Highly poisonous Mandrake has a long, parsniplike root that can grow into a humanlike form, and a rosette of leaves with pale purple flowers which become round, yellow, pineapple-scented fruits.

• **USES** Mandrake root was a sedative for depression, anxiety, and insomnia and later an anesthetic for surgery, with the leaves used externally for pain relief. Both root and leaf tea produce initial excitement and then torpor, giving the plant an aphrodisiac reputation and role in fertility. It became a witches' hexing herb, and the link with flying probably came from Mandrake's hallucinatory effect. It is a homeopathic treatment for asthma and coughs.

• **REMARK** Mandrake root is one of the oldest narcotics.

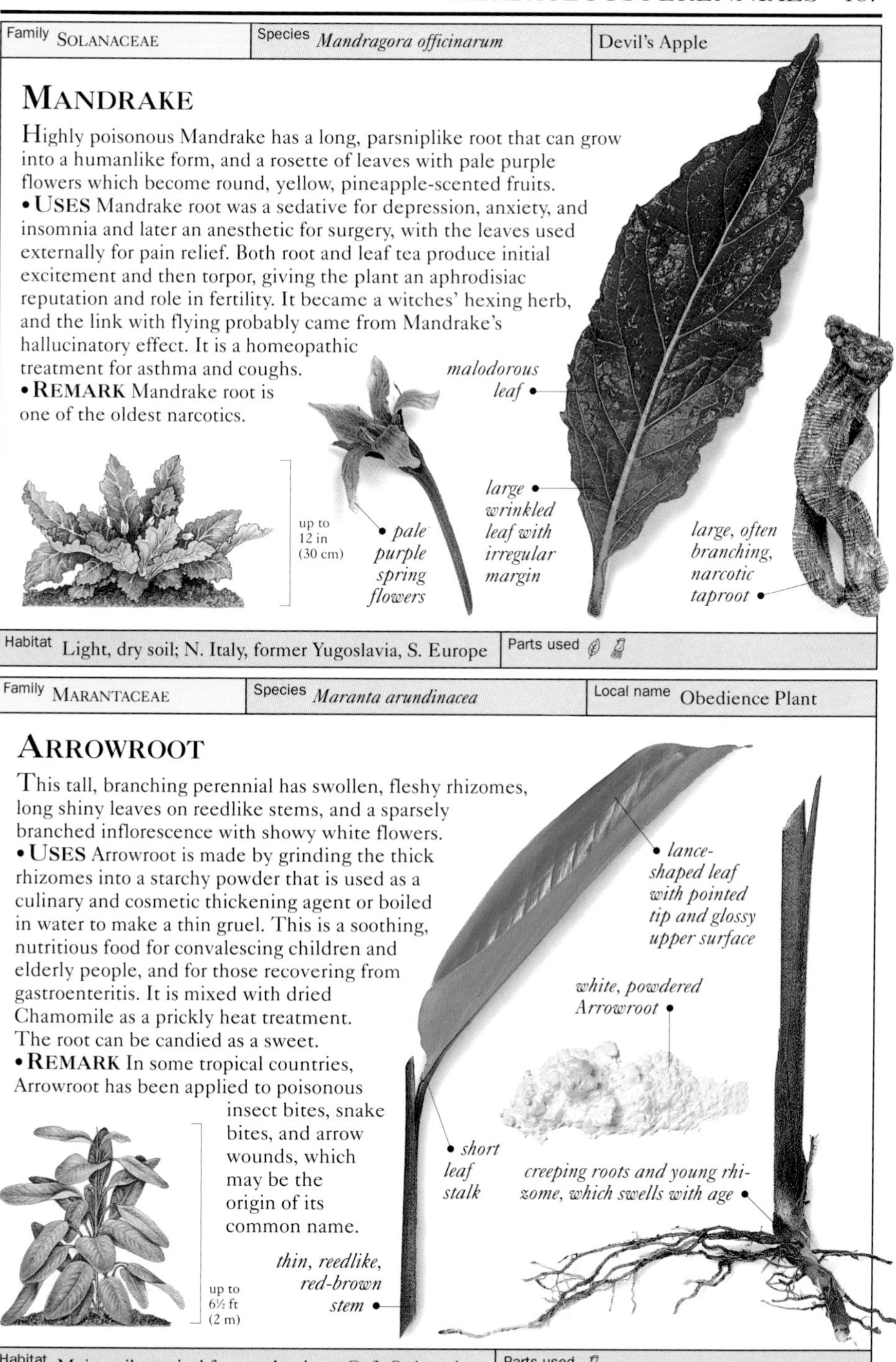
up to 12 in (30 cm)
pale purple spring flowers
malodorous leaf
large wrinkled leaf with irregular margin
large, often branching, narcotic taproot
up to 6½ ft (2 m)
thin, reedlike, red-brown stem
short leaf stalk
lance-shaped leaf with pointed tip and glossy upper surface
white, powdered Arrowroot
creeping roots and young rhizome, which swells with age

Habitat Light, dry soil; N. Italy, former Yugoslavia, S. Europe	Parts used

Family MARANTACEAE	Species *Maranta arundinacea*	Local name Obedience Plant

ARROWROOT

This tall, branching perennial has swollen, fleshy rhizomes, long shiny leaves on reedlike stems, and a sparsely branched inflorescence with showy white flowers.

• **USES** Arrowroot is made by grinding the thick rhizomes into a starchy powder that is used as a culinary and cosmetic thickening agent or boiled in water to make a thin gruel. This is a soothing, nutritious food for convalescing children and elderly people, and for those recovering from gastroenteritis. It is mixed with dried Chamomile as a prickly heat treatment. The root can be candied as a sweet.

• **REMARK** In some tropical countries, Arrowroot has been applied to poisonous insect bites, snake bites, and arrow wounds, which may be the origin of its common name.

Habitat Moist soil, tropical forest, clearings; C. & S. America	Parts used

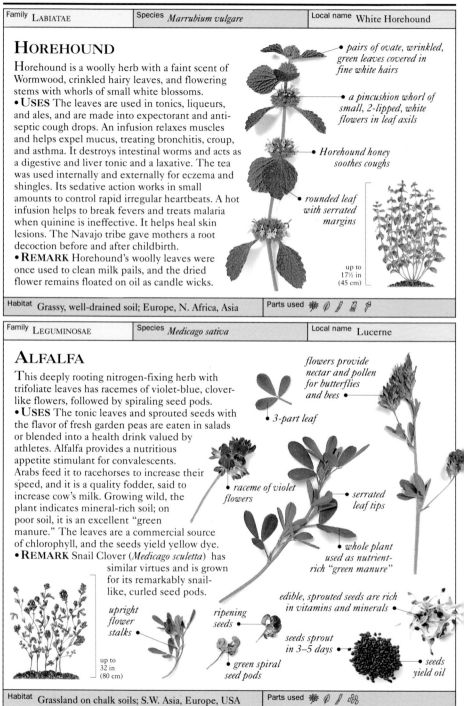

Family LABIATAE	Species *Marrubium vulgare*	Local name White Horehound

HOREHOUND

Horehound is a woolly herb with a faint scent of Wormwood, crinkled hairy leaves, and flowering stems with whorls of small white blossoms.

• **USES** The leaves are used in tonics, liqueurs, and ales, and are made into expectorant and antiseptic cough drops. An infusion relaxes muscles and helps expel mucus, treating bronchitis, croup, and asthma. It destroys intestinal worms and acts as a digestive and liver tonic and a laxative. The tea was used internally and externally for eczema and shingles. Its sedative action works in small amounts to control rapid irregular heartbeats. A hot infusion helps to break fevers and treats malaria when quinine is ineffective. It helps heal skin lesions. The Navajo tribe gave mothers a root decoction before and after childbirth.

• **REMARK** Horehound's woolly leaves were once used to clean milk pails, and the dried flower remains floated on oil as candle wicks.

pairs of ovate, wrinkled, green leaves covered in fine white hairs

a pincushion whorl of small, 2-lipped, white flowers in leaf axils

Horehound honey soothes coughs

rounded leaf with serrated margins

up to 17½ in (45 cm)

Habitat Grassy, well-drained soil; Europe, N. Africa, Asia	Parts used

Family LEGUMINOSAE	Species *Medicago sativa*	Local name Lucerne

ALFALFA

This deeply rooting nitrogen-fixing herb with trifoliate leaves has racemes of violet-blue, clover-like flowers, followed by spiraling seed pods.

• **USES** The tonic leaves and sprouted seeds with the flavor of fresh garden peas are eaten in salads or blended into a health drink valued by athletes. Alfalfa provides a nutritious appetite stimulant for convalescents. Arabs feed it to racehorses to increase their speed, and it is a quality fodder, said to increase cow's milk. Growing wild, the plant indicates mineral-rich soil; on poor soil, it is an excellent "green manure." The leaves are a commercial source of chlorophyll, and the seeds yield yellow dye.

• **REMARK** Snail Clover (*Medicago sculetta*) has similar virtues and is grown for its remarkably snail-like, curled seed pods.

flowers provide nectar and pollen for butterflies and bees

3-part leaf

raceme of violet flowers

serrated leaf tips

whole plant used as nutrient-rich "green manure"

up to 32 in (80 cm)

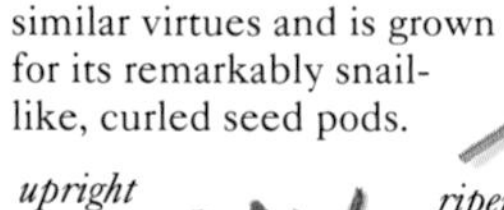

upright flower stalks

ripening seeds

green spiral seed pods

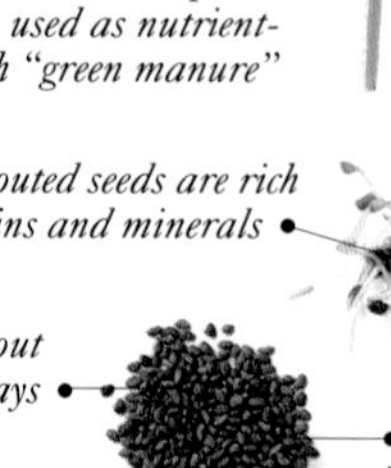

edible, sprouted seeds are rich in vitamins and minerals

seeds sprout in 3–5 days

seeds yield oil

Habitat Grassland on chalk soils; S.W. Asia, Europe, USA	Parts used

Family LABIATAE	Species *Melissa officinalis*	Local name Melissa

LEMON BALM

This bushy herb has square stems, lemon-scented foliage, and late-summer flowers that mature from white or yellow to pale blue.
• **USES** Fresh leaves add a delicate flavor to many dishes, oils, vinegars, and liqueurs, provide a relaxing bath, soothe insect bites, and make a sedative and tonic tea. This tea has a reputation for giving longevity and soothes headaches, indigestion, and nausea. Extracts of Lemon Balm are antiviral and help clean and heal wounds by starving bacteria of oxygen. The refreshing, antidepressant essential oil helps some eczema and allergy sufferers.
• **REMARK** It attracts bees, and if rubbed on empty hives will encourage new tenants.

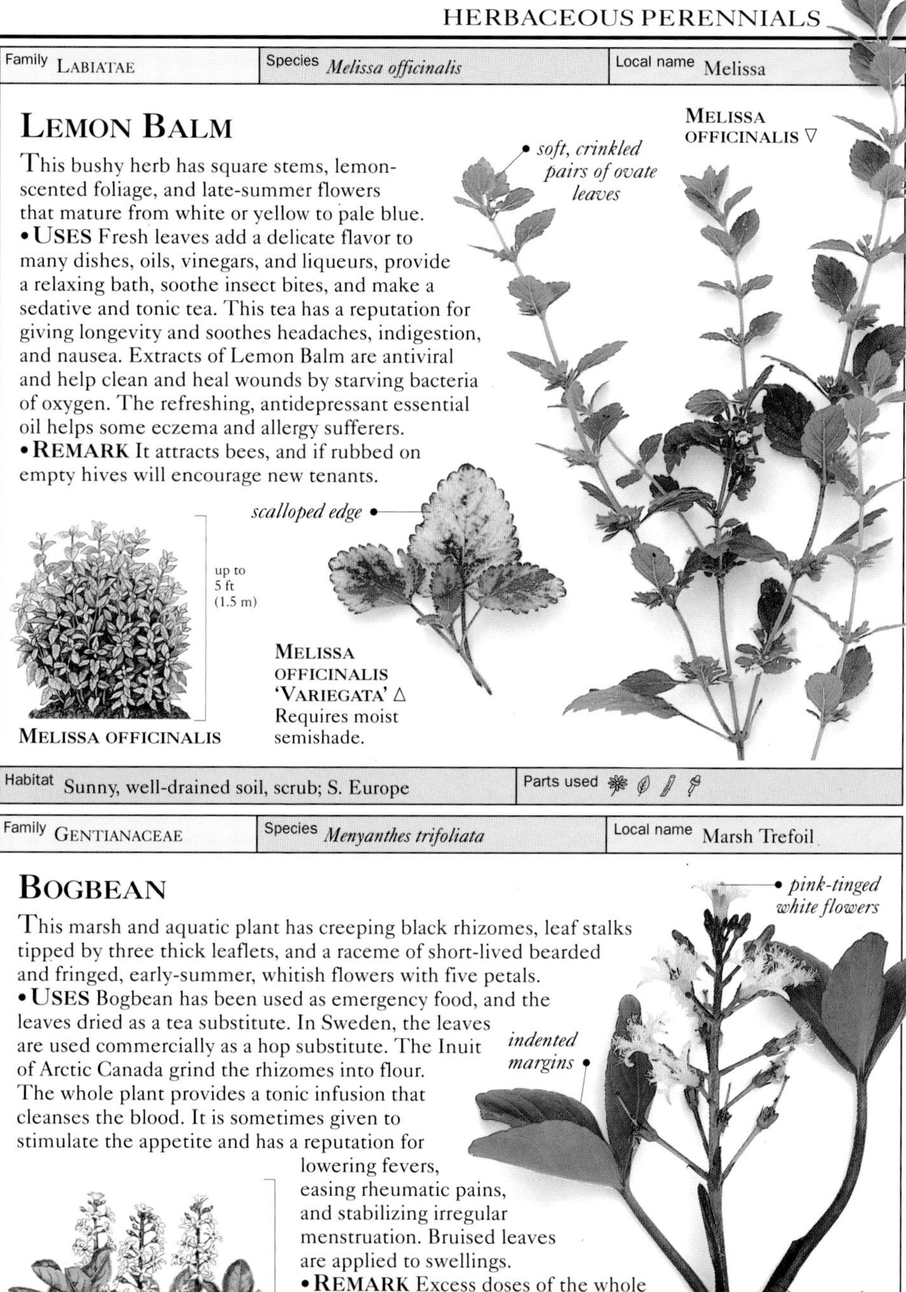
soft, crinkled pairs of ovate leaves
scalloped edge
up to 5 ft (1.5 m)

MELISSA OFFICINALIS ▽

MELISSA OFFICINALIS 'VARIEGATA' △ Requires moist semishade.

MELISSA OFFICINALIS

Habitat Sunny, well-drained soil, scrub; S. Europe	Parts used

Family GENTIANACEAE	Species *Menyanthes trifoliata*	Local name Marsh Trefoil

BOGBEAN

This marsh and aquatic plant has creeping black rhizomes, leaf stalks tipped by three thick leaflets, and a raceme of short-lived bearded and fringed, early-summer, whitish flowers with five petals.
• **USES** Bogbean has been used as emergency food, and the leaves dried as a tea substitute. In Sweden, the leaves are used commercially as a hop substitute. The Inuit of Arctic Canada grind the rhizomes into flour. The whole plant provides a tonic infusion that cleanses the blood. It is sometimes given to stimulate the appetite and has a reputation for lowering fevers, easing rheumatic pains, and stabilizing irregular menstruation. Bruised leaves are applied to swellings.
• **REMARK** Excess doses of the whole plant may cause vomiting and diarrhea.

pink-tinged white flowers

indented margins

purple-green coloring

leaf stalk bearing 3 leaflets sheathes onto rhizome

up to 10 in (25 cm)

Habitat Water & water margins; northern temperate zones	Parts used

Family LABIATAE	Species *Mentha* species	Local name Erba Santa Maria

MINTS

Most mints, including the best known Spearmint and Peppermint, are creeping plants that hybridize easily, producing infinite variations. They have erect, square, branching stems, aromatic foliage, and flowers in leaf axils.

• **USES** Spearmint, Peppermint, and Applemint flavor sauces, vinegar, vegetables, desserts, and julep, and are crystallized. Their teas are popular in the alcohol-free Arab world. Spearmint and Peppermint oils have a mild anesthetic action, and a cool, refreshing taste. They flavor candy, drinks, cigarettes, toothpastes, and medicines. Mints are stimulant, aid digestion, and reduce flatulence. Peppermint has additional antiseptic, antiparasitic, antiviral, and sweat-inducing properties. It is included in ointments and cold remedies and is given for headaches and other aches and pains. In an inhalation the essential oil treats shock and nausea and improves concentration.

excellent clean spearmint flavor

wrinkly leaf

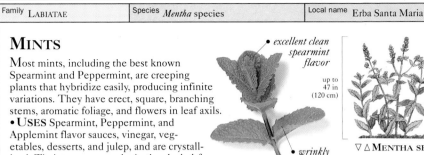

△ MENTHA SPICATA 'MOROCCAN'
Moroccan Spearmint relieves spasms.

up to 47 in (120 cm)

▽ △ MENTHA SPICATA

square stem

▽ MENTHA REQUIENII
Corsican Mint forms a cushion of tiny, peppermint-scented leaves with miniature flowers.

bright green leaf

lilac flower

serrated margin

◁ MENTHA SUAVEOLENS 'VARIEGATA'
Variegated Applemint has cream-edged leaves. Continues growing into early winter.

cream edging

apple-scented leaf

MENTHA SUAVEOLENS ▷
Applemint has regularly toothed, bright green leaves, good in fruit salads.

hairy leaf

MENTHA X SMITHIANA 'RUBRA' ▽
Red Raripila Mint has leaves with a sweet spearmint flavor, used in salads, desserts, and drinks.

pointed, dark green leaves

toothed leaves

healthy purple stem

gold splash

smooth leaves

△ MENTHA X GRACILIS 'VARIEGATA'
Ginger Mint has gold-splashed leaves with a mild fruity, ginger flavor.

▽ MENTHA SPICATA 'CRISPATA'
Curly Mint has crinkled, deep green leaves, with a subtle savory spearmint flavor.

curled margin

Habitat Rich soils, sun, moisture; Eurasia, Africa	Parts used ❀ 🍃 💧

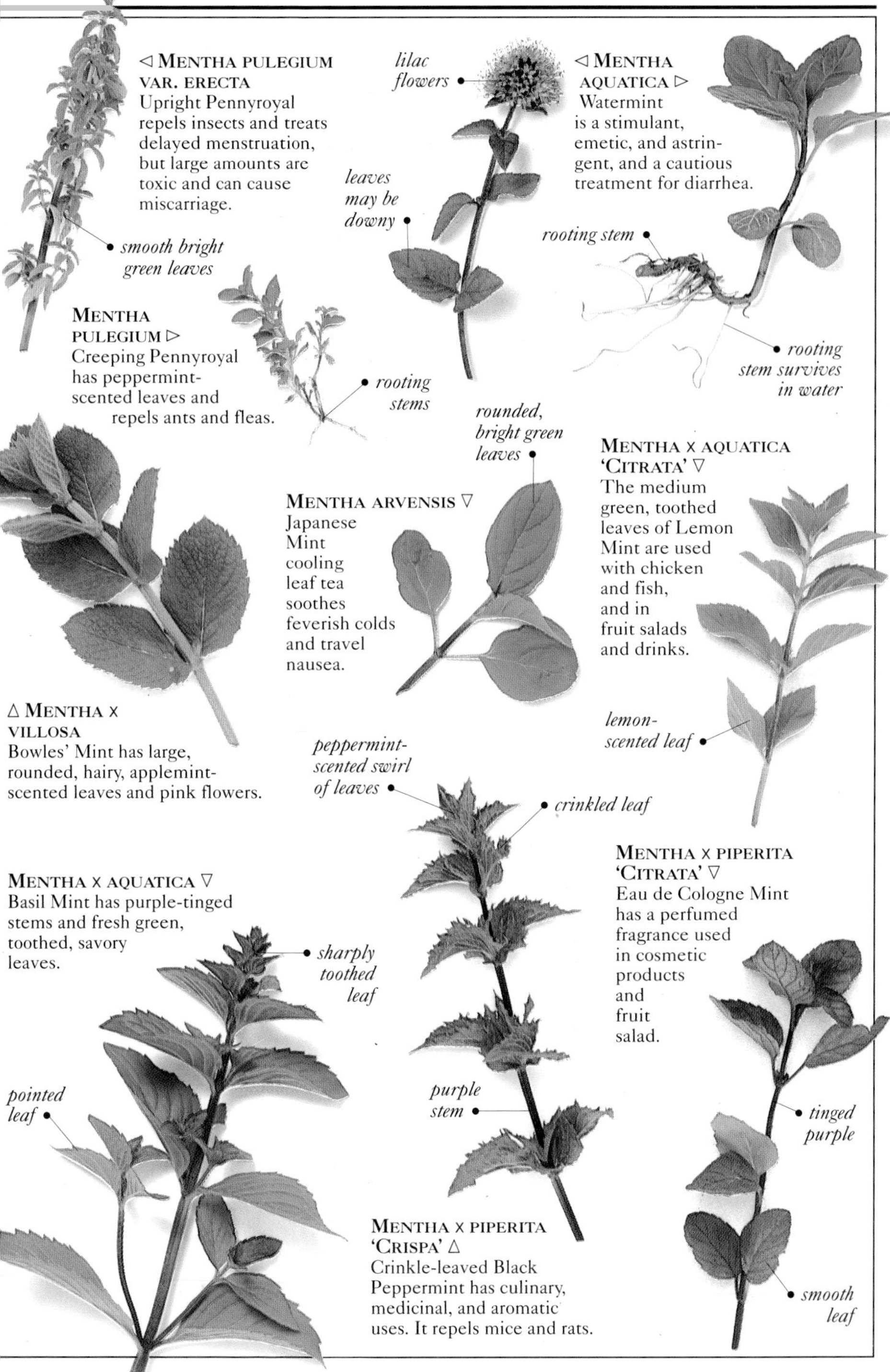
smooth bright green leaves
rooting stems
lilac flowers
leaves may be downy
rooting stem
rooting stem survives in water
rounded, bright green leaves
lemon-scented leaf
peppermint-scented swirl of leaves
crinkled leaf
sharply toothed leaf
pointed leaf
purple stem
tinged purple
smooth leaf

◁ **Mentha pulegium var. erecta**
Upright Pennyroyal repels insects and treats delayed menstruation, but large amounts are toxic and can cause miscarriage.

Mentha pulegium ▷
Creeping Pennyroyal has peppermint-scented leaves and repels ants and fleas.

◁ **Mentha aquatica** ▷
Watermint is a stimulant, emetic, and astringent, and a cautious treatment for diarrhea.

△ **Mentha x villosa**
Bowles' Mint has large, rounded, hairy, applemint-scented leaves and pink flowers.

Mentha arvensis ▽
Japanese Mint cooling leaf tea soothes feverish colds and travel nausea.

Mentha x aquatica 'Citrata' ▽
The medium green, toothed leaves of Lemon Mint are used with chicken and fish, and in fruit salads and drinks.

Mentha x aquatica ▽
Basil Mint has purple-tinged stems and fresh green, toothed, savory leaves.

Mentha x piperita 'Citrata' ▽
Eau de Cologne Mint has a perfumed fragrance used in cosmetic products and fruit salad.

Mentha x piperita 'Crispa' △
Crinkle-leaved Black Peppermint has culinary, medicinal, and aromatic uses. It repels mice and rats.

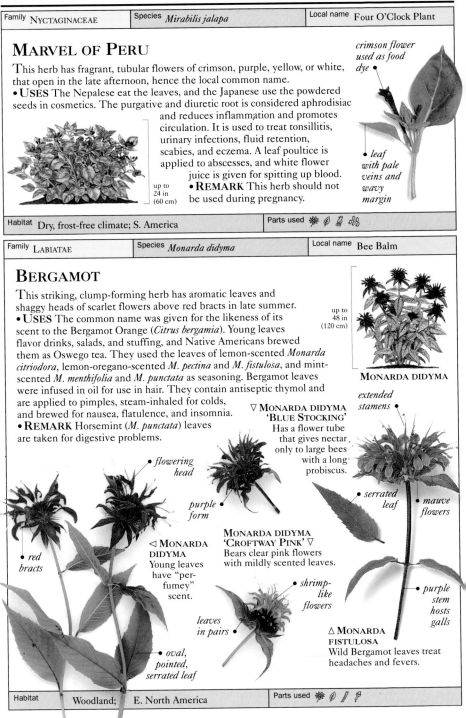

Family NYCTAGINACEAE	Species *Mirabilis jalapa*	Local name Four O'Clock Plant

MARVEL OF PERU

This herb has fragrant, tubular flowers of crimson, purple, yellow, or white, that open in the late afternoon, hence the local common name.
• **USES** The Nepalese eat the leaves, and the Japanese use the powdered seeds in cosmetics. The purgative and diuretic root is considered aphrodisiac and reduces inflammation and promotes circulation. It is used to treat tonsillitis, urinary infections, fluid retention, scabies, and eczema. A leaf poultice is applied to abscesses, and white flower juice is given for spitting up blood.
• **REMARK** This herb should not be used during pregnancy.

up to 24 in (60 cm)

crimson flower used as food dye
leaf with pale veins and wavy margin

Habitat Dry, frost-free climate; S. America	Parts used

Family LABIATAE	Species *Monarda didyma*	Local name Bee Balm

BERGAMOT

This striking, clump-forming herb has aromatic leaves and shaggy heads of scarlet flowers above red bracts in late summer.
• **USES** The common name was given for the likeness of its scent to the Bergamot Orange (*Citrus bergamia*). Young leaves flavor drinks, salads, and stuffing, and Native Americans brewed them as Oswego tea. They used the leaves of lemon-scented *Monarda citriodora*, lemon-oregano-scented *M. pectina* and *M. fistulosa*, and mint-scented *M. menthifolia* and *M. punctata* as seasoning. Bergamot leaves were infused in oil for use in hair. They contain antiseptic thymol and are applied to pimples, steam-inhaled for colds, and brewed for nausea, flatulence, and insomnia.
• **REMARK** Horsemint (*M. punctata*) leaves are taken for digestive problems.

up to 48 in (120 cm)

MONARDA DIDYMA

extended stamens

▽ MONARDA DIDYMA 'BLUE STOCKING'
Has a flower tube that gives nectar only to large bees with a long probiscus.

purple form

flowering head
red bracts
oval, pointed, serrated leaf

◁ MONARDA DIDYMA
Young leaves have "perfumey" scent.

MONARDA DIDYMA 'CROFTWAY PINK' ▽
Bears clear pink flowers with mildly scented leaves.

shrimp-like flowers
leaves in pairs
serrated leaf
mauve flowers
purple stem hosts galls

△ MONARDA FISTULOSA
Wild Bergamot leaves treat headaches and fevers.

Habitat Woodland; E. North America	Parts used

Family LILIACEAE	Species *Muscari comosum*	Local name Purse Tassel

TASSEL HYACINTH

Three to seven narrow, channeled, fleshy leaves arise from the Tassel Hyacinth bulb. In spring, a thin flowering stem grows with olive-brown fertile flowers, topped by a plume of violet-blue sterile flowers.

• **USES** In Greece, the edible bulbs are gathered in spring and boiled to remove their bitter taste. They have similar qualities to onions and are pickled in vinegar. Medicinally, they are stimulant and diuretic.

• **REMARK** The edible bulb is sold in the USA as *cipollino*.

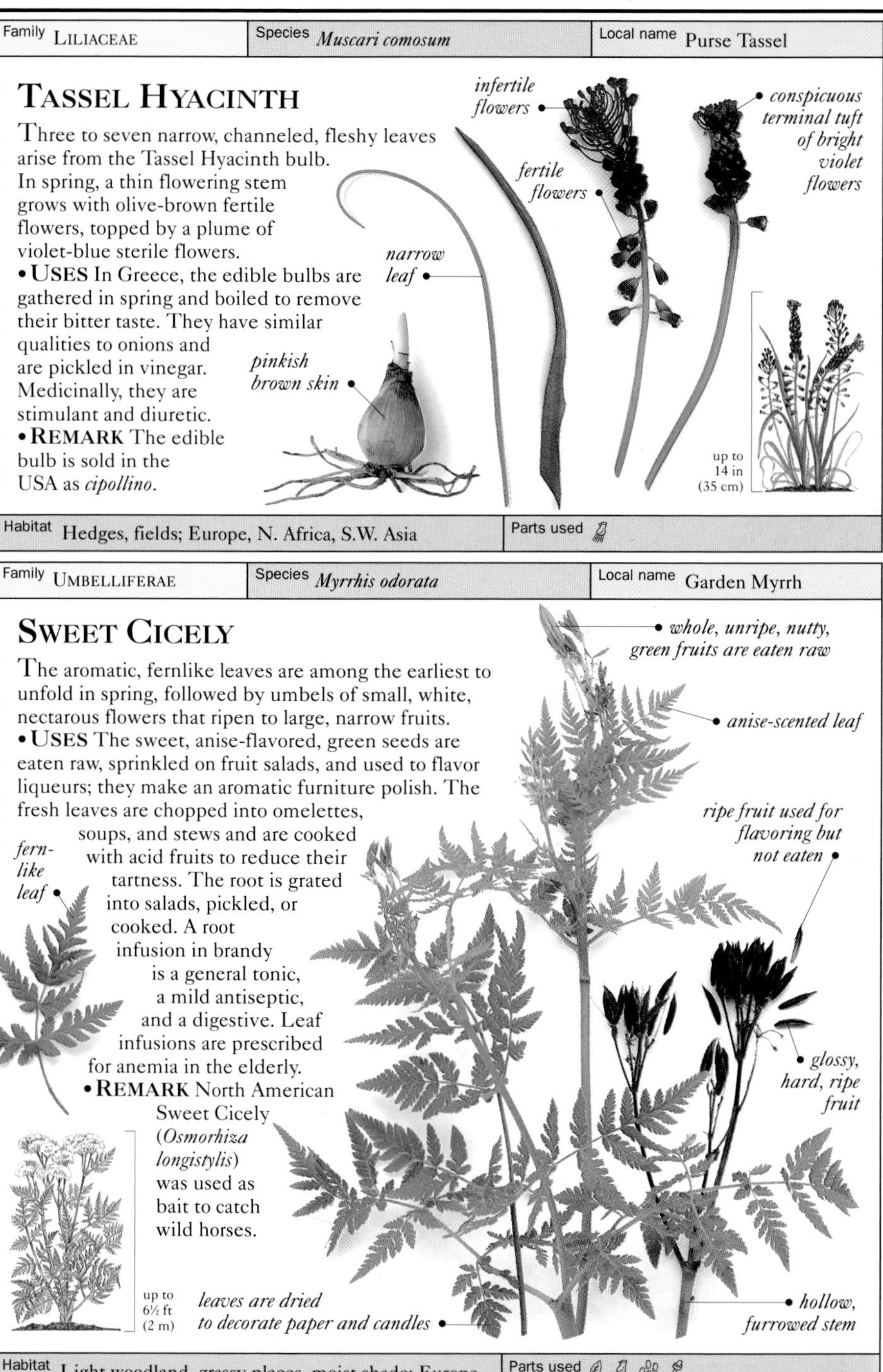

infertile flowers
conspicuous terminal tuft of bright violet flowers
fertile flowers
narrow leaf
pinkish brown skin
up to 14 in (35 cm)
whole, unripe, nutty, green fruits are eaten raw
anise-scented leaf
ripe fruit used for flavoring but not eaten
fern-like leaf
glossy, hard, ripe fruit
up to 6½ ft (2 m)
leaves are dried to decorate paper and candles
hollow, furrowed stem

Habitat Hedges, fields; Europe, N. Africa, S.W. Asia	Parts used

Family UMBELLIFERAE	Species *Myrrhis odorata*	Local name Garden Myrrh

SWEET CICELY

The aromatic, fernlike leaves are among the earliest to unfold in spring, followed by umbels of small, white, nectarous flowers that ripen to large, narrow fruits.

• **USES** The sweet, anise-flavored, green seeds are eaten raw, sprinkled on fruit salads, and used to flavor liqueurs; they make an aromatic furniture polish. The fresh leaves are chopped into omelettes, soups, and stews and are cooked with acid fruits to reduce their tartness. The root is grated into salads, pickled, or cooked. A root infusion in brandy is a general tonic, a mild antiseptic, and a digestive. Leaf infusions are prescribed for anemia in the elderly.

• **REMARK** North American Sweet Cicely (*Osmorhiza longistylis*) was used as bait to catch wild horses.

Habitat Light woodland, grassy places, moist shade; Europe	Parts used

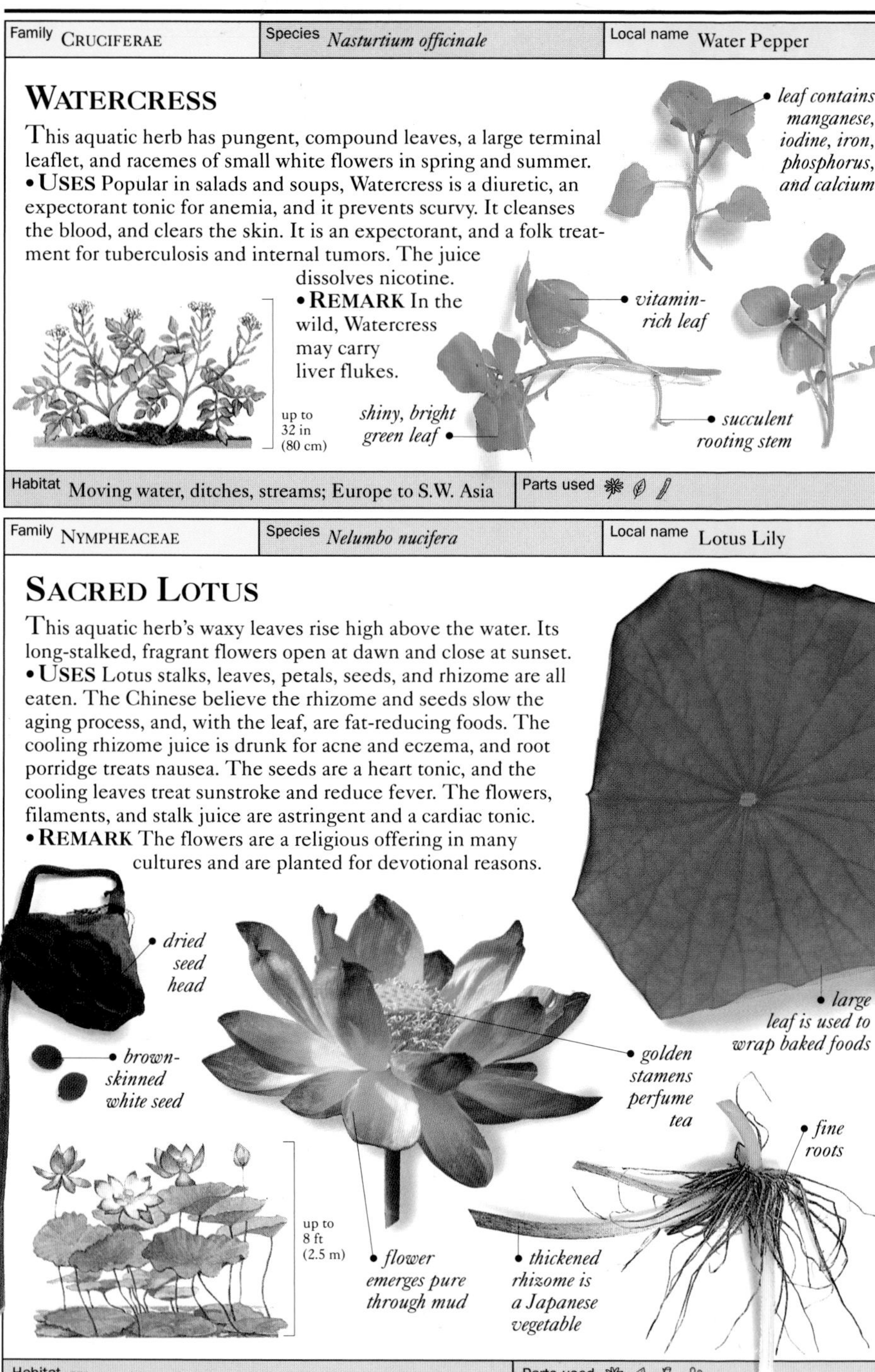
leaf contains manganese, iodine, iron, phosphorus, and calcium
vitamin-rich leaf
shiny, bright green leaf
succulent rooting stem
up to 32 in (80 cm)
dried seed head
brown-skinned white seed
golden stamens perfume tea
large leaf is used to wrap baked foods
fine roots
up to 8 ft (2.5 m)
flower emerges pure through mud
thickened rhizome is a Japanese vegetable

Family CRUCIFERAE	Species *Nasturtium officinale*	Local name Water Pepper

WATERCRESS

This aquatic herb has pungent, compound leaves, a large terminal leaflet, and racemes of small white flowers in spring and summer.

• **USES** Popular in salads and soups, Watercress is a diuretic, an expectorant tonic for anemia, and it prevents scurvy. It cleanses the blood, and clears the skin. It is an expectorant, and a folk treatment for tuberculosis and internal tumors. The juice dissolves nicotine.

• **REMARK** In the wild, Watercress may carry liver flukes.

Habitat Moving water, ditches, streams; Europe to S.W. Asia	Parts used

Family NYMPHEACEAE	Species *Nelumbo nucifera*	Local name Lotus Lily

SACRED LOTUS

This aquatic herb's waxy leaves rise high above the water. Its long-stalked, fragrant flowers open at dawn and close at sunset.

• **USES** Lotus stalks, leaves, petals, seeds, and rhizome are all eaten. The Chinese believe the rhizome and seeds slow the aging process, and, with the leaf, are fat-reducing foods. The cooling rhizome juice is drunk for acne and eczema, and root porridge treats nausea. The seeds are a heart tonic, and the cooling leaves treat sunstroke and reduce fever. The flowers, filaments, and stalk juice are astringent and a cardiac tonic.

• **REMARK** The flowers are a religious offering in many cultures and are planted for devotional reasons.

Habitat Warm rivers & lakes; S.E. Asia to Australia	Parts used

Family LABIATAE	Species *Nepeta cataria*	Local name Catnep

CATNIP

This herb has aromatic leaves and whorled spikes of two-lipped, white spotted-lavender flowers, enjoyed by bees.

• **USES** The root and leaf scent, minty with cat pheromone overtones, intoxicates cats and repels rats and flea beetles. Tender leaves are added to salads and flavor meat. They can also be brewed as tea and were used before China tea was imported. The leaves and flowering tops treat colds, calm upset stomachs, reduce fevers, and soothe headaches and scalp irritations. Their mild, sedative action soothes babies with colic. The leaves are used in a poultice for bruises and are put into cat toys.

• **REMARK** When smoked, leaves give mild euphoria with no harmful effects.

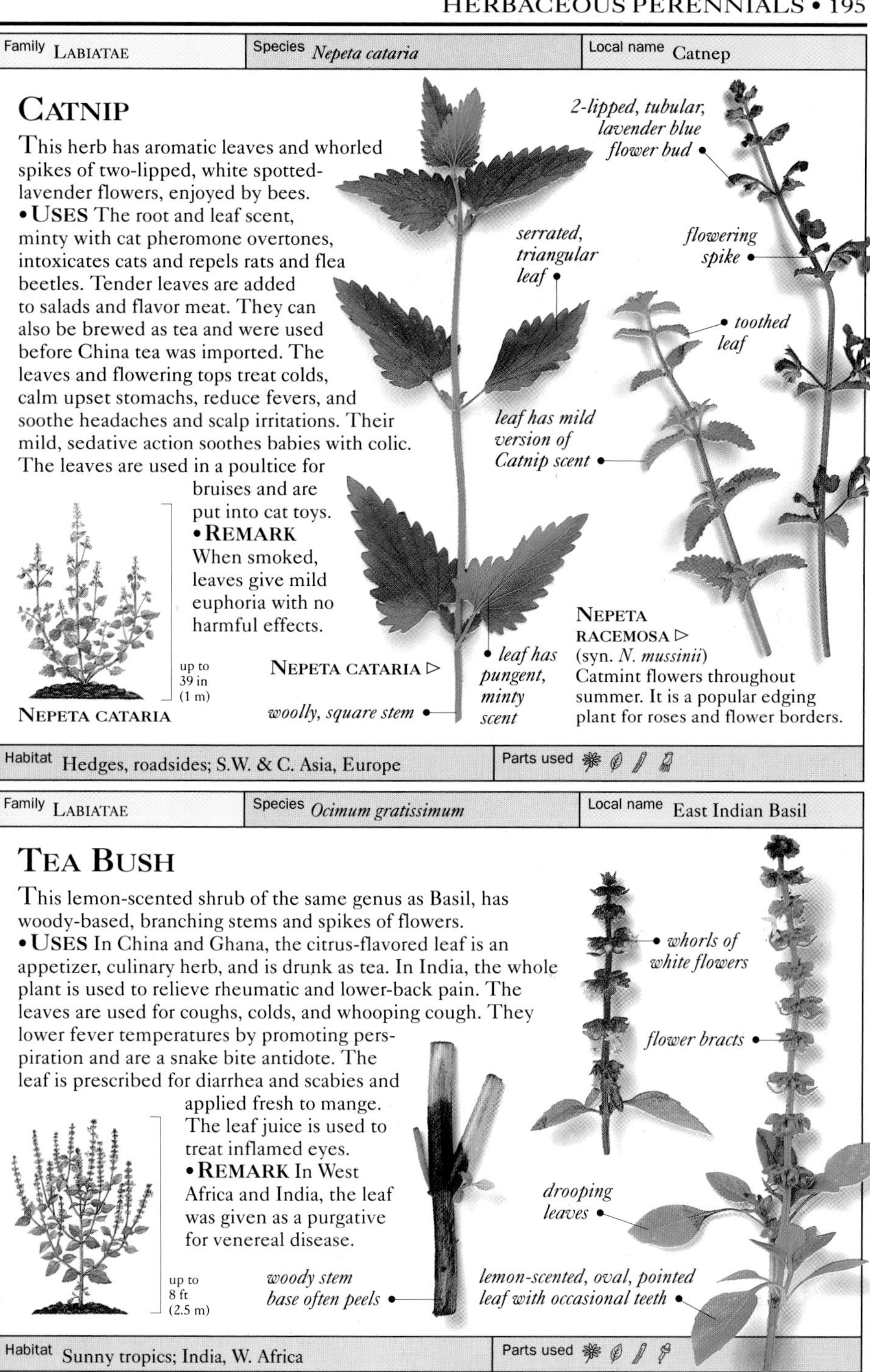
2-lipped, tubular, lavender blue flower bud
serrated, triangular leaf
flowering spike
toothed leaf
leaf has mild version of Catnip scent
leaf has pungent, minty scent
woolly, square stem
up to 39 in (1 m)
whorls of white flowers
flower bracts
drooping leaves
woody stem base often peels
lemon-scented, oval, pointed leaf with occasional teeth
up to 8 ft (2.5 m)

NEPETA CATARIA

NEPETA CATARIA ▷

NEPETA RACEMOSA ▷ (syn. *N. mussinii*) Catmint flowers throughout summer. It is a popular edging plant for roses and flower borders.

Habitat Hedges, roadsides; S.W. & C. Asia, Europe	Parts used

Family LABIATAE	Species *Ocimum gratissimum*	Local name East Indian Basil

TEA BUSH

This lemon-scented shrub of the same genus as Basil, has woody-based, branching stems and spikes of flowers.

• **USES** In China and Ghana, the citrus-flavored leaf is an appetizer, culinary herb, and is drunk as tea. In India, the whole plant is used to relieve rheumatic and lower-back pain. The leaves are used for coughs, colds, and whooping cough. They lower fever temperatures by promoting perspiration and are a snake bite antidote. The leaf is prescribed for diarrhea and scabies and applied fresh to mange. The leaf juice is used to treat inflamed eyes.

• **REMARK** In West Africa and India, the leaf was given as a purgative for venereal disease.

Habitat Sunny tropics; India, W. Africa	Parts used

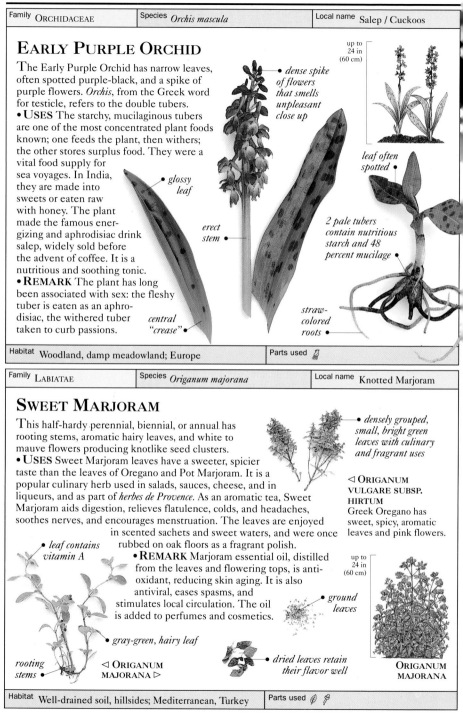

Family ORCHIDACEAE	Species *Orchis mascula*	Local name Salep / Cuckoos

EARLY PURPLE ORCHID

The Early Purple Orchid has narrow leaves, often spotted purple-black, and a spike of purple flowers. *Orchis*, from the Greek word for testicle, refers to the double tubers.

• **USES** The starchy, mucilaginous tubers are one of the most concentrated plant foods known; one feeds the plant, then withers; the other stores surplus food. They were a vital food supply for sea voyages. In India, they are made into sweets or eaten raw with honey. The plant made the famous energizing and aphrodisiac drink salep, widely sold before the advent of coffee. It is a nutritious and soothing tonic.

• **REMARK** The plant has long been associated with sex: the fleshy tuber is eaten as an aphrodisiac, the withered tuber taken to curb passions.

dense spike of flowers that smells unpleasant close up

glossy leaf

erect stem

central "crease"

up to 24 in (60 cm)

leaf often spotted

2 pale tubers contain nutritious starch and 48 percent mucilage

straw-colored roots

Habitat Woodland, damp meadowland; Europe	Parts used

Family LABIATAE	Species *Origanum majorana*	Local name Knotted Marjoram

SWEET MARJORAM

This half-hardy perennial, biennial, or annual has rooting stems, aromatic hairy leaves, and white to mauve flowers producing knotlike seed clusters.

• **USES** Sweet Marjoram leaves have a sweeter, spicier taste than the leaves of Oregano and Pot Marjoram. It is a popular culinary herb used in salads, sauces, cheese, and in liqueurs, and as part of *herbes de Provence*. As an aromatic tea, Sweet Marjoram aids digestion, relieves flatulence, colds, and headaches, soothes nerves, and encourages menstruation. The leaves are enjoyed in scented sachets and sweet waters, and were once rubbed on oak floors as a fragrant polish.

• **REMARK** Marjoram essential oil, distilled from the leaves and flowering tops, is antioxidant, reducing skin aging. It is also antiviral, eases spasms, and stimulates local circulation. The oil is added to perfumes and cosmetics.

densely grouped, small, bright green leaves with culinary and fragrant uses

◁ **ORIGANUM VULGARE SUBSP. HIRTUM**
Greek Oregano has sweet, spicy, aromatic leaves and pink flowers.

leaf contains vitamin A

gray-green, hairy leaf

rooting stems

◁ **ORIGANUM MAJORANA** ▷

ground leaves

dried leaves retain their flavor well

up to
24 in
(60 cm)

ORIGANUM MAJORANA

Habitat Well-drained soil, hillsides; Mediterranean, Turkey	Parts used

Family LABIATAE	Species *Origanum onites*	Local name French Marjoram

POT MARJORAM

This mound-forming, small perennial shrub has reddish stems, late-summer flowers, and aromatic, savory green leaves of a color that falls between the gray-green of Sweet Marjoram and the darker Oregano. The new spring leaves tend toward golden green.

• **USES** The leaves are generally milder than Oregano, especially when grown in hot countries. They are included in *bouquet garni*, rubbed onto roasting meat, blended with peppers and garlic, and used with tomatoes, cheese, eggs, and fish. Stems laid across barbecue charcoal add a faint flavor to food.

• **REMARK** The flowers will attract butterflies and bees to the garden, and seed heads provide winter fare for birds.

O. ONITES 'AUREUM' ▷ Clump-forming Golden Marjoram, 24 in (60 cm) tall, has stalkless upper leaves. *O. vulgare* 'Aureum' is similar but grows to 12 in (30 cm).

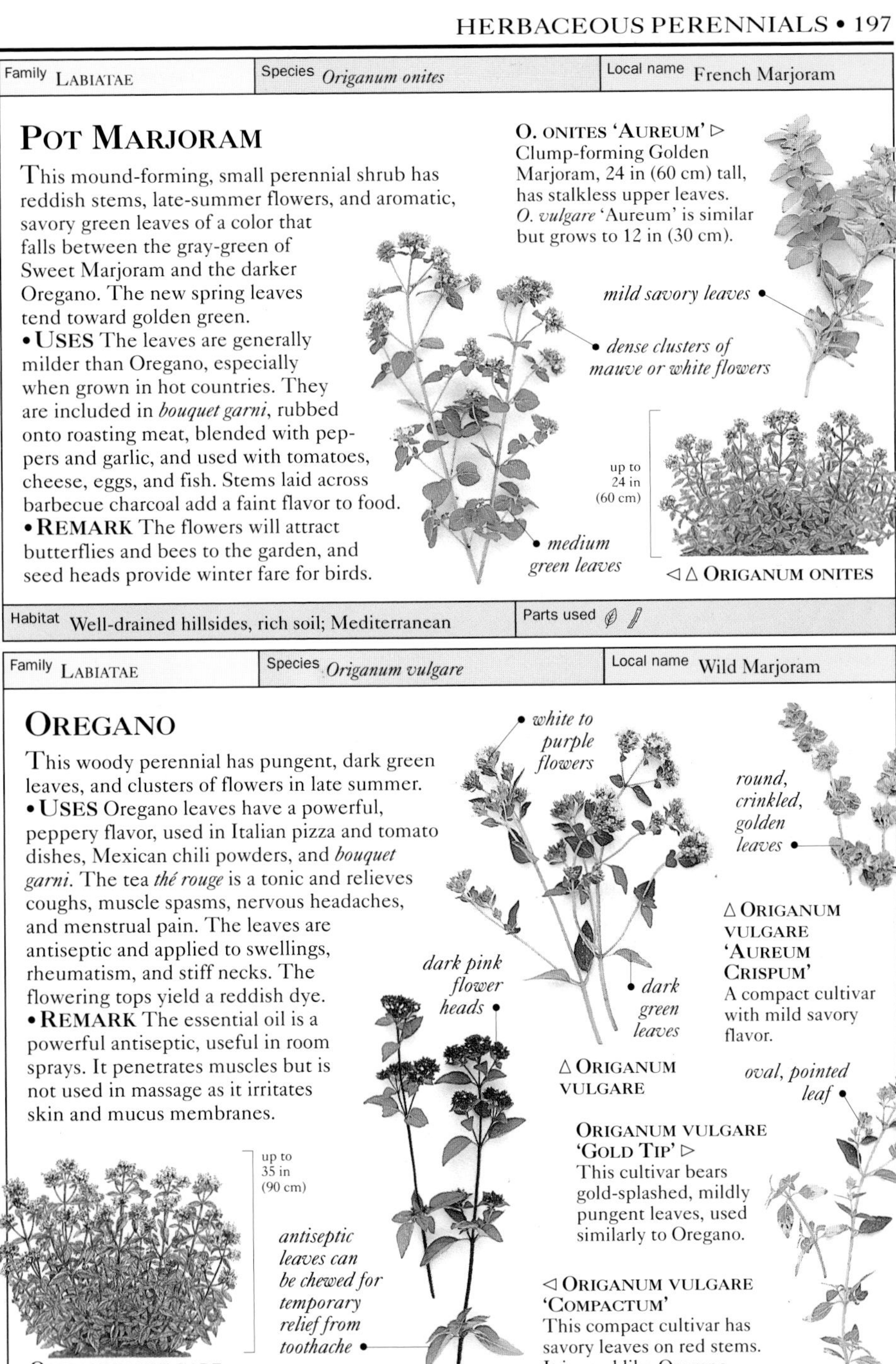
mild savory leaves
dense clusters of mauve or white flowers
medium green leaves
up to 24 in (60 cm)

◁ △ ORIGANUM ONITES

Habitat Well-drained hillsides, rich soil; Mediterranean	Parts used

Family LABIATAE	Species *Origanum vulgare*	Local name Wild Marjoram

OREGANO

This woody perennial has pungent, dark green leaves, and clusters of flowers in late summer.

• **USES** Oregano leaves have a powerful, peppery flavor, used in Italian pizza and tomato dishes, Mexican chili powders, and *bouquet garni*. The tea *thé rouge* is a tonic and relieves coughs, muscle spasms, nervous headaches, and menstrual pain. The leaves are antiseptic and applied to swellings, rheumatism, and stiff necks. The flowering tops yield a reddish dye.

• **REMARK** The essential oil is a powerful antiseptic, useful in room sprays. It penetrates muscles but is not used in massage as it irritates skin and mucus membranes.

white to purple flowers
round, crinkled, golden leaves
dark pink flower heads
dark green leaves
oval, pointed leaf
up to 35 in (90 cm)
antiseptic leaves can be chewed for temporary relief from toothache

△ **ORIGANUM VULGARE 'AUREUM CRISPUM'** A compact cultivar with mild savory flavor.

△ ORIGANUM VULGARE

ORIGANUM VULGARE 'GOLD TIP' ▷ This cultivar bears gold-splashed, mildly pungent leaves, used similarly to Oregano.

◁ **ORIGANUM VULGARE 'COMPACTUM'** This compact cultivar has savory leaves on red stems. It is used like Oregano.

ORIGANUM VULGARE

Habitat Open woodland, hillsides, rough grassland; Europe	Parts used

Family OXALIDACEAE	Species *Oxalis acetosella*	Local name Cuckoo Bread

WOOD SORREL

Wood Sorrel has a creeping rhizome, three-part leaves, and lilac-veined white flowers. The leaves and flowers droop at night.
• **USES** The leaves have a sharp, acidic flavor that gives zest to salads and sauces. An astringent, diuretic infusion treats fevers and urinary problems and is prepared as a soothing external wash for rashes and boils. Native Americans used it to remove cancerous growths from lips, and fed the root to horses to increase their speed.
• **REMARK** It is dangerous in large quantities and is not used in cases of gastritis, rheumatism, or gout.

Habitat Shady woodland; North America, Europe, Asia	Parts used

Family PAEONIACEAE	Species *Paeonia lactiflora*	Local name Bar-cher

CHINESE PEONY

This bushy herb has thick, tuberous roots, compound leaves with wavy margins, and fragrant white, pink, or red summer flowers with gold stamens.
• **USES** Chinese Peony roots are immunostimulant, reduce blood pressure, pain, spasms, and inflammation, and improve blood flow to the uterus. The Chinese consider red Peony root, Chi Shao, blood cooling and analgesic, and white Peony root, Bai Shao, as blood nourishing and a liver tonic, treating liver and uterine congestion, anemia, and beautifying the skin.
• **REMARK** Moutan Peony root bark cools the blood, stimulates circulation, and reduces wound clots, menstrual irregularities, fevers, and boils. Research confirms it is antibiotic and lowers blood pressure. It is used with red Chinese Peony root in a successful children's eczema treatment.

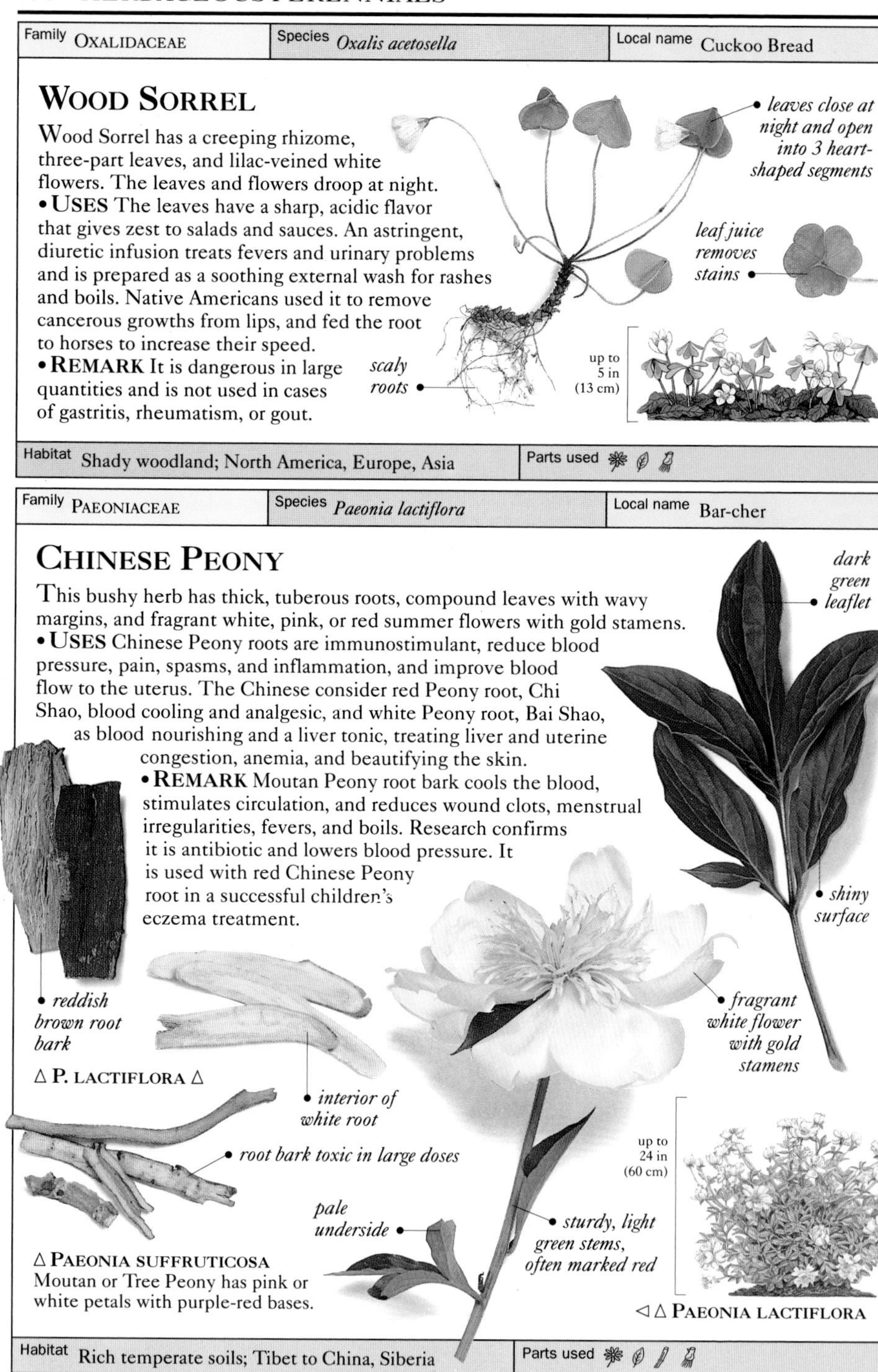
• leaves close at night and open into 3 heart-shaped segments
leaf juice removes stains •
scaly roots •
up to 5 in (13 cm)
dark green leaflet
• shiny surface
• reddish brown root bark
• interior of white root
• fragrant white flower with gold stamens
• root bark toxic in large doses
pale underside •
• sturdy, light green stems, often marked red
up to 24 in (60 cm)

△ P. LACTIFLORA △

△ PAEONIA SUFFRUTICOSA
Moutan or Tree Peony has pink or white petals with purple-red bases.

◁ △ PAEONIA LACTIFLORA

Habitat Rich temperate soils; Tibet to China, Siberia	Parts used

Family PAEONIACEAE	Species *Paeonia officinalis*	Local name King of Flowers

PEONY

This herb has medium green, indented foliage, and sumptuous, fragrant, summer blossoms in purple-red, pink, or white. Peony derives its name from Pæon, the physician of the Greek gods.
• **USES** In Japan, where the plant is considered the "food of dragons," the flowers are eaten as a vegetable. In 14th-century England, the seeds were used as a culinary spice, infused in mead for a drink to prevent nightmares, and strung in a necklace as a protective charm. The root was made into beads on which children cut their teeth. The roots are a tonic and antispasmodic and became a popular treatment for head and nerve disorders, including epilepsy. The dried petals are added to potpourri.
• **REMARK** Peony can be poisonous and should be given only by qualified persons.

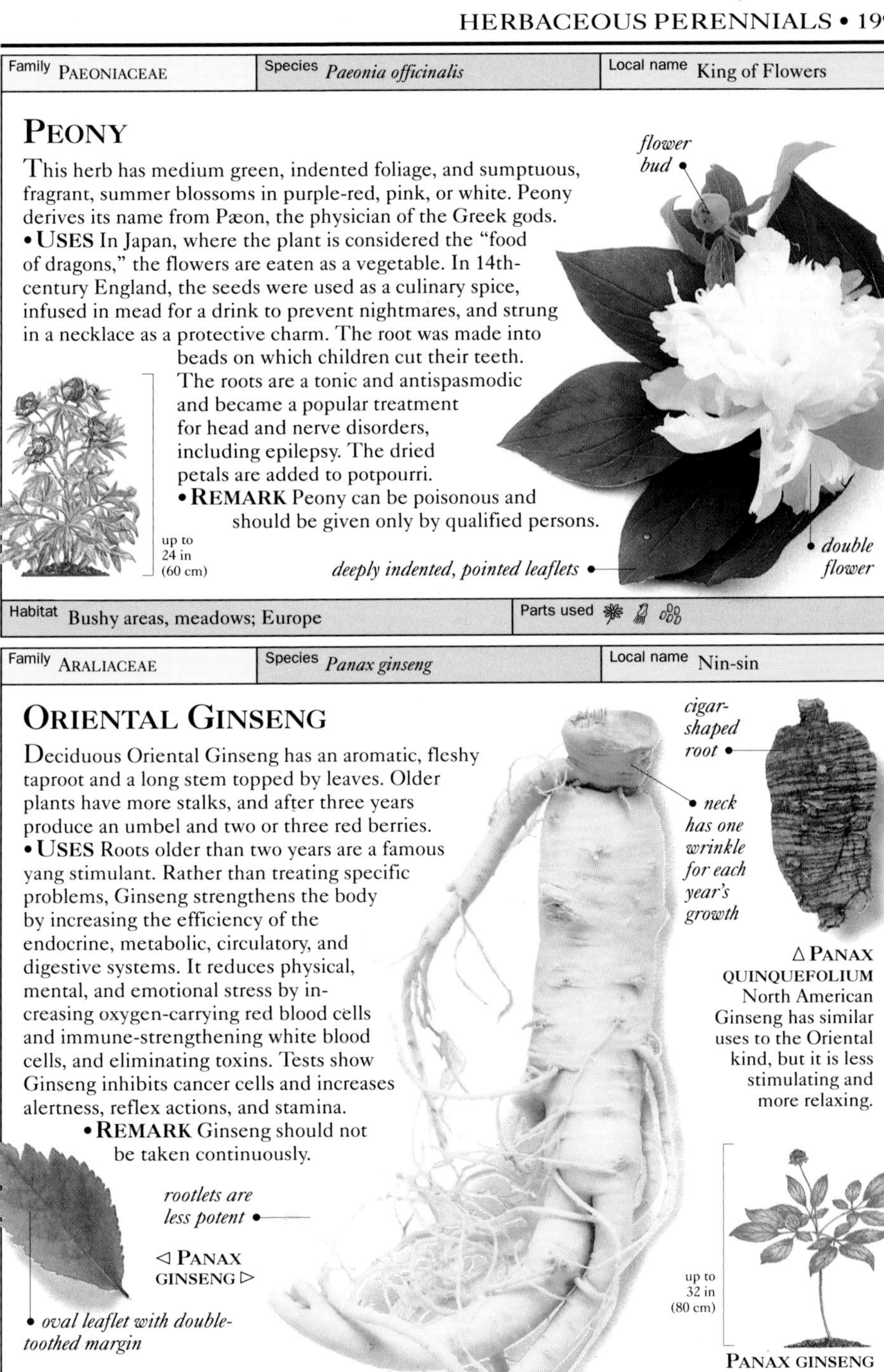

flower bud
double flower
deeply indented, pointed leaflets
up to 24 in (60 cm)

Habitat Bushy areas, meadows; Europe	Parts used

Family ARALIACEAE	Species *Panax ginseng*	Local name Nin-sin

ORIENTAL GINSENG

Deciduous Oriental Ginseng has an aromatic, fleshy taproot and a long stem topped by leaves. Older plants have more stalks, and after three years produce an umbel and two or three red berries.
• **USES** Roots older than two years are a famous yang stimulant. Rather than treating specific problems, Ginseng strengthens the body by increasing the efficiency of the endocrine, metabolic, circulatory, and digestive systems. It reduces physical, mental, and emotional stress by increasing oxygen-carrying red blood cells and immune-strengthening white blood cells, and eliminating toxins. Tests show Ginseng inhibits cancer cells and increases alertness, reflex actions, and stamina.
• **REMARK** Ginseng should not be taken continuously.

cigar-shaped root
neck has one wrinkle for each year's growth
rootlets are less potent
oval leaflet with double-toothed margin
up to 32 in (80 cm)

△ PANAX QUINQUEFOLIUM North American Ginseng has similar uses to the Oriental kind, but it is less stimulating and more relaxing.

◁ PANAX GINSENG ▷

PANAX GINSENG

Habitat Mountains, humus-rich soil; N.E. China, Korea	Parts used

Family LILIACEAE	Species *Paris quadrifolia*	Local name One Berry

HERB PARIS

This rhizomatous herb has a single stalk crowned by a whorl of four leaves through which grow a yellow-green flower and a purple berry.

• **USES** The root is a toxic narcotic once used to treat gout, cramps, and rheumatism. Seed and leaf juice were applied to tumors. The fresh plant is an antidote to arsenic and is now used in homeopathy.

• **REMARK** The root of *Paris chinensis* treats asthma and tubercular meningitis and is being tested in lung cancer therapy.

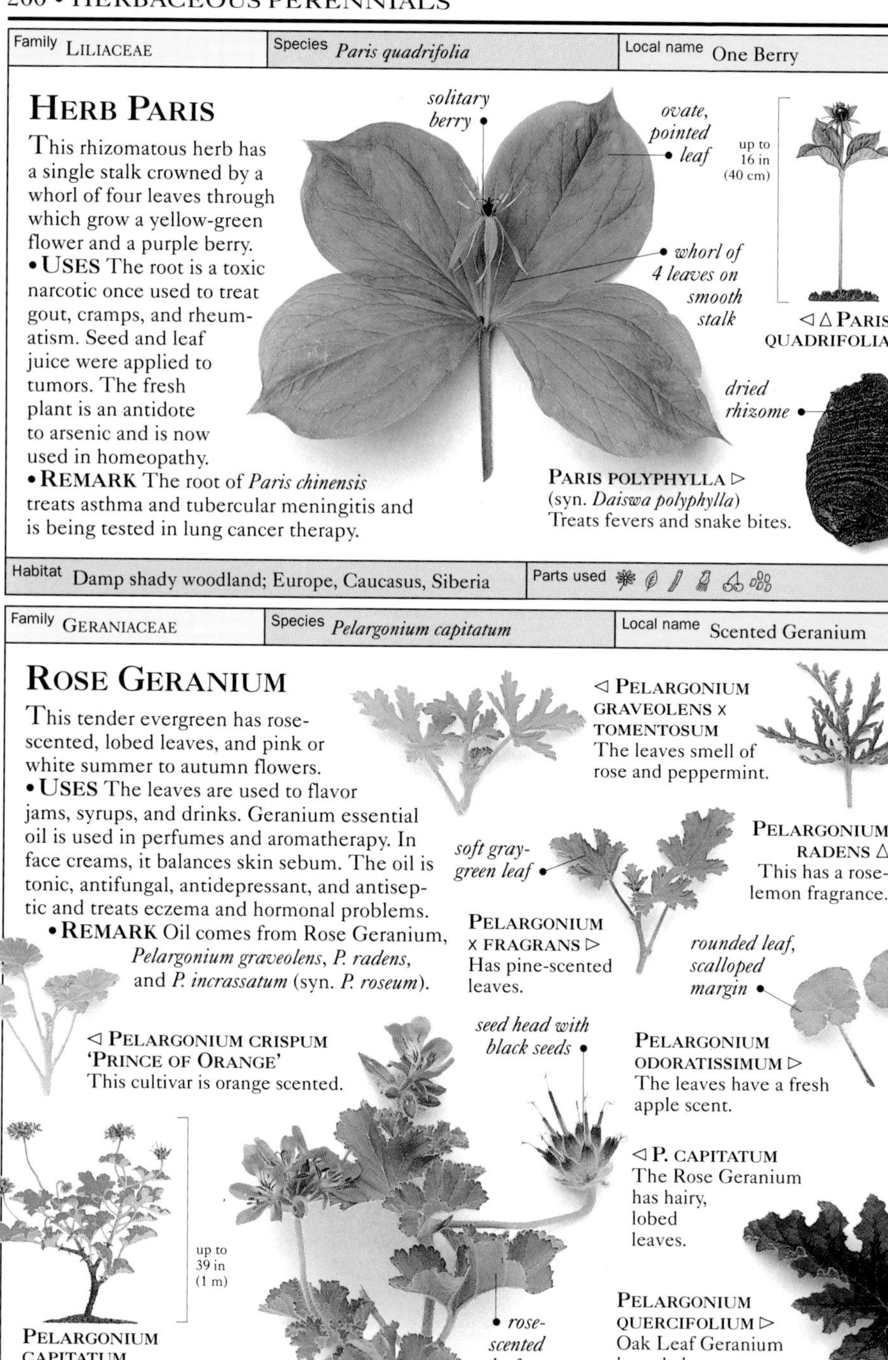

solitary berry
ovate, pointed leaf
up to 16 in (40 cm)
whorl of 4 leaves on smooth stalk
dried rhizome
soft gray-green leaf
rounded leaf, scalloped margin
seed head with black seeds
up to 39 in (1 m)
rose-scented leaf

◁ △ PARIS QUADRIFOLIA

PARIS POLYPHYLLA ▷ (syn. *Daiswa polyphylla*) Treats fevers and snake bites.

Habitat Damp shady woodland; Europe, Caucasus, Siberia	Parts used

Family GERANIACEAE	Species *Pelargonium capitatum*	Local name Scented Geranium

ROSE GERANIUM

This tender evergreen has rose-scented, lobed leaves, and pink or white summer to autumn flowers.

• **USES** The leaves are used to flavor jams, syrups, and drinks. Geranium essential oil is used in perfumes and aromatherapy. In face creams, it balances skin sebum. The oil is tonic, antifungal, antidepressant, and antiseptic and treats eczema and hormonal problems.

• **REMARK** Oil comes from Rose Geranium, *Pelargonium graveolens*, *P. radens*, and *P. incrassatum* (syn. *P. roseum*).

◁ PELARGONIUM GRAVEOLENS X TOMENTOSUM The leaves smell of rose and peppermint.

PELARGONIUM RADENS △ This has a rose-lemon fragrance.

PELARGONIUM X FRAGRANS ▷ Has pine-scented leaves.

◁ PELARGONIUM CRISPUM 'PRINCE OF ORANGE' This cultivar is orange scented.

PELARGONIUM ODORATISSIMUM ▷ The leaves have a fresh apple scent.

◁ P. CAPITATUM The Rose Geranium has hairy, lobed leaves.

PELARGONIUM CAPITATUM

PELARGONIUM QUERCIFOLIUM ▷ Oak Leaf Geranium has a balsam scent.

Habitat Sand dunes, coastal hillsides, sun; S. Africa	Parts used

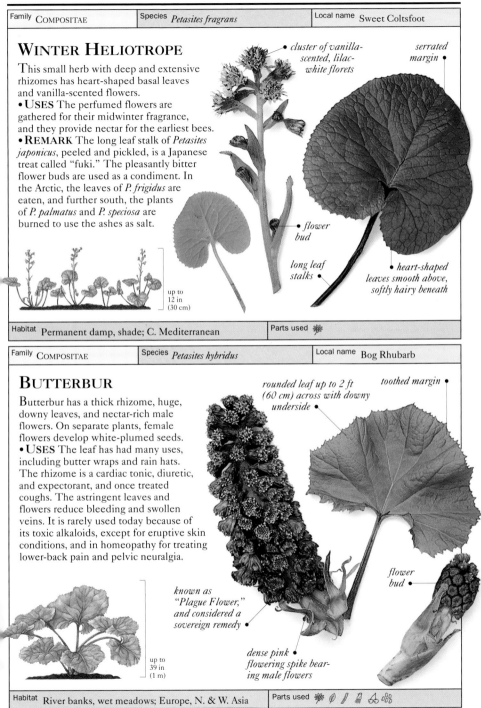

Family COMPOSITAE	Species *Petasites fragrans*	Local name Sweet Coltsfoot

WINTER HELIOTROPE

This small herb with deep and extensive rhizomes has heart-shaped basal leaves and vanilla-scented flowers.

• **USES** The perfumed flowers are gathered for their midwinter fragrance, and they provide nectar for the earliest bees.

• **REMARK** The long leaf stalk of *Petasites japonicus*, peeled and pickled, is a Japanese treat called "fuki." The pleasantly bitter flower buds are used as a condiment. In the Arctic, the leaves of *P. frigidus* are eaten, and further south, the plants of *P. palmatus* and *P. speciosa* are burned to use the ashes as salt.

cluster of vanilla-scented, lilac-white florets
serrated margin
flower bud
long leaf stalks
heart-shaped leaves smooth above, softly hairy beneath
up to 12 in (30 cm)
rounded leaf up to 2 ft (60 cm) across with downy underside
toothed margin
flower bud
known as "Plague Flower," and considered a sovereign remedy
dense pink flowering spike bearing male flowers
up to 39 in (1 m)

Habitat Permanent damp, shade; C. Mediterranean	Parts used

Family COMPOSITAE	Species *Petasites hybridus*	Local name Bog Rhubarb

BUTTERBUR

Butterbur has a thick rhizome, huge, downy leaves, and nectar-rich male flowers. On separate plants, female flowers develop white-plumed seeds.

• **USES** The leaf has had many uses, including butter wraps and rain hats. The rhizome is a cardiac tonic, diuretic, and expectorant, and once treated coughs. The astringent leaves and flowers reduce bleeding and swollen veins. It is rarely used today because of its toxic alkaloids, except for eruptive skin conditions, and in homeopathy for treating lower-back pain and pelvic neuralgia.

Habitat River banks, wet meadows; Europe, N. & W. Asia	Parts used

Family GRAMINEAE	Species *Phragmites australis*	Local name Carrizo

REED GRASS

Reed Grass (syn. *Phragmites communis*) has sturdy stems with a long leaf blade and plumes of silky, purple-brown flowers.
• **USES** Native Americans use the tiny reddish seeds to make gruel; boil young shoots as vegetables; grind the roots into flour; eat the sweet sap; and toast the powdery, moistened stems which puff like marshmallows. In China, the rhizome and roots are given for nausea, urinary problems, arthritis, and fever thirst.
• **REMARK** Reed Grass has an important future in organic sewage treatment as it absorbs impurities from water.

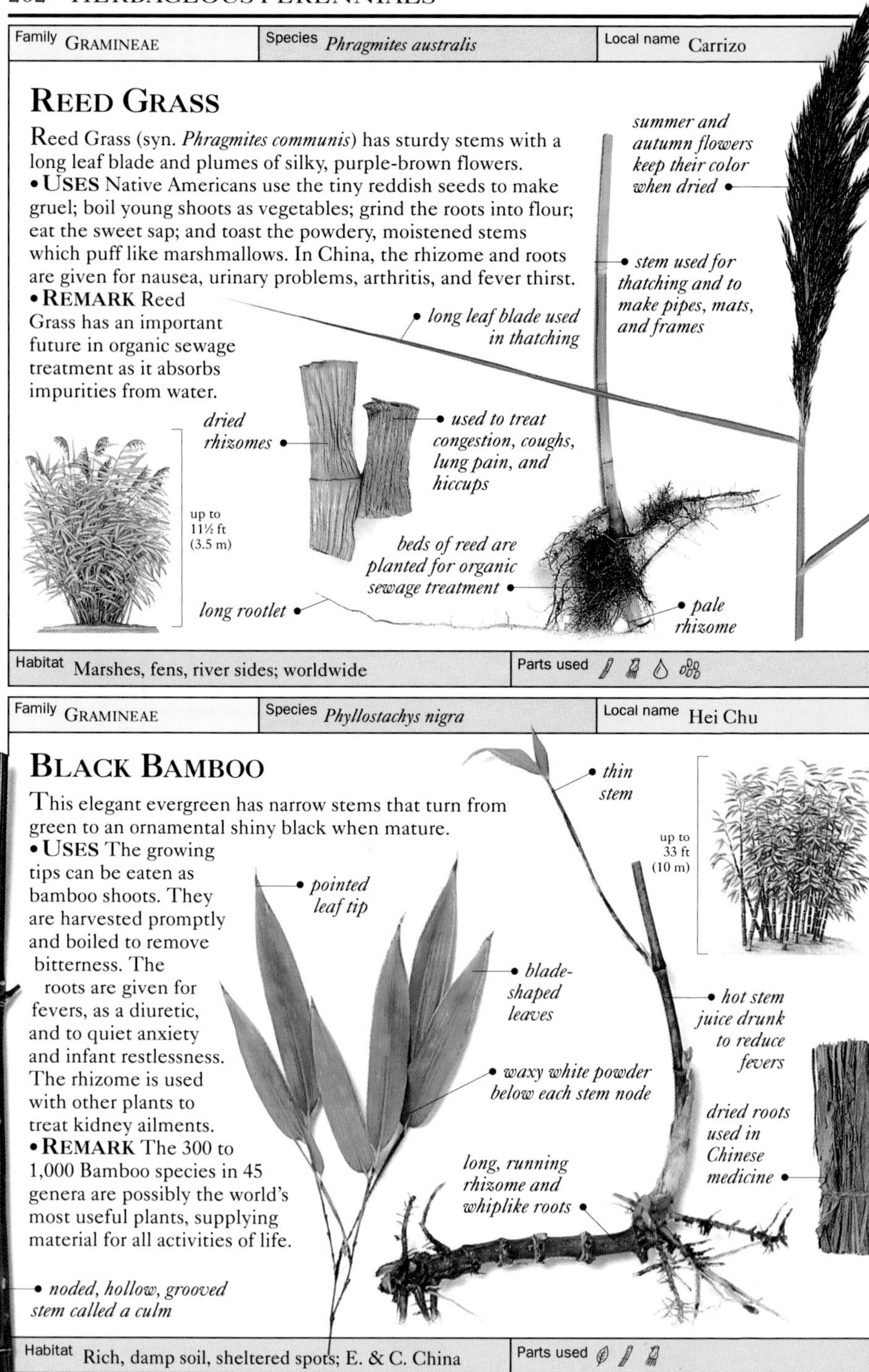

summer and autumn flowers keep their color when dried
stem used for thatching and to make pipes, mats, and frames
long leaf blade used in thatching
dried rhizomes
used to treat congestion, coughs, lung pain, and hiccups
up to 11½ ft (3.5 m)
beds of reed are planted for organic sewage treatment
long rootlet
pale rhizome

Habitat Marshes, fens, river sides; worldwide	Parts used

Family GRAMINEAE	Species *Phyllostachys nigra*	Local name Hei Chu

BLACK BAMBOO

This elegant evergreen has narrow stems that turn from green to an ornamental shiny black when mature.
• **USES** The growing tips can be eaten as bamboo shoots. They are harvested promptly and boiled to remove bitterness. The roots are given for fevers, as a diuretic, and to quiet anxiety and infant restlessness. The rhizome is used with other plants to treat kidney ailments.
• **REMARK** The 300 to 1,000 Bamboo species in 45 genera are possibly the world's most useful plants, supplying material for all activities of life.

thin stem
up to 33 ft (10 m)
pointed leaf tip
blade-shaped leaves
hot stem juice drunk to reduce fevers
waxy white powder below each stem node
dried roots used in Chinese medicine
long, running rhizome and whiplike roots
noded, hollow, grooved stem called a culm

Habitat Rich, damp soil, sheltered spots; E. & C. China	Parts used

Family PHYTOLACCACEAE	Species *Phytolacca americana*	Local name Pigeon Berry

POKEWEED

This purple-stemmed, toxic herb has fetid foliage and white or pinkish flowers, followed by green berries, ripening to dark purple.

• **USES** Shoots are eaten after long boiling. The anti-inflammatory root is given for swollen throat glands. It is purgative and narcotic, expels phlegm, soothes arthritis, kills sperm, and, with the leaf, treats fungal infections.

• **REMARK** Research has found a component of Pokeweed that is useful to the immune system, and proteins that inhibit flu, herpes, and leukemia.

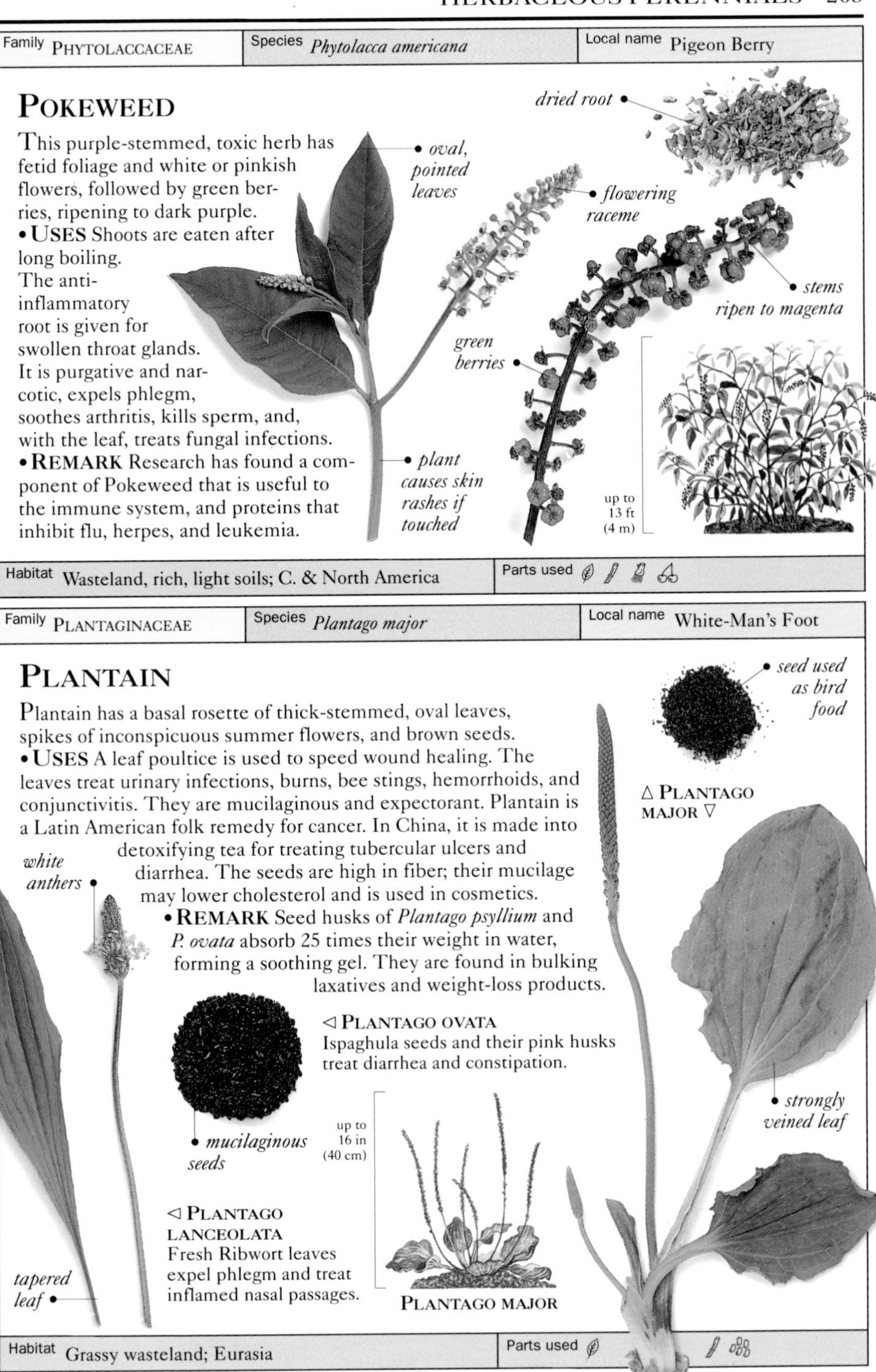
dried root
oval, pointed leaves
flowering raceme
stems ripen to magenta
green berries
plant causes skin rashes if touched
up to 13 ft (4 m)
seed used as bird food
△ PLANTAGO MAJOR ▽
white anthers
strongly veined leaf
mucilaginous seeds
up to 16 in (40 cm)
tapered leaf
PLANTAGO MAJOR

Habitat Wasteland, rich, light soils; C. & North America | Parts used

Family PLANTAGINACEAE	Species *Plantago major*	Local name White-Man's Foot

PLANTAIN

Plantain has a basal rosette of thick-stemmed, oval leaves, spikes of inconspicuous summer flowers, and brown seeds.

• **USES** A leaf poultice is used to speed wound healing. The leaves treat urinary infections, burns, bee stings, hemorrhoids, and conjunctivitis. They are mucilaginous and expectorant. Plantain is a Latin American folk remedy for cancer. In China, it is made into detoxifying tea for treating tubercular ulcers and diarrhea. The seeds are high in fiber; their mucilage may lower cholesterol and is used in cosmetics.

• **REMARK** Seed husks of *Plantago psyllium* and *P. ovata* absorb 25 times their weight in water, forming a soothing gel. They are found in bulking laxatives and weight-loss products.

◁ PLANTAGO OVATA
Ispaghula seeds and their pink husks treat diarrhea and constipation.

◁ PLANTAGO LANCEOLATA
Fresh Ribwort leaves expel phlegm and treat inflamed nasal passages.

Habitat Grassy wasteland; Eurasia | Parts used

Family CAMPANULACEAE	Species *Platycodon grandiflorum*	Local name Chinese Bell Flower

BALLOON FLOWER

Balloon Flower has a fleshy taproot, upright stems with a milky juice, serrated leaves, and white to purple-blue, balloonlike flowers, inflated in bud. • **USES** In China and Japan, the tender leaves are eaten in salads, and the roots loosen lung and throat phlegm, stop coughing, reduce swelling and inflammation, and promote pus drainage. They are prescribed for colds, bronchitis, pneumonia, pleurisy, and lung abscesses. • **REMARK** The poisonous roots are treated before use.

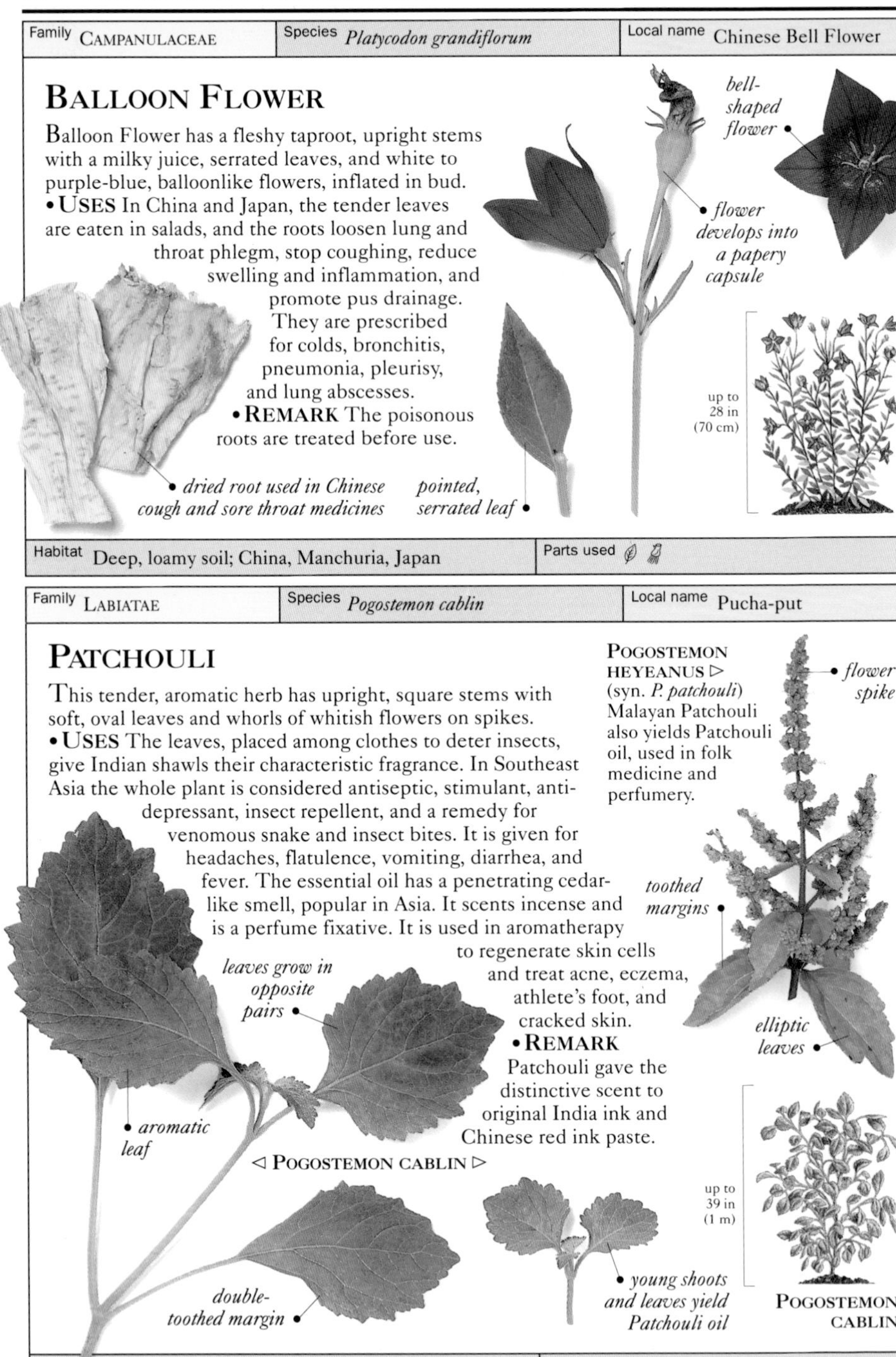
bell-shaped flower
flower develops into a papery capsule
up to 28 in (70 cm)
dried root used in Chinese cough and sore throat medicines
pointed, serrated leaf
POGOSTEMON HEYEANUS ▷
flower spike
toothed margins
elliptic leaves
leaves grow in opposite pairs
aromatic leaf
◁ POGOSTEMON CABLIN ▷
up to 39 in (1 m)
double-toothed margin
young shoots and leaves yield Patchouli oil
POGOSTEMON CABLIN

Habitat Deep, loamy soil; China, Manchuria, Japan	Parts used

Family LABIATAE	Species *Pogostemon cablin*	Local name Pucha-put

PATCHOULI

This tender, aromatic herb has upright, square stems with soft, oval leaves and whorls of whitish flowers on spikes. • **USES** The leaves, placed among clothes to deter insects, give Indian shawls their characteristic fragrance. In Southeast Asia the whole plant is considered antiseptic, stimulant, antidepressant, insect repellent, and a remedy for venomous snake and insect bites. It is given for headaches, flatulence, vomiting, diarrhea, and fever. The essential oil has a penetrating cedar-like smell, popular in Asia. It scents incense and is a perfume fixative. It is used in aromatherapy to regenerate skin cells and treat acne, eczema, athlete's foot, and cracked skin. • **REMARK** Patchouli gave the distinctive scent to original India ink and Chinese red ink paste.

POGOSTEMON HEYEANUS ▷ (syn. *P. patchouli*) Malayan Patchouli also yields Patchouli oil, used in folk medicine and perfumery.

Tropical or subtropical conditions; S.E. Asia, India	Parts used

Family POLEMONIACEAE	Species *Polemonium caeruleum*	Local name Greek Valerian

JACOB'S LADDER

This herb has stems of pinnate leaves, and dense clusters of blue flowers with yellow stamens in early summer.

• **USES** The whole plant was once listed in European pharmacopeias for its astringent and blood-purifying properties as a treatment for syphilis and rabies, but it is no longer used medicinally. Boiled in Olive oil, it makes a mens' hair dressing, and a black dye.

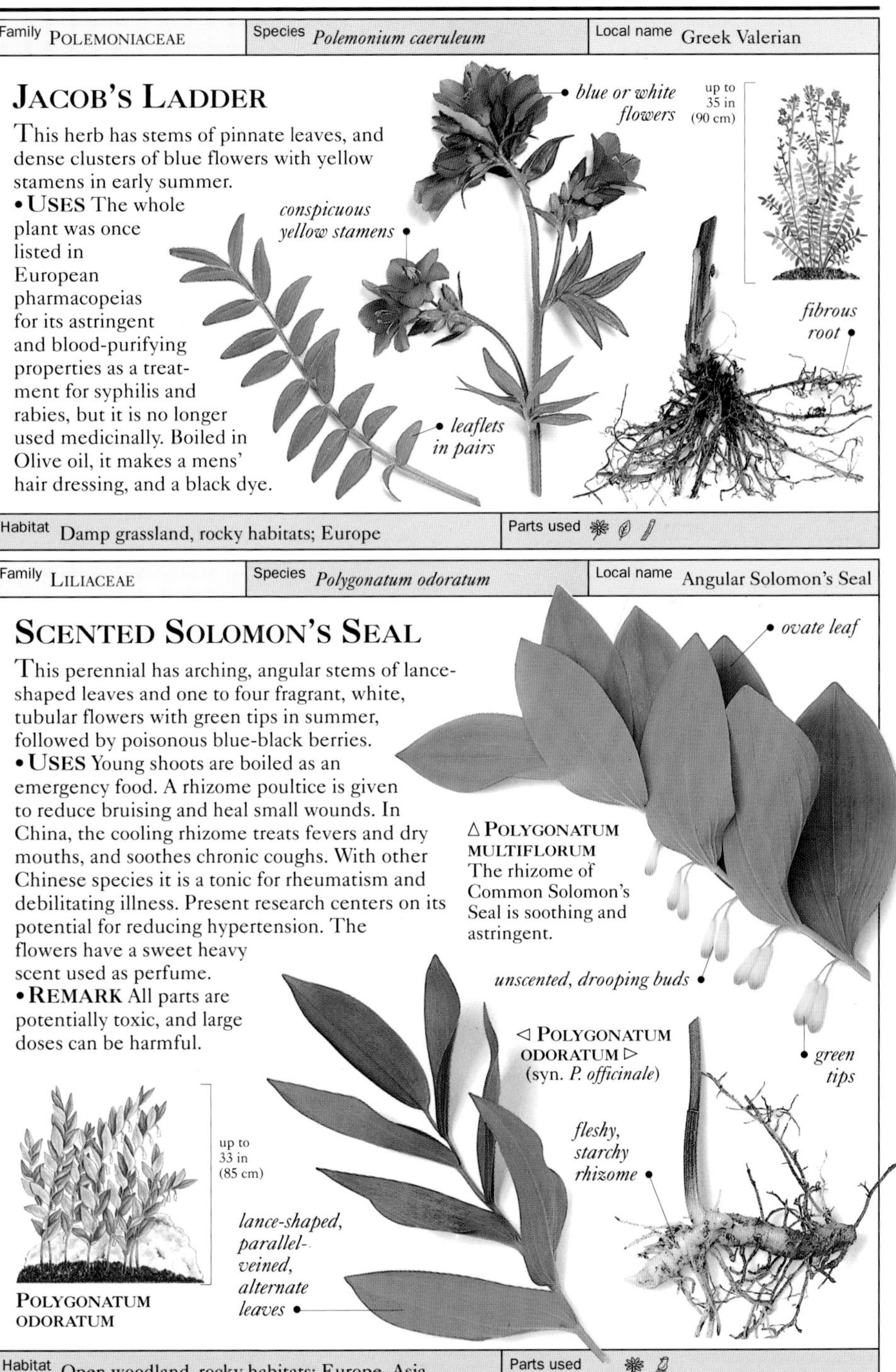

blue or white flowers
up to 35 in (90 cm)
conspicuous yellow stamens
fibrous root
leaflets in pairs
ovate leaf
unscented, drooping buds
green tips
fleshy, starchy rhizome
lance-shaped, parallel-veined, alternate leaves
up to 33 in (85 cm)

Habitat Damp grassland, rocky habitats; Europe	Parts used

Family LILIACEAE	Species *Polygonatum odoratum*	Local name Angular Solomon's Seal

SCENTED SOLOMON'S SEAL

This perennial has arching, angular stems of lance-shaped leaves and one to four fragrant, white, tubular flowers with green tips in summer, followed by poisonous blue-black berries.

• **USES** Young shoots are boiled as an emergency food. A rhizome poultice is given to reduce bruising and heal small wounds. In China, the cooling rhizome treats fevers and dry mouths, and soothes chronic coughs. With other Chinese species it is a tonic for rheumatism and debilitating illness. Present research centers on its potential for reducing hypertension. The flowers have a sweet heavy scent used as perfume.

• **REMARK** All parts are potentially toxic, and large doses can be harmful.

△ POLYGONATUM MULTIFLORUM The rhizome of Common Solomon's Seal is soothing and astringent.

◁ POLYGONATUM ODORATUM ▷ (syn. *P. officinale*)

POLYGONATUM ODORATUM

Habitat Open woodland, rocky habitats; Europe, Asia	Parts used

Family POLYGONACEAE	Species *Polygonum bistorta*	Local name Snakeweed

BISTORT

Bistort has a stout rhizome, oval base leaves, and triangular stem leaves with dense flower spikes.

• **USES** The shoots and soaked rhizomes are cooked as a tonic. The leaves and roots treat cuts; a root gargle helps mouth ulcers, phlegm, and bleeding gums; and an enema infusion treats diarrhea. The rhizomes were used in soups and stews by the Cheyenne tribe.

• **REMARK** *Polygonum multiflorum* is a climbing vine with tonic, laxative, antispasmodic, antibacterial tubers, used in China to treat dizziness, tetanus, cramps, and prematurely gray hair, and to increase mental clarity.

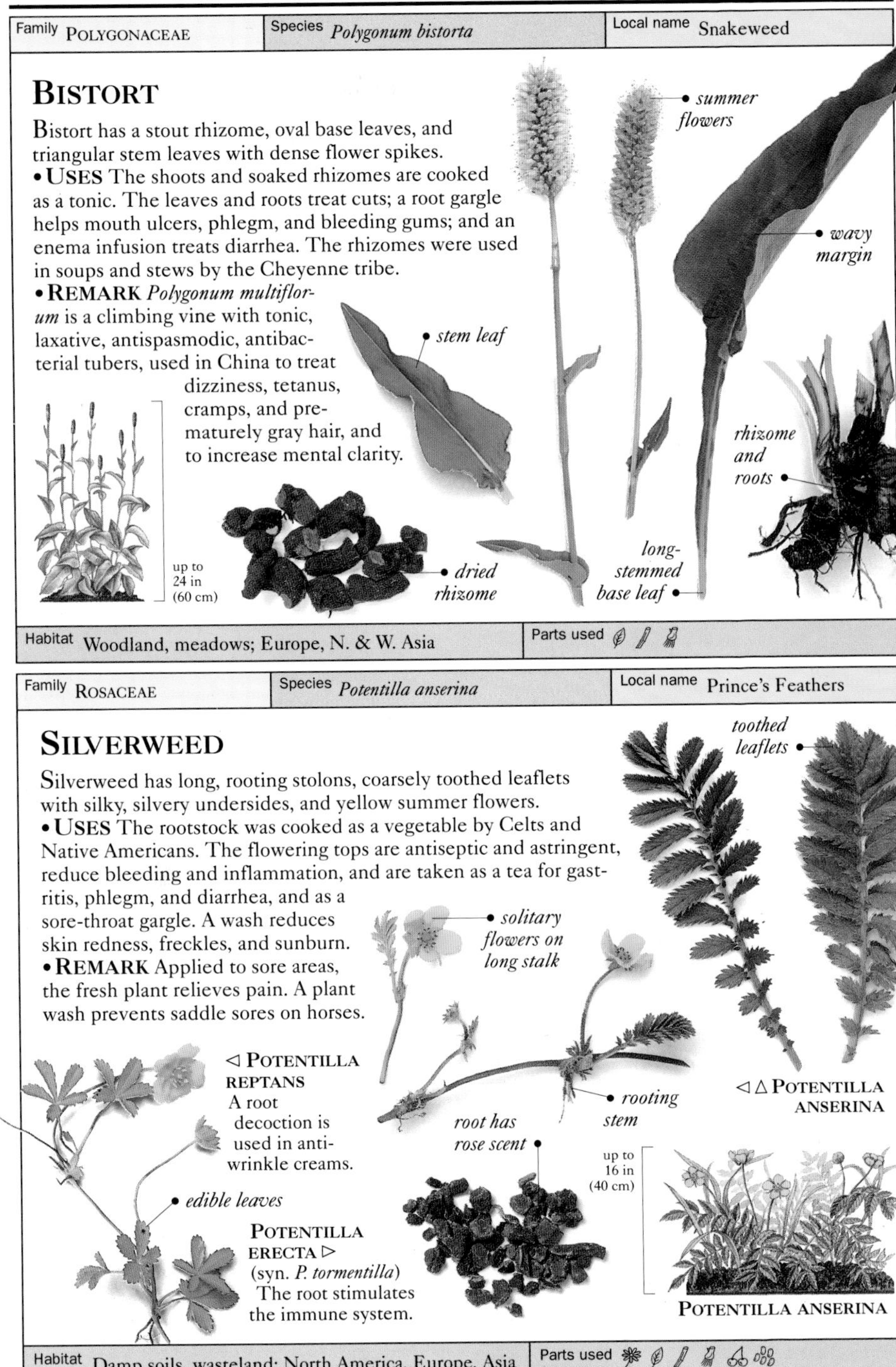

summer flowers
wavy margin
stem leaf
rhizome and roots
up to 24 in (60 cm)
dried rhizome
long-stemmed base leaf
toothed leaflets
solitary flowers on long stalk
rooting stem
root has rose scent
edible leaves
up to 16 in (40 cm)

Habitat Woodland, meadows; Europe, N. & W. Asia	Parts used

Family ROSACEAE	Species *Potentilla anserina*	Local name Prince's Feathers

SILVERWEED

Silverweed has long, rooting stolons, coarsely toothed leaflets with silky, silvery undersides, and yellow summer flowers.

• **USES** The rootstock was cooked as a vegetable by Celts and Native Americans. The flowering tops are antiseptic and astringent, reduce bleeding and inflammation, and are taken as a tea for gastritis, phlegm, and diarrhea, and as a sore-throat gargle. A wash reduces skin redness, freckles, and sunburn.

• **REMARK** Applied to sore areas, the fresh plant relieves pain. A plant wash prevents saddle sores on horses.

◁ **POTENTILLA REPTANS** A root decoction is used in anti-wrinkle creams.

POTENTILLA ERECTA ▷ (syn. *P. tormentilla*) The root stimulates the immune system.

◁ △ **POTENTILLA ANSERINA**

POTENTILLA ANSERINA

Habitat Damp soils, wasteland; North America, Europe, Asia	Parts used

Family PRIMULACEAE	Species *Primula veris*	Local name Paigle

COWSLIP

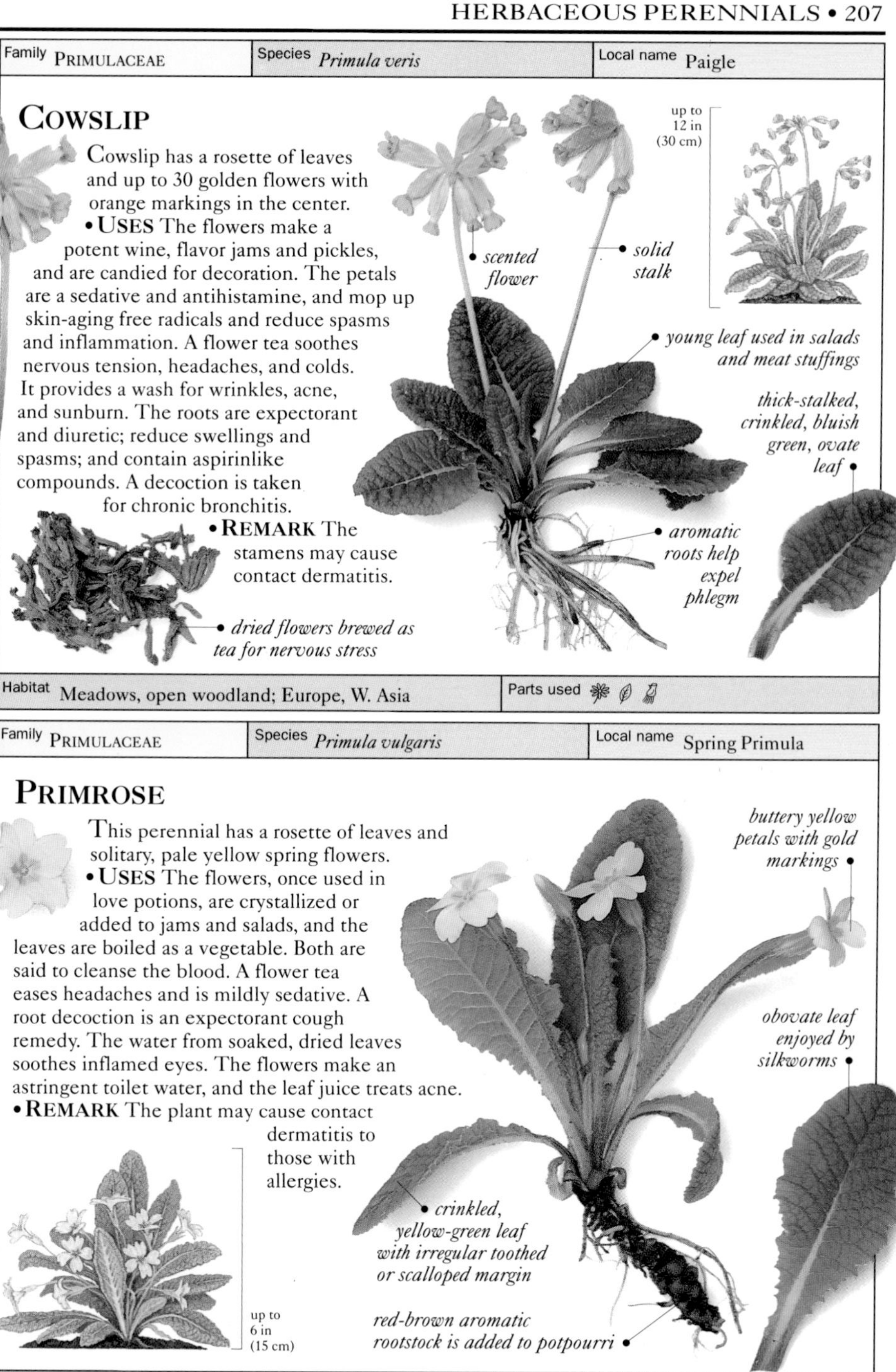

up to
12 in
(30 cm)
scented
flower
solid
stalk
young leaf used in salads
and meat stuffings
thick-stalked,
crinkled, bluish
green, ovate
leaf
aromatic
roots help
expel
phlegm
dried flowers brewed as
tea for nervous stress
buttery yellow
petals with gold
markings
obovate leaf
enjoyed by
silkworms
crinkled,
yellow-green leaf
with irregular toothed
or scalloped margin
up to
6 in
(15 cm)
red-brown aromatic
rootstock is added to potpourri

Cowslip has a rosette of leaves and up to 30 golden flowers with orange markings in the center.

• **USES** The flowers make a potent wine, flavor jams and pickles, and are candied for decoration. The petals are a sedative and antihistamine, and mop up skin-aging free radicals and reduce spasms and inflammation. A flower tea soothes nervous tension, headaches, and colds. It provides a wash for wrinkles, acne, and sunburn. The roots are expectorant and diuretic; reduce swellings and spasms; and contain aspirinlike compounds. A decoction is taken for chronic bronchitis.

• **REMARK** The stamens may cause contact dermatitis.

Habitat Meadows, open woodland; Europe, W. Asia	Parts used

Family PRIMULACEAE	Species *Primula vulgaris*	Local name Spring Primula

PRIMROSE

This perennial has a rosette of leaves and solitary, pale yellow spring flowers.

• **USES** The flowers, once used in love potions, are crystallized or added to jams and salads, and the leaves are boiled as a vegetable. Both are said to cleanse the blood. A flower tea eases headaches and is mildly sedative. A root decoction is an expectorant cough remedy. The water from soaked, dried leaves soothes inflamed eyes. The flowers make an astringent toilet water, and the leaf juice treats acne.

• **REMARK** The plant may cause contact dermatitis to those with allergies.

Habitat Moist shady woods, grassy banks; W. & S. Europe	Parts used

Family LABIATAE	Species *Prunella vulgaris*	Local name Prunella / Xia ku cao

SELF HEAL

This perennial has creeping rooting stems with upright flowering stems, oval to diamond-shaped leaves, and compact heads of purple-blue flowers in summer or autumn.

• **USES** The aerial parts are astringent and antiseptic and may reduce blood pressure. They treat sore throats, bleeding gums, hemorrhoids, and heavy menstruation. In China, the antiseptic, cooling flower spikes are considered a liver and gallbladder stimulant, and treat the symptoms associated with an unbalanced liver, including hypertension and conjunctivitis.

• **REMARK** This herb's common name indicates its long history of first-aid use on fresh wounds.

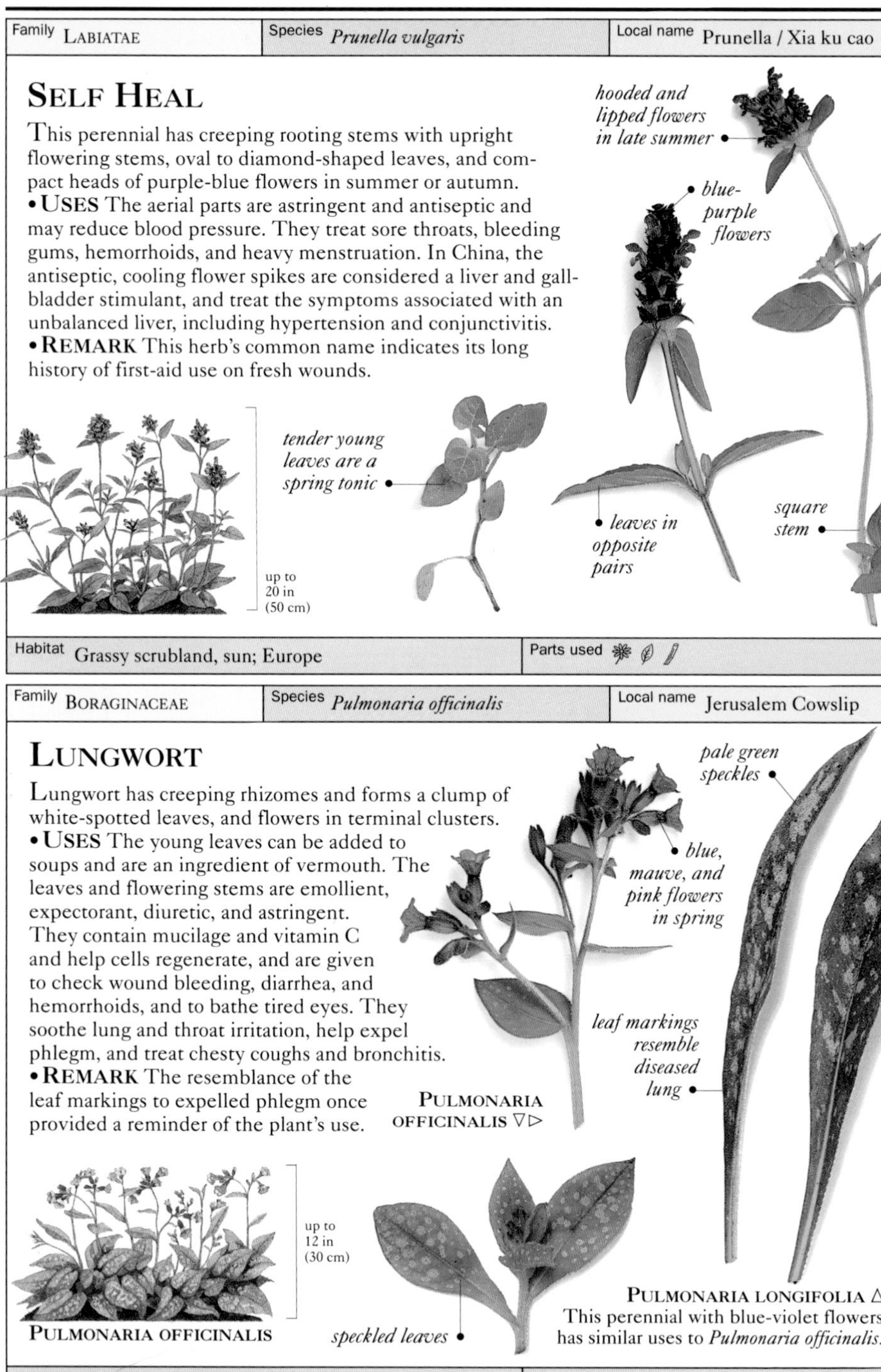
hooded and lipped flowers in late summer
blue-purple flowers
tender young leaves are a spring tonic
leaves in opposite pairs
square stem
up to 20 in (50 cm)
pale green speckles
blue, mauve, and pink flowers in spring
leaf markings resemble diseased lung
up to 12 in (30 cm)
speckled leaves

Habitat Grassy scrubland, sun; Europe	Parts used

Family BORAGINACEAE	Species *Pulmonaria officinalis*	Local name Jerusalem Cowslip

LUNGWORT

Lungwort has creeping rhizomes and forms a clump of white-spotted leaves, and flowers in terminal clusters.

• **USES** The young leaves can be added to soups and are an ingredient of vermouth. The leaves and flowering stems are emollient, expectorant, diuretic, and astringent. They contain mucilage and vitamin C and help cells regenerate, and are given to check wound bleeding, diarrhea, and hemorrhoids, and to bathe tired eyes. They soothe lung and throat irritation, help expel phlegm, and treat chesty coughs and bronchitis.

• **REMARK** The resemblance of the leaf markings to expelled phlegm once provided a reminder of the plant's use.

PULMONARIA OFFICINALIS ▽▷

PULMONARIA OFFICINALIS

PULMONARIA LONGIFOLIA △
This perennial with blue-violet flowers has similar uses to *Pulmonaria officinalis.*

Habitat Woods, hedges, rich soil, shade; Europe	Parts used

Family	Species	Local name
RANUNCULACEAE	*Pulsatilla vulgaris*	Windflower

PASQUEFLOWER

Pulsatilla vulgaris (syn. *Anemone pulsatilla*) has soft hairs, a rosette of finely divided leaves, and bell-shaped spring flowers that become feathery seed heads.

• **USES** *Pasque* is old French for Easter when the plant flowers. Poisonous when fresh, the dried aerial parts are sedative and reduce pain, nervous stress, and spasms. Herbalists give them for tension, headaches, exhaustion, earache, and neuralgia.

• **REMARK** The fresh plant should be used by qualified personnel only.

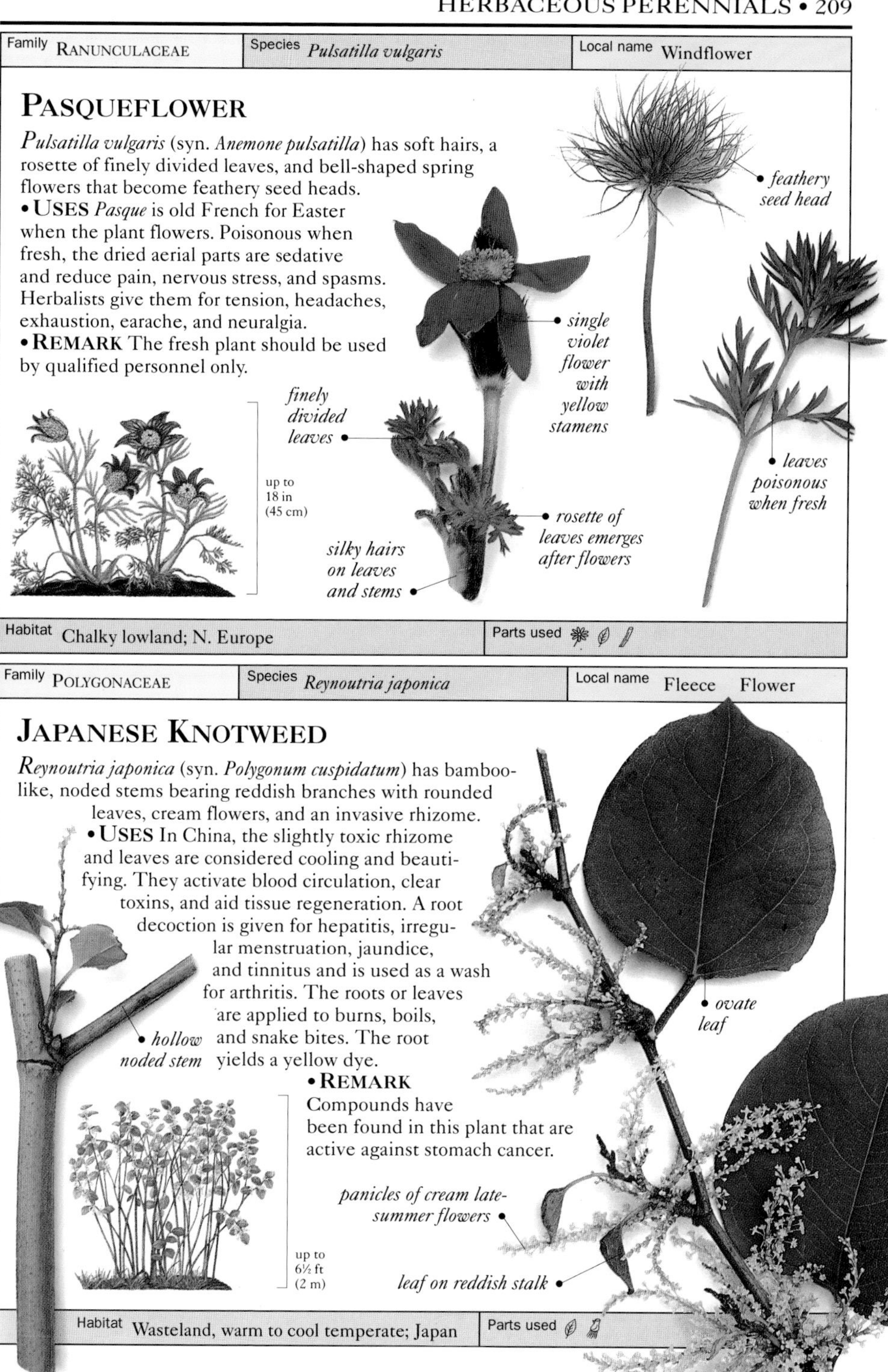

feathery seed head
single violet flower with yellow stamens
leaves poisonous when fresh
finely divided leaves
up to 18 in (45 cm)
rosette of leaves emerges after flowers
silky hairs on leaves and stems
hollow noded stem
ovate leaf
up to 6½ ft (2 m)
panicles of cream late-summer flowers
leaf on reddish stalk

Habitat	Parts used
Chalky lowland; N. Europe	

Family	Species	Local name
POLYGONACEAE	*Reynoutria japonica*	Fleece Flower

JAPANESE KNOTWEED

Reynoutria japonica (syn. *Polygonum cuspidatum*) has bamboo-like, noded stems bearing reddish branches with rounded leaves, cream flowers, and an invasive rhizome.

• **USES** In China, the slightly toxic rhizome and leaves are considered cooling and beautifying. They activate blood circulation, clear toxins, and aid tissue regeneration. A root decoction is given for hepatitis, irregular menstruation, jaundice, and tinnitus and is used as a wash for arthritis. The roots or leaves are applied to burns, boils, and snake bites. The root yields a yellow dye.

• **REMARK** Compounds have been found in this plant that are active against stomach cancer.

Habitat	Parts used
Wasteland, warm to cool temperate; Japan	

Family POLYGONACEAE	Species *Rheum officinale*	Local name Chinese Rhubarb

MEDICINAL RHUBARB

This thick-rhizomed perennial has large long-stalked leaves and a tall branched stem of densely clustered, small, green-white flowers in summer. • **USES** The leaf stalks are edible and mildly laxative, but this variety is not the usual Garden Rhubarb (*Rheum* x *cultorum*). The rhizome is a purgative irritant used for constipation, although in small amounts its astringency treats diarrhea and is an appetite and digestive stimulant added to tonic wines. In China, the rhizome is used to disperse blood clots, to cleanse the liver, and to treat jaundice, fevers, and abdominal pain. It is applied as an antiseptic, anti-inflammatory compress for boils, ulcers, and burns. Chinese researchers have identified properties that inhibit cancer cells. The rhizome removes rust stains, de-scales pans, and yields a yellow dye. Rhubarb (*Rheum palmatum*) shares the same medicinal properties.

• **REMARK** The Rhubarb rhizome has been used in Chinese medicine for almost 3,000 years.

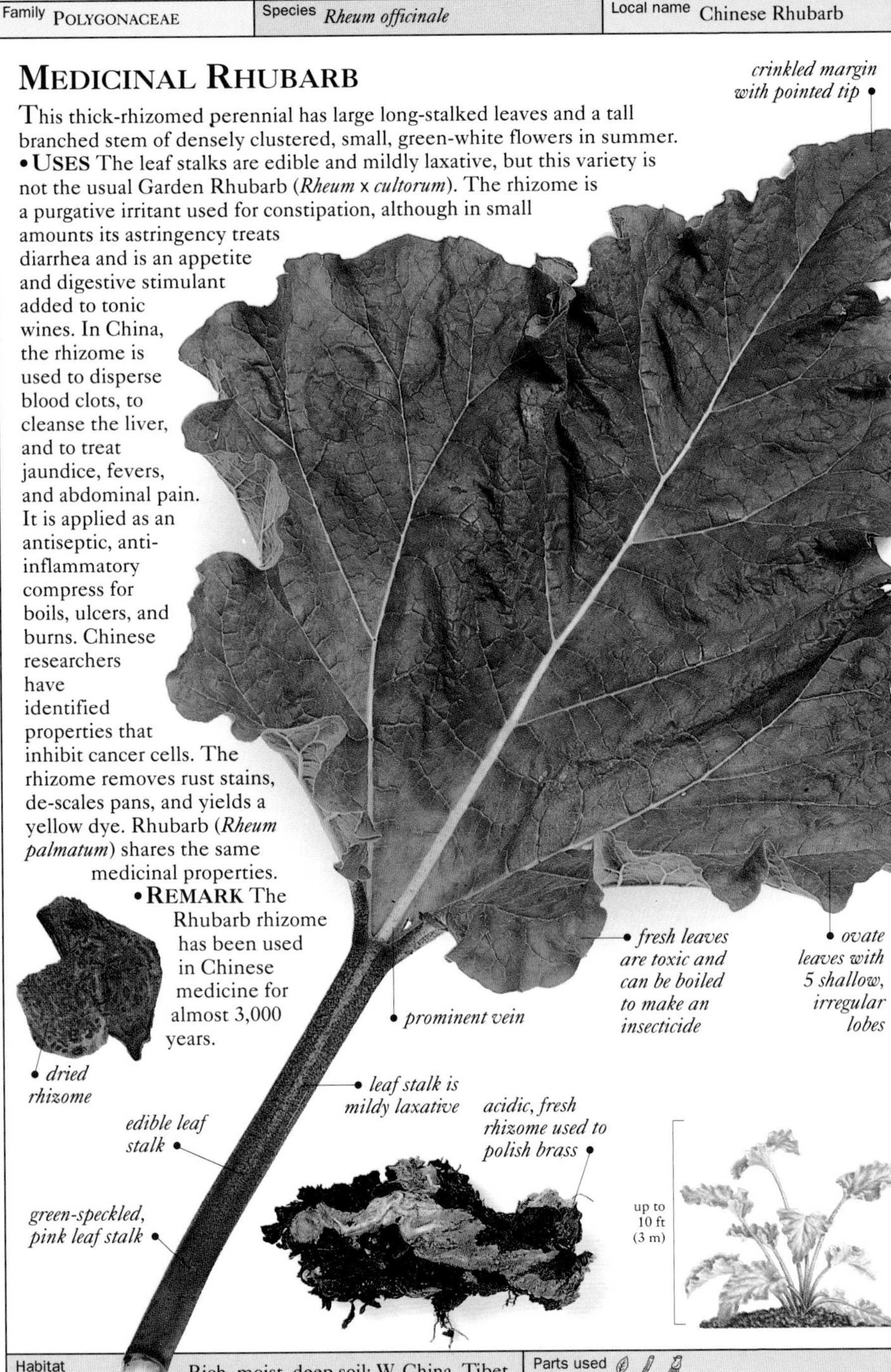
crinkled margin with pointed tip
fresh leaves are toxic and can be boiled to make an insecticide
ovate leaves with 5 shallow, irregular lobes
prominent vein
dried rhizome
leaf stalk is mildy laxative
acidic, fresh rhizome used to polish brass
edible leaf stalk
green-speckled, pink leaf stalk
up to 10 ft (3 m)

Habitat	Rich, moist, deep soil; W. China, Tibet	Parts used

Family CRASSULACEAE	Species *Rhodiola rosea*	Local name Midsummer Men

ROSE-ROOT

This variable herb has a thick branching rhizome; small fleshy leaves, sometimes tinged red; and scentless, greeny yellow flower heads appearing in summer.

• **USES** The leaves of this Arctic plant (syn. *Sedum rosea*) are a valuable food source, eaten in oil by the Inuit, and as a salad by Laplanders. The fresh root is scentless but when dried smells of roses. It was added to a skin tonic called "poor man's rosewater" and sprinkled on clothes to give a faint perfume. The whole plant when hung inside to deter insects stayed fresh for weeks. Modern plants give less scent.

• **REMARK** Known as Golden Root in Siberia, it is infused to treat coughs and ease pain. It causes mild euphoria and hangovers if taken in excess.

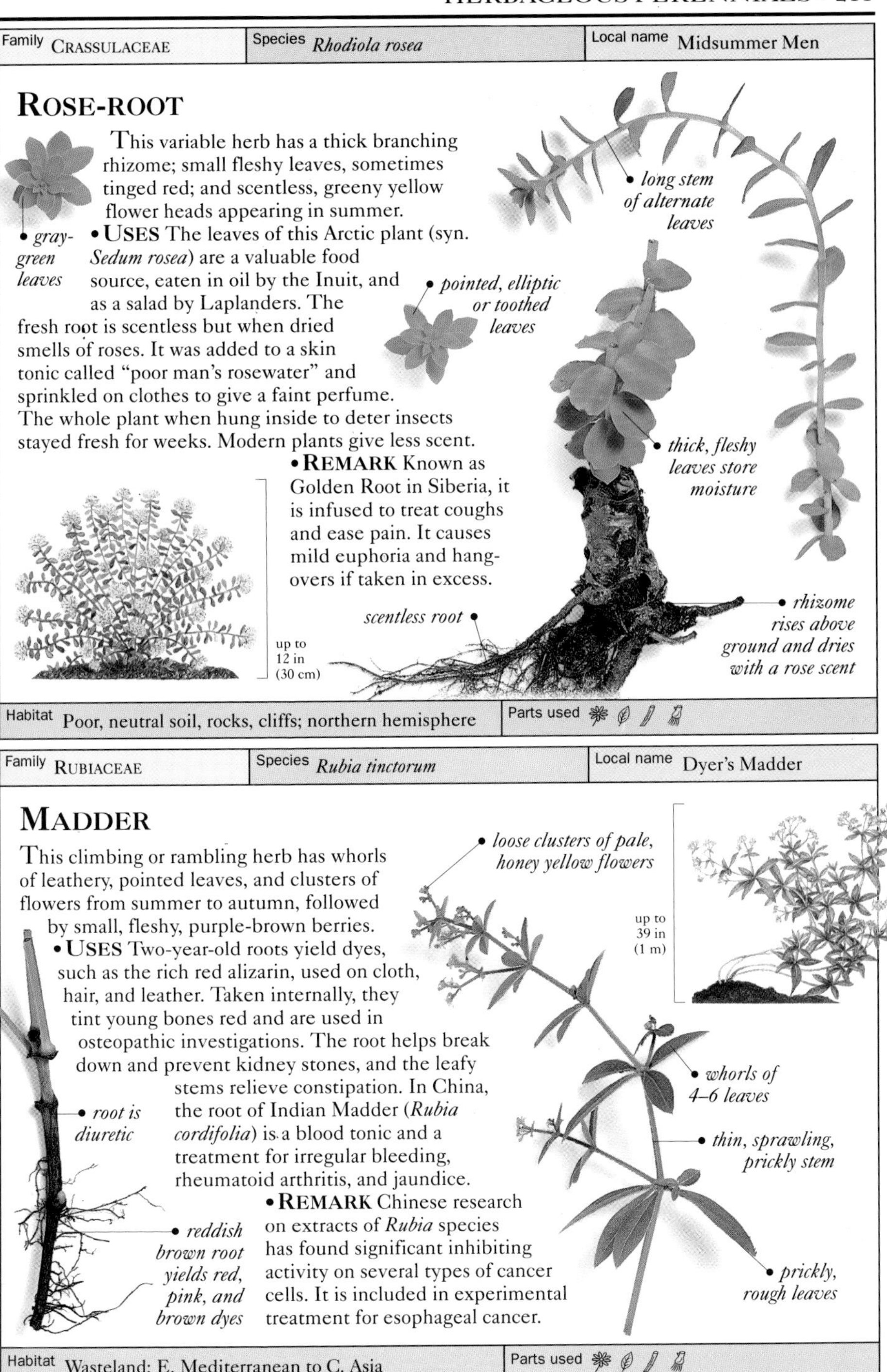

• gray-green leaves
• long stem of alternate leaves
• pointed, elliptic or toothed leaves
• thick, fleshy leaves store moisture
up to 12 in (30 cm)
scentless root •
• rhizome rises above ground and dries with a rose scent
• loose clusters of pale, honey yellow flowers
up to 39 in (1 m)
• whorls of 4–6 leaves
• thin, sprawling, prickly stem
• prickly, rough leaves
• root is diuretic
• reddish brown root yields red, pink, and brown dyes

Habitat Poor, neutral soil, rocks, cliffs; northern hemisphere	Parts used

Family RUBIACEAE	Species *Rubia tinctorum*	Local name Dyer's Madder

MADDER

This climbing or rambling herb has whorls of leathery, pointed leaves, and clusters of flowers from summer to autumn, followed by small, fleshy, purple-brown berries.

• **USES** Two-year-old roots yield dyes, such as the rich red alizarin, used on cloth, hair, and leather. Taken internally, they tint young bones red and are used in osteopathic investigations. The root helps break down and prevent kidney stones, and the leafy stems relieve constipation. In China, the root of Indian Madder (*Rubia cordifolia*) is a blood tonic and a treatment for irregular bleeding, rheumatoid arthritis, and jaundice.

• **REMARK** Chinese research on extracts of *Rubia* species has found significant inhibiting activity on several types of cancer cells. It is included in experimental treatment for esophageal cancer.

Habitat Wasteland; E. Mediterranean to C. Asia	Parts used

Family POLYGONACEAE	Species *Rumex acetosa*	Local name Little Vinegar Plant

BROAD-LEAF SORREL

Broad-leaf Sorrel has tall stems with fresh green, arrow-shaped leaves, and red-green flower spikes in summer.

• **USES** The vitamin-rich leaves are bland in spring, but as their sharp, refreshing taste develops they offer zest to salads, soups, sauces, omelettes, meat, fish, and poultry; they can be cooked like spinach with one change of water. The leaves quench thirst, reduce fevers, and are taken as a diuretic tea for some kidney and liver problems. A leaf poultice treats acne, mouth ulcers, boils, and infected wounds, and the root is a mild laxative. Leaf juice will bleach rust, mold, and ink stains from linen, wicker, and silver.

• **REMARK** The root of Yellow Dock (*Rumex crispus*) treats psoriasis and constipation.

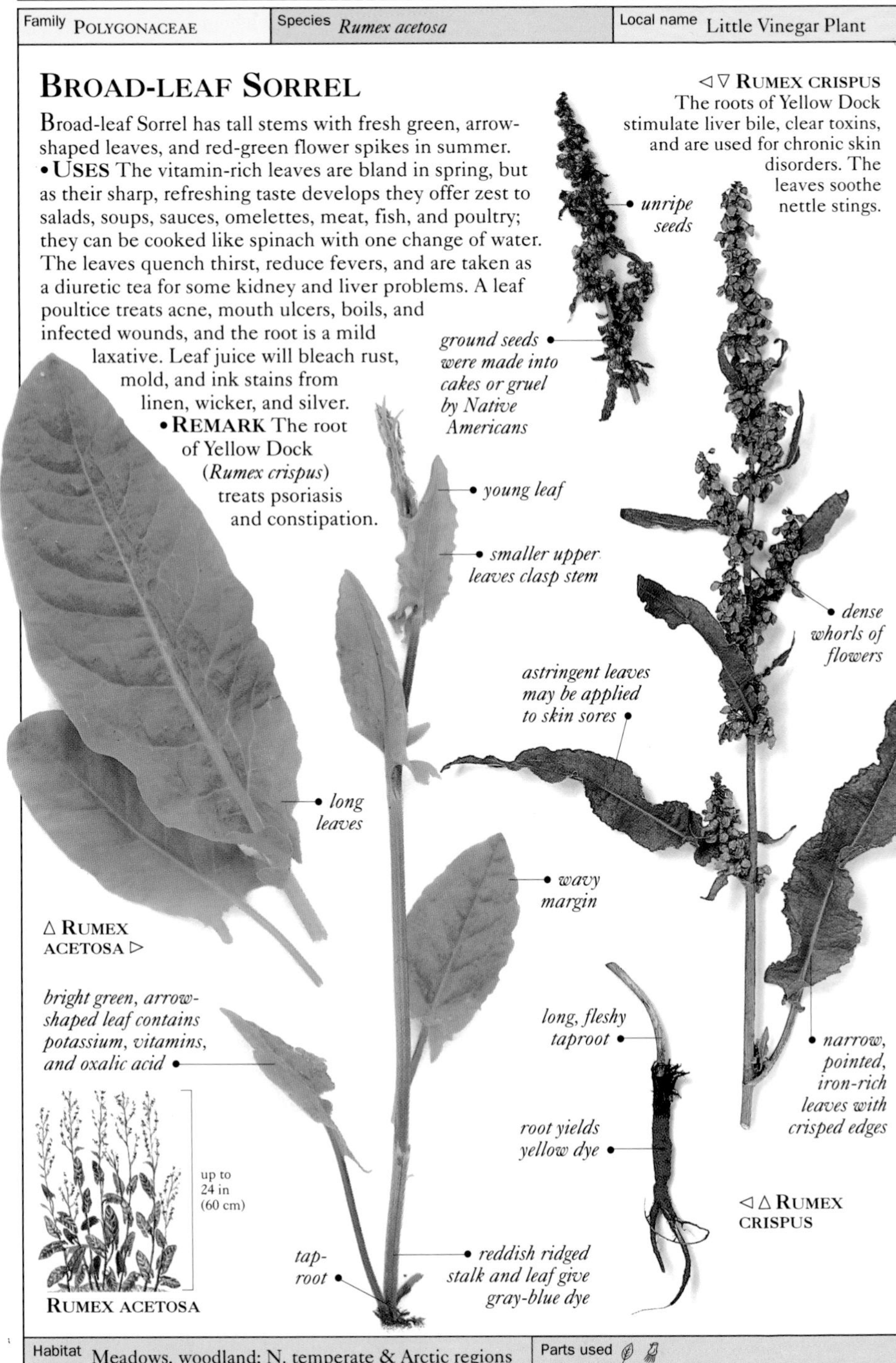
unripe seeds
ground seeds were made into cakes or gruel by Native Americans
young leaf
smaller upper leaves clasp stem
dense whorls of flowers
astringent leaves may be applied to skin sores
long leaves
wavy margin
bright green, arrow-shaped leaf contains potassium, vitamins, and oxalic acid
long, fleshy taproot
narrow, pointed, iron-rich leaves with crisped edges
root yields yellow dye
up to 24 in (60 cm)
tap-root
reddish ridged stalk and leaf give gray-blue dye

◁ ▽ RUMEX CRISPUS The roots of Yellow Dock stimulate liver bile, clear toxins, and are used for chronic skin disorders. The leaves soothe nettle stings.

△ RUMEX ACETOSA ▷

RUMEX ACETOSA

◁ △ RUMEX CRISPUS

Habitat Meadows, woodland; N. temperate & Arctic regions	Parts used

Family POLYGONACEAE	Species *Rumex scutatus*	Local name French Sorrel

BUCKLER-LEAF SORREL

This low-growing herb has prostrate and upright stems of shield-shaped leaves with occasional silver patches and pointed lobes. Insignificant summer flower spikes ripen with pinkish brown fruits.

• **USES** Buckler-leaf Sorrel is popular in salads for its mild but succulent lemon piquancy and its attractive leaf size. It is used like Broad-leaf Sorrel and favored for sorrel soup, sandwiches, and blending into yogurt drinks.

• **REMARK** It should be avoided by those with arthritis or kidney stones.

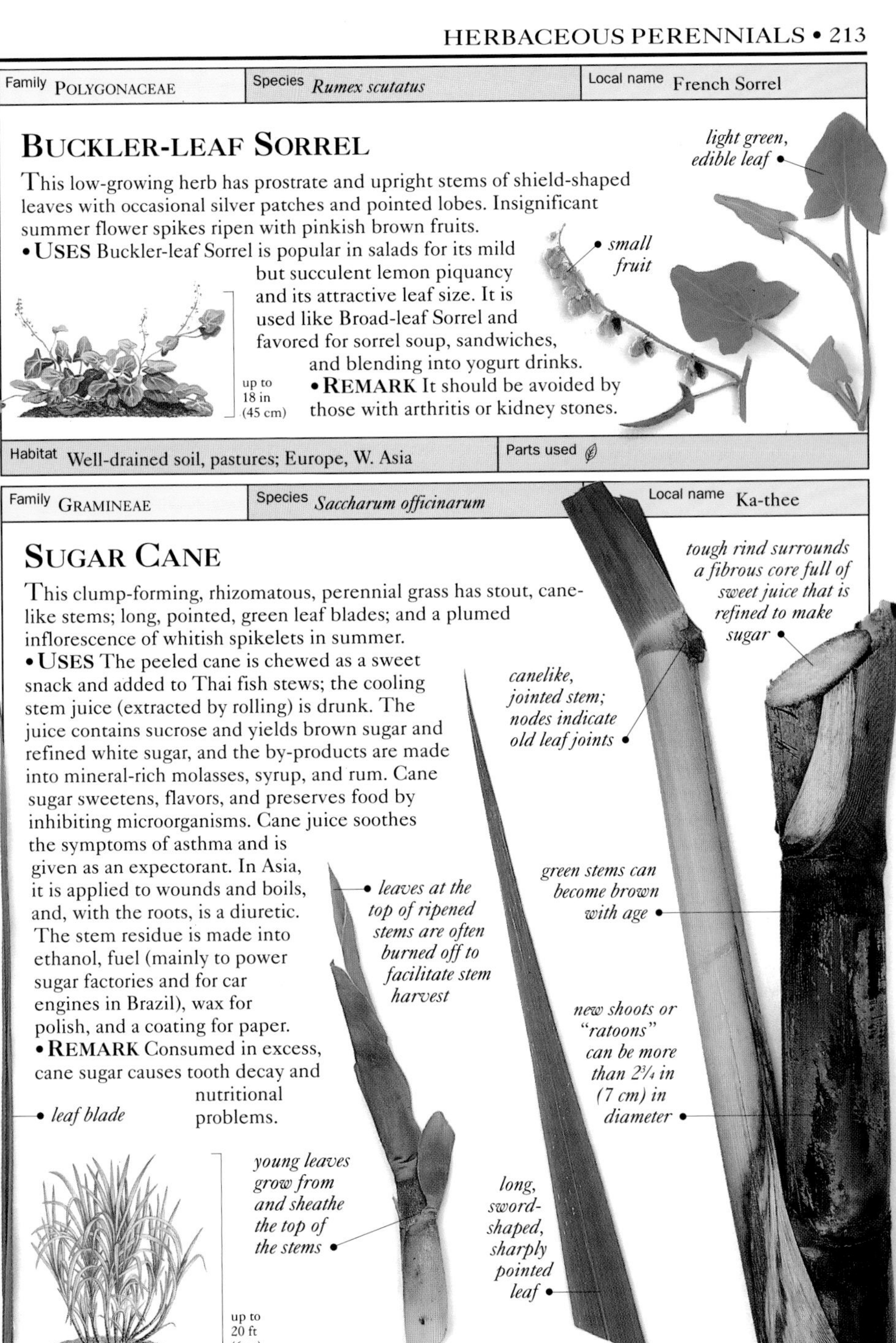
light green, edible leaf
small fruit
up to 18 in (45 cm)
tough rind surrounds a fibrous core full of sweet juice that is refined to make sugar
canelike, jointed stem; nodes indicate old leaf joints
leaves at the top of ripened stems are often burned off to facilitate stem harvest
green stems can become brown with age
new shoots or "ratoons" can be more than 2¾ in (7 cm) in diameter
leaf blade
young leaves grow from and sheathe the top of the stems
long, sword-shaped, sharply pointed leaf
up to 20 ft (6 m)

Habitat Well-drained soil, pastures; Europe, W. Asia	Parts used

Family GRAMINEAE	Species *Saccharum officinarum*	Local name Ka-thee

SUGAR CANE

This clump-forming, rhizomatous, perennial grass has stout, cane-like stems; long, pointed, green leaf blades; and a plumed inflorescence of whitish spikelets in summer.

• **USES** The peeled cane is chewed as a sweet snack and added to Thai fish stews; the cooling stem juice (extracted by rolling) is drunk. The juice contains sucrose and yields brown sugar and refined white sugar, and the by-products are made into mineral-rich molasses, syrup, and rum. Cane sugar sweetens, flavors, and preserves food by inhibiting microorganisms. Cane juice soothes the symptoms of asthma and is given as an expectorant. In Asia, it is applied to wounds and boils, and, with the roots, is a diuretic. The stem residue is made into ethanol, fuel (mainly to power sugar factories and for car engines in Brazil), wax for polish, and a coating for paper.

• **REMARK** Consumed in excess, cane sugar causes tooth decay and nutritional problems.

Habitat Cultivated land, rich soils; tropical S.E. Asia	Parts used

Family PAPAVERACEAE	Species *Sanguinaria canadensis*	Local name Indian Paint

BLOOD ROOT

Blood Root has a creeping rhizome and single, large leaves, folded at first, through which the white flowers emerge in spring.

• **USES** The rhizome yields an orange-red dye once used by Native Americans as a body paint and insect repellent. Although toxic, the rhizome is expectorant, tonic, antibacterial, and antiviral. It is a local anesthetic, and is given in small doses for chronic coughs, sore throats, fevers, and skin infections.

• **REMARK** Recent research has focused on its potential as a skin cancer treatment.

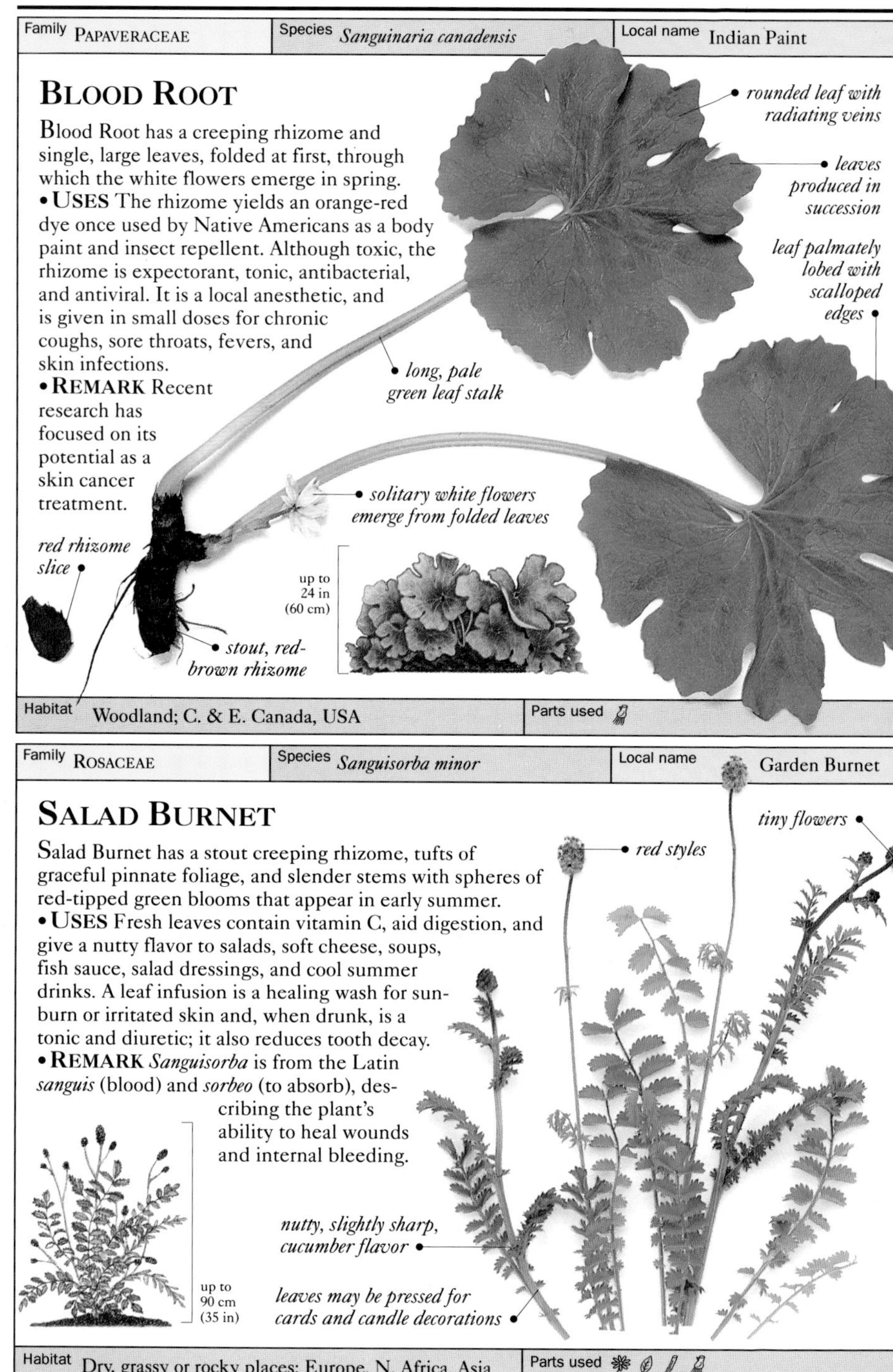
rounded leaf with radiating veins
leaves produced in succession
leaf palmately lobed with scalloped edges
long, pale green leaf stalk
solitary white flowers emerge from folded leaves
red rhizome slice
up to 24 in (60 cm)
stout, red-brown rhizome
tiny flowers
red styles
nutty, slightly sharp, cucumber flavor
leaves may be pressed for cards and candle decorations
up to 90 cm (35 in)

Habitat Woodland; C. & E. Canada, USA	Parts used

Family ROSACEAE	Species *Sanguisorba minor*	Local name Garden Burnet

SALAD BURNET

Salad Burnet has a stout creeping rhizome, tufts of graceful pinnate foliage, and slender stems with spheres of red-tipped green blooms that appear in early summer.

• **USES** Fresh leaves contain vitamin C, aid digestion, and give a nutty flavor to salads, soft cheese, soups, fish sauce, salad dressings, and cool summer drinks. A leaf infusion is a healing wash for sunburn or irritated skin and, when drunk, is a tonic and diuretic; it also reduces tooth decay.

• **REMARK** *Sanguisorba* is from the Latin *sanguis* (blood) and *sorbeo* (to absorb), describing the plant's ability to heal wounds and internal bleeding.

Habitat Dry, grassy or rocky places; Europe, N. Africa, Asia	Parts used

Family UMBELLIFERAE	Species *Sanicula europaea*	Local name Wood Sanicle

SANICLE

Sanicle has a creeping rhizome; palmately lobed leaves; and erect, slender stems with white or pale pink summer flowers followed by fruits with hooked bristles.

• **USES** An infusion of leaves, stems, and roots is given for diarrhea, as a blood purifier to improve the skin, and once treated coughs, urinary and liver disorders, internal bleeding, and stomach or intestine inflammation. It is gargled for sore throats, applied as a compress for bruises, and is added to baths to detoxify the skin.

• **REMARK** The common name is from the Latin *sanus*, meaning "sound, whole, or healthy."

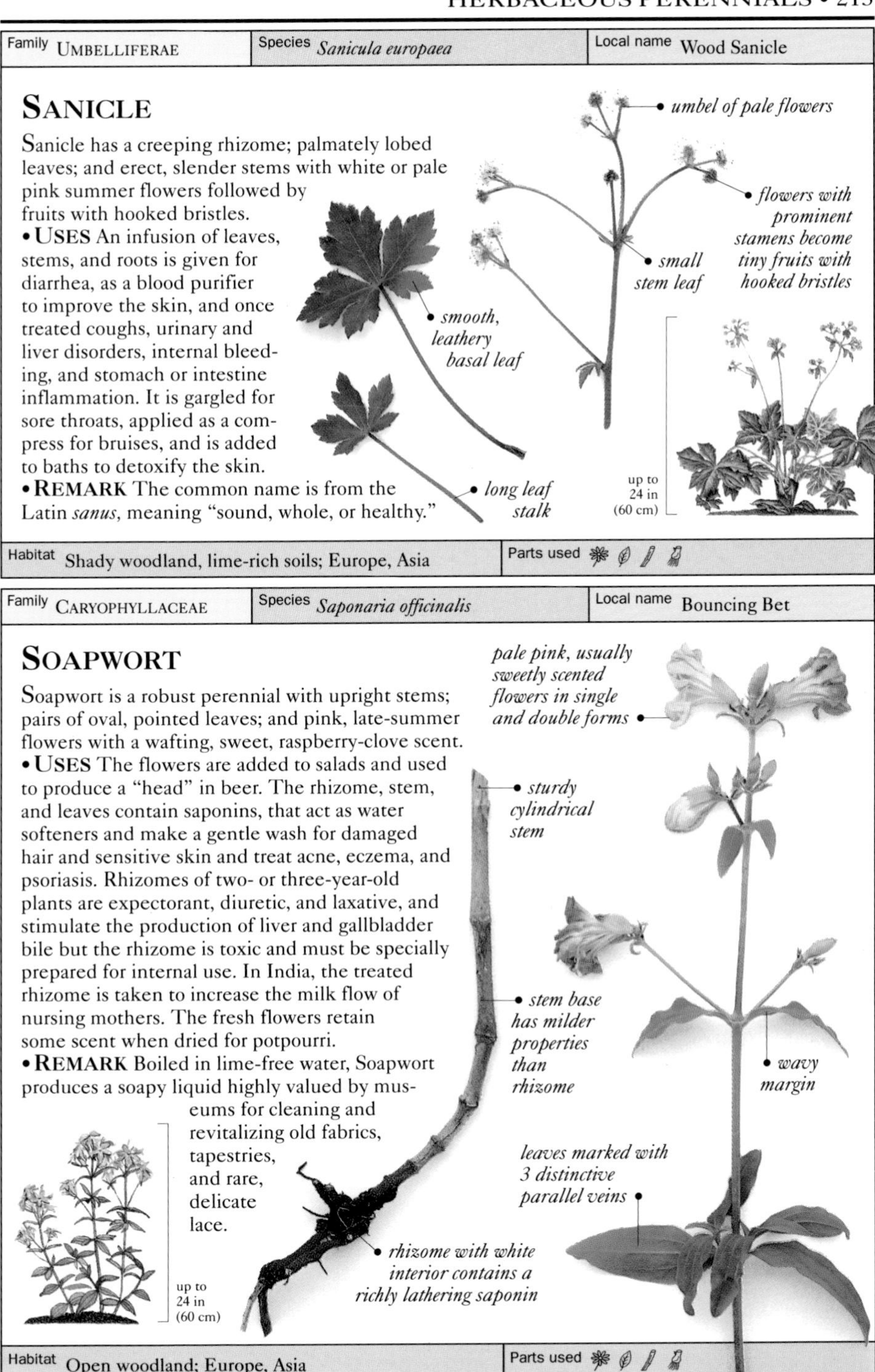
umbel of pale flowers
flowers with prominent stamens become tiny fruits with hooked bristles
small stem leaf
smooth, leathery basal leaf
long leaf stalk
up to 24 in (60 cm)
pale pink, usually sweetly scented flowers in single and double forms
sturdy cylindrical stem
stem base has milder properties than rhizome
wavy margin
leaves marked with 3 distinctive parallel veins
rhizome with white interior contains a richly lathering saponin
up to 24 in (60 cm)

Habitat Shady woodland, lime-rich soils; Europe, Asia	Parts used

Family CARYOPHYLLACEAE	Species *Saponaria officinalis*	Local name Bouncing Bet

SOAPWORT

Soapwort is a robust perennial with upright stems; pairs of oval, pointed leaves; and pink, late-summer flowers with a wafting, sweet, raspberry-clove scent.

• **USES** The flowers are added to salads and used to produce a "head" in beer. The rhizome, stem, and leaves contain saponins, that act as water softeners and make a gentle wash for damaged hair and sensitive skin and treat acne, eczema, and psoriasis. Rhizomes of two- or three-year-old plants are expectorant, diuretic, and laxative, and stimulate the production of liver and gallbladder bile but the rhizome is toxic and must be specially prepared for internal use. In India, the treated rhizome is taken to increase the milk flow of nursing mothers. The fresh flowers retain some scent when dried for potpourri.

• **REMARK** Boiled in lime-free water, Soapwort produces a soapy liquid highly valued by museums for cleaning and revitalizing old fabrics, tapestries, and rare, delicate lace.

Habitat Open woodland; Europe, Asia	Parts used

Family SCROPHULARIACEAE	Species *Scrophularia nodosa*	Local name Rosenoble

KNOTTED FIGWORT

This herb has narrow, pointed stem leaves, wider base leaves, green and purple-brown summer flowers, and small, round seed capsules.

• **USES** Figwort is a blood-cleansing tonic with a diuretic and pain-relieving action suited to the skin and lymph system. It was traditionally given for scrofula and gangrene, and today is drunk or applied as a poultice for swollen lymph glands, itching eczema, psoriasis, swellings, boils, and small wounds. It is a heart stimulant and should be avoided by those with a rapid heartbeat.

• **REMARK** The root of Chinese *Scrophularia buergeriana* is a heart tonic and treats malarial and typhoid fever.

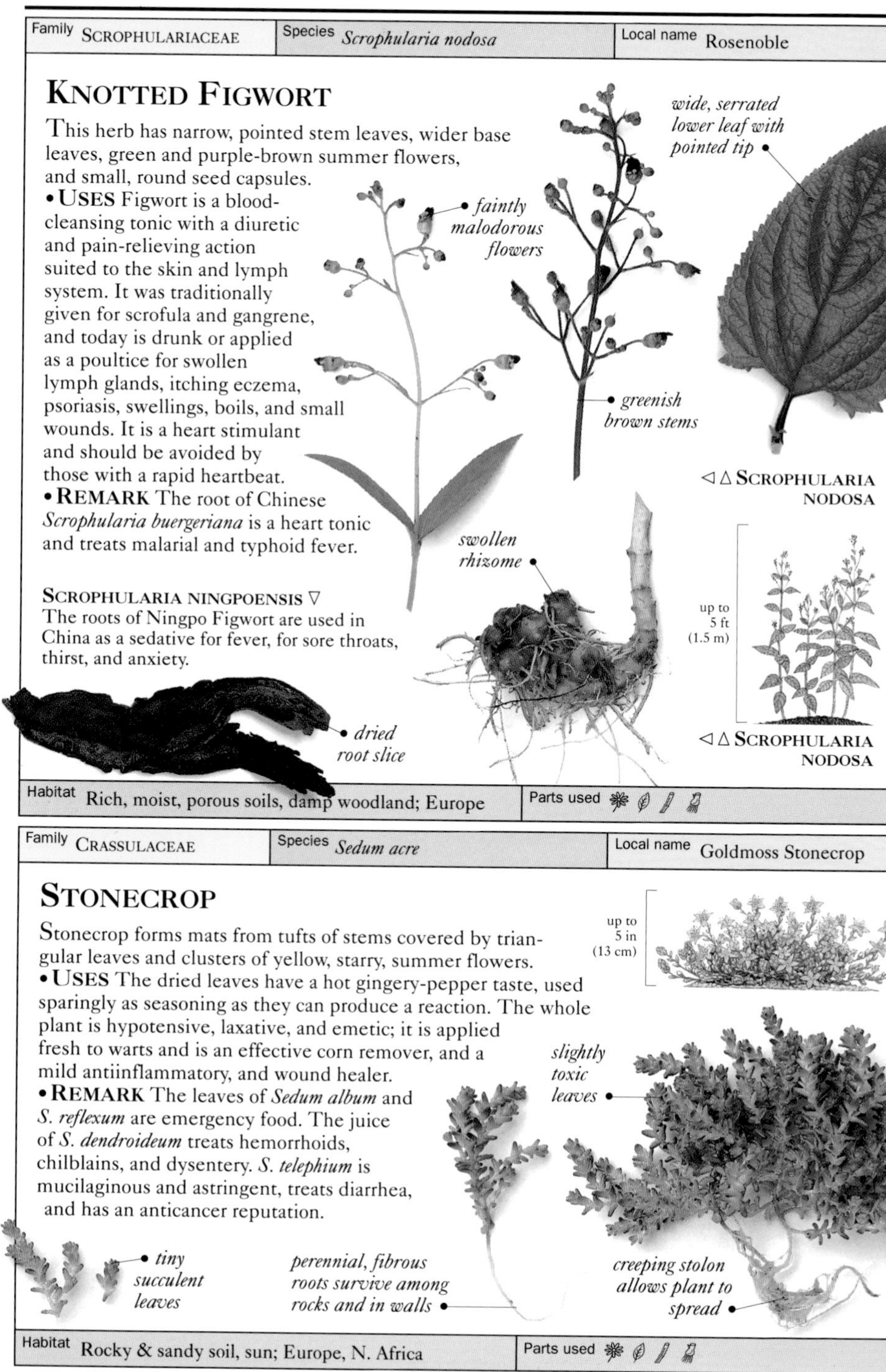

faintly malodorous flowers
wide, serrated lower leaf with pointed tip
greenish brown stems
swollen rhizome
up to 5 ft (1.5 m)
dried root slice
perennial, fibrous roots survive among rocks and in walls
slightly toxic leaves
creeping stolon allows plant to spread
tiny succulent leaves
up to 5 in (13 cm)

◁ △ SCROPHULARIA NODOSA

◁ △ SCROPHULARIA NODOSA

SCROPHULARIA NINGPOENSIS ▽
The roots of Ningpo Figwort are used in China as a sedative for fever, for sore throats, thirst, and anxiety.

Habitat Rich, moist, porous soils, damp woodland; Europe	Parts used

Family CRASSULACEAE	Species *Sedum acre*	Local name Goldmoss Stonecrop

STONECROP

Stonecrop forms mats from tufts of stems covered by triangular leaves and clusters of yellow, starry, summer flowers.

• **USES** The dried leaves have a hot gingery-pepper taste, used sparingly as seasoning as they can produce a reaction. The whole plant is hypotensive, laxative, and emetic; it is applied fresh to warts and is an effective corn remover, and a mild antiinflammatory, and wound healer.

• **REMARK** The leaves of *Sedum album* and *S. reflexum* are emergency food. The juice of *S. dendroideum* treats hemorrhoids, chilblains, and dysentery. *S. telephium* is mucilaginous and astringent, treats diarrhea, and has an anticancer reputation.

Habitat Rocky & sandy soil, sun; Europe, N. Africa	Parts used

Family LABIATAE	Species *Scutellaria lateriflora*	Local name Mad Dog Skullcap

VIRGINIA SKULLCAP

This hardy perennial has branching stems of oval to triangular leaves and tubular, blue summer flowers.

• **USES** Virginia Skullcap calms the nerves and is a tonic. The aerial parts are sedative and antispasmodic, and were once given for epilepsy and rabies. A tea is now taken for anxiety, depression, nervous exhaustion, premenstrual syndrome, rheumatism, and neuralgia. It has potential in reducing the withdrawal symptoms of Valium and other barbiturates, of alcohol, and in easing the pain of multiple sclerosis.

• **REMARK** Tests on the root of Huang Qin (*Scutellaria Baicalensis*) confirm it lowers blood pressure. *S. barbata* inhibits some cancer cells.

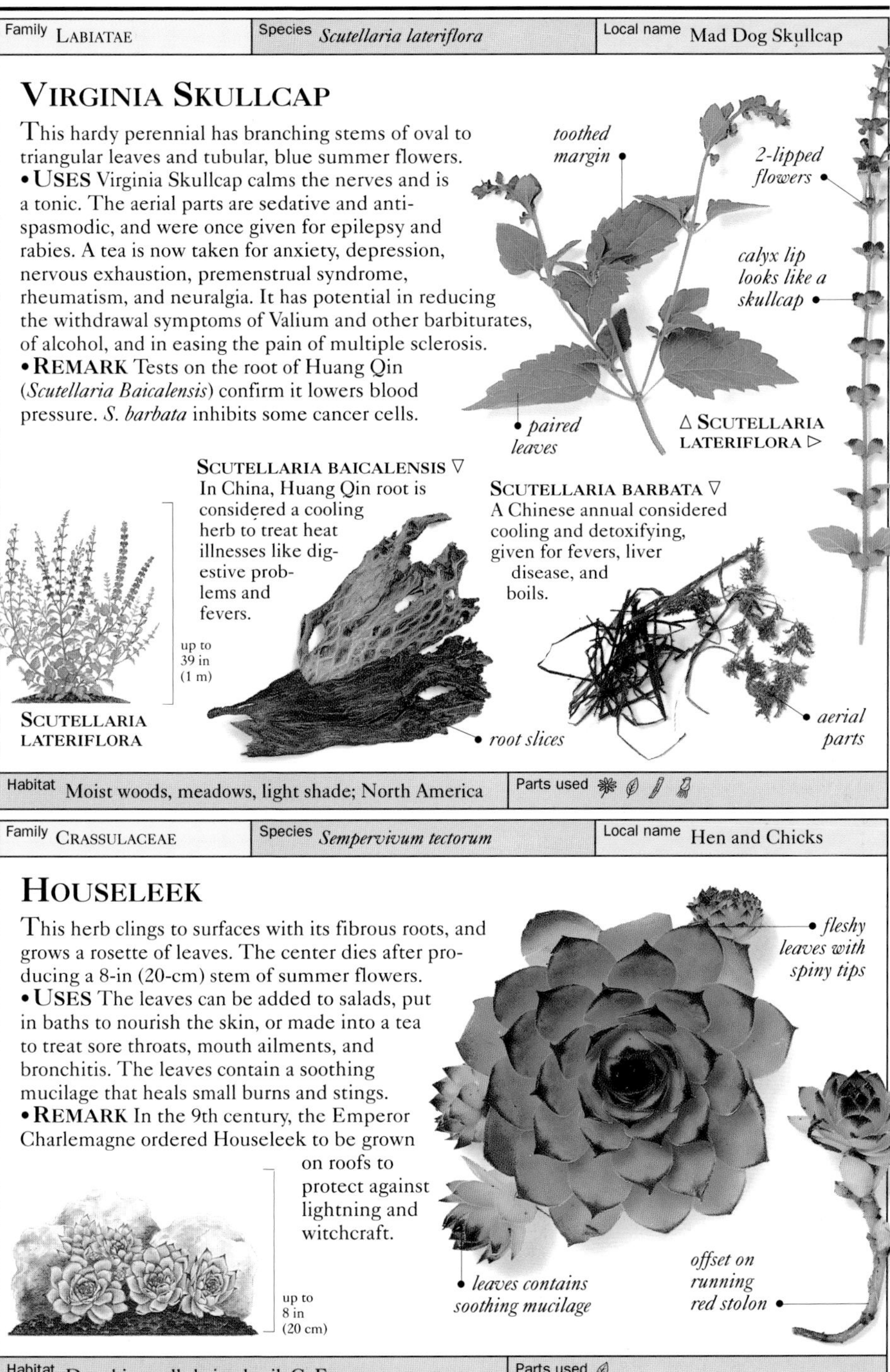

toothed margin
2-lipped flowers
calyx lip looks like a skullcap
paired leaves
△ SCUTELLARIA LATERIFLORA ▷
up to 39 in (1 m)
SCUTELLARIA LATERIFLORA
root slices
aerial parts
fleshy leaves with spiny tips
leaves contains soothing mucilage
offset on running red stolon
up to 8 in (20 cm)

SCUTELLARIA BAICALENSIS ▽ In China, Huang Qin root is considered a cooling herb to treat heat illnesses like digestive problems and fevers.

SCUTELLARIA BARBATA ▽ A Chinese annual considered cooling and detoxifying, given for fevers, liver disease, and boils.

Habitat Moist woods, meadows, light shade; North America	Parts used

Family CRASSULACEAE	Species *Sempervivum tectorum*	Local name Hen and Chicks

HOUSELEEK

This herb clings to surfaces with its fibrous roots, and grows a rosette of leaves. The center dies after producing a 8-in (20-cm) stem of summer flowers.

• **USES** The leaves can be added to salads, put in baths to nourish the skin, or made into a tea to treat sore throats, mouth ailments, and bronchitis. The leaves contain a soothing mucilage that heals small burns and stings.

• **REMARK** In the 9th century, the Emperor Charlemagne ordered Houseleek to be grown on roofs to protect against lightning and witchcraft.

Habitat Dry, thin, well-drained soil; C. Europe	Parts used

Family UMBELLIFERAE	Species *Sium sisarum*	Local name Chervin

SKIRRET

Skirret has aromatic roots and branched stems bearing elegant, pointed leaflets and umbels of white flowers in summer.

• **USES** The young spring shoots and slender roots are steamed or stir-fried; roots are added to stews, pickled to serve with cold meats, or roasted as a coffee substitute. The clustered, gray-skinned, swollen roots of *Sium sisarum* var. *sisarum* have the best flavor. The roots have been prescribed to promote urine, cleanse the bladder, treat jaundice and other liver disorders, and to relieve chest complaints.

• **REMARK** The plant looks dangerously similar to deadly Water Hemlock.

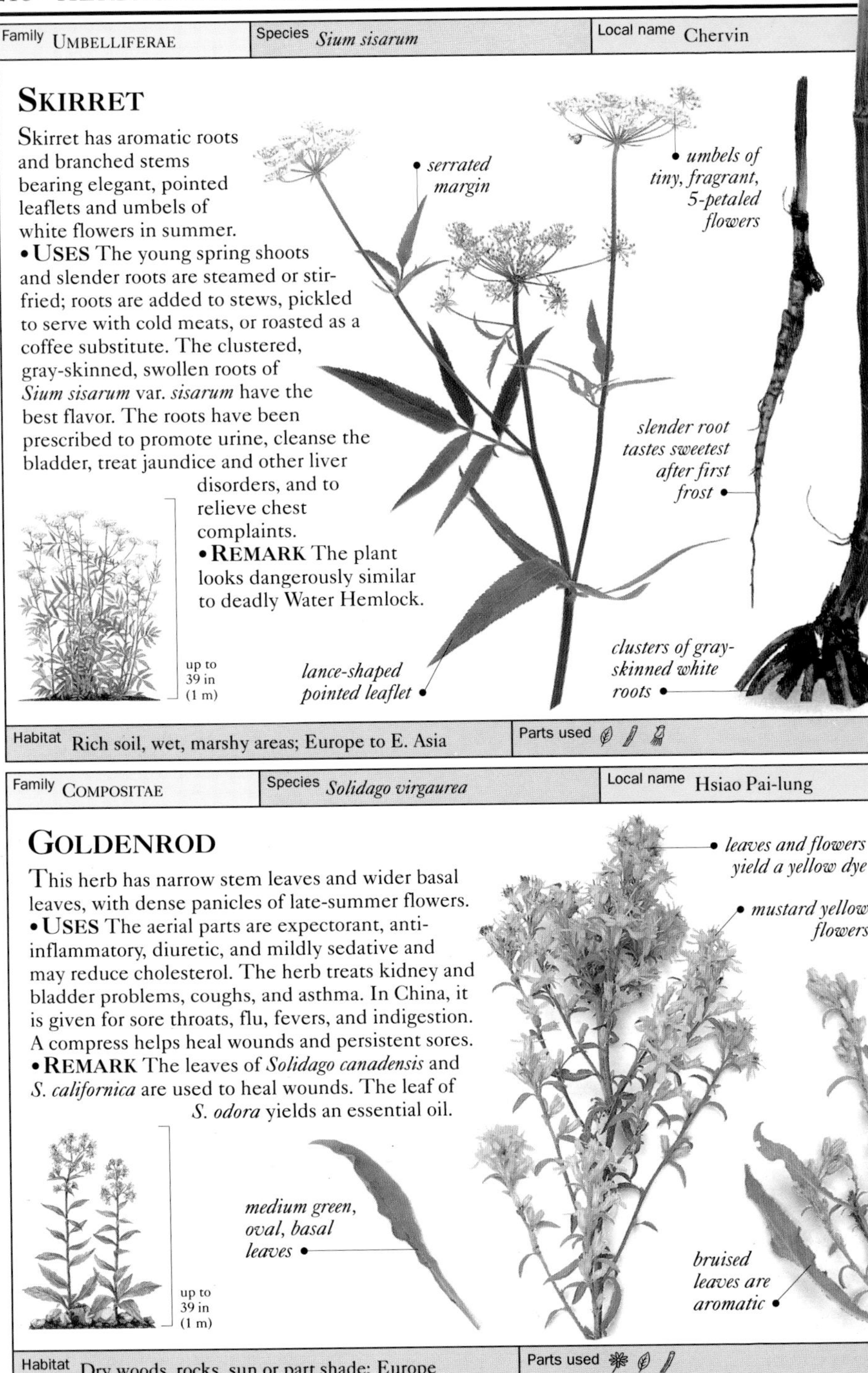
serrated margin
umbels of tiny, fragrant, 5-petaled flowers
slender root tastes sweetest after first frost
clusters of gray-skinned white roots
lance-shaped pointed leaflet
up to 39 in (1 m)
leaves and flowers yield a yellow dye
mustard yellow flowers
medium green, oval, basal leaves
bruised leaves are aromatic
up to 39 in (1 m)

Habitat Rich soil, wet, marshy areas; Europe to E. Asia	Parts used

Family COMPOSITAE	Species *Solidago virgaurea*	Local name Hsiao Pai-lung

GOLDENROD

This herb has narrow stem leaves and wider basal leaves, with dense panicles of late-summer flowers.

• **USES** The aerial parts are expectorant, anti-inflammatory, diuretic, and mildly sedative and may reduce cholesterol. The herb treats kidney and bladder problems, coughs, and asthma. In China, it is given for sore throats, flu, fevers, and indigestion. A compress helps heal wounds and persistent sores.

• **REMARK** The leaves of *Solidago canadensis* and *S. californica* are used to heal wounds. The leaf of *S. odora* yields an essential oil.

Habitat Dry woods, rocks, sun or part shade; Europe	Parts used

Family LABIATAE	Species *Stachys officinalis*	Local name Bishop's Wort

WOOD BETONY

Wood Betony has faintly pungent, scalloped, hairy leaves, and spikes of pale magenta summer flowers.

• **USES** The aerial parts provide a tea substitute and are added to tonics and herbal cigarettes. An infusion is mildly sedative and cleansing and is a nerve and circulation tonic for migraine, anxiety, indigestion, drunkenness, and difficult labor. It has potential as a cerebral tonic.

• **REMARK** Wood Betony was an Anglo-Saxon protective charm.

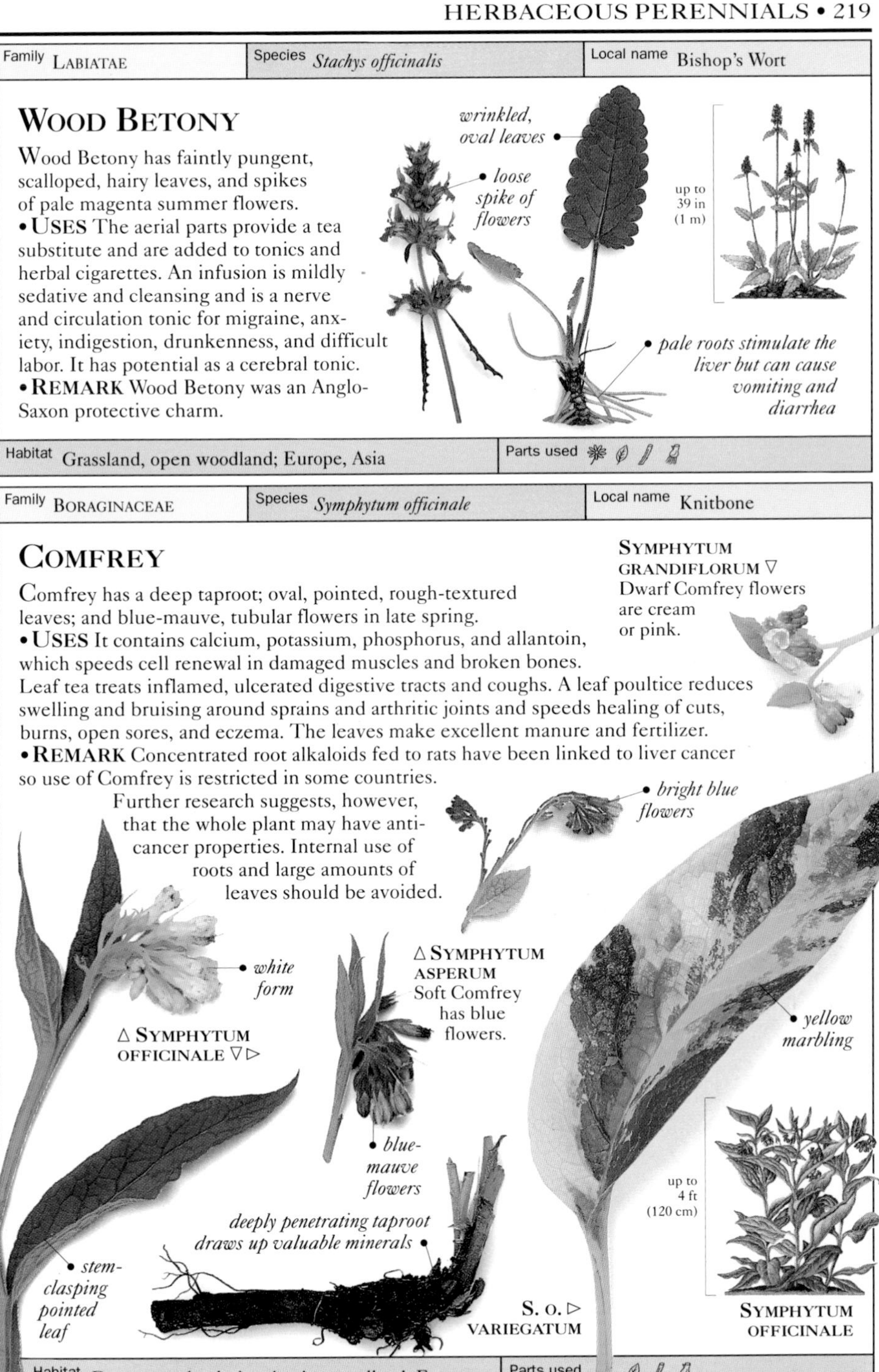
wrinkled, oval leaves
loose spike of flowers
up to 39 in (1 m)
pale roots stimulate the liver but can cause vomiting and diarrhea

Habitat Grassland, open woodland; Europe, Asia	Parts used

Family BORAGINACEAE	Species *Symphytum officinale*	Local name Knitbone

COMFREY

Comfrey has a deep taproot; oval, pointed, rough-textured leaves; and blue-mauve, tubular flowers in late spring.

• **USES** It contains calcium, potassium, phosphorus, and allantoin, which speeds cell renewal in damaged muscles and broken bones. Leaf tea treats inflamed, ulcerated digestive tracts and coughs. A leaf poultice reduces swelling and bruising around sprains and arthritic joints and speeds healing of cuts, burns, open sores, and eczema. The leaves make excellent manure and fertilizer.

• **REMARK** Concentrated root alkaloids fed to rats have been linked to liver cancer so use of Comfrey is restricted in some countries. Further research suggests, however, that the whole plant may have anti-cancer properties. Internal use of roots and large amounts of leaves should be avoided.

SYMPHYTUM GRANDIFLORUM ▽ Dwarf Comfrey flowers are cream or pink.

△ **SYMPHYTUM ASPERUM** Soft Comfrey has blue flowers.

△ **SYMPHYTUM OFFICINALE** ▽ ▷

S. O. ▷ **VARIEGATUM**

SYMPHYTUM OFFICINALE

bright blue flowers
white form
yellow marbling
blue-mauve flowers
deeply penetrating taproot draws up valuable minerals
stem-clasping pointed leaf
up to 4 ft (120 cm)

Habitat Damp grassland, river banks, woodland; Europe	Parts used

Family COMPOSITAE	Species *Tanacetum balsamita*	Local name Costmary / Bible Leaf

ALECOST

Alecost has pointed, oval, scalloped, silvery green leaves and small heads of yellow disk florets, sometimes with white outer ray florets.
• **USES** The leaves give a sharp tang to salads, soups, game stuffing, and fruitcakes and have a refreshing spearmint scent. Before the use of hops they were used to clear, flavor, and preserve ale. The leaves scent linen and potpourri; they are balsamic, preservative, and antiseptic. A leaf rinse or crushed leaf soothes burns and stings. The tea relieves colds, phlegm, upset stomachs, and cramps and was once taken to ease childbirth.
• **REMARK** Puritans carried the minty leaf in their Bibles to allay hunger during long sermons.

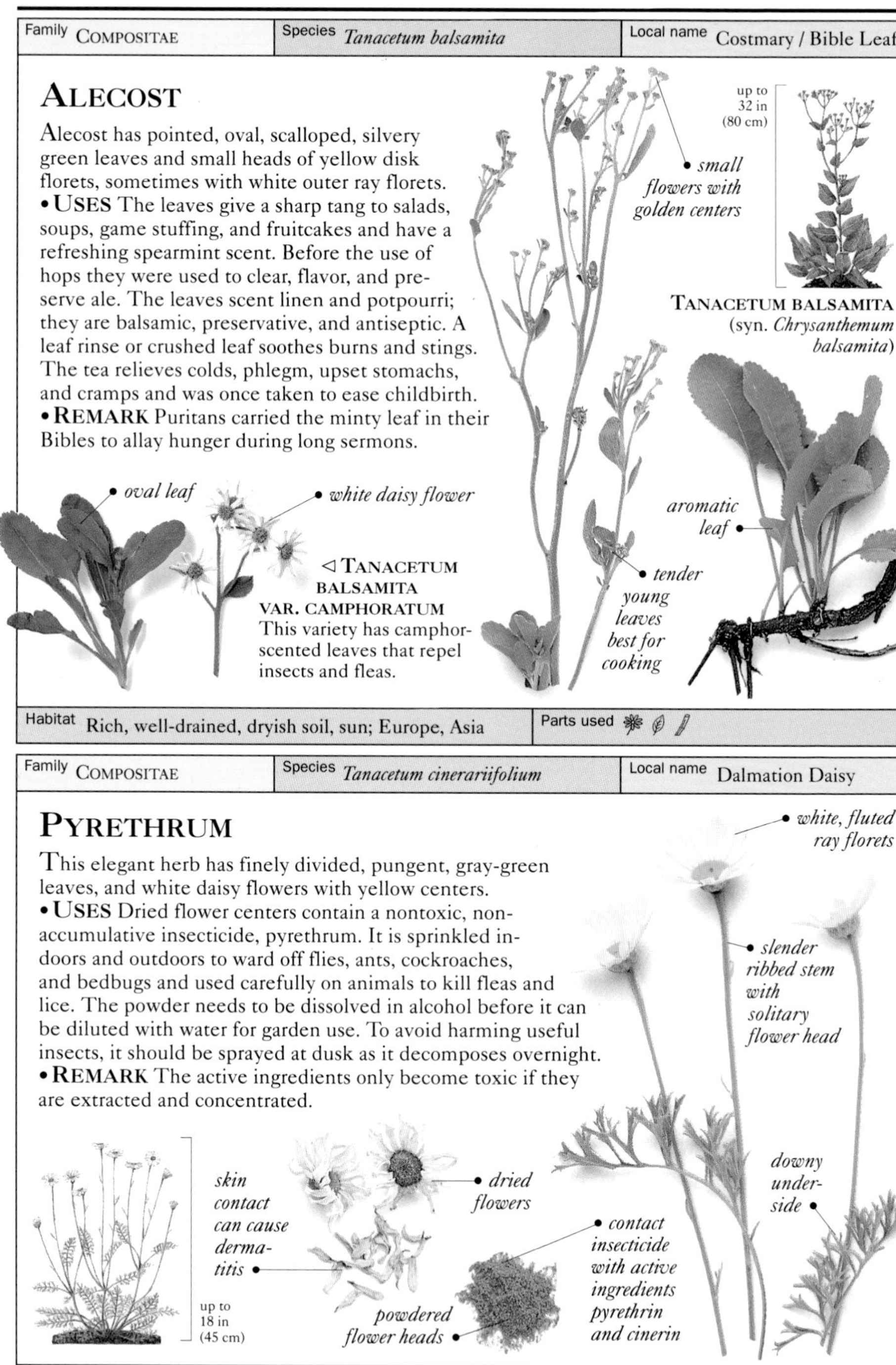

small flowers with golden centers
up to 32 in (80 cm)
oval leaf
white daisy flower
aromatic leaf
tender young leaves best for cooking
white, fluted ray florets
slender ribbed stem with solitary flower head
skin contact can cause dermatitis
dried flowers
contact insecticide with active ingredients pyrethrin and cinerin
downy underside
powdered flower heads
up to 18 in (45 cm)

TANACETUM BALSAMITA (syn. *Chrysanthemum balsamita*)

◁ TANACETUM BALSAMITA VAR. CAMPHORATUM
This variety has camphor-scented leaves that repel insects and fleas.

Habitat Rich, well-drained, dryish soil, sun; Europe, Asia	Parts used

Family COMPOSITAE	Species *Tanacetum cinerariifolium*	Local name Dalmation Daisy

PYRETHRUM

This elegant herb has finely divided, pungent, gray-green leaves, and white daisy flowers with yellow centers.
• **USES** Dried flower centers contain a nontoxic, non-accumulative insecticide, pyrethrum. It is sprinkled indoors and outdoors to ward off flies, ants, cockroaches, and bedbugs and used carefully on animals to kill fleas and lice. The powder needs to be dissolved in alcohol before it can be diluted with water for garden use. To avoid harming useful insects, it should be sprayed at dusk as it decomposes overnight.
• **REMARK** The active ingredients only become toxic if they are extracted and concentrated.

Habitat Alkaline, well-drained, rocky soil, sun; S.E. Europe	Parts used

Family COMPOSITAE	Species *Tanacetum parthenium*	Local name Featherfoil

FEVERFEW

Semievergreen Feverfew has pungent, divided, medium to yellow-green leaves and white daisy flowers appearing in summer.

• **USES** The leaves add a bitter tang to food and are found in digestive apertifs. They relax blood vessels, reduce inflammation, and are mildly sedative. Feverfew's importance lies in its success in reducing some migraines. Chewed daily its accumulative effect is to reduce headache pains and inhibit the secretion of a compound implicated in migraine and arthritis; infused flowering tops are applied to ease headaches and arthritic swellings. A tea is taken for tinnitus and irregular periods and to cleanse the uterus after childbirth.

• **REMARK** Fresh leaves can irritate the mouth.

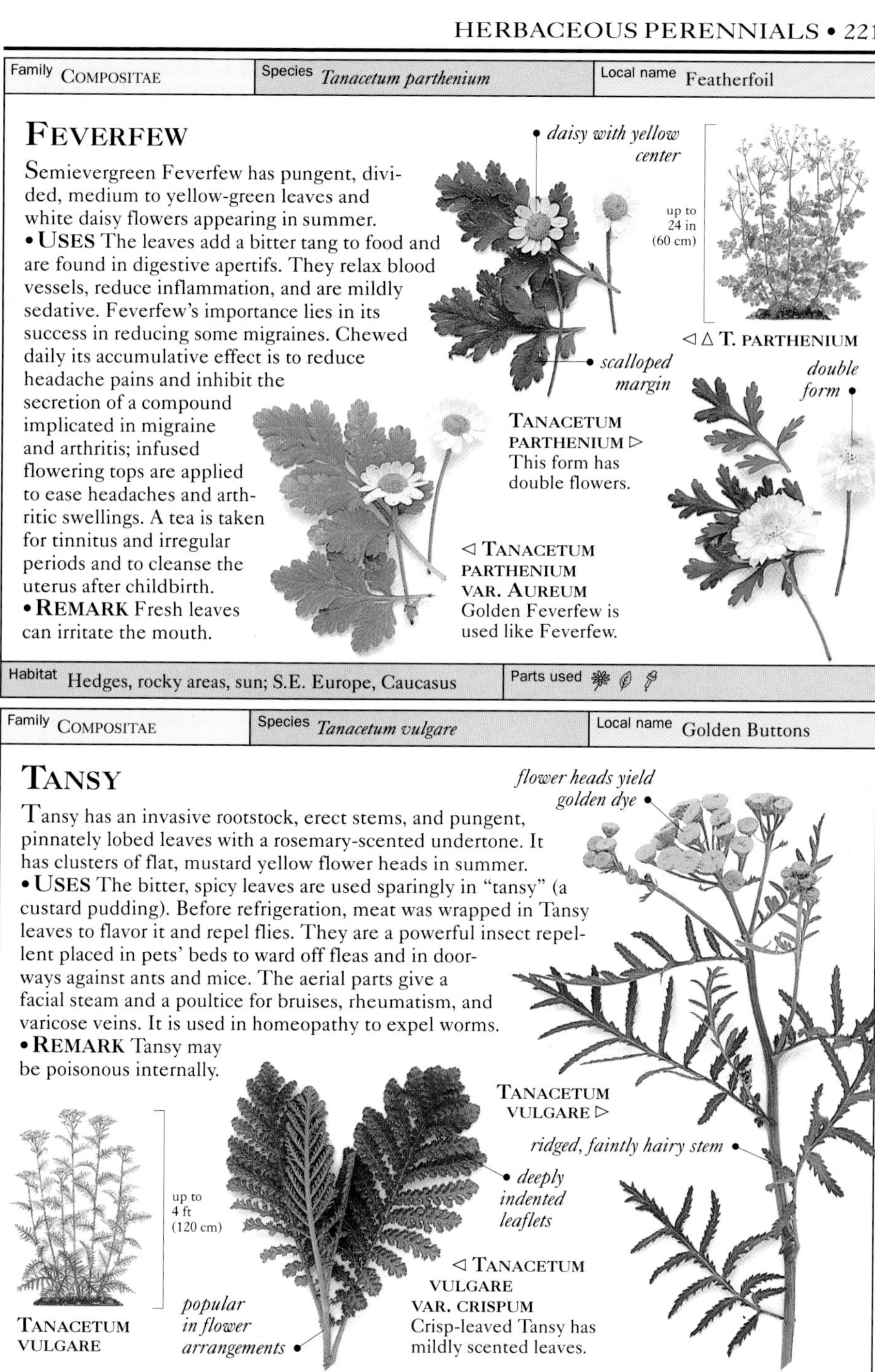
daisy with yellow center
up to 24 in (60 cm)
◁ △ T. PARTHENIUM
scalloped margin
double form
flower heads yield golden dye
ridged, faintly hairy stem
deeply indented leaflets
up to 4 ft (120 cm)
popular in flower arrangements

TANACETUM PARTHENIUM ▷ This form has double flowers.

◁ TANACETUM PARTHENIUM VAR. AUREUM Golden Feverfew is used like Feverfew.

Habitat Hedges, rocky areas, sun; S.E. Europe, Caucasus	Parts used

Family COMPOSITAE	Species *Tanacetum vulgare*	Local name Golden Buttons

TANSY

Tansy has an invasive rootstock, erect stems, and pungent, pinnately lobed leaves with a rosemary-scented undertone. It has clusters of flat, mustard yellow flower heads in summer.

• **USES** The bitter, spicy leaves are used sparingly in "tansy" (a custard pudding). Before refrigeration, meat was wrapped in Tansy leaves to flavor it and repel flies. They are a powerful insect repellent placed in pets' beds to ward off fleas and in doorways against ants and mice. The aerial parts give a facial steam and a poultice for bruises, rheumatism, and varicose veins. It is used in homeopathy to expel worms.

• **REMARK** Tansy may be poisonous internally.

TANACETUM VULGARE ▷

TANACETUM VULGARE

◁ TANACETUM VULGARE VAR. CRISPUM Crisp-leaved Tansy has mildly scented leaves.

Habitat Hedges, dry soil, sun or light shade; Europe	Parts used

Family COMPOSITAE	Species *Taraxacum sect. Ruderalia* species	Local name Fairy Clock

DANDELION

This hardy herb has rosettes of oblong, deeply toothed leaves. Golden flowers, often striped with brown, from spring to autumn, are followed by balls of tufted seeds.

• **USES** The flowers are made into wine, the buds are pickled, and the leaves, rich in vitamins A and C and minerals, are eaten in salads. The leaves are a powerful diuretic, treating urinary disorders and fluid retention without depleting body potassium. They detoxify the blood, so are given for acne and eczema. The white sap treats warts and corns. The root reduces inflammation and is an important liver stimulant used for jaundice, gallstones, and rheumatic joints. The roots yield a magenta dye.

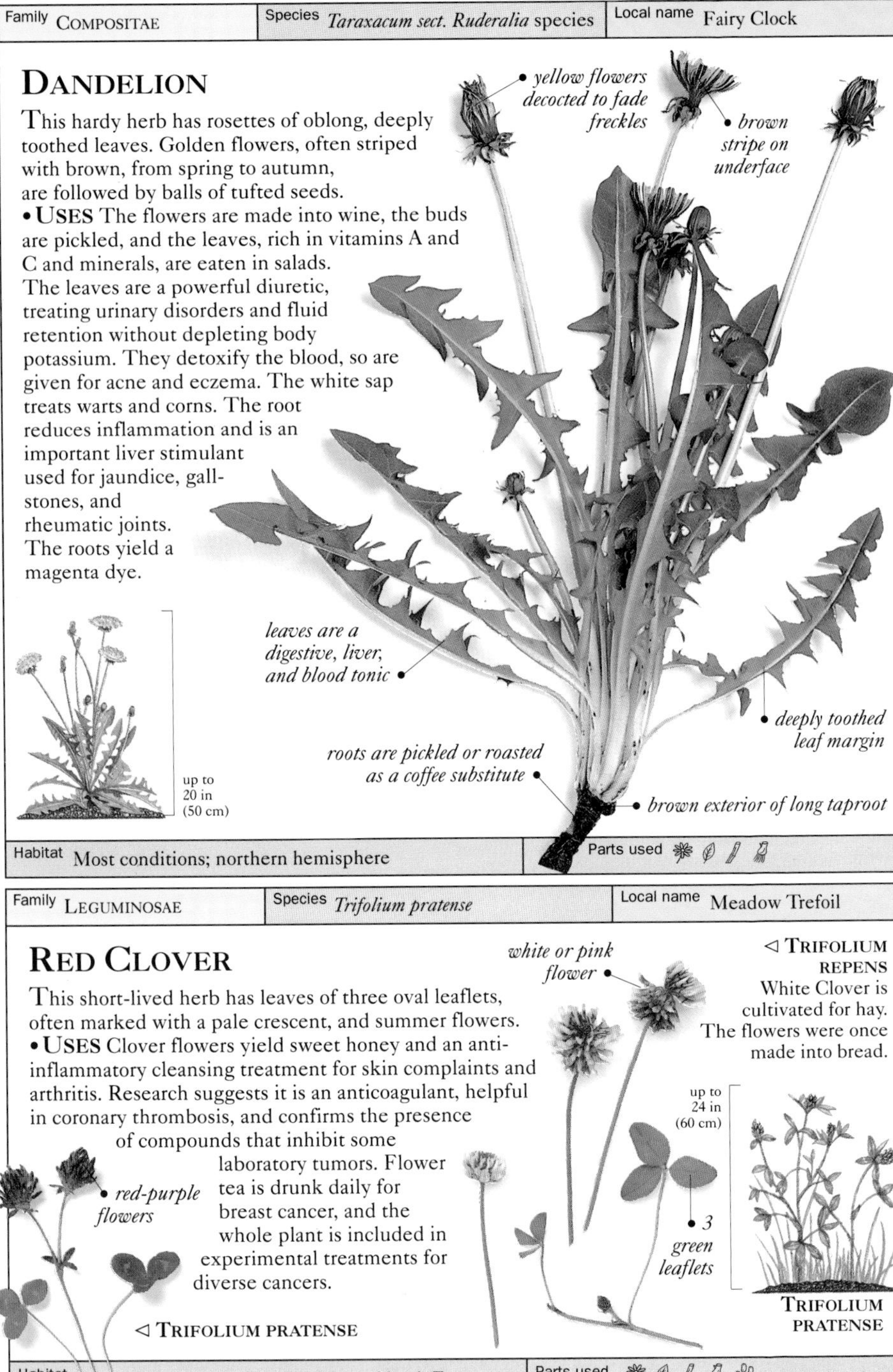

yellow flowers decocted to fade freckles
brown stripe on underface
leaves are a digestive, liver, and blood tonic
deeply toothed leaf margin
roots are pickled or roasted as a coffee substitute
brown exterior of long taproot
up to 20 in (50 cm)
white or pink flower
red-purple flowers
3 green leaflets
up to 24 in (60 cm)

Habitat Most conditions; northern hemisphere	Parts used

Family LEGUMINOSAE	Species *Trifolium pratense*	Local name Meadow Trefoil

RED CLOVER

This short-lived herb has leaves of three oval leaflets, often marked with a pale crescent, and summer flowers.

• **USES** Clover flowers yield sweet honey and an anti-inflammatory cleansing treatment for skin complaints and arthritis. Research suggests it is an anticoagulant, helpful in coronary thrombosis, and confirms the presence of compounds that inhibit some laboratory tumors. Flower tea is drunk daily for breast cancer, and the whole plant is included in experimental treatments for diverse cancers.

◁ TRIFOLIUM REPENS White Clover is cultivated for hay. The flowers were once made into bread.

◁ TRIFOLIUM PRATENSE

TRIFOLIUM PRATENSE

Habitat Moist, grassy places, cultivated land; Europe	Parts used

Family LABIATAE	Species *Teucrium chamaedrys*	Local name Common Germander

WALL GERMANDER

This small evergreen shrub has faintly aromatic, lobed leaves and whorls of purple-pink flowers in late summer.

• **USES** Aerial parts are digestive and included in tonic wines and vermouth. The herb is diuretic and antiseptic, promotes perspiration, reduces phlegm and inflammation, and is under research for use in reducing fatty deposits and healing ulcers. An infusion treats inflammation and once treated gout and rheumatism. A Wall Germander and Green Tea mix was found to be effective in weight control, but long-term use may damage the liver.

• **REMARK** Cat Thyme (*Teucrium marum*) is a Mediterranean rock garden plant, attractive to cats. *T. viscidum* is used in China for internal bleeding, snake bite, wounds, and arthritis.

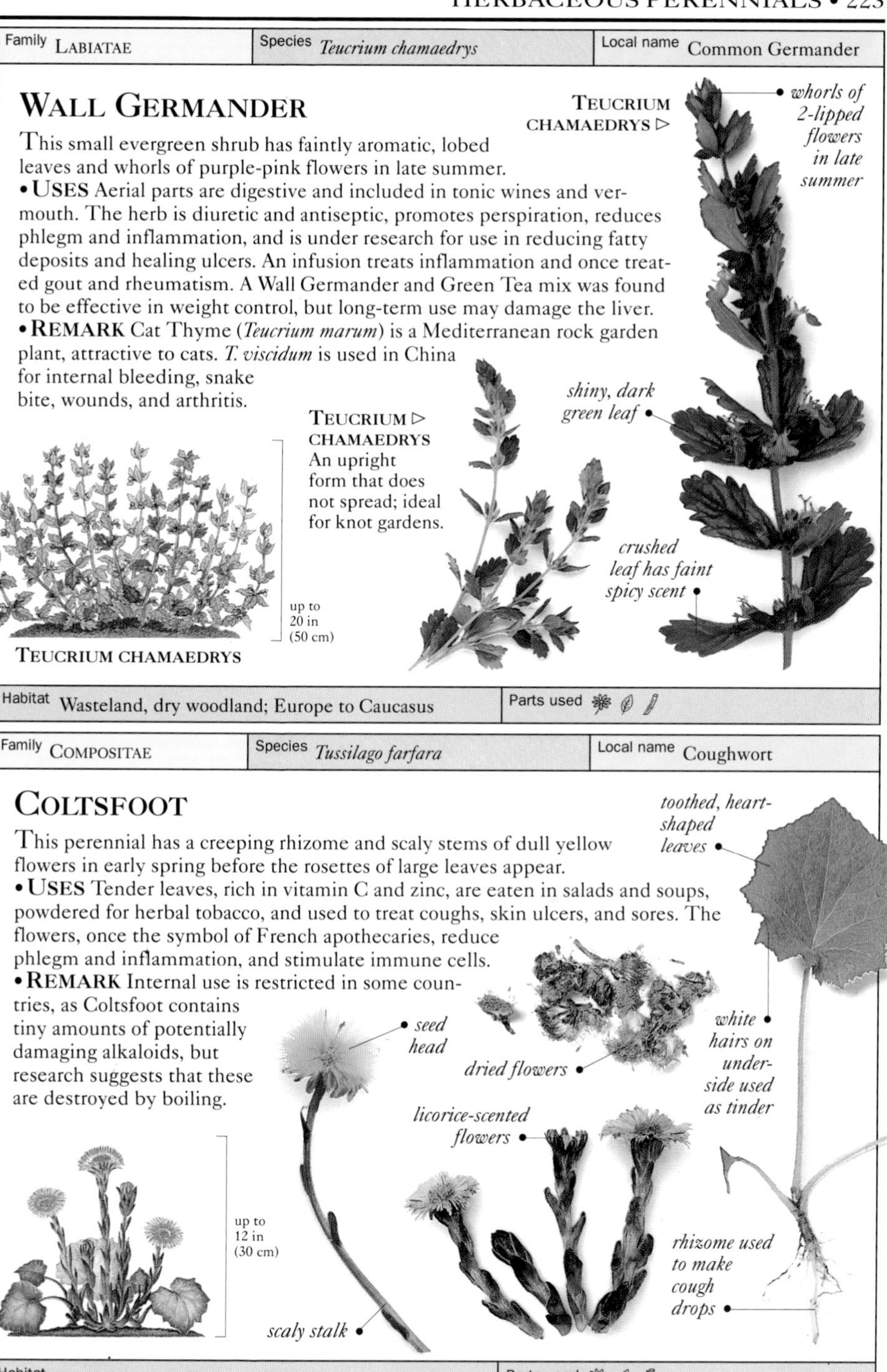
TEUCRIUM CHAMAEDRYS ▷
whorls of 2-lipped flowers in late summer
shiny, dark green leaf
crushed leaf has faint spicy scent
TEUCRIUM ▷ CHAMAEDRYS
An upright form that does not spread; ideal for knot gardens.
up to 20 in (50 cm)
TEUCRIUM CHAMAEDRYS

Habitat Wasteland, dry woodland; Europe to Caucasus	Parts used

Family COMPOSITAE	Species *Tussilago farfara*	Local name Coughwort

COLTSFOOT

This perennial has a creeping rhizome and scaly stems of dull yellow flowers in early spring before the rosettes of large leaves appear.

• **USES** Tender leaves, rich in vitamin C and zinc, are eaten in salads and soups, powdered for herbal tobacco, and used to treat coughs, skin ulcers, and sores. The flowers, once the symbol of French apothecaries, reduce phlegm and inflammation, and stimulate immune cells.

• **REMARK** Internal use is restricted in some countries, as Coltsfoot contains tiny amounts of potentially damaging alkaloids, but research suggests that these are destroyed by boiling.

toothed, heart-shaped leaves
seed head
dried flowers
white hairs on underside used as tinder
licorice-scented flowers
up to 12 in (30 cm)
rhizome used to make cough drops
scaly stalk

Habitat Damp habitats; Europe, W. & N. Asia, N. Africa	Parts used

Family URTICACEAE	Species *Urtica dioica*	Local name Common Nettle

STINGING NETTLE

Nettles have a vigorous creeping rhizome, serrated leaves covered in stinging hairs, and tiny flowers in summer.
• **USES** Young leaves and shoots, rich in vitamins and minerals, are cooked as greens and brewed for beer or an iron-rich tonic tea for anemia. The leaves are a valuable fertilizer. The plant is diuretic, digestive, and astringent, stimulates circulation, and clears uric acid, relieving arthritis, gout, and eczema. A poultice treats eczema, burns, cuts, and hemorrhoids. The seeds were given for tuberculosis and to treat the lungs after bronchitis.
• **REMARK** Heating or drying removes the leaves' sting.

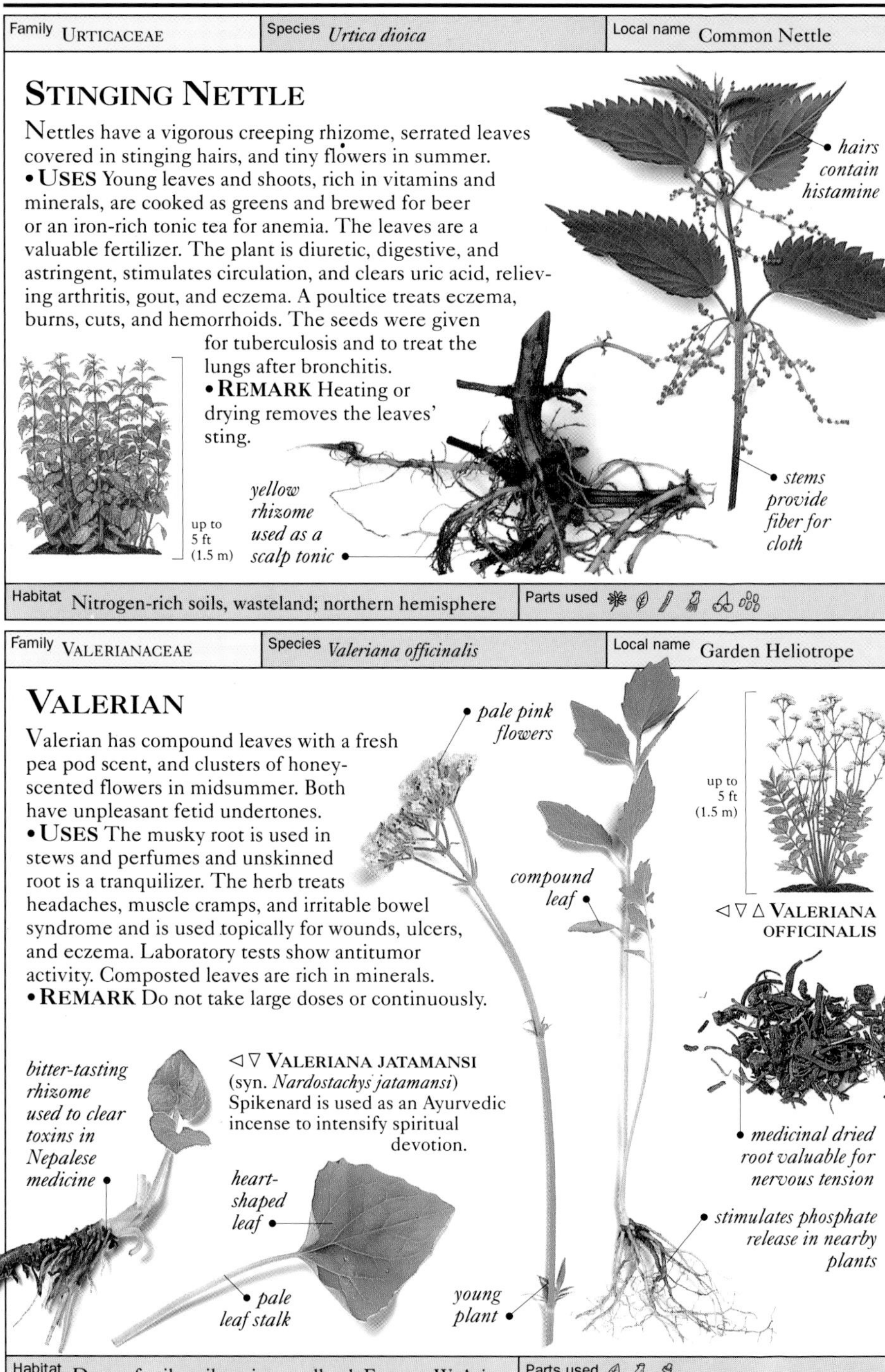

hairs contain histamine
up to 5 ft (1.5 m)
yellow rhizome used as a scalp tonic
stems provide fiber for cloth
pale pink flowers
compound leaf
up to 5 ft (1.5 m)
bitter-tasting rhizome used to clear toxins in Nepalese medicine
heart-shaped leaf
pale leaf stalk
young plant
medicinal dried root valuable for nervous tension
stimulates phosphate release in nearby plants

Habitat Nitrogen-rich soils, wasteland; northern hemisphere	Parts used

Family VALERIANACEAE	Species *Valeriana officinalis*	Local name Garden Heliotrope

VALERIAN

Valerian has compound leaves with a fresh pea pod scent, and clusters of honey-scented flowers in midsummer. Both have unpleasant fetid undertones.
• **USES** The musky root is used in stews and perfumes and unskinned root is a tranquilizer. The herb treats headaches, muscle cramps, and irritable bowel syndrome and is used topically for wounds, ulcers, and eczema. Laboratory tests show antitumor activity. Composted leaves are rich in minerals.
• **REMARK** Do not take large doses or continuously.

◁ ▽ △ VALERIANA OFFICINALIS

◁ ▽ VALERIANA JATAMANSI (syn. *Nardostachys jatamansi*) Spikenard is used as an Ayurvedic incense to intensify spiritual devotion.

Habitat Damp, fertile soil, moist woodland; Europe, W. Asia	Parts used

Family VERBENACEAE	Species *Verbena officinalis*	Local name Holy Wort

VERVAIN

This hardy perennial has deeply cut lower leaves and smooth upper leaves, with small, dense spikes of pale lilac-pink, midsummer flowers. • **USES** An ancient, sacred herb of purification, visions, and love potions, it was included in liqueurs and aphrodisiacs. A leaf decoction makes a hair tonic and an eyewash. The aerial parts are a liver stimulant and a nerve tonic and increase breast milk. Flowering tops are infused to treat depression, insomnia, nervous headaches, jaundice, urinary problems, and stomach, bowel, and menstrual cramps. A poultice treats wounds and skin ulcers. • **REMARK** Tests have shown possible heart-strengthening and antitumor activity.

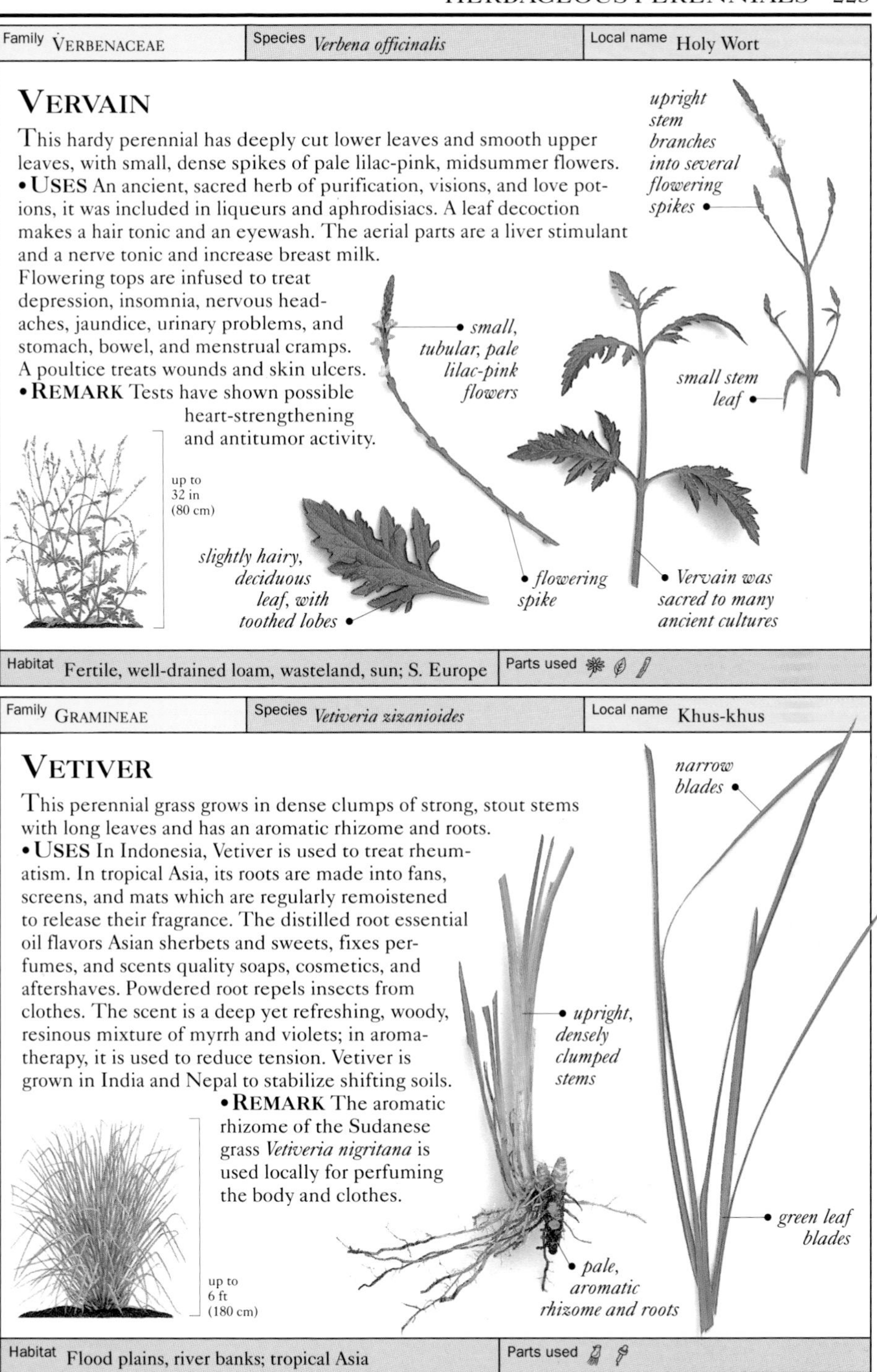
upright stem branches into several flowering spikes
small, tubular, pale lilac-pink flowers
small stem leaf
up to 32 in (80 cm)
slightly hairy, deciduous leaf, with toothed lobes
flowering spike
Vervain was sacred to many ancient cultures
narrow blades
upright, densely clumped stems
green leaf blades
pale, aromatic rhizome and roots
up to 6 ft (180 cm)

Habitat Fertile, well-drained loam, wasteland, sun; S. Europe	Parts used

Family GRAMINEAE	Species *Vetiveria zizanioides*	Local name Khus-khus

VETIVER

This perennial grass grows in dense clumps of strong, stout stems with long leaves and has an aromatic rhizome and roots. • **USES** In Indonesia, Vetiver is used to treat rheumatism. In tropical Asia, its roots are made into fans, screens, and mats which are regularly remoistened to release their fragrance. The distilled root essential oil flavors Asian sherbets and sweets, fixes perfumes, and scents quality soaps, cosmetics, and aftershaves. Powdered root repels insects from clothes. The scent is a deep yet refreshing, woody, resinous mixture of myrrh and violets; in aromatherapy, it is used to reduce tension. Vetiver is grown in India and Nepal to stabilize shifting soils. • **REMARK** The aromatic rhizome of the Sudanese grass *Vetiveria nigritana* is used locally for perfuming the body and clothes.

Habitat Flood plains, river banks; tropical Asia	Parts used

Family VIOLACEAE | Species *Viola odorata* | Local name Little Faces

SWEET VIOLET

This stemless perennial has scalloped, heart-shaped leaves and violet or white, sweetly scented flowers from winter to spring.

• **USES** The crystallized flowers flavor sweets and liqueurs and are tossed in salads with the leaves. All parts contain active ingredients. Decocted flowers make an eyewash, and leaf tea treats varicose veins. The flower syrup is antiseptic and a mild laxative, and with the leaves treats coughs, headaches, and insomnia. The root treats bronchitis. The leaves are a folk remedy for breast and lung cancer.

• **REMARK** The aerial parts of Heartsease are cleansing and are a circulation and immune system stimulant, used for chronic skin complaints.

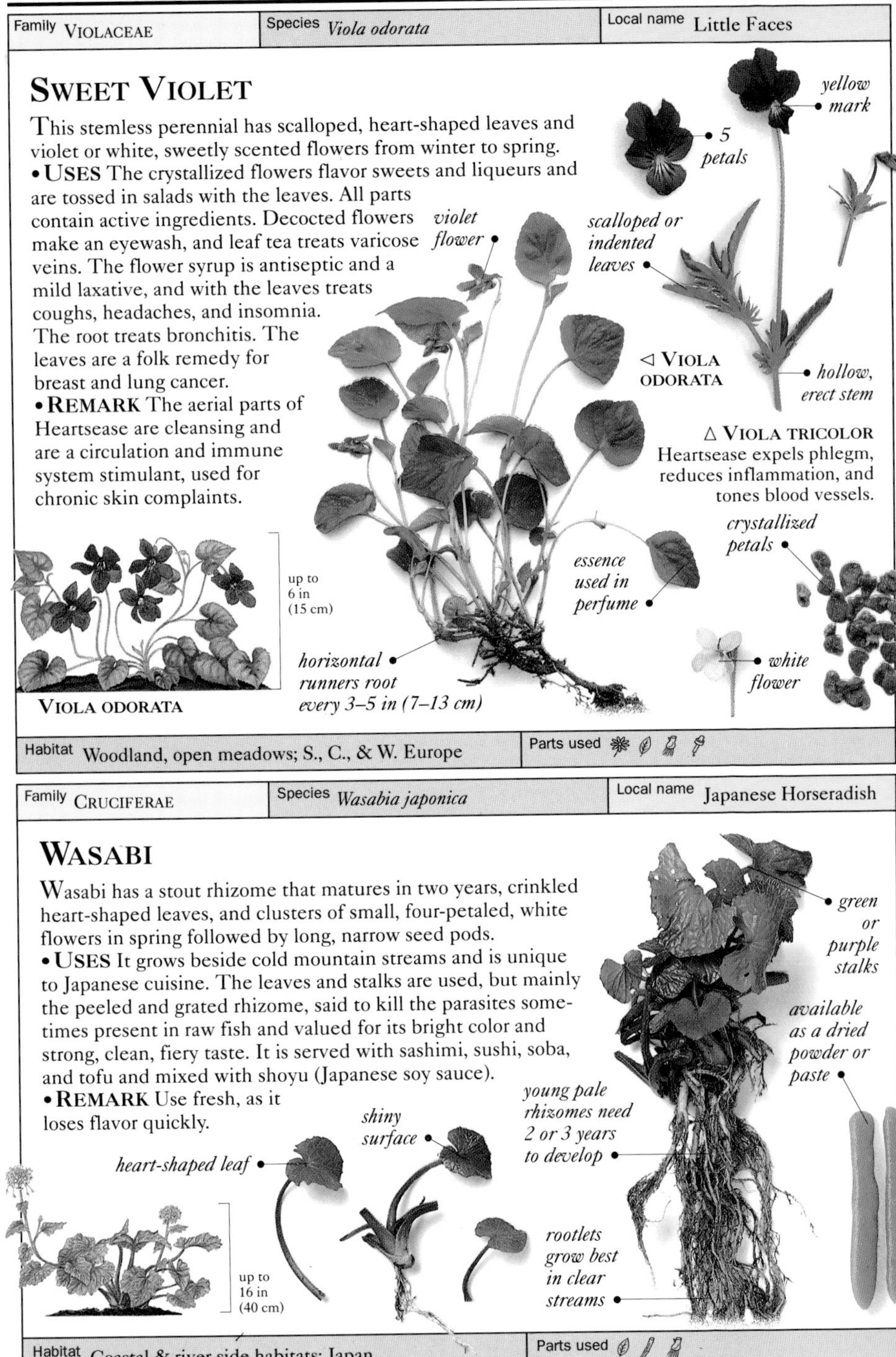
yellow mark
5 petals
scalloped or indented leaves
violet flower
hollow, erect stem
essence used in perfume
crystallized petals
white flower
horizontal runners root every 3–5 in (7–13 cm)
up to 6 in (15 cm)
green or purple stalks
available as a dried powder or paste
young pale rhizomes need 2 or 3 years to develop
shiny surface
heart-shaped leaf
rootlets grow best in clear streams
up to 16 in (40 cm)

◁ VIOLA ODORATA

△ VIOLA TRICOLOR
Heartsease expels phlegm, reduces inflammation, and tones blood vessels.

VIOLA ODORATA

Habitat Woodland, open meadows; S., C., & W. Europe | Parts used

Family CRUCIFERAE | Species *Wasabia japonica* | Local name Japanese Horseradish

WASABI

Wasabi has a stout rhizome that matures in two years, crinkled heart-shaped leaves, and clusters of small, four-petaled, white flowers in spring followed by long, narrow seed pods.

• **USES** It grows beside cold mountain streams and is unique to Japanese cuisine. The leaves and stalks are used, but mainly the peeled and grated rhizome, said to kill the parasites sometimes present in raw fish and valued for its bright color and strong, clean, fiery taste. It is served with sashimi, sushi, soba, and tofu and mixed with shoyu (Japanese soy sauce).

• **REMARK** Use fresh, as it loses flavor quickly.

Habitat Coastal & river side habitats; Japan | Parts used

Family ZINGIBERACEAE	Species *Zingiber officinale*	Local name Jiang

GINGER

Ginger has an aromatic rhizome, erect stems of two ranks, lance-shaped leaves, and spikes of white flowers. • **USES** The rhizome is used fresh, dried, pickled, and preserved. Essential to Asian dishes, it is used elsewhere in desserts and cordials. The shoots, leaves, and inflorescences of *Zingiber officinale*, *Z. mioga*, and *Z. zerumbet* are eaten raw or cooked. Crystallized or infused Ginger suppresses nausea. A steam inhalation treats colds and lung infections. Ginger tea eases indigestion and flatulence, and reduces fever. One drop of the root essential oil in a massage blend helps relieve muscular pain, rheumatism, lumbago, and fatigue.
• **REMARK** Use only in small doses to prevent morning sickness.

up to
5 ft
(1.5 m)
ALPINIA ZERUMBET ▷
The inflorescence of Shell Ginger is similar to the rare "true" Ginger flower.
inflorescence becomes pendulous
long, narrow, pointed leaves
fragrant flower
stem with long-lasting inflorescence
hollow stem with reddish base
aromatic rhizome
leafy, reedlike stem with 2 ranks of leaves
ground ginger used in Asian spice blends and to flavor cakes and confectionery
knobbly, yellowish, fresh rhizome also known as Green Ginger

Habitat Lowland rain forest; tropical Asia	Parts used

ANNUALS AND BIENNIALS

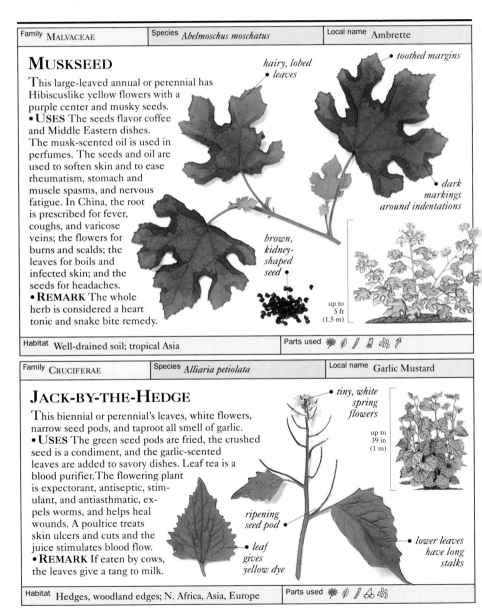

Family MALVACEAE	Species *Abelmoschus moschatus*	Local name Ambrette

MUSKSEED

This large-leaved annual or perennial has Hibiscuslike yellow flowers with a purple center and musky seeds.
• **USES** The seeds flavor coffee and Middle Eastern dishes. The musk-scented oil is used in perfumes. The seeds and oil are used to soften skin and to ease rheumatism, stomach and muscle spasms, and nervous fatigue. In China, the root is prescribed for fever, coughs, and varicose veins; the flowers for burns and scalds; the leaves for boils and infected skin; and the seeds for headaches.
• **REMARK** The whole herb is considered a heart tonic and snake bite remedy.

hairy, lobed leaves
toothed margins
dark markings around indentations
brown, kidney-shaped seed
up to 5 ft (1.5 m)

Habitat Well-drained soil; tropical Asia	Parts used

Family CRUCIFERAE	Species *Alliaria petiolata*	Local name Garlic Mustard

JACK-BY-THE-HEDGE

This biennial or perennial's leaves, white flowers, narrow seed pods, and taproot all smell of garlic.
• **USES** The green seed pods are fried, the crushed seed is a condiment, and the garlic-scented leaves are added to savory dishes. Leaf tea is a blood purifier. The flowering plant is expectorant, antiseptic, stimulant, and antiasthmatic, expels worms, and helps heal wounds. A poultice treats skin ulcers and cuts and the juice stimulates blood flow.
• **REMARK** If eaten by cows, the leaves give a tang to milk.

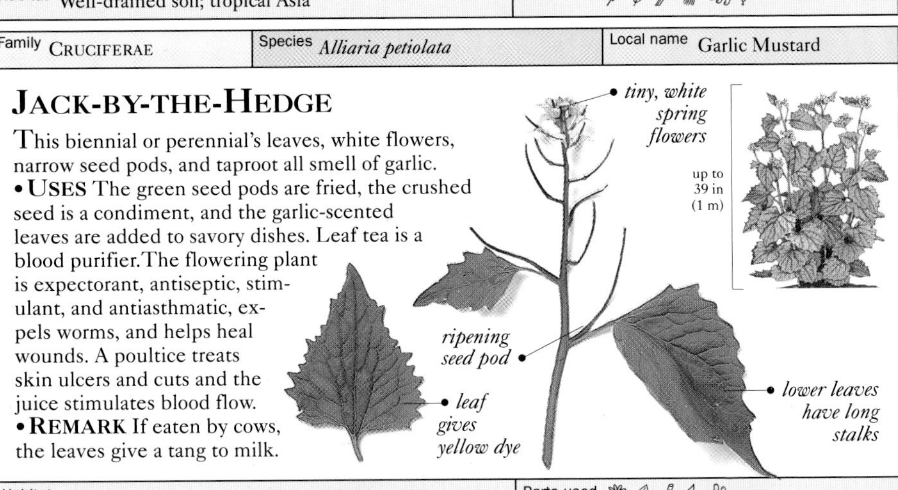
tiny, white spring flowers
up to 39 in (1 m)
ripening seed pod
leaf gives yellow dye
lower leaves have long stalks

Habitat Hedges, woodland edges; N. Africa, Asia, Europe	Parts used

Family COMPOSITAE	Species *Ambrosia artemisiifolia*	Local name American Ragweed

COMMON RAGWEED

This annual has dissected Artemisialike leaves and erect spikes of green, inconspicuous, drooping flower heads in summer and autumn.

• **USES** Native Americans use crushed leaves on insect stings and infections. The leaves are infused for a scalp wash to treat skin diseases and applied as a poultice to infected wounds or eyes. The astringent leaf tea treats abdominal cramps, constipation, vomiting, pneumonia, and fevers. Root tea treats menstrual problems. The seed case is a potential source of oil.

• **REMARK** Ragweed is said to cause 90 percent of pollen-induced allergies in the USA. The pollen of this and Giant Ragweed (*Ambrosia trifida*) is harvested for treatments for Ragweed allergies. The leaf of *A. psilostachya* is burned in Native American sweat lodges.

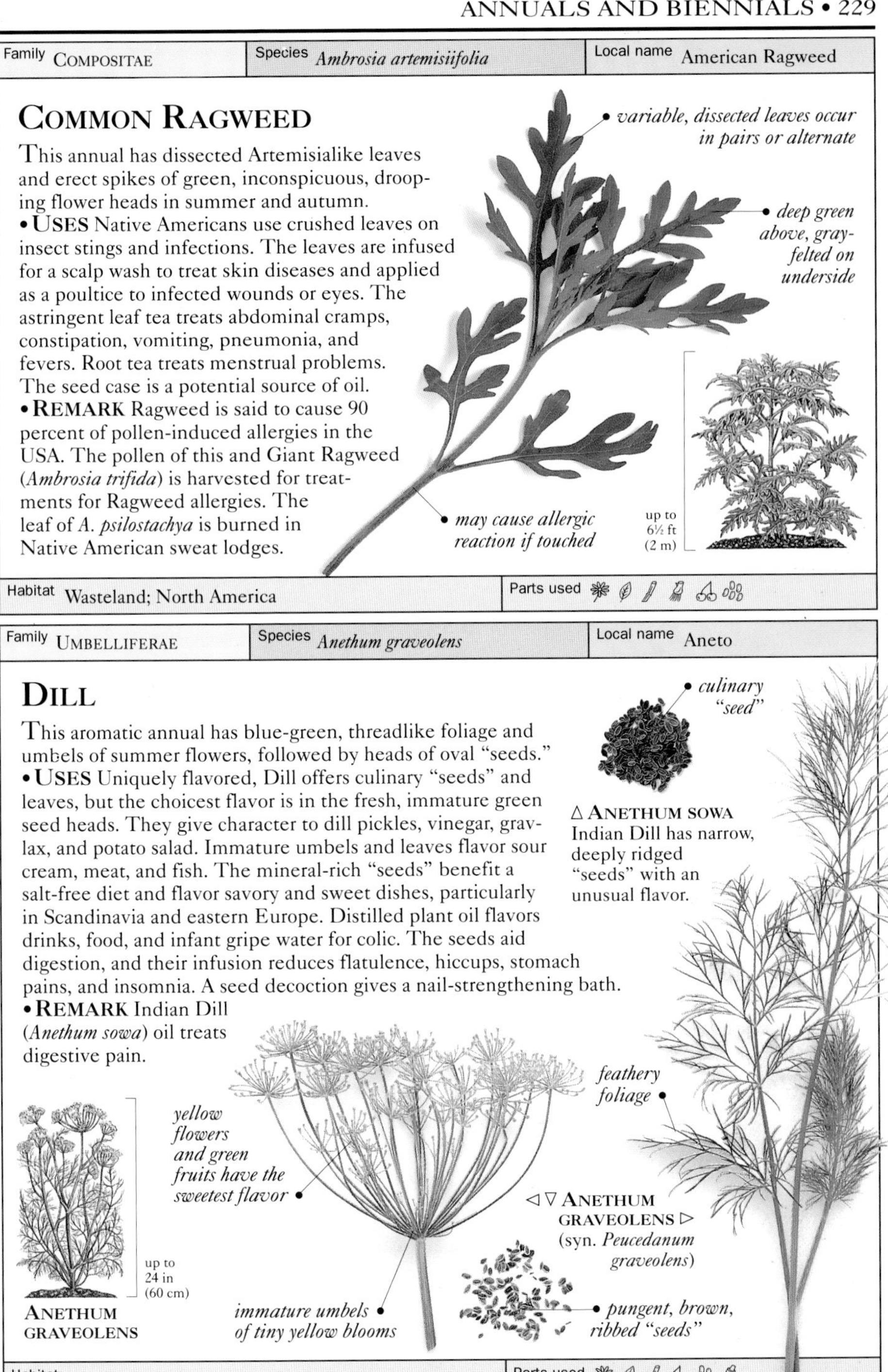

variable, dissected leaves occur in pairs or alternate
deep green above, gray-felted on underside
may cause allergic reaction if touched
up to 6½ ft (2 m)
culinary "seed"
feathery foliage
yellow flowers and green fruits have the sweetest flavor
immature umbels of tiny yellow blooms
pungent, brown, ribbed "seeds"
up to 24 in (60 cm)

Habitat Wasteland; North America	Parts used

Family UMBELLIFERAE	Species *Anethum graveolens*	Local name Aneto

DILL

This aromatic annual has blue-green, threadlike foliage and umbels of summer flowers, followed by heads of oval "seeds."

• **USES** Uniquely flavored, Dill offers culinary "seeds" and leaves, but the choicest flavor is in the fresh, immature green seed heads. They give character to dill pickles, vinegar, gravlax, and potato salad. Immature umbels and leaves flavor sour cream, meat, and fish. The mineral-rich "seeds" benefit a salt-free diet and flavor savory and sweet dishes, particularly in Scandinavia and eastern Europe. Distilled plant oil flavors drinks, food, and infant gripe water for colic. The seeds aid digestion, and their infusion reduces flatulence, hiccups, stomach pains, and insomnia. A seed decoction gives a nail-strengthening bath.

• **REMARK** Indian Dill (*Anethum sowa*) oil treats digestive pain.

△ **ANETHUM SOWA** Indian Dill has narrow, deeply ridged "seeds" with an unusual flavor.

◁ ▽ **ANETHUM GRAVEOLENS** ▷ (syn. *Peucedanum graveolens*)

ANETHUM GRAVEOLENS

Habitat Rich, well-drained soil; S. Europe to India	Parts used

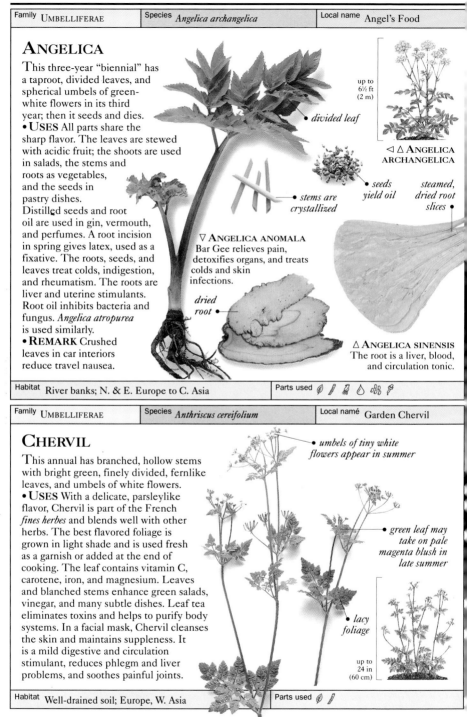

Family UMBELLIFERAE	Species *Angelica archangelica*	Local name Angel's Food

ANGELICA

This three-year "biennial" has a taproot, divided leaves, and spherical umbels of green-white flowers in its third year; then it seeds and dies.

• **USES** All parts share the sharp flavor. The leaves are stewed with acidic fruit; the shoots are used in salads, the stems and roots as vegetables, and the seeds in pastry dishes. Distilled seeds and root oil are used in gin, vermouth, and perfumes. A root incision in spring gives latex, used as a fixative. The roots, seeds, and leaves treat colds, indigestion, and rheumatism. The roots are liver and uterine stimulants. Root oil inhibits bacteria and fungus. *Angelica atropurea* is used similarly.

• **REMARK** Crushed leaves in car interiors reduce travel nausea.

• *divided leaf*

up to 6½ ft (2 m)

◁ △ ANGELICA ARCHANGELICA

• *seeds yield oil*

• *stems are crystallized*

steamed, dried root slices •

▽ ANGELICA ANOMALA
Bar Gee relieves pain, detoxifies organs, and treats colds and skin infections.

dried root •

△ ANGELICA SINENSIS
The root is a liver, blood, and circulation tonic.

Habitat River banks; N. & E. Europe to C. Asia	Parts used

Family UMBELLIFERAE	Species *Anthriscus cereifolium*	Local namé Garden Chervil

CHERVIL

This annual has branched, hollow stems with bright green, finely divided, fernlike leaves, and umbels of white flowers.

• **USES** With a delicate, parsleylike flavor, Chervil is part of the French *fines herbes* and blends well with other herbs. The best flavored foliage is grown in light shade and is used fresh as a garnish or added at the end of cooking. The leaf contains vitamin C, carotene, iron, and magnesium. Leaves and blanched stems enhance green salads, vinegar, and many subtle dishes. Leaf tea eliminates toxins and helps to purify body systems. In a facial mask, Chervil cleanses the skin and maintains suppleness. It is a mild digestive and circulation stimulant, reduces phlegm and liver problems, and soothes painful joints.

• umbels of tiny white flowers appear in summer
• green leaf may take on pale magenta blush in late summer
• lacy foliage
up to 24 in (60 cm)

Habitat Well-drained soil; Europe, W. Asia	Parts used

Family UMBELLIFERAE | Species *Apium graveolens* | Local name Wild Celery

SMALLAGE

This celery-scented biennial has a taproot, a rosette of leaves in its first year, and leafy stems with umbels of green to creamy white summer flowers followed by "seeds" in its second year.

• **USES** The "seeds" are added to savory dishes and ground as a salt substitute. The leaves, rich in mineral salts and vitamins, are eaten in salads, cream cheese, stews, and stuffing. The leaves and stalks stimulate enzymes to digest nutrients, while the seeds and their distilled oil help clear toxins from the system and reduce swelling, easing arthritis and gout. The whole plant provides fiber, and Chinese tests confirm that a tincture reduces hypertension, is antifungal, and a sedative.

• **REMARK** It may be mildly toxic and is safer in cooked dishes. Cooking also reduces its bitterness.

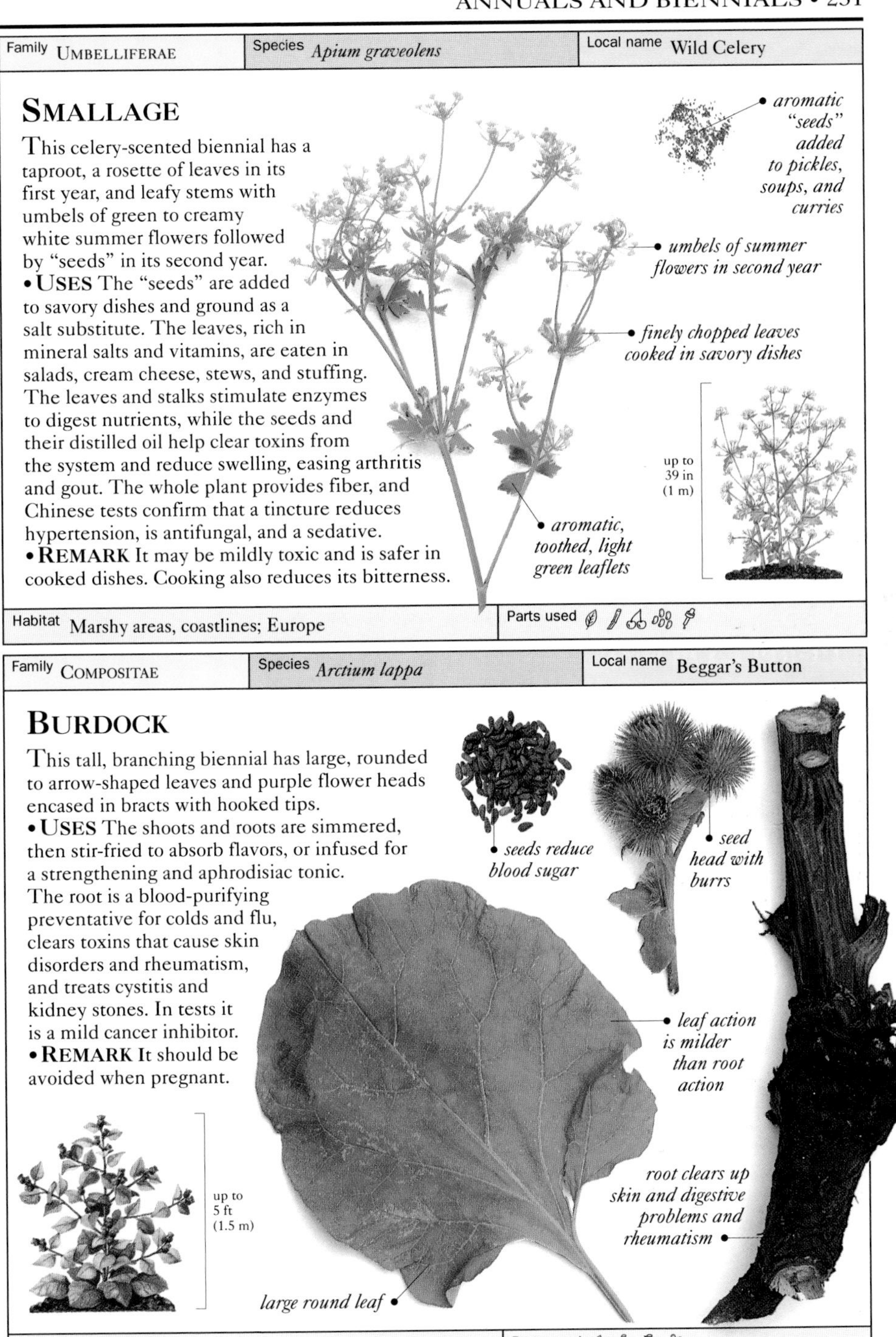
aromatic "seeds" added to pickles, soups, and curries
umbels of summer flowers in second year
finely chopped leaves cooked in savory dishes
up to 39 in (1 m)
aromatic, toothed, light green leaflets
seeds reduce blood sugar
seed head with burrs
leaf action is milder than root action
root clears up skin and digestive problems and rheumatism
up to 5 ft (1.5 m)
large round leaf

Habitat Marshy areas, coastlines; Europe | Parts used

Family COMPOSITAE | Species *Arctium lappa* | Local name Beggar's Button

BURDOCK

This tall, branching biennial has large, rounded to arrow-shaped leaves and purple flower heads encased in bracts with hooked tips.

• **USES** The shoots and roots are simmered, then stir-fried to absorb flavors, or infused for a strengthening and aphrodisiac tonic. The root is a blood-purifying preventative for colds and flu, clears toxins that cause skin disorders and rheumatism, and treats cystitis and kidney stones. In tests it is a mild cancer inhibitor.

• **REMARK** It should be avoided when pregnant.

Habitat Well-drained soil, woodland, partial shade; Europe | Parts used

Family COMPOSITAE	Species *Artemisia annua*	Local name Sweet Annie

SWEET WORMWOOD

This annual has feathery foliage, loose panicles of flower heads from summer onward, and red stems in autumn.

• **USES** In IndoChina, the herb treats jaundice, dysentery, and skin complaints. Chinese herbalists recommend it to stop wound bleeding and to help new muscle growth, although they warn of possible side effects. It is used by the Chinese army to prevent malaria and Chinese research has isolated an antimalarial compound, QHS (quinghaosu), or artemisinin, which treats drug-resistant strains. The seeds treat eye disease.

• **REMARK** Biennial *Artemisia apiacea* is considered a beautifying nutriment in China as it clears toxins. It is also taken to prevent and treat malaria.

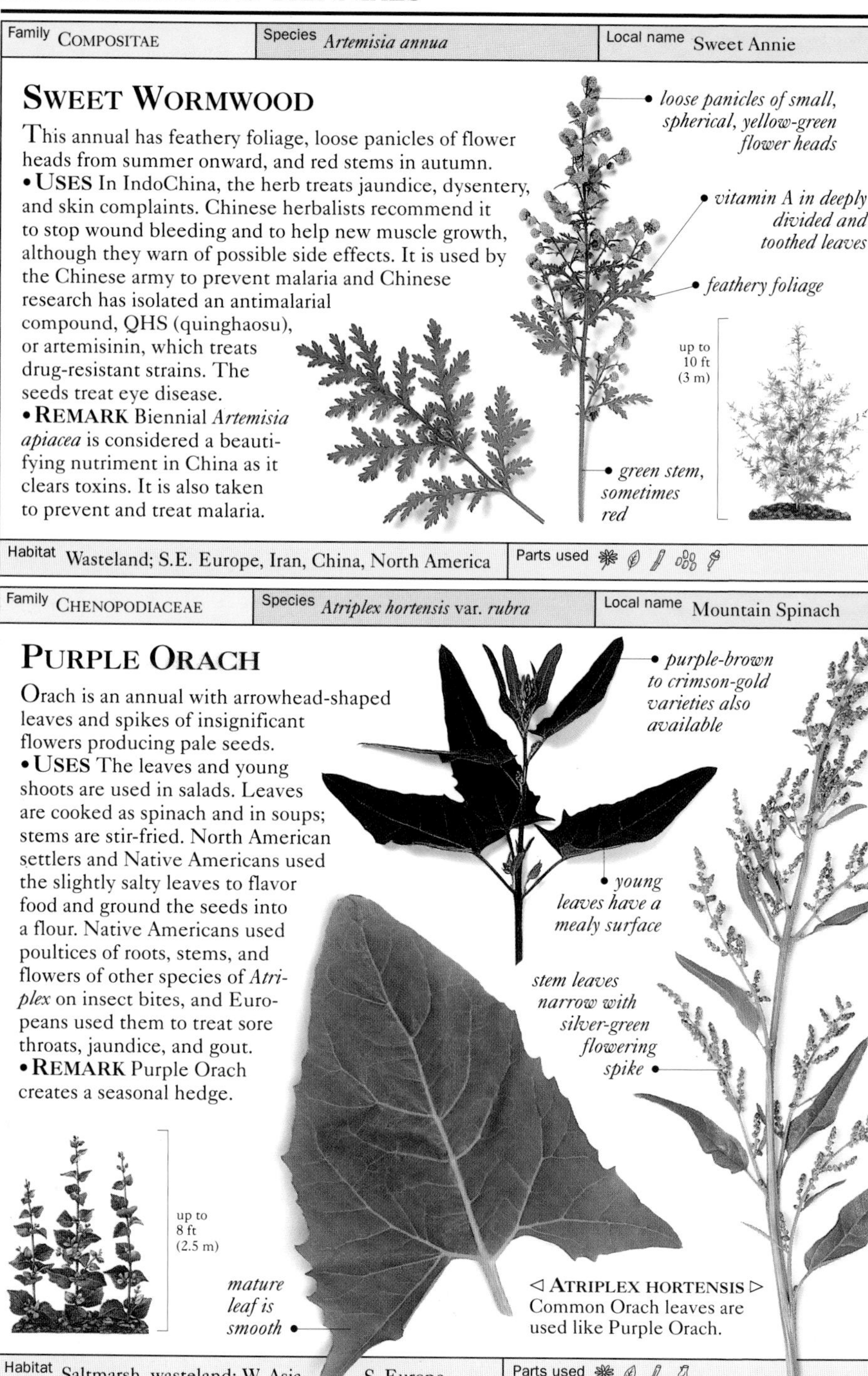

loose panicles of small, spherical, yellow-green flower heads
vitamin A in deeply divided and toothed leaves
feathery foliage
up to 10 ft (3 m)
green stem, sometimes red
purple-brown to crimson-gold varieties also available
young leaves have a mealy surface
stem leaves narrow with silver-green flowering spike
up to 8 ft (2.5 m)
mature leaf is smooth

Habitat Wasteland; S.E. Europe, Iran, China, North America	Parts used

Family CHENOPODIACEAE	Species *Atriplex hortensis* var. *rubra*	Local name Mountain Spinach

PURPLE ORACH

Orach is an annual with arrowhead-shaped leaves and spikes of insignificant flowers producing pale seeds.

• **USES** The leaves and young shoots are used in salads. Leaves are cooked as spinach and in soups; stems are stir-fried. North American settlers and Native Americans used the slightly salty leaves to flavor food and ground the seeds into a flour. Native Americans used poultices of roots, stems, and flowers of other species of *Atriplex* on insect bites, and Europeans used them to treat sore throats, jaundice, and gout.

• **REMARK** Purple Orach creates a seasonal hedge.

◁ ATRIPLEX HORTENSIS ▷ Common Orach leaves are used like Purple Orach.

Habitat Saltmarsh, wasteland; W. Asia, S. Europe	Parts used

Family GRAMINEAE	Species *Avena sativa*	Local name Groats

OATS

This annual has upright stems, bladelike leaves, and loose panicles of spikelets made of three florets which form grain.

• **USES** Oats, rich in vitamin E, minerals, and protein, are a food tonic for the heart, nerves, and thymus gland. Oat bran, now available in bread, helps reduce cholesterol. A decoction of the ripe plant treats depression, menopausal estrogen deficiency, persistent colds, and the debility of shingles and muscular sclerosis. Rolled oats make oatmeal. Fine oatmeal is an exfoliating body rub and a soothing wash for dry skin and eczema.

• **REMARK** Used in Ayurvedic medicine to cure addictions, but Western tests have had conflicting results.

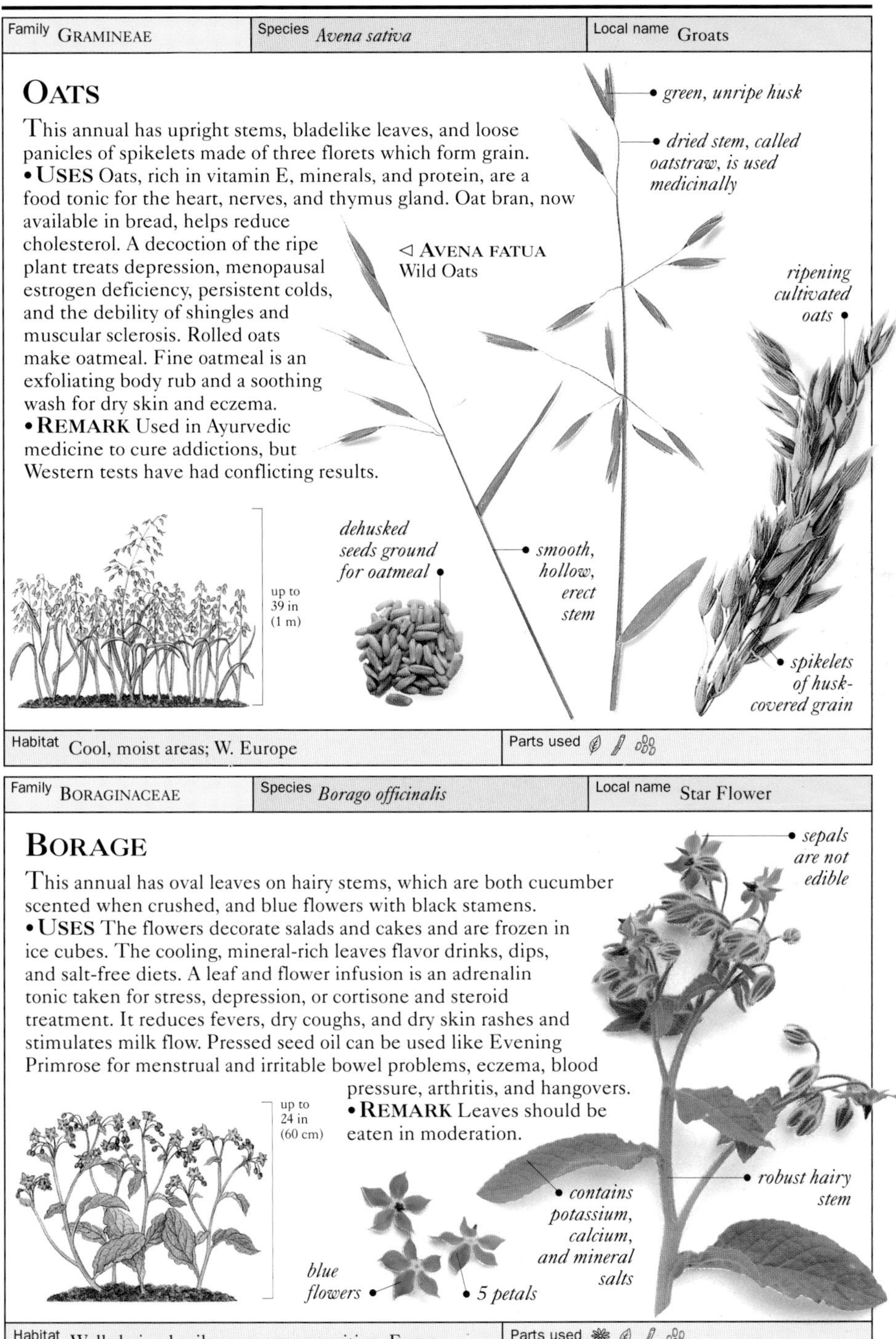

• green, unripe husk
• dried stem, called oatstraw, is used medicinally
◁ AVENA FATUA Wild Oats
ripening cultivated oats •
dehusked seeds ground for oatmeal •
• smooth, hollow, erect stem
• spikelets of husk-covered grain
up to 39 in (1 m)
• sepals are not edible
up to 24 in (60 cm)
• robust hairy stem
• contains potassium, calcium, and mineral salts
blue flowers •
• 5 petals

Habitat Cool, moist areas; W. Europe	Parts used

Family BORAGINACEAE	Species *Borago officinalis*	Local name Star Flower

BORAGE

This annual has oval leaves on hairy stems, which are both cucumber scented when crushed, and blue flowers with black stamens.

• **USES** The flowers decorate salads and cakes and are frozen in ice cubes. The cooling, mineral-rich leaves flavor drinks, dips, and salt-free diets. A leaf and flower infusion is an adrenalin tonic taken for stress, depression, or cortisone and steroid treatment. It reduces fevers, dry coughs, and dry skin rashes and stimulates milk flow. Pressed seed oil can be used like Evening Primrose for menstrual and irritable bowel problems, eczema, blood pressure, arthritis, and hangovers.

• **REMARK** Leaves should be eaten in moderation.

Habitat Well-drained soil, open, sunny position; Europe	Parts used

Family CRUCIFERAE	Species *Brassica nigra*	Local name Moutarde Noire

BLACK MUSTARD

This annual has bright green oval leaves, clusters of four-petaled, yellow summer flowers, and dark brown seeds.
• **USES** Black Mustard seed has the strongest flavor and was used to make most mustards, but as it is difficult to harvest mechanically it has been replaced by Brown Mustard. Mustard becomes pungent only when the crushed seeds are mixed with cold water to activate the appropriate enzymes. Boiling water, applied to dormant enzymes, kills them, vinegar inhibits them, and both create a weak aroma but bitter taste. Mustard seeds stimulate circulation, which invited their use in love potions. They treat bronchitis, give a warming footbath, and, in a mustard poultice, reduce inflammation treating chilblains and rheumatism. The oil is a lubricant.
• **REMARK** In China, Brown Mustard seed is used to treat colds, stomach problems, abscesses, rheumatism, lumbago, and ulcers. Leaves treat bladder inflammation.

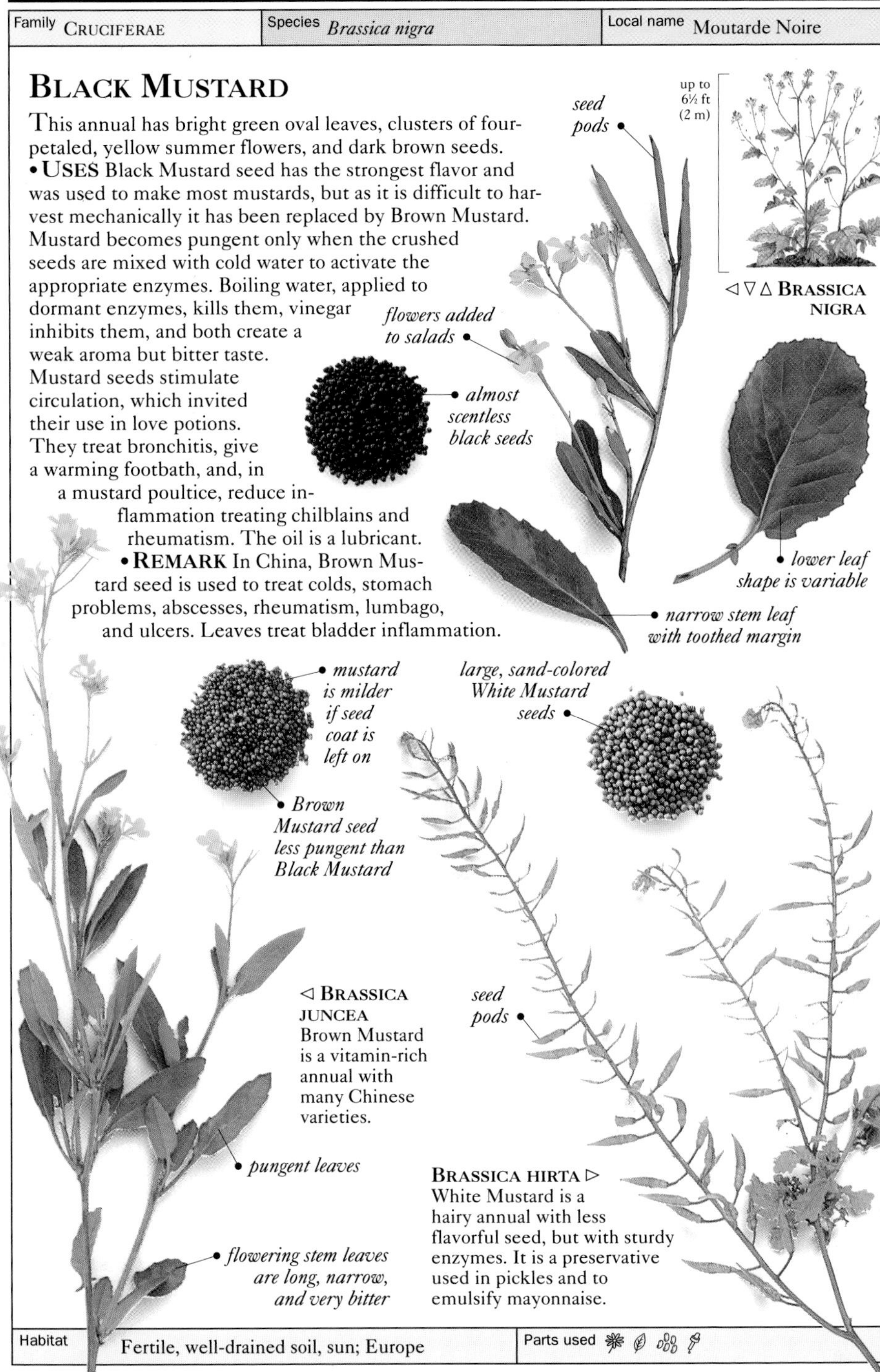

up to 6½ ft (2 m)
seed pods
flowers added to salads
almost scentless black seeds
lower leaf shape is variable
narrow stem leaf with toothed margin
mustard is milder if seed coat is left on
Brown Mustard seed less pungent than Black Mustard
large, sand-colored White Mustard seeds
seed pods
pungent leaves
flowering stem leaves are long, narrow, and very bitter

◁ ▽ △ **BRASSICA NIGRA**

◁ **BRASSICA JUNCEA**
Brown Mustard is a vitamin-rich annual with many Chinese varieties.

BRASSICA HIRTA ▷
White Mustard is a hairy annual with less flavorful seed, but with sturdy enzymes. It is a preservative used in pickles and to emulsify mayonnaise.

Habitat Fertile, well-drained soil, sun; Europe	Parts used

Family CRUCIFERAE	Species *Brassica oleracea*	Local name Colewort

WILD CABBAGE

Wild Cabbage is an annual or perennial with a woody base, a rosette of large, closely packed, lobed leaves, flowering stems with narrow leaves, and yellow summer flowers.

• **USES** The nutritional leaves, eaten raw, stir-fried, or steamed, contain minerals and vitamins A, B_1, B_2, and C. The leaves are a tonic aid to digestion. A poultice of raw leaves eases arthritis, muscle strain, and headaches. It inhibits bacteria and speeds tissue growth on wounds, skin ulcers, and infected spots. Wild Cabbage relieves nerve pain and may detoxify the liver. Recent tests show that the leaf juice eases stomach ulcers.

• **REMARK** "Lorenzo's oil" from Rape (*Brassica napus*) seed seems to reduce the onset of ALD, a rare, fatal, boyhood disease that attacks the nervous system.

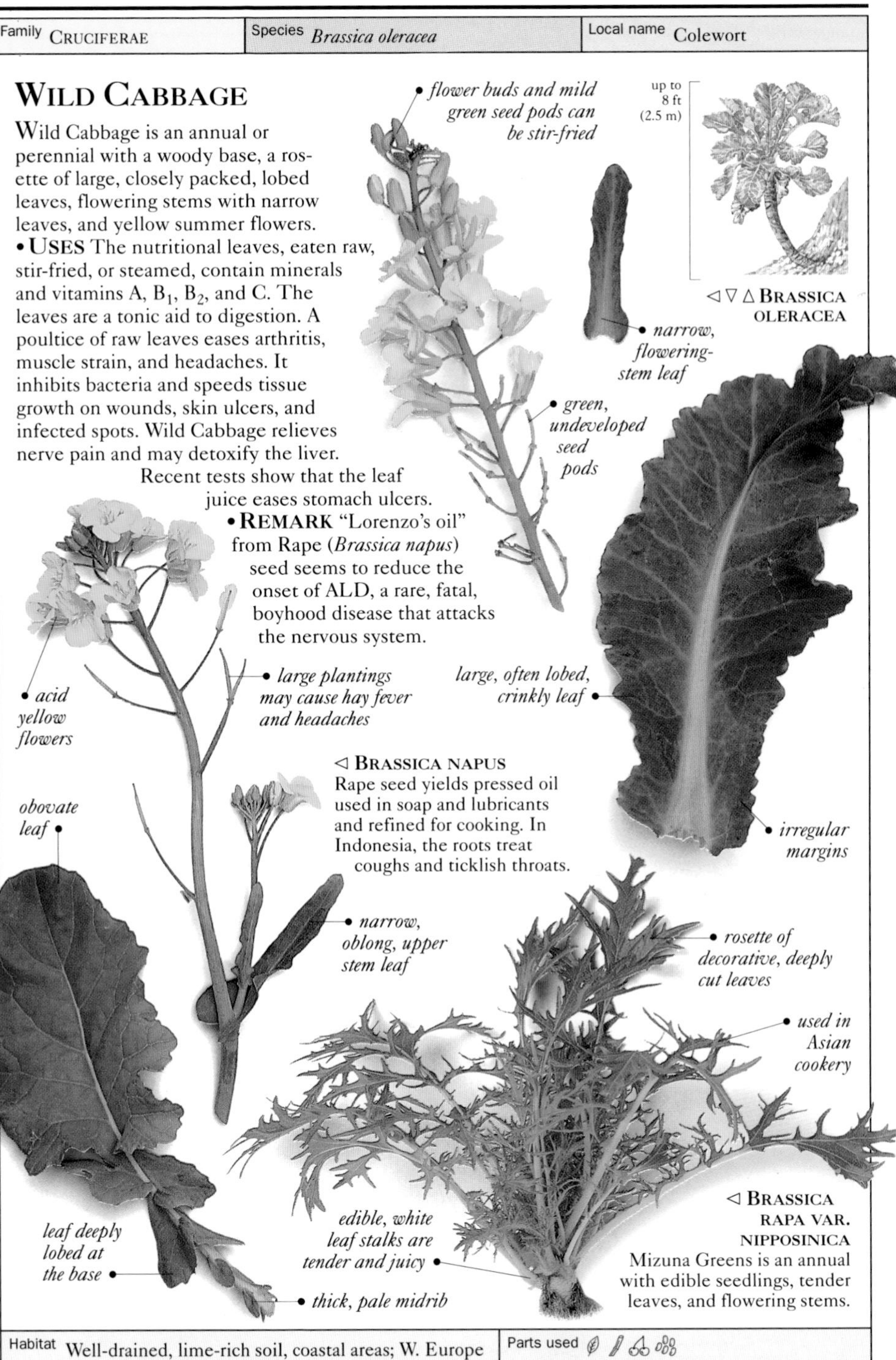
flower buds and mild green seed pods can be stir-fried
up to 8 ft (2.5 m)
narrow, flowering-stem leaf
green, undeveloped seed pods
large, often lobed, crinkly leaf
irregular margins
acid yellow flowers
large plantings may cause hay fever and headaches
obovate leaf
narrow, oblong, upper stem leaf
rosette of decorative, deeply cut leaves
used in Asian cookery
edible, white leaf stalks are tender and juicy
leaf deeply lobed at the base
thick, pale midrib

◁ ▽ △ BRASSICA OLERACEA

◁ BRASSICA NAPUS
Rape seed yields pressed oil used in soap and lubricants and refined for cooking. In Indonesia, the roots treat coughs and ticklish throats.

◁ BRASSICA RAPA VAR. NIPPOSINICA
Mizuna Greens is an annual with edible seedlings, tender leaves, and flowering stems.

Habitat Well-drained, lime-rich soil, coastal areas; W. Europe	Parts used

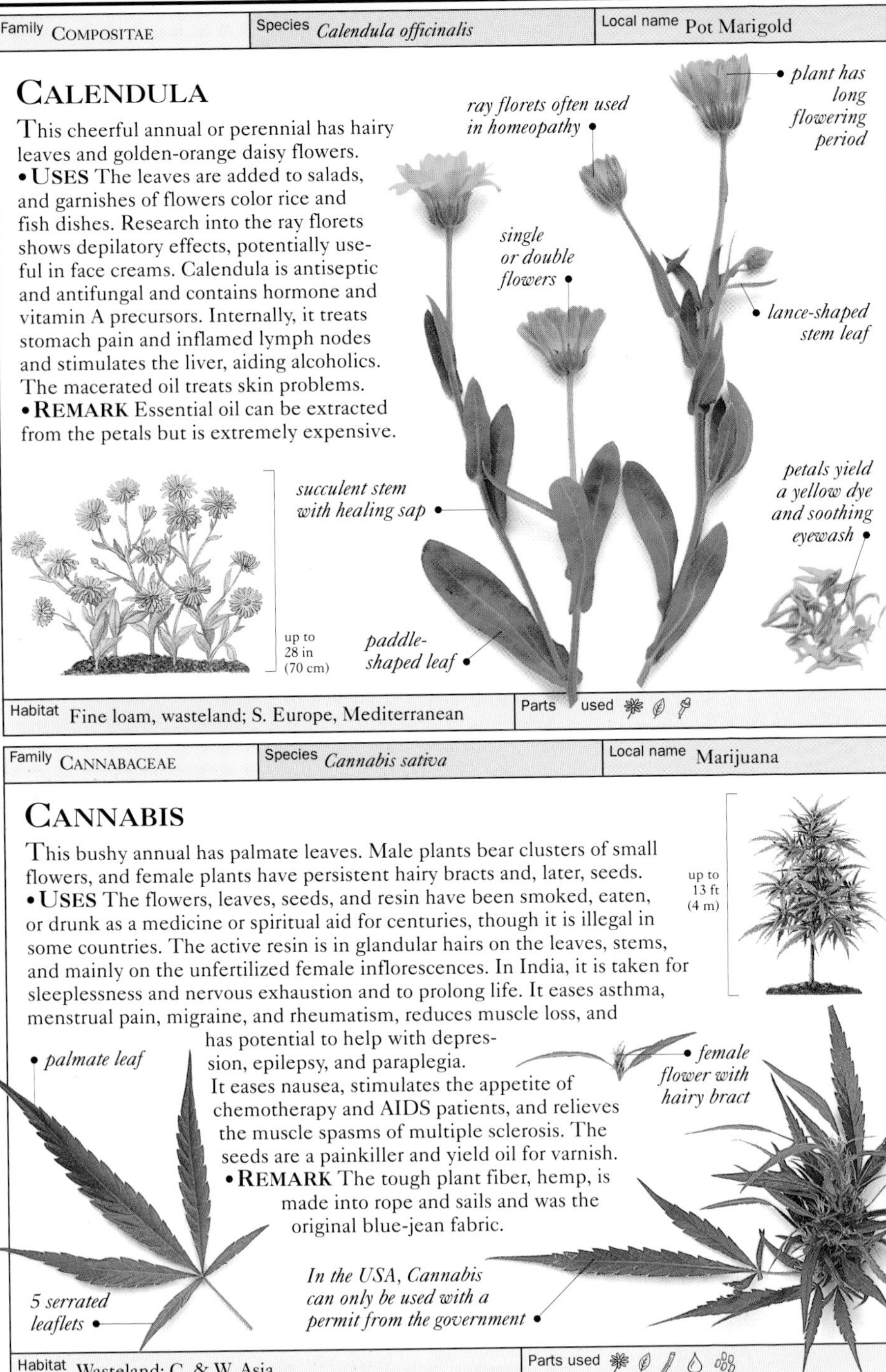
ray florets often used in homeopathy
plant has long flowering period
single or double flowers
lance-shaped stem leaf
succulent stem with healing sap
petals yield a yellow dye and soothing eyewash
up to 28 in (70 cm)
paddle-shaped leaf
up to 13 ft (4 m)
palmate leaf
female flower with hairy bract
5 serrated leaflets
In the USA, Cannabis can only be used with a permit from the government

Family COMPOSITAE	Species *Calendula officinalis*	Local name Pot Marigold

CALENDULA

This cheerful annual or perennial has hairy leaves and golden-orange daisy flowers.
• **USES** The leaves are added to salads, and garnishes of flowers color rice and fish dishes. Research into the ray florets shows depilatory effects, potentially useful in face creams. Calendula is antiseptic and antifungal and contains hormone and vitamin A precursors. Internally, it treats stomach pain and inflamed lymph nodes and stimulates the liver, aiding alcoholics. The macerated oil treats skin problems.
• **REMARK** Essential oil can be extracted from the petals but is extremely expensive.

Habitat Fine loam, wasteland; S. Europe, Mediterranean	Parts used

Family CANNABACEAE	Species *Cannabis sativa*	Local name Marijuana

CANNABIS

This bushy annual has palmate leaves. Male plants bear clusters of small flowers, and female plants have persistent hairy bracts and, later, seeds.
• **USES** The flowers, leaves, seeds, and resin have been smoked, eaten, or drunk as a medicine or spiritual aid for centuries, though it is illegal in some countries. The active resin is in glandular hairs on the leaves, stems, and mainly on the unfertilized female inflorescences. In India, it is taken for sleeplessness and nervous exhaustion and to prolong life. It eases asthma, menstrual pain, migraine, and rheumatism, reduces muscle loss, and has potential to help with depression, epilepsy, and paraplegia. It eases nausea, stimulates the appetite of chemotherapy and AIDS patients, and relieves the muscle spasms of multiple sclerosis. The seeds are a painkiller and yield oil for varnish.
• **REMARK** The tough plant fiber, hemp, is made into rope and sails and was the original blue-jean fabric.

Habitat Wasteland; C. & W. Asia	Parts used

Family SOLANACEAE	Species *Capsicum annuum*	Local name Capsicum

SWEET PEPPER

For a cook there are two types of pepper: sweet and hot; but the botanical divisions are more complex. *Capsicum annuum* is an annual or short-lived perennial with one flower in each leaf axil and includes sweet and hot peppers. *C. frutescens* is a perennial with up to three flowers per leaf joint and has smaller, pungent chilies. Both have branching stems with oval, pointed leaves and fruits in a variety of shapes, colors, and tastes.

• **USES** Sweet peppers (chilies), rich in vitamin C and a digestive stimulant, are chopped in salads, cooked, and pickled. Hot peppers enliven bland foods and give heat to curries. The pungent capsaicin of chilies stimulates circulation and sensory nerves, "disinfects" food, and eases sore throats. The infused oil gives a warming massage for rheumatism, cold limbs, and neuralgia.

• **REMARK** Capsaicin eases shingles and may prevent a fatal swallowing disorder of the elderly.

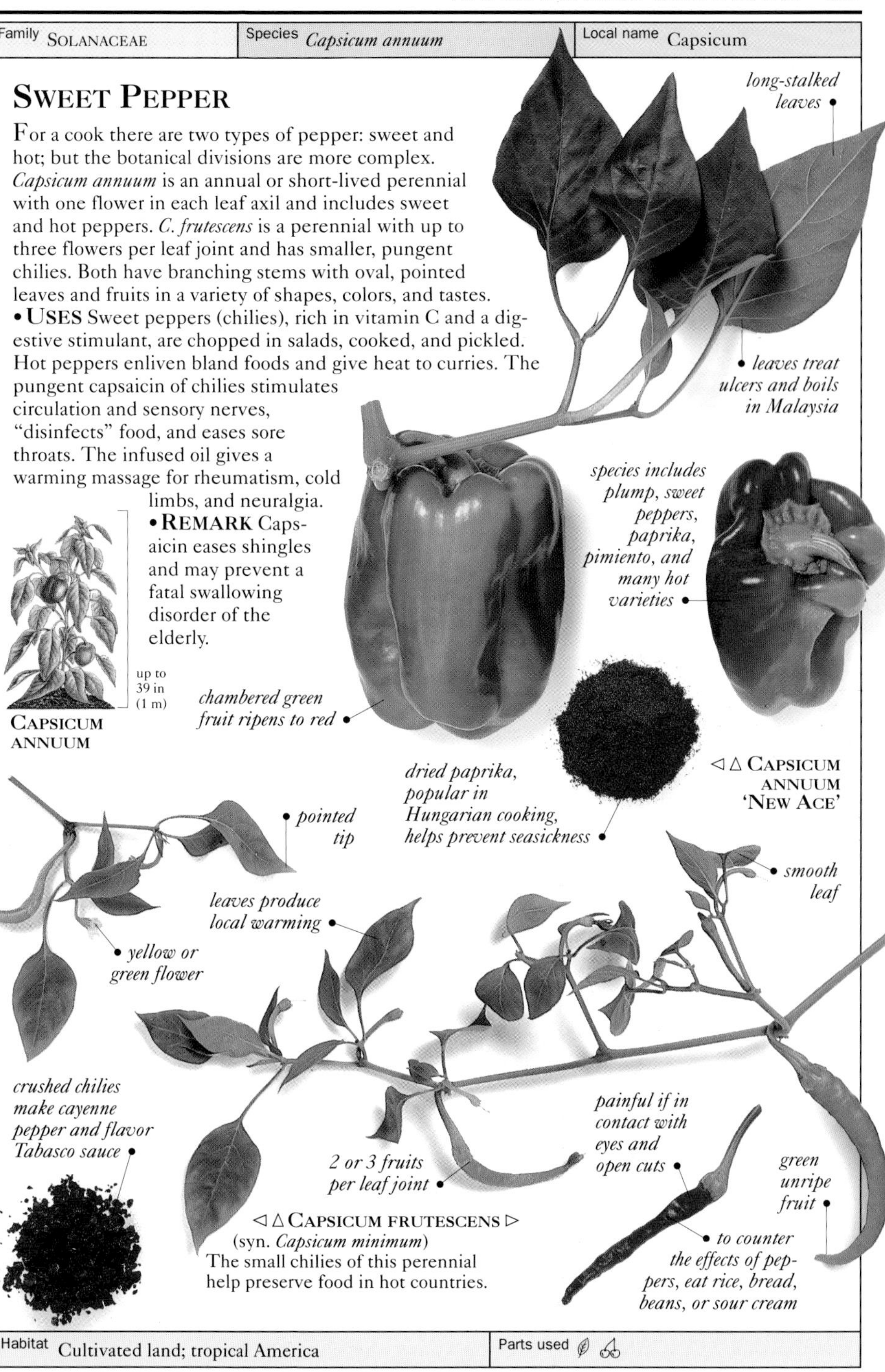

up to 39 in (1 m)
CAPSICUM ANNUUM
long-stalked leaves
leaves treat ulcers and boils in Malaysia
species includes plump, sweet peppers, paprika, pimiento, and many hot varieties
chambered green fruit ripens to red
dried paprika, popular in Hungarian cooking, helps prevent seasickness
◁ △ CAPSICUM ANNUUM 'NEW ACE'
pointed tip
smooth leaf
leaves produce local warming
yellow or green flower
crushed chilies make cayenne pepper and flavor Tabasco sauce
2 or 3 fruits per leaf joint
painful if in contact with eyes and open cuts
green unripe fruit
to counter the effects of peppers, eat rice, bread, beans, or sour cream

◁ △ CAPSICUM FRUTESCENS ▷
(syn. *Capsicum minimum*)
The small chilies of this perennial help preserve food in hot countries.

Habitat Cultivated land; tropical America	Parts used

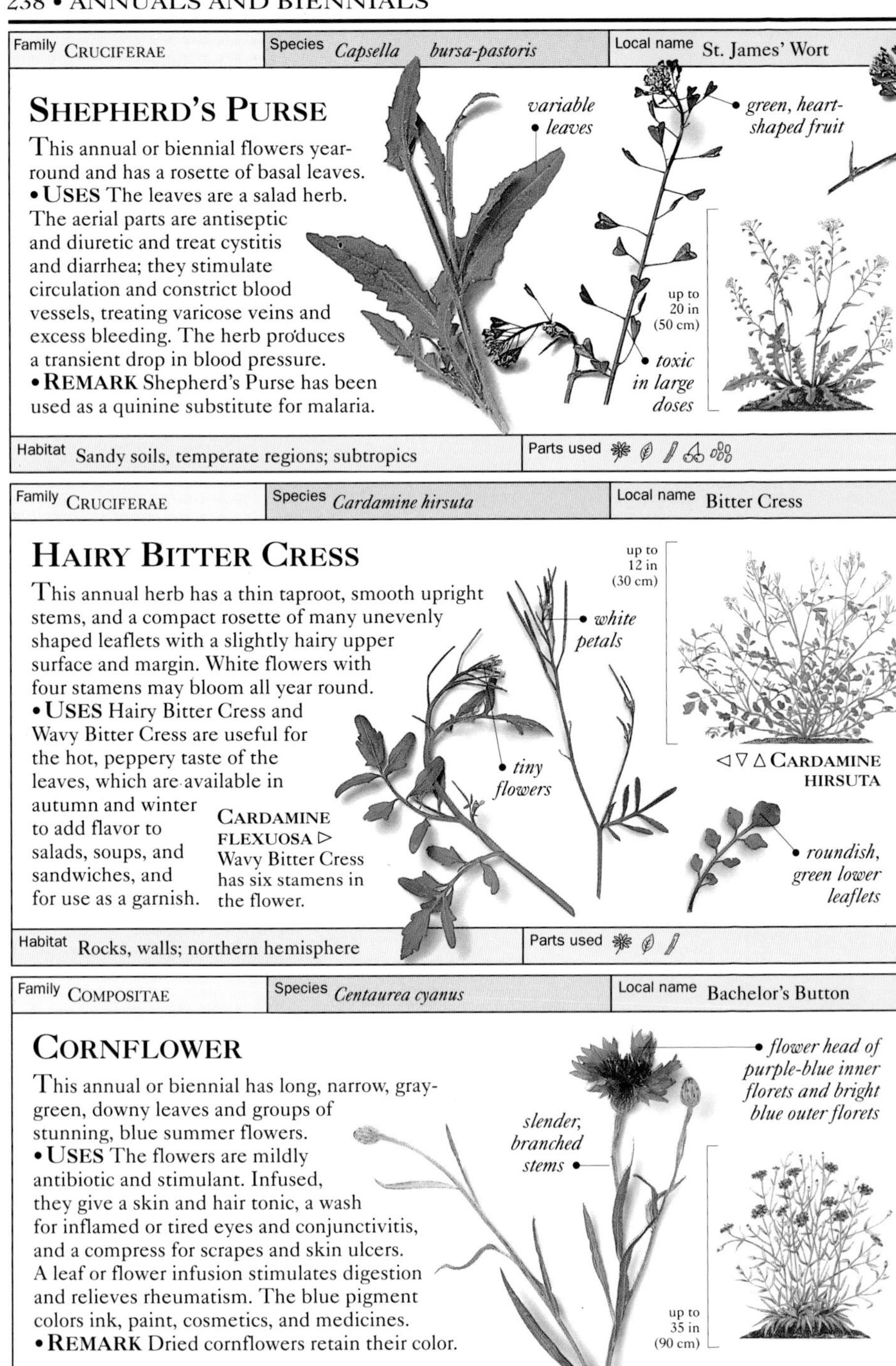
variable leaves
green, heart-shaped fruit
up to 20 in (50 cm)
toxic in large doses
up to 12 in (30 cm)
white petals
tiny flowers
roundish, green lower leaflets
flower head of purple-blue inner florets and bright blue outer florets
slender, branched stems
up to 35 in (90 cm)

Family CRUCIFERAE | Species *Capsella bursa-pastoris* | Local name St. James' Wort

SHEPHERD'S PURSE

This annual or biennial flowers year-round and has a rosette of basal leaves.

• **USES** The leaves are a salad herb. The aerial parts are antiseptic and diuretic and treat cystitis and diarrhea; they stimulate circulation and constrict blood vessels, treating varicose veins and excess bleeding. The herb produces a transient drop in blood pressure.

• **REMARK** Shepherd's Purse has been used as a quinine substitute for malaria.

Habitat Sandy soils, temperate regions; subtropics | Parts used

Family CRUCIFERAE | Species *Cardamine hirsuta* | Local name Bitter Cress

HAIRY BITTER CRESS

This annual herb has a thin taproot, smooth upright stems, and a compact rosette of many unevenly shaped leaflets with a slightly hairy upper surface and margin. White flowers with four stamens may bloom all year round.

• **USES** Hairy Bitter Cress and Wavy Bitter Cress are useful for the hot, peppery taste of the leaves, which are available in autumn and winter to add flavor to salads, soups, and sandwiches, and for use as a garnish.

CARDAMINE FLEXUOSA ▷ Wavy Bitter Cress has six stamens in the flower.

◁ ▽ △ CARDAMINE HIRSUTA

Habitat Rocks, walls; northern hemisphere | Parts used

Family COMPOSITAE | Species *Centaurea cyanus* | Local name Bachelor's Button

CORNFLOWER

This annual or biennial has long, narrow, gray-green, downy leaves and groups of stunning, blue summer flowers.

• **USES** The flowers are mildly antibiotic and stimulant. Infused, they give a skin and hair tonic, a wash for inflamed or tired eyes and conjunctivitis, and a compress for scrapes and skin ulcers. A leaf or flower infusion stimulates digestion and relieves rheumatism. The blue pigment colors ink, paint, cosmetics, and medicines.

• **REMARK** Dried cornflowers retain their color.

Habitat Wasteland; northern temperate regions | Parts used

Family UMBELLIFERAE | Species *Carum carvi* | Local name Karawya

CARAWAY

Caraway is a hardy biennial with finely cut feathery leaves, umbels of small flower heads in midsummer, and capsules containing two curved narrow seeds.

• **USES** The seeds are a popular spice, especially in central Europe. They enhance pork, goulash, sauerkraut, cheese, and pickles and are added to cooking cabbage to reduce the smell. They flavor breads and cakes and are eaten raw or sugar-coated as Caraway comfits after a spicy meal. They sweeten the breath, aid digestion, and relieve flatulence. Chopped leaves are added to soups and salads, and the root is cooked as a vegetable. Essential oil, distilled from the seeds, flavors candy, gin, the liqueur *Kümmel*, and mouthwashes, and scents soaps and aftershaves. The seeds are antiseptic and a vermifuge.

• **REMARK** Caraway seeds have been used in cooking since the Stone Age.

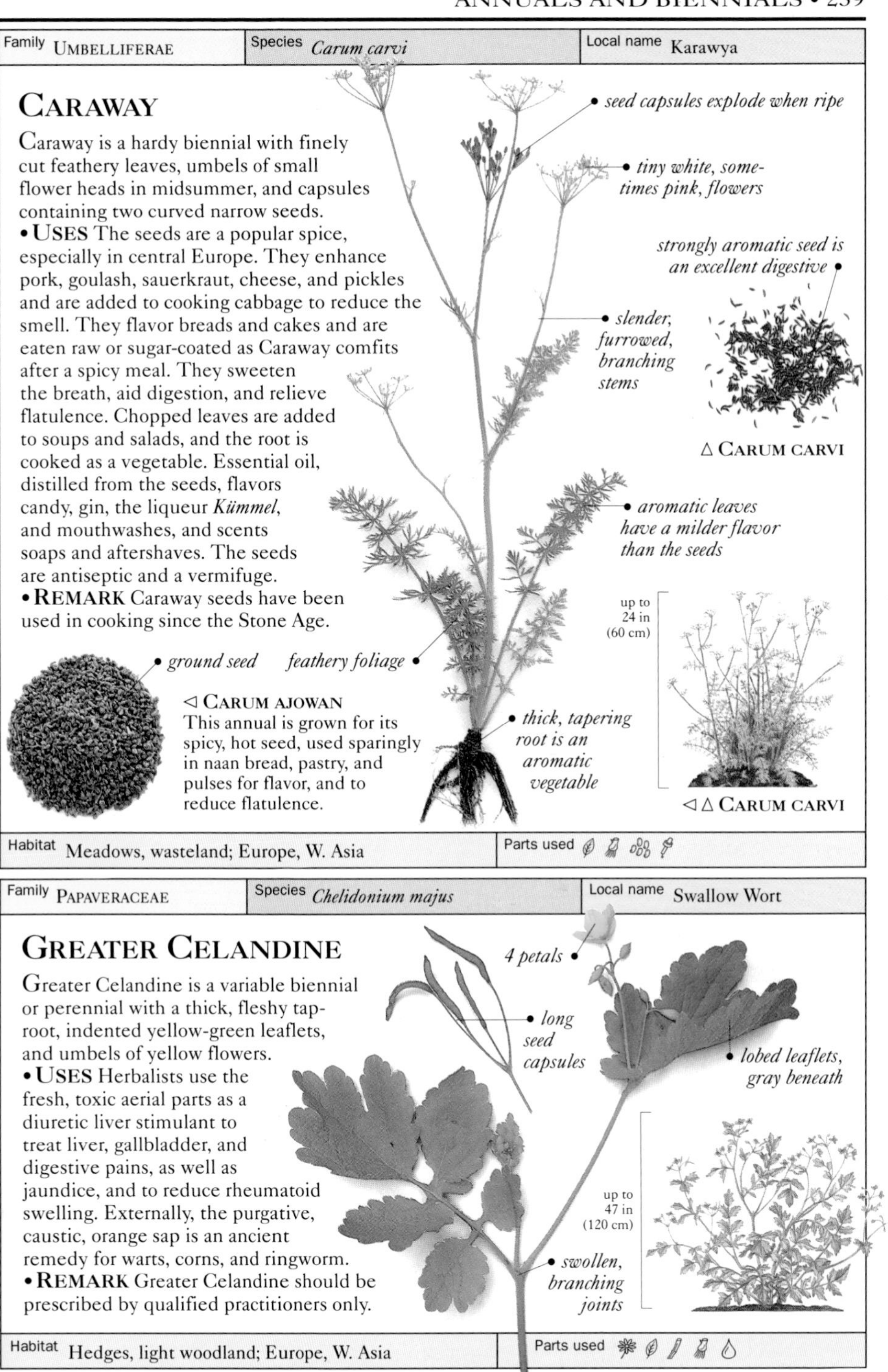

seed capsules explode when ripe
tiny white, sometimes pink, flowers
strongly aromatic seed is an excellent digestive
slender, furrowed, branching stems
aromatic leaves have a milder flavor than the seeds
up to 24 in (60 cm)
ground seed
feathery foliage
thick, tapering root is an aromatic vegetable
4 petals
long seed capsules
lobed leaflets, gray beneath
up to 47 in (120 cm)
swollen, branching joints

△ CARUM CARVI

◁ CARUM AJOWAN
This annual is grown for its spicy, hot seed, used sparingly in naan bread, pastry, and pulses for flavor, and to reduce flatulence.

◁ △ CARUM CARVI

Habitat Meadows, wasteland; Europe, W. Asia | Parts used

Family PAPAVERACEAE | Species *Chelidonium majus* | Local name Swallow Wort

GREATER CELANDINE

Greater Celandine is a variable biennial or perennial with a thick, fleshy tap-root, indented yellow-green leaflets, and umbels of yellow flowers.

• **USES** Herbalists use the fresh, toxic aerial parts as a diuretic liver stimulant to treat liver, gallbladder, and digestive pains, as well as jaundice, and to reduce rheumatoid swelling. Externally, the purgative, caustic, orange sap is an ancient remedy for warts, corns, and ringworm.

• **REMARK** Greater Celandine should be prescribed by qualified practitioners only.

Habitat Hedges, light woodland; Europe, W. Asia | Parts used

Family CHENOPODIACEAE | Species *Chenopodium ambrosioides* | Local name Epazote

AMERICAN WORMSEED

This annual, or short-lived perennial, has pungent, spear-shaped, deeply toothed leaves, green summer flowers, and small dry fruits. • **USES** The leaves season soup, corn, beans, and shellfish in Mexico and are brewed for "Jesuit Tea," but the herb's main use is to expel intestinal worms from humans and animals. All parts contain a worm-repelling compound, ascaridole, but the fruit and the chenopodium oil distilled from it are most potent and toxic. Locally called "Herba Sancti Mariæ," the leaf is used to expel phlegm and treat asthma. Some Amazon tribes take it to encourage breast milk. The Maya tribe of Yucatan use the whole plant as a flavoring. • **REMARK** American Wormseed is poisonous and should be used by qualified practitioners only.

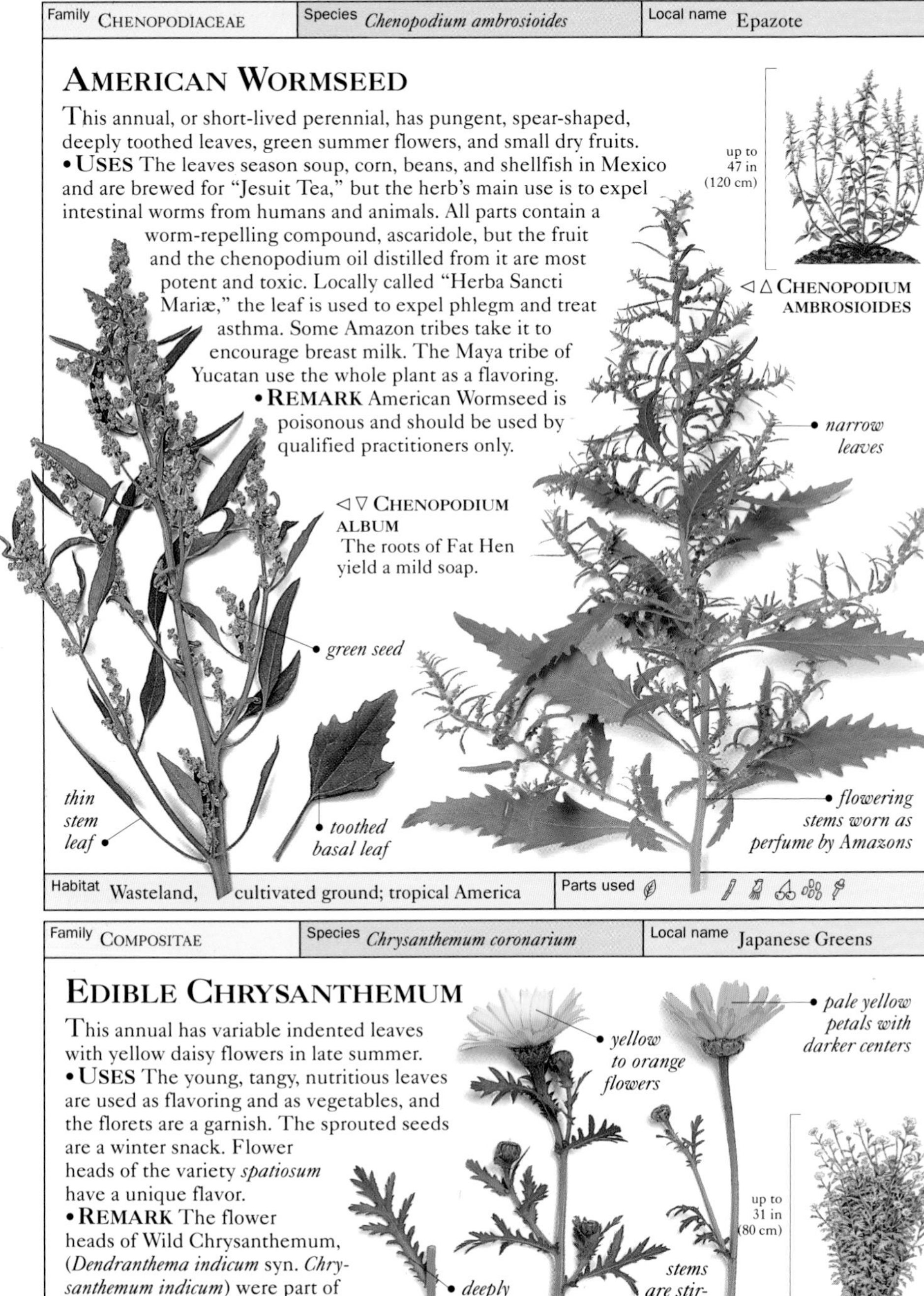
up to
47 in
(120 cm)
narrow leaves
green seed
thin stem leaf
toothed basal leaf
flowering stems worn as perfume by Amazons
yellow to orange flowers
pale yellow petals with darker centers
deeply toothed leaf
stems are stir-fried
up to
31 in
(80 cm)

◁ △ CHENOPODIUM AMBROSIOIDES

◁ ▽ CHENOPODIUM ALBUM
The roots of Fat Hen yield a mild soap.

Habitat Wasteland, cultivated ground; tropical America | Parts used

Family COMPOSITAE | Species *Chrysanthemum coronarium* | Local name Japanese Greens

EDIBLE CHRYSANTHEMUM

This annual has variable indented leaves with yellow daisy flowers in late summer. • **USES** The young, tangy, nutritious leaves are used as flavoring and as vegetables, and the florets are a garnish. The sprouted seeds are a winter snack. Flower heads of the variety *spatiosum* have a unique flavor. • **REMARK** The flower heads of Wild Chrysanthemum, (*Dendranthema indicum* syn. *Chrysanthemum indicum*) were part of the Taoist elixir of immortality.

Habitat Moist, fertile soil, sun; Mediterranean | Parts used

Family LEGUMINOSAE	Species *Cicer arietinum*	Local name Egyptian Pea

CHICK PEA

This annual has upright or trailing stems with paired oval leaflets, white or violet pealike flowers, and short, oval pods containing smooth seeds.

• **USES** Young green pods are eaten. The protein-rich ripe peas readily absorb other flavors and are used in India fresh or dried in soups, hummus, and vegetable stews. Ground seed flour is called gram flour and is made into bread and sweets. The sprouted seeds are eaten, and the roasted root has been powdered for skin packs and used as a coffee substitute.

• **REMARK** Seed pod hairs may irritate skin on contact.

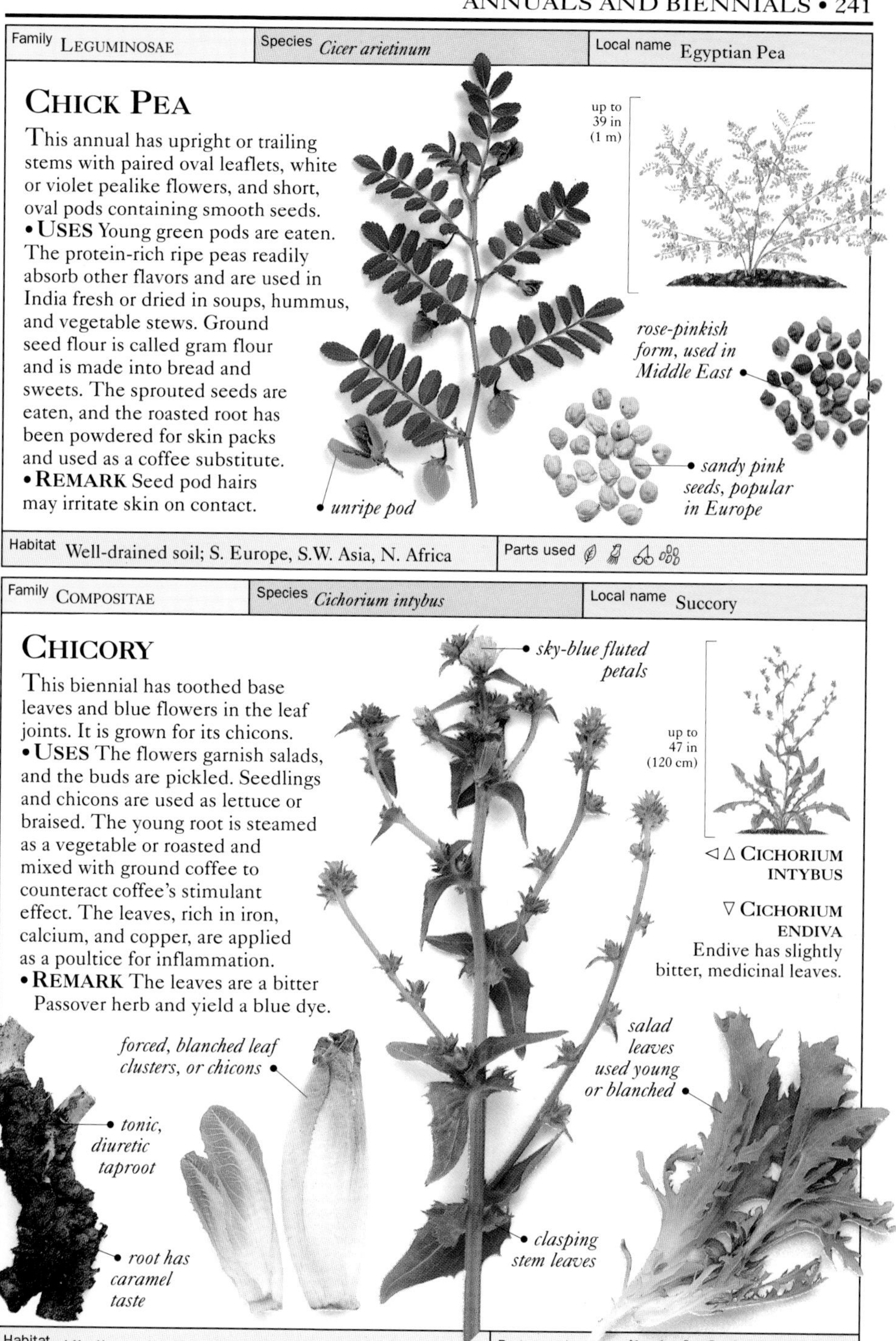

up to 39 in (1 m)
rose-pinkish form, used in Middle East
sandy pink seeds, popular in Europe
unripe pod
sky-blue fluted petals
up to 47 in (120 cm)
forced, blanched leaf clusters, or chicons
salad leaves used young or blanched
tonic, diuretic taproot
root has caramel taste
clasping stem leaves

Habitat Well-drained soil; S. Europe, S.W. Asia, N. Africa	Parts used

Family COMPOSITAE	Species *Cichorium intybus*	Local name Succory

CHICORY

This biennial has toothed base leaves and blue flowers in the leaf joints. It is grown for its chicons.

• **USES** The flowers garnish salads, and the buds are pickled. Seedlings and chicons are used as lettuce or braised. The young root is steamed as a vegetable or roasted and mixed with ground coffee to counteract coffee's stimulant effect. The leaves, rich in iron, calcium, and copper, are applied as a poultice for inflammation.

• **REMARK** The leaves are a bitter Passover herb and yield a blue dye.

◁ △ CICHORIUM INTYBUS

▽ CICHORIUM ENDIVA
Endive has slightly bitter, medicinal leaves.

Habitat Alkaline soils; Europe, W. Asia, N. Africa	Parts used

Family COMPOSITAE	Species *Cnicus benedictus*	Local name Sacred Thistle

HOLY THISTLE

Holy Thistle (*Cnicus benedictus* syns. *Carduus benedicta, Carbenia benedicta*) is a hairy annual with red stems, spiny-toothed leaves, and summer to autumn flower heads.

• **USES** The leaves, flower heads, and roots are edible, and the aerial parts add bitterness to liqueurs. The plant is taken as a tonic to purify and strengthen circulation. Small doses treat digestive problems and infections, expel phlegm, and are applied to wounds. The seeds were once a source of oil.

• **REMARK** Large doses cause vomiting.

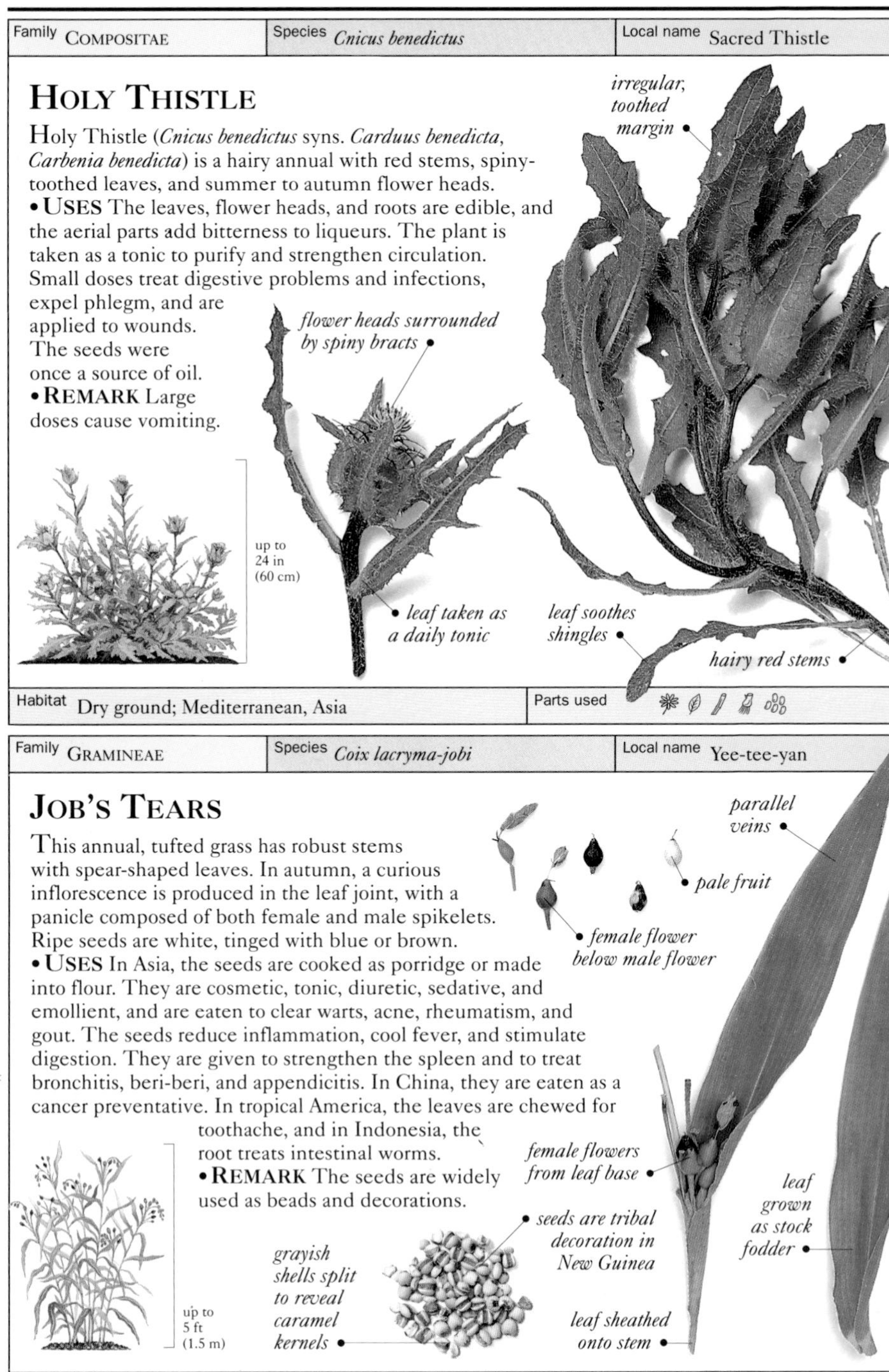

irregular, toothed margin
flower heads surrounded by spiny bracts
up to 24 in (60 cm)
leaf taken as a daily tonic
leaf soothes shingles
hairy red stems
parallel veins
pale fruit
female flower below male flower
female flowers from leaf base
leaf grown as stock fodder
seeds are tribal decoration in New Guinea
grayish shells split to reveal caramel kernels
leaf sheathed onto stem
up to 5 ft (1.5 m)

Habitat Dry ground; Mediterranean, Asia	Parts used

Family GRAMINEAE	Species *Coix lacryma-jobi*	Local name Yee-tee-yan

JOB'S TEARS

This annual, tufted grass has robust stems with spear-shaped leaves. In autumn, a curious inflorescence is produced in the leaf joint, with a panicle composed of both female and male spikelets. Ripe seeds are white, tinged with blue or brown.

• **USES** In Asia, the seeds are cooked as porridge or made into flour. They are cosmetic, tonic, diuretic, sedative, and emollient, and are eaten to clear warts, acne, rheumatism, and gout. The seeds reduce inflammation, cool fever, and stimulate digestion. They are given to strengthen the spleen and to treat bronchitis, beri-beri, and appendicitis. In China, they are eaten as a cancer preventative. In tropical America, the leaves are chewed for toothache, and in Indonesia, the root treats intestinal worms.

• **REMARK** The seeds are widely used as beads and decorations.

Habitat Moist soils; S.E. Asia	Parts used

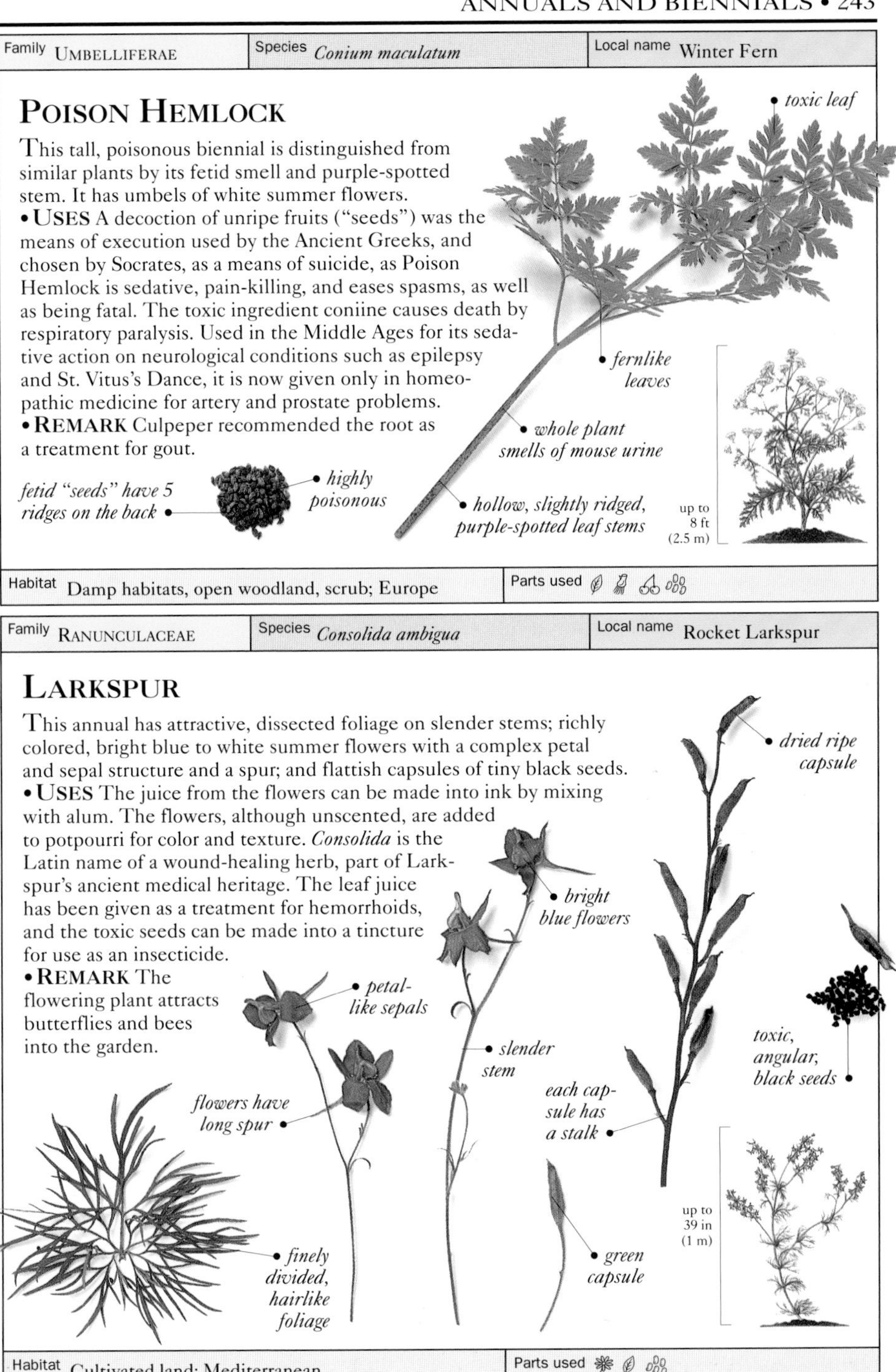

Family UMBELLIFERAE | Species *Conium maculatum* | Local name Winter Fern

POISON HEMLOCK

This tall, poisonous biennial is distinguished from similar plants by its fetid smell and purple-spotted stem. It has umbels of white summer flowers.

• **USES** A decoction of unripe fruits ("seeds") was the means of execution used by the Ancient Greeks, and chosen by Socrates, as a means of suicide, as Poison Hemlock is sedative, pain-killing, and eases spasms, as well as being fatal. The toxic ingredient coniine causes death by respiratory paralysis. Used in the Middle Ages for its sedative action on neurological conditions such as epilepsy and St. Vitus's Dance, it is now given only in homeopathic medicine for artery and prostate problems.

• **REMARK** Culpeper recommended the root as a treatment for gout.

toxic leaf
fernlike leaves
whole plant smells of mouse urine
hollow, slightly ridged, purple-spotted leaf stems
highly poisonous
fetid "seeds" have 5 ridges on the back
up to 8 ft (2.5 m)

Habitat Damp habitats, open woodland, scrub; Europe | Parts used

Family RANUNCULACEAE | Species *Consolida ambigua* | Local name Rocket Larkspur

LARKSPUR

This annual has attractive, dissected foliage on slender stems; richly colored, bright blue to white summer flowers with a complex petal and sepal structure and a spur; and flattish capsules of tiny black seeds.

• **USES** The juice from the flowers can be made into ink by mixing with alum. The flowers, although unscented, are added to potpourri for color and texture. *Consolida* is the Latin name of a wound-healing herb, part of Larkspur's ancient medical heritage. The leaf juice has been given as a treatment for hemorrhoids, and the toxic seeds can be made into a tincture for use as an insecticide.

• **REMARK** The flowering plant attracts butterflies and bees into the garden.

dried ripe capsule
bright blue flowers
petal-like sepals
slender stem
toxic, angular, black seeds
each capsule has a stalk
flowers have long spur
finely divided, hairlike foliage
green capsule
up to 39 in (1 m)

Habitat Cultivated land; Mediterranean | Parts used

Family UMBELLIFERAE	Species *Coriandrum sativum*	Local name Chinese Parsley

CORIANDER

The whole of this annual is pungently aromatic, with lobed lower and finely cut upper foliage, summer flowers, and round seeds in ribbed beige coats.

• **USES** The pungent leaves are widely used in Middle Eastern and Asian cuisine. The mildly-narcotic seed is popular in pickles, ratatouille, curries, and liqueurs. The root is added to curries and the stem to beans and soups. It was an Egyptian aphrodisiac and a wine flavoring for the Greeks. The seed is a mild sedative, aids digestion, reduces flatulence, and eases migraines.

• **REMARK** The spicy essential oil, distilled from the seeds, is used in perfumes and incense, flavors medicines and toothpaste, and is added to massage oil for facial neuralgia and cramps.

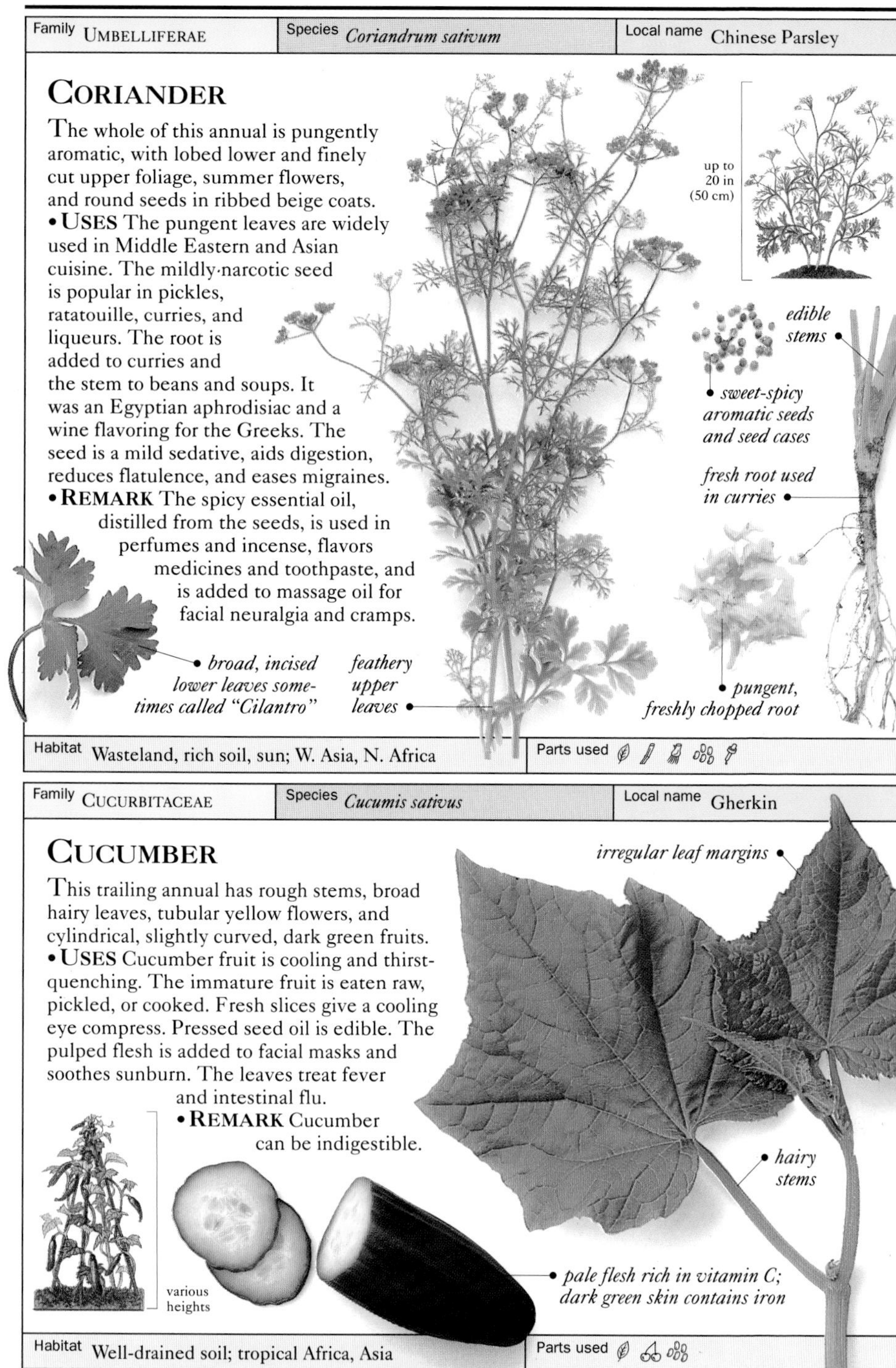
up to 20 in (50 cm)
edible stems
sweet-spicy aromatic seeds and seed cases
fresh root used in curries
broad, incised lower leaves sometimes called "Cilantro"
feathery upper leaves
pungent, freshly chopped root
irregular leaf margins
hairy stems
various heights
pale flesh rich in vitamin C; dark green skin contains iron

Habitat Wasteland, rich soil, sun; W. Asia, N. Africa	Parts used

Family CUCURBITACEAE	Species *Cucumis sativus*	Local name Gherkin

CUCUMBER

This trailing annual has rough stems, broad hairy leaves, tubular yellow flowers, and cylindrical, slightly curved, dark green fruits.

• **USES** Cucumber fruit is cooling and thirst-quenching. The immature fruit is eaten raw, pickled, or cooked. Fresh slices give a cooling eye compress. Pressed seed oil is edible. The pulped flesh is added to facial masks and soothes sunburn. The leaves treat fever and intestinal flu.

• **REMARK** Cucumber can be indigestible.

Habitat Well-drained soil; tropical Africa, Asia	Parts used

Family CUCURBITACEAE | Species *Cucurbita pepo* | Local name Squash

PUMPKIN

This trailing annual has sprawling prickly stems, tendrils opposite large leaves, large orange-yellow male flowers in leaf axils, female flowers on stalks, and green to orange fruits.

• **USES** The species includes pumpkins, squashes, and zucchinis. The flowers are stuffed or battered and the flesh cooked in sweet and savory dishes. Nutritious pumpkin seeds are roasted for snacks and are considered a longevity food in China. The seeds yield a culinary oil and help expel intestinal worms.

• **REMARK** Seeds of *Cucurbita moschata* var. *toonas*, *C. pepo*, and *C. maxima* expel worms and prevent prostate trouble.

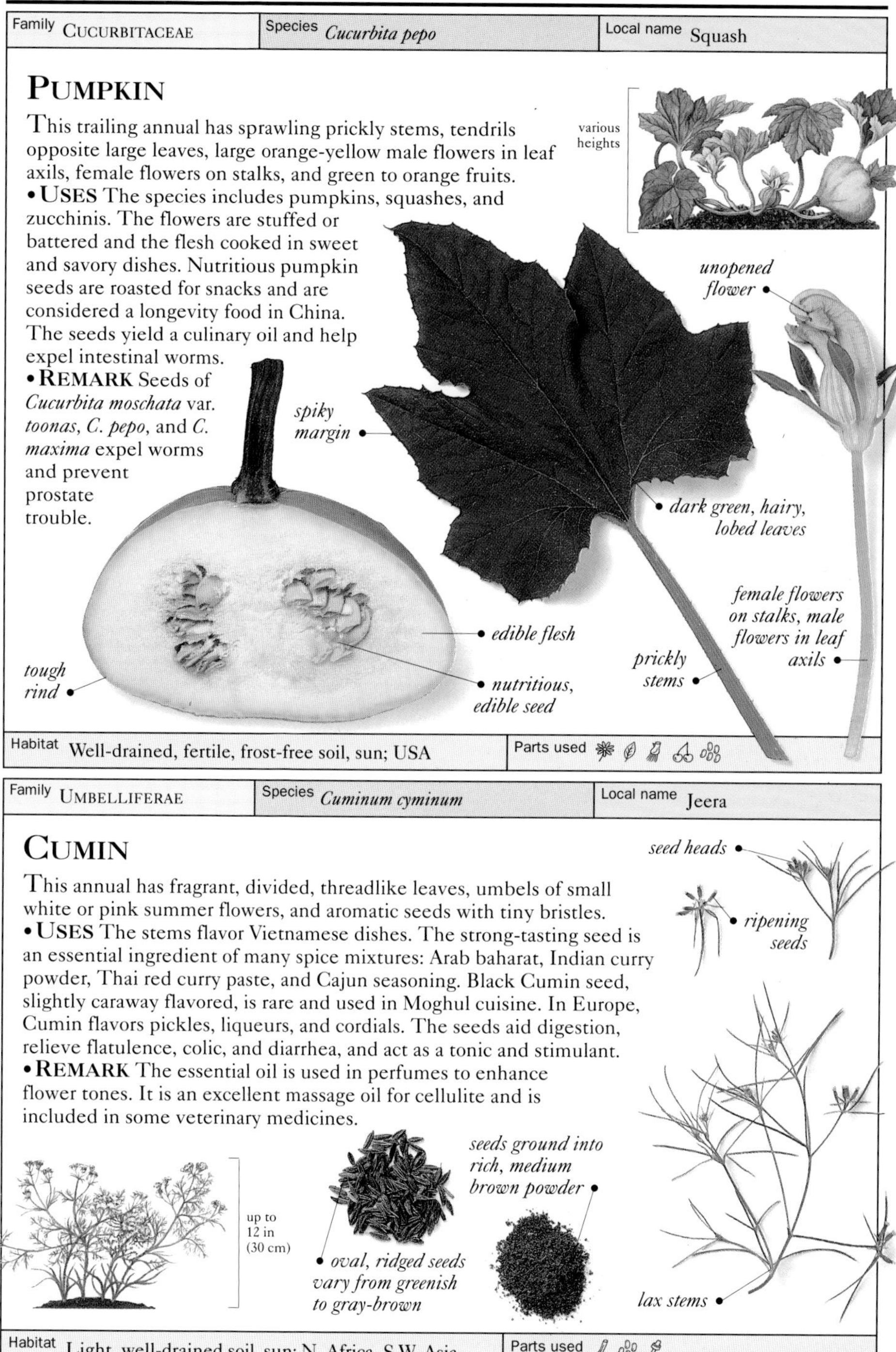
various heights
unopened flower
spiky margin
dark green, hairy, lobed leaves
female flowers on stalks, male flowers in leaf axils
edible flesh
prickly stems
tough rind
nutritious, edible seed
seed heads
ripening seeds
up to 12 in (30 cm)
seeds ground into rich, medium brown powder
oval, ridged seeds vary from greenish to gray-brown
lax stems

Habitat Well-drained, fertile, frost-free soil, sun; USA | Parts used

Family UMBELLIFERAE | Species *Cuminum cyminum* | Local name Jeera

CUMIN

This annual has fragrant, divided, threadlike leaves, umbels of small white or pink summer flowers, and aromatic seeds with tiny bristles.

• **USES** The stems flavor Vietnamese dishes. The strong-tasting seed is an essential ingredient of many spice mixtures: Arab baharat, Indian curry powder, Thai red curry paste, and Cajun seasoning. Black Cumin seed, slightly caraway flavored, is rare and used in Moghul cuisine. In Europe, Cumin flavors pickles, liqueurs, and cordials. The seeds aid digestion, relieve flatulence, colic, and diarrhea, and act as a tonic and stimulant.

• **REMARK** The essential oil is used in perfumes to enhance flower tones. It is an excellent massage oil for cellulite and is included in some veterinary medicines.

Habitat Light, well-drained soil, sun; N. Africa, S.W. Asia | Parts used

white, yellow, or purple flowers
large leaf
spiky seed pod
toxic brown seeds
seeds are hallucinogenic
large leaf with incised margin, smoked in asthma cigarettes
up to 2 m (6½ ft)
purple flower
tap-root
fine leaf
up to 39 in (1 m)

Family SOLANACEAE | Species *Datura stramonium* | Local name Jimson Weed

THORN APPLE

This annual has musky leaves, strangely scented trumpet-shaped flowers, and spiky fruit capsules.

• **USES** The leaves of Thorn Apple and Hindu Datura relieve asthmatic spasms and excessive salivation; the flowers are an anesthetic for tooth decay and minor operations. Both herbs help nervous disorders and numbness, and their roots and flowers, applied externally, ease rheumatism. Thorn Apple contains the alkaloid hyoscine, used as a truth serum and to prevent travel sickness. It was a prophecy plant of the Delphic oracle.

• **REMARK** Thorn Apple is poisonous, causing insanity or even death.

△ DATURA STRAMONIUM

△ DATURA METEL ▷ The Hindu Datura is used in Ayurvedic medicine for some mental illness.

◁ DATURA STRAMONIUM

DATURA STRAMONIUM

Habitat Fertile wasteland; the Americas | Parts used

Family UMBELLIFERAE | Species *Daucus carota* | Local name Wild Carrot

QUEEN ANNE'S LACE

This biennial has a long taproot, a hairy stem with segmented leaves, and umbels of white to purple-tinged flowers with a purple flower in the center and divided bracts beneath.

• **USES** The roots of *Daucus carota* subsp. *sativus*, rich in vitamin C and carotene, are a source of orange dye, a coffee substitute, and a syrup. The seeds are a folk remedy "morning after" treatment; their essence is used in liqueurs and perfumery. The roots kill bacteria and lower blood pressure. A herb tea acts as a diuretic and urinary antiseptic.

Habitat Rough grassland, coastal cliffs; Europe to India | Parts used

Family SCROPHULARIACEAE	Species *Digitalis lanata*	Local name Witches' Gloves

GRECIAN FOXGLOVE

This biennial or perennial has purple-tinged stems with narrow leaves, terminating in a raceme of pinky beige, tubular flowers in summer.

• **USES** The drugs digitoxin and digoxin are prepared from the leaves of this species and are used in medicine for heart disease; they increase the strength of heart contractions without increasing oxygen consumption (acting as stimulants) and regulate the heartbeat. The compounds were discovered in the Common Foxglove, but compounds in Grecian Foxglove are up to four times as potent. The leaves of Straw Foxglove are less dangerous, as their effects are not cumulative. The leaves have been prescribed for epilepsy and tumors.

• **REMARK** The plant is poisonous and should be used by qualified personnel only.

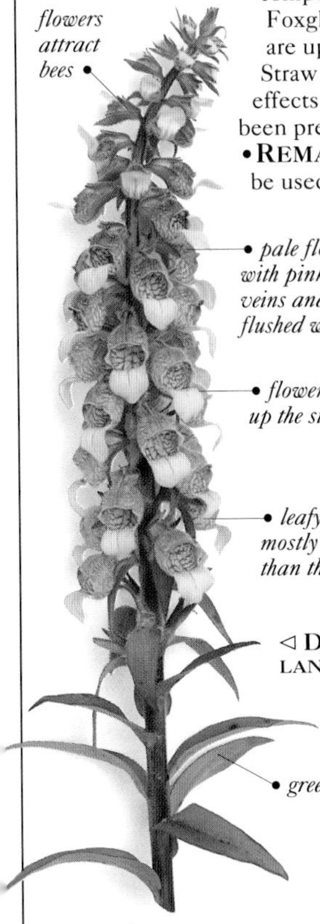

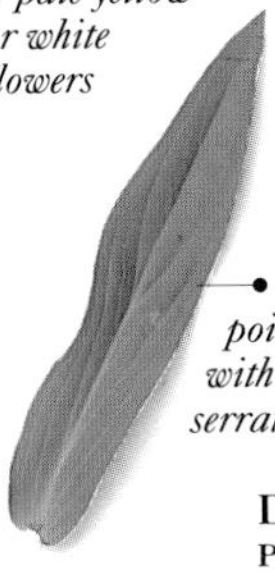

DIGITALIS PURPUREA ▷ Common Foxglove is the other main species from which drugs are prepared.

unopened flower
purple to white flowers
spotted interior

flowers attract bees
pale flower with pink-brown veins and pink-flushed white lip
flowers open up the stem
leafy bracts mostly shorter than the flowers
green leaves with reddish vein

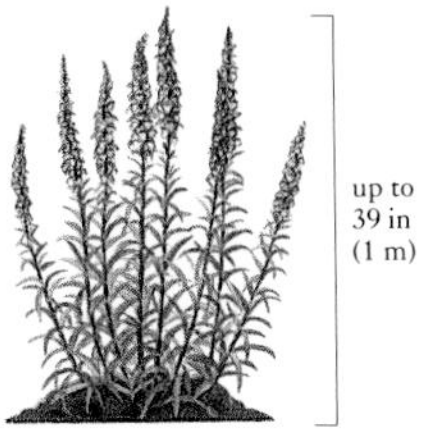

◁ DIGITALIS LANATA

◁ DIGITALIS LUTEA Straw Foxglove is a perennial with pale yellow to white flowers. The leaf glycosides are used in heart drugs.

pale yellow or white flowers
narrow, pointed leaf with finely serrated edge

DIGITALIS PURPUREA ▽▷

oval, pointed, textured, basal leaf with finely serrated margin

up to 39 in (1 m)

DIGITALIS LANATA

smooth, bright green stem and leaves

DIGITALIS LUTEA ▷

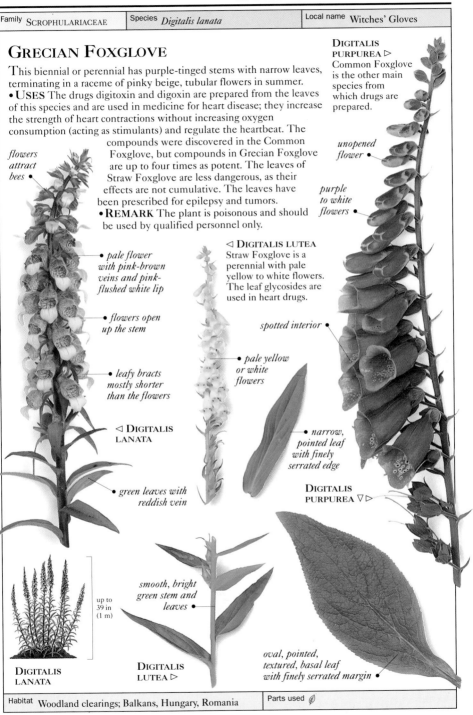

Habitat Woodland clearings; Balkans, Hungary, Romania	Parts used

Family DIPSACACEAE	Species *Dipsacus fullonum*	Local name Brushes and Combs

COMMON TEASEL

This biennial's first-year rosette of leaves grows a tall stem in the second year, with spiny, summer flowers.

• **USES** In Gypsy medicine the water collected in leaf joints treats irritated eyes, reduces dark circles, and soothes wrinkles. The cleansing root treats sties and whitlows, and is a liver and stomach tonic. The spiny bracteoles of Fuller's Teasel end in a hook with a resilience perfect for combing wool. Although largely replaced by wire, their exact resistance cannot be duplicated, and they are still used for specialist cloth such as billiard baize.

• **REMARK** The root of *Dipsacus japonicus* is given for rheumatoid pain, cancer of the breast, and irregular menstruation.

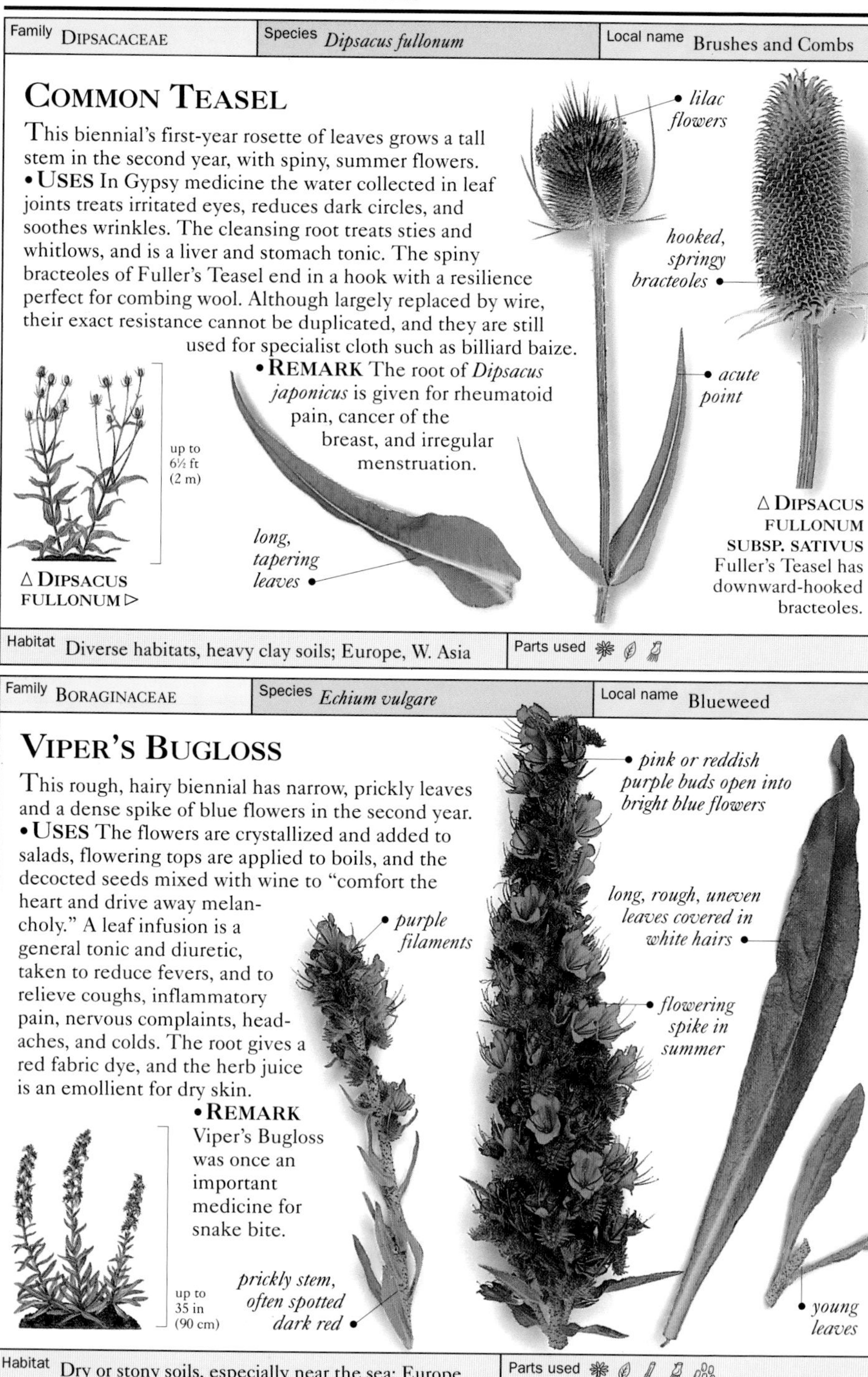

lilac flowers
hooked, springy bracteoles
acute point
long, tapering leaves
up to 6½ ft (2 m)
pink or reddish purple buds open into bright blue flowers
long, rough, uneven leaves covered in white hairs
purple filaments
flowering spike in summer
prickly stem, often spotted dark red
young leaves
up to 35 in (90 cm)

△ DIPSACUS FULLONUM ▷

△ DIPSACUS FULLONUM SUBSP. SATIVUS Fuller's Teasel has downward-hooked bracteoles.

Habitat Diverse habitats, heavy clay soils; Europe, W. Asia	Parts used

Family BORAGINACEAE	Species *Echium vulgare*	Local name Blueweed

VIPER'S BUGLOSS

This rough, hairy biennial has narrow, prickly leaves and a dense spike of blue flowers in the second year.

• **USES** The flowers are crystallized and added to salads, flowering tops are applied to boils, and the decocted seeds mixed with wine to "comfort the heart and drive away melancholy." A leaf infusion is a general tonic and diuretic, taken to reduce fevers, and to relieve coughs, inflammatory pain, nervous complaints, headaches, and colds. The root gives a red fabric dye, and the herb juice is an emollient for dry skin.

• **REMARK** Viper's Bugloss was once an important medicine for snake bite.

Habitat Dry or stony soils, especially near the sea; Europe	Parts used

Family CRUCIFERAE	Species *Eruca vesicaria* subsp. *sativa*	Local name Roquette / Arugula

ROCKET SALAD

This annual has variable, mainly lance-shaped leaves, and four-petaled cream flowers in late spring and early summer.
• **USES** The young leaves have a refreshing tangy spiciness, but maturity and hot sun produce a strong, bitter flavor. The leaves are added to salads and sauces, or steamed. The flowers have a mild version of the leaf flavor. The leaves are diuretic, are taken for stomach upsets, and are rubbed on the skin as rouge as they cause reddening.
• **REMARK** In India, the seed oil (Jamba oil) is used as a lubricant or for pickling, or it is stored to remove the acrid taste and used for cooking.

cream flowers with purple veins
variable leaves
leaves grown quickly in cool moist conditions are less bitter
small brown seeds used like mustard
up to 39 in (1 m)

Habitat Wasteland, waysides; Mediterranean	Parts used

Family UMBELLIFERAE	Species *Eryngium maritimum*	Local name Sea Holm

SEA HOLLY

This biennial or short-lived perennial has stiff, spiny leaves and metallic blue summer flowers.
• **USES** The young leaves, leaf buds, and shoots are edible. Mineral-rich autumn roots flavor vegetables and preserves and are candied as "eryngoes," popular in the 18th century as a tonic, cough remedy, and aphrodisiac. A root poultice is applied as a tissue regenerator, and a decoction is given for cystitis, urethritis, and inflamed prostate glands.
• **REMARK** *Eryngium foetidum* is grown near doorways because its scent repels snakes.

clusters of tiny flowers with spiny bracts beneath
silvery leaves
spiny lobes
△ ERYNGIUM MARITIMUM
plant unpleasantly scented
finely toothed, basal leaf
whorls of small stem leaves
up to 24 in (60 cm)
ERYNGIUM MARITIMUM

ERYNGIUM FOETIDUM △▷
Perennial Coriander has malodorous roots that flavor soup and meat stews.

Habitat Sandy soil, sun, coastal areas; Europe	Parts used

Family PAPAVERACEAE	Species *Eschscholzia californica*	Local name Cup of Gold

CALIFORNIA POPPY

This variable annual to short-lived perennial has feathery foliage and velvety, golden-orange flower petals that close in dull weather.

• **USES** Native Americans ate the leaves boiled or roasted on hot stones and used the aerial parts as a tranquilizer, particularly for toothache. The whole plant oxygenates the circulatory system and helps the body absorb vitamin A. Its calming action has gained popularity in Europe, where it is given for hyperactivity, sleeplessness, and coughs in children and is included in preparations for insomnia in adults. Dried leaves and flowers are smoked for mild euphoria with no known side effects.

• **REMARK** Now the state flower of California, it is one of the Californian Flower Remedies (similar to Bach Flower Remedies) and is given to assist in emotional cleansing.

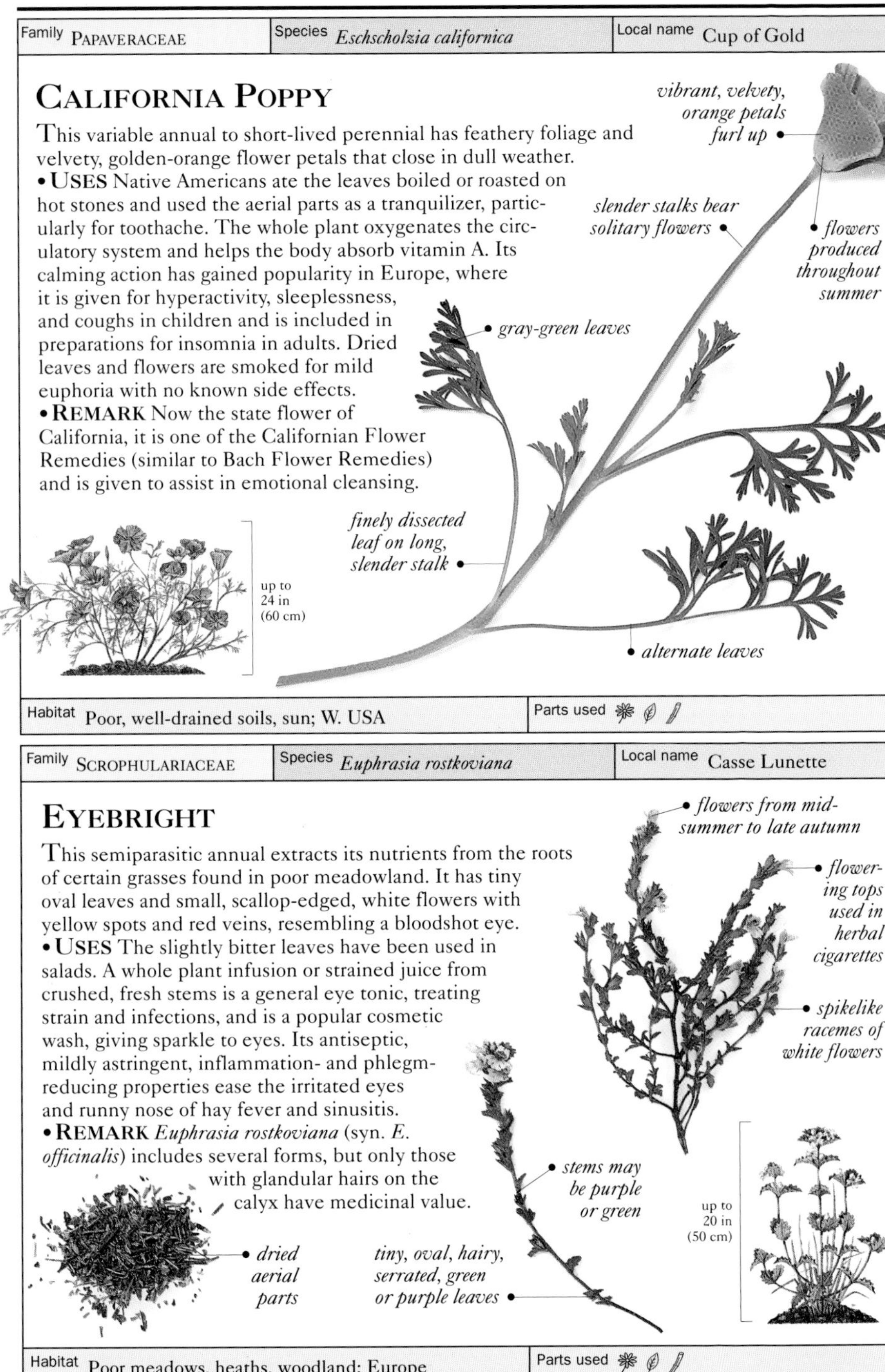
vibrant, velvety, orange petals furl up
slender stalks bear solitary flowers
flowers produced throughout summer
gray-green leaves
finely dissected leaf on long, slender stalk
up to 24 in (60 cm)
alternate leaves
flowers from mid-summer to late autumn
flower-ing tops used in herbal cigarettes
spikelike racemes of white flowers
stems may be purple or green
up to 20 in (50 cm)
dried aerial parts
tiny, oval, hairy, serrated, green or purple leaves

Habitat Poor, well-drained soils, sun; W. USA	Parts used

Family SCROPHULARIACEAE	Species *Euphrasia rostkoviana*	Local name Casse Lunette

EYEBRIGHT

This semiparasitic annual extracts its nutrients from the roots of certain grasses found in poor meadowland. It has tiny oval leaves and small, scallop-edged, white flowers with yellow spots and red veins, resembling a bloodshot eye.

• **USES** The slightly bitter leaves have been used in salads. A whole plant infusion or strained juice from crushed, fresh stems is a general eye tonic, treating strain and infections, and is a popular cosmetic wash, giving sparkle to eyes. Its antiseptic, mildly astringent, inflammation- and phlegm-reducing properties ease the irritated eyes and runny nose of hay fever and sinusitis.

• **REMARK** *Euphrasia rostkoviana* (syn. *E. officinalis*) includes several forms, but only those with glandular hairs on the calyx have medicinal value.

Habitat Poor meadows, heaths, woodland; Europe	Parts used

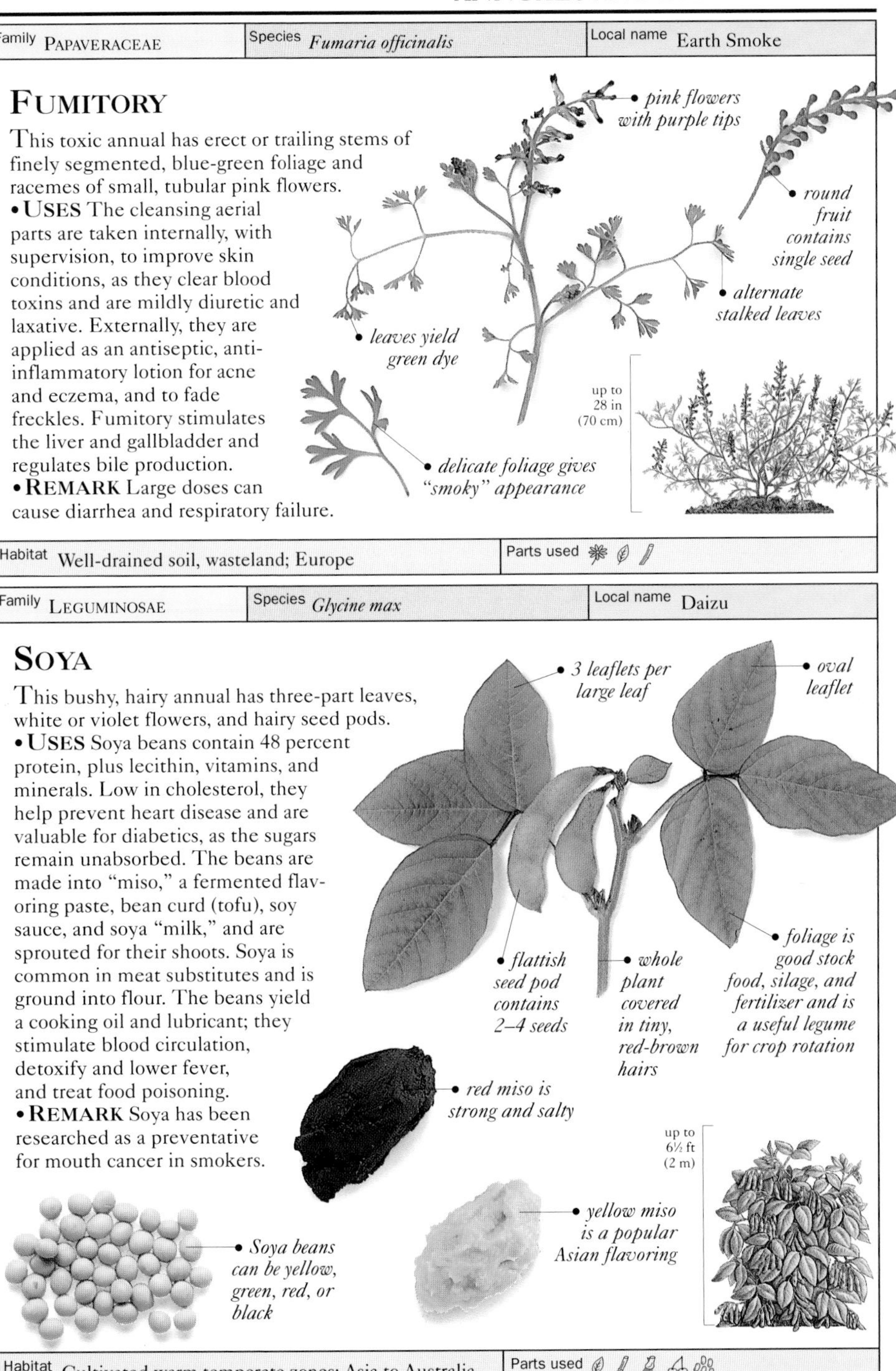
pink flowers with purple tips
round fruit contains single seed
alternate stalked leaves
leaves yield green dye
delicate foliage gives "smoky" appearance
up to 28 in (70 cm)
3 leaflets per large leaf
oval leaflet
flattish seed pod contains 2–4 seeds
whole plant covered in tiny, red-brown hairs
foliage is good stock food, silage, and fertilizer and is a useful legume for crop rotation
red miso is strong and salty
up to 6½ ft (2 m)
Soya beans can be yellow, green, red, or black
yellow miso is a popular Asian flavoring

Family PAPAVERACEAE	Species *Fumaria officinalis*	Local name Earth Smoke

FUMITORY

This toxic annual has erect or trailing stems of finely segmented, blue-green foliage and racemes of small, tubular pink flowers.

• **USES** The cleansing aerial parts are taken internally, with supervision, to improve skin conditions, as they clear blood toxins and are mildly diuretic and laxative. Externally, they are applied as an antiseptic, anti-inflammatory lotion for acne and eczema, and to fade freckles. Fumitory stimulates the liver and gallbladder and regulates bile production.

• **REMARK** Large doses can cause diarrhea and respiratory failure.

Habitat Well-drained soil, wasteland; Europe	Parts used

Family LEGUMINOSAE	Species *Glycine max*	Local name Daizu

SOYA

This bushy, hairy annual has three-part leaves, white or violet flowers, and hairy seed pods.

• **USES** Soya beans contain 48 percent protein, plus lecithin, vitamins, and minerals. Low in cholesterol, they help prevent heart disease and are valuable for diabetics, as the sugars remain unabsorbed. The beans are made into "miso," a fermented flavoring paste, bean curd (tofu), soy sauce, and soya "milk," and are sprouted for their shoots. Soya is common in meat substitutes and is ground into flour. The beans yield a cooking oil and lubricant; they stimulate blood circulation, detoxify and lower fever, and treat food poisoning.

• **REMARK** Soya has been researched as a preventative for mouth cancer in smokers.

Habitat Cultivated warm temperate zones; Asia to Australia	Parts used

Family RUBIACEAE	Species *Hedyotis diffusa*	Local name Snake Tongue Grass

SPREADING HEDYOTIS

This spreading annual has branched stems of opposite pairs of linear leaves and tiny, pale pink flowers in the leaf axils.
• **USES** The aerial parts detoxify and tone the blood; reduce fevers, swelling, and inflammation; are diuretic; treat jaundice, snake bite, appendicitis, bronchitis, sore throats, liver, and urinary problems. They are applied to boils, infected skin, and traumatic bruises. Plant juice is taken for intestinal disorders
• **REMARK** Chinese tests confirm that *Hedyotis diffusa* and five other species have anticancer activity.

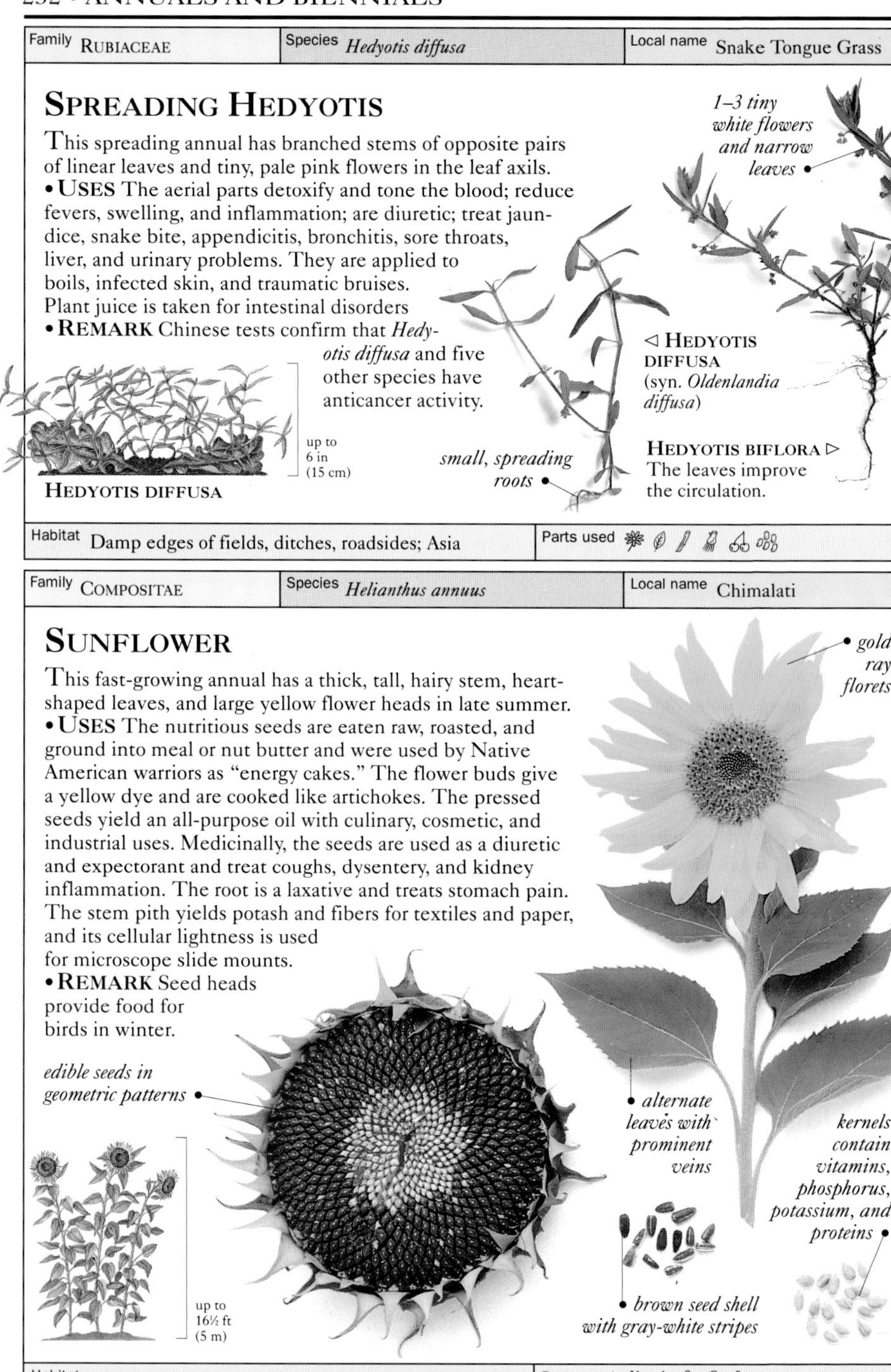

up to 6 in (15 cm)
small, spreading roots
1–3 tiny white flowers and narrow leaves
gold ray florets
edible seeds in geometric patterns
up to 16½ ft (5 m)
alternate leaves with prominent veins
kernels contain vitamins, phosphorus, potassium, and proteins
brown seed shell with gray-white stripes

HEDYOTIS DIFFUSA

◁ HEDYOTIS DIFFUSA (syn. *Oldenlandia diffusa*)

HEDYOTIS BIFLORA ▷ The leaves improve the circulation.

Habitat Damp edges of fields, ditches, roadsides; Asia	Parts used

Family COMPOSITAE	Species *Helianthus annuus*	Local name Chimalati

SUNFLOWER

This fast-growing annual has a thick, tall, hairy stem, heart-shaped leaves, and large yellow flower heads in late summer.
• **USES** The nutritious seeds are eaten raw, roasted, and ground into meal or nut butter and were used by Native American warriors as "energy cakes." The flower buds give a yellow dye and are cooked like artichokes. The pressed seeds yield an all-purpose oil with culinary, cosmetic, and industrial uses. Medicinally, the seeds are used as a diuretic and expectorant and treat coughs, dysentery, and kidney inflammation. The root is a laxative and treats stomach pain. The stem pith yields potash and fibers for textiles and paper, and its cellular lightness is used for microscope slide mounts.
• **REMARK** Seed heads provide food for birds in winter.

Habitat Fertile, well-drained soil, sun; USA	Parts used

Family GRAMINEAE	Species *Hordeum vulgare*	Local name Six-rowed Barley

BARLEY

This annual grass has straight stems, long, sheathed leaves, and grouped spikelets that produce husk-covered seeds with a characteristic upward "bristle."

• **USES** Barley has been cultivated for thousands of years; today the nutritious grain is made into cereals and meal and polished as Pearl Barley for soups and stews. Malted Barley is used to brew beer, whisky, and gin. Brewer's yeast and vitamin-rich yeast extract are by-products. Malt extract and Barley foods and water aid convalescence and soothe internal passages, easing throat and gastrointestinal irritation. In China, Barley is given for poor appetite and digestion. A poultice of cooked Barley is applied to sores, and the germinated grain treats bronchitis. It is skin-refining and softening and is used in facial masks.

• **REMARK** Two-rowed Barley, a strain of the same species, is the main malting Barley and has similar uses.

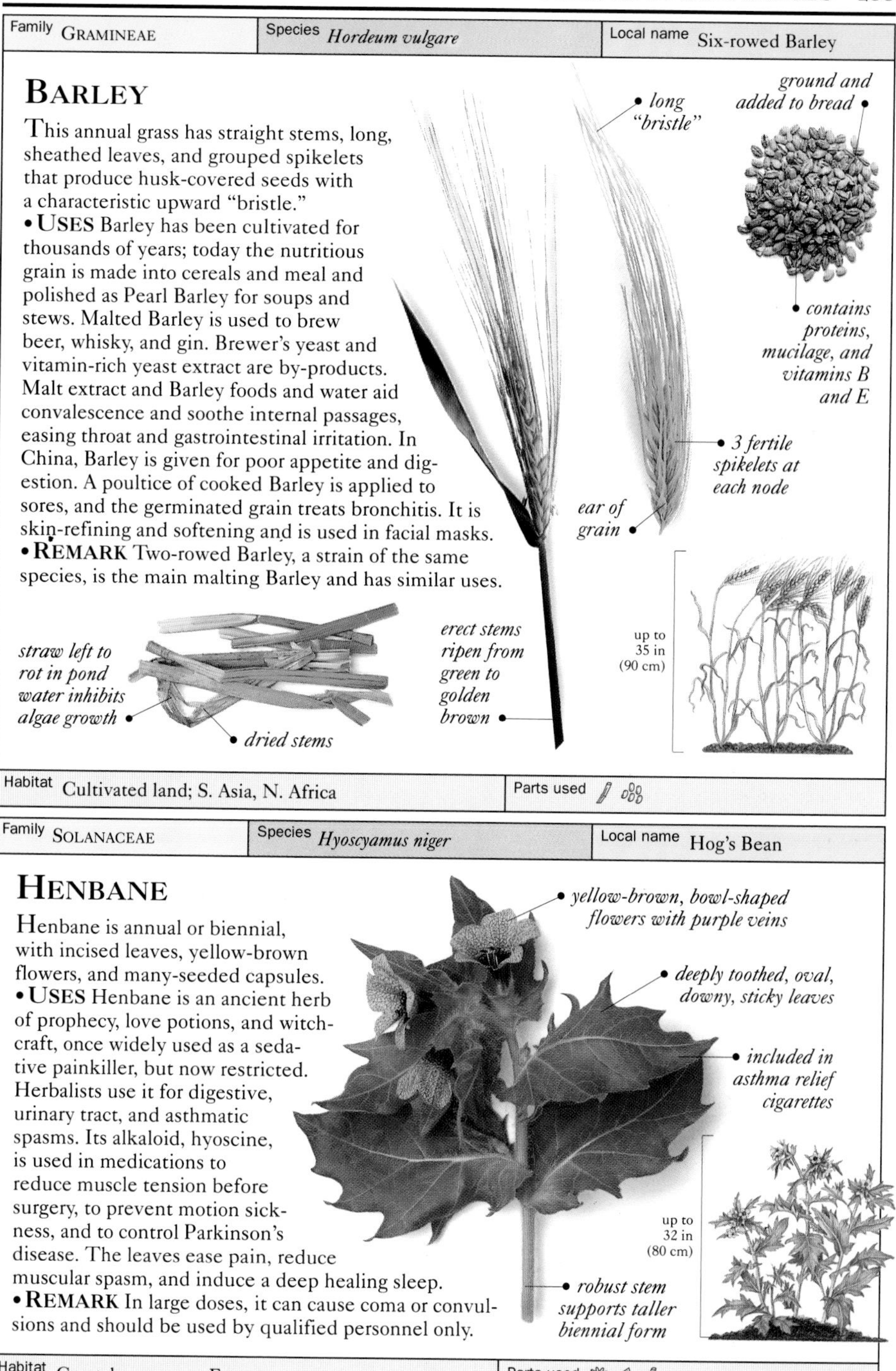
long "bristle"
ground and added to bread
contains proteins, mucilage, and vitamins B and E
3 fertile spikelets at each node
ear of grain
up to 35 in (90 cm)
erect stems ripen from green to golden brown
straw left to rot in pond water inhibits algae growth
dried stems
yellow-brown, bowl-shaped flowers with purple veins
deeply toothed, oval, downy, sticky leaves
included in asthma relief cigarettes
up to 32 in (80 cm)
robust stem supports taller biennial form

Habitat Cultivated land; S. Asia, N. Africa	Parts used

Family SOLANACEAE	Species *Hyoscyamus niger*	Local name Hog's Bean

HENBANE

Henbane is annual or biennial, with incised leaves, yellow-brown flowers, and many-seeded capsules.

• **USES** Henbane is an ancient herb of prophecy, love potions, and witchcraft, once widely used as a sedative painkiller, but now restricted. Herbalists use it for digestive, urinary tract, and asthmatic spasms. Its alkaloid, hyoscine, is used in medications to reduce muscle tension before surgery, to prevent motion sickness, and to control Parkinson's disease. The leaves ease pain, reduce muscular spasm, and induce a deep healing sleep.

• **REMARK** In large doses, it can cause coma or convulsions and should be used by qualified personnel only.

Habitat Coastal areas, sun; Europe	Parts used

Family BALSAMINACEAE	Species *Impatiens balsamina*	Local name Trigger Plant

GARDEN BALSAM

Annual Garden Balsam has pink stems, dark green leaves, white spurred flowers, and explosive seed pods that violently expel ripe seeds.

• **USES** In parts of Asia, the crushed aerial parts, mixed with turmeric, salt, and oil, are used like Henna to paint temporary reddish patterns on fingernails and skin. In Indonesia, the leaf is a treatment for swellings, ulcers, and cuts.

• **REMARK** The leaves of four species – *Impatiens burtonii* and *I. irvingii* of Central Africa, *I. noli-tangere* the "Touch-Me-Not" of China, Japan, and Europe, and *I. platypetala* of Malaysia – are used locally as antiseptic treatments for wounds and skin diseases.

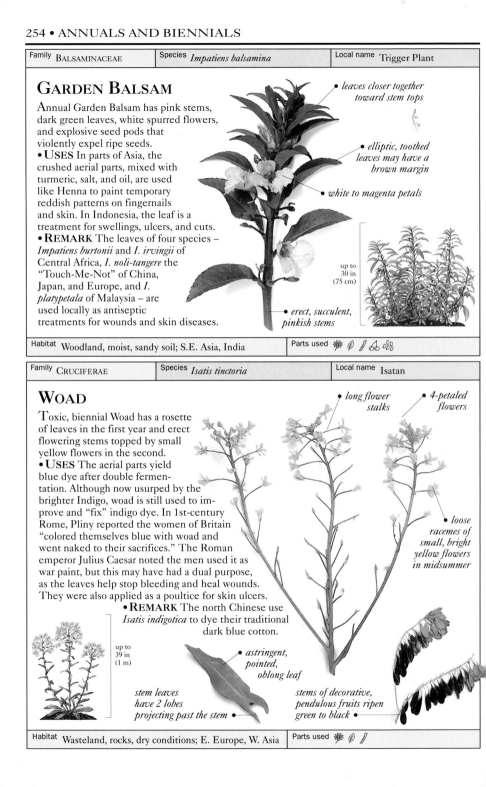

leaves closer together toward stem tops

elliptic, toothed leaves may have a brown margin

white to magenta petals

erect, succulent, pinkish stems

up to 30 in (75 cm)

Habitat Woodland, moist, sandy soil; S.E. Asia, India	Parts used

Family CRUCIFERAE	Species *Isatis tinctoria*	Local name Isatan

WOAD

Toxic, biennial Woad has a rosette of leaves in the first year and erect flowering stems topped by small yellow flowers in the second.

• **USES** The aerial parts yield blue dye after double fermentation. Although now usurped by the brighter Indigo, woad is still used to improve and "fix" indigo dye. In 1st-century Rome, Pliny reported the women of Britain "colored themselves blue with woad and went naked to their sacrifices." The Roman emperor Julius Caesar noted the men used it as war paint, but this may have had a dual purpose, as the leaves help stop bleeding and heal wounds. They were also applied as a poultice for skin ulcers.

• **REMARK** The north Chinese use *Isatis indigotica* to dye their traditional dark blue cotton.

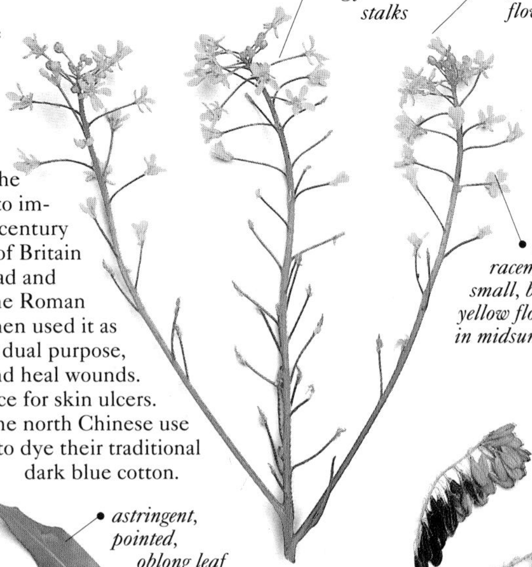

long flower stalks

4-petaled flowers

loose racemes of small, bright yellow flowers in midsummer

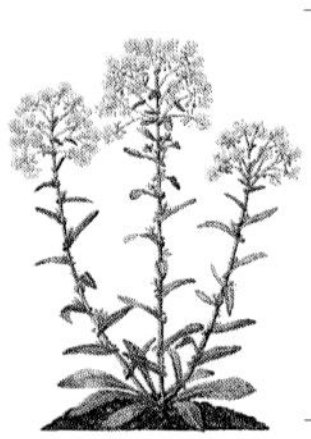

up to 39 in (1 m)

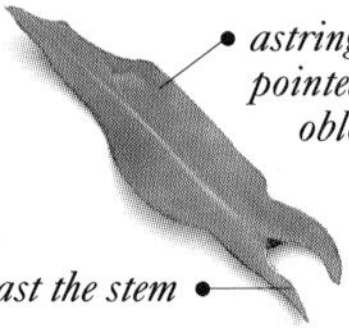

astringent, pointed, oblong leaf

stem leaves have 2 lobes projecting past the stem

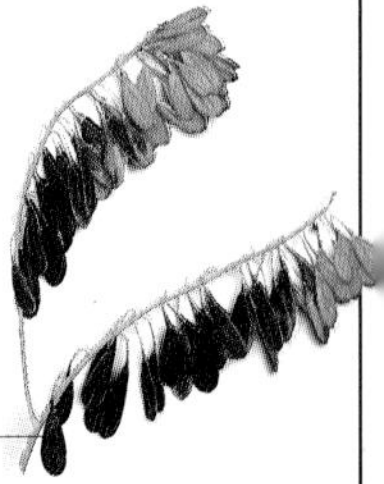

stems of decorative, pendulous fruits ripen green to black

Habitat Wasteland, rocks, dry conditions; E. Europe, W. Asia	Parts used

Family COMPOSITAE	Species *Lactuca virosa*	Local name Poor Man's Opium

BITTER LETTUCE

This annual or biennial has yellow flowers, oblong leaves, fetid roots, and black, hairy-winged fruits.
• **USES** The whole plant contains a milky juice that dries reddish brown and tastes and smells like opium. This latex and the leaves reduce blood sugar levels and are sedative, pain-relieving, and expectorant, but in excess can cause insomnia and stimulate sexual urges. Bitter Lettuce juice treats irritable coughs, whooping cough, bronchitis, and anxiety and, when diluted, is applied to acne or weather-damaged skin to soften and reduce soreness. It is found in soaps, lotions, and bath products.
• **REMARK** Salad Lettuce has had the bitterness, and hence most medicinal virtues, bred out of it.

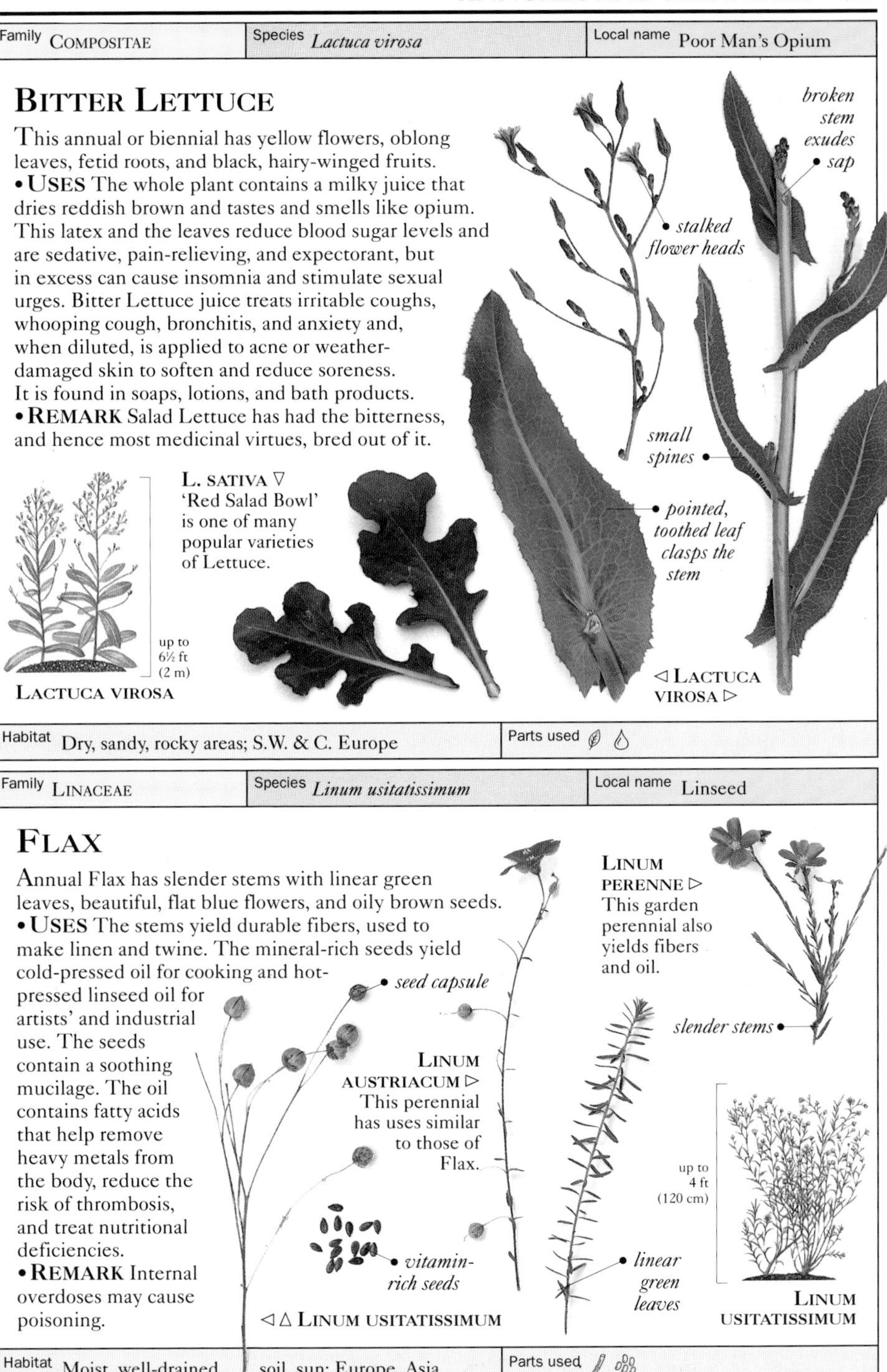

broken stem exudes sap
stalked flower heads
small spines
pointed, toothed leaf clasps the stem
up to 6½ ft (2 m)
seed capsule
slender stems
vitamin-rich seeds
linear green leaves
up to 4 ft (120 cm)

L. SATIVA ▽ 'Red Salad Bowl' is one of many popular varieties of Lettuce.

LACTUCA VIROSA

◁ LACTUCA VIROSA ▷

Habitat Dry, sandy, rocky areas; S.W. & C. Europe	Parts used

Family LINACEAE	Species *Linum usitatissimum*	Local name Linseed

FLAX

Annual Flax has slender stems with linear green leaves, beautiful, flat blue flowers, and oily brown seeds.
• **USES** The stems yield durable fibers, used to make linen and twine. The mineral-rich seeds yield cold-pressed oil for cooking and hot-pressed linseed oil for artists' and industrial use. The seeds contain a soothing mucilage. The oil contains fatty acids that help remove heavy metals from the body, reduce the risk of thrombosis, and treat nutritional deficiencies.
• **REMARK** Internal overdoses may cause poisoning.

LINUM PERENNE ▷ This garden perennial also yields fibers and oil.

LINUM AUSTRIACUM ▷ This perennial has uses similar to those of Flax.

◁ △ LINUM USITATISSIMUM

LINUM USITATISSIMUM

Habitat Moist, well-drained, soil, sun; Europe, Asia	Parts used

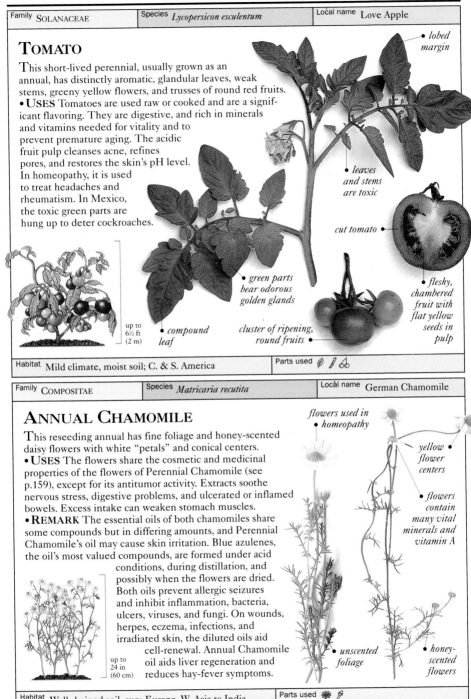

Family SOLANACEAE	Species *Lycopersicon esculentum*	Local name Love Apple

TOMATO

This short-lived perennial, usually grown as an annual, has distinctly aromatic, glandular leaves, weak stems, greeny yellow flowers, and trusses of round red fruits.
• **USES** Tomatoes are used raw or cooked and are a significant flavoring. They are digestive, and rich in minerals and vitamins needed for vitality and to prevent premature aging. The acidic fruit pulp cleanses acne, refines pores, and restores the skin's pH level. In homeopathy, it is used to treat headaches and rheumatism. In Mexico, the toxic green parts are hung up to deter cockroaches.

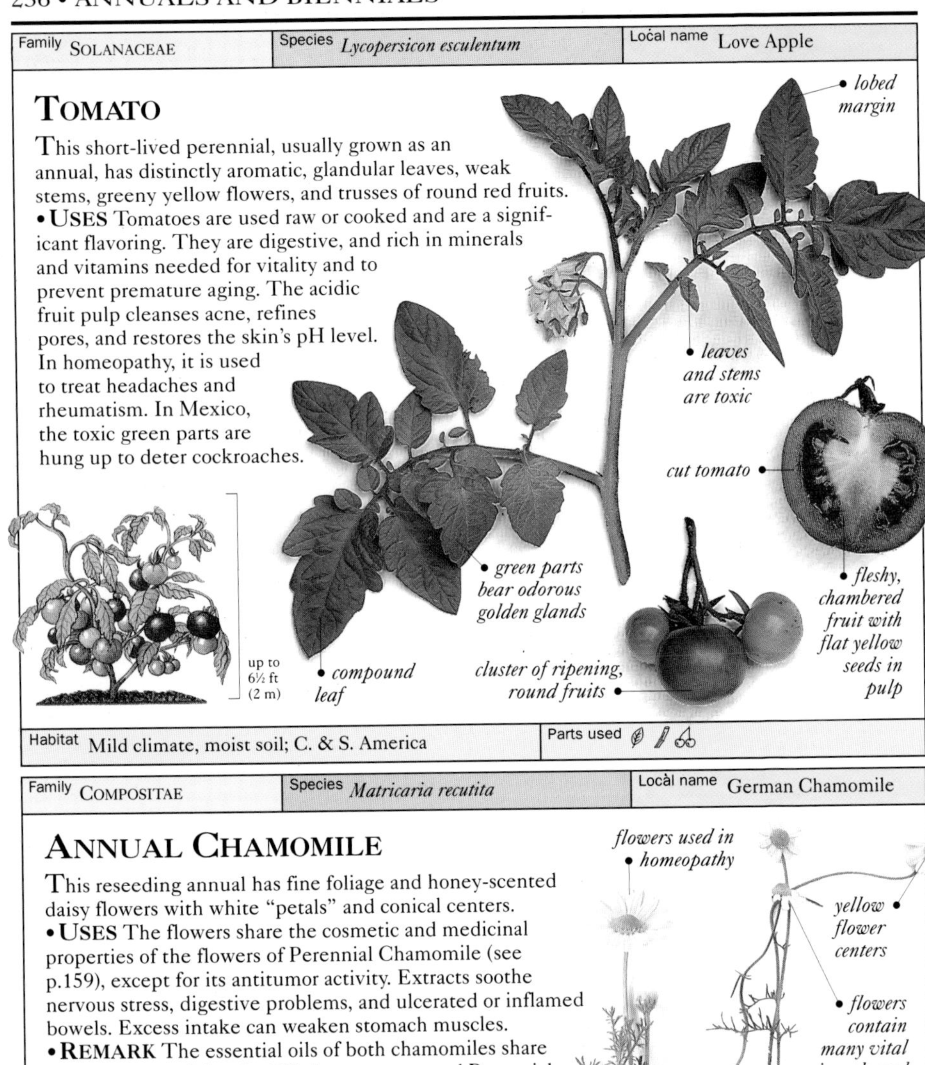
lobed margin
leaves and stems are toxic
cut tomato
green parts bear odorous golden glands
fleshy, chambered fruit with flat yellow seeds in pulp
up to 6½ ft (2 m)
compound leaf
cluster of ripening, round fruits

Habitat Mild climate, moist soil; C. & S. America	Parts used

Family COMPOSITAE	Species *Matricaria recutita*	Local name German Chamomile

ANNUAL CHAMOMILE

This reseeding annual has fine foliage and honey-scented daisy flowers with white "petals" and conical centers.
• **USES** The flowers share the cosmetic and medicinal properties of the flowers of Perennial Chamomile (see p.159), except for its antitumor activity. Extracts soothe nervous stress, digestive problems, and ulcerated or inflamed bowels. Excess intake can weaken stomach muscles.
• **REMARK** The essential oils of both chamomiles share some compounds but in differing amounts, and Perennial Chamomile's oil may cause skin irritation. Blue azulenes, the oil's most valued compounds, are formed under acid conditions, during distillation, and possibly when the flowers are dried. Both oils prevent allergic seizures and inhibit inflammation, bacteria, ulcers, viruses, and fungi. On wounds, herpes, eczema, infections, and irradiated skin, the diluted oils aid cell-renewal. Annual Chamomile oil aids liver regeneration and reduces hay-fever symptoms.

up to 24 in (60 cm)

flowers used in homeopathy
yellow flower centers
flowers contain many vital minerals and vitamin A
unscented foliage
honey-scented flowers

Habitat Well-drained soil, sun; Europe, W. Asia to India	Parts used

Family LEGUMINOSAE	Species *Melilotus officinalis*	Local name Yellow Sweet Clover

MELILOT

This biennial has weakly upright stems, a compound leaf of three finely toothed leaflets, conspicuous stipules at the stem junction, and slender stalks of honey-scented flowers. • **USES** The leaves and seeds flavor Gruyere cheese and Polish vodka, flower nectar yields quality honey, the dried leaf yields scent, and the seeds are antibiotic. A leaf tea soothes indigestion, headaches, insomnia, and muscle stress and is used as a mild sedative. A leaf poultice is antiseptic. Melilot is given as a blood tonic for varicose veins and to reduce thrombosis risk, and it may treat lymphoedema. It is made into an anticoagulant.

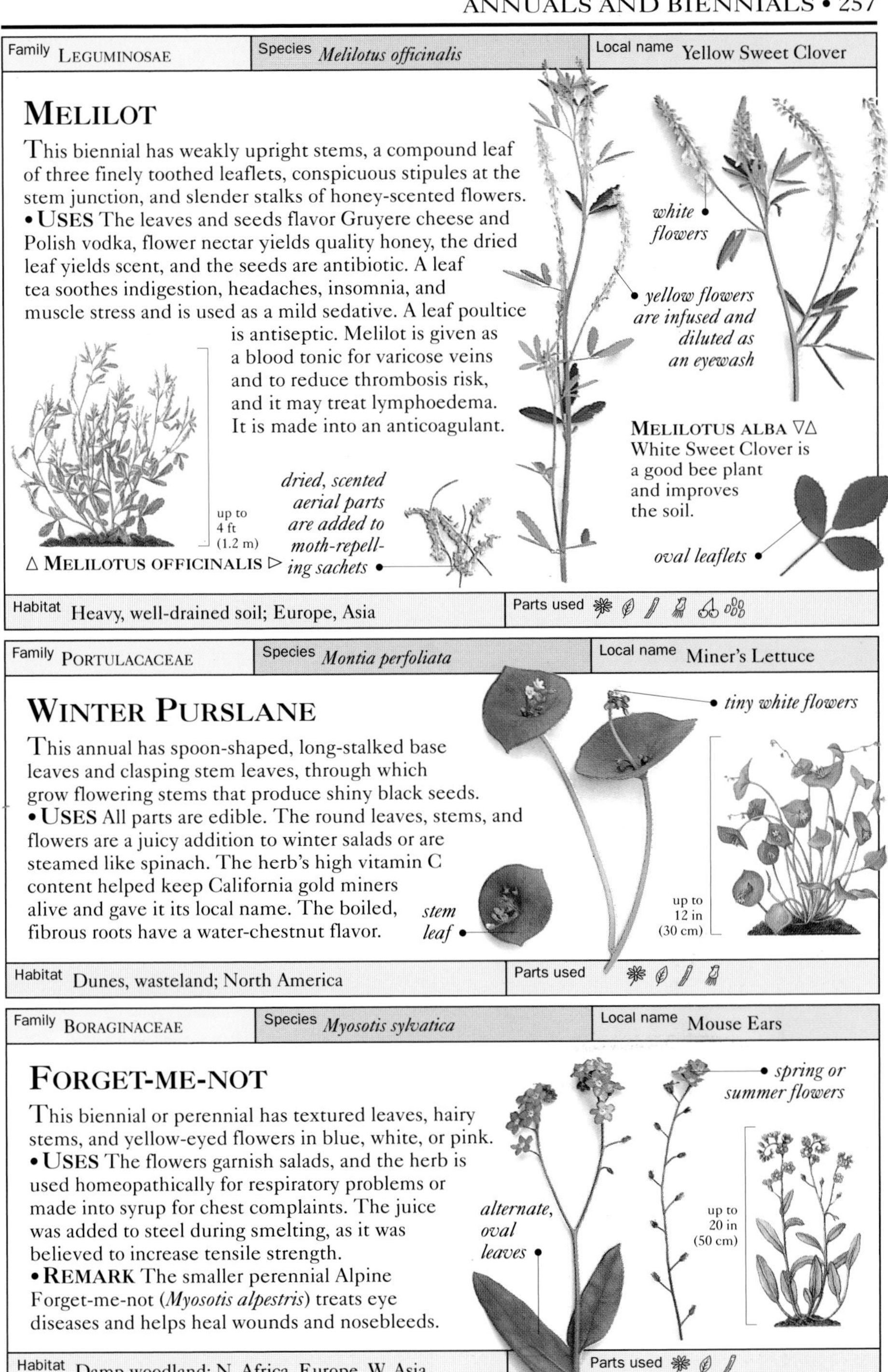

up to 4 ft (1.2 m)
△ MELILOTUS OFFICINALIS ▷
dried, scented aerial parts are added to moth-repelling sachets
white flowers
yellow flowers are infused and diluted as an eyewash
oval leaflets
tiny white flowers
up to 12 in (30 cm)
stem leaf
spring or summer flowers
alternate, oval leaves
up to 20 in (50 cm)

MELILOTUS ALBA ▽△
White Sweet Clover is a good bee plant and improves the soil.

Habitat Heavy, well-drained soil; Europe, Asia	Parts used

Family PORTULACACEAE	Species *Montia perfoliata*	Local name Miner's Lettuce

WINTER PURSLANE

This annual has spoon-shaped, long-stalked base leaves and clasping stem leaves, through which grow flowering stems that produce shiny black seeds. • **USES** All parts are edible. The round leaves, stems, and flowers are a juicy addition to winter salads or are steamed like spinach. The herb's high vitamin C content helped keep California gold miners alive and gave it its local name. The boiled, fibrous roots have a water-chestnut flavor.

Habitat Dunes, wasteland; North America	Parts used

Family BORAGINACEAE	Species *Myosotis sylvatica*	Local name Mouse Ears

FORGET-ME-NOT

This biennial or perennial has textured leaves, hairy stems, and yellow-eyed flowers in blue, white, or pink. • **USES** The flowers garnish salads, and the herb is used homeopathically for respiratory problems or made into syrup for chest complaints. The juice was added to steel during smelting, as it was believed to increase tensile strength.
• **REMARK** The smaller perennial Alpine Forget-me-not (*Myosotis alpestris*) treats eye diseases and helps heal wounds and nosebleeds.

Habitat Damp woodland; N. Africa, Europe, W. Asia	Parts used

Family SOLANACEAE	Species *Nicandra physaloides*	Local name Apple of Peru

SHOO-FLY

This free-branching annual has large, oval leaves with wavy or toothed margins. The bell-shaped, lilac blue flowers become papery pods, each containing a berry, with seeds capable of dormancy for decades.

• **USES** Shoo-Fly is grown for its decorative flowers and seed pods and because it may repel flies when growing in confined spaces. More successfully, the leaf is applied as an insecticide to kill flies.

• **REMARK** The leaves of the Shoo-Fly are used to eradicate head lice.

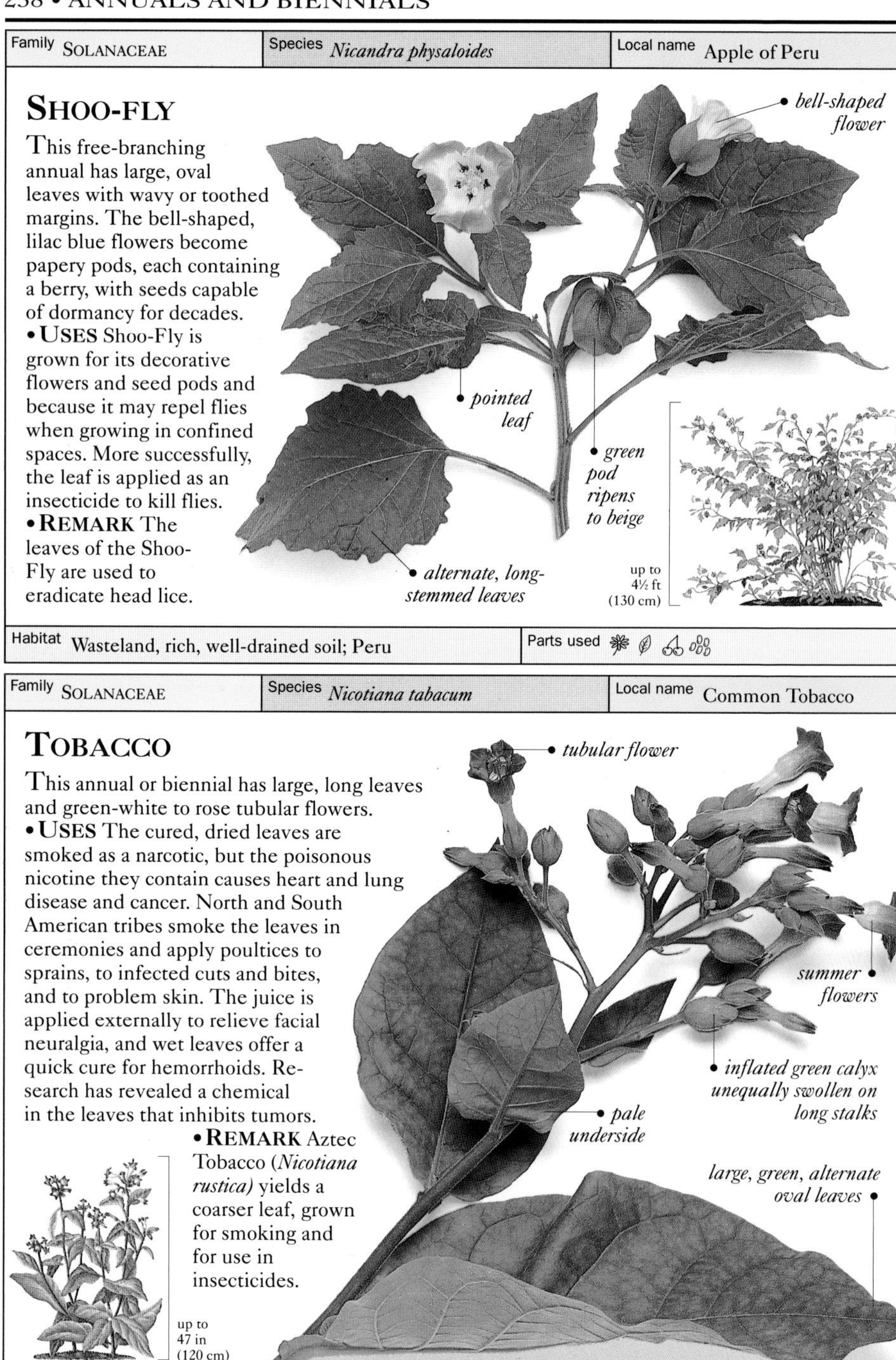

bell-shaped flower
pointed leaf
green pod ripens to beige
alternate, long-stemmed leaves
up to 4½ ft (130 cm)
tubular flower
summer flowers
inflated green calyx unequally swollen on long stalks
pale underside
large, green, alternate oval leaves
up to 47 in (120 cm)

Habitat Wasteland, rich, well-drained soil; Peru | Parts used

Family SOLANACEAE	Species *Nicotiana tabacum*	Local name Common Tobacco

TOBACCO

This annual or biennial has large, long leaves and green-white to rose tubular flowers.

• **USES** The cured, dried leaves are smoked as a narcotic, but the poisonous nicotine they contain causes heart and lung disease and cancer. North and South American tribes smoke the leaves in ceremonies and apply poultices to sprains, to infected cuts and bites, and to problem skin. The juice is applied externally to relieve facial neuralgia, and wet leaves offer a quick cure for hemorrhoids. Research has revealed a chemical in the leaves that inhibits tumors.

• **REMARK** Aztec Tobacco (*Nicotiana rustica)* yields a coarser leaf, grown for smoking and for use in insecticides.

Habitat Rich soil; N.E. Argentina, Bolivia | Parts used

Family RANUNCULACEAE	Species *Nigella sativa*	Local name Roman Coriander

NIGELLA

This annual has feathery foliage, gray-blue flowers, and inflated pods of black seeds.

• **USES** The strawberry-scented seeds have a peppery nutmeg taste popular in India, Egypt, Greece, and Turkey. Fresh or dry roasted Nigella seeds flavor curries, vegetables, and pulses. In India, they are used to repel insects from clothes and are given to treat intestinal worms and nerve defects, to reduce flatulence, induce sweating, and stimulate breast milk.

• **REMARK** The warm, ground seed was once used in sweet powders and sniffed to restore a lost sense of smell.

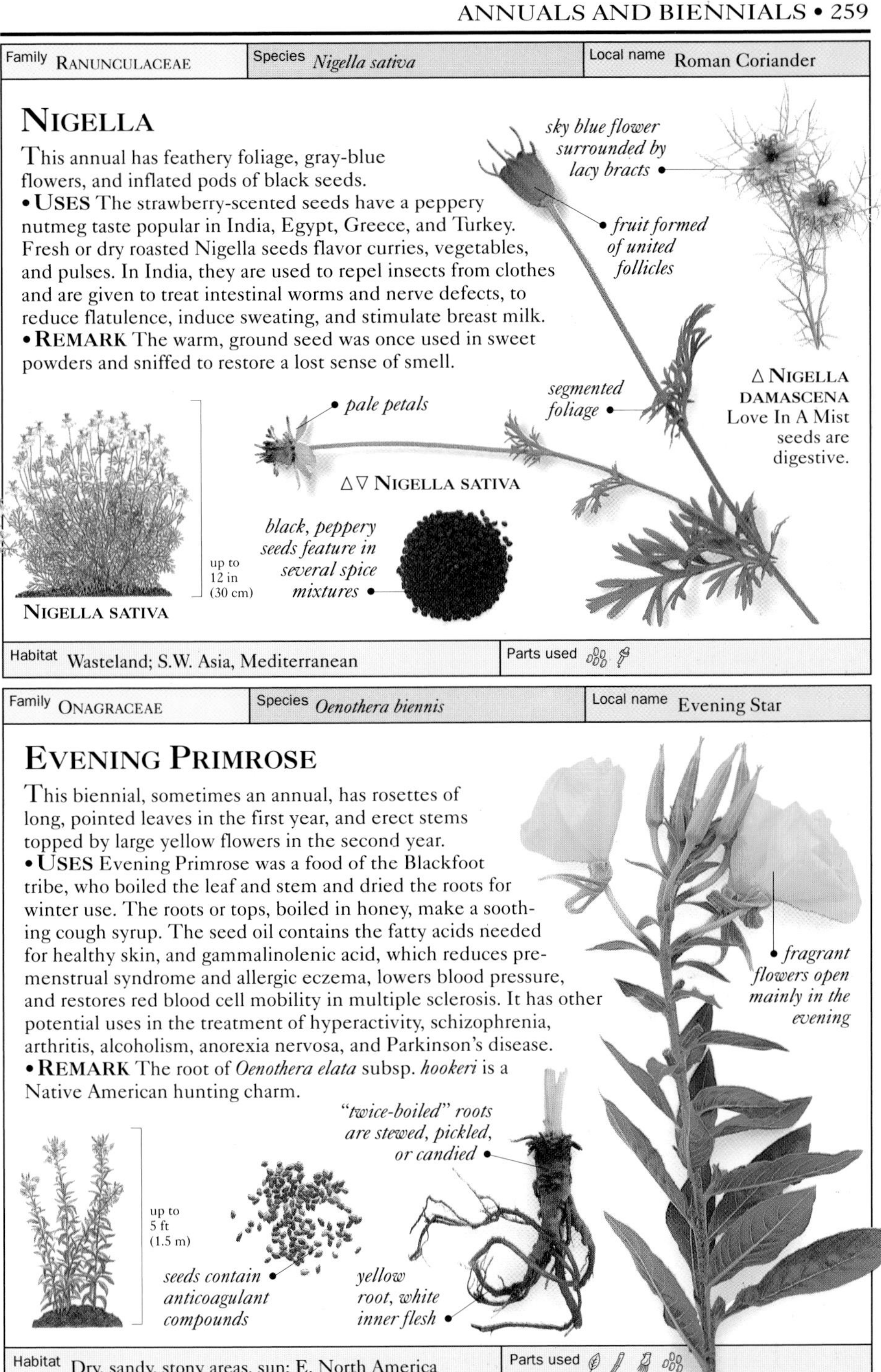
sky blue flower surrounded by lacy bracts
fruit formed of united follicles
segmented foliage
pale petals
△ NIGELLA DAMASCENA Love In A Mist seeds are digestive.
△▽ NIGELLA SATIVA
black, peppery seeds feature in several spice mixtures
up to 12 in (30 cm)
NIGELLA SATIVA

Habitat Wasteland; S.W. Asia, Mediterranean	Parts used

Family ONAGRACEAE	Species *Oenothera biennis*	Local name Evening Star

EVENING PRIMROSE

This biennial, sometimes an annual, has rosettes of long, pointed leaves in the first year, and erect stems topped by large yellow flowers in the second year.

• **USES** Evening Primrose was a food of the Blackfoot tribe, who boiled the leaf and stem and dried the roots for winter use. The roots or tops, boiled in honey, make a soothing cough syrup. The seed oil contains the fatty acids needed for healthy skin, and gammalinolenic acid, which reduces premenstrual syndrome and allergic eczema, lowers blood pressure, and restores red blood cell mobility in multiple sclerosis. It has other potential uses in the treatment of hyperactivity, schizophrenia, arthritis, alcoholism, anorexia nervosa, and Parkinson's disease.

• **REMARK** The root of *Oenothera elata* subsp. *hookeri* is a Native American hunting charm.

fragrant flowers open mainly in the evening
"twice-boiled" roots are stewed, pickled, or candied
up to 5 ft (1.5 m)
seeds contain anticoagulant compounds
yellow root, white inner flesh

Habitat Dry, sandy, stony areas, sun; E. North America	Parts used

Family LABIATAE	Species *Ocimum basilicum*	Local name Garden Basil / Tulsi

SWEET BASIL

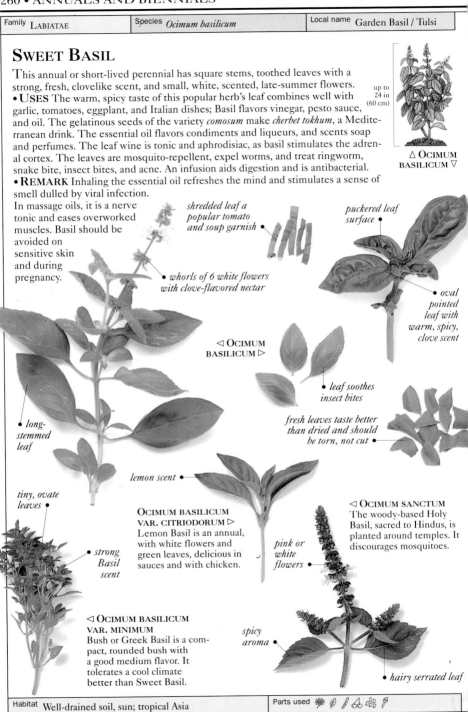

This annual or short-lived perennial has square stems, toothed leaves with a strong, fresh, clovelike scent, and small, white, scented, late-summer flowers.
• **USES** The warm, spicy taste of this popular herb's leaf combines well with garlic, tomatoes, eggplant, and Italian dishes; Basil flavors vinegar, pesto sauce, and oil. The gelatinous seeds of the variety *comosum* make *cherbet tokhum*, a Mediterranean drink. The essential oil flavors condiments and liqueurs, and scents soap and perfumes. The leaf wine is tonic and aphrodisiac, as basil stimulates the adrenal cortex. The leaves are mosquito-repellent, expel worms, and treat ringworm, snake bite, insect bites, and acne. An infusion aids digestion and is antibacterial.
• **REMARK** Inhaling the essential oil refreshes the mind and stimulates a sense of smell dulled by viral infection. In massage oils, it is a nerve tonic and eases overworked muscles. Basil should be avoided on sensitive skin and during pregnancy.

up to 24 in (60 cm)

△ OCIMUM BASILICUM ▽

shredded leaf a popular tomato and soup garnish

puckered leaf surface

whorls of 6 white flowers with clove-flavored nectar

oval pointed leaf with warm, spicy, clove scent

◁ OCIMUM BASILICUM ▷

leaf soothes insect bites

long-stemmed leaf

fresh leaves taste better than dried and should be torn, not cut

lemon scent

tiny, ovate leaves

OCIMUM BASILICUM VAR. CITRIODORUM ▷
Lemon Basil is an annual, with white flowers and green leaves, delicious in sauces and with chicken.

◁ OCIMUM SANCTUM
The woody-based Holy Basil, sacred to Hindus, is planted around temples. It discourages mosquitoes.

strong Basil scent

pink or white flowers

◁ OCIMUM BASILICUM VAR. MINIMUM
Bush or Greek Basil is a compact, rounded bush with a good medium flavor. It tolerates a cool climate better than Sweet Basil.

spicy aroma

hairy serrated leaf

Habitat Well-drained soil, sun; tropical Asia	Parts used

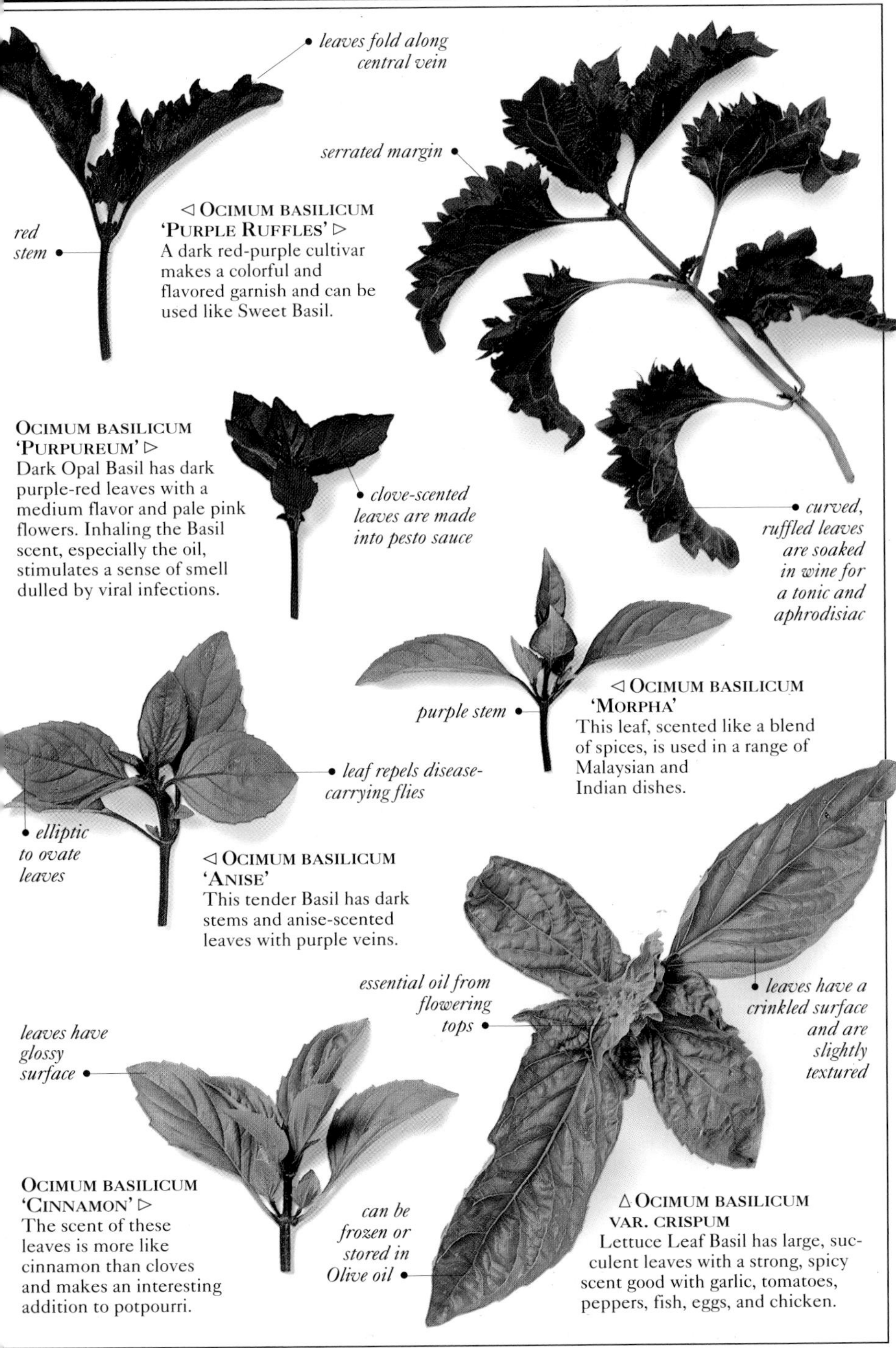
leaves fold along central vein
serrated margin
red stem
clove-scented leaves are made into pesto sauce
curved, ruffled leaves are soaked in wine for a tonic and aphrodisiac
purple stem
leaf repels disease-carrying flies
elliptic to ovate leaves
essential oil from flowering tops
leaves have a crinkled surface and are slightly textured
leaves have glossy surface
can be frozen or stored in Olive oil

◁ OCIMUM BASILICUM 'PURPLE RUFFLES' ▷
A dark red-purple cultivar makes a colorful and flavored garnish and can be used like Sweet Basil.

OCIMUM BASILICUM 'PURPUREUM' ▷
Dark Opal Basil has dark purple-red leaves with a medium flavor and pale pink flowers. Inhaling the Basil scent, especially the oil, stimulates a sense of smell dulled by viral infections.

◁ OCIMUM BASILICUM 'MORPHA'
This leaf, scented like a blend of spices, is used in a range of Malaysian and Indian dishes.

◁ OCIMUM BASILICUM 'ANISE'
This tender Basil has dark stems and anise-scented leaves with purple veins.

OCIMUM BASILICUM 'CINNAMON' ▷
The scent of these leaves is more like cinnamon than cloves and makes an interesting addition to potpourri.

△ OCIMUM BASILICUM VAR. CRISPUM
Lettuce Leaf Basil has large, succulent leaves with a strong, spicy scent good with garlic, tomatoes, peppers, fish, eggs, and chicken.

Family COMPOSITAE	Species *Onopordum acanthium*	Local name Cotton Thistle

SCOTCH THISTLE

This tall, imposing biennial has spiny winged stems, spiny, toothed leaves covered with fine white down, and thistle flower heads with purple-pink or white florets.

• **USES** The Scotch Thistle's large flower heads can be boiled or steamed and served with butter, after removing the outer bracts. The young stems are blanched and peeled, eaten raw with oil and vinegar, or steamed and eaten hot. The seeds once produced oil for cooking and lamps, and the down of leaves and stems was collected as pillow stuffing. The leaf juice was taken as a cancer treatment and applied to skin ulcers, and a root decoction was used to reduce mucus discharges.

• **REMARK** The Thistle is the emblem of Scotland.

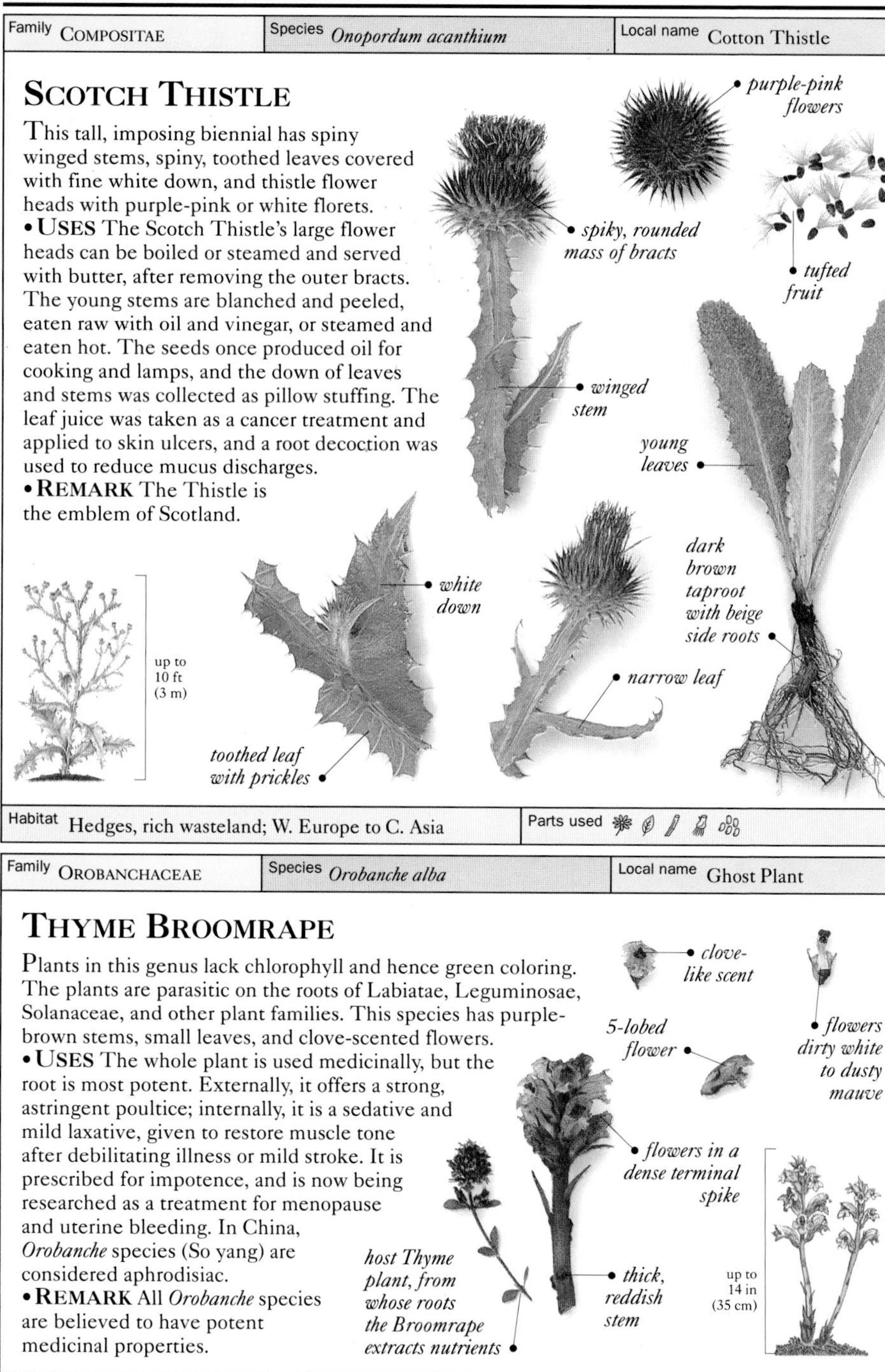
purple-pink flowers
spiky, rounded mass of bracts
tufted fruit
winged stem
young leaves
white down
dark brown taproot with beige side roots
narrow leaf
toothed leaf with prickles
up to 10 ft (3 m)
clove-like scent
5-lobed flower
flowers dirty white to dusty mauve
flowers in a dense terminal spike
host Thyme plant, from whose roots the Broomrape extracts nutrients
thick, reddish stem
up to 14 in (35 cm)

Habitat Hedges, rich wasteland; W. Europe to C. Asia	Parts used

Family OROBANCHACEAE	Species *Orobanche alba*	Local name Ghost Plant

THYME BROOMRAPE

Plants in this genus lack chlorophyll and hence green coloring. The plants are parasitic on the roots of Labiatae, Leguminosae, Solanaceae, and other plant families. This species has purple-brown stems, small leaves, and clove-scented flowers.

• **USES** The whole plant is used medicinally, but the root is most potent. Externally, it offers a strong, astringent poultice; internally, it is a sedative and mild laxative, given to restore muscle tone after debilitating illness or mild stroke. It is prescribed for impotence, and is now being researched as a treatment for menopause and uterine bleeding. In China, *Orobanche* species (So yang) are considered aphrodisiac.

• **REMARK** All *Orobanche* species are believed to have potent medicinal properties.

Habitat Temperate, rocky regions on shrubs; Europe, China	Parts used

Family GRAMINEAE	Species *Oryza sativa*	Local name Ine

RICE

This annual has long, narrow leaf blades and arching stems carrying grouped spikelets of grains encased in husks.

• **USES** Easily digested, Rice is the staple diet of half the world; it comes long-, medium-, or short-grained. Rice *congee* (porridge) counters heavy feasting and is a cooling dish with medicinal uses. Rice is fermented into *sake* (Rice wine). Rice flour is a face powder base, the roots treat fever sweating, and the sprouts relieve indigestion and strengthen the stomach and spleen. The straw is made into hats.

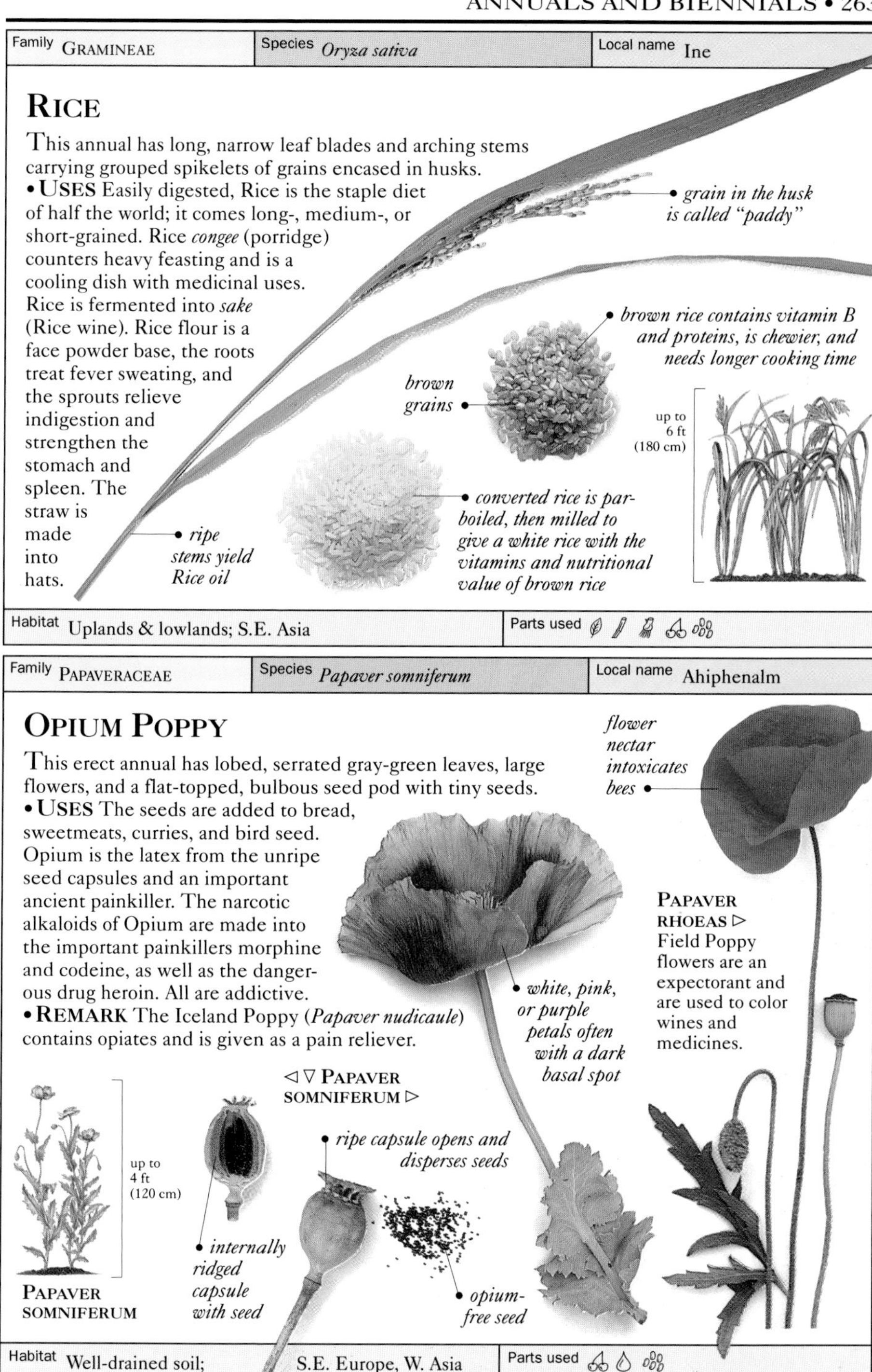

grain in the husk is called "paddy"
brown rice contains vitamin B and proteins, is chewier, and needs longer cooking time
brown grains
up to 6 ft (180 cm)
converted rice is par-boiled, then milled to give a white rice with the vitamins and nutritional value of brown rice
ripe stems yield Rice oil
flower nectar intoxicates bees
white, pink, or purple petals often with a dark basal spot
ripe capsule opens and disperses seeds
up to 4 ft (120 cm)
internally ridged capsule with seed
opium-free seed

Habitat Uplands & lowlands; S.E. Asia	Parts used

Family PAPAVERACEAE	Species *Papaver somniferum*	Local name Ahiphenalm

OPIUM POPPY

This erect annual has lobed, serrated gray-green leaves, large flowers, and a flat-topped, bulbous seed pod with tiny seeds.

• **USES** The seeds are added to bread, sweetmeats, curries, and bird seed. Opium is the latex from the unripe seed capsules and an important ancient painkiller. The narcotic alkaloids of Opium are made into the important painkillers morphine and codeine, as well as the dangerous drug heroin. All are addictive.

• **REMARK** The Iceland Poppy (*Papaver nudicaule*) contains opiates and is given as a pain reliever.

PAPAVER RHOEAS ▷ Field Poppy flowers are an expectorant and are used to color wines and medicines.

◁ ▽ PAPAVER SOMNIFERUM ▷

PAPAVER SOMNIFERUM

Habitat Well-drained soil; S.E. Europe, W. Asia	Parts used

Family UMBELLIFERAE	Species *Petroselinium crispum*	Local name Persil

PARSLEY

Parsley is a taprooted biennial with solid stems of triangular, toothed, and curled leaves divided into three segments, umbels of tiny cream summer flowers, and aromatic "seeds."

• **USES** Vitamin- and mineral-rich leaves and stems are added to salads and savory dishes. Parsley is used in *bouquet garni* and eaten to freshen breath. Leaf infusions are a tonic for hair, skin, and eyes. The leaves are eaten as a vegetable in the Middle East. The root is used in soups and stews. The leaves, root, and seeds are diuretic, scavenge skin-aging free radicals, and reduce the release of histamine. They relieve rheumatism, aid digestion, and tone uterine muscles after birth. Leaf poultices soothe sprains and cuts.

• **REMARK** Grown near roses, it improves their health and scent.

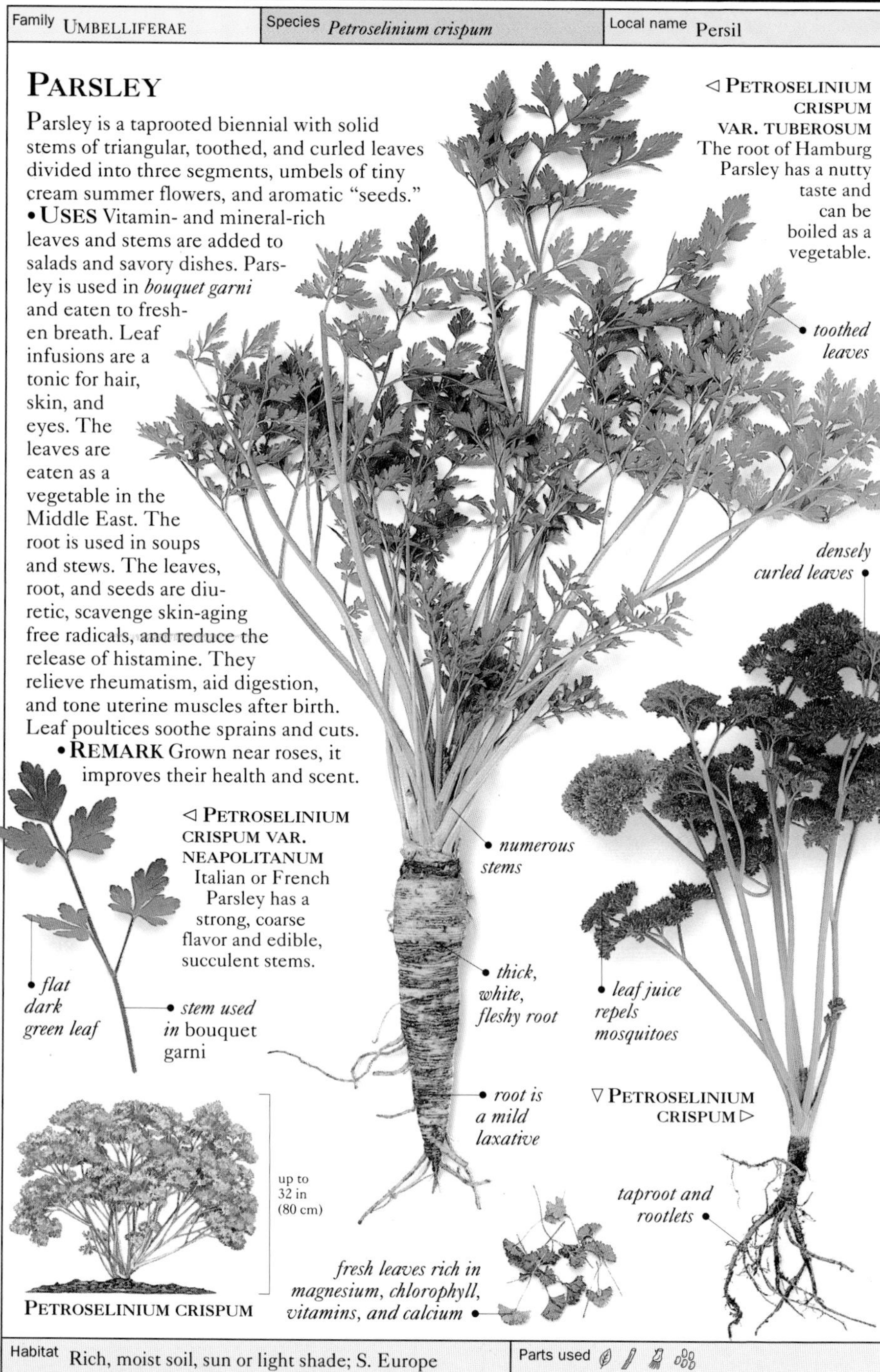
◁ PETROSELINIUM CRISPUM VAR. TUBEROSUM
The root of Hamburg Parsley has a nutty taste and can be boiled as a vegetable.
toothed leaves
densely curled leaves
numerous stems
thick, white, fleshy root
root is a mild laxative
leaf juice repels mosquitoes
▽ PETROSELINIUM CRISPUM ▷
taproot and rootlets
◁ PETROSELINIUM CRISPUM VAR. NEAPOLITANUM
Italian or French Parsley has a strong, coarse flavor and edible, succulent stems.
flat dark green leaf
stem used in bouquet garni
up to 32 in (80 cm)
fresh leaves rich in magnesium, chlorophyll, vitamins, and calcium

PETROSELINIUM CRISPUM

Habitat Rich, moist soil, sun or light shade; S. Europe	Parts used

Family HYDROPHYLLACEAE	Species *Phacelia tanacetifolia*	Local name Fiddleneck

TANSY PHACELIA

This annual is covered in minute stiff hairs. It has segmented leaves and dense curled cymes of nectar-rich, lavender-blue flowers.

• **USES** Tansy Phacelia is planted in rows between crops as the nectar feeds aphid-eating hoverflies; it also attracts pollinating bees. The nectar of Tansy Phacelia yields delicious honey. In autumn, the plant is plowed back into the soil as "green manure."

• **REMARK** This combination of Tansy Phacelia's virtues reduces the need for chemical insecticides and fertilizer. Plantings may also replace nutrients being taken from the soil.

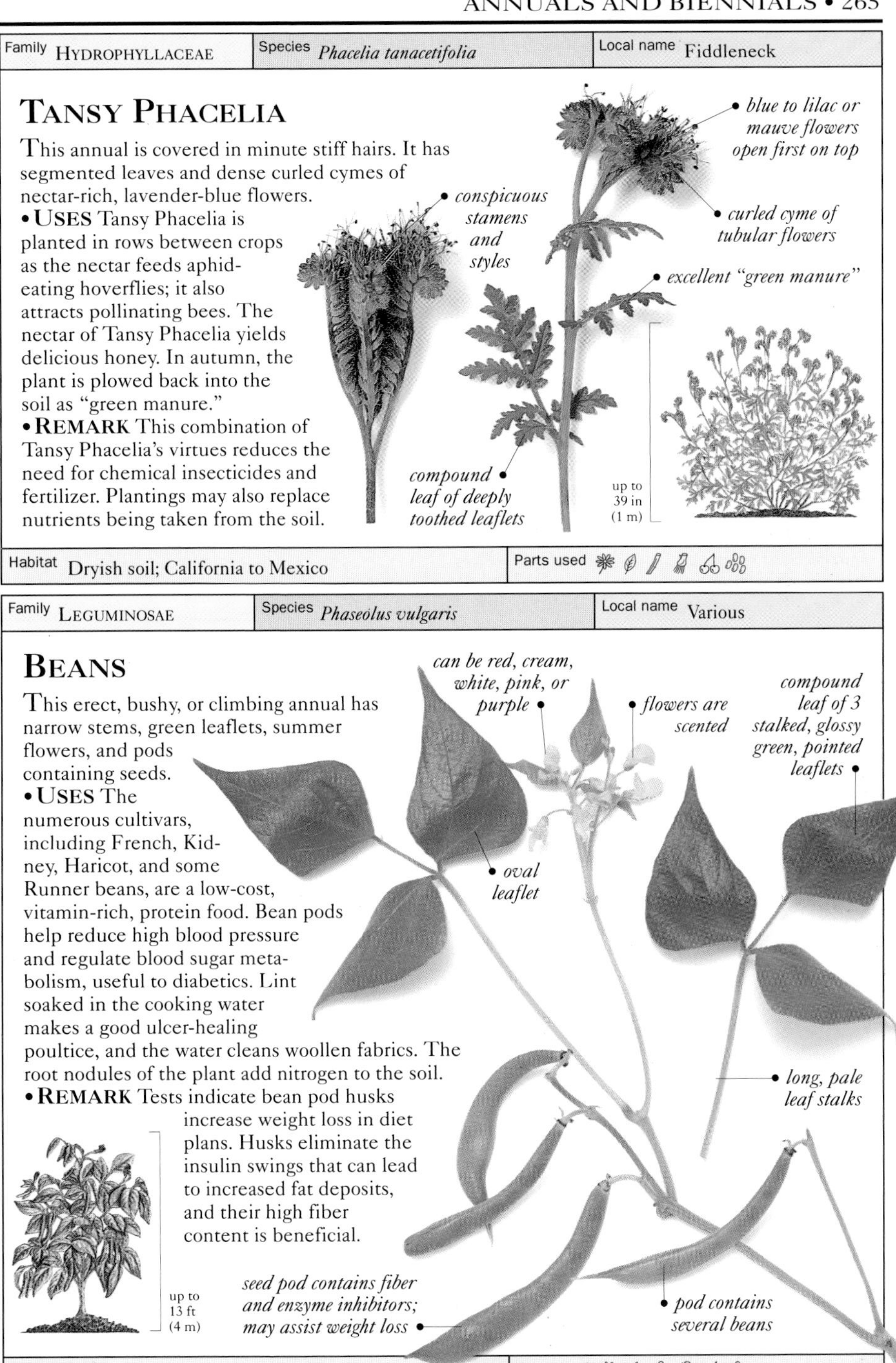

conspicuous stamens and styles
blue to lilac or mauve flowers open first on top
curled cyme of tubular flowers
excellent "green manure"
compound leaf of deeply toothed leaflets
up to 39 in (1 m)
can be red, cream, white, pink, or purple
flowers are scented
compound leaf of 3 stalked, glossy green, pointed leaflets
oval leaflet
long, pale leaf stalks
seed pod contains fiber and enzyme inhibitors; may assist weight loss
pod contains several beans
up to 13 ft (4 m)

Habitat Dryish soil; California to Mexico	Parts used

Family LEGUMINOSAE	Species *Phaseolus vulgaris*	Local name Various

BEANS

This erect, bushy, or climbing annual has narrow stems, green leaflets, summer flowers, and pods containing seeds.

• **USES** The numerous cultivars, including French, Kidney, Haricot, and some Runner beans, are a low-cost, vitamin-rich, protein food. Bean pods help reduce high blood pressure and regulate blood sugar metabolism, useful to diabetics. Lint soaked in the cooking water makes a good ulcer-healing poultice, and the water cleans woollen fabrics. The root nodules of the plant add nitrogen to the soil.

• **REMARK** Tests indicate bean pod husks increase weight loss in diet plans. Husks eliminate the insulin swings that can lead to increased fat deposits, and their high fiber content is beneficial.

Habitat Sun, good soil; Tropical Americas	Parts used

Family UMBELLIFERAE	Species *Pimpinella anisum*	Local name Aniseed

ANISE

Anise has sweetly aromatic leaves, rounded at the base and narrower on the stem, with umbels of flowers followed by aromatic fruits.

• **USES** Popular in European, Arabic, and Indian cooking, whole or crushed seeds add sweet, spicy flavor to desserts, candies, pickles, curries, and spirits such as *Pernod*, *Anisette*, *Ricard*, *ouzo*, and *arrak*. The flowers and leaves are used in fruit salads, the stem and roots in sweet soups. In cooking or infused as a tea, the seeds aid digestion, quell nausea, and ease flatulence and colic. Anise is used in cough mixtures, as it is expectorant and soothes spasms of irritant coughs and bronchial problems. It promotes estrogen production and is used to encourage breast milk, ease childbirth, and stimulate libido. In tests, it has significantly increased liver regeneration in rats.

• **REMARK** Tiny amounts of the essential oil, produced from the seeds, are added to toothpastes, perfumes, and mouthwashes, and are used to mask bitter medicines, but in large amounts Anise is highly toxic.

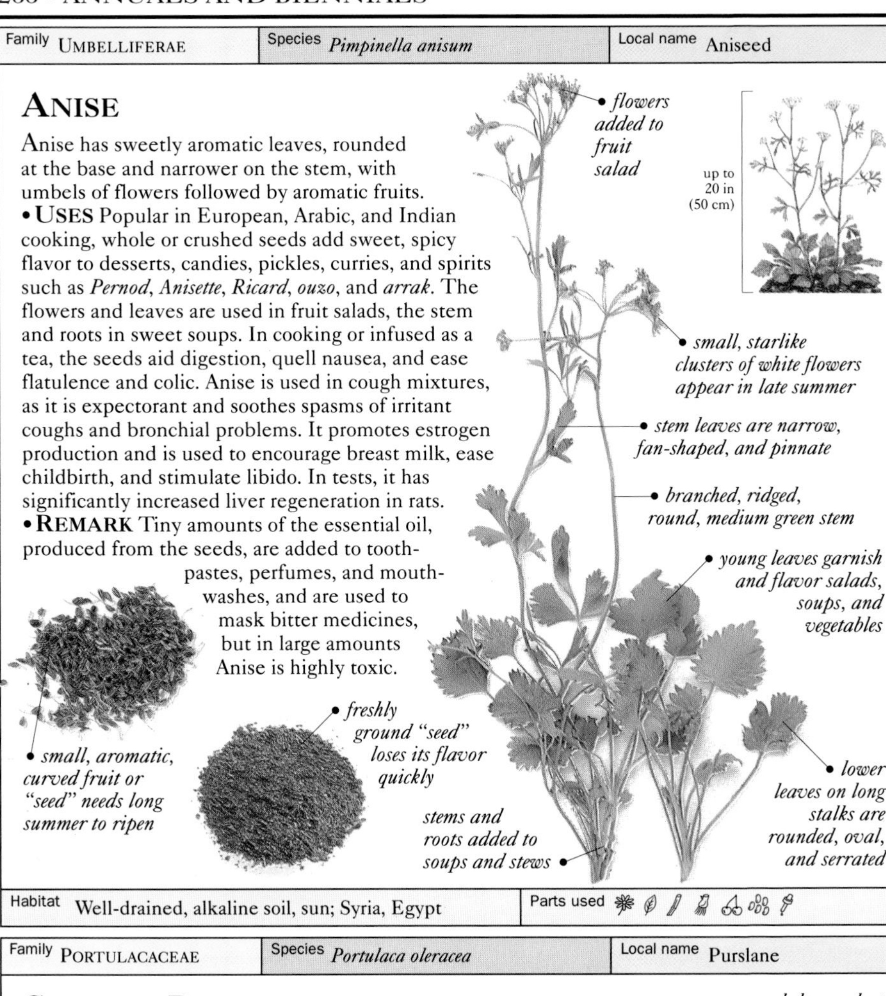
flowers added to fruit salad
up to 20 in (50 cm)
small, starlike clusters of white flowers appear in late summer
stem leaves are narrow, fan-shaped, and pinnate
branched, ridged, round, medium green stem
young leaves garnish and flavor salads, soups, and vegetables
freshly ground "seed" loses its flavor quickly
small, aromatic, curved fruit or "seed" needs long summer to ripen
stems and roots added to soups and stews
lower leaves on long stalks are rounded, oval, and serrated

Habitat Well-drained, alkaline soil, sun; Syria, Egypt	Parts used

Family PORTULACACEAE	Species *Portulaca oleracea*	Local name Purslane

SUMMER PURSLANE

This annual has thick, fleshy pink to green stems, succulent leaves, and bright yellow midsummer flowers with sensitive stamens.

• **USES** Rich in iron and vitamin C, the crunchy, cooling leaves and stems blend well with spicier salad herbs. They make a succulent pickle and are cooked as a vegetable and are added to soups. The dried seed is ground and added to flour. In China, the whole plant is given for diarrhea and urinary infections and to reduce fevers. In Indonesia, it is prescribed for cardiac weakness, and the seed and fruit for breathing difficulties. The juice treats skin diseases.

rounded, succulent leaves

leaves make a soothing, cooling poultice

up to 12 in (30 cm)

small, easily spreading roots make the plant mat-forming

Habitat Well-drained light soil, shelter, sun; India, Eurasia	Parts used

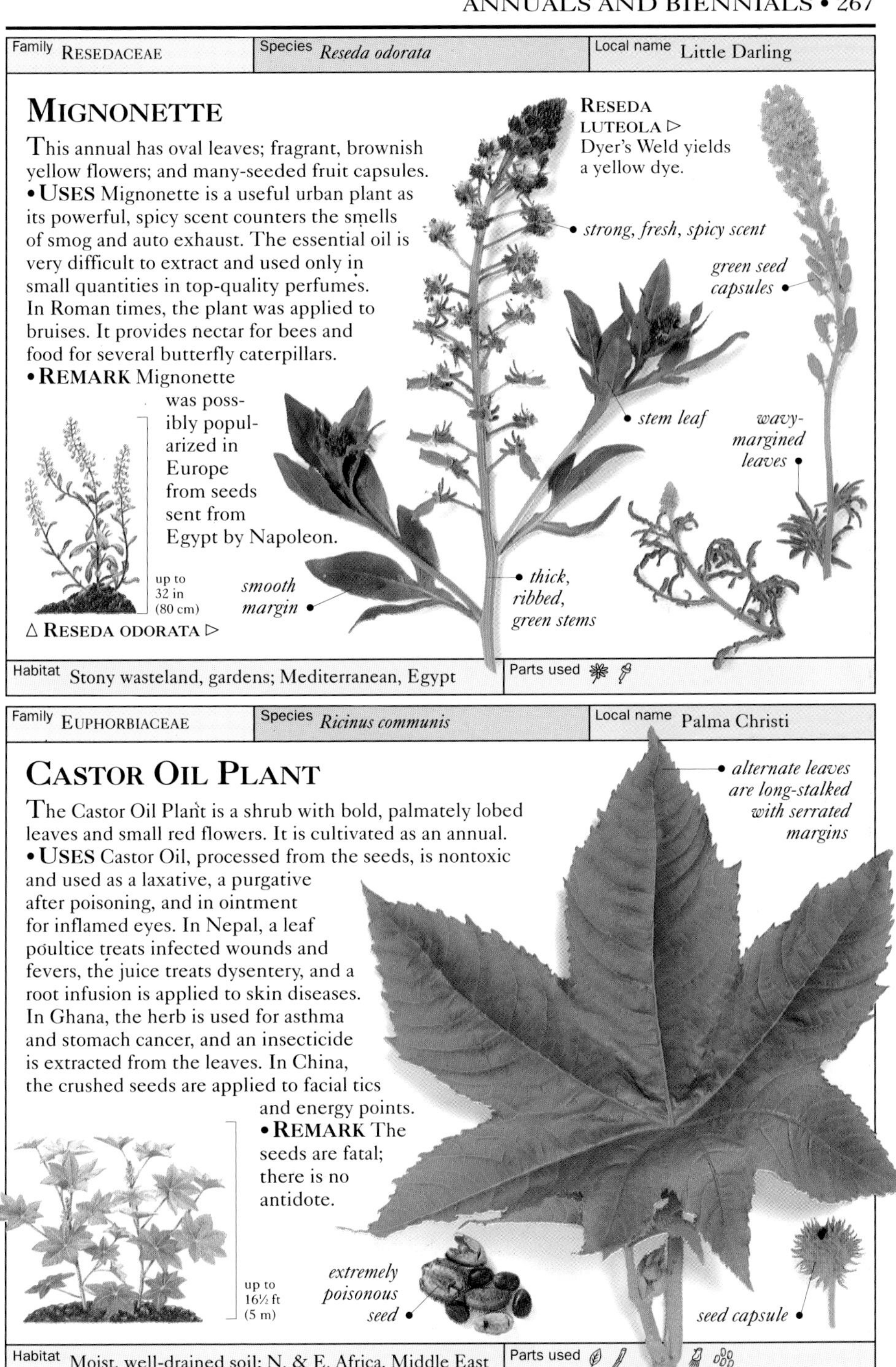
strong, fresh, spicy scent
green seed capsules
stem leaf
wavy-margined leaves
thick, ribbed, green stems
smooth margin
up to 32 in (80 cm)
alternate leaves are long-stalked with serrated margins
extremely poisonous seed
seed capsule
up to 16½ ft (5 m)

Family RESEDACEAE | Species *Reseda odorata* | Local name Little Darling

MIGNONETTE

This annual has oval leaves; fragrant, brownish yellow flowers; and many-seeded fruit capsules.

• **USES** Mignonette is a useful urban plant as its powerful, spicy scent counters the smells of smog and auto exhaust. The essential oil is very difficult to extract and used only in small quantities in top-quality perfumes. In Roman times, the plant was applied to bruises. It provides nectar for bees and food for several butterfly caterpillars.

• **REMARK** Mignonette was possibly popularized in Europe from seeds sent from Egypt by Napoleon.

△ RESEDA ODORATA ▷

RESEDA LUTEOLA ▷ Dyer's Weld yields a yellow dye.

Habitat Stony wasteland, gardens; Mediterranean, Egypt | Parts used

Family EUPHORBIACEAE | Species *Ricinus communis* | Local name Palma Christi

CASTOR OIL PLANT

The Castor Oil Plant is a shrub with bold, palmately lobed leaves and small red flowers. It is cultivated as an annual.

• **USES** Castor Oil, processed from the seeds, is nontoxic and used as a laxative, a purgative after poisoning, and in ointment for inflamed eyes. In Nepal, a leaf poultice treats infected wounds and fevers, the juice treats dysentery, and a root infusion is applied to skin diseases. In Ghana, the herb is used for asthma and stomach cancer, and an insecticide is extracted from the leaves. In China, the crushed seeds are applied to facial tics and energy points.

• **REMARK** The seeds are fatal; there is no antidote.

Habitat Moist, well-drained soil; N. & E. Africa, Middle East | Parts used

Family CHENOPODIACEAE	Species *Salicornia europaea*	Local name Marsh Samphire

GLASSWORT

This upright annual has woody brown stems and succulent, jointed branches. Minute green flowers appear in autumn.

• **USES** The juicy, salty, mineral-rich stems are like Samphire and are eaten when ripe and green. They can be pickled or eaten like asparagus: boiled and served hot with butter or cold with vinaigrette. Seeds were once ground into flour, and the whole plant was burned for its ash, barilla, used in glass- and soapmaking.

• **REMARK** Cattle relish its high salt content.

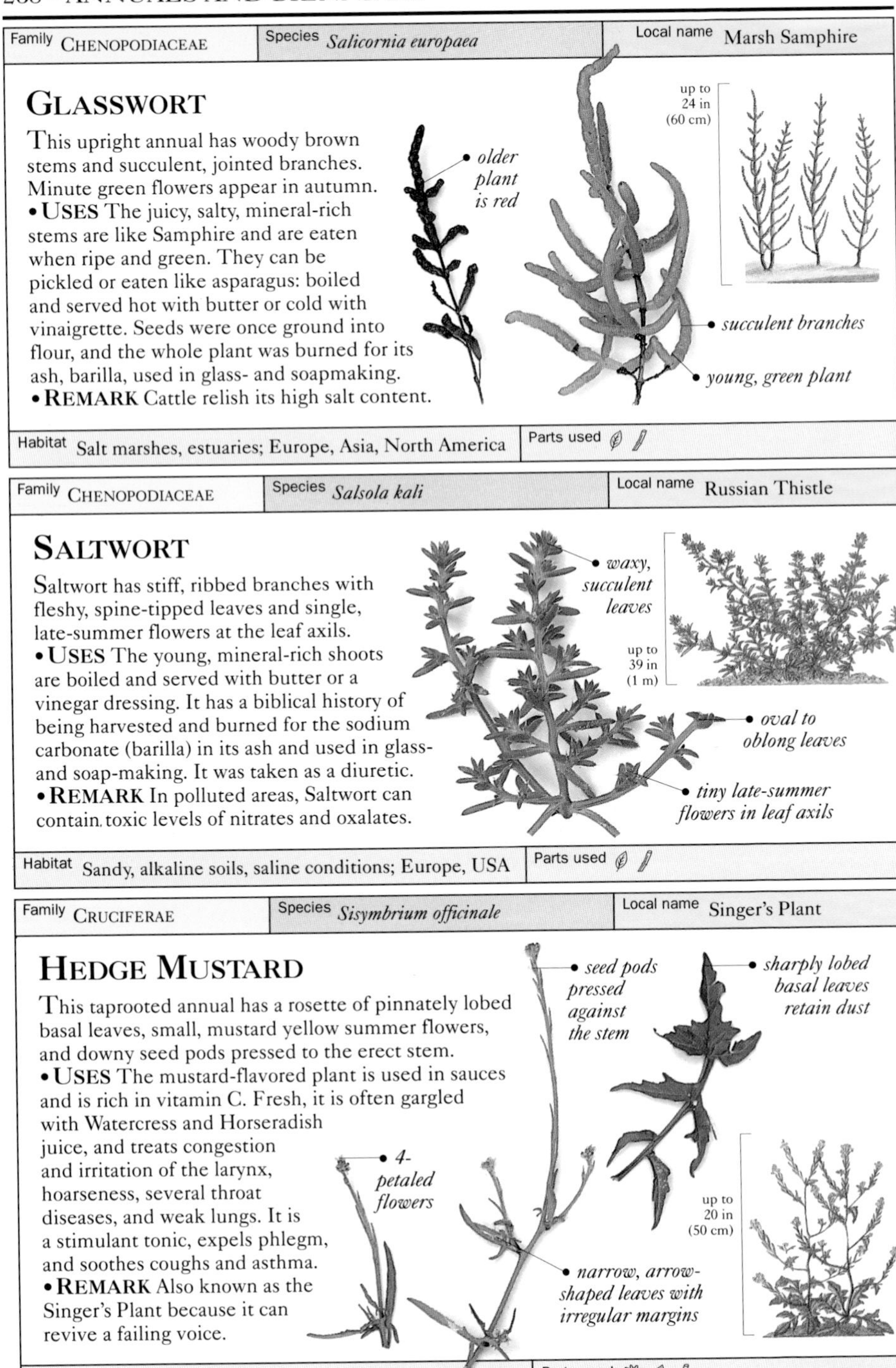
older plant is red
up to 24 in (60 cm)
succulent branches
young, green plant
waxy, succulent leaves
up to 39 in (1 m)
oval to oblong leaves
tiny late-summer flowers in leaf axils
seed pods pressed against the stem
sharply lobed basal leaves retain dust
4-petaled flowers
up to 20 in (50 cm)
narrow, arrow-shaped leaves with irregular margins

Habitat Salt marshes, estuaries; Europe, Asia, North America	Parts used

Family CHENOPODIACEAE	Species *Salsola kali*	Local name Russian Thistle

SALTWORT

Saltwort has stiff, ribbed branches with fleshy, spine-tipped leaves and single, late-summer flowers at the leaf axils.

• **USES** The young, mineral-rich shoots are boiled and served with butter or a vinegar dressing. It has a biblical history of being harvested and burned for the sodium carbonate (barilla) in its ash and used in glass- and soap-making. It was taken as a diuretic.

• **REMARK** In polluted areas, Saltwort can contain toxic levels of nitrates and oxalates.

Habitat Sandy, alkaline soils, saline conditions; Europe, USA	Parts used

Family CRUCIFERAE	Species *Sisymbrium officinale*	Local name Singer's Plant

HEDGE MUSTARD

This taprooted annual has a rosette of pinnately lobed basal leaves, small, mustard yellow summer flowers, and downy seed pods pressed to the erect stem.

• **USES** The mustard-flavored plant is used in sauces and is rich in vitamin C. Fresh, it is often gargled with Watercress and Horseradish juice, and treats congestion and irritation of the larynx, hoarseness, several throat diseases, and weak lungs. It is a stimulant tonic, expels phlegm, and soothes coughs and asthma.

• **REMARK** Also known as the Singer's Plant because it can revive a failing voice.

Habitat Wasteland; temperate Europe	Parts used

Family PEDALIACEAE	Species *Sesamum indicum*	Local name Bene / Til

SESAME

This annual has a single erect stem, oval leaves, a scented, tubular, purple to white flower in the leaf axils, and long seed capsules that burst when ripe.
• **USES** The nutritious nutty seed, enhanced by dry roasting, is sprinkled on bread, pastries, and stir-fries, and ground for halva and tahini paste. The aromatic seed oil, pressed and refined, is popular in Chinese cooking. It is used in margarine, sunscreens, ointments, and laxatives. In Indonesia, the leaves are given for vertigo, gonorrhea, and diarrhea. In China, seeds and oil treat weak kidneys and livers, coughs, rheumatism, paralysis, and incontinence. A cologne is made from the flowers.
• **REMARK** The oil is stable and will keep for years without turning rancid, even in hot climates.

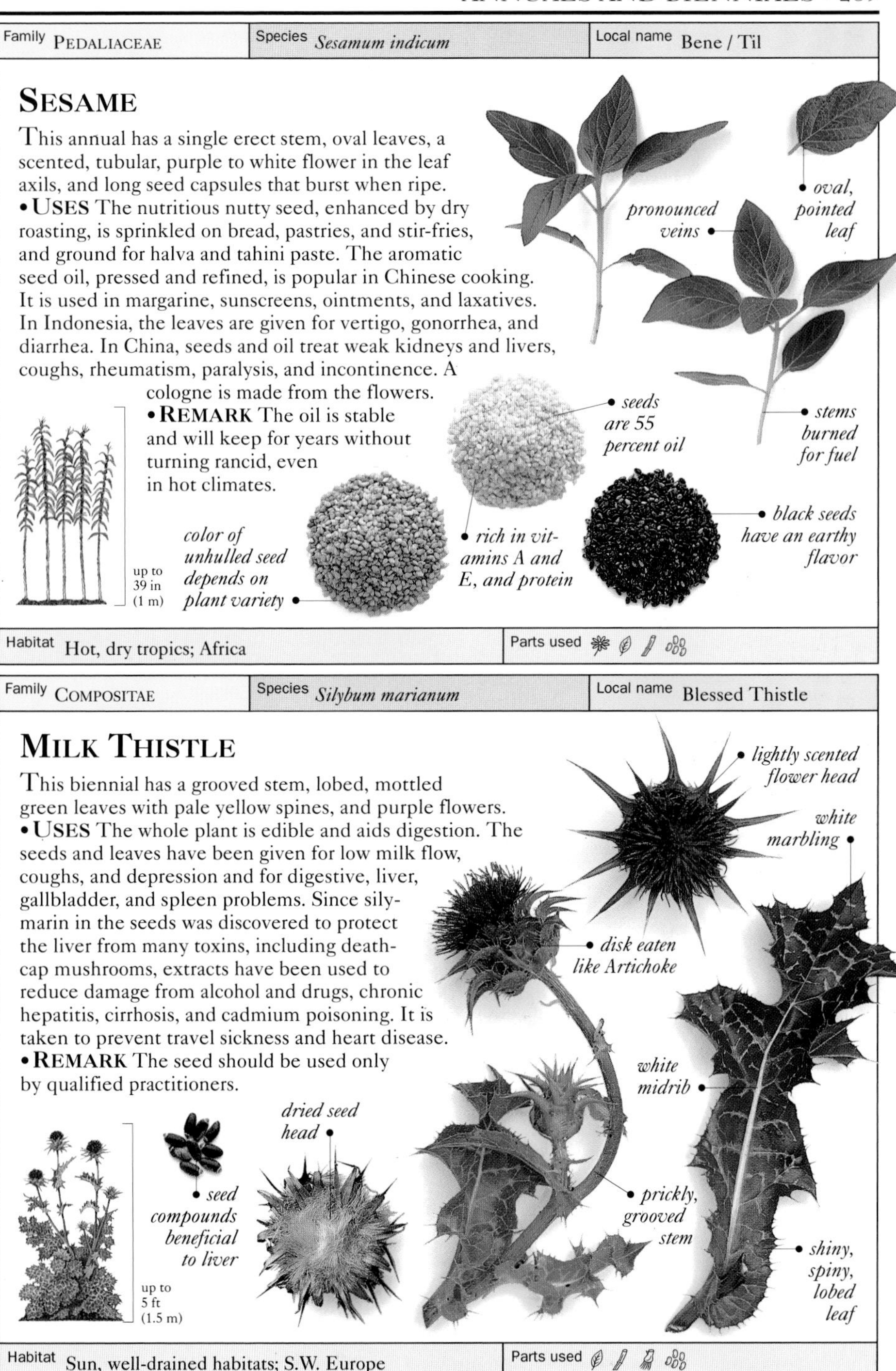
oval, pointed leaf
pronounced veins
seeds are 55 percent oil
stems burned for fuel
up to 39 in (1 m)
color of unhulled seed depends on plant variety
rich in vitamins A and E, and protein
black seeds have an earthy flavor
lightly scented flower head
white marbling
disk eaten like Artichoke
white midrib
dried seed head
seed compounds beneficial to liver
prickly, grooved stem
shiny, spiny, lobed leaf
up to 5 ft (1.5 m)

Habitat Hot, dry tropics; Africa	Parts used

Family COMPOSITAE	Species *Silybum marianum*	Local name Blessed Thistle

MILK THISTLE

This biennial has a grooved stem, lobed, mottled green leaves with pale yellow spines, and purple flowers.
• **USES** The whole plant is edible and aids digestion. The seeds and leaves have been given for low milk flow, coughs, and depression and for digestive, liver, gallbladder, and spleen problems. Since silymarin in the seeds was discovered to protect the liver from many toxins, including death-cap mushrooms, extracts have been used to reduce damage from alcohol and drugs, chronic hepatitis, cirrhosis, and cadmium poisoning. It is taken to prevent travel sickness and heart disease.
• **REMARK** The seed should be used only by qualified practitioners.

Habitat Sun, well-drained habitats; S.W. Europe	Parts used

Family UMBELLIFERAE	Species *Smyrnium olusatrum*	Local name Black Lovage

ALEXANDERS

This aromatic biennial has glossy, serrated-edged leaves and umbels of nectar-rich, yellow spring flowers, followed by dark fruits, or "seeds."
• **USES** Blanched young stems are steamed; the flowers are made into fritters; and tender leaves and pickled flower buds flavor fish dishes, salads, soups, and stews. The aromatic "seed" is ground as pepper or added to potpourri, and the parsnip-flavored root is boiled or candied. All parts promote appetite and aid digestion. The roots are mildly diuretic, the leaves supply vitamin C, the "seed" reduces spasms, and the plant juice is used to wash cuts.

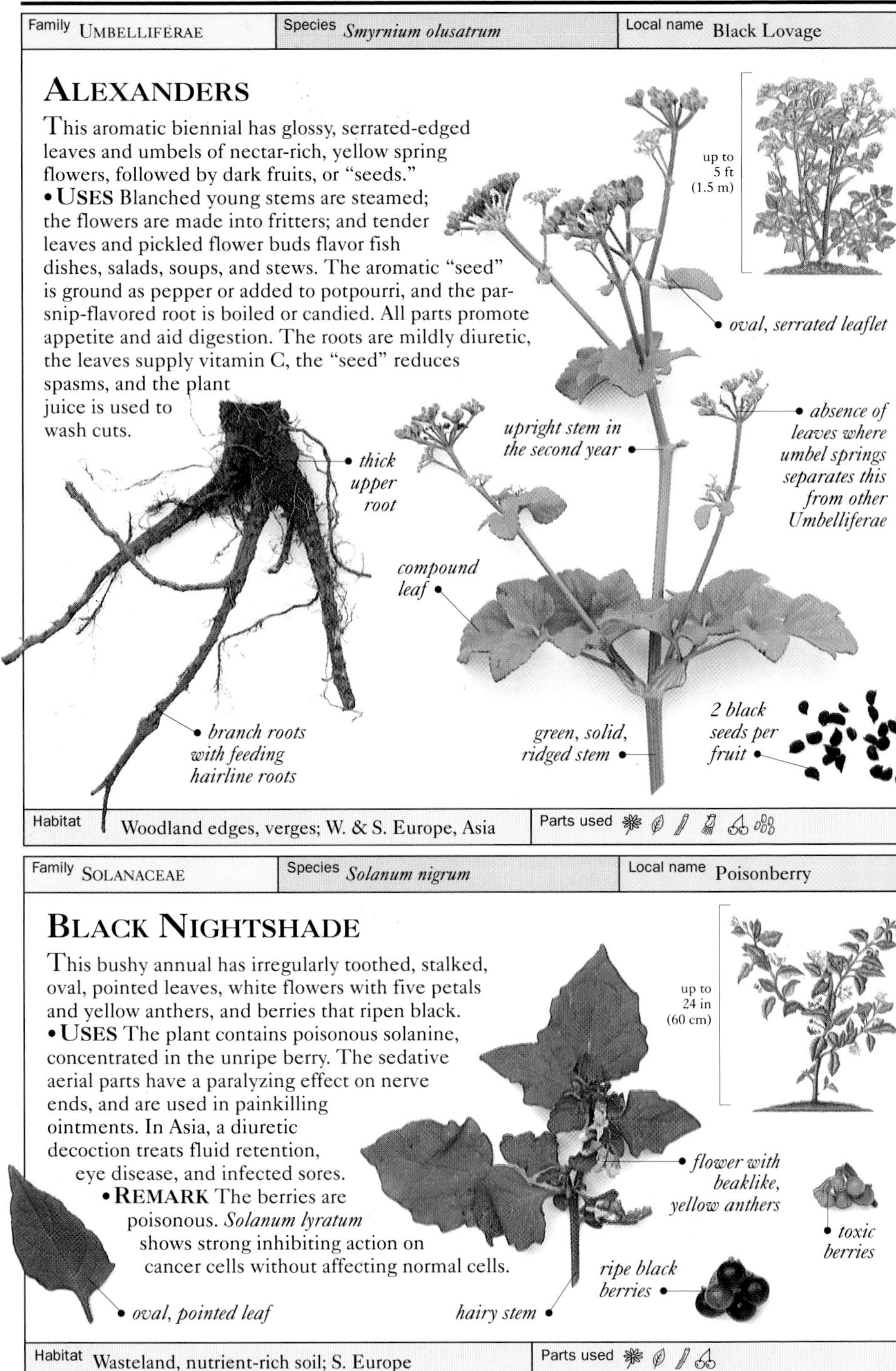
up to
5 ft
(1.5 m)
oval, serrated leaflet
absence of leaves where umbel springs separates this from other Umbelliferae
upright stem in the second year
thick upper root
compound leaf
branch roots with feeding hairline roots
green, solid, ridged stem
2 black seeds per fruit
up to
24 in
(60 cm)
flower with beaklike, yellow anthers
toxic berries
ripe black berries
oval, pointed leaf
hairy stem

Habitat Woodland edges, verges; W. & S. Europe, Asia	Parts used

Family SOLANACEAE	Species *Solanum nigrum*	Local name Poisonberry

BLACK NIGHTSHADE

This bushy annual has irregularly toothed, stalked, oval, pointed leaves, white flowers with five petals and yellow anthers, and berries that ripen black.
• **USES** The plant contains poisonous solanine, concentrated in the unripe berry. The sedative aerial parts have a paralyzing effect on nerve ends, and are used in painkilling ointments. In Asia, a diuretic decoction treats fluid retention, eye disease, and infected sores.
• **REMARK** The berries are poisonous. *Solanum lyratum* shows strong inhibiting action on cancer cells without affecting normal cells.

Habitat Wasteland, nutrient-rich soil; S. Europe	Parts used

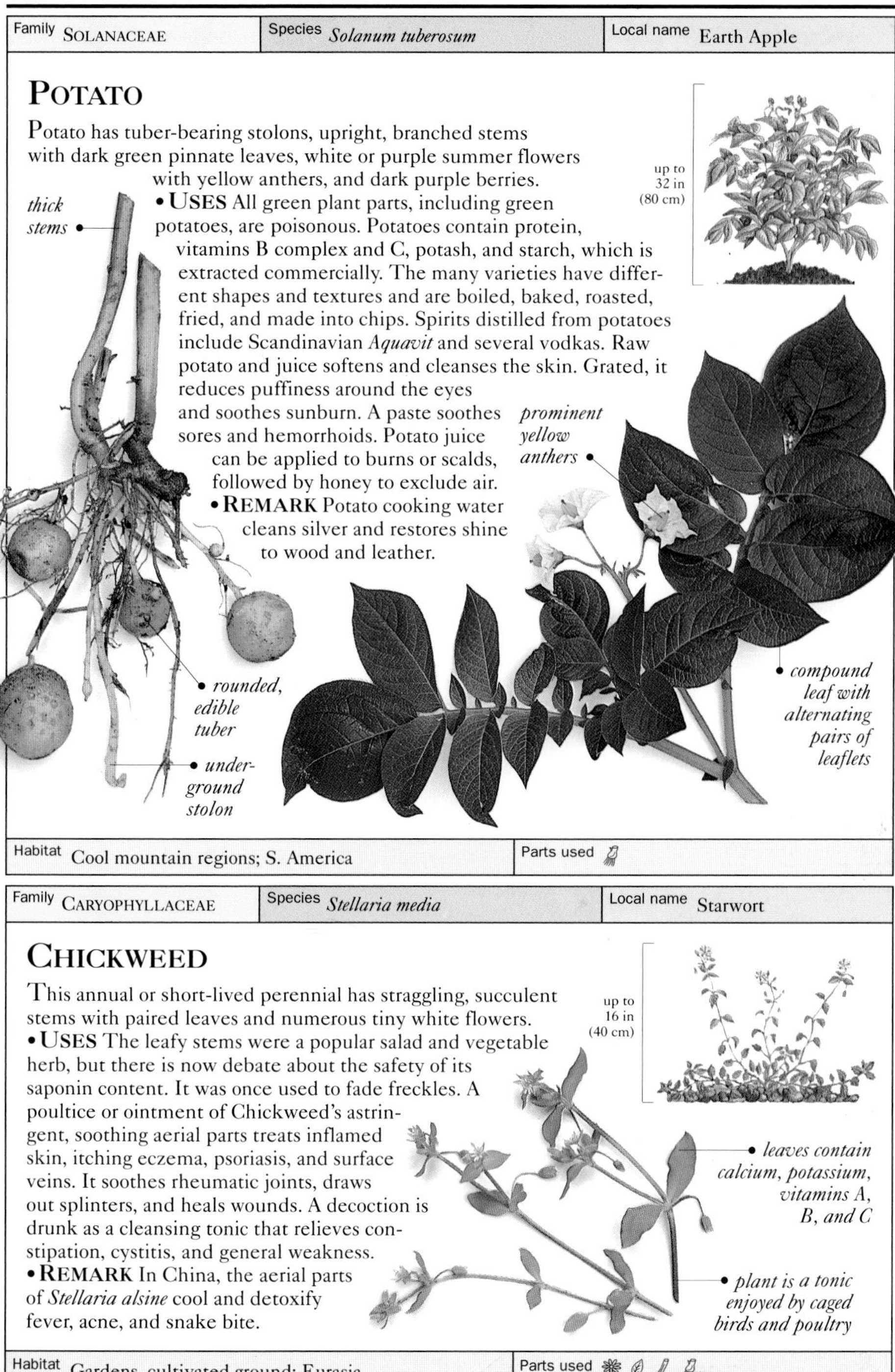
up to
32 in
(80 cm)
thick stems
prominent yellow anthers
rounded, edible tuber
under-ground stolon
compound leaf with alternating pairs of leaflets
up to
16 in
(40 cm)
leaves contain calcium, potassium, vitamins A, B, and C
plant is a tonic enjoyed by caged birds and poultry

Family SOLANACEAE	Species *Solanum tuberosum*	Local name Earth Apple

POTATO

Potato has tuber-bearing stolons, upright, branched stems with dark green pinnate leaves, white or purple summer flowers with yellow anthers, and dark purple berries.

• **USES** All green plant parts, including green potatoes, are poisonous. Potatoes contain protein, vitamins B complex and C, potash, and starch, which is extracted commercially. The many varieties have different shapes and textures and are boiled, baked, roasted, fried, and made into chips. Spirits distilled from potatoes include Scandinavian *Aquavit* and several vodkas. Raw potato and juice softens and cleanses the skin. Grated, it reduces puffiness around the eyes and soothes sunburn. A paste soothes sores and hemorrhoids. Potato juice can be applied to burns or scalds, followed by honey to exclude air.

• **REMARK** Potato cooking water cleans silver and restores shine to wood and leather.

Habitat Cool mountain regions; S. America	Parts used

Family CARYOPHYLLACEAE	Species *Stellaria media*	Local name Starwort

CHICKWEED

This annual or short-lived perennial has straggling, succulent stems with paired leaves and numerous tiny white flowers.

• **USES** The leafy stems were a popular salad and vegetable herb, but there is now debate about the safety of its saponin content. It was once used to fade freckles. A poultice or ointment of Chickweed's astringent, soothing aerial parts treats inflamed skin, itching eczema, psoriasis, and surface veins. It soothes rheumatic joints, draws out splinters, and heals wounds. A decoction is drunk as a cleansing tonic that relieves constipation, cystitis, and general weakness.

• **REMARK** In China, the aerial parts of *Stellaria alsine* cool and detoxify fever, acne, and snake bite.

Habitat Gardens, cultivated ground; Eurasia	Parts used

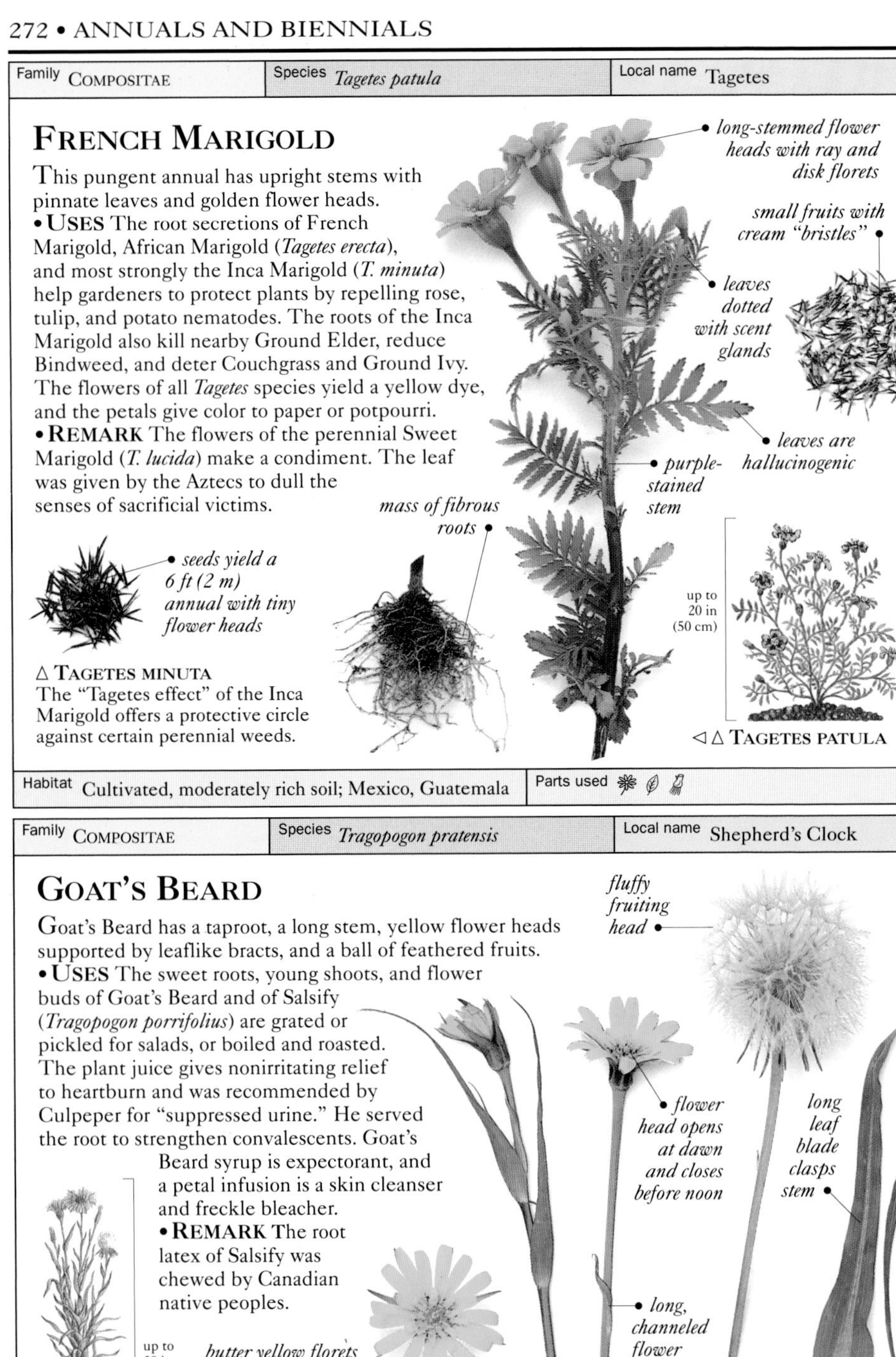

Family COMPOSITAE	Species *Tagetes patula*	Local name Tagetes

FRENCH MARIGOLD

This pungent annual has upright stems with pinnate leaves and golden flower heads.

• **USES** The root secretions of French Marigold, African Marigold (*Tagetes erecta*), and most strongly the Inca Marigold (*T. minuta*) help gardeners to protect plants by repelling rose, tulip, and potato nematodes. The roots of the Inca Marigold also kill nearby Ground Elder, reduce Bindweed, and deter Couchgrass and Ground Ivy. The flowers of all *Tagetes* species yield a yellow dye, and the petals give color to paper or potpourri.

• **REMARK** The flowers of the perennial Sweet Marigold (*T. lucida*) make a condiment. The leaf was given by the Aztecs to dull the senses of sacrificial victims.

long-stemmed flower heads with ray and disk florets
small fruits with cream "bristles"
leaves dotted with scent glands
leaves are hallucinogenic
purple-stained stem
mass of fibrous roots
seeds yield a 6 ft (2 m) annual with tiny flower heads
up to 20 in (50 cm)

△ TAGETES MINUTA
The "Tagetes effect" of the Inca Marigold offers a protective circle against certain perennial weeds.

◁ △ TAGETES PATULA

Habitat Cultivated, moderately rich soil; Mexico, Guatemala	Parts used

Family COMPOSITAE	Species *Tragopogon pratensis*	Local name Shepherd's Clock

GOAT'S BEARD

Goat's Beard has a taproot, a long stem, yellow flower heads supported by leaflike bracts, and a ball of feathered fruits.

• **USES** The sweet roots, young shoots, and flower buds of Goat's Beard and of Salsify (*Tragopogon porrifolius*) are grated or pickled for salads, or boiled and roasted. The plant juice gives nonirritating relief to heartburn and was recommended by Culpeper for "suppressed urine." He served the root to strengthen convalescents. Goat's Beard syrup is expectorant, and a petal infusion is a skin cleanser and freckle bleacher.

• **REMARK** The root latex of Salsify was chewed by Canadian native peoples.

fluffy fruiting head
flower head opens at dawn and closes before noon
long leaf blade clasps stem
long, channeled flower stem
up to 28 in (70 cm)
butter yellow florets have notched tips

Habitat Grassland, wasteland; Europe, USA	Parts used

Family LEGUMINOSAE	Species *Trifolium incarnatum*	Local name Italian Clover

CRIMSON CLOVER

This annual has nitrogen-fixing root nodules, leaves of three rounded leaflets, and heads of crimson flowers.
• **USES** The sweet, scarlet florets are sprinkled in salads. Their high nectar content gives a delicate tonic tea and sought-after clover honey. The herb is a protein-rich fodder and a valuable "green manure." All clover leaves are indigestible and can cause bloating unless soaked for several hours in salty water or boiled for up to 10 minutes to yield a nutritious vegetable.
• **REMARK** The leaves of Aztec Clover (*Trifolium amabile*) and *T. ciliolatum* are also eaten raw or cooked.

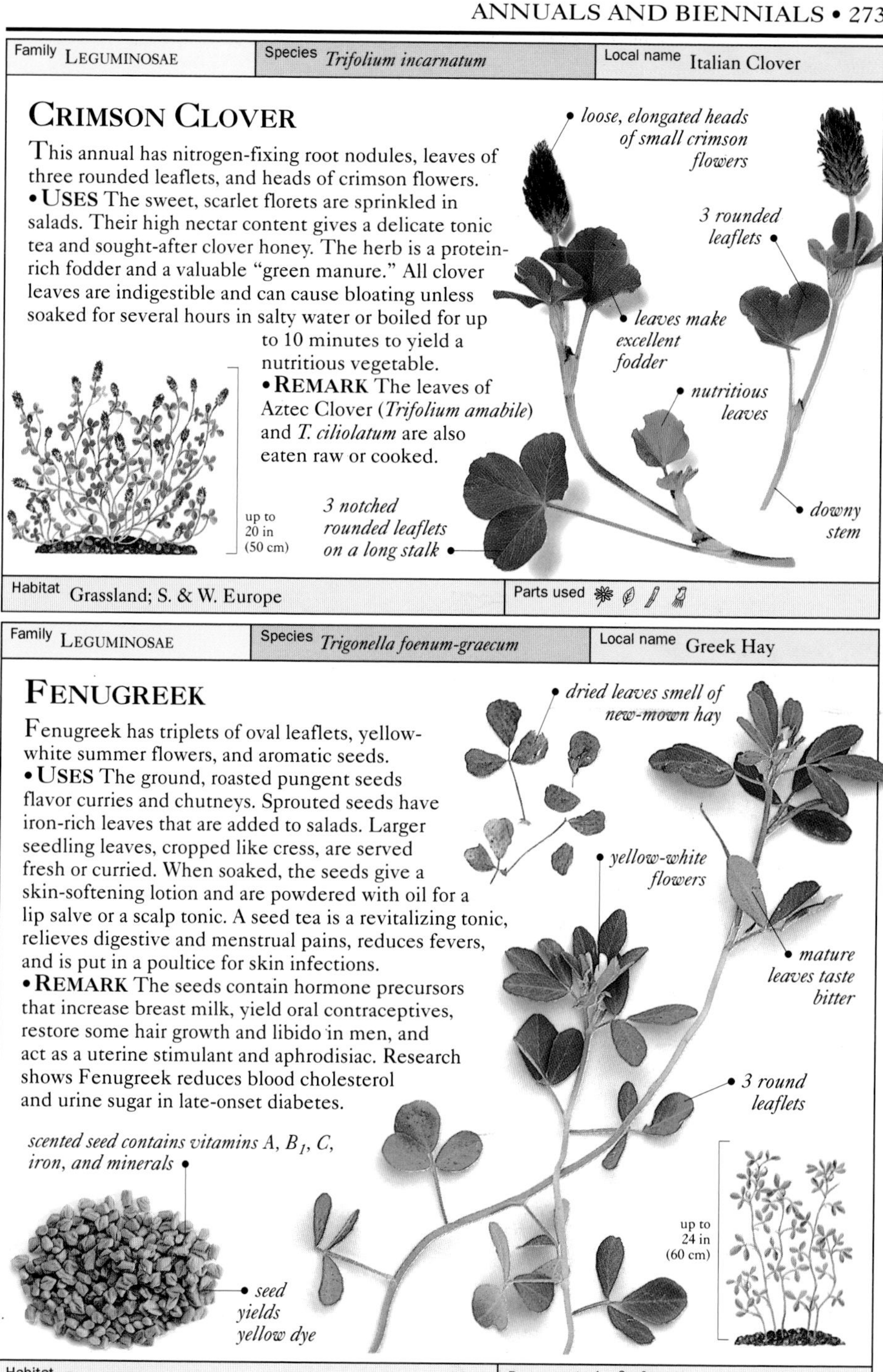

up to
20 in
(50 cm)
loose, elongated heads of small crimson flowers
3 rounded leaflets
leaves make excellent fodder
nutritious leaves
downy stem
3 notched rounded leaflets on a long stalk

Habitat Grassland; S. & W. Europe	Parts used

Family LEGUMINOSAE	Species *Trigonella foenum-graecum*	Local name Greek Hay

FENUGREEK

Fenugreek has triplets of oval leaflets, yellow-white summer flowers, and aromatic seeds.
• **USES** The ground, roasted pungent seeds flavor curries and chutneys. Sprouted seeds have iron-rich leaves that are added to salads. Larger seedling leaves, cropped like cress, are served fresh or curried. When soaked, the seeds give a skin-softening lotion and are powdered with oil for a lip salve or a scalp tonic. A seed tea is a revitalizing tonic, relieves digestive and menstrual pains, reduces fevers, and is put in a poultice for skin infections.
• **REMARK** The seeds contain hormone precursors that increase breast milk, yield oral contraceptives, restore some hair growth and libido in men, and act as a uterine stimulant and aphrodisiac. Research shows Fenugreek reduces blood cholesterol and urine sugar in late-onset diabetes.

dried leaves smell of new-mown hay
yellow-white flowers
mature leaves taste bitter
3 round leaflets
scented seed contains vitamins A, B_1, C, iron, and minerals
seed yields yellow dye
up to
24 in
(60 cm)

Habitat Dry grassland, hillsides; S. Europe, Asia	Parts used

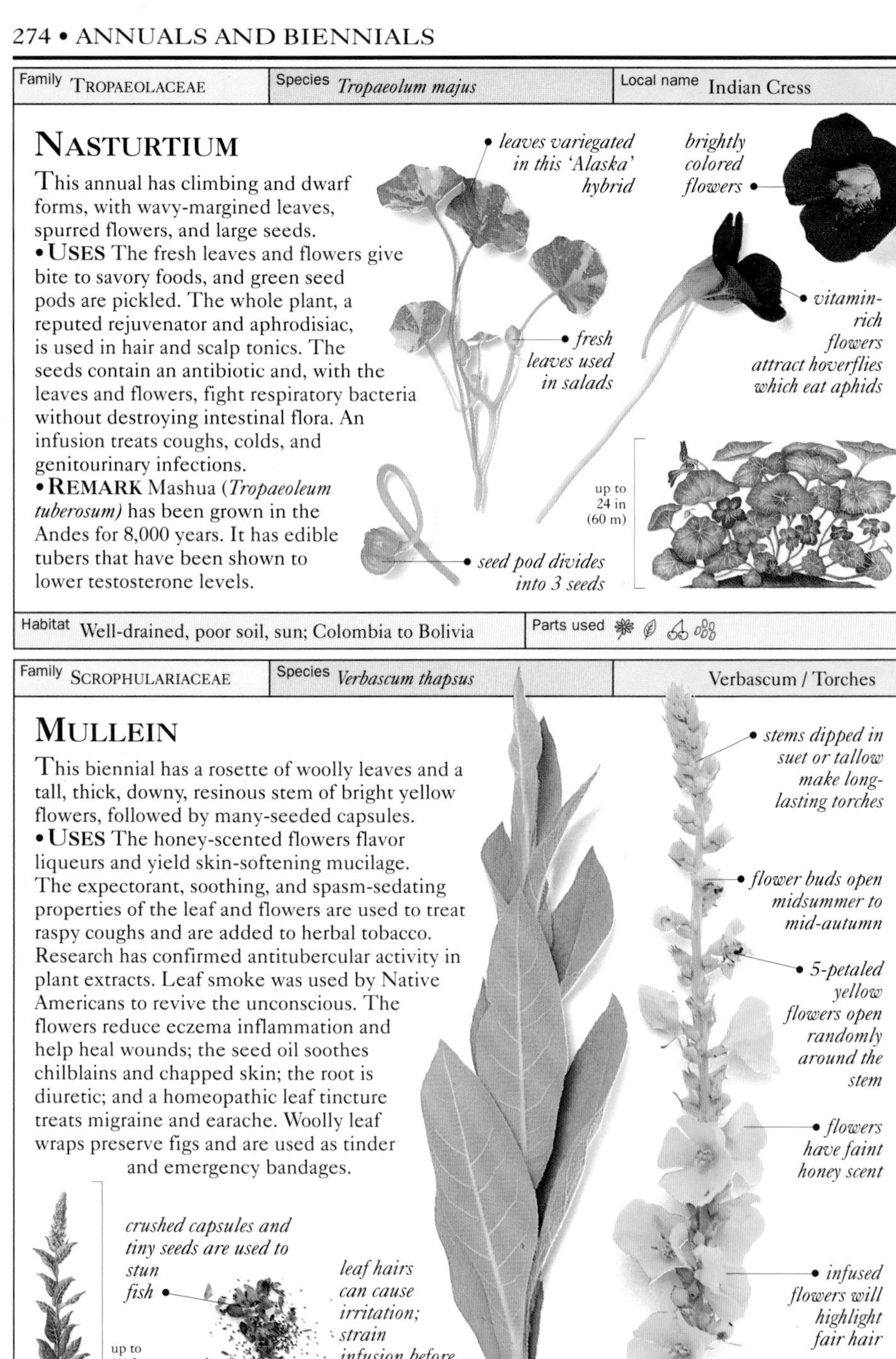

leaves variegated in this 'Alaska' hybrid
brightly colored flowers
vitamin-rich flowers attract hoverflies which eat aphids
fresh leaves used in salads
up to 24 in (60 m)
seed pod divides into 3 seeds
stems dipped in suet or tallow make long-lasting torches
flower buds open midsummer to mid-autumn
5-petaled yellow flowers open randomly around the stem
flowers have faint honey scent
infused flowers will highlight fair hair
crushed capsules and tiny seeds are used to stun fish
leaf hairs can cause irritation; strain infusion before drinking
up to 6½ ft (2 m)

Family TROPAEOLACEAE	Species *Tropaeolum majus*	Local name Indian Cress

NASTURTIUM

This annual has climbing and dwarf forms, with wavy-margined leaves, spurred flowers, and large seeds.

• **USES** The fresh leaves and flowers give bite to savory foods, and green seed pods are pickled. The whole plant, a reputed rejuvenator and aphrodisiac, is used in hair and scalp tonics. The seeds contain an antibiotic and, with the leaves and flowers, fight respiratory bacteria without destroying intestinal flora. An infusion treats coughs, colds, and genitourinary infections.

• **REMARK** Mashua (*Tropaeoleum tuberosum)* has been grown in the Andes for 8,000 years. It has edible tubers that have been shown to lower testosterone levels.

Habitat Well-drained, poor soil, sun; Colombia to Bolivia	Parts used

Family SCROPHULARIACEAE	Species *Verbascum thapsus*	Verbascum / Torches

MULLEIN

This biennial has a rosette of woolly leaves and a tall, thick, downy, resinous stem of bright yellow flowers, followed by many-seeded capsules.

• **USES** The honey-scented flowers flavor liqueurs and yield skin-softening mucilage. The expectorant, soothing, and spasm-sedating properties of the leaf and flowers are used to treat raspy coughs and are added to herbal tobacco. Research has confirmed antitubercular activity in plant extracts. Leaf smoke was used by Native Americans to revive the unconscious. The flowers reduce eczema inflammation and help heal wounds; the seed oil soothes chilblains and chapped skin; the root is diuretic; and a homeopathic leaf tincture treats migraine and earache. Woolly leaf wraps preserve figs and are used as tinder and emergency bandages.

Habitat Dry, gravelly hillsides, woodland; Europe, Asia	Parts used

Family CARYOPHYLLACEAE	Species *Vaccaria hispanica*	Local name Cow Cockle

FORBIDDEN PALACE FLOWER

Common in China's Imperial Palace grounds, this annual has upright, forked stems of medium green narrow leaves, pink to dark purple flowers, and capsules that open to release dark, round seeds.

• **USES** The seeds stimulate blood circulation, treat abscesses and skin ulcers, are decocted for breast pain or inflammation, and given for benign breast tumors. They regulate and induce menstruation and are given for delayed labor and lactation in China.

• **REMARK** It is valued as milk-increasing cattle fodder (its name is from *vacca*, Latin for "cow"), and is included in wildflower meadows. Its presence in bird seed mixes has resulted in wider sowing.

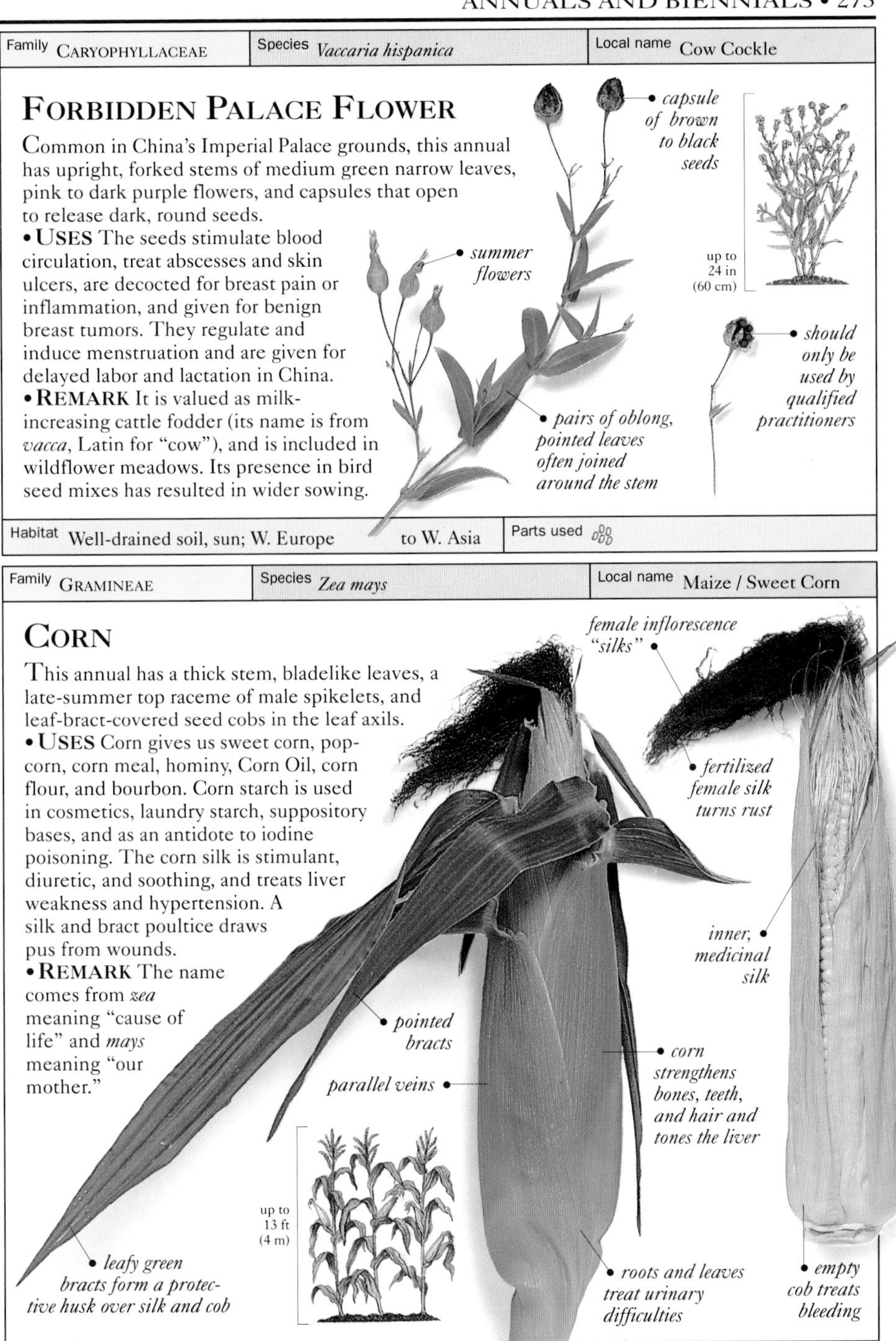
capsule of brown to black seeds
up to 24 in (60 cm)
summer flowers
should only be used by qualified practitioners
pairs of oblong, pointed leaves often joined around the stem
female inflorescence "silks"
fertilized female silk turns rust
inner, medicinal silk
pointed bracts
corn strengthens bones, teeth, and hair and tones the liver
parallel veins
up to 13 ft (4 m)
leafy green bracts form a protective husk over silk and cob
roots and leaves treat urinary difficulties
empty cob treats bleeding

Habitat Well-drained soil, sun; W. Europe to W. Asia	Parts used

Family GRAMINEAE	Species *Zea mays*	Local name Maize / Sweet Corn

CORN

This annual has a thick stem, bladelike leaves, a late-summer top raceme of male spikelets, and leaf-bract-covered seed cobs in the leaf axils.

• **USES** Corn gives us sweet corn, popcorn, corn meal, hominy, Corn Oil, corn flour, and bourbon. Corn starch is used in cosmetics, laundry starch, suppository bases, and as an antidote to iodine poisoning. The corn silk is stimulant, diuretic, and soothing, and treats liver weakness and hypertension. A silk and bract poultice draws pus from wounds.

• **REMARK** The name comes from *zea* meaning "cause of life" and *mays* meaning "our mother."

Habitat Warm, sunny, sheltered sites; C. America	Parts used

VINES

Family LEGUMINOSAE	Species *Abrus precatorius*	Local name Indian Licorice

ABRUS

This vinelike, leguminous climber has mauve peaflowers, equally pinnate compound leaves, and pods of glossy, red, black-spotted seeds.

• **USES** An Ayurvedic herb, Abrus contains sweet glycyrrhizin, found in Licorice. It is a diuretic and an aphrodisiac and treats rheumatism. The sweet leaves are chewed for coughs and sore throats and treat asthma, intestinal problems, heart disease, and bleeding. The seeds are sold by Asian herbalists as a contraceptive.

• **REMARK** The attractive but fatally poisonous seeds are now made into necklaces.

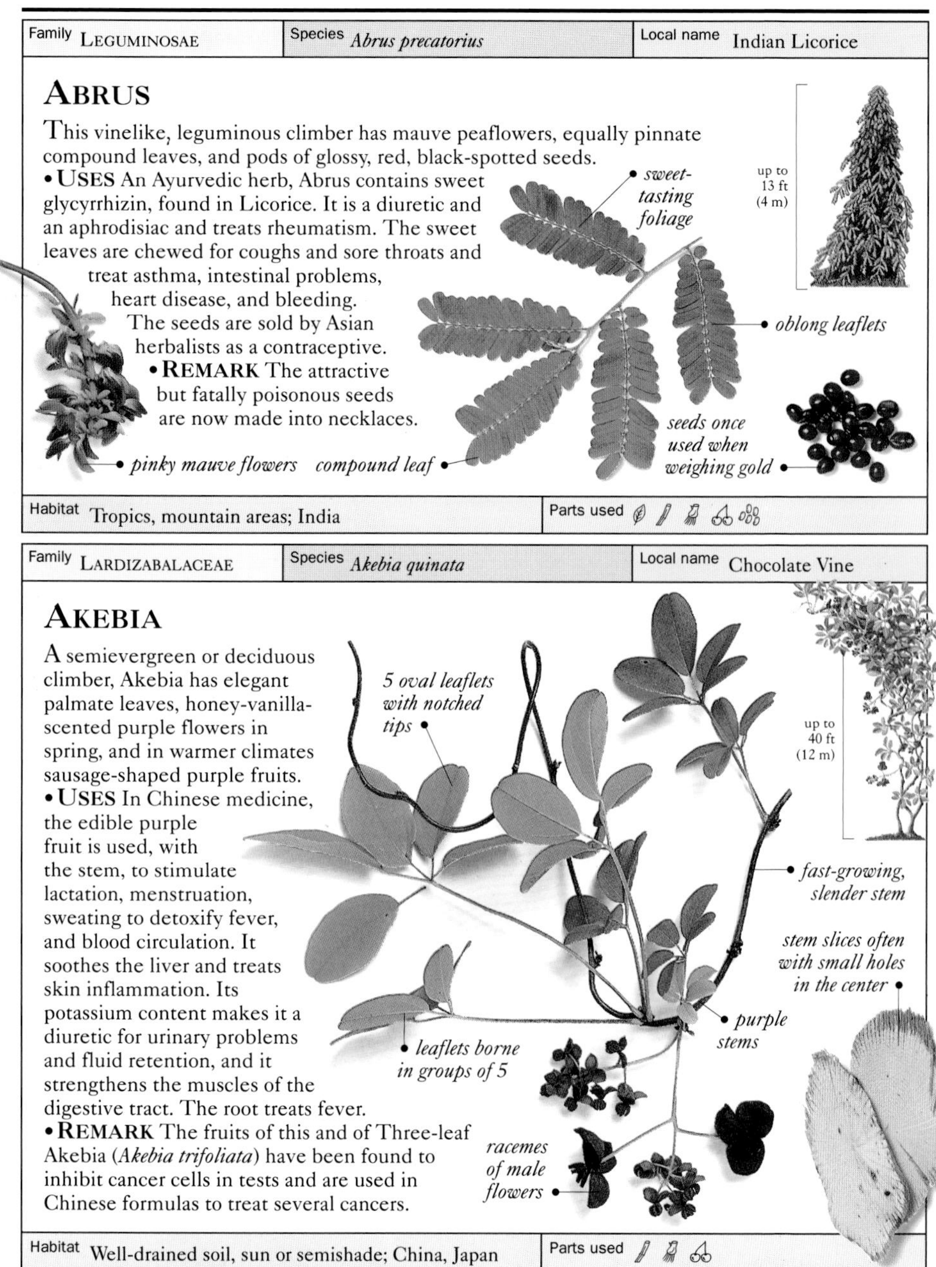
sweet-tasting foliage
up to 13 ft (4 m)
oblong leaflets
seeds once used when weighing gold
pinky mauve flowers
compound leaf

Habitat Tropics, mountain areas; India	Parts used

Family LARDIZABALACEAE	Species *Akebia quinata*	Local name Chocolate Vine

AKEBIA

A semievergreen or deciduous climber, Akebia has elegant palmate leaves, honey-vanilla-scented purple flowers in spring, and in warmer climates sausage-shaped purple fruits.

• **USES** In Chinese medicine, the edible purple fruit is used, with the stem, to stimulate lactation, menstruation, sweating to detoxify fever, and blood circulation. It soothes the liver and treats skin inflammation. Its potassium content makes it a diuretic for urinary problems and fluid retention, and it strengthens the muscles of the digestive tract. The root treats fever.

• **REMARK** The fruits of this and of Three-leaf Akebia (*Akebia trifoliata*) have been found to inhibit cancer cells in tests and are used in Chinese formulas to treat several cancers.

5 oval leaflets with notched tips
up to 40 ft (12 m)
fast-growing, slender stem
stem slices often with small holes in the center
purple stems
leaflets borne in groups of 5
racemes of male flowers

Habitat Well-drained soil, sun or semishade; China, Japan	Parts used

Family MALPIGHIACEAE	Species *Banisteriopsis caapi*	Local name Caapi / Yage

AYAHUASCA

This tropical woody liana has smooth brown bark, oval pointed leaves that are dark green when mature, a pink inflorescence, and a winged seed pod.

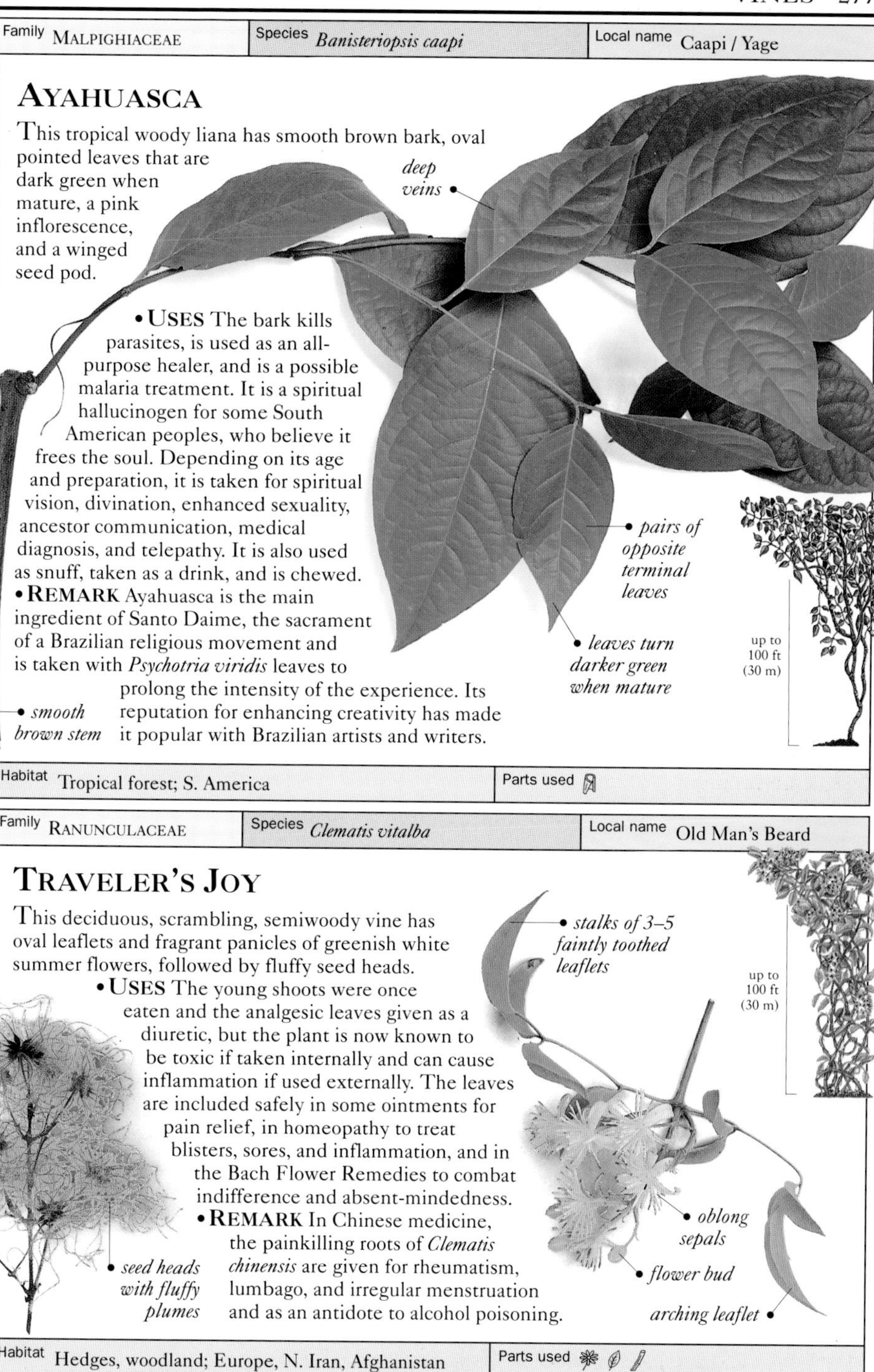
deep veins
pairs of opposite terminal leaves
leaves turn darker green when mature
smooth brown stem
up to 100 ft (30 m)
stalks of 3–5 faintly toothed leaflets
up to 100 ft (30 m)
oblong sepals
flower bud
arching leaflet
seed heads with fluffy plumes

• **USES** The bark kills parasites, is used as an all-purpose healer, and is a possible malaria treatment. It is a spiritual hallucinogen for some South American peoples, who believe it frees the soul. Depending on its age and preparation, it is taken for spiritual vision, divination, enhanced sexuality, ancestor communication, medical diagnosis, and telepathy. It is also used as snuff, taken as a drink, and is chewed.

• **REMARK** Ayahuasca is the main ingredient of Santo Daime, the sacrament of a Brazilian religious movement and is taken with *Psychotria viridis* leaves to prolong the intensity of the experience. Its reputation for enhancing creativity has made it popular with Brazilian artists and writers.

Habitat Tropical forest; S. America	Parts used

Family RANUNCULACEAE	Species *Clematis vitalba*	Local name Old Man's Beard

TRAVELER'S JOY

This deciduous, scrambling, semiwoody vine has oval leaflets and fragrant panicles of greenish white summer flowers, followed by fluffy seed heads.

• **USES** The young shoots were once eaten and the analgesic leaves given as a diuretic, but the plant is now known to be toxic if taken internally and can cause inflammation if used externally. The leaves are included safely in some ointments for pain relief, in homeopathy to treat blisters, sores, and inflammation, and in the Bach Flower Remedies to combat indifference and absent-mindedness.

• **REMARK** In Chinese medicine, the painkilling roots of *Clematis chinensis* are given for rheumatism, lumbago, and irregular menstruation and as an antidote to alcohol poisoning.

Habitat Hedges, woodland; Europe, N. Iran, Afghanistan	Parts used

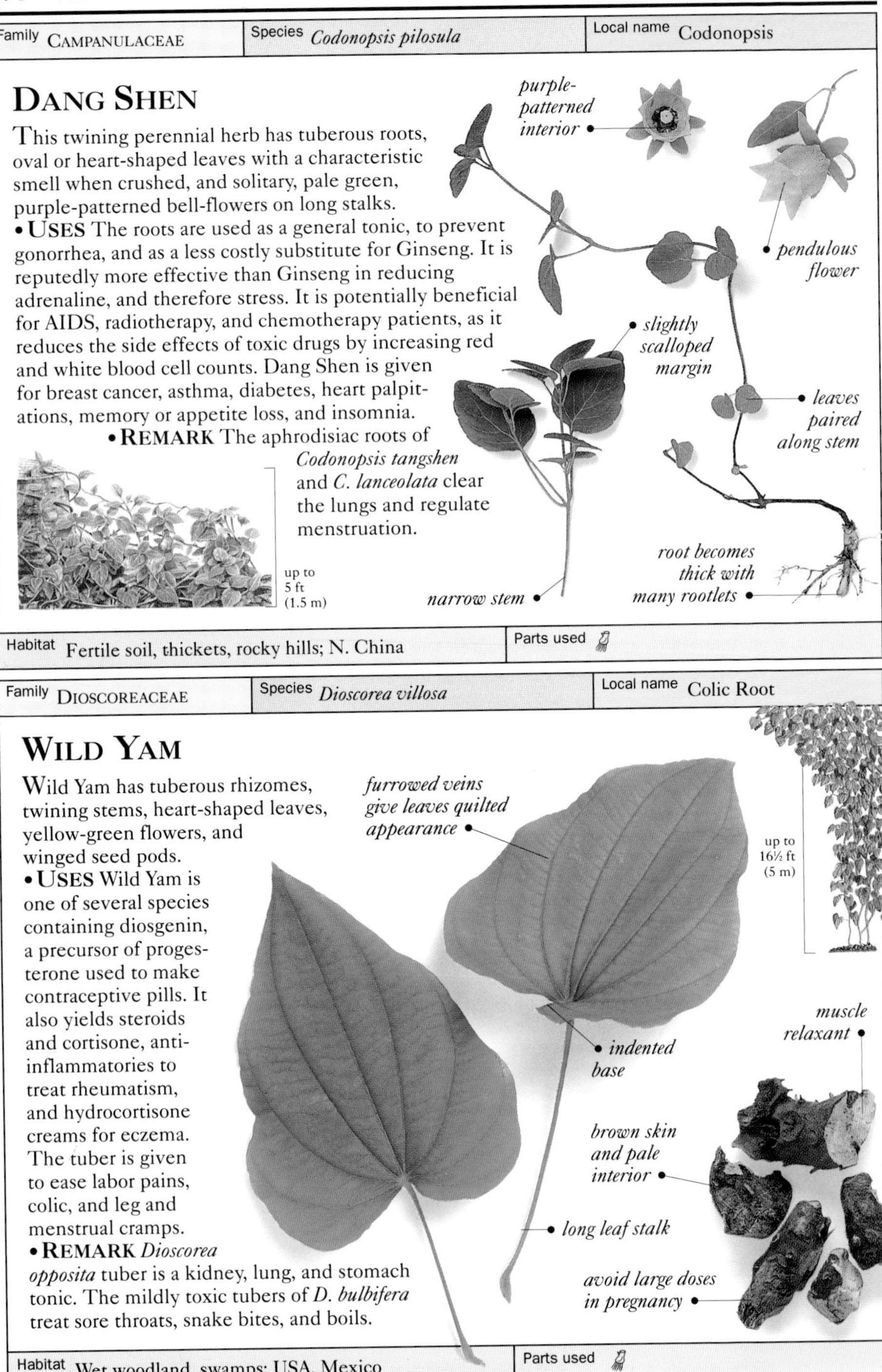
purple-patterned interior
pendulous flower
slightly scalloped margin
leaves paired along stem
root becomes thick with many rootlets
narrow stem
up to 5 ft (1.5 m)
furrowed veins give leaves quilted appearance
up to 16½ ft (5 m)
muscle relaxant
indented base
brown skin and pale interior
long leaf stalk
avoid large doses in pregnancy

Family CAMPANULACEAE | Species *Codonopsis pilosula* | Local name Codonopsis

DANG SHEN

This twining perennial herb has tuberous roots, oval or heart-shaped leaves with a characteristic smell when crushed, and solitary, pale green, purple-patterned bell-flowers on long stalks.

• **USES** The roots are used as a general tonic, to prevent gonorrhea, and as a less costly substitute for Ginseng. It is reputedly more effective than Ginseng in reducing adrenaline, and therefore stress. It is potentially beneficial for AIDS, radiotherapy, and chemotherapy patients, as it reduces the side effects of toxic drugs by increasing red and white blood cell counts. Dang Shen is given for breast cancer, asthma, diabetes, heart palpitations, memory or appetite loss, and insomnia.

• **REMARK** The aphrodisiac roots of *Codonopsis tangshen* and *C. lanceolata* clear the lungs and regulate menstruation.

Habitat Fertile soil, thickets, rocky hills; N. China | Parts used

Family DIOSCOREACEAE | Species *Dioscorea villosa* | Local name Colic Root

WILD YAM

Wild Yam has tuberous rhizomes, twining stems, heart-shaped leaves, yellow-green flowers, and winged seed pods.

• **USES** Wild Yam is one of several species containing diosgenin, a precursor of progesterone used to make contraceptive pills. It also yields steroids and cortisone, anti-inflammatories to treat rheumatism, and hydrocortisone creams for eczema. The tuber is given to ease labor pains, colic, and leg and menstrual cramps.

• **REMARK** *Dioscorea opposita* tuber is a kidney, lung, and stomach tonic. The mildly toxic tubers of *D. bulbifera* treat sore throats, snake bites, and boils.

Habitat Wet woodland, swamps; USA, Mexico | Parts used

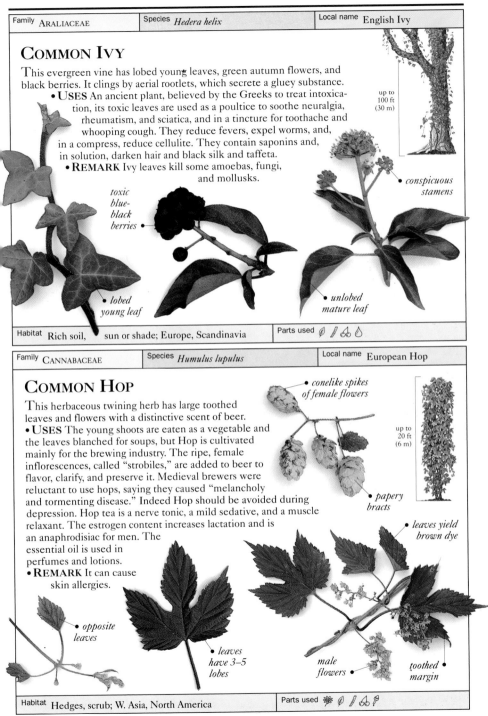

Family ARALIACEAE	Species *Hedera helix*	Local name English Ivy

COMMON IVY

This evergreen vine has lobed young leaves, green autumn flowers, and black berries. It clings by aerial rootlets, which secrete a gluey substance.

• **USES** An ancient plant, believed by the Greeks to treat intoxication, its toxic leaves are used as a poultice to soothe neuralgia, rheumatism, and sciatica, and in a tincture for toothache and whooping cough. They reduce fevers, expel worms, and, in a compress, reduce cellulite. They contain saponins and, in solution, darken hair and black silk and taffeta.

• **REMARK** Ivy leaves kill some amoebas, fungi, and mollusks.

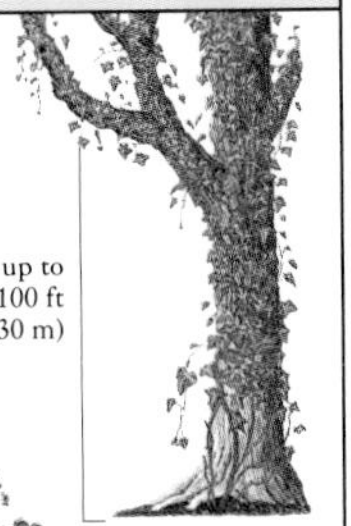

toxic blue-black berries

conspicuous stamens

up to 100 ft (30 m)

lobed young leaf

unlobed mature leaf

Habitat Rich soil, sun or shade; Europe, Scandinavia	Parts used

Family CANNABACEAE	Species *Humulus lupulus*	Local name European Hop

COMMON HOP

This herbaceous twining herb has large toothed leaves and flowers with a distinctive scent of beer.

• **USES** The young shoots are eaten as a vegetable and the leaves blanched for soups, but Hop is cultivated mainly for the brewing industry. The ripe, female inflorescences, called "strobiles," are added to beer to flavor, clarify, and preserve it. Medieval brewers were reluctant to use hops, saying they caused "melancholy and tormenting disease." Indeed Hop should be avoided during depression. Hop tea is a nerve tonic, a mild sedative, and a muscle relaxant. The estrogen content increases lactation and is an anaphrodisiac for men. The essential oil is used in perfumes and lotions.

• **REMARK** It can cause skin allergies.

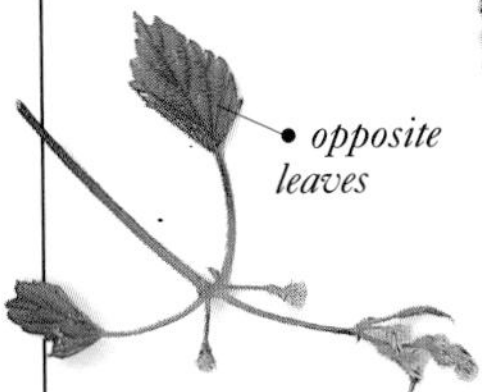

conelike spikes of female flowers

up to 20 ft (6 m)

papery bracts

leaves yield brown dye

opposite leaves

leaves have 3–5 lobes

male flowers

toothed margin

Habitat Hedges, scrub; W. Asia, North America	Parts used

Family CONVOLVULACEAE	Species *Ipomoea hederacea*	Local name Tlililtzin / Piule

MORNING GLORY

This usually hairy, annual vine has three or five lobed, long-stalked leaves and trumpet-shaped flowers.

• **USES** The whole plant, especially the roots, is purgative. The dried, ripe seeds are hallucinogenic and toxic, and are used in Asia to expel worms and treat constipation, as a diuretic, and to promote menstruation.

• **REMARK** Water Spinach (*Ipomoea aquatica*) is eaten to treat general weakness and coughs. *I. tricolor* and *I. violacea* seeds have compounds similar to LSD and were taken in sacred Aztec rituals.

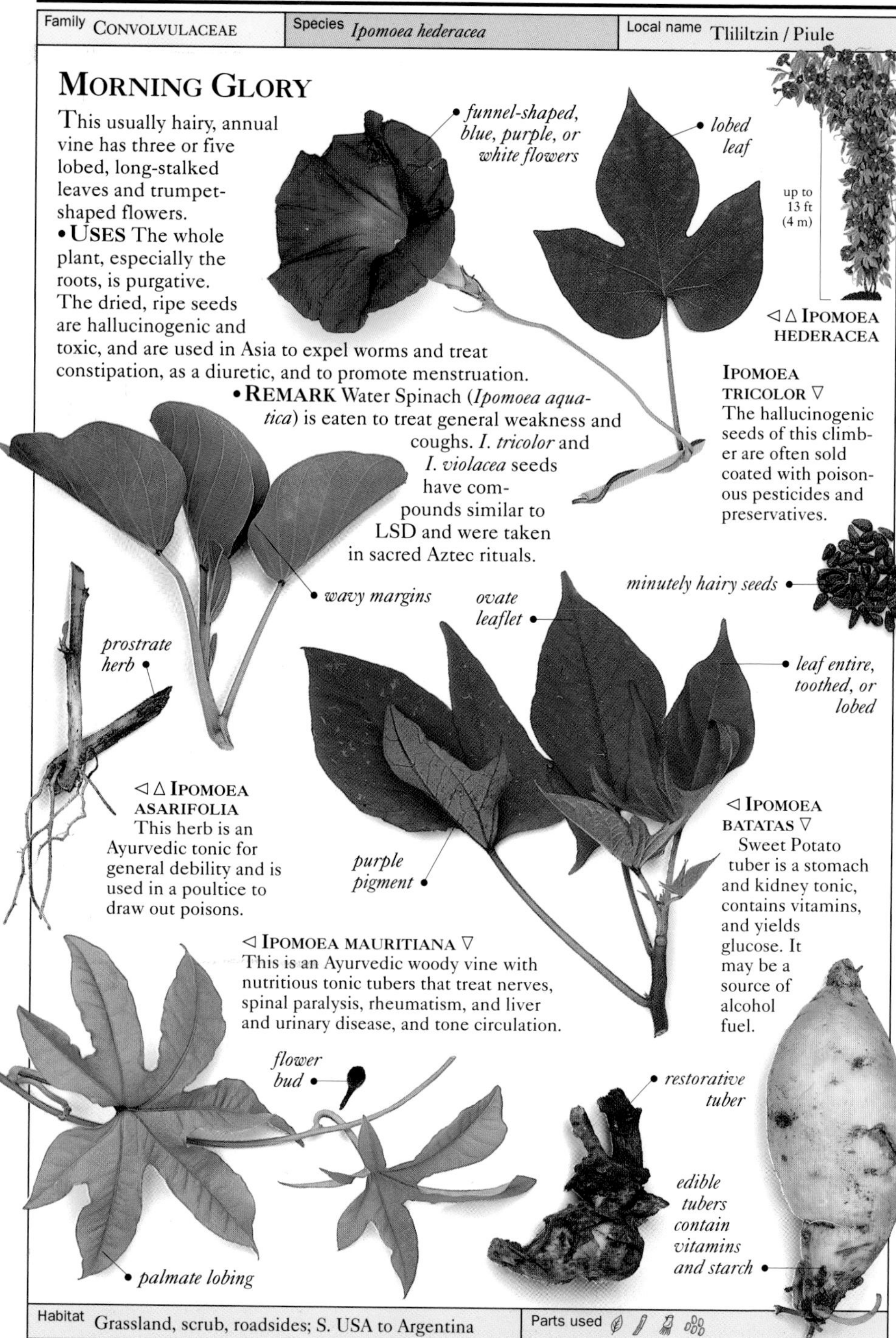
funnel-shaped, blue, purple, or white flowers
lobed leaf
up to 13 ft (4 m)
wavy margins
prostrate herb
ovate leaflet
minutely hairy seeds
leaf entire, toothed, or lobed
purple pigment
flower bud
restorative tuber
edible tubers contain vitamins and starch
palmate lobing

◁ △ **IPOMOEA HEDERACEA**

IPOMOEA TRICOLOR ▽
The hallucinogenic seeds of this climber are often sold coated with poisonous pesticides and preservatives.

◁ △ **IPOMOEA ASARIFOLIA**
This herb is an Ayurvedic tonic for general debility and is used in a poultice to draw out poisons.

◁ **IPOMOEA BATATAS** ▽
Sweet Potato tuber is a stomach and kidney tonic, contains vitamins, and yields glucose. It may be a source of alcohol fuel.

◁ **IPOMOEA MAURITIANA** ▽
This is an Ayurvedic woody vine with nutritious tonic tubers that treat nerves, spinal paralysis, rheumatism, and liver and urinary disease, and tone circulation.

Habitat Grassland, scrub, roadsides; S. USA to Argentina	Parts used

Family OLEACEAE	Species *Jasminum sambac*	Local name Sambac

ARABIAN JASMINE

This evergreen vine has glossy leaves and an almost continuous show of fragrant white flowers.

• **USES** In Asia, the flowers scent desserts and add fragrance to Chinese tea. In Thailand, Jasmine garlands are used in traditional Buddhist ceremonies and as a sign of respect. In India, Yellow Jasmine is offered to Shiva and Ganesh. In Southeast Asia, the flower tea is an eyewash and the leaves and roots soothe fever and burns.

• **REMARK** Common Jasmine is a source of essential oil and a main perfumery component. Aromatherapists find it antidepressant and relaxing. It can help dry or sensitive skin and tiredness.

clustered flowers
up to 6½ ft (2 m)
flowers appear from summer to early autumn
flower bud
yellow summer flowers
ovate to pointed leaflets
up to 7 leaflets
fragrant flowers
ovate-elliptic leaf
dried flower buds
up to 13 ft (4 m)

◁ △ JASMINUM SAMBAC

△ JASMINUM HUMILE
The leaves of the Yellow Jasmine shrub treat sinus problems and cold sores.

JASMINUM OFFICINALE ▷
Common Jasmine is a deciduous shrub with strongly scented, white summer flowers.

Habitat Tropical areas; India, S.E. Asia	Parts used

Family CAPRIFOLIACEAE	Species *Lonicera japonica*	Local name Gold and Silver Flower

JAPANESE HONEYSUCKLE

This evergreen or semievergreen has hairy leaves and fragrant spring to summer flowers that open white and turn yellow, followed by poisonous black berries.

• **USES** As a Chinese cooling herb, the flowers and stems are used in summer drinks. They are given to treat diarrhea, as a diuretic, and to cool fevers. Tests have confirmed the plant's ability to raise or lower blood sugar and its antibacterial and detoxifying properties are used to treat flu, coughs, laryngitis, boils, swollen lymph glands, and food poisoning.

Habitat Sun or part shade; Japan, Korea, Manchuria, China	Parts used

Family CUCURBITACEAE | Species *Luffa cylindrica* | Local name Vegetable Sponge

SMOOTH LOOFAH

This annual vine has conspicuous female flowers, yellow male flowers, and smooth, cylindrical fruits.

• **USES** The flower buds, shoots, leaves, and fruits are eaten; the seeds yield edible oil. The flowers and gourds are steeped to make a drink for throat and lung problems and leaf juice is applied to rashes. The painkilling fruit fiber treats uterine bleeding, hemorrhoids, and dysentery.

• **REMARK** When dried, soaked, and bleached the fruit reveals the loofah, used for scrubbing the skin and cleaning dishes and as a shock absorber.

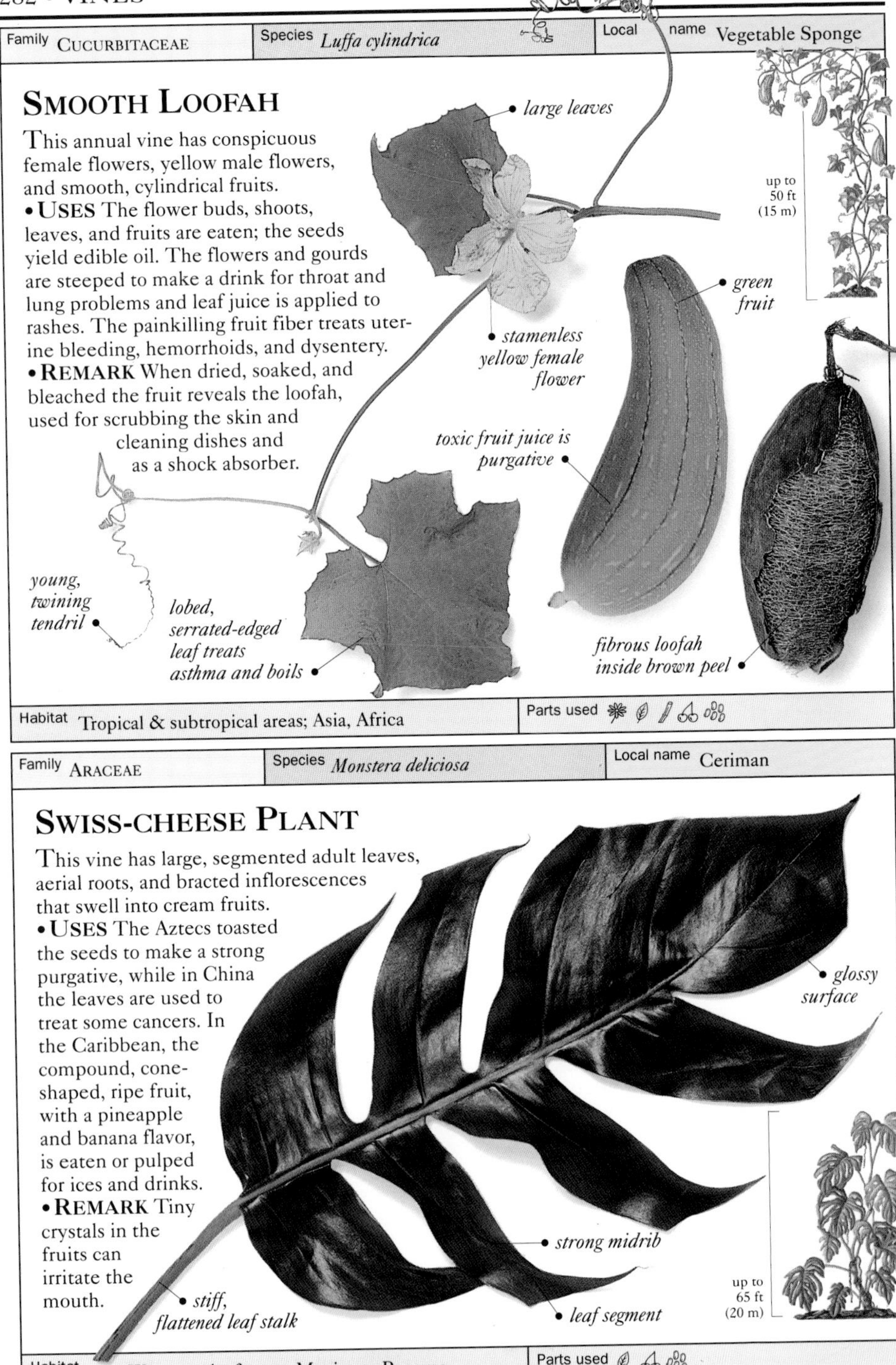
large leaves
up to
50 ft
(15 m)
green
fruit
stamenless
yellow female
flower
toxic fruit juice is
purgative
young,
twining
tendril
lobed,
serrated-edged
leaf treats
asthma and boils
fibrous loofah
inside brown peel
glossy
surface
strong midrib
stiff,
flattened leaf stalk
leaf segment
up to
65 ft
(20 m)

Habitat Tropical & subtropical areas; Asia, Africa | Parts used

Family ARACEAE | Species *Monstera deliciosa* | Local name Ceriman

SWISS-CHEESE PLANT

This vine has large, segmented adult leaves, aerial roots, and bracted inflorescences that swell into cream fruits.

• **USES** The Aztecs toasted the seeds to make a strong purgative, while in China the leaves are used to treat some cancers. In the Caribbean, the compound, cone-shaped, ripe fruit, with a pineapple and banana flavor, is eaten or pulped for ices and drinks.

• **REMARK** Tiny crystals in the fruits can irritate the mouth.

Habitat Warm, moist forests; Mexico to Panama | Parts used

Family PIPERACEAE	Species *Piper nigrum*	Local name Vine Pepper

BLACK PEPPER

This perennial vine has stout stems, white flowering spikes, and green to dark red fruits.
• **USES** Black, green, and white pepper are all made from the berries, taken at different stages of maturity and processed differently. Now used worldwide, Black Pepper's value was an incentive to early trade voyagers. The alkaloid piperine in pepper stimulates saliva and gastric juices, aiding digestion and killing bacteria. The diuretic fruit treats flatulence, colic, rheumatism, headaches, and diarrhea.
• **REMARK** The essential oil gives commercial foods pepper flavor without the pungency and adds spicy notes to perfumes. In massage oils, it is stimulating and toning.

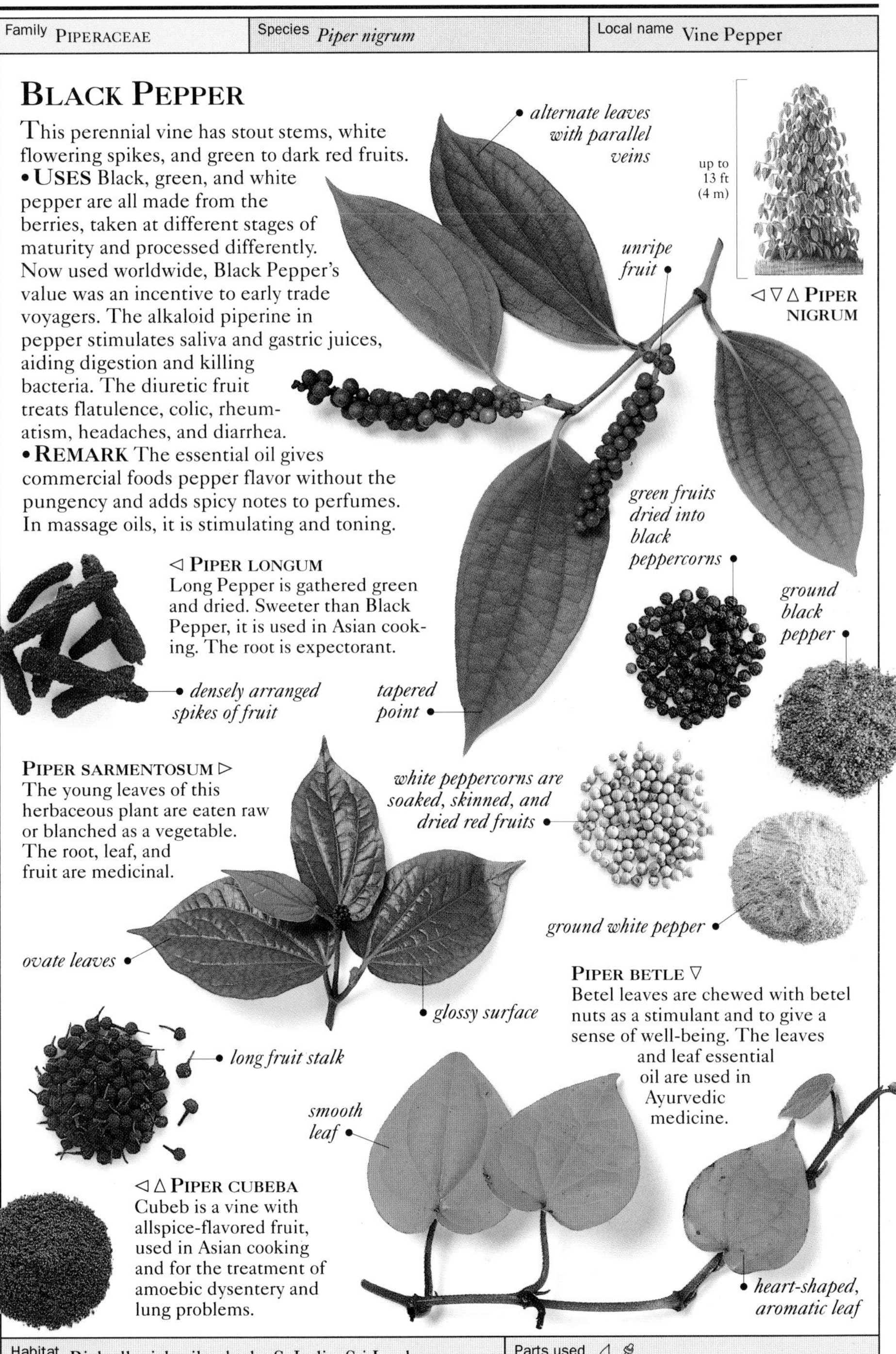

alternate leaves with parallel veins
up to 13 ft (4 m)
unripe fruit
green fruits dried into black peppercorns
ground black pepper
densely arranged spikes of fruit
tapered point
white peppercorns are soaked, skinned, and dried red fruits
ground white pepper
ovate leaves
glossy surface
long fruit stalk
smooth leaf
heart-shaped, aromatic leaf

◁ ▽ △ PIPER NIGRUM

◁ PIPER LONGUM
Long Pepper is gathered green and dried. Sweeter than Black Pepper, it is used in Asian cooking. The root is expectorant.

PIPER SARMENTOSUM ▷
The young leaves of this herbaceous plant are eaten raw or blanched as a vegetable. The root, leaf, and fruit are medicinal.

PIPER BETLE ▽
Betel leaves are chewed with betel nuts as a stimulant and to give a sense of well-being. The leaves and leaf essential oil are used in Ayurvedic medicine.

◁ △ PIPER CUBEBA
Cubeb is a vine with allspice-flavored fruit, used in Asian cooking and for the treatment of amoebic dysentery and lung problems.

Habitat Rich alluvial soils, shade; S. India, Sri Lanka	Parts used

Family PASSIFLORACEAE	Species *Passiflora incarnata*	Local name Maypop

WILD PASSION FLOWER

This herbaceous vine has trilobed leaves, long tendrils, cream to lavender flowers with long violet filaments, and yellow-skinned fruits.

• **USES** The juicy oval fruit has fragrant, edible white pulp made into refreshing drinks and ice creams. Native Americans used the whole plant to treat swollen and irritated eyes, and the root as a general tonic. The leaves give a nonaddictive, nondepressant sedative for insomnia and anxiety, to prevent rapid heartbeat, and to reduce high blood pressure. They relieve the muscle spasm of asthma, epilepsy, and irritable bowel syndrome, and, in a compress, soothe burns and skin irritations.

• **REMARK** The *Passiflora* genus contains Grenadilla fruits, including the prized Sweet Grenadilla (*P. ligularis*), Purple Grenadilla (*P. edulis*), Yellow Grenadilla (*P. laurifolia*), and Banana Passion Fruit (*P. mollissima*).

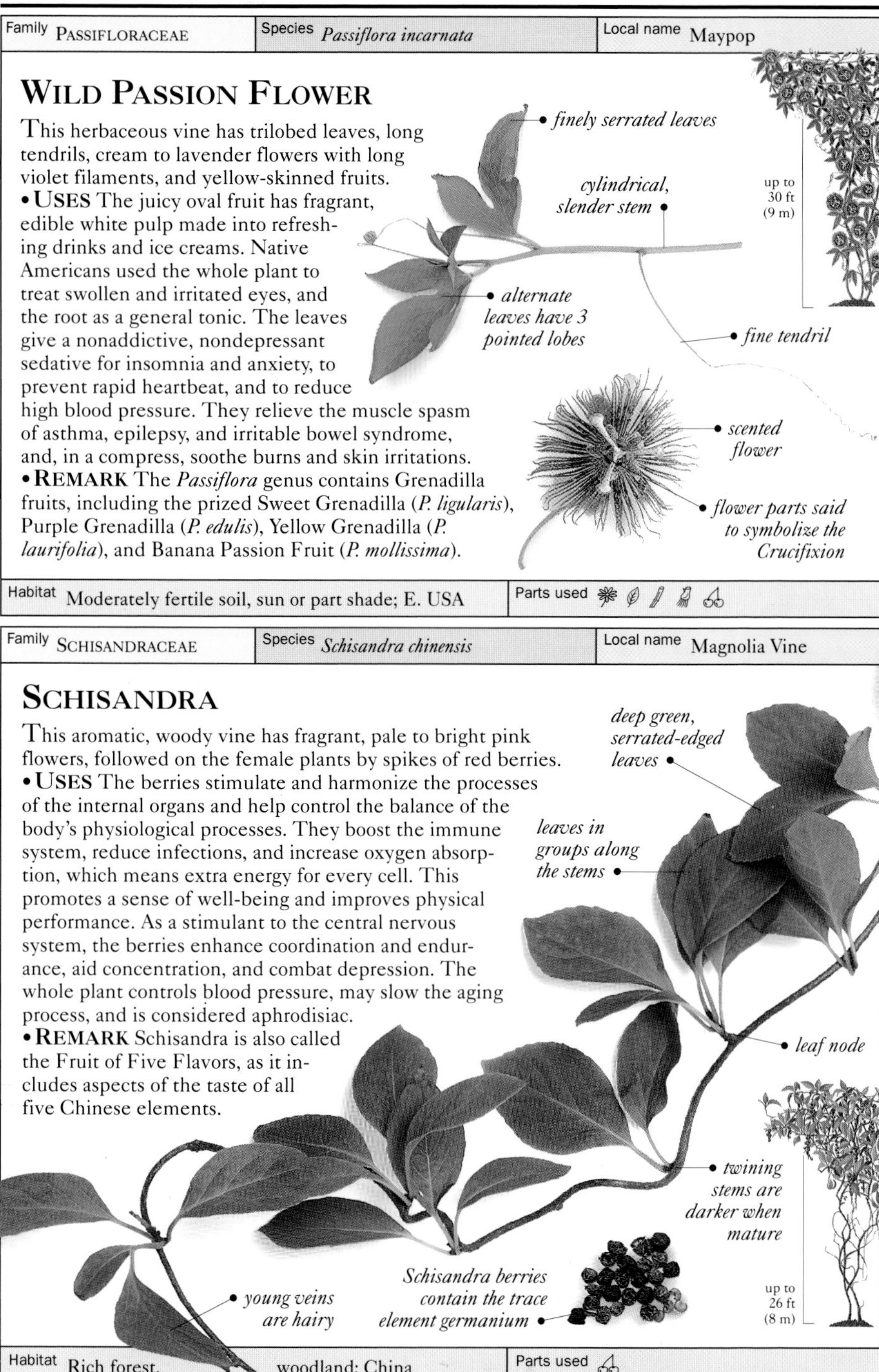
finely serrated leaves
cylindrical, slender stem
up to 30 ft (9 m)
alternate leaves have 3 pointed lobes
fine tendril
scented flower
flower parts said to symbolize the Crucifixion
deep green, serrated-edged leaves
leaves in groups along the stems
leaf node
twining stems are darker when mature
up to 26 ft (8 m)
Schisandra berries contain the trace element germanium
young veins are hairy

Habitat Moderately fertile soil, sun or part shade; E. USA	Parts used

Family SCHISANDRACEAE	Species *Schisandra chinensis*	Local name Magnolia Vine

SCHISANDRA

This aromatic, woody vine has fragrant, pale to bright pink flowers, followed on the female plants by spikes of red berries.

• **USES** The berries stimulate and harmonize the processes of the internal organs and help control the balance of the body's physiological processes. They boost the immune system, reduce infections, and increase oxygen absorption, which means extra energy for every cell. This promotes a sense of well-being and improves physical performance. As a stimulant to the central nervous system, the berries enhance coordination and endurance, aid concentration, and combat depression. The whole plant controls blood pressure, may slow the aging process, and is considered aphrodisiac.

• **REMARK** Schisandra is also called the Fruit of Five Flavors, as it includes aspects of the taste of all five Chinese elements.

Habitat Rich forest, woodland; China	Parts used

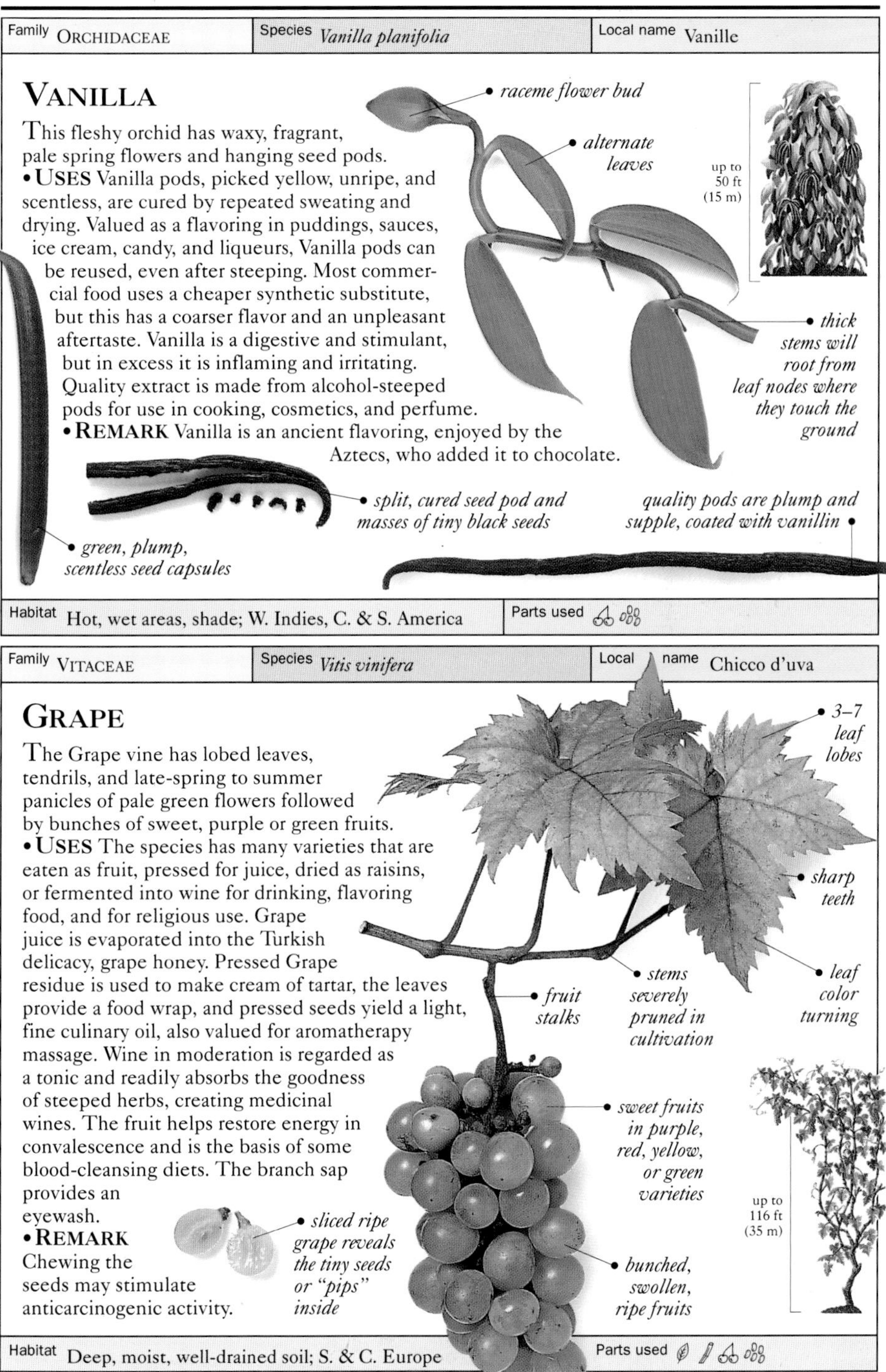
raceme flower bud
alternate leaves
up to 50 ft (15 m)
thick stems will root from leaf nodes where they touch the ground
split, cured seed pod and masses of tiny black seeds
quality pods are plump and supple, coated with vanillin
green, plump, scentless seed capsules
3–7 leaf lobes
sharp teeth
stems severely pruned in cultivation
fruit stalks
leaf color turning
sweet fruits in purple, red, yellow, or green varieties
up to 116 ft (35 m)
sliced ripe grape reveals the tiny seeds or "pips" inside
bunched, swollen, ripe fruits

Family ORCHIDACEAE	Species *Vanilla planifolia*	Local name Vanille

VANILLA

This fleshy orchid has waxy, fragrant, pale spring flowers and hanging seed pods. • **USES** Vanilla pods, picked yellow, unripe, and scentless, are cured by repeated sweating and drying. Valued as a flavoring in puddings, sauces, ice cream, candy, and liqueurs, Vanilla pods can be reused, even after steeping. Most commercial food uses a cheaper synthetic substitute, but this has a coarser flavor and an unpleasant aftertaste. Vanilla is a digestive and stimulant, but in excess it is inflaming and irritating. Quality extract is made from alcohol-steeped pods for use in cooking, cosmetics, and perfume. • **REMARK** Vanilla is an ancient flavoring, enjoyed by the Aztecs, who added it to chocolate.

Habitat Hot, wet areas, shade; W. Indies, C. & S. America	Parts used

Family VITACEAE	Species *Vitis vinifera*	Local name Chicco d'uva

GRAPE

The Grape vine has lobed leaves, tendrils, and late-spring to summer panicles of pale green flowers followed by bunches of sweet, purple or green fruits. • **USES** The species has many varieties that are eaten as fruit, pressed for juice, dried as raisins, or fermented into wine for drinking, flavoring food, and for religious use. Grape juice is evaporated into the Turkish delicacy, grape honey. Pressed Grape residue is used to make cream of tartar, the leaves provide a food wrap, and pressed seeds yield a light, fine culinary oil, also valued for aromatherapy massage. Wine in moderation is regarded as a tonic and readily absorbs the goodness of steeped herbs, creating medicinal wines. The fruit helps restore energy in convalescence and is the basis of some blood-cleansing diets. The branch sap provides an eyewash. • **REMARK** Chewing the seeds may stimulate anticarcinogenic activity.

Habitat Deep, moist, well-drained soil; S. & C. Europe	Parts used

OTHER HERBS

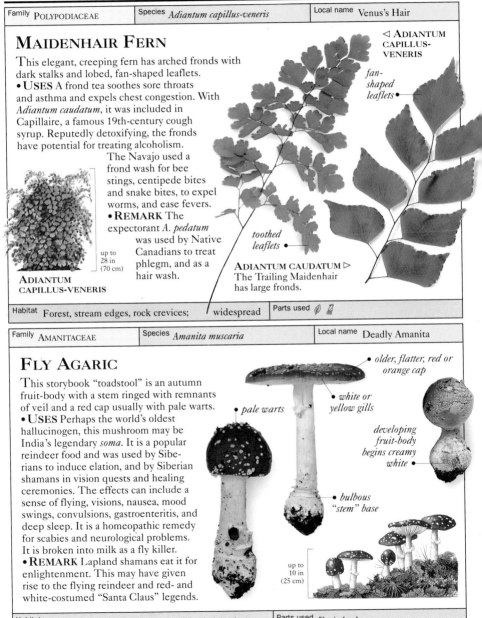

Family	Species	Local name
POLYPODIACEAE	*Adiantum capillus-veneris*	Venus's Hair

MAIDENHAIR FERN

This elegant, creeping fern has arched fronds with dark stalks and lobed, fan-shaped leaflets.

• **USES** A frond tea soothes sore throats and asthma and expels chest congestion. With *Adiantum caudatum*, it was included in Capillaire, a famous 19th-century cough syrup. Reputedly detoxifying, the fronds have potential for treating alcoholism. The Navajo used a frond wash for bee stings, centipede bites and snake bites, to expel worms, and ease fevers.

• **REMARK** The expectorant *A. pedatum* was used by Native Canadians to treat phlegm, and as a hair wash.

up to 28 in (70 cm)

ADIANTUM CAPILLUS-VENERIS

◁ ADIANTUM CAPILLUS-VENERIS

fan-shaped leaflets

toothed leaflets

ADIANTUM CAUDATUM ▷ The Trailing Maidenhair has large fronds.

Habitat	Parts used
Forest, stream edges, rock crevices; widespread	

Family	Species	Local name
AMANITACEAE	*Amanita muscaria*	Deadly Amanita

FLY AGARIC

This storybook "toadstool" is an autumn fruit-body with a stem ringed with remnants of veil and a red cap usually with pale warts.

• **USES** Perhaps the world's oldest hallucinogen, this mushroom may be India's legendary *soma*. It is a popular reindeer food and was used by Siberians to induce elation, and by Siberian shamans in vision quests and healing ceremonies. The effects can include a sense of flying, visions, nausea, mood swings, convulsions, gastroenteritis, and deep sleep. It is a homeopathic remedy for scabies and neurological problems. It is broken into milk as a fly killer.

• **REMARK** Lapland shamans eat it for enlightenment. This may have given rise to the flying reindeer and red- and white-costumed "Santa Claus" legends.

older, flatter, red or orange cap
pale warts
white or yellow gills
developing fruit-body begins creamy white
bulbous "stem" base
up to 10 in (25 cm)

Habitat	Parts used
Thin forests with Birch; Europe, North America	Fruit-body

Family	Species	Local name
Clavicipitaceae	*Claviceps purpurea*	Secale Cornuti

Ergot

A parasitic fungus, Ergot produces an over-wintering sclerotium with a violet crust and unpleasant scent.

• **Uses** Ergot was given by midwives in medieval times to stimulate contractions during childbirth. Doctors still use extracts for this purpose, as a vasoconstrictor to relieve migraines, and as a basis for psychiatric drugs; LSD was first isolated from Ergot.

• **Remark** Ergot is thought to be responsible for the behaviour which brought about the Salem witch trials. It was also probably used in rituals of the Ancient Greek Eleusinian Mysteries. The milling of Ergot-infected grain in Medieval times caused mass poisoning, with epileptic or gangrenous symptoms.

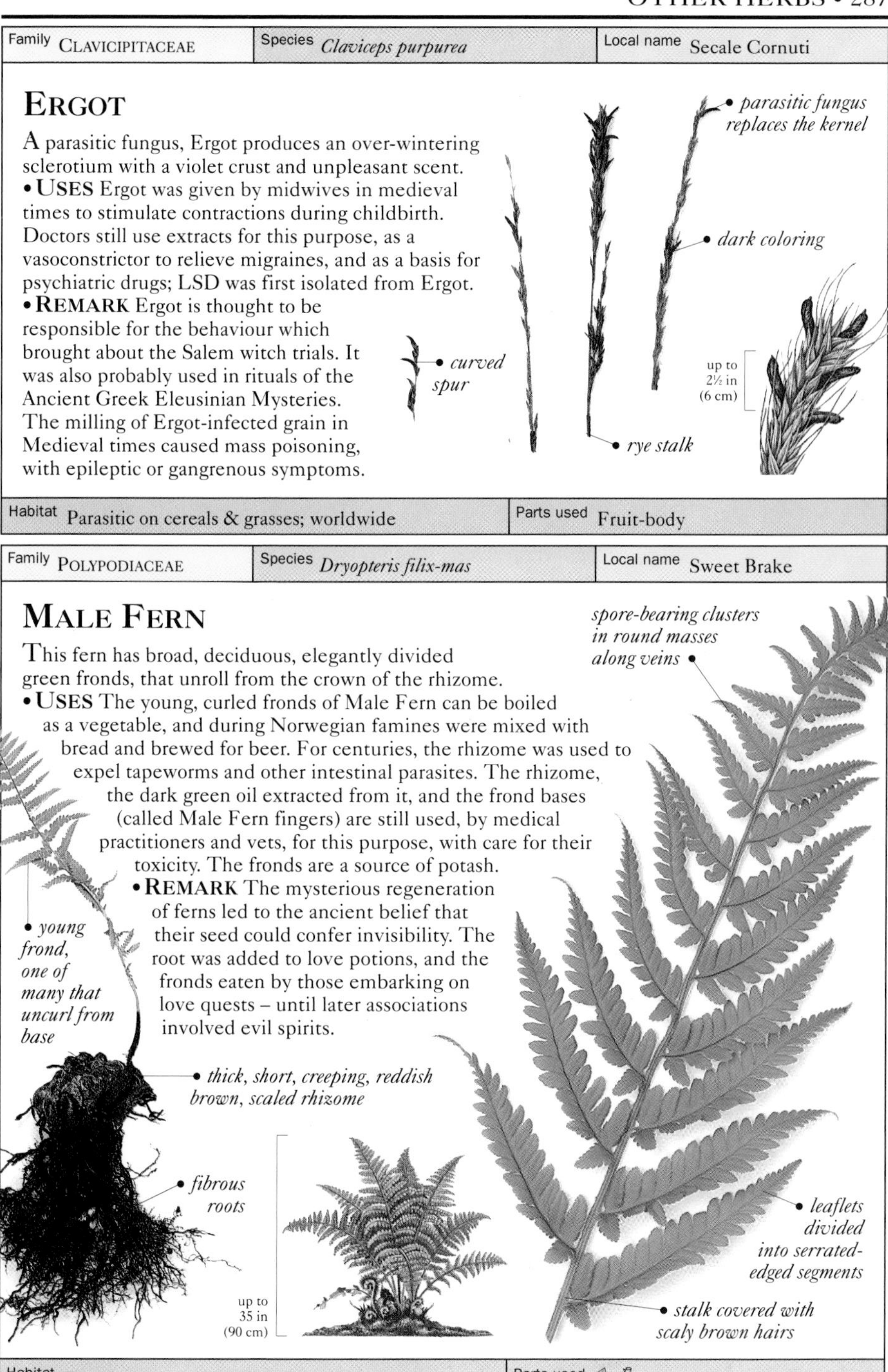
parasitic fungus replaces the kernel
dark coloring
curved spur
up to 2½ in (6 cm)
rye stalk
spore-bearing clusters in round masses along veins
young frond, one of many that uncurl from base
thick, short, creeping, reddish brown, scaled rhizome
fibrous roots
up to 35 in (90 cm)
leaflets divided into serrated-edged segments
stalk covered with scaly brown hairs

Habitat	Parts used
Parasitic on cereals & grasses; worldwide	Fruit-body

Family	Species	Local name
Polypodiaceae	*Dryopteris filix-mas*	Sweet Brake

Male Fern

This fern has broad, deciduous, elegantly divided green fronds, that unroll from the crown of the rhizome.

• **Uses** The young, curled fronds of Male Fern can be boiled as a vegetable, and during Norwegian famines were mixed with bread and brewed for beer. For centuries, the rhizome was used to expel tapeworms and other intestinal parasites. The rhizome, the dark green oil extracted from it, and the frond bases (called Male Fern fingers) are still used, by medical practitioners and vets, for this purpose, with care for their toxicity. The fronds are a source of potash.

• **Remark** The mysterious regeneration of ferns led to the ancient belief that their seed could confer invisibility. The root was added to love potions, and the fronds eaten by those embarking on love quests – until later associations involved evil spirits.

Habitat	Parts used
Damp woods, hedges; North America, Eurasia	

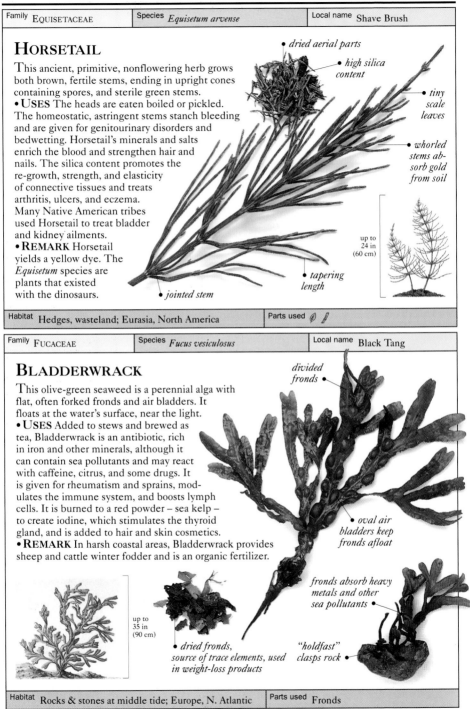

Family EQUISETACEAE	Species *Equisetum arvense*	Local name Shave Brush

HORSETAIL

This ancient, primitive, nonflowering herb grows both brown, fertile stems, ending in upright cones containing spores, and sterile green stems.

• **USES** The heads are eaten boiled or pickled. The homeostatic, astringent stems stanch bleeding and are given for genitourinary disorders and bedwetting. Horsetail's minerals and salts enrich the blood and strengthen hair and nails. The silica content promotes the re-growth, strength, and elasticity of connective tissues and treats arthritis, ulcers, and eczema. Many Native American tribes used Horsetail to treat bladder and kidney ailments.

• **REMARK** Horsetail yields a yellow dye. The *Equisetum* species are plants that existed with the dinosaurs.

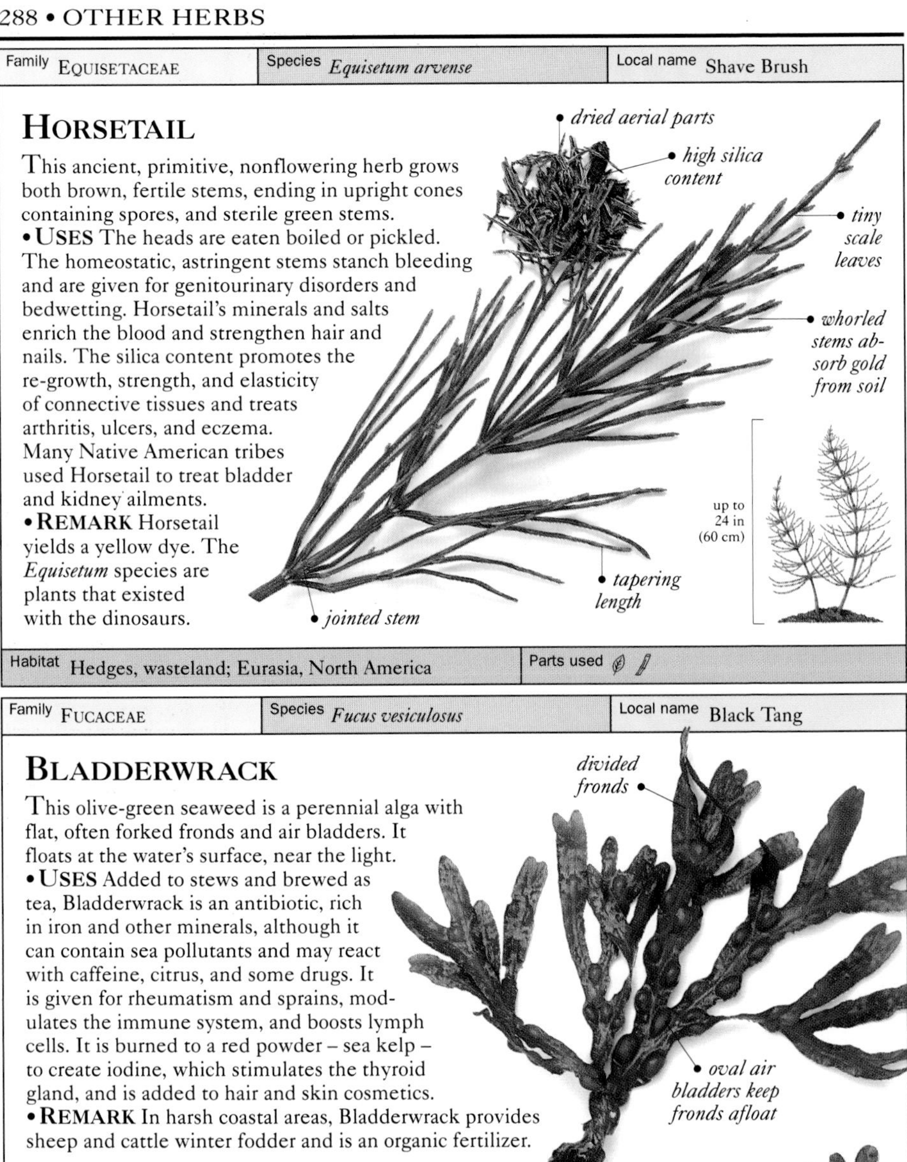
dried aerial parts
high silica content
tiny scale leaves
whorled stems absorb gold from soil
up to 24 in (60 cm)
tapering length
jointed stem
divided fronds
oval air bladders keep fronds afloat
fronds absorb heavy metals and other sea pollutants
up to 35 in (90 cm)
dried fronds, source of trace elements, used in weight-loss products
"holdfast" clasps rock

Habitat Hedges, wasteland; Eurasia, North America	Parts used

Family FUCACEAE	Species *Fucus vesiculosus*	Local name Black Tang

BLADDERWRACK

This olive-green seaweed is a perennial alga with flat, often forked fronds and air bladders. It floats at the water's surface, near the light.

• **USES** Added to stews and brewed as tea, Bladderwrack is an antibiotic, rich in iron and other minerals, although it can contain sea pollutants and may react with caffeine, citrus, and some drugs. It is given for rheumatism and sprains, modulates the immune system, and boosts lymph cells. It is burned to a red powder – sea kelp – to create iodine, which stimulates the thyroid gland, and is added to hair and skin cosmetics.

• **REMARK** In harsh coastal areas, Bladderwrack provides sheep and cattle winter fodder and is an organic fertilizer.

Habitat Rocks & stones at middle tide; Europe, N. Atlantic	Parts used Fronds

Family GANODERMATACEAE	Species *Ganoderma lucidum*	Local name Ling Zhi

REISHI MUSHROOM

This fungus has a long-stalked, shiny, chestnut-brown fruit-body. The laterally attached, hard-crusted cap is kidney- to fan-shaped, with concentric furrows, rusty spores, and off-white to dull brown pores, through which the spores are released.

• **USES** A Taoist "Elixir of Life," the legendary "Mushroom of Deathlessness," and once reserved for the Emperor, Reishi has a long association with longevity and increased spiritual energy. It is said to improve circulation and reduce heart strain, while lowering blood pressure. It is calming and pain-relieving, given to ease arthritis, asthma, bronchitis, allergies, and insomnia. It boosts the immune system and reduces skin-aging free radicals by 50 percent.

• **REMARK** In China, Reishi is prescribed for various forms of cancer, and it is being researched in Japan.

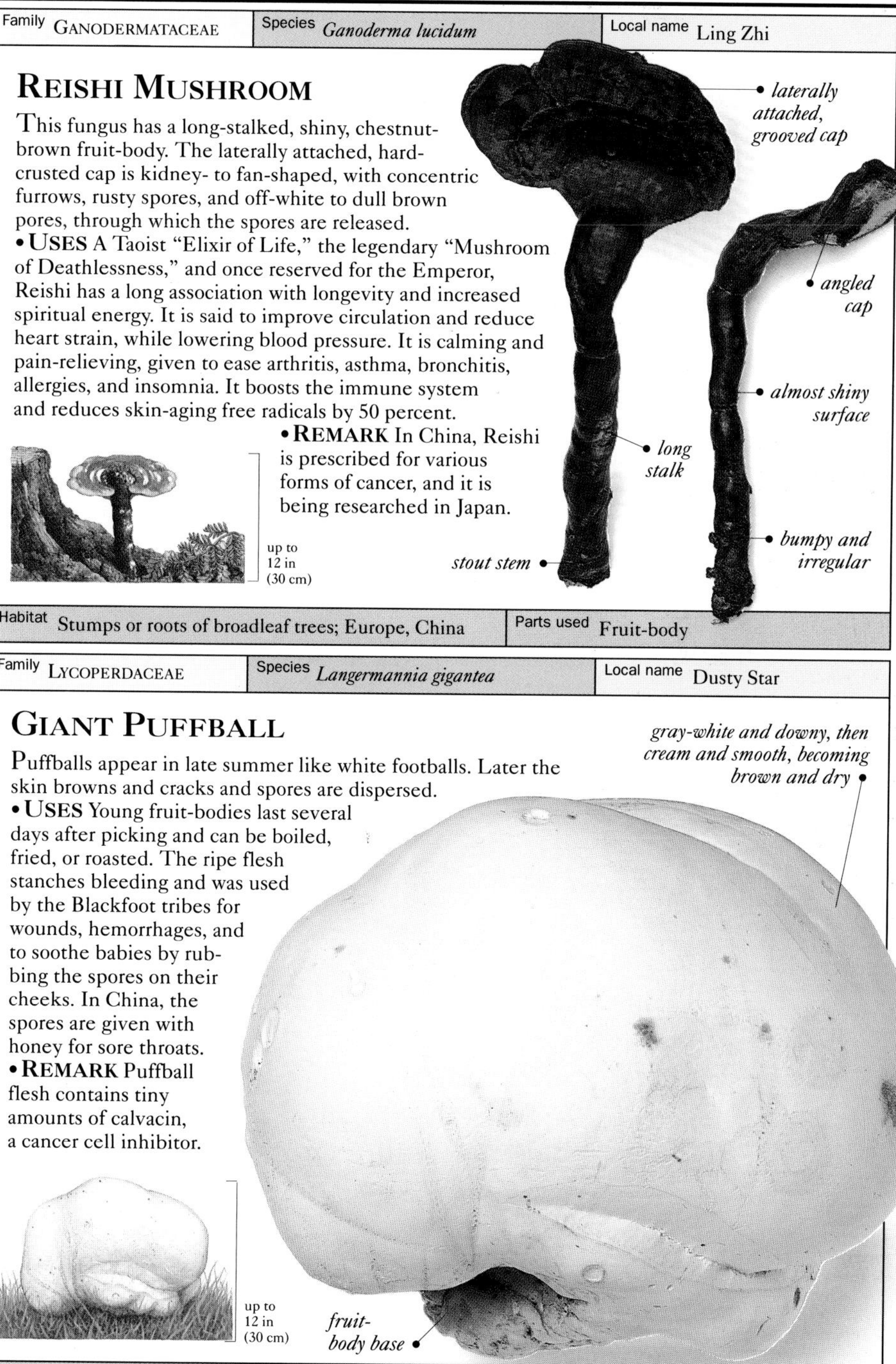
laterally attached, grooved cap
angled cap
almost shiny surface
long stalk
bumpy and irregular
stout stem
up to 12 in (30 cm)
gray-white and downy, then cream and smooth, becoming brown and dry
fruit-body base
up to 12 in (30 cm)

Habitat Stumps or roots of broadleaf trees; Europe, China	Parts used Fruit-body

Family LYCOPERDACEAE	Species *Langermannia gigantea*	Local name Dusty Star

GIANT PUFFBALL

Puffballs appear in late summer like white footballs. Later the skin browns and cracks and spores are dispersed.

• **USES** Young fruit-bodies last several days after picking and can be boiled, fried, or roasted. The ripe flesh stanches bleeding and was used by the Blackfoot tribes for wounds, hemorrhages, and to soothe babies by rubbing the spores on their cheeks. In China, the spores are given with honey for sore throats.

• **REMARK** Puffball flesh contains tiny amounts of calvacin, a cancer cell inhibitor.

Habitat Grassy areas, wood edges; Europe, North America	Parts used Fruit-body

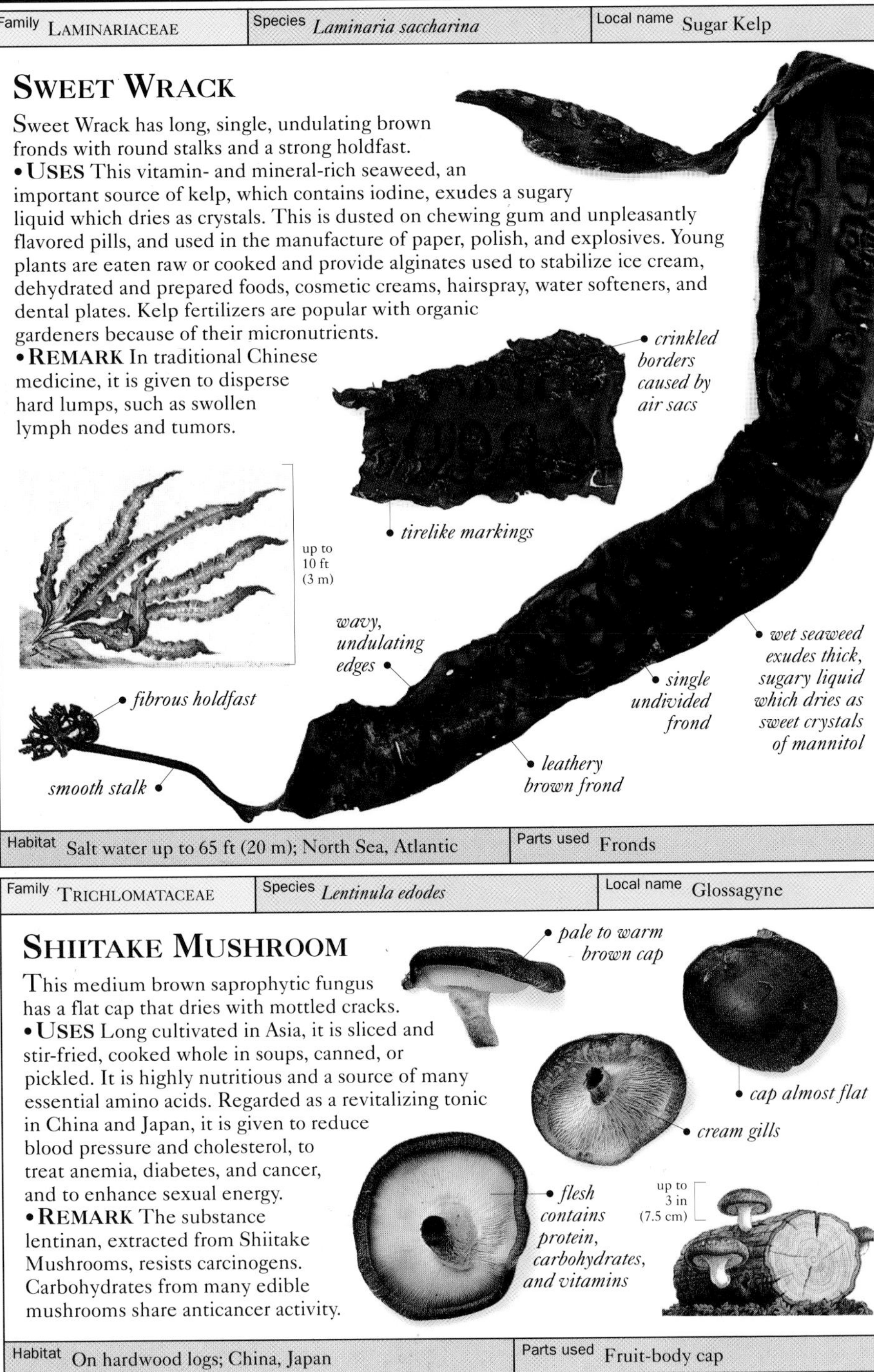
crinkled borders caused by air sacs
tirelike markings
up to 10 ft (3 m)
wavy, undulating edges
fibrous holdfast
smooth stalk
single undivided frond
leathery brown frond
wet seaweed exudes thick, sugary liquid which dries as sweet crystals of mannitol
pale to warm brown cap
cap almost flat
cream gills
flesh contains protein, carbohydrates, and vitamins
up to 3 in (7.5 cm)

Family LAMINARIACEAE	Species *Laminaria saccharina*	Local name Sugar Kelp

SWEET WRACK

Sweet Wrack has long, single, undulating brown fronds with round stalks and a strong holdfast.

• **USES** This vitamin- and mineral-rich seaweed, an important source of kelp, which contains iodine, exudes a sugary liquid which dries as crystals. This is dusted on chewing gum and unpleasantly flavored pills, and used in the manufacture of paper, polish, and explosives. Young plants are eaten raw or cooked and provide alginates used to stabilize ice cream, dehydrated and prepared foods, cosmetic creams, hairspray, water softeners, and dental plates. Kelp fertilizers are popular with organic gardeners because of their micronutrients.

• **REMARK** In traditional Chinese medicine, it is given to disperse hard lumps, such as swollen lymph nodes and tumors.

Habitat Salt water up to 65 ft (20 m); North Sea, Atlantic	Parts used Fronds

Family TRICHLOMATACEAE	Species *Lentinula edodes*	Local name Glossagyne

SHIITAKE MUSHROOM

This medium brown saprophytic fungus has a flat cap that dries with mottled cracks.

• **USES** Long cultivated in Asia, it is sliced and stir-fried, cooked whole in soups, canned, or pickled. It is highly nutritious and a source of many essential amino acids. Regarded as a revitalizing tonic in China and Japan, it is given to reduce blood pressure and cholesterol, to treat anemia, diabetes, and cancer, and to enhance sexual energy.

• **REMARK** The substance lentinan, extracted from Shiitake Mushrooms, resists carcinogens. Carbohydrates from many edible mushrooms share anticancer activity.

Habitat On hardwood logs; China, Japan	Parts used Fruit-body cap

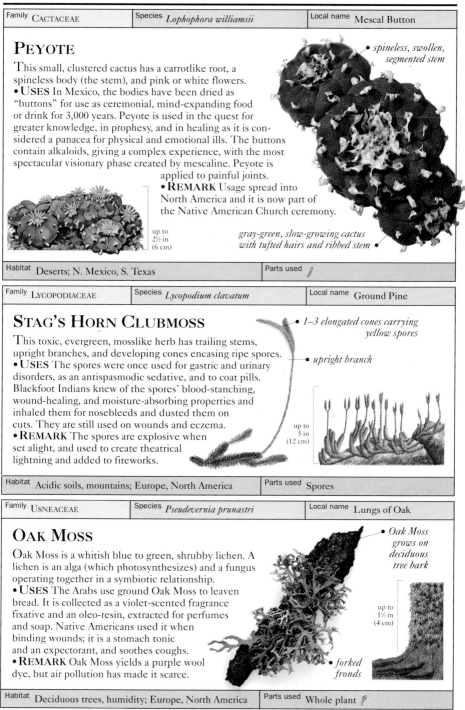

Family CACTACEAE	Species *Lophophora williamsii*	Local name Mescal Button

PEYOTE

This small, clustered cactus has a carrotlike root, a spineless body (the stem), and pink or white flowers.
• **USES** In Mexico, the bodies have been dried as "buttons" for use as ceremonial, mind-expanding food or drink for 3,000 years. Peyote is used in the quest for greater knowledge, in prophesy, and in healing as it is considered a panacea for physical and emotional ills. The buttons contain alkaloids, giving a complex experience, with the most spectacular visionary phase created by mescaline. Peyote is applied to painful joints.
• **REMARK** Usage spread into North America and it is now part of the Native American Church ceremony.

spineless, swollen, segmented stem

gray-green, slow-growing cactus with tufted hairs and ribbed stem

up to 2½ in (6 cm)

Habitat Deserts; N. Mexico, S. Texas	Parts used

Family LYCOPODIACEAE	Species *Lycopodium clavatum*	Local name Ground Pine

STAG'S HORN CLUBMOSS

This toxic, evergreen, mosslike herb has trailing stems, upright branches, and developing cones encasing ripe spores.
• **USES** The spores were once used for gastric and urinary disorders, as an antispasmodic sedative, and to coat pills. Blackfoot Indians knew of the spores' blood-stanching, wound-healing, and moisture-absorbing properties and inhaled them for nosebleeds and dusted them on cuts. They are still used on wounds and eczema.
• **REMARK** The spores are explosive when set alight, and used to create theatrical lightning and added to fireworks.

1–3 elongated cones carrying yellow spores

upright branch

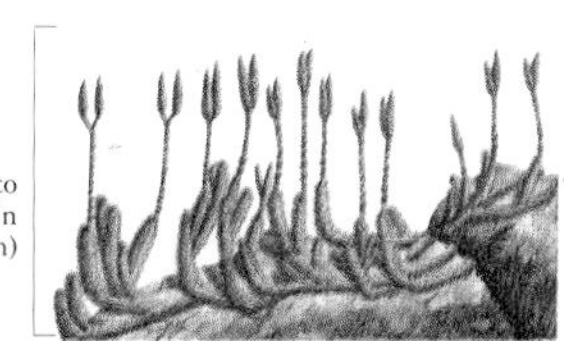

up to 5 in (12 cm)

Habitat Acidic soils, mountains; Europe, North America	Parts used Spores

Family USNEACEAE	Species *Pseudevernia prunastri*	Local name Lungs of Oak

OAK MOSS

Oak Moss is a whitish blue to green, shrubby lichen. A lichen is an alga (which photosynthesizes) and a fungus operating together in a symbiotic relationship.
• **USES** The Arabs use ground Oak Moss to leaven bread. It is collected as a violet-scented fragrance fixative and an oleo-resin, extracted for perfumes and soap. Native Americans used it when binding wounds; it is a stomach tonic and an expectorant, and soothes coughs.
• **REMARK** Oak Moss yields a purple wool dye, but air pollution has made it scarce.

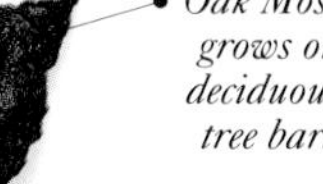

Oak Moss grows on deciduous tree bark

forked fronds

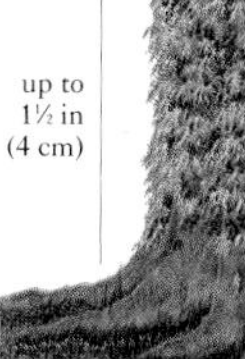

up to 1½ in (4 cm)

Habitat Deciduous trees, humidity; Europe, North America	Parts used Whole plant

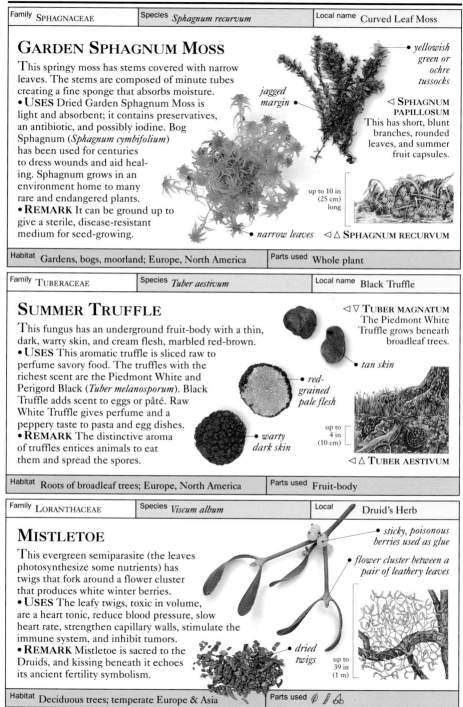

Family SPHAGNACEAE	Species *Sphagnum recurvum*	Local name Curved Leaf Moss

GARDEN SPHAGNUM MOSS

This springy moss has stems covered with narrow leaves. The stems are composed of minute tubes creating a fine sponge that absorbs moisture.

• **USES** Dried Garden Sphagnum Moss is light and absorbent; it contains preservatives, an antibiotic, and possibly iodine. Bog Sphagnum (*Sphagnum cymbifolium*) has been used for centuries to dress wounds and aid healing. Sphagnum grows in an environment home to many rare and endangered plants.

• **REMARK** It can be ground up to give a sterile, disease-resistant medium for seed-growing.

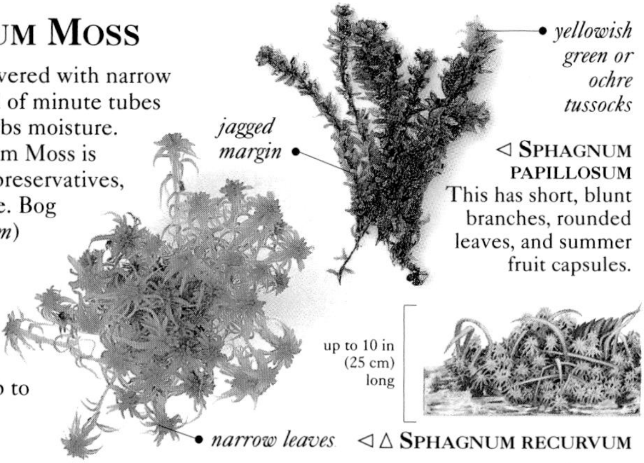

jagged margin

yellowish green or ochre tussocks

◁ SPHAGNUM PAPILLOSUM
This has short, blunt branches, rounded leaves, and summer fruit capsules.

up to 10 in (25 cm) long

narrow leaves

◁ △ SPHAGNUM RECURVUM

Habitat Gardens, bogs, moorland; Europe, North America	Parts used Whole plant

Family TUBERACEAE	Species *Tuber aestivum*	Local name Black Truffle

SUMMER TRUFFLE

This fungus has an underground fruit-body with a thin, dark, warty skin, and cream flesh, marbled red-brown.

• **USES** This aromatic truffle is sliced raw to perfume savory food. The truffles with the richest scent are the Piedmont White and Perigord Black (*Tuber melanosporum*). Black Truffle adds scent to eggs or pâté. Raw White Truffle gives perfume and a peppery taste to pasta and egg dishes.

• **REMARK** The distinctive aroma of truffles entices animals to eat them and spread the spores.

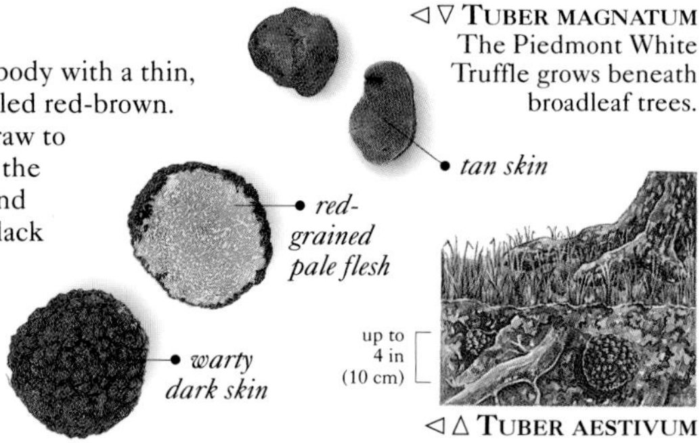

◁ ▽ TUBER MAGNATUM
The Piedmont White Truffle grows beneath broadleaf trees.

tan skin

red-grained pale flesh

warty dark skin

up to 4 in (10 cm)

◁ △ TUBER AESTIVUM

Habitat Roots of broadleaf trees; Europe, North America	Parts used Fruit-body

Family LORANTHACEAE	Species *Viscum album*	Local Druid's Herb

MISTLETOE

This evergreen semiparasite (the leaves photosynthesize some nutrients) has twigs that fork around a flower cluster that produces white winter berries.

• **USES** The leafy twigs, toxic in volume, are a heart tonic, reduce blood pressure, slow heart rate, strengthen capillary walls, stimulate the immune system, and inhibit tumors.

• **REMARK** Mistletoe is sacred to the Druids, and kissing beneath it echoes its ancient fertility symbolism.

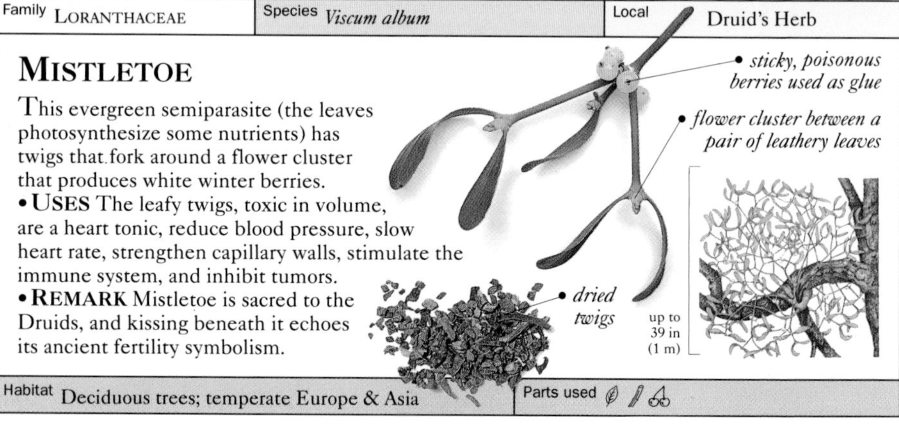
sticky, poisonous berries used as glue
flower cluster between a pair of leathery leaves
dried twigs
up to 39 in (1 m)

Habitat Deciduous trees; temperate Europe & Asia	Parts used

Glossary

Many plant parts and active ingredients are explained in the introduction on pages 10–27. Words printed in **bold** type are defined elsewhere in the glossary.

• **Analgesic**
A pain reliever.
• **Antibiotic**
That which destroys or inhibits the growth of microorganisms.
• **Astringent**
A substance that causes contraction of tissues by binding proteins.
• **Balsamic**
Having a resinous scent.
• **Basal**
Of the base; leaf or **inflorescence** joined at ground level.
• **Berry**
A one- to many-seeded fruit with pulpy flesh and skin.
• **Bipinnate**
When the divisions of a **pinnate** leaf are, themselves, **pinnate**.
• **Bract**
A small modified protective leaf at the base of a flower.
• **Calyx**
Sterile flower parts, called **sepals**, that surround the petals.
• **Capsule**
A dry fruit with one or more seeds. When ripe, it splits open and the seeds escape through pores or slits.
• **Catkin**
A pendulous **inflorescence** made up of tiny stalked flowers.
• **Compound**
A leaf or flower cluster with a branched main axis.
• **Corymb**
Flat-topped **inflorescence** in which outer flowers open first.
• **Coumarin**
A plant substance that gives the scent of new-mown hay when dried. Anticoagulant, it may cause hemorrhaging if taken internally.
• **Cyme**
A broad flower cluster in which the main stem and side branches grow flowers; it may form a curve.
• **Deciduous**
A plant that sheds its leaves at the end of the growing season.
• **Demulcent**
A substance that soothes inflamed internal body tissue. Used externally, it is called an **emollient**.
• **Disk floret**
Small, tubular, central florets of a daisylike flower.
• **Dissected leaf**
A leaf with deeply cut margins.
• **Elliptic**
An oval leaf, pointed at both ends.
• **Emollient**
See **Demulcent**.
• **Expectorant**
A substance that assists lungs to cough up phlegm.
• **Filament**
Either the stalk of a stamen, or any threadlike part of a plant.
• **Floret**
A flower unit in an **inflorescence** such as grass spikes or daisies.
• **Flower head**
Compact terminal cluster of stalkless flowers.
• **Free radicals**
Loose oxygen atoms that crosslink molecules to create nonelastic bonds. They may age skin.
• **Frond**
The leaf of a fern or palm tree.
• **Fruit-body**
Visible spore-producing part of a fungus. In mushrooms it is made up of the cap and stipe (stem).
• **Half-hardy**
A plant that may not survive extremely cold weather.
• **Hardy**
A plant capable of surviving winter outdoors without protection.
• **Inflorescence**
The arrangement of flowers and their leaves on a stem.
• **Lanceolate**
Lancelike leaf, wider at the base.
• **Legume**
The seed pod or the plant of the Leguminosae family, which yields nitrogen **nodes** on its roots.
• **Lobed**
Leaves that are slightly divided; each division is rounded in shape.
• **Mordant**
A chemical applied to fabrics to bind with and fix dye colors.
• **Node**
A point on a stem from which leaves or shoots arise.
• **Obovate**
Leaves that are paddle-shaped, widest above the middle.
• **Ovate**
Leaves that are egg-shaped.
• **Palmate**
Three or more leaflets arising from the same point.
• **Panicle**
A branched cluster of stalked flowers.
• **Pinnate**
Three or more pairs of leaflets in two opposite rows along a common stalk. May have a terminal leaflet.
• **Pod**
A dry fruit, usually a long cylinder enclosing several seeds, that splits down two sides when ripe.
• **Prostrate**
Growing flat along the ground.
• **Raceme**
Unbranched flower cluster, usually pyramid-shaped with stalked flowers on an elongated axis.
• **Ray floret**
Outer ring of petals on a daisylike **flower head**.
• **Receptacle**
Enlarged end of a stem that bears the flower parts.
• **Rootstock**
The entire root system.
• **Sepal**
A petal-like leaf. A ring of sepals surrounds and protects the flower bud, forming the **calyx**.
• **Spike**
An elongated **inflorescence** of stalkless individual flowers.
• **Subshrub**
A low-growing shrub with a woody base and soft stems.
• **Subspecies**
A species subdivision; distinct in structure but can interbreed with other species members.
• **Succulent**
Thickly cellular and fleshy.
• **Tender**
A plant that is not frost-hardy.
• **Tendril**
A slender, twining organ formed to help the plant cling to a support.
• **Umbel**
An **inflorescence** where flowers arise from the same point and have stalks the same length.
• **Variegated**
Leaves with secondary markings.
• **Veil**
A mushroom membrane that encloses the young fruit-body.
• **Vermifuge**
That which kills intestinal worms.

INDEX

C

D

M

Q

R

S

T

U

V

W

XYZ

ACKNOWLEDGMENTS

THE AUTHOR would like to pay the highest tribute to the DK team for its focus on quality, with special thanks to Charlotte Davies, Mustafa Sami, and Colin Walton; to Dr. Pat Griggs and Holly Shimizu for their botanical knowledge; and to Neil Fletcher and Matthew Ward. Thanks also to my assistant Catriona MacFarlane for correlating the research; and to Louisa Bird for supervising my herb garden.

Many people around the world contributed to the collection of this herbal information: special thanks to Prof. Kaminee Vaidya and Judith Chase in Nepal; W. K. Premawansa of Peradeniya Botanical Garden, Sri Lanka; the remarkable herbalist/driver "Lucky", and Dr. Danister Perera of the Siddhayurvedic Pharmaceutical Co. Ltd., Sri Lanka; Ibu Gedong Bagoes Oka, Bali; Dr. Wee Yeow Chin and Prof. N. B. Abdul Karim of the University of Singapore; Mr Lim of PTE Chinese Medicine Co.; Cao Heng of Hangzou, China; Mina and Shiro Mishima, Ma Suo Shimota, and Seizaburo Hemmi, the Medicinal Plants Garden, Japan; Sumaia and Umaia Farid Ismail of Manaus, Amazonas, Brazil; Godsman Ellis and the Mayan healer Don Eligio of Belize; Anamette Olsen of Denmark; Grethe Gerhardsen Træland of Norway; Vivienne Boulton for Southern Africa; Dr. Anne Anderson of the Cree Nation, Alberta, Canada.

Thanks to my husband J. Roger Lowe for his unfailing support and wisdom, and to my four sons, each for their unique contribution.

I would like to dedicate this book to Manuel Incra Mamani, an Aymara Indian of Bolivia who was killed for revealing the secrets of the best quinine tree to foreigners, thereby saving millions of lives from malaria.

DORLING KINDERSLEY would like to thank: Julia Pashley for picture research; Michael Allaby for compiling the index; Damien Moore for additional editorial assistance; Neal Cobourne for the jacket design; East West Herbs Ltd; David Sleigh, Wellingham Walled Herb Garden; Compton & Compton; Tony Murdock, "Overbecks" Museum and Garden; Selsey Herb Farm; Dr. Richard N. Lester, The University of Birmingham; the staff of the University Botanic Garden, Cambridge, The Royal Botanic Gardens, Kew, Chelsea Physic Garden, and The Botanic Garden, Singapore; Dr. D. B. Sumithraarachchi, Peradeniya Botanical Garden, Sri Lanka; The Lindley Library, Royal Horticultural Society.

Photographs by Neil Fletcher and Matthew Ward, except: Peter Anderson: 23cr; 56bl; 63cb fruit; 70br; 96tr; 96br; 102br; 104t; 145b; 155br; 179bc; 186t; 223tr; 232br; 238b; 246cl; 247l; 247r; 253b; 258t; 281cl; 281cr; 284b; 287br; Kathie Atkinson: 92cl; 93bl; Lesley Bremness: 7tr; 31b; Bridgeman Art Library/Bodleian Library Ash 1431 folio 15v-16r: 6b; Martin Cameron: 13bl; 17bc; 19bl; 25bl; 27b steps; Bruce Coleman/Gerald Cubitt: 194bc flower; Bruce Coleman: 253tc stem; Compix/A&J Somaya: 29tc; Eric Crichton: 7bl; Andrew de Lory 29bc flower; Philip Dowell: 13c; 25tr; 122 except cl; 230b; 241tr seeds; 251bl seeds; 253tr seeds; 263c dried; Steve Gorton: 11cl; 21cl; 23b bottle; 27cl; 28bcl; 54tr; 81tr; 109tr dried; 114bl dried; 118 tr dried; 128tr pods; 130cl; 149tc dried; 149br dried; 152c dried; 160bc; 168br; 187tr dried; 199bc root; 199bl leal; 203cr seeds; 233cr; 246tc seeds; 253tcr seed stem; 255bc; 267bc seeds; 278br dried; 286br dried; 288t; Derek Hall: 179tr, Robert Harding Picture Library/ European Magazines Ltd.: 22br; Dave King: 9; 11br; 14cr; 15c petals; 17cl; 27c; 61b; 82bl; 87cr beans; 97br; 108 except bc variegated; 112-113 except br; 116b; 120cl dried petals; 120br hips; 124-125; 126t; 127t; 127c; 132; 133 except tr; 136c; 139bcr tall stems; 140b; 141tr; 142 except bl; 143 except tc; 145tc; 148bc; 150; 151t, 151br; 159b; 160cl; 166t; 168bl; 170cr; 171; 172tr; 182b except dried; 184br; 185tc flower; 189t; 190 except tc, bl; 191 except tc, tr, c, bl; 192bl; 195tc; 196b; 197; 199t, 200b; 214b; 215b; 212cl; 218t; 219cr flowers; 220tr; 220b; 221; 223tc; 226tc; 229br; 230tc; 231t; 233b; 234bl; 236t; 239t; 241b; 244tc; 252b; 255cl; 255bl; 256 br; 257tc; 259tr; 259b; 262cr; 263br; 264bl; 264br; 266tc; 270t; 272tr; 273br; 274t; 274bl; 274br; Colin Leftley: 46cl; 47bl; 234br; 235br; 264c; 265b; Rory Lowe: back flap; 30bl; 30br; David Murray: 12cr; 15br; 18l; 24cr; 30tr; 30cl; 59tr dried; 60tc berries; 69br fruit; 83bc bark; 86cr pod; 96bl dried; 127bl; 127br; 148br root; 164tr; 193b; 234 seeds; 237cr dried; 237bl dried; 244cl; 244cr; 251bc paste; 260cl; 260c; 260cr; 261tr; 266cl seeds; 273bl seeds; 283cr dried; Martin Norris: 16cl seeds; 19l; 24b dried; 46b; 68bcr; 119bl seeds; 144b roots; 169c seeds; 169br; 226br paste; 239cl seeds; 259c seeds; 263bl; 269c seeds; 283cl dried; 283bl dried; 285c dried; Roger Phillips: 87c butter; 115tl; 118bl fruit; 134tr fruit; Potter's Herbal Supplies, Wigan: 8tr; Still Pictures/Bojan Brecelj: 8b, Still Pictures/Edward Parker: 21br; Colin Walton: 8cl; 12cl; 12c; 13cl; 13tr; 14c; 15tc; 16bl; 17tc; 17cr; 17br; 18cl; 18cr; 19tc; 19tr; 19cl; 19cr; 19r; 20cr; 21tc; 21tr; 21cl; 21cr; 21r; 22c dried; 24tr equipment; 25tl; 25c dried; 25br; 28tr; 28bcr; 28cr; 29tl; 29tr; 29cr; 29br; 31t; 129tc seeds; 152cr; 152b; 158tr; 188br sprouts & seeds; 193tc bulb; 196 tr roots; 216b; 229cr seeds; 243cl seeds; 244b; 244b; 249c seeds; 253cl straw; 269tr; 269bl dried; 272cl seeds; 280cr seeds; 284t flower; 284b seeds.

Illustrations by Laura Andrew; 168; 170; 203; 204t; 205t; 211t; 212; 213t; 242b; 271b; 272t; 273; Evelyn Binns; 9; 95b; 124b; 125; 126; 127; 146; 171; 172b; 181t; 182t; 185b; 195; 209b; 218b; 219t; 220; 221; 230; 231; 232; 234; 236b; 238t; 238b; 239t; 240t; 241t; 250b; 254b; 266t; 267b;Julia Cobbold; 97b; 101b; 104b; 118t; 128t; 130b; 138b; 193b; 196b; 197; 198b; 199t; 228t; 229; 235; 264; 270t; 275t; Joanne Cowne; 145; 147t; 148t; 153b; 154t; 157t; 186t; 214b; 215b; 216t; 222; 255t; Myra Giles; 267t; 277t; 292c; Ruth Hall; 117b; 157b; 175t; 214t; 215t; 219b; 223b; 252t; 258b; 268b; 270b; 274t; 282b; Tim Hayward: 36t; 38b; 39; 40t; 46; 48; 49; 50t; 53; 55; 56; 57; 58b; 62; 63; 71; 72; 74; 75; 76; 77; 78t; 79b; 82; 84t; 85b; 86t; 87t; 90t; 93b; 94b; 95t; 103b; 105b; 107b; 110t; 115b; 131b; Philippa Lumber; 268t; 280; 284; 291b; Stephen McLean; 10br *Langermannia*; 277b; 281; 289b; David More; 10cl *Alnus*; 34; 35; 37; 38t; 41; 42; 43t; 44b; 51b; 54; 58t; 59b; 64; 65; 66; 67t; 68; 69; 70; 71; 80t; 81t; 83t; 90b; 91; 92; 93; 99b; 100; 103t; 132; 133; 140b; 141; 148b; 149b; 156b; 158b; 159b; 161b; 238c; Leighton Moses; 10bcl *Piper*; 276b; 278t; 283; 288b; 290t; Sue Oldfield; 32; 33; 36b; 40b; 43b; 44t; 45; 50b; 51t; 52; 59t; 60; 61; 67b; 68b; 73; 78b; 79t; 80b; 81b; 83b; 84b; 85t; 86b; 87b; 88; 89; 97t; 98; 99t; 101t; 102t; 103t; 109t; 111; 114; 116t; 119; 129b; 130t; 131t; 153t; 202b; Liz Pepperell; 12; 14 line; 16; 18; 20; 128b; 136; 142; 150; 151; 154b; 158t; 166t; 172t; 173; 179; 180; 181b; 182b; 183b; 189b; 192; 202t; 228b; 240b; Valerie Price; 102b; 147b; 149t;159t; 160b; 183t; 184; 201; 211b; 226b; 239b; 241b; 243; 244t; 245b; 246; 247; 248; 249t; 250t; 251t; 252b; 253b; 257t; 257c; 259b; 262t; 263b; 265t; 266b; Michelle Ross; 10c *Camellia*; 10bl *Lycopersicon*; 14 colour; 94t; 96; 106; 104t; 109b; 110b; 118b; 120; 122; 123; 124t; 129t; 134t; 135; 137; 138t; 139b; 140t; 155b; 162t; 163; 166b; 174 175b; 176b 177 178; 186b; 187t;189t; 190; 194t; 196t; 198t; 200t; 206b; 223t; 233; 236t; 244b; 245t; 253t; 256; 257b; 260; 263t; 269t; 275b; 276t; 286b; 289t; 290b; Hayley Simmons; 10bcr *Dryopteris*; 285t; 286t; 287b; 292t; Catherine Slade; 112; 115t; 116b; 117t; Jenny Steer; 279b; 282t; 287t; 288t; 292b; Rebekah Thorpe; 274b; 278b; 279t; 291c; Jonathon Tyler; 285b; Barbara Walker; 10cr; 105t; 107t; 134b; 139t; 144; 152t; 155t; 156t; 162b; 169b; 176t; 185t; 193t; 194b; 199b; 200b; 207; 208; 209t; 216b; 217t; 218t; 224; 225; 226t; 227; 242t; 249b; 254t; 255b; 258t; 259t; 262b; 268c; 269b; 291t; Wendy Webb; 152b; Debra Woodward; 160t; 161t; 164; 165; 167; 169t; 187b; 188; 204b; 205b; 206t; 210; 213b; 217b; 237; 251b; 265b; 266b; 271t; 272b.

Endpaper illustrations by Caroline Church.